DICKENS
STUDIES
ANNUAL

Essays on Victorian Fiction

VOLUME
18

Edited by
Michael Timko, Fred Kaplan,
and Edward Guiliano

AMS PRESS
NEW YORK

DICKENS STUDIES ANNUAL
ISSN 0084-9812

COPYRIGHT © 1989 by AMS Press, Inc.
Dickens Studies Annual: Essays on Victorian Fiction is published in cooperation with Queens College and the Graduate Center, CUNY.

International Standard Book Number
Series: 0-404-18520-7
Vol. 18: 0-404-18538-X

Dickens Studies Annual: Essays on Victorian Fiction welcomes essay and monograph-length contributions on Dickens as well as on other Victorian novelists and on the history or aesthetics of Victorian fiction. All manuscripts should be double-spaced, including footnotes, which should be grouped at the end of the submission, and should be prepared according to the format used in this journal. An editorial decision can usually be reached more quickly if two copies are submitted. The preferred editions for citations from Dickens' works are the Clarendon and the Norton Critical when available, otherwise the Oxford Illustrated Dickens or the Penguin.

Please send submission to the Editors, *Dickens Studies Annual*, Room 1522. Graduate School and University Center, City University of New York, 33 West 42nd Street, New York, N.Y. 10036: please send subscription inquiries to AMS Press, Inc., 56 East 13th Street, New York, N.Y. 10003.

Manufactured in the United States of America

All AMS books are printed on acid-free paper that meets the guidelines
for performance and durability of the Committee on Production Guidelines
for Book Longevity of the Council on Library Resources.

Contents

v

List of Illustrations

Preface

The depth, breadth, and variety of the essays and reviews in *DSA* 18 are further evidence of the wide interest of the Annual and the gratifying response of scholars and critics to that interest. Dickens, of course, continues to be the major "figure," as he should, but the other authors represented in this volume—Scott, Thackeray, and the Brontës—attest the continuing attraction that Victorian fiction in general and authors other than Dickens continue to have for those concerned with nineteenth-century literature. A glance at some of the titles themselves serves as a gauge to this depth and variety: "Dickens and Shipwreck," "Dickens and Opera," "Writing as a Woman: Dickens, *Hard Times,* and Feminine Discourses," "Faith's Incubus: The Influence of Sir Walter Scott's Folklore on 'Young Goodman Brown,' " "William Thackeray's Fiction and Caroline Norton's Biography: Narrative Matrix of Feminist Legal Reform." Interest in nineteenth-century fiction is alive and well, and *DSA* 18 is proof of it.

The editors continue to be grateful for the good services of the members of the editorial and advisory boards. Special thanks go to those who wrote the comprehensive review essays that constitute one of the outstanding features of each volume: Kathleen Blake (Brontës) and George Worth (Dickens). We also thank, for special kinds of services, Murray Baumgarten, John Jordan, and the participants in the annual Santa Cruz Dickens Conference. Ed Marx, the editorial assistant from CUNY, deserves special mention.

We note and express our gratidude to those in administrative posts in different institutions who continue to provide supports of various kinds, administrative and financial: Chancellor Joseph Murphy, CUNY; President Harold Proshansky, Provost Stephen Cahn, and Executive Officer, Ph.D. Program in English, Martin Stevens, the Graduate School and University Center; Dean of Humanities Michael Spitzer, The New York Institute of Technology; President Shirley Strum Kenny, Dean John Reilly, and Chair, English Department, Charles Molesworth, Queens College. Finally, our appreciation to our collaborators at AMS Press: Gabriel Hornstein, president, and William Long, editor.

—THE EDITORS.

Notes on Contributors

KATHLEEN BLAKE is Professor of English at the University of Washington and the author of *Play, Games, and Sport, The Literary Works of Lewis Carroll, Love and the Woman Question in Victorian Literature, The Art of Self-Postponement*, and articles in the field of nineteenth-century British literature. She has edited *Approaches to Teaching George Eliot's Middlemarch*, forthcoming in the *MLA Approaches to Teaching World Literature* series.

ROBERT BLEDSOE teaches in the English Department of the University of Texas at El Paso. His articles on Victorian literature have appeared in journals such as *PMLA, Victorian Studies, Studies in the Novel*, and *The Dickensian*.

JEAN FERGUSON CARR is an Assistant Professor of English at the University of Pittsburgh. She was textual editor for two volumes of *The Collected Works of R. W. Emerson* (Harvard University Press, 1979, 1983) and has published essays on Dickens, Austen, and on McGuffey's *Readers* and literacy. She is co-editor of a book series on composition and cultural studies at University of Pittsburgh Press and is currently working on a book on nineteenth-century American literacy and letters.

MICAEL M. CLARKE teaches English and Women's Studies at Loyola University of Chicago. She has published articles on Thackeray in *Texas Studies in Literature and Language, Works and Days*, and *Victorian Periodicals Review*, and is currently writing an annotated bibliography of Thackeray criticism and a book on women in Thackeray's fiction. She also wrote the entry on Caroline Norton in *Victorian Britain: An Encyclopedia*.

JOHN P. FRAZEE is Associate Professor of Literature and Director of the Division of Humanities and Fine Arts at The University of Texas of the Permian Basin. In addition to his work on Dickens, he has published articles on George Orwell and Thackeray. His current research includes several articles in progress on Dickensian topics.

RUTH D. JOHNSTON teaches English and Film at Pace University, New York. Her teaching and research (including the essay in this volume) explore the relations between narrative and visual structures from a feminist perspective informed by psychoanalytic theory and semiology.

JOHN O. JORDAN is Associate Professor of English and Director of the Dickens Project at the University of California, Santa Cruz.

GERHARD JOSEPH, Professor of English at Lehman College and the Graduate School of The City University of New York, has written *Tennysonian Love: The Strange Diagonal,* and articles on a wide variety of nineteenth-century subjects. He is completing a second book on Tennyson entitled *Weaving Tennyson.*

ADRIANE LAPOINTE is Assistant Professor of English at Auburn University, where she teaches Nineteenth-Century English Novel, an occasional class in Dickens, and much composition. She has just completed as essay on Conan Doyle's *A Study in Scarlet,* and is looking forward in her next project to an extended encounter with the novels of Wilkie Collins.

BARBARA FASS LEAVY, Associate Professor of English at Queens College, brings together many of her interests in her essay on Collins's *The Woman in White.* She is the author of *La Belle Dame sans Merci and the Aesthetics of Romanticism* (1974) and is presently working on a companion volume on the Demon Lover motif. Her works on demonology in the fairy tale and also on the history of British psychology during the Victorian age have been presented at the Research Seminars of the History of Psychiatry Section of the New York Hospital-Cornell Medical College at which she is a participating member.

CAROL HANBERY MACKAY, Associate Professor of English at the University of Texas at Austin, is author of *Soliloquy in Nineteenth-Century Fiction* and editor-introducer of *The Two Thackerays* and *Dramatic Dickens.* She is currently engaged in a book-length study of Victorian novelists, melodrama, and the lure of the theater.

JULIET MCMASTER is University Professor of English at the University of Alberta, and a Fellow of the Royal Society of Canada. She is the author of *Thackeray: The Major Novels* (1971), *Jane Austen on Love* (1978), *Trollope's Palliser Novels* (1978), and *Dickens the Designer* (1988), and co-author with

R. D. McMaster of *The Novel from Sterne to James*. She is currently working on a study of body and character in the eighteenth-century novel.

NANCY AYCOCK METZ is an Associate Professor of English at Virginia Polytechnic Institute and State University. She has published articles and reviews on Dickens, Trollope, and Victorian social history.

ROBERT NEWSOM is Professor of English at the University of California, Irvine. He is the author of several articles on Dickens as well as *Dickens on the Romantic Side of Familiar Things: Bleak House and the Novel Tradition* (1977; rpt. 1988) and *A Likely Story: Probability and Play in Fiction* (1988). He is at work on a book about Victorian ethics and the novel.

WILLIAM J. PALMER teaches literature and film at Purdue University. His *Tradition, Art, and the Loneliness of Selfhood: The Fiction of John Fowles* was the first book written about that contemporary novelist. His *The Films of the Seventies: A Social History* was published in 1988.

GRAHAME SMITH is Senior Lecturer in English Studies at the University of Stirling. He has taught at UCLA, the University of Wales (Swansea) and the University of Malawi. His major publications include *Dickens, Money and Society, The Novel and Society: from Defoe to George Eliot* and *The Achievement of Graham Greene*.

SARAH WINTER is in comparative literature at Yale University. She is working on a dissertation entitled "Tragedies of Gender: Freud, Jane Harrison, H. D., Proust, Myrivilis."

GEORGE J. WORTH is Professor of English at the University of Kansas. Among his publications are two books on Dickens: *Dickensian Melodrama* (1978) and Great Expectations: *An Annotated Bibliography* (1986). "Recent Dickens Studies: 1987" is his second contribution to the *Dickens Studies Annual;* his "Mr. Wopsle's Hamlet: 'Something Too Much of This' " appeared in *DSA* 17.

The Purloined Handkerchief

John O. Jordan

> Handkerchief! confessions! handkerchief! To confess, and
> be hanged for his labor. First, to be hanged, and then to
> confess: I tremble at it.
>
> *Othello* IV.1. 37–40.

The topic of this essay is a small but revealing aspect of Dickens' *Oliver Twist* (1837–39): namely, the motif of pocket-handkerchiefs in the book. The title, ''The Purloined Handkerchief,'' aims not only at the scenes of pocket picking and handkerchief thieving in the novel but also, somewhat more obliquely, at Edgar Allan Poe's celebrated detective story of 1845, ''The Purloined Letter,'' and at the important body of critical commentary that Poe's story has received in recent years, notably in essays by Jacques Lacan, Jacques Derrida, and Barbara Johnson.[1] The term ''purloined'' derives largely from this critical tradition. The verb ''to purloin'' (from the Anglo-French *pur + loigner*) means to set aside or delay and hence, by extension, to steal; but as Lacan insists with respect to Poe (Muller and Richardson, 43), the word should properly retain something of its original sense of retardation and displacement in addition to the more straightforward notion of theft, and it is with this broader sense of its meaning that the word is used here. Like the letter in Poe's story, the handkerchiefs in *Oliver Twist* are displaced from their original location and made to circulate through the text and illustrations of the book along a complex network of communication and exchange. To describe some of the features of this network, its circuitry so to speak, will be a principal goal of this paper.

Pocket-handkerchiefs abound in *Oliver Twist*. Nearly every major character in the book handles, carries, or wears some form of handkerchief during the course of the narrative. Over fifty separate instances of the word ''handkerchief'' or its near-synonyms (''neckerchief,'' ''cravat''; also the slang terms

1

"fogle" and "wipe") occur in the text, and if we include references to other woven materials such as veils, shrouds, curtains, blankets, coverlets, and so forth, then the number is even greater. In addition, handkerchiefs figure prominently in Cruikshank's illustrations to the novel. At least half of the twenty-four plates in the book contain or suggest the presence of a handkerchief. Moreover, the novel appears at times deliberately to flaunt its preoccupation with handkerchiefs, presenting them not just singly but in astonishing profusion.

The abundance of pocket-handkerchiefs in *Oliver Twist* is of course in large part a function of the plot and of Dickens' decision to place his young protagonist in Fagin's gang of juvenile London pickpockets, for whom the theft of handkerchiefs represents a chief source of livelihood. The importance of handkerchiefs in the thieves' domestic economy is evident in the description of Oliver's first arrival at Fagin's den.

> [Fagin] was dressed in a greasy flannel gown, with his throat bare; and seemed to be dividing his attention between the frying pan and a clothes-horse: over which a great number of silk handkerchiefs were hanging. . . .
> "We are very glad to see you Oliver—very," said the Jew. "Dodger, take off the sausages; and draw a tub near the fire for Oliver. Ah, you're a-staring at the pocket-handkerchiefs! eh, my dear? There are a good many of 'em, ain't there? We've just looked 'em out, ready for the wash; that's all, Oliver; that's all. Ha! ha! ha!"[2]

Oliver finds many things to wonder at in his new surroundings, but, as Fagin observes and as Cruikshank's illustration for this scene also suggests, what astonishes him most is the profusion of handkerchiefs. The reader immediately recognizes what Oliver fails to understand: namely, that the handkerchiefs are stolen. Oliver's failure to grasp this fact reveals more than just his naiveté, however. Ignorance here is a sign of goodness. Because his heart and mind are innocent, the idea of theft never occurs to him. Indeed, it is only much later, when he actually witnesses a crime, that the meaning of the handkerchiefs becomes clear. Until then, they remain morally neutral objects in what he mistakenly construes as a game.

A few chapters later, in a companion scene to the one just cited, the narrative follows Fagin through the streets of London to another point along the route traced by handkerchiefs through the text of the book.

> Near to the spot on which Snow Hill and Holborn Hill meet, there opens: upon the right hand as you come out of the city, a narrow and dismal alley leading to Saffron Hill. In its filthy shops are exposed for sale huge bunches of second-hand silk handkerchiefs, of all sizes and patterns; for here reside the traders

who purchase them from pickpockets. Hundreds of these handkerchiefs hang dangling from pegs outside the windows, or flaunting from the door-posts; and the shelves, within, are piled with them. Confined as the limits of Field Lane are, it has its barber, its coffee-shop, its beer-shop, and its fried-fish warehouse. It is a commercial colony of itself: the emporium of petty larceny: visited at early morning, and setting-in of dusk, by silent merchants, who traffic in dark back-parlours; and who go as strangely as they come. Here, the clothesman, the shoe-vamper, and the rag-merchant, display their goods, as sign-boards to the petty thief; here, stores of old iron and bones, and heaps of mildewy fragments of woolen-stuff and linen, rust and rot in the grimy cellars.

(162)

Here we have the documentary urban journalist at work, the Dickens of *Sketches by Boz*, describing a real London street—Field Lane—for the benefit of middle-class readers who have presumably never seen it. Unlike Oliver in the preceding passage, the narrative voice here has no difficulty grasping the significance of the many handkerchiefs on display. They are "sign-boards" that advertise to both buyer and seller the particular form of commerce conducted within. As such, they belong to a larger class of cultural signs that the narrator records and interprets in conjunction with his project of documenting city life. As in the earlier passage, the very excess of pocket-handkerchiefs in the text calls attention to their status as signifiers in need of interpretation and thus reinforces the handkerchief motif in the book.

In addition to documenting a particular class of petty criminals, the handkerchiefs in *Oliver Twist* are themselves part of a specific social and historical formation.[3] During the 1820s and 30s, when the action of *Oliver Twist* presumably takes place, handkerchiefs continued, as they had throughout the eighteenth century, to be an important fashion accessory for well-to-do persons of both sexes. Fine handkerchiefs were considered articles of luxury, hence their value to thieves and receivers of stolen goods such as Fagin. Preferably made of silk, but also of cambric and fine muslin, dress handkerchiefs frequently bore the "marks" or initials of their owners embroidered into the fabric. Women's handkerchiefs were usually white, often with fancy lace borders and other examples of fine needlework, while men's handkerchiefs, especially snuff handkerchiefs, were more likely to be dark and to bear a printed pattern or design.[4]

Men's handkerchiefs of the period were quite large by modern standards, averaging more than thirty inches square; women's handkerchiefs, though somewhat smaller, also tended to be large. Since the eighteenth century, men generally carried handkerchiefs in the pockets of their trousers, waistcoats, or topcoats, bringing the term pocket-handkerchief into common parlance as a result. Ladies carried their handkerchiefs in a bag or reticule tied round the waist on top of the skirt. From a pickpocket's perspective, the most easily accessible place from which to take a handkerchief was probably the tail-pocket of a gentleman's long-tailed coat. It is from this location, as we see in Cruikshank's illustration, that the Artful Dodger and Charley Bates lift a handkerchief from the distracted Mr. Brownlow, while Oliver looks on in horrified amazement.

In addition to dress handkerchiefs of the kind I have been describing, the late eighteenth and early nineteenth century saw an increase in the use of handkerchiefs by people of the lower classes. The power loom and the availability of cheap cotton from America, together with improved dyeing techniques, made it possible for relatively inexpensive cotton handkerchiefs to be owned by all but the poorest members of society. Thus, although there are no handkerchiefs in the workhouse, when Oliver runs away from the undertaker's house, he does have a handkerchief in which to tie up his few articles of clothing. Likewise, the charity boy Noah Claypole arrives in London with his belongings tied in a handkerchief. Servants also have handkerchiefs. For example, we are told that Giles, the butler in Mrs. Maylie's house, wipes his eyes "with a blue cotton pocket-handkerchief dotted with white spots" (222). This distinctive pattern identifies it as a "belcher" handkerchief, so named in honor of the early nineteenth-century prize fighter, Jim Belcher, who wore neckerchiefs of this design.

The thieves also carry handkerchiefs—ordinary cotton ones worn characteristically around the neck rather than carried in the pocket. Bill Sikes, for example, wears "a dirty belcher handkerchief round his neck" (76); flash Toby Crackit wears an orange neckerchief (140); and Charley Bates explains the slang term "scragged" to Oliver by giving a "pantomimic representation" that involves holding the end of his neckerchief in the air and dropping his head on his shoulder so as to indicate "that scragging and hanging were one and the same thing" (118). Only Fagin, whose throat is bare, lacks the distinctive neckerchief that is virtually a badge of membership in the gang.[5] Thus, although they steal silk handkerchiefs, the thieves do not normally wear them, the one exception to this rule being the occasion when Fagin dresses up like an old gentleman in order to teach Oliver the pocket-handkerchief "game." Fagin's own handkerchief, however, is an old cotton one in which he ties up his gold coins (94).

What begins to emerge from these examples is something like a rudimentary dress code in the book with respect to handkerchiefs. Silk handkerchiefs, carried in the pocket, are the property of the upper classes. Ordinary cotton handkerchiefs, often worn about the neck, belong to the lower classes, especially the thieves. Thieves wear neckerchiefs, the neckerchief being an article of working-class attire used for protection against the sun and for wiping away sweat. Sailors, agricultural laborers, and boxers wear neckerchiefs; gentlemen wear ''neckcloths'' and ''cravats,'' ancestors of the present-day necktie. This code perhaps helps to explain why Mr. Bumble, a lower-class character whose role as beadle aligns him politically with the upper classes, should have two handkerchiefs: one in his pocket, which he daintily spreads over his knees when he takes tea with Mrs. Corney so as ''to prevent the crumbs from sullying the splendour of his shorts'' (149)—a parodic imitation of upper-class gentility; and another that he takes from inside his hat to wipe his brow (22). There are, of course, exceptions to the handkerchief code. Both Grimwig and Monks, two upper-class characters, wear neckerchiefs, though the case of Monks is complicated by his close association with the thieves and by the special reason he has for covering his throat.

One other aspect of early nineteenth-century handkerchief history deserves mention at this point: a development that I shall call the ''textualization'' of the handkerchief. The invention of the roller or cylinder printing machine by Thomas Bell in 1785 was of tremendous importance for the British textile industry at the turn of the century (Braun-Ronsdorf, 34). Printed handkerchiefs, which had previously been relatively difficult and expensive to manufacture, now became mass-produced articles. In addition to decorative patterns such as the blue and white belcher design, one finds an increasing number of utilitarian, commemorative, literary, and political motifs represented upon nineteenth-century handkerchiefs. Maps, statistical tables, poems, political caricatures, and scenes depicting important social and historical events appear with regularity. Handkerchiefs thus become texts as well as textiles, objects to be read and interpreted as well as used in connection with some bodily function.

The ''textualization'' of handkerchiefs of course begins long before the nineteenth century with the use of embroidered initials, names, and decorative motifs (like the strawberry pattern in *Othello* [III.3.435]), but it is not until the industrial age that this practice becomes so elaborate or widespread. Dickens was well aware of these new developments in handkerchief production, as he was of nearly every commercial and technological innovation of the age. In *Nicholas Nickleby* (1838–39), for example, the novel that immediately followed *Oliver Twist*, he describes one of the boys who is about to leave with Squeers for Dotheboys Hall as sobbing and ''rubbing his face very hard with the Beggar's Petition in printed calico'' (*Nickleby*, 91).

Likewise, in *Dombey and Son* (1846–48), a decade after *Oliver Twist*, he mentions something called "the Strangers' Map of London, . . . printed (with a view to pleasant and commodious reference) on pocket handkerchiefs" (*Dombey*, 65). Although *Oliver Twist* contains no references to printed hand- kerchiefs of this sort, I believe that the idea of the handkerchief as a printed document or text is implicit in the novel and shall return to this point later in the paper.

From the examples already cited, it will be clear that *Oliver Twist* is full of handkerchiefs to an extent that both reflects the tremendous increase in handkerchief production around and after the turn of the century and at the same time exceeds the requirements of any documentary or mimetic realism on Dickens' part. As they reappear and pass from one context to another, handkerchiefs take on increasing thematic and figural significance in the novel. Thus, although their importance as a commodity is evident, they seem as well to have symbolic or exchange value in the book, circulating like a form of currency in the thieves' underground economy. As we have seen, handkerchiefs also function as indicators of social class and gender in the book. Their distribution follows a semiotic system or dress code that may owe something to the philosophy of clothes elaborated in Carlyle's *Sartor Resartus* (1833–34) but that lends itself as well to analysis in terms of Roland Barthes' *Systeme de la mode*.

That Dickens was attempting to develop some kind of philosophy of cloth- ing in the book is evident from a passage at the end of the opening chapter, in which the narrator moralizes upon the newly born Oliver's first entry into clothes:

> What an excellent example of the power of dress, young Oliver Twist was! Wrapped in the blanket which had hitherto formed his only covering, he might have been the child of a nobleman or a beggar; it would have been hard for the haughtiest stranger to have assigned him his proper station in society. But now that he was enveloped in the old calico robes which had grown yellow in the same service, he was badged and ticketed, and fell into his place at once—a parish child—the orphan of a workhouse—the humble half-starved drudge—to be cuffed and buffeted through the world—despised by all, and pitied by none.
>
> (3)

Several important points concerning the "power of dress" emerge from this passage. First, clothes are a powerful way of marking social distinctions in a class society; second, power itself is often vested in clothing or social roles rather than in the person, as we see later on in the book from the example of Mr. Bumble, who loses every vestige of authority when he takes off his beadle's cocked hat, laced coat, and cane (239); and finally, dress codes function not just as a differential system of classification but as a means of social control whereby institutions like the workhouse identify and regulate ("badge" and "ticket") members of the lower classes. The exercise of this control begins in the workhouse with the naming, dressing, and subsequent selling of parish orphans as apprentices; it takes its ultimate form in the power of the state over life and death–that is, in the operation of the gallows, which, as Fagin notes, changes "strong and vigorous men to dangling heaps of clothes" (360).

Not surprisingly, then, in a book so preoccupied with handkerchiefs, the power of the state in *Oliver Twist* extends to the absurd length of an attempt by the workhouse board of governors to forbid the possession of pocket-handkerchiefs by any inmate. When the gentleman in the white waistcoat predicts that one day Oliver will come to be hung, the narrator responds with the following ironic comment:

> It appears, at first sight, not unreasonable to suppose, that, if he had entertained a becoming feeling of respect for the prediction of the gentleman in the white waistcoat, he would have established that sage individual's prophetic character, once and for ever, by tying one end of his pocket-handkerchief to a hook in the wall, and attaching himself to the other. To the performance of this feat, however, there was one obstacle: namely, that pocket-handkerchiefs being decided articles of luxury, had been, for all future times and ages, removed from the noses of paupers by the express order of the board, in council assembled: solemnly given and pronounced under their hands and seals.
>
> (12).

The connection between pocket-handkerchiefs and hanging that appears in this passage is another important aspect of the handkerchief motif in the book.[6] The thieves of course all live in constant fear of the gallows. Their nervousness on this score is evident in their frequent joking references to public execution and in the colorful figurative language they use in order to avoid pronouncing the word "hanging." Instead, they say things like "scragged" (118) and "dance upon nothing"[7] (261). Bill Sikes, who has more to fear than anyone at the hands of "Jack Ketch," betrays his anxiety by means of hostile attacks on other people's throats. He threatens to "stop [Oliver's] windpipe"[8] (82), takes his knife to Fagin's throat (93), and leaves bruises on Nancy's "neck and arms" (132). "Wolves tear your throats!" is his most violent oath in the book (179), and he attempts to drown his dog by tying a stone to its throat with a handkerchief and throwing them in the river (329–330).

As these and other examples indicate, the throat is an extremely sensitive part of the anatomy in *Oliver Twist* precisely because it is the focus of so much physical and verbal aggression. It is little wonder then that the thieves make such efforts to protect their throats by wearing handkerchiefs around the neck. These neckerchiefs perform a double and almost contradictory function, however. In addition to protecting a sensitive part of the body, they also serve as a constant reminder of the noose that is figuratively always around the thieves' necks: the "cravat" (293), as Fagin sardonically calls it at one point. Fagin's bare throat suggests his greater vulnerability to the danger that threatens them all, a danger reinforced linguistically throughout the novel by the pun lurking in the first syllable of the the word "handkerchief." If handkerchiefs are "*hang*-crchiefs" and if petty larceny is a capital crime (as it was within recent memory, until the Larceny Act of 1808), then the game to which Oliver is introduced at Fagin's and in which Dodger and the other boys are old hands is one where they are invited to play with their own mortality.

The association between handkerchiefs and hanging is confirmed both verbally and visually in *Oliver Twist*. In the passage already discussed describing Oliver's first arrival at Fagin's den, the silk handkerchiefs are said to be "*hanging*" (emphasis mine) over a clothes-horse, and in the companion scene-describing Field Lane they "*hang dangling* from pegs outside the windows" (emphasis mine). The hanging motif is further reinforced in the illustration that accompanies the first of these scenes. On the wall adjacent to the cascade of handkerchiefs we can recognize a small popular print in which three bodies are shown hanging from a gallows. The hang/handkerchief pun is also apparent in Charley Bates's dumb-show explanation of the word "scragged." Here again, Cruikshank's illustration for the scene repeats and thus corroborates the evidence of the verbal text.

The thieves' obsessive fear of hanging may point toward other anxieties as well. Dianne Sadoff, for example, has argued that the thieves' tenderness about the neck represents the displacement upward of a repressed castration anxiety that structures the entire novel (Sadoff, 212–14). For Sadoff, metaphors of castration at once repress and repeat Oedipal fantasies that underlie Oliver's story. Handkerchiefs and neckerchiefs can thus be understood as signifiers that mark the place of a conspicuous absence in the text—that of the phallus. Likewise, handkerchief stealing can be viewed as a defensive strategy whereby the original conflict is displaced but in which the substitute symptom—pocket picking—repeats in symbolic form the conflict it was intended to resolve.

Castration anxiety is not the only motive for narration in *Oliver Twist*. If handkerchiefs signal a conspicuous absence in the text, then we should consider them as well in relation to Oliver's status as an orphan. Oliver's lack of parents, or rather the lack of any evidence as to their identity, is of course a central mystery that the plot works initially to obscure but ultimately to clear up to achieve narrative closure. The search for parents and for parental substitutes is thus an important motivating force behind the story. It is perhaps too much, however, to say that Oliver himself engages actively in this search. Indeed, he remains remarkably passive throughout the book, ready to attach himself to almost any adult figure that the plot tosses his way, but hardly ever an active participant in initiating such attachments. The search for his father, for example, is carried out on Oliver's behalf by a committee of (mostly) older men, all of them aligned in various ways with the paternal order and the rule of law. The place of Oliver's missing father is marked in the text by a series of written documents—the will, the letter, and the ring given by him to Oliver's mother with her name inscribed inside. All of these, along with other unnamed ''proofs'' (351), have been either stolen or destroyed by Monks and his mother in their effort to conceal Oliver's paternal origin. They constitute what we might call the ''purloined letters'' of the novel, and they must be recovered before the plot can come to a close.

The place of Oliver's missing mother is marked in the text not so much by documents and inscriptions, although these exist, as by a series of woven materials such as blankets, curtains, shrouds, and of course handkerchiefs, that appear regularly throughout the novel. These materials are similar but not identical to what the psychoanalytic literature calls ''transitional objects''—that is, objects that take the place of the absent mother and help the child to master the trauma of separation from her. Typically these include such things as the child's teddy bear or blanket—soft, malleable objects that recall the maternal breast and that the child can use as a comforting substitute when the mother is away. The transitional objects in *Oliver Twist* do not always provide comfort, however, but serve instead as reminders or premonitions of the mother's death.

The trail marked by these reminders of maternal death begins in the workhouse with the ''patchwork coverlet'' (2) thrown over the body of his dying mother and continues with the ''old blanket'' (31) that covers the corpse of the poor woman whose home Oliver visits in the company of the undertaker. It includes the curtain from behind which Mrs. Bedwin's ''motherly'' face appears at Mr. Brownlow's house (67), as well as the figurative ''dusky curtain'' or ''shroud'' (61) that hangs over Brownlow's memory and keeps him from recognizing the resemblance between Oliver's face and the portrait of Agnes Fleming hanging on the wall. The portrait itself, painted on "canvas" (70), is another instance of the motif, as is the rug that Bill Sikes throws over the body of the murdered Nancy (323). Less obvious examples include the wallpaper in Brownlow's house, whose "intricate pattern" (69) Oliver traces with his eyes in the still of the night as if attempting to make out on the wall the image of his lost mother's face, an image that materializes for him the next morning when he sees the portrait. The white handkerchief that passes from Rose Maylie, who almost dies, to Nancy, who holds it up in an effort to ward off Bill Sikes' murderous assault, is another instance of the motif, the handkerchief here serving as a link among the three "sisters"—Rose, Nancy, and Agnes—each of whom briefly occupies the place of Oliver's mother in the book.

The signifying chain that unites these various examples comes to an end in the concluding image of the novel: the white marble tablet with the name "Agnes" inscribed upon it (368). White like the handkerchief and positioned like the portrait and the wallpaper patterns on the wall, the tablet achieves a permanency that the other objects lack and that promises therefore to bring the chain of substitutions to a close. The fact, however, that the inscription is incomplete—like the ring, it lacks a second name—and that it marks a grave without a corpse may indicate that the tablet is only a temporary resting place in the endless process of signification. Indeed, the closure achieved here seems not only unstable but also transparently ideological in its motivation. The marble tablet enshrines Agnes Fleming safely within the bourgeois order that prevails at the novel's end. It thus prevents the search for Oliver's mother from going back to the anonymous pauper's grave at the workhouse where her body presumably lies, and in this way it helps to shield the institution —as well as Oliver's dead father—from any charge of responsibility or neglect in the matter of her death.

Among the many pocket-handkerchiefs that dot the text of *Oliver Twist*, none is so distinctive as the one that Nancy holds aloft at the moment when Bill Sikes bludgeons her to death. Nancy's handkerchief is memorable on several accounts, not the least of which is the strong contrast it presents to the phallic violence of Sikes. Hers is specifically a female-gendered handkerchief—white, as if to suggest that the purity of her womanly "nature" remains unstained despite the sordid conditions in which she lives. Moreover, since it comes from Rose Maylie, the handkerchief signifies the sisterly bond that unites two women of different social classes who are nevertheless alike in their devotion to Oliver. The handkerchief also seems imbued with religious significance, for as she lifts it "towards Heaven" Nancy "breathe[s] one prayer for mercy to her Maker" (322-23).[9]

It is important to recall that Nancy acquires the handkerchief from Rose Maylie not as a simple gift but in exchange for the information about Oliver that she provides to the Maylie group. Nancy will not sell her story, refusing the money that they offer as a reward, but requests from Rose instead some personal memento—a glove or handkerchief. The fact that it is exchanged for a story suggests that the handkerchief has story value of its own, as a female subtext or intertext in a narrative ostensibly about the progress of a parish boy. When Sikes strikes through the handkerchief with his club, he is attempting to cancel the woman's story, but he succeeds only in driving it underground. He represses it (just as he covers Nancy's body with the rug), but it will not stay hidden. The story dogs him, literally, in the form of the mongrel that follows and finally betrays him to the mob. Even the handkerchief returns to haunt him. In Cruikshank's illustration of the scene in which Sikes falls to his death, we see not only the belcher handkerchief around his neck and the hangman's noose that awaits his fall, but in the background, hanging from a pole, a large white square cloth, mentioned in the text only as an absence —"the linen that is never there" (339)—but traceable nonetheless back to Nancy and to Rose. Although repressed, the female subtext returns to assert its power in the end.

One further suggestion concerning Nancy's handkerchief merits consideration at this point. The scenes between Sikes and Nancy in the final one-quarter of the novel represent, I believe, Dickens' attempt to retell the story of *Othello*, with Bill Sikes in the role of the murderer, Nancy as Desdemona, and Fagin as the cunning, manipulative Iago who drives Sikes to commit the deed.[10] "You won't be—too—violent, Bill?" he says after confronting Sikes with the evidence of Nancy's betrayal (321). The handkerchief that Nancy lifts toward Heaven in the murder scene is thus, I would suggest, an intertextual allusion to the lost or purloined handkerchief that serves as the focus of Othello's sexual jealousy. Nancy's unexpected and futile gesture with the handkerchief has its motive partly at least in Shakespeare's play, in Desdemona's equally futile wish to prove her innocence by returning to her husband the missing object that has come to symbolize for him her sexual infidelity.

The hypothesis that Dickens may have been attempting a Newgate *Othello* in *Oliver Twist* is not entirely without foundation. Dickens was of course familiar with all of Shakespeare's work, both as a reader and as a theater-goer. His friend Macready often played the part of Othello and was in fact performing it in 1838, just as Dickens was putting the finishing touches to his novel.[11] Moreover, Dickens appears to have taken a particular interest in *Othello* during the 1830s. We know that in 1833, for example, at the age of 21, he wrote and produced a burlesque theatrical version of *Othello* entitled *O'Thello*, in which his father took a leading role. Only a few manuscript fragments of this burlesque have survived. Similarly, the satirical sketch of 1834 entitled "Mrs. Joseph Porter," reprinted two years later in *Sketches by Boz*, deals with the hilarious and unsuccessful attempt to mount an amateur theatrical production of *Othello*. The scenes between Sikes and Nancy in *Oliver Twist* thus may well be another effort to revise Shakespeare's tragedy, this time as melodrama rather than burlesque or farce. If this hypothesis is correct, it may also help to explain the shift in narrative perspective that takes place toward the end of the book, when the novel's point of view moves inside the guilty consciousness of Sikes, creating greater sympathy for him and making him, if not a tragic hero, at least briefly the protagonist of a Victorian melodrama.

Finally, and at the risk of giving an overly figural reading to the book, I would submit that Oliver himself is a purloined handkerchief circulating through the text of the novel and waiting to be claimed by his rightful owner. To view Oliver in this way is to consider him not so much a character as a narrative function—a small but valuable piece of portable property shuttled about the story by forces outside of his control, including the narrator, until he settles more or less permanently in the Maylie household.

Certainly, from the hour of his birth onward, Oliver is treated more like an object than a human child. " 'You needn't mind sending up to me, if the child cries, nurse' said the surgeon. . . . 'It's very likely it *will* be troublesome. Give it a little gruel if it is!' " (2). The narrator himself ironically adopts the language of the workhouse in order to satirize its treatment of people as commodities, calling Oliver an "item of mortality" (1) and "an article direct from the manufactory of the Devil himself" (13). If at times Oliver figures as a small piece of manufactured goods, he is also, in Bumble's delightfully mixed metaphor, a strange species of neckerchief: "a porochial 'prentis, who is at present a dead-weight; a millstone, as I may say; round the porochial throat" (21).

Like a handkerchief, Oliver seems at first to be little more than a blank space on which others can inscribe their mark of ownership. Bumble gives him the memorable name by which he is known, using the arbitrary, impersonal rule of the alphabet as one guide and his own inadvertent talent for metaphor as another. The police officer who brings Oliver before Mr. Fang, the magistrate, gives him his other name: Tom White. Both names reflect in different ways the namegiver's attempt to classify the boy and insert him in a narrative. "Twist" suggests the hangman's rope and thus the often-repeated prediction that "this boy will be hung." "Tom White" is of course a generic name (recalling Tom Jones), used here to indicate obscure origin and social inconsequence. At the same time, the name suggests that whiteness is an important quality in the boy. Its connotations include both moral purity and genteel birth, both of which Oliver turns out to possess in ample amounts, as well as the inviting and somewhat feminized blankness that leads so many characters to try and leave their mark on him. White, we recall, is also the color of women's handkerchiefs.[12]

Fagin too attempts to impose an identity on Oliver, but not by giving him a name. Rather, he seeks to inscribe a narrative of crime on Oliver's blankness by telling him exciting stories about robbery and giving him the Newgate Calendar to read. In this way he hopes to "blacken" (120) Oliver's soul—an echo of Dickens' blacking factory experience, perhaps. Oliver appears to be a *tabula rasa* unmarked by experience, and he is often described as having a face of perfect innocence. His body is physically unmarked as well. The proof of his identity does not depend, like that of Fielding's Joseph Andrews, on the discovery of a strawberry mark upon his breast. Instead, it his brother Monks who bears the identifying mark, in this case of evil—a birthmark located, significantly, on his throat.

Although he seems at first to be a blank handkerchief, Oliver in fact turns out to be a printed one. In the opening chapter of the book, Oliver's mother "imprint[s] her cold white lips passionately on [his] forehead" (2) only a moment before she dies, and this mark apparently remains with him through the rest of the novel.[13] A crucial scene for this reading of Oliver's character is the one in which he is set to work by Fagin "picking the marks out of the pocket-handkerchiefs" (56). The task that Fagin assigns him is in fact the same one that Fagin is engaged to perform upon the boy—to remove the mark of origin from his soul. Oliver is a pocket-handkerchief that bears the mark of its owner, the dead mother whose spirit serves as Oliver's guardian angel. The question of whether that mark is indelible or can be effaced and another printed in its place is raised by the terms of the father's will. Oliver can inherit only if it can be shown that in his minority he should never have "stained" his name with any public act of dishonor, meanness, cowardice, or wrong (351).

The question of "marks" and "stains," of genetic traits and environmental determinants, arises in connection with other characters in the book. Rose, Nancy, Sikes, and Monks are all "marked" characters in one way or another.

Indeed, the novel seems to revert at times to an almost literal understanding of the idea of "character" as a graphic sign or glyph. For example, the female pauper who announces the death of Old Sally in the workhouse has a face that "resembled more the grotesque shaping of some wild pencil, than the work of Nature's hand" (152). Character in this sense is something written or printed on the body, a textual effect like the designs and patterns printed upon nineteenth-century handkerchiefs.

The handkerchiefs in *Oliver Twist* belong both to a material economy of production and exchange and to a symbolic economy of representation. I have tried to show the presence of both economies in the book as well as some of the connections between them. The history and sociology of handkerchiefs in Britain from the eighteenth through the early nineteenth century provides a useful context for understanding the different kinds of handkerchiefs that appear in the book. In particular, the dramatic increase in handkerchief production at the end of the century, brought about by the new industrial technology, may help to explain the presence of so many handkerchiefs in *Oliver Twist* as well as their availability for the complex thematic treatment that Dickens gives to the handkerchief motif.

Handkerchiefs are integral to the plot and to the narrative project of documenting London's criminal classes. They carry a range of thematic significance, especially in relation to hanging and to issues of power and social control. They are also one of the chief means by which the novel represents its own text-making practice. The circulation of handkerchiefs, like the regular displacement of the letter in Poe's story, is a figure for the process of narration itself. So long as handkerchiefs remain in circulation, the story continues. When they stop, the story ends.

In his "Seminar on 'The Purloined Letter,' " Lacan draws the conclusion that "a letter always arrives at its destination" (Muller and Richardson, 53). One might argue similarly with respect to *Oliver Twist* that a purloined handkerchief always reaches its destination as well. Indeed, the story of Oliver suggests that a handkerchief usually ends up back in its owner's pocket. The story of Oliver's mother, however, suggests otherwise. If the marble tablet on the church wall provides a fitting emblem of closure and containment, refiguring Rose Maylie's white handkerchief after its violent passage through the scene of Nancy's murder, this image of reconciliation is offset by the figure of Agnes Fleming's restless "shade" hovering about the church, and even more so, in the final words of the novel, by the narrator's memory of the living woman as "weak and erring" (368). Despite his evident wish to recover and redeem the fallen woman, the narrator's language here recalls the transgressive sexual desire that generated the entire story as well as the weary, footsore vagrant who gives birth to Oliver in the novel's opening chapter. "Erring"—that is, wandering[14]—she remains an outsider to the final scene of domestic bliss.

The novel's effort to reach closure thus contains the elements of its own undoing, an undoing that Derrida would attribute to the process of "dissemination" and that he views as inherent in the structure of the signifier. To paraphrase Derrida's reformulation of Lacan (Muller and Richardson, 187), it is not that the handkerchief never arrives at its destination, but that it belongs to the structure of the handkerchief to be capable, always, of not arriving. In *Oliver Twist*, the handkerchief that arrives, but at the same time does not fully arrive, is female.

NOTES

1. These and other related essays have recently been collected and published together, along with the text of Poe's story, in *The Purloined Poe: Lacan, Derrida, and Psychoanalytic Reading*, eds. John P. Muller and William J. Richardson (Baltimore, Md.: Johns Hopkins University Press, 1987).
2. Charles Dickens, *Oliver Twist*, ed. Kathleen Tillotson (Oxford: Clarendon Press, 1966), p. 50. All references hereafter are to this edition and appear parenthetically in the text.
3. Here and in the following paragraphs, I have drawn on M. Braun-Ronsdorf, *The History of the Handkerchief* (Leigh-on-Sea, England: F. Lewis, 1967).
4. The presence of so many snuff-takers is one of the features that gives *Oliver Twist* its eighteenth-century atmosphere. Snuff users in the book range from the middle-class characters like Brownlow and Grimwig down to the two old crones in the workhouse. Mr. Sowerberry, the undertaker, offers snuff to Bumble from a little box in the shape of a coffin, and the Artful Dodger is transported for having taken what Charley Bates describes as "a common twopenny-halfpenny sneeze box" (295). Cruikshank's illustration of the scene where "Oliver escapes being bound to a Sweep" shows Mr. Limbkins indifferently taking a pinch of snuff as Oliver falls on his knees to plead with the magistrate.
5. Significantly in this respect, the action intended to confirm Oliver's initiation into the gang begins with his acquisition of a neckerchief. Just as he leaves with Sikes on the ill-fated expedition to Chertsey, Nancy "threw him a handkerchief to tie round his throat" (134). Though intended as an act of kindness toward the boy, this gesture—with its hint of the hangman's noose—has sinister implications for Oliver's future.
6. To my knowledge, Robert L. Patten was the first to comment on this connection (Patten, 219–20). Juliet McMaster also discusses this aspect of the handkerchief motif in a chapter that came to my attention after the present essay was written (McMaster, 45–51).
7. I have preserved the Manuscript reading here. The Clarendon edition omits the pasage in which this phrase appears, but includes it in a textual note.

8. Again I have preserved the Manuscript reading. The Clarendon edition reads "stop his mouth."

9. Morris Golden suggests that Dickens may be recalling in this scene the gesture made by Clarissa, who, when Lovelace attempts to achieve a reconciliation three days after the rape, holds up to Heaven the "innocent" marriage license whose terms Lovelace has violated by his assault upon her body (Golden, 77, n.6).

10. For a more extended discussion of parallels between the two works, see the essays by Alfred Harbage and Laurence Senelick.

11. See Dickens's letter to Mrs. W. C. Macready, dated (by the editors) October 4, 1838, in which he declines a dinner invitation because of his "resolution to shut myself up so stricly with Oliver Twist, as not to enter the doors of Covent Garden Theatre since the opening night, despite Hamlet and Othello" (Pilgrim *Letters*, vol. 1: 440).

12. Mr. Grimwig also calls attention to Oliver's fair skin when he classifies him as a "mealy" boy (that is, pale) rather than a "beef-faced" one. "Mealy" of course anticipates Maylie.

13. Michael Ragussis makes a similar point about "bodily writing" in *Oliver Twist* (Ragussis, 39–40).

14. For this reading of the novel's ending, I am indebted to an unpublished essay by Hilary Schor.

WORKS CITED

Braun-Ronsdorf, M. *The History of the Handkerchief.* Leigh-on-Sea, England: F. Lewis, 1967.

Dickens, Charles. *Dombey and Son.* Ed. Alan Horsman. Oxford: Clarendon Press, 1974.

———. *The Letters of Charles Dickens.* Eds. Madeline House and Graham Storey. Vol. 1. Pilgrim Edition. Oxford: Clarendon Press, 1965.

———. *Nicholas Nickleby.* Ed. Michael Slater. Harmondsworth, England: Penguin, 1978.

———. *Oliver Twist.* Ed. Kathleen Tillotson. Oxford: Clarendon Press, 1966.

Golden, Morris. "Dickens, Oliver, and Boz." *Dickens Quarterly* 4 (1987): 65–77.

Harbage, Alfred. "Shakespeare and the Early Dickens." In *Shakespeare: Aspects of Influence.* Ed. G. B. Evans. Cambridge, Mass.: Harvard University Press, 1967, pp. 109–34.

McMaster, Juliet. *Dickens the Designer.* Totowa, N. J.: Barnes & Noble, 1987.

Muller, John P. and Richardson, William J., eds. *The Purloined Poe: Lacan, Derrida, and Psychoanalytic Reading.* Baltimore: Johns Hopkins University Press, 1987.

Patten, Robert L. "Capitalism and Compassion in *Oliver Twist*," *Studies in the Novel* 1 (1969): 207–21.

Ragussis, Michael. *Acts of Naming: The Family Plot in Fiction*. New York and Oxford: Oxford University Press, 1986.

Sadoff, Dianne. "*Locus Suspectus*: Narrative, Castration, and the Uncanny." *Dickens Studies Annual* 13 (1984): 207–30.

Schor, Hilary. " 'But for Babbling Drabs': The Shadow of Female Narrative in *Oliver Twist*," unpublished essay, n.d.

Senelick, Laurence. "Traces of *Othello* in *Oliver Twist*." *Dickensian* 70 (1974): 97–102.

Little Nell Once More:
Absent Fathers in
The Old Curiosity Shop

Adriane LaPointe

To talk about Little Nell is almost invariably to attack her or to explain her away; Nell puts even those disposed favorably toward *The Old Curiosity Shop* on the defensive. George Ford, for example, feels compelled to qualify his initial assertion that Nell is ''worthy of resurrection'' with the assurance that this is ''not because [he believes] a fresh appreciation [of her] is required'' (Ford, 55). Ford is understandably anxious to establish himself as one who comes to resurrect Nell, not to praise her: his essay demonstrates that although she was tremendously popular in Dickens' lifetime, Nell has been the ''inevitable whipping-girl'' of Dickens' oeuvre ever since (71). Oscar Wilde's famous observation that ''one must have a heart of stone to read the death of Nell without laughing'' (Pearson, 208) comes immediately to mind, and Ford himself describes her death quite succinctly as ''inexcusably dreadful.'' Perhaps even more damningly, G. K. Chesterton remarks that ''it is not the death of Little Nell, but the life of Little Nell,'' that he objects to (Chesterton, 54), and Aldous Huxley describes Nell's history as ''distressing in its ineptitude and vulgar sentimentality'' (Huxley, 57).

When modern critics like Ford or Spilka bring Nell to our attention, then, they usually do so not to debate her worth, but either to justify her existence in terms of Dickens' own psychic needs, or to account for the remarkable disparity between our negative reaction to her and the enthusiasm felt for her by Dickens' contemporaries. My purposes in this essay are somewhat different. I will not only address the issue of Nell's (un)popularity, but suggest what is still mildly unthinkable—that a fresh appreciation of Nell as something more than a Victorian social phenomenon is indeed possible with a clearer understanding of both her personal significance to Dickens, and her role in *The Old Curiosity Shop*. While Nell does indeed owe her being to two of the central events of his life, in his fictive recreation of those experiences, Dickens grapples with issues not only of the greatest importance to his Victorian peers, but of continued relevance to us today.[1]

Nell's shortcomings as a character are commonly attributed to Dickens' identification of her with his beloved sister-in-law, Mary Hogarth, who died three years before he began the novel. Dickens both idolized and idealized Mary; he described her as "the chief solace of his labours,"[2] and expressed his belief that "so perfect a creature never breathed."[3]

As Edgar Johnson observes, if Dickens idealized Mary "into the unattainable of perfection, it was no doubt partly because she was in fact unattainable"; there were indeed "natural boundaries to the development of Dickens' feelings for his adoring sister-in-law" (1:200). But idealization is also a way of setting or enforcing boundaries; Dickens' idealized image of Mary allowed him to enjoy an intense, but safely asexual, intimacy with her. The extremity of his claims for her perfection—"she had not a fault"—can thus be said to correspond to the strength of his attraction to her (Nonesuch *Letters*, 1:259).

That there is a connection between Nell and Mary Hogarth is obvious, but that it is not in fact a matter of simple identification is evident if we compare the striking features of their lives and deaths. Mary did not suffer in life like Nell, and although she, too, died young, she underwent no Nell-like decline or illness. She collapsed after an evening at the theater and died the next day—in Dickens' arms—of unsuspected heart disease at the age of seventeen. *Dickens* was the one who suffered: the intensity and duration of his grief are legendary. I am suggesting that Nell is less an embodiment of Mary Hogarth than an embodiment of Dickens himself experiencing Mary Hogarth's death. His grief, and more importantly, his survivor's sense of the randomness, meaninglessness, and injustice of such a death, are, as I will argue a bit further on, enacted in Nell's life, and indeed in all of *The Old Curiosity Shop*.

Dickens' choice to represent his own adult experience of bereavement in the suffering of a child rather than an adult suggests, however, that he is influenced in *The Old Curiosity Shop* by more than Mary Hogarth's death. Describing his original vision of the novel in his preface to the First Cheap Edition (1848), Dickens writes,

I had it always in my fancy to surround the lonely figure of the child with

grotesque and wild, but not impossible companions, and to gather about her
innocent face and pure intentions, associates as strange and uncongenial as the
grim objects that are about her bed when her history is first foreshadowed.

(42)

If, as we will see, the general victimization of Nell represents Dickens' own
adult experience of bereavement-as-victimization, Nell's projected predicament also parallels that of another young child whose (grand)father failed to
provide for him, and who suffered (he felt) unjustly amidst "strange and
uncongenial" associates and surroundings. I speak, of course, of Dickens
himself, and of the months he spent in the blacking warehouse in the company
of Bob Fagin and "Poll" Green. We know that this experience, like the loss
of Mary Hogarth, haunted Dickens for the rest of his life: he writes " 'My
old way home [from the warehouse] by the Borough made me cry long after
my eldest child could speak' " (Forster, 1:33). With the exception of the
autobiographical fragment written in 1845 or 1846 and confided to Forster,
he remained silent on the subject; his wife and children first learned of it
when Forster published the biography after Dickens' death (Johnson, 45).

The neglect Dickens suffered as a child and the loss of his beloved sister-
in-law are of course quite distinct experiences, but the fact that they are
brought together in *The Old Curiosity Shop* establishes—obviously enough—that
Dickens in some way connected them. I will argue that in each instance
Dickens experienced a loss which can be seen as a deprivation for which the
father is responsible. The responsibility of a father-figure for the victimization
of Dickens through Mary Hogarth's death is not immediately obvious (and
I will spend the bulk of this paper arguing for it), but the father is quite clearly
responsible for the deprivation Dickens suffered while employed in the blacking warehouse.

When the Dickens family first moved from Chatham to Camden Town,
Dickens was of necessity removed from his old school, but he was not placed
in a new school as he had expected. John Dickens, " 'in the ease of his
temper, and straitness of his means . . . appeared to have utterly lost at this
time the idea of educating' " his son (Forster, 13). When the offer came to
place the boy in the blacking warehouse, John accepted. Charles's sister
Fanny, however, received a scholarship to the Royal Academy of Music,
where she remained throughout the family troubles. To Dickens, the blacking
warehouse seemed the end of all his hopes of education, and he " 'could not
bear to think of [him]self—beyond the reach of such honorable emulation and
success' " as that achieved by Fanny (Forster, 31). The young Dickens had
an "extraordinary desire to learn and distinguish himself," and this was

associated with his desire to rise in society; he found the "descent into drudging among common boys with uncouth manners . . . unspeakably humiliating" (Johnson, 33). By putting him to work and neglecting his education, the father lowered his son's present, and possibly future social status, destroying—Dickens believed—his capacity to become the man he wanted to be.[4]

> "No words can express the secret agony of my soul as I . . . felt my early hopes of growing up to be a learned and distinguished man, crushed in my breast. The deep remembrance of the sense I had of being utterly neglected and hopeless; of the shame I felt in my position; of the misery it was to my young heart to believe that, day by day, what I had learned, and thought, and delighted in, and raised my fancy and my emulation up by, was passing away from me, never to be brought back any more; cannot be written."
>
> (Forster, 22)

This passage is bracketed by denial of its own existence and power. Even as he writes his account of the blacking warehouse episode, Dickens insists that such an account "cannot be written," that "no words" can describe what his words go on to describe very effectively. The present passage asserts its non-existence, strives to absent itself, thus reflecting both the shame Dickens felt as a child, and the reason for the shame: his sense of inadequacy, loss. Dickens' choice of a little girl to represent this experience in *The Old Curiosity Shop* reflects this sense of himself as maimed, as characterized by absence—specifically, the feeling that in his warehouse experience, in being deprived of an education, in being deprived (as he thought) of his chance to rise in the world, he had suffered a sort of "castration" at the hands of his father.[5]

Like the young Dickens deprived of education, Nell is characteristically associated with absence. Walking through the town to which she and the grandfather have come with Mrs. Jarley, Nell observes the moon

> shining down upon the old gateway of the town, leaving the low archway very black, and dark; and with a mingled sensation of curiosity and fear, she slowly approached the gate, and stood still to look up at it, wondering to see how dark, and grim, and old, and cold, it looked.
> There was an empty niche from which some old statue had fallen or been carried away hundreds of years ago, and she was thinking what strange people it must have looked down upon when it stood there, and how many hard struggles might have taken place, and how many murders might have been done, upon that silent spot.
>
> (276)

Nell is contemplating an absence here, and insofar as she reflects upon what the absent statue must have seen, identifying herself with it. This perception of the self as missing from a proper place parallels Dickens' strong sense that he had fallen from his own proper station.[6] As Nell continues to watch, withdrawn "into a dark corner," afraid to move and silent as the statue once was, a figure appears under the archway—Quilp, "showing in the moonlight like some monstrous image that had come down from its niche" (276–78).[7] The adult Quilp is also missing from his proper place (literally, London, and figuratively, the niche)—like John Dickens, who had essentially vacated his proper paternal role even before he took up residence in the Marshalsea. (I will discuss Quilp's role as father at some length later in the essay.) In his absence from a proper superintending (elevated) position, the father is become "monstrous"—that is, Quilp.

The absent statue reappears at the Valiant Soldier in Nell's dream of "falling from high towers, and waking with a start and in great terror" (301). When she awakens from her fitful sleep to see the "figure in the room" as she saw Quilp's figure beneath the arch, she is once again the silent (absent) watching statue: with "no voice to cry for help, no power to move, [she] lay still, watching it" (301). And again Nell's perception of her own absence or removal from a proper place/position, of herself *as* an absence, is associated with the absence of a father-figure—here, the grandfather—from *his* proper place. As the figure by the bed, as well as the "figure" that silently watches Nell earlier in the passageway, the grandfather is identified, like his grand-daughter and Quilp, with the absent statue. This "figure" is not a presence, but a present absence; in both instances his identity as the figure is, or could be, established by absence. Nell attempts to identify the first figure by the absence of one of the party from the main room, and actually identifies the second by the grandfather's absence from his "smooth and empty bed" (300, 302). The identification of the grandfather with absence is hardly limited to this one episode. Master Humphrey muses on the grandfather's repeated absence from home at the beginning of the book (55),[8] and Nell muses over the grandfather's literal and figurative (mental) absences throughout. While reflecting on the old man's "vacancy," Nell "withdraw[s] into some secret place"—that is, absents herself in response to *his* absence—and prays "that he might be restored" (289). To be restored in this sense means of course to have one's intellect returned, but the choice of words also suggests a return home. To be re*stored* would be to be back in the Old Curiosity Shop, to be present.[9] We are continually reminded, by the title, and by the events of the other part of the novel, of the absence of Nell and the grandfather from home.[10]

If Nell is the neglected/bereaved Dickens, the grandfather is, then, quite obviously the absent (homeless, nameless, maternal *grand*)father, responsible, and yet not responsible for the child's sufferings, not monstrous, like Quilp, but pitiable, feeble. John Dickens, with his "ease of . . . temper," was clearly such an absent, inadequate father even when he was present, and he was of course quite literally absent from home in the Marshalsea for the worst of Dickens' blacking warehouse experience. Like Nell's, the young Charles's absence from home is the direct result of the father's impotence and improvidence— of the father's absence.

But the father's absence from Dickens' childish world was so powerful in its consequences, so absolute, that it could be fully represented in *The Old Curiosity Shop* only by the Absolute. The absent father who allowed the young Dickens to suffer in the blacking warehouse and seemingly cut off his chances to rise in the world is symbolized by and conflated with the absent Father who deprived Dickens—or allowed him to be deprived—of Mary Hogarth.[11] Dickens' hostility toward his father is embodied not only in the inadequacy of Nell's grandfather, but in the indifference of her Heavenly Father—the same Father culpable in Mary Hogarth's death. *The Old Curiosity Shop* becomes, as a result of this conflation, more than the working-out of a personal hurt. Dickens shows Nell ultimately persecuted/neglected not by any human agency, not by a Fagin or Bumble, but by the Almighty, and in so doing adds his voice to the great Victorian dialogue on the question of God's existence, and the role of Providence in our lives.

Nell's sufferings, and by extension all unfairness and unearned sorrow, are either meaningful, actively intended by God, or accidental, as much a matter of chance as the grandfather's card game—that is, caused by God's absence. *The Old Curiosity Shop* is shaped by conflicting desires—the desire to find meaning in the experience of pain, to identify meaning with God's agency, and to believe that the God who presumably motivates every event is perfectly just and benevolent—that is, by the desire to both attack and justify the father. Dickens' inability to reconcile these desires leads not only to the dual structure of the novel, but to a variety of striking contradictions and dichotomies within each part. Not the least of these is the contrast between the story of Nell's life, which reads like *Jude the Obscure*, and the account of her death, which reads rather more like *The Pilgrim's Progress*. At the center of *The Old Curiosity Shop* we find not presence, but absence—the absence not only of Nell's literal, personal father, but of the figurative Father, of a God whose presence would give meaning not only to the experience of death, but to the experience of survival.

If the world were run by an absolutely benevolent God, we would expect the grandfather's original gambling scheme to succeed. His motives are good, and his cause is indeed just.

> "I am no gambler," cried the old man fiercely. "I call Heaven to witness that I never played for gain of mine, or love of play; that at every piece I staked, I whispered to myself that orphan's name and called on Heaven to bless the venture, which it never did. Whom did it prosper? Who were those with whom I played? Men who lived by plunder, profligacy, and riot, squandering their gold in doing ill and propagating vice and evil. My winnings would have been bestowed on a young sinless child whose life they would have sweetened and made happy . . . who would not have hoped in such a cause—tell me that; now who would not have hoped as I did?"
>
> (126–27)

Nell and her grandfather move through a world which, for all its allegorical feel, is "realistic" in the sense that good is not consistently rewarded, and injustice frequently prevails. If Dickens is not to falsify this reality, if he is not to show Nell's goodness rewarded with good fortune, he must find a respectable motive for her suffering. He must show God to be cruel and unjust in inflicting it on her, or he must deny God's presence in her life. Unable, like Ivan Karamazov, to imagine a good reason for a child's pain (Nell's no more than his own), and equally unable to believe in an actively vicious deity, he chooses to deny God's involvement, to assert God's absence. Nell and her grandfather move through a mechanical world, a world in which events are not motivated. Like the grandfather's game of chance, Nell's fate is governed during their travels, not by the direct action of the God to whom she appeals, but by a fortune that prospers profligates. In this part of the novel, "fortune" and "chance" are simply euphemisms for God's absence. " 'God help us!' cried the child. 'Oh! what hard fortune brought us here!' " (245).

The absence of God's agency from their lives is underscored by the comparison Dickens invites between their travels and Christian's in *The Pilgrim's Progress*. We are told that Nell has

> an old copy of the Pilgrim's Progress, with strange plates, upon a shelf at home . . . [and that as] she looked back upon the place they had left, one part of it came strongly on her mind.
> "Dear grandfather," she said, "only that this place is prettier and a great deal better than the real one, if that in the book is like it, I feel as if we were both Christian, and laid down on this grass all the cares and troubles we brought with us; never to take them up again"
>
> (175).

The incident which Nell recalls is the removal of Christian's burden of guilt

and sin before the cross; he is at that time given a roll representing the promise
of salvation. This certainty of God's love, and of God's agency in his life,
is Christian's mainstay and comfort. God is continually present to him, and
every aspect of his experience is therefore meaningful.

Nell's relationship with her heavenly Father is very different. While she
clearly believes, she neither trusts implicitly in Him to right things, nor
assumes that all things happen as part of some divine plan. This attitude
contrasts not only with Christian's, but with the attitudes of characters in
other Dickens novels. When Rose Maylie lies ill in *Oliver Twist*, Mrs. Maylie,
her adoptive mother, is able to comfort herself and Oliver with the following
reflection:

> "I have seen enough . . . to know that it is not always the youngest and best
> who are spared to those that love them; but this should give us comfort in our
> sorrow; for Heaven is just; and such things teach us, impressively, that there
> is a brighter world than this; and that the passage to it is speedy. God's will
> be done!"
>
> (296)

The assumption underlying this circular argument is obviously that things fall
out as they do not by accident, but by the will of Heaven. In other words,
an event as seemingly fortuitous as Rose's sudden illness is *motivated* by a
present God. Mrs. Maylie says, " 'God's will be done!' " with the conviction
that it will be for the best, however it may seem to us, but Nell can only
speak conditionally of God's mercy.[12] Mercy is only one possible outcome
in the game of chance that is her life.

> "Oh! if we live to reach the country once again, if we get clear of these dreadful
> places though it is only to lie down and die, with what a grateful heart I shall
> thank God for so much mercy!"
>
> (422)

Nell is hedging her bets here, rather as if she had taken to heart the grandfather's warning that "fortune will not bear chiding" (295). She phrases her
rather pathetic wish cautiously, laying no blame for their present predicament,
and avoiding any direct request. While she would be grateful for God's mercy,
she will be neither disappointed nor reproachful if it is denied. Unlike the
grandfather, who can never accept the possible absence of God's hand, Nell
is well aware that God need not prosper them, that He may choose to take
a hand in neither the game nor their lives. And He is indeed absent at crucial
moments. Although Neil urges the old man to pray "to Heaven, to save us
from such deeds" as the robbery of Mrs. Jarley, it is Nell herself who saves

them, and she is, significantly, "inspired" to do so not by God, but by terror (405). Similarly, the schoolmaster reflects with amazement that Nell has "heroically persevered under all doubts and dangers . . . sustained," not by the grace of God, but "by strong affection and the consciousness of rectitude *alone*" (435, my emphasis). Perhaps most strikingly of all, in her greatest extremity on the Birmingham/Wolverhampton road, Nell has

> no resource but the poor man's gift [some pennies], and no encouragement but that which flowed from her own heart, and its sense of the truth and right of what she did.[13]
>
> (422)

The comfort of God's love, the encouragement of any belief that things must happen for the best in God's creation, are as conspicuously absent here from Nell's thoughts, and from Dickens' thoughts about her, as God Himself is from her world. This contrasts quite sharply with Christian's conviction in the Valley of the Shadow of Death that he can rely on God's protection.

Dickens clearly does not intend us to regard Nell's lack of conviction as wrongheadedness; we are shown no reason why she should feel differently. Nell is the moral touchstone of the novel, and there can be no question that her sufferings, unlike those of Christian, represent neither a grappling with doubt nor yet a trial of faith. As Qualls observes, Nell "is the Romantic child who will never need ask with Christian, 'What shall I do to be saved?' " (98–99). Although Nell feels like Christian as she looks back on London, she has no burden of guilt to lay down.

As all this suggests, Nell may refrain from reproaching God for His absence, but Dickens, the author who has banished Him, cannot. The futility of characters' appeals and references to Him constitutes a kind of authorial attack. Dickens' hostility is also evident in speeches like that of the fire-tender, who wonders why the fire, his god, failed to help his dying father (420), and in Mrs. Jarley's response to Miss Monflathers's insults:

> Mrs. Jarley's wrath on first learning that she had been threatened with the indignity of Stocks and Penance, passed all description. The genuine and only Jarley exposed to public scorn, jeered by children, and flouted by beadles! "I am a'most inclined," said Mrs. Jarley, bursting with the fulness of her anger and the weakness of her means of revenge "to turn atheist when I think of it!"
>
> (313)

Miss Monflathers's threats prove to Mrs. Jarley that all is not right with the world. The very suggestion of the possibility of such monstrous injustice leads her to doubt (momentarily) the existence of God; it seems to Mrs. Jarley that a world in which such injustice is possible cannot be presided over by a just Being. This is a comic version of the central problem posed by the story of Nell's life, and Mrs. Jarley's is the response that Dickens, no more anxious to be atheist than overt father-killer, must himself avoid. But authorial hostility is perhaps most evident in the words of Isaac List, as he encourages the grandfather to rob Mrs. Jarley:

> "Certainly," Isaac List struck in, "if this good lady as keeps the wax-works has money, and does keep it in a tin box when she goes to bed, and doesn't lock her door for fear of fire, it seems a easy thing; quite a Providence, *I* should call it—but then I've been religiously brought up."
>
> (401)

Dickens is taking a jab at people who pervert the idea of Providence to justify their own ends, but clearly the very mention of Providence here speaks scathingly of either its absence or its malice. List is not entirely unjustified in the construction he puts on the situation: the temptation that falls once again into the path of the weak old man and so blights the improving prospects of his grandchild seems more purposefully contrived, more motivated—more *intended*, albeit for ill—than any other event in Nell's life up to this point. The reader's choice here is seemingly between a deliberately absent God, or one who is actively cruel.

The idea of God's indifference or absence may be preferable to the idea of a vicious deity, but it is finally too disturbing to be given free reign, even in fiction. The rules of the game begin to change near the end of Nell's story; the travellers run across the schoolmaster, now equipped to care for them, and it is

> concluded that Nell and her grandfather should accompany him to the village whither he was bound, and that he should endeavour to find them some humble occupation by which they could subsist. "We shall be sure to succeed," said the schoolmaster, heartily. "The cause is too good a one to fail."
>
> (435)

Although the schoolmaster reasons here much as the grandfather did when formulating his gambling scheme, the narrative now bears out such reasoning. The schoolmaster's timely reappearance is not, however, described as an answer to the sufferers' prayers or an instance of God's mercy, but as a "fortunate chance" (432). To introduce God's agency at this point would be to throw His earlier absence into the sharpest relief; Dickens cannot show God's agency in Nell's life without showing Him to be the author of injustice. For this reason Dickens cannot find meaning in her suffering. He can and does, however, motivate, and hence find meaning in, her death. As we have seen with Rose Maylie, the fictional fact or threat of death can be reconciled rather easily with belief in a present, loving God.

> Of every tear that sorrowing mortals shed on such green graves, some good is born, some gentler nature comes. In the Destroyer's steps there spring up bright creations that defy his power, and his dark path becomes a way of light to Heaven.
>
> (659)

The existence of an afterlife is of course beyond proving or disproving; we have the evidence of our senses to tell us that this world is frequently unjust, but the blank page of death allows Dickens to project onto it what he and his readers want most to see. Dickens uses Nell's death to argue both that God is present, and that He is benevolent. As there is precious little evidence of either God's agency or His benevolence in her life, Dickens must push the argument very hard. This leads him to equate the death he has painted so harshly elsewhere in the novel with birth itself:

> Where were the traces of her early cares, her sufferings, and fatigues? All gone. Sorrow was dead indeed in her, but peace and perfect happiness were born; imaged in her tranquil beauty and repose.[14]
>
> (654)

Although the grandfather has described death as "that doom which is dealt out so unequally" (128), death turns out in *The Old Curiosity Shop* to be dealt with a sort of equality, or at least reason, after all, and the dealer is God. The "living dead may remain above ground while the young and beautiful die, but this is because the young are most deserving of the joy of heaven (658). Nell's death is presented to us as a blessing, a comprehensible act of justice; she and the little scholar die to be reborn in a better world.

> "It is not . . . on earth that Heaven's justice ends. Think what it is compared with the World to which her young spirit has winged its early flight, and say, if one deliberate wish expressed in solemn terms above this bed could call her back to life, which of us would utter it!"
>
> (654)

What remains unequal and unexplained is the way in which *life*, specifically, Nell's life, is dealt out. The bulk of the novel quite simply invalidates the consolation Dickens insists upon by her bier.[15] The conflict which Sucksmith observes between genuine pathos and "uncompromising insistence on consolation" in Dickens' treatment of Nell's death is thus a product of the larger conflict between visions of Nell's life: between Nell as a victim of injustice—a vision terrifying as well as pathetic in that it implies a world abandoned by God—and Nell as the favored child of a loving Father.[16] Nell's death is a retreat from the meaninglessness consequent upon God's (malevolent) absence into the reassuring assertion of His (benevolent) presence, an assertion, therefore, of His ability to substitute for the absent/inadequate earthly father.

If Nell's life embodies Dickens' doubts about God's agency in the world, the stories of Kit, Dick Swiveller, and Quilp reflect his desire to believe in it. These stories assert the active presence of God (and hence symbolically, the father), His power, and, most importantly, His benevolence. They in fact threaten to crowd out the other plot line and take over the novel.[17]

Injustice is not a serious threat in the largely comic world of these characters. The virtuous Kit spends time in jail, but his sufferings are painted lightly; we know that he will eventually be restored to the esteem of the Garlands and be allowed to live happily ever after with Barbara. We know just as surely that the quintessentially evil Quilp will come to no good—and are thus free to regret that he comes to so much bad. Such injustices as Kit's incarceration and Quilp's success are temporary, and are clearly attributable to human agency—Kit's imprisonment and loss of reputation are the direct results of the machinations of Quilp and the Brasses, and Quilp himself prevails upon the world through his own efforts. By contrast, justice is served, and virtue rewarded, providentially. Chance, the result of God's absence in Nell's story, is (in quotation marks) evidence of God's presence in this part of *The Old Curiosity Shop*. Kit's meeting with his patrons is fortuitous, and he is saved from transportation not so much by the Marchioness or by a concerted effort on anyone's part, as by a chain of coincidences beginning with the Marchioness's fear of fire, and culminating in Dick Swiveller's timely recovery.[18] Quilp meets his end through no human agency, but through a poetically just accident. Dick's reform is rewarded (in a pointedly more limited way than unsullied goodness would have been) by the death of his well-to-do aunt just when he needs money most.

Dick Swiveller's relationship with God the Father stands in particularly striking contrast to Nell's. Though James Kincaid maintains that Dick's attitude toward destiny "smacks too much of the attitude of Nell" (101), it is in fact a precise inversion of it. That the Fate or Destiny to which Dick refers familiarly on one occasion as "my buck" is a comic version of God is clearly evinced by "the circumstance of Mr. Swiveller directing his observations to the ceiling'' (331, 330). Dick does *not* rant and rave at destiny like a stage hero; he addresses his destiny with something more like filial disrespect—and Quilp's offer to the contrary, God is the only father Dick has (236–37).

> "What shall I be next? Shall I be a convict in a felt hat and a grey suit, trotting about a dockyard with . . . the order of the garter on my leg, restrained from chafing my ankle by a twisted belcher handkerchief? Shall I be that? Will that do, or is it too genteel? Whatever you please, have it your own way of course."
>
> (330)

Dick responds to his experience, in fact, as we can only wish Nell would respond to hers, laying the blame for all his problems squarely at the feet of Destiny. Because he attributes agency in his life to God only in the form of a personified destiny, Dick can effectively question His actions, cast aspersions upon, and attribute less than praiseworthy motives to Him with impunity.

The various "staggerers" under which Dick reels—loss of support, loss of home, loss of "friend," and so on—are, however, the result not of God's absence, but of his own weaknesses. Dick has indeed knocked himself down, and although hostility toward God the Father would be appropriate in Nell, it is foolish in Dick. Dick's railings thus serve simultaneously as an outlet for authorial hostility toward the present but malicious, or benevolent but absent God, and as evidence that such hostility is misplaced. Dick must learn to identify responsibility for the evils of his world with human rather than supernatural agency. He begins to do this after his first lengthy conversation with the Marchioness leads him to reflect not only on the pathos, but on the peculiarity of her circumstances.

> "This Marchioness," said Mr. Swiveller, folding his arms, "is a very extraordinary person—surrounded by mysteries, ignorant of the taste of beer, unacquainted with her own name (which is less remarkable), and taking a limited view of society through the keyholes of doors—can these things be her destiny, or has some unknown person started an opposition to the decrees of fate? It is a most inscrutable and unmitigated staggerer!"
>
> (532)

The questions Dick ponders about the Marchioness are of course very like those raised by Nell's experiences, but in this part of the novel such questions are more easily answered. We know that Sally Brass is responsible for the Marchioness's sufferings, and we eventually see Providence acting here—through the finding of the key, and Dick's illness—to set things right. And Dick's inheritance allows him to elevate the Marchioness in the same way, if on a smaller scale, that the grandfather longed to elevate Nell: "And she shall

walk in silk attire, and siller have to spare, or may I never rise from this bed
again!'' (612). This part of the novel is concerned primarily with the problems
of life rather than with loss through death, and so when God the father acts
benevolently toward Dick the penitent son, Dickens can bring it to the sort
of satisfyingly just conclusion not possible in the other part.

But the perverse ill-chance or "anti-providence" that prevails in the
Father's absence and dominates Nell's story is present in this part of the novel
as well. Quilp deliberately perpetrates, and hence motivates, the kind of event
that is accidental, meaningless, and unmotivated in Nell's experience. Like
the absent God of Nell's story, he is impervious to appeal and devoid of
human sympathy, capable of telling his poor meek little wife with complete
sincerity, ''I'm glad you're cold. I'm glad you've lost your way. I'm glad
your eyes are red with crying. It does my heart good to see your little nose
so pinched and frosty'' (615). Quilp is at the same time precisely *un*like the
God whose absence shapes Nell's life in that he is unquestionably present,
an easily identifiable agent whose actions are motivated and intentional. When
the grandfather falls in with gamblers at the Valiant Soldier, we, like Nell,
see it as ill-fortune, an evil coincidence; we cannot motivate the incident
without impugning God. When, on the other hand, Quilp shows up at Little
Bethel, or the inn of Mrs. Jarley's town, we know that there is more than
mere coincidence involved:

> "Would the gentleman like this room?" said a voice, as a little out-of-the-
> way door at the foot of the well-staircase flew briskly open and a head popped
> out . . . and there he stood . . . looking like the evil genius of the cellars come
> from under-ground upon some work of mischief.
> "Would you do me the honour?" said Quilp.
> "I prefer being alone," replied the single gentleman.
> "Oh!" said Quilp. And with that, he darted in again with one jerk and
> clapped the little door to, like a figure in a Dutch clock when the hour strikes.
> (447)

Quilp in fact thinks of himself as, and wishes to be, the "evil genius" of
Nell and her grandfather (619). He is not, of course, although his malice is
quite equal to the task: that role is reserved, insofar as the choice to absent
Himself from the world is deliberate, for the absent God. Although a number
of critics cite Quilp's persecution as the cause of Nell's suffering—Lindsay,
for example, refers to ''Quilp, whose lust drives the girl to her death''
(193)—this is clearly an overstatement. Nell certainly fears Quilp, but she
originally sees in the prospect of flight only ''a return of the simple pleasures
they had once enjoyed, a relief from the gloomy solitude in which she had

lived, an escape from the heartless people by whom she had been surrounded in her late time of trial, the restoration of the old man's health and peace, and a life of tranquil happiness'' (48). While she fears that Quilp will attempt to trace them, she is equally suspicious of many other people who might try (with good reason, the reader thinks) to put her grandfather in a madhouse.

If Quilp is not the evil genius of Nell and the grandfather, his role in *The Old Curiosity Shop* is nonetheless God's reduced to human proportions (23). It is appropriate that when his elaborate plan for Kit's downfall comes to fruition, Quilp, the significant presence and evil genius of his own part of the novel, should pronounce his ''Blessings on all the world!'' out a tavern window (550). The effects of God's absence from Nell's world indeed parallel those of Quilp's presence in his. As God is a bad (absent) father to Nell, for example, Quilp is a bad father to the Marchioness, and to Dick Swiveller, his eventual son-in-law (236–37).[19] Quilp tells the single gentleman at one point, ''You think I'm a conjuror, sir . . . If I was, I should tell my own fortune—and make it'' (451). Quilp does indeed make his own fortune, acting as his own Providence until the moment of his death—a death which he has in a sense foretold as well as contrived (616). Quilp's death has been described as Dickens' revenge for the death of Nell.[20] It can perhaps better be read as Dickens' destruction in effigy of the absent God (father) responsible for Nell's fate during life, as an attack on the father become monstrous in his present absence, as an assertion of the existence of a *present* God capable of meting out justice to that monstrous human personation of His absent Self.

The Old Curiosity Shop is not, of course, the only novel in which Dickens is influenced by the events of his childhood or the loss of Mary Hogarth. *Oliver Twist* also deals with the vulnerability of the fatherless child and with the wasting of a young woman, but while Dickens represents his experience of neglect in the character of Oliver, Rose Maylie is a simple representation of Mary rather than of Dickens's own experience of loss. Dickens is thus unable to resolve his feelings about Mary in his treatment of Rose. Edgar Johnson suggests that Dickens in fact ''found himself unable to carry out his original intention of having Rose Maylie die'' because of his grief over Mary's death (208). Nell, in contrast, *can* die because she is not Mary, but Dickens, the grieving adult Dickens and the maimed Dickens of childhood. Nell in fact *must* die so that the whole Dickens can reach maturity; her death paves the way not only for Dickens' most clearly autobiographical characters, Pip and David Copperfield, but for Dick Swiveller, to grow into full manhood. As Nell, the victim of God the absent Father, and embodiment of the inadequacy consequent upon the earthly father's absence, dies to prove His presence, Dick, the hostile son, recognizes the baselessness of his anger with the Father and becomes a man, marrying the Marchioness, a comic Nell whom he has, significantly, sent to school. This son becomes good father and husband both.

Important in light of Dickens' efforts to come to terms with the two most significant experiences of his life, *The Old Curiosity Shop* is of equal importance as both an exploration of experientially meaningless and unjust aspects of existence, and an attempt to reconcile them with the idea of a present, benevolent deity. This task is always difficult, and particularly so at a time in which, as Carlyle observed, the

> sum of man's misery is that he feel himself crushed under the Juggernaut wheels, and know that Juggernaut is no divinity, but a dead mechanical idol.
>
> (xxviii, 4–5)

Nell, in life, is representative of the human condition in a godless, non-providential, and hence mechanical world.

We are today perhaps less inclined to see the victim of such a world as deserving of so much unmitigated pity; the modern reader of Nell's story is more likely to feel anger—with Nell, for her tolerance; with the grandfather, for his self-indulgence; and with Dickens himself for his "persecution" of the heroine. But the anger we may feel with the manipulative author is more properly directed at the God whose characteristic actions he is representing—fiction being, as Dickens wrote, "but a little imitation" of "the ways of Providence" (Nonesuch *Letters*, 3:125). For Dickens's contemporaries, a great deal less comfortable with the idea of hostility toward God than we are, extreme pity and affection for Nell were expressions of partisanship directed *against* God, and hence equivalent in some respects to our own probable irritation with the author.

But precisely inasmuch as Dickens' contemporary readers were troubled by, and resented God for, Nell's suffering, they were anxious for a reassertion of His power and benevolence, in whatever terms. The great good of the benevolent God's reappearance more than outweighs the evil of Nell's death, and in fact invests the idea of death with a goodness it has resolutely NOT had throughout the novel (146, 343, 418). The copious tears which Nell's death caused to flow were not, then, exclusively tears of grief or pain, but also tears of relief. A genuine catharsis had taken place for Victorian readers; a drama of meaninglessness had become a tragedy.[21] The anxiety raised by their own participation and acquiescence in doubt and hostility had been relieved by a timely retreat into what was, perversely, the happiest ending possible—an ending which was consistent with the reality of suffering Dickens had represented in Nell's life, but which invested the final moment of that life with meaning and the evidence of God's paternal presence.

The modern reader who holds Dickens responsible for Nell's fate can only be repelled by the presentation of her life and death. But for the modern reader who recognizes the role of God as both providential force and symbolic father in Nell's life, *The Old Curiosity Shop* can emerge as a powerful and moving drama of the present absence of both God and the father in our own lives.

NOTES

1. As Sylvère Monod suggests (384), recent critics have indeed tended to look more kindly on Nell. But their approach still tends to be sociological than thematic. See, for example, John Kucich's excellent article, "Death Worship among the Victorians: *The Old Curiosity Shop*" which argues for the novel as "the greatest example of [the] Victorian death dynamic" (59). He suggests that *The Old Curiosity Shop* legitimizes "desires for death by merging them with a positive cultural ideal" (58).
2. Notice of explanation to missing installment of *Oliver Twist* in Bentley's *Miscellany*, June, 1837.
3. Letter to Thomas Beard [17 May 1837]. (*The Letters of Charles Dickens*, Pilgrim Ed. Vol. 1:659).
4. The death of the Little Scholar represents the death of Dickens' own "very clever" scholarly self (*OCS*, 251). This death is also possibly an attempt on Dickens' part to justify the motives of his parents in removing him from school—particularly those of his mother, who wanted him kept at work longer than his father. The grand*mother* of the little scholar believes that study is responsible for the illness that kills him, that study is dangerous (259).
5. It is as well a sort of revenge on Fanny, whose contrasting success "unmanned" the boy further. Nell signifies in a variety of (even contradictory) ways.
6. Nell's identification with the statue here is foreshadowed earlier in the novel when Kit stands "In the Shadow of an archway" outside the Old Curiosity Shop, looking up at the window at which the child was accustomed to sit but from which she is absent (129–30). Nell eventually finds her own "niche" in the window of the house she assumes when she fills the "vacant post" in the village where she dies (480, 483). But she is particularly characterized by present absence even here: "the roughest among [the schoolboys] was sorry if he missed her in her usual place upon his way to school, and would turn out of the path to ask for her at the latticed window." It is not made clear exactly where this usual place is—"sitting in the church" (amongst the statues and relics), or in the window/niche itself (508). (It seems unlikely that this "niche" and the latticed window are actually the same, but as the niche is the only window mentioned in the initial description of the house, such an association seems excusable.) Elevation and absences come together again at the end of the novel: the "feeling . . . abroad which raised the child above" the villagers is clearly conditioned

by her impending absence in death, and figuratively elevates her, as her fondness for the church tower literally elevates her, to an even loftier position than that once occupied by the absent statue (509, 494).

7. The silence associated with the statue's inability to speak, to comment on its observations, is also significant. The young Dickens feared that both his lack of education and his relegation to a lower social station could keep him—unlike the songstress-scholar Fanny—silent, could take from his hand the pen with which he would later describe the "many hard struggles" and "many murders" about which the statue is doubly silent in its absence. Dickens' insistence (Forster, 22) that he cannot express his feelings about the blacking warehouse experience is particularly noteworthy in this context.

8. Master Humphrey describes Nell, in the grandfather's absence, as "alone, unwatched, uncared for (save by angels)" (55). The parenthetical angels clearly count for very little—and as we will see, it is most significant that Master Humphrey does not refer to God here.

9. There is some suggestion that Nell and the grandfather *are* "restored" in their new home at the end of the novel, although if they do become temporarily present, it is only to become absent again—Nell in death, and the grandfather in imbecility. As many critics have observed, their surroundings are similarly gothic, and the schoolmaster tells Nell she " 'would have looked at [the house] more *curiously* yet' " if she had known that it was to be hers (480, my emphasis).

10. Note also the emphasis on their absence from places they have been along the way—as, for example, from Mrs. Jarley's—cf. 298, 301, 444–45.

11. These "deprivations" are also clearly "castrations." Lacan argues that the Name of the Father inevitably castrates the child as it divides him/her from (the possibility/illusion of) union with the (maternal) other. Dickens' deep desire to be buried with Mary Hogarth (a desire baulked by the laws of both propriety and consanguinity) reflects the intensity of his desire for (re)union with her, and suggests the extent to which the loss of this young sister-in-law through the agency (or, as we will see, absence) of God, the law-giving, authoritarian embodiment of the Name of the Father, reenacts this original castration. Dickens's desire to see the castration as a result of the Father's absence rather than presence suggests both his identification with the Father's law-giving, ordering role and his allegiance to the logocentrism described by Derrida as predicated upon the notion of presence. John Dickens' conduct in the blacking warehouse episode can be seen as more unreconstructedly Freudian castration; the father reduces the son to his own level of economic and social impotence as he destroys the boy's potential to be a "learned and distinguished"—that is, potent—"man."

12. Even Mrs. Maylie's remarks are open to question; as William Veeder has pointed out to me, she "may lie."

13. Note the similar pattern of negation in Dickens' description of his experience in the blacking warehouse: "[I received] no advice, no counsel, no encouragement, no consolation, no support, from anyone that I can call to mind, so help me God" (Forster, 24). The association of God with "help" here is significant, because clearly God helped Dickens in his need no more than He helps Nell in hers. When Nell thinks of love and protection, she does not think of God: "If we were in the country now . . . we should find some good old tree, stretching out his green arms as if he loved us, and nodding and rustling as if he would have us fall asleep, thinking of him while he watched" (415).

14. Perhaps even more striking is his earlier confusion of decay and purity: Nell finds

the air in the village church simultaneously "laden with decay, [and] purified by time of all its grosser particles" (493). Clearly the paradoxical association of spiritual transcendence and physical decay in death were troubling Dickens.

15. We know that Dickens was himself unsatisfied by this consolation. As she told Forster, "I can't preach to myself the schoolmaster's consolation, though I try" [Letter of ?8 January, 1841, 2:181]. It is noteworthy, too, that directly after he has delivered his famous dissertation on death to Nell, Mr. Marton, now in receipt of 35 pounds annually, is referred to as "the *poor* schoolmaster" (503, my emphasis). Must we not read the "poor" here in emotional terms? The schoolmaster is an object for pity, presumably because of his great need to believe in the comforting doctrine he offers.

16. Nell's death is an often-cited example of the Victorian preoccupation with dead and dying children. See, for example, Stone. For more on Victorian literary treatments of death, see Stewart.

17. "All the while we are exploring peace, serenity and, ultimately, death in the country, Dickens keeps straining to offer us instead all of the interest and energy and life of the city slickers, hustlers and hucksters, and the reading experience we have is of being lured off into that more lively world, and then being reluctantly dragged back to the central world of serenity and death. The *Old Curiosity Shop* that we read and re-read is not the one Dickens wrote, but the one he could not quite write: the novel he strains and sometimes delivers—the world of life and energy and comedy that goes on in spite of the death at the centre" (Horton, 121). Readers who respond like Horton are shying away from confrontation with potential meaninglessness in giving preference to the "lively" half of the novel, with its illusion of Providential control.

18. The little servant's perfectly reasonable fear for her safety in the event of fire (which leads her to the discovery of the key, which ultimately leads to her liberation from the Brasses' and Kit's liberation from prison) is reminiscent of Mrs. Jarley's fear of fire, the fire-tender's love of fire, and Quilp's predilection for "fiery" hot liquor (226, 481, 568).

19. Sadoff suggests that "the novel names Quilp 'father,' " but this is true primarily as Quilp represents God, the absent Father (15). And although we learn something of Nell's genealogy in *The Old Curiosity Shop*, we learn next to nothing about her literal *paternity*. The grandfather is not, as Sadoff says, "Grandfather Trent" (20). The father's absence can only be dealt with on an absolute scale.

20. "When [Quilp] is eventually brought to heel he is punished not as a result of the inevitable logic of plot within the novel, but by an arbitrary end whose brutality can be seen as part-reflection of Dickens's revenge for the death of Nell. (Easson, "Introduction." *OCS*, 18).

21. Nell's "death is a tragedy of the true sort, that which softens, and yet strengthens and elevates." "The Province of Tragedy—Bulwer and Dickens." *Westminster Review* 47.1 (April 1847):6.

WORDS CITED

Carlyle, Thomas. *The Centenary Edition of the works of Thomas Carlyle*. New York: Scribners, 1896–1901.

Chesterton, G. K. *Appreciations and Criticisms of Dickens*. New York: E.P. Dutton, 1911.

Dickens, Charles. *The Letters of Charles Dickens*. Ed. Walter Dexter. Bloomsbury: Nonesuch Press, 1938.

————. *The Letters of Charles Dickens*. Eds. Madeline House and Graham Storey. Pilgrim Edition. Vol. 1. Oxford: Clarendon Press, 1965.

————. *Oliver Twist*. Ed. Peter Fairclough. New York: Penguin, 1966.

————. *The Old Curiosity Shop*. Ed. Angus Easson. New York: Penguin, 1972.

Ford, George H. "Little Nell: The Limits of Explanatory Criticism." *Dickens and His Readers*. Princeton, N.J.: Princeton Press, 1955.

Forster, John. *The Life of Dickens*. Vol. 1. London: Dent, 1966.

Horton, Susan R. *The Reader in the Dickens World*. Pittsburgh, Pa.: University of Pittsburgh Press, 1981.

Huxley, Aldous. *Vulgarity in Literature*. London: Chatto & Windus, 1930.

Johnson, Edgar. *Charles Dickens: His Tragedy and Triumph*. Vol. 1. Boston: Little, Brown, 1952.

Kincaid, James. *Dickens and the Rhetoric of Laughter*. London: Oxford University Press, 1971.

Kucich, John. "Death Worship among the Victorians." *PMLA* 95:1 (1980):58–72.

Lindsey, Jack. *Charles Dickens: A Biographical and Critical Study*. London: Dakers, 1950.

Monod, Sylvère. "Recent Dickens Studies: 1981." *Dickens Studies Annual* 12 (1983):357–385.

Pearson, Hesketh. *Oscar Wilde*. New York: Harper, 1946.

Qualls, Barry V. *The Secular Pilgrims of Victorian Fiction*. Cambridge: Cambridge University Press, 1982.

Sadoff, Diane. *"Monsters of Affection": Dickens, Eliot and Bronte on Fatherhood*. Baltimore, Md.: Johns Hopkins University Press, 1982.

Stewart, Garrett. *Death Sentences*. Cambridge, Mass.: Harvard University Press, 1984.

Stone, Donald D. *The Romantic Impulse in Victorian Fiction*. Cambridge, Mass.: Harvard University Press, 1980.

Sucksmith, H. P. *The Narrative Art of Charles Dickens*. Oxford: University Press, 1970.

Dickens and Shipwreck

William J. Palmer

In 1805 the East Indiaman *Earl of Abergavenny*, under the command of
Captain John Wordsworth, wrecked on the rocks off Portland Bill. Two
hundred fifty lives were lost to the sea. Immediately, news reports and in-
terviews with at least two of the survivors appeared in the London papers.
Only eight days after the shipwreck, a forty-nine-page pamphlet account of
the *Earl of Abergavenny*'s demise was published. The next year another
chapbook on this particular wreck was published and the story was also
included in an important anthology of shipwreck narratives (Huntress, x). All
of this appeared, as well as three poems about the wreck written by Captain
Wordsworth's brother. And *we* think that the paperback houses got the Warren
Commission report or the Watergate transcripts into print fast?

In 1826 the *Frances Mary* out of New Brunswick for Liverpool ran into
fierce storms, became a dismasted hulk, and drifted helplessly in the North
Atlantic because her cargo of lumber would not sink. The passengers and
crew, starving, took to cannibalism to survive:

> James Frier was working his passage home, under a promise of marriage to
> Ann Saunders, the female passenger . . . who, when she heard of Frier's death,
> shrieked a loud yell, then snatching a cup from . . . the mate, cut her late
> intended husband's throat and drank his blood! insisting that she had the greatest
> right to it.
>
> (Huntress, xviii)

Ann Saunders survived the wreck of the *Frances Mary*, but the husband she
ultimately took must have thought twice about coming home from the pub
later than expected.

Between 1793 and 1849, the Royal Navy lost four hundred seventeen
vessels not including vessels lost during the Napoleonic wars. Seventy-one

of these four hundred seventeen Royal Navy shipwrecks cost the lives of all on board; for example, five hundred ninety lives lost when the *Hero* sank off Jutland in 1811 (Huntress, xx).

In 1838, the following title was published in London: *Shipwreck of the Stirling Castle, containing a Faithful Narrative of the Dreadful Sufferings of the Crew, and the Cruel Murder of Captain Fraser by the Savages. Also the Horrible Barbarity of the Cannibals inflicted upon the Captain's Widow, whose Unparalleled Sufferings are stated by herself, and corroborated by the Other Survivors* (Fowles, 8). That title is a bit long, but it surely does catch one's attention.

In 1847, the *Son and Heir* bound for Barbadoes sank in the pages of Dickens's novel *Dombey and Son,* triggering the domino effect which would result in the eventual failure of the great London trading house of that book's title. And, in 1850, "a schooner from Spain or Portugal, laden with fruit and wine" (Ch. 55) broke up and sank close to shore just off Yarmouth in the pages of *David Copperfield* claiming the lives of all on board and at least one rescuer.[1]

Those are just a mentioning of some of the more famous shipwrecks of the Victorian age and an indication of the fascination, both morbid and pragmatic, of the whole society with what was the most frequent and frequently reported disaster of the time.

I. THE SHIPWRECK FACTS

There were excellent reasons why shipwrecks were a subject of such intense national interest, of such conscientious reportage and literary exploitation, during the Victorian age. The most obvious reason was their frequency as a natural and man-made disaster. Earthquakes, volcanic eruptions, floods, wars, revolutions, plagues, only happened and were reported in England once or twice per century, but violent storms at sea and the shipwrecks they caused happened almost every day and claimed large numbers of lives and inflicted huge losses of property. One statistic can be projected out to indicate just how elemental a fact of English life shipwrecks were. In the short period of five years between 1864 and 1869, "the Lloyd's registers give a world loss of 10,000 sailing ships. In 1856 alone 1153 ships were lost round the British coast. . . . In *one* day of a great gale in 1859, 195 ships foundered; another 298 ships were lost in the terrible November of 1893" (Fowles, 7).

Even more shocking, however, are the statistics which chronicle the loss of life attributable to shipwrecks in that age. In 1800 the *Queen Charlotte* went down with a loss of 673 of 859 passengers and crew. Four Hundred of 500 died in the wreck of the *Invincible* in 1801; 731 of 738 on the *St. George* in 1803; and 587 of 593 on the *Defence* in 1811. In the 1860s, *The Book of the Ocean*, which compiled statistics of shipwrecks, states: "In England, it is calculated that about five thousand natives of the British Isles yearly perish at sea" (Huntress, xix).

Why did so many ships sink and why were so many lives lost? In his book, *British Shipping*, R. H. Thornton, after enumerating at length all the things that can go wrong with a ship at sea, flatly states: "In short the fast-sailing, full-rigged ship remains about the most dangerous vehicle ever invented by man" (49). But sailing ships were not just inherently dangerous by species, too often they were dangerous by inadequacy, neglect, and even criminal intent. John Fowles, in his essay *Shipwrecks*, argues that "[b]efore Samuel Plimsoll's Merchant Shipping Act of 1876 [ships] were often sent out criminally overladen, undermanned and rotten-timbered. Sailors had a name for these: coffin-ships. On a lee-shore or in heavy seas that was only too often precisely what they were—and also precisely what their astutely over-insured owners hoped they would be" (9).

But such staggering numbers of British ships did not sink only because they were defective. They also sank due to the ineptitude of their captains, the inexperience of their crews, and the underdevelopment of their navigational equipment and knowledge. In the course of the debate over the repeal of the protectionist Navigation Laws in 1849 the following analysis of the state of the British shipping industry surfaces:

> For the truth is that since the end of the Napoleonic Wars, British shipowners had done little or nothing to advance their industry. . . . With the one exception of the Indian Trade, where the East India Company had at least established some conception of a disciplined service, the industry had failed to develop any general standard of professional competence or *amour-propre*. . . . With roads and railways underdeveloped, our coastal traffic was enormous. No finer seamen could be found, nor more jealous of their craft, than the sturdy illiterates who fought their little brigs in all weathers between London and the Tyne. But the supply was not inexhaustible and there was little to attract it to the hazards and hardships of deep sea trading. In 1843 the Foreign Office issued a circular to all Consuls asking for a comparison of British and Foreign seamen . . . Mr. Consul Hesketh of Rio De Janeiro remarked dryly that he had reached the conclusion "that British shipmasters are frequently entrusted with commands or voyages requiring more knowledge of the scientific department of navigation than they possess . . ." [the conclusion drawn from this survey was that] "the persons placed in charge of British ships were too frequently unfit for their

duties, and while many of them were so habitually addicted to drunkenness as
to be altogether incompetent, not a few were almost without education.''
(Thornton, 37–39)

Thornton in his history of *British Shipping* characterized Victorian seamen
as "the rum-soaked illiterates of 1843 . . . the so-called master mariners,
who could not read a chart" (215). Not only were there bad ships and
overmatched, undertrained seamen, but there also weren't enough lighthouses.
Before 1800, along the whole Cornwall coast, one of the most dangerous reef
configurations in the world, there were only four lighthouses and two of
those—the Lizard and St. Agnes in the Scillies—were undependable coal-
cresset beacons. The most important lighthouse on the south coast of England,
the Bishop's Rock, did not go into operation until 1858 (Fowles, 7).

The inherent danger of sailing ships and seafaring: bad boats, bad seamen,
poor navigational equipment, especially lighthouses, lack of real education
in navigational skills, were all reasons for the astounding frequency of shipwrecks and their prominence in Victorian life. But another factor also contributed to the larger numbers which appear in those statistics. The loss of
ships and the loss of life was shockingly high simply because of a significant
increase in sea-going volume in the late eighteenth and the nineteenth centuries. More ships than ever before sailed out more often than ever before
carrying more cargo and more passengers than ever before, hence more sank
and more lives were lost than ever before. The main reasons for this large
and sudden increase in volume were emigration to America and the rapid
growth of America as a purchaser of British manufactured goods. By 1835,
"Europe was sending 50,000 emigrants per year to America and, yearly, the
Irish sailed by the thousands from Liverpool to New York" (Thornton, 7).
Further, "in the decade following 1845 over two and one half million persons
sailed from British ports alone, a vast increase on the annual average of about
70,000 from the whole of Europe in the decade before" (Thornton, 29). From
1787 to 1860 there was tremendous expansion of the import-export figures
out of the port of Liverpool. By 1852, for example, Liverpool was exporting
452,000 tons of coal overseas, 116,000 tons coastwise and to Ireland, and
1,000 million yards of piece-goods to all parts of the world (Hyde, 40–41).
Emigration and trade fed the maw of shipwreck frequency which in turn fed
the maw of Victorian curiosity, sensationalism and imagination.

In a certain cold way, all of these aforementioned statistics explain the
Victorian preoccupation with shipwrecks, but, in a more human way, that
Victorian fascination for shipwreck news and shipwreck myth was also fed
by the very real and personal effects that this staggering number of shipwrecks

had upon the Victorian population and the society itself. When a shipwreck occurred, the ship was lost, the cargo lost, lives lost, profits lost, jobs lost, mail lost, investment capital lost, and insurance lost. Albeit there might be some positive effects to salvage wreckers, shipbuilding outfitters, and smart insurers, in no way could the positive ever outweigh the negative effects of a shipwreck. In other words, a shipwreck set up a ripple effect which spread throughout all levels of Victorian society and touched the lives of countless people in large and small, economic and human, ways.

Of course, the major human loss was the lives of loved ones or the instant extermination of whole families emigrating to the New World. The sea and the ships that sailed her were England's life blood and the history of the sea was part of everyone's personal history. Thus, every time there was a shipwreck, its impact was felt in the hearts of the people as well as in the pocketbooks of the merchants and insurance underwriters, but it was also felt in the basic day-to-day survival of the nation.

In the nineteenth century the British economy was totally dependent upon the British shipping industry and the British shipping industry was dependent upon three basic strengths:

> a) The strong industrial position of the United Kingdom itself, based on free access to the markets of the world for foodstuffs and raw materials;
> b) a world-wide Empire with well-distributed coaling stations and ports of call;
> c) a large coal export trade which provided ships with outward freights which would otherwise be lacking.
>
> (Zimmerman, 223–24)

In the mid-nineteenth century, England's life blood flowed in a vein-artery closed system. Coal pumping out; foodstuffs and raw materials (such as cotton) constantly flowing in. Shipwrecks were the clots that slowed the pulse of the nation, clogged life styles, the economy, the production capability of the most industrial nation in the world.

England's dependence upon shipping had to be a two-way flow system in order for any national benefit or personal profit to occur. It worked in this way: the "majority of ships taking coal from England and Wales . . . bring back to England . . . lumber from the White Sea or Scandinavia, grain from the Black Sea, cotton from Egypt, ore from Spain. Coal, in other words, holds the balance against a variety of imports, thereby giving the carrying trade if not all-around employment, at least much better employment than would be the case in the absence of coal" (Zimmerman, 230). In 1850, more than 3.2 million tons of coal left the ports of the United Kingdom (Zimmer-

man, 226) and that coal was all there was, in most cases, to subsidize the
return freight service, especially from distant ports, which was where all the
profits and national benefits (for example, supply of food, raw materials for
industry, employment) accrued. As an unknown writer of the seventeenth
century wrote: "The coal trade is indeed the refuge and mother of our entire
shipping industry" (Zimmerman, 223). Thus, another major ripple from a
major shipwreck was the temporary loss of a supply of either profits or
materials within the British capital and industrial system.

A third major ripple would run through the London financial community.
When a shipwreck triggers this type of ripple effect, the ones most quickly
affected after the crew, the shipowner, and the family of the crew are the
maritime insurance underwriters. In the aftermath of any shipwreck, the insurers were immediately notified and their investigations of the cause, the
action of captain and crew, and the value of lost property and cargo were set
in motion. The history and underwriting of marine insurance in the nineteenth
century worked rather differently from the sort of insurance experience most
people take for granted in the late twentieth century. A policy for a certain
amount was not simply taken out with a single company or agent. When a
ship went to sea, it could be underwritten by as many as 100 to 200 different
marine insurance underwriters, who were quartered under the umbrella of the
Lloyd's of London marine insurance exchange.

The history of Lloyd's of London is well known but deserves brief recounting. Because of the uncertainty of the mails and the non-existence of
newspapers, almost all shipping news and intelligence in the seventeenth
century had to be disseminated by word of mouth. Owners of vessels, sea
captains, merchants, anyone interested in shipping intelligence gathered at
certain coffee shops to exchange news and gather information on current
events affecting their interests. In the 1680s and 90s the Coffee House of one
Edward Lloyd became *the* most important centre for gaining information
concerning shipping matters. By the 1730s the concept of professional shipping underwriter had come into existence and Lloyd's Coffee House was
London's major marine insurance center. In 1734 the then proprietor of
Lloyd's Coffee House established and published a newspaper, *Lloyd's List*,
which was devoted exclusively to shipping intelligence. By 1760 the first
Register of Shipping was published by the "Society of Underwriters" at
Lloyd's Coffee House who had, in a sense, incorporated. In 1779 seventy
merchants, underwriters and brokers at Lloyd's banded together at a hundred
pounds a head to build an exchange where they could conduct the marine
intelligence and insurance business. By the turn of the nineteenth century the

shipping insurance industry had fully outgrown its coffee house beginnings and was a rather streamlined financial institution in London (Beeman, 14–15).

A Captain Robert Dollar, whose ship was wrecked at sea, describes how his Lloyd's policy was set up:

> The ship was insured for One Hundred Eighty Thousand Pounds. I had a Lloyd's policy for it, and on the back of it there were 103 different signatures for various amounts. Some for a hundred pounds, some fifty pounds, some five hundred pounds, and so on. Lloyd's had taken their insurance and then re-issued it and marked it all on the back; so each paid the amount that was on it in his name.
>
> (Zimmerman, 378)

The importance of marine insurance to the British shipping industry and the British economy in the last three centuries is staggering. Without marine insurance,

> only the wealthiest individuals and corporations could afford to risk their vessels on the high seas; without it only such commodities as afford a wide margin of profit could enter into world trade; without it many lands, which today are the homes of millions, would be deserted. Industries would be lacking raw materials; and raw materials would rot for want of transportation. Marine insurance is the basis of credit, without which commercial loans to importers and exporters would be impossible. Marine insurance bears to commerce the relation of bodyguard rather than senile attendant.
>
> (Zimmerman, 363)

It stands to reason, then, that the underwriters on the Lloyd's exchange had to have the best information concerning ships that were sound, not "coffin ships" ("ships overloaded and overinsured, the destruction of which meant more to their owners than their safe arrival" Zimmerman, 355); captains who were competent; and the circumstances of any shipwreck that did occur. When a ship was wrecked and the insurance had to be paid, the rule of Lloyd's was very clearly defined: "every Member independently of his actual underwriting funds at Lloyd's is liable up to the last penny of his entire personal fortune outside Lloyd's for the due fulfillment of his underwriting obligations and *thereafter* his Policyholders have first call on his deposit" (Beeman, 6).

Early in *Our Mutual Friend*, Veneering "institutes an original comparison between the country and a ship, pointedly calling the ship the Vessel of State, and the Minister the Man at the Helm. . . . 'And, gentlemen, when the timbers of the Vessel of the State are unsound and the Man at the Helm is unskillful, would these great Marine Insurers, who rank among our world-famed merchant-princes—would they insure her, gentlemen? Would they underwrite her? Would they incur risk in her? . . . No!'" (2.3).

A fourth major ripple in English society was the effect that a shipwreck would have upon employment. At the turn of the nineteenth century, under government subsidization (principally the East India Dock Acts of 1799, 1800, 1802), the West India and East India dock systems turned London into the greatest of all European ports and stimulated the drastic expansion of the British cargo fleets. The Port of London's elaborate dock system as we know it today was fully in place by 1830 (Broodbank, 100). Simultaneously, the Liverpool dock system was being similarly expanded (Hyde, 8). Ironically, the larger, more complex docking systems of these two major English ports not only increased British shipping, but also increased the number of shipwrecks. Collisions, explosions, fires, and small boat injuries were not uncommon in these new, crowded dock areas. In-port accidents were, in fact, so commonplace that laws were written to deal with this particular type of shipwreck. The regulations for the West India docks in the Port of London read:

> Vessels were not to navigate the docks under sail. . . . Vessels were to unload immediately on entrance into the docks. Explosives were not allowed in the docks, and combustible materials were only allowed twelve hours on the quays . . . penalties incurred by seamen or lightermen were recoverable from the masters or owners.
>
> (Broodbank, 100)

Yet, with the expansion of the London and Liverpool dock system came a parallel expansion of the work force which supported the huge British shipping industry. When a British ship, or any ship which frequented British ports, wrecked or sank, the impact of that disaster was felt not only by those involved directly with that particular ship, but also by an army of support personnel involved in the docking, loading, unloading, outfitting, maintenance, and provisioning of that ship. The in-port workforce begins with the pilots, watermen, and lightermen, who guide the ships into the docks and do small transport work, and progresses to the dockside personnel such as the wharfingers (clerks responsible for the consignment documents), the superintendent, the stevedores, and the

> dockers [who] work in gangs of seventeen men of whom some are on the quay, trucking cargo to the ship's side and slipping under it the stout rope slings in readiness to be picked up by the hook of the ship's fall. On deck there will be a winchman . . . and down in the hold will be the remainder of the gang who receive the cargo and stow it. A gang, then, is a self-contained unit and, given time enough, could load a whole ship. Our ship, however, has six hatches and could probably work twelve gangs simultaneously without danger or confusion . . . a half-day is the minimum period of engagement for a docker.
>
> (Thornton, 144)

A shipwreck would have the effect of depriving this whole support structure of a portion of their employment.

II. THE SHIPWRECK LITERATURE

In *Dombey and Son*, Dickens is quite aware of the ripple effect in both financial and human terms set off by the shipwreck of the *Son and Heir*. Carker, the novel's villain, shows little concern for the effect of that shipwreck upon the House of Dombey and Son when he remarks, "The underwriters suffer a considerable loss. We are very sorry. No help! Such is life!" (450). But later in the novel the shipwreck of the *Son and Heir* becomes a metaphor for the fall of the House of Dombey itself:

> Through a whole year, the famous House of Dombey and Son had fought . . . against the infatuation of its head, who would not contract its enterprises by a hair's breadth and would not listen to a word of warning that the ship he strained so hard against the storm, was weak and could not bear it. The year was out, and the great House was down.
>
> (Ch. 58)

The ineptitude of the captain, the complexity of the financial storm and finally the breaking down of the ship all cause the wreck of the House of Dombey and affect all who are concerned with that house. As evidenced later by the all-encompassing fog in *Bleak House*, Dickens chooses metaphors which can set in motion exactly these kinds of cross-cultural ripple effects. Shipwrecks are ideal for his purposes.

The Victorian fascination with shipwrecks and all of the lore which surrounds them can be explained by arguments of statistical frequency and social ripple effect, but the fascination was also fueled by the Victorian media. Within the limited context of shipwreck media dissemination, there were, in the nineteenth century, two major outlets. First, newspapers: the major newspapers of the day all had shipping intelligence sections while some special interest newspapers were devoted solely either to shipping intelligence or to the reporting of shipping disasters. Second, shipwreck narratives: these were generally first-person accounts of shipwrecks and of the survivors' ensuing trials and tribulations. They appeared under a number of different formats: individual books, chapbooks, broadsides devoted to a single shipwreck, anthologies of shipwreck narratives, and shipwreck novels.

By Dickens' time, newspaper reportage of shipping intelligence and shipwreck coverage was a long-standing staple of most newspapers. While the

London *Times, The Daily News* (in which Dickens held a proprietary interest, in expectation at least, and for which he wielded editorial power) and Dickens' own tabloid *The Household Narrative* had regular sections devoted solely to shipping intelligence and disaster reports, there were smaller periodicals devoted solely to shipping news and shipwreck coverage. For example, *Lloyd's List*, begun in 1734 and "published without interruption ever since . . . is, apart from the official *London Gazette* published by the government, the oldest surviving newspaper in London" (Beeman, 15). In Dickens' time, while the major newspapers had regular sections of "criminal intelligence" and shipping intelligence which included shipwreck reportage, "the comprehensive reporting of recent crimes and disasters . . . became a staple of the cheap newspaper. The waywardness of man and Providence was a double blessing to early Victorian popular journalism, for not only was the supply of such material inexhaustible; so too was the common man's appetite for it" (Altick, 344). These specialized periodicals were: "The *Naval Chronicle* (1799–1818) [which] included narratives of shipwrecks and disasters. . . . *Chronicles of the Sea* (London, 1838–40) consisted of 119 weekly numbers . . . apparently devoted exclusively to maritime disasters" (Huntress, xii).

While there was certainly no shortage of up-to-the-minute news reports of shipwrecks in Victorian England, one of the two most popular genres of nonfiction prose was the shipwreck narrative, published in either single publication or anthology form. Since the beginnings of print, shipwreck narratives have been prominent in the demands of the English common reader. This was especially true in the nineteenth century. Hakluyt's *Voyages*, for example, one of the top ten best sellers of Shakespeare's age (Altick, 21), was still being reprinted and selling strongly in Dickens' age. By the mid-nineteenth century, Hakluyt's *Voyages* had been superseded by more modern, more sensational anthologies of shipwreck narratives such as Archibald Duncan's *The Mariner's Chronicle* in six volumes published in 1804 which became *the* basic source for many of the other shipwreck narrative anthologies of the nineteenth century (Huntress, x) including Cook's *Voyages* (Altick, 119, 218), and Hall's *Voyages* (Altick, 269). In fact, throughout his *English Common Reader*, Richard Altick consistently refers to the popularity of voyage and shipwreck non-fiction. For example, in 1826 the whole printing business of Archibald Constable was rescued from bankruptcy by the success of a reprint of Basil Hall's *Voyages* (Altick, 268–69). Similarly, whenever Altick offers his different versions of Victorian best-seller lists, shipwreck narratives are always well represented. In 1849, a Buckinghamshire clergyman described the most popular books in his local lending library: "we require duplicates over and over again of such works as Bunyan's *Pilgrim's Progress, Robinson Crusoe*, Cook's *Voyages*, and works of that description" (Altick, 220). In 1838 the London Statistical Society tabulated the holdings of ten Westminister lending libraries. Shipwreck narratives, "voyages" as they were most often called, were the second highest in number of holdings. "Sir Walter Scott and his imitators" compiled a total of 166 volumes and "Voyages" was second with 136 volumes (Altick, 217). In 1883, school children were still required by public school inspectors such as Matthew Arnold to read "extracts from standard authors, or from 'such works as *Robinson Crusoe, Voyages* . . . or Biographies of eminent men' " (Altick, 160).

Among Dickens' own characters, shipwreck narratives were also very popular. In *Dombey and Son*, Solomon Gills and his nephew Walter Gay are well versed in the shipwreck narratives of their day. On a snug night in the Wooden Midshipman, old Sol and young Walter sit before the fire and talk of the sea and of famous shipwrecks as if reciting some familiar litany:

> ". . . why when the Charming Sally went down in the—
>
> "In the Baltic Sea, in the dead of the night, five and twenty minutes past twelve when the captain's watch stopped in his pocket; he lying dead against the main mast—on the fourteenth of February, seventeen forty-nine!" cried Walter with great animation.
>
> "Aye, to be sure!" cried old Sol, "quite right! Then, there were five hundred casks of such wine aboard; and all hands (except the first mate, first lieutenant, two seamen, and a lady in a leaky boat) going to work to stave the casks, got drunk and died drunk, singing 'Rule Brittannia,' when she settled and went down, and ending in one awful scream in chorus.
>
> "But when the George the Second drove ashore, Uncle, on the coast of Cornwall, in a dismal gale, two hours before daybreak, on the fourth of March, 'seventy one, she had near two hundred horses aboard: and the horses breaking loose down below, early in the gale, and tearing to and fro, and trampling each other to death, made such noises, and set up such human cries, that the crew believing the ship to be full of devils, some of the best men, losing heart and head, went overboard in despair, and only two were left alive, at last, to tell the tale.
>
> "And when," said old Sol, "when the Polyphemus. . . .
>
> "Private West India Trader, burden three hundred and fifty tons, Captain John Brown of Deptford. Owners, Wiggs and Co.," cried Walter.
>
> (Ch.4)

Dickens goes on for almost two full pages in this vein with old Sol and Walter reciting the names of the wrecked ships, the circumstances of the disasters, even the cargoes and officers and owners. The shipwrecks which old Sol and Walter so animatedly remember, of the *Charming Sally*, the

George the Second and the *Polyphemus*, are all shipwrecks of the late eighteenth century which they could only have learned about from reading the shipwreck anthologies of the day. For young Walter, these shipwrecks are romantic events in history and he knows his history of the sea quite well.

Thus, the shipwreck narratives, either in the Victorian media or in the many anthologies of such narratives, were readily available and enthusiastically read and studied especially by young Englishmen who fancied themselves one day going to sea in ships as so many of their ancestors and countrymen had always done. However, by far the most popular shipwreck narrative among the English common readers and among Dickens' own characters was not a work of non-fiction prose found in a newspaper, a shipping intelligencer, or a shipwreck narrative anthology. Rather, it was Daniel Defoe's classic work of shipwreck fiction, *Robinson Crusoe*:

> The common reader has always relished a good story, and nowhere has the taste been more pronounced than on the very fringes of the literate public, to which no other form of reading has an equal appeal. Small shopkeepers, artisans and domestic servants—people who had gone to school for only two or three years—at the beginning of the century had devoured *Robinson Crusoe* and the narratives that imitated it, notably *The Adventures of Phillip Quarll*.
>
> (Altick, 63)

All through the Victorian age the popularity of *Robinson Crusoe* held up; "cottages had their little shelf of worn and precious books, family possessions passed down through a century or more—the Bible, *Robinson Crusoe*, . . ." (Altick, 95). In 1867 *Robinson Crusoe* was still mandatory reading for any Victorian school child. One commentator remarked quite negatively, "It is as if we were to begin the teaching of our children with Milton's *Paradise Lost*, and then advance them to *Robinson Crusoe* . . ." (Altick, 159). In fact, in the 1850s, "penny books about Jack the Giantkiller, and . . . Robinson Crusoe" (Altick, 169), were the scorn of schoolteachers. Thus, the shipwreck narrative of *Robinson Crusoe* was a sort of universal furnishing of the Victorian consciousness, like ornamental table legs and lace antimacassars.

Allusions to *Robinson Crusoe* are also everywhere in the canon of Charles Dickens. Of all the well-known shipwreck narratives, it is by far his favorite. Early in *The Pickwick Papers*, Mr. Pickwick embarks on an ill-fated bird shoot with his host who "carrying both guns like a second Robinson Crusoe, led the way" (Ch. 7). In *The Old Curiosity Shop*, after his return from the dead and his return to being a "devil-may-care bachelor" when he judges his wife's mourning of his supposed death not up to his standards, Quilp sets up housekeeping in his counting house at the wharf, which he characterizes as "a country-house like Robinson Crusoe" (Ch. 50).

Defoe's novel is, perhaps, *the* strongest literary influence upon *Martin Chuzzlewit*. Early in the novel, as Tom Pinch explores the city of Salisbury, he is drawn to a shop "where children's books were sold and where poor Robinson Crusoe stood alone in his might, with dog and hatchet, goatskin cap and fowling-piece, calmly surveying Philip Quarll and the host of imitators round him and calling Mr. Pinch to witness that he of all the crowd impressed one solitary footprint on the shore of boyish memory" (Ch. 5). Not only does this passage confirm Richard Altick's assertions concerning the prominence of shipwreck narratives, specifically *Robinson Crusoe*, in Victorian book-stores and libraries (both lending and private), but it also prefigures the ironic shipwreck narrative which will serve as the experiential fulcrum of this text, the bitter and debilitating shipwreck of young Martin and Mark in the fallen Eden of America. Later in *Martin Chuzzlewit*, like Crusoe and his man Friday, Martin and Mark Tapley look for the first time upon Eden; it was a "flat morass, bestrewn with fallen timber; a marsh on which the good growth of the earth seemed to have been wrecked and cast away" (Ch. 23). Other characters in *Martin Chuzzlewit* refer easily to their favorite work of shipwreck narrative. In his bombastic speech, General Choke refers to "the naked visitors to Crusoe's island" (Ch. 21) and, when John Westlock seeks to calm Tom Pinch's fears of imposing, he refers to his rooms as "nothing but a few little bachelor contrivances! The sort of impromptu arrangements that might have suggested themselves to Phillip Quarll or Robinson Crusoe" (Ch. 36).

Finally, near the end of the first half of the Dickens canon, old Sol Gills decries to his nephew, Walter Gay, the manner in which the new technological world is passing the sheltered but isolated world of the Wooden Midshipman: "not being like the Savages who came on Robinson Crusoe's Island, we can't live on a man who asks for change for a sovereign" (Ch. 4). The footprints of Defoe's *Robinson Crusoe* appear in almost every Dickens novel just as they appear all across the consciousness of Victorian society.

John Fowles offers a romantic psychological speculation as to why the English love their shipwrecks, their shipwreck narratives, and their shipwreck lore so much:

> There is, from dry land, great poetry and drama about the shipwreck; but no sailor would let me suggest that the amusement of an audience is the heart of the matter. That heart lies, as it always has and always will, in the terror and despair, in the drowned, in the appalling suffering of the survived, the bravery of the rescuers. We should never forget that; and yet . . . I should like to go

now into the calmer, though deeper and darker, waters of why the spectacle
of the shipwreck is so pleasing—why, in short, there is a kind of Cornish
wrecker in every single one of us.

. . . I'm not sure the most important reaction is not the instinctive: thank
God this did not happen to me. In other words, we derive from the spectacle
of calamity a sense of personal survival—as also, however tenuously, intimations of the metaphysical sea of hazard on which we all sail.

(9–10)

Keith Huntress explains the Victorian fascination for shipwrecks and shipwreck narratives in much less psychological and much more popular and
practical terms:

The primary appeal was, and is, that of adventure and suspense in narrative.
The years 1650–1860 made up the peak period for the wooden sailing ship in
commerce and in war. . . . Sailors made up a significant portion of the labor
force in both England and America, and ship owners and ship captains were
important people of the times. Major sea battles decided the destinies of nations;
major explorations had the same fascination as the moon flights of our own
times with the same sudden extensions of the boundaries of knowledge; and
the sea was dangerous and therefore always interesting.

(xiii-xiv)

Thus, for all of these reasons—the statistical frequency of shipwrecks, the
wide ripple effect of shipwrecks through Victorian society, the extensive
shipwreck reports in the popular press, the availability and great popularity
of true shipwreck narratives as well as shipwreck fiction—the shipwreck had
become for the late eighteenth and the whole nineteenth century a fascination
bordering upon a cultural preoccupation. Therefore, it is not at all unexpected
or the least bit surprising that the most popular and widely read novelist of
the Victorian age, the one Victorian novelist who most conscientiously mon-
itored the temper of his times and employed the interests of that Victorian
temper in his art, should share and repeatedly exploit that fascination.

Dickens' consistent and imaginative use of shipwrecks in all manner of
metaphorical constructs from *Barnaby Rudge* on is one of the clearest attes-
tations to the power of his alchemic imagination, that facility he possessed
to search out, record, and remember in detail the most commonplace events,
people, verbal exchanges, and cultural phenomena, and, like the mythical
alchemist, to transform all of that data garnered in the course of his daily
life, greedily harvested out of his frenzied night prowling of the city's streets,
into the imaginative stuff of his fiction. To steal an apt phrase from Muriel
Spark's *The Prime of Miss Jean Brodie*, Dickens progressively in his canon
became an expert practitioner in ''The Transfiguration of the Commonplace''

(Ch. 6). By the late 1840s, due to the strong cultural interest of his time and his own personal interest in the subject, shipwrecks became for him one of the most available base metals upon which he worked the magic of his alchemic imagination. He gathered a wealth of fact and lore about shipwrecks and transfigured that material into the images, sustained metaphors, myths, and apocalyptic events of his fiction.[2]

Evidence of what would later become Dickens' shipwreck fascination surfaces slowly in his early works. It appears infrequently as little more than an isolated simile in these early novels, yet it is there. As little Oliver, having escaped from Sowerberry and the Bumbles, walks toward London, he receives aid from an "old lady, who had a shipwrecked grandson wandering barefoot in some distant part of the earth" (Ch. 7). In *Nicholas Nickleby*, as Ralph Nickleby moves relentlessly toward suicide in his garret room, his turbulent emotional state is described in terms of a shipwreck seascape. He is tossed in a psychological "whirlwind of passion and regret" and his mind is like "a stormy maddened sea" (Ch. 62).

Though there are but a few shipwreck images in *The Old Curiosity Shop*, too few for them to be considered a thematic motif, Dickens' language of shipwreck is becoming more elaborate, his shipwreck similes more direct and extended. Sampson Brass's frowning face, for example, becomes "one of nature's beacons, warning of those who navigated the shoals of the World, or of that dangerous strait the Law, and admonishing them to seek less treacherous harbours and try their fortune elsewhere" (Ch. 35). Later, as Nell and her grandfather wander destitute in the mean streets of a fiery industrial city, Dickens describes them as "feeling amidst the crowd a solitude which has no parallel but in the thirst of the shipwrecked mariner, who, tossed to and fro upon the billows of a mighty ocean, his red eyes blinded by looking on the water which hems him in on every side, has not one drop to cool his burning tongue" (Ch. 44). Thus, in the early canon, though the shipwreck images are isolated and infrequent, they are nonetheless developing from mere offhand analogies to more elaborate similes to eloquent extended analogies.

III. DICKENS'S SHIPWRECK METAPHORS AND THEIR SOURCE

By the early 1840s, Dickens begins to use the concept of shipwreck as metaphor and motif in much more substantial ways in *Barnaby Rudge, Martin Chuzzlewit* and the aforementioned *Dombey and Son*. In *Barnaby Rudge*, the controlling analogy which Dickens chooses to describe the religious and political upheaval of the Gordon Riots is that of a violent storm, of nature gone mad. With the same kind of romantic linking of violent man and violent nature that Emily Brontë accomplished in *Wuthering Heights*, Dickens foreshadows the riots that are to come:

> There are times when, the elements being in unusual commotion, those who are bent on daring enterprises, or agitated by great thoughts, whether of good or evil, feel a mysterious sympathy with the tumult of nature, and are roused into corresponding violence. In the midst of thunder, lightning, and storm, many tremendous deeds have been committed; men, self-possessed before, have given sudden loose to passions they could no longer control.
>
> (Ch. 2)

This passage in *Barnaby Rudge* is especially valuable not only as a prefiguration of the language used to describe the Gordon Riots later in that novel but also as a preview of the much more mythic and sophisticated storm and shipwreck metaphors which Dickens will later create to embody the French Revolution in *A Tale of Two Cities*.

Later in *Barnaby Rudge*, the Gordon Riots are repeatedly described as a violent storm, an upheaval of nature which is normally benign, but intermixed with and secondary to this storm analogy is a motif of shipwreck images. Just prior to the outbreak of the Gordon Riots, the city of London is buffeted by a winter storm: "Each humble tavern by the waterside, had its group of uncouth figures round the hearth, who talked of vessels foundering at sea, and all hands lost; related many a dismal tale of shipwreck and drowned men" (Ch. 33). When the riots begin, the crowd, armed with all manner of household weapons, follows their mad leaders, "roaring and chafing like an angry sea" (Ch. 63).

At the center of *Martin Chuzzlewit* lies the broad satire of American life and the shipwreck of Martin and Mark in the pestilent American Eden. Dickens employs the following "coffin ship" ironic image to portray the voracious greed which he sees as a main cause of the shipwreck of American society: "The more of that worthless ballast, honour and fair-dealing, which any man cast overboard from the ship of his Good Name and Good Intent, the more ample storage room he had for dollars" (Ch. 16).

In *Barnaby Rudge* and *Martin Chuzzlewit*, the use of shipwreck similes has increased in volume, but it is in *Dombey and Son* that Dickens first employs the metaphor of shipwreck as a controlling motif. Beyond the copious knowledge of shipwreck fact and lore which Old Sol Gills and his nephew Walter Gay so gleefully bandy about in the snug parlor of the Wooden Midshipman,

Shipwreck woodcut

Shipwreck woodcut

"Explosion of the Helen McGregor at Memphis on the Mississippi," cartoon, *The Times* (London) 1830

Sunken ship

the whole language of the novel recurringly depends upon the imagery of shipwreck for the presentation of its social and moral commentary. As will be the case in *Bleak House* two novels later, two houses, the great merchant House of Dombey and the small commercial chandlery of the Wooden Midshipman, provide the two poles of action in the novel. Both of *Dombey and Son*'s houses are portrayed as ships wrecked on the shoals of materialistic Victorian society. At the end of *Dombey and Son*'s first chapter, Mrs. Dombey dies in the act of insuring the continuity of family ownership of her husband's great merchant house, and, "clinging fast to that slight spar within her arms, the mother drifted out upon the dark and unknown sea that rolls round all the world" (Ch. 1). In the course of the novel, both houses are shipwrecked, with their captains suffering grave personal losses, their surviving crews, Walter Gay and Florence Dombey, being set adrift and marooned in isolation until the respective captains find and rescue them from their estrangements from the safe harbor of Victorian family life.

The shipwreck metaphor and its function in *Dombey and Son* is quite obvious in its implication, much more obvious and less interesting than its use in Dickens' later novels. The whole meaning of the motif turns on the obvious word play upon the shipwreck of the House of Dombey's merchant ship, the *Son and Heir*. Leaving the port of London, "upon her voyage went the Son and Heir, as hopefully and trippingly as many another son and heir, gone down, had started on his way before her" (Ch. 20). When Sol Gills and Florence Dombey are told that "they have never had a ship on that voyage so long unheard of" (Ch. 23) and begin to worry about Walter, the whole inanimate skyline of the city of London comes alive to the terrible fear of shipwreck: "The weathercocks on spires and housetops were mysterious with hints of stormy wind and pointed, like so many ghostly fingers, out to dangerous seas, where fragments of great wrecks were drifting, perhaps, and helpless men were rocked upon them into a sleep as deep as the unfathomable waters" (Ch. 23). Houses and ships and people all must undergo shipwreck and rescue in this novel as Captain Cuttle puts it, "there's been uncommon bad weather in them latitudes, there's no denyin', and they have drove and drove and been beat off, may be t'other side of the world. But the ship's a good ship, and the lad's a good lad; and it ain't easy, thank the Lord . . . to break up hearts of oak, whether they're in brigs or buzzums" (Ch. 23). Finally, when the "Shipping Intelligence" (Ch. 32) of every newspaper in London reports the sinking of the *Son and Heir*, "the whole world of Captain Cuttle had been drowned" (Ch. 33).

In *Dombey and Son* the shipwreck of the *Son and Heir* is but the objective correlative for the ongoing shipwrecks of the emotional worlds of the novel's central characters. Captain Cuttle is like some Shakespearean fool who babbles on about the perils of the sea yet whose words, within the context of the novel's action, predict human outcomes. Though but another Dickensian grotesque, Captain Cuttle gives good advice to Florence, who has been cast adrift by everyone whom she ever loved. He advises her to ride out the storm and "stand by" (Ch. 49) on her desert island until the wind changes and she is rescued. By the end of the novel, this is exactly what happens. As will be the case for Esther Summerson, for Little Dorrit and for Lizzie Hexam, later cast adrift, Florence Dombey's patience is rewarded and she is rescued from her shipwrecked state by reawakened love.

Though violent storms at sea and shipwrecks are employed as analogs to the situations, both physical and emotional, of the characters in *Dombey and Son*, it is with the ultimate shipwreck of the House of Dombey that this motif passes out of the descriptive realm of imagery and into the thematic realm of controlling metaphor. By the end of *Dombey and Son*, the language of shipwreck is no longer just a verbal tool or a plotting device; Dickens' alchemic imagination has transfigured it into a prophetic metaphor for what can happen in an age ruled by pride and materialism: "the ship he strained so hard against the storm was weak and could not bear it. The year was out and the great House was down" (Ch. 58).

There is a clear and definite reason why the imagery of shipwreck in Dickens' canon begins to prove more substantial, becomes a major alloy in the forge of his alchemic imagination, right at about the time of *Barnaby Rudge* and *Dombey and Son* and continuing consistently on in different forms through the novels of the 1850s. That reason lies in the fact that shipwrecks had become significantly more prominent in his everyday life. That reason can be found in Dickens' strong editorial commitment to his newspaper work during that time. Since there are relatively few sea-going or shipwreck images and metaphors in Dickens' early novels prior to *Barnaby Rudge* and *Dombey and Son*, the quickening of his interest in this particular metaphorical construct can be dated accurately to the mid-1840s, the time of his journalistic prime.

Dickens was founding editor of the *Daily News*. He became a contributor to Forster's editorship of the *Daily News* after 1846. By 1850, he was the founding editor of *Household Words*, soon accompanied by the monthly supplement *The Household Narrative of Current Events*, a news magazine. Dickens was, therefore, more familiar with the "shipping intelligence" which was a staple of every London newspaper and most periodicals than he had been prior to the time.

In the early numbers of *Household Words* Dickens included a number of feature articles on shipwrecks, shipwreck issues, and the ripple effects of shipwrecks upon English life. In an article titled "A Sea-Side Churchyard" (7 Dec. 1850), the writer contemplates the gravestones of all of the residents of a coastal town who have died by shipwreck. In "Lighthouses and Light-boats" (11 Jan. 1851), the writer states, "the sudden withdrawal of a single 'light' from an important position would . . . be the cause of hundreds of shipwrecks in a single night." An earlier *Household Words* article, "The Preservation of Life from Shipwreck," (3 Aug. 1850) had explored a similar political shipwreck issue. This article calls for the planning and training for better procedures for rescue when shipwrecks occur and mirrors Dickens' consciousness of the shipwreck rescue situation which he had already so powerfully described in the deaths of Steerforth and Ham in *David Copper-field*.

Shipwrecks even have a way of sneaking into articles on completely different subjects. In "On Duty with Inspector Field" (14 June 1851) Dickens goes on a tour of the London underworld with Inspector Field of the Metropolitan Protectives and enters a house in which all of the rooms "were decorated with nautical subjects. Wrecks, engagements, ships on fire, ships passing lighthouses on iron-bound coasts, ships blowing up, ships going down, ships running ashore . . . sailors and ships in every variety of peril, constitute the illustrations of fact."

In two other feature articles, "Life and Luggage" (8 Nov. 1851) and "A Sea-Coroner" (13 Mar. 1852), Dickens' writers quote shipwreck statistics from Parliamentary bluebooks as arguments for legislation regarding better rescue procedures and more lighthouses as a means of reducing the shocking loss of life from shipwrecks around the English coast. In "Life and Luggage," referring to 1850, the writer notes that

[L]ast year, six hundred and eighty-one English and Foreign vessels were wrecked on the coasts, and within the seas of the British Isles. Of these, two hundred and seventy-seven were total wrecks; eighty-four were sunk by leaks and collisions. . . . As nearly as can be ascertained, seven hundred and eighty lives were lost. . . . In the single month of March, 1850, not less than one hundred and thirty-four vessels were wrecked on our coasts, or the average for the month of more than *four a day*. . . . no doubt, many [shipwrecks] occur which never appear in *Lloyd's Lists* or other public records. They are lost at sea with every soul on board.

In "The Sea-Coroner," shipwreck statistics again bolster the argument:

In the Parliamentary Report on Shipwrecks for the year 1836, the loss of property in British shipping wrecked or foundered at sea, is estimated on an average of six years, at three millions sterling per annum. . . . The annual loss of life by the wreck or foundering of British vessels at sea is estimated at one thousand persons each year.

All of these numbers were leveled at the terrible irony of the methods and motives of shipwreck salvage and rescue which Dickens set out to expose in *Household Words*. In "Life and Luggage," the title of which clearly defines that irony, the writer argues:

While our system of lighthouses, lightboats, and beacons, and the matchless judgement, skill and daring of our boatmen, on many parts of the coast, are the admiration of all, whether natives or foreigners, who have any opportunities of experiencing or testing their merits, there has at the very same time existed the fact, that the preservation from shipwreck of a man's portmanteau receives, as a lawful demand, a proportionate reward—and the preservation of his human trunk, nothing whatever.

All during Dickens' career as a journalist he was involved with political causes which attempted to expose and change the savagery of everyday English life: public hangings, government bureaucracy, labor and educational inequities, and shipwreck salvage regulations. He used *Household Words* as a forum in his many attempts to transfigure the commonplace, to make fairer and civilize what he saw as the accepted barbarism and inhumanity of so many aspects of English life, including the astounding number of lives lost in shipwrecks.

By 1852, articles about shipwrecks and the use of shipwrecks as a source for descriptive analogy had become a recurring motif in *Household Words*. "Margaret Fuller" (24 April 1852) describes the shipwreck that took her life and the lives of all her family. In "The Life of Poor Jack" (21 May 1853) the dangerous carelessness of shipboard life is indicated and the writer ends by stating that the "consequences of all this carelessness is, as I find in my blue books, that of every seventeen sailors who die, twelve are drowned or lost by shipwreck."

By late 1853, *Household Words* had begun to publish shipwreck fiction. Two shipwreck stories (31 Dec. 1853 and Feb. 1854) were published within two months of each other. Late in 1854, a two-part anthology of true shipwreck narratives entitled "The Lost Arctic Voyages" (2 Dec. and 9 Dec. 1854) proved extremely popular with *Household Words* readers. These articles simply describe a series of Arctic shipwrecks, but they are important because they serve as immediate sources and influences upon the imagery of two works with which Dickens was to involve himself, *The Frozen Deep* and *A Tale of Two Cities.*

Finally, in "When the Wind Blows" (24 March 1855) and "Wrecks at Sea" (11 Aug. 1855) the magazine returns to statistical polemic to expose the hazards of shipwreck on the English coast, a subject which by this time had become almost a preoccupation of this magazine. When *The Household Narrative of Current Events* was installed as a monthly supplement to *Household Words*, a whole section of this news tabloid was devoted to "Narratives of Accident and Disaster" which each month listed shipwrecks individually with whatever information was available.

Thus, at the time that Charles Dickens was creating stunning scenes of shipwreck and metaphorical constructs of shipwreck imagery in his novels *Dombey and Son, David Copperfield, Hard Times,* and *A Tale of Two Cities,* his obsession with shipwreck facts and shipwreck narratives was also very evident in his everyday journalistic work. He took all of the shipwreck information that he absorbed in his editing first of the *Daily News,* and then *Household Words* and *The Household Narrative of Current Events,* passed it through the magic of his alchemic imagination and thus transfigured it into the symbolic stuff of his fiction.

IV. SHIPWRECKED LIVES, SHIPWRECKED WORLDS: *DAVID COPPERFIELD*

George P. Landow in *Images of Crisis: Literary Iconology,* has written the seminal work on the description and symbolic function of shipwrecks in the literature of the last 240 years. In that study, Landow presents both a theory defining the literary iconology of shipwrecks as well as a great deal of applied criticism analyzing the meaning of shipwreck scenes, images, and metaphors in major works. For some inexplicable reason, however, Landow does little with the novels of Charles Dickens. Landow even fails to remark upon the most famous and elaborate shipwreck in the Dickens canon, the shipwreck off Yarmouth in *David Copperfield.*

Perhaps one reason why Landow does not spend much time with Dickens involves the difference between iconology which combines metaphorical signification with religious signification and imagery. While for Landow shipwrecks and shipwreck language consistently present an iconology of existential and spiritual crisis, for Dickens, shipwrecks form, in different novels, images of apocalypse and desolation (as sin the famous shipwreck of *David Cop-*

perfield), images of social and existential abandonment, alienation and emptiness (as in *Hard Times*), images of utter social and political chaos leading to social apocalypse (as in *A Tale of Two Cities*), and, finally, images of retribution and rescue embodying the sort of religious iconic significance which Landow espouses (as in Dickens' last completed novel, *Our Mutual Friend*).

The controlling shipwreck imagery of *David Copperfield* demonstrates Dickens' employment of this motif to signify, both metaphorically and objectively, the apocalyptic violation and desolation of nature (including human nature) due to one man's immoral tampering with the natural world of the Victorian concepts of family and social class. In the prefigurative construction of their controlling metaphors culminating in their apocalyptic resolutions, Dickens's *David Copperfield* and George Eliot's *The Mill on the Floss* are nearly identical in both structure and theme. Four-fifths of the way through each of these novels, the controlling imagery—of shipwreck in *David Copperfield* and of flood in *The Mill on the Floss*—builds to a violent apocalyptic scene which sweeps away all pretense of human control, free will, aspiration and redemption to leave its victims either physically or spiritually dead to the world around them.

In both novels, when the apocalyptic event subsides, the victims who have been swept away in the grip of its terrible force wash up upon a desolate beach of the sort repeatedly described in the poems of Matthew Arnold as representations of the moral desolation of the Victorian world (compare "Dover Beach," and "To Marguerite"). For Steerforth, Ham, and David (who powerless looks on), the desolation of the apocalyptic shipwreck is complete, offers only the waxen after-image of human beings shipwrecked, drowned and washed up on the beach like the broken spars and shattered hulls of fragile barks caught in the violent maelstrom of their emotional lives in an unemotional age. David is their witness, the failed salvager of the moral shipwreck of his age. He can only stand by and claim the corpses once the apocalypse has spun its victims through its vortex.

The flood in *The Mill on the Floss* and the shipwreck near the end of *David Copperfield* are the inevitable deconstructions of fragile, ill-designed, morally shaky worlds. Maggie Tulliver is a flirt, but her flirtations with the men in her life are nothing in comparison to her flirtation with the narrow catwalks of Victorian morality. When she repeatedly walks too near the edge in her sexual flirtations, it becomes inevitable that she must slip and be swept away. When Steerforth plots a course that not only ignores the charted meridians of Victorian morality but also the chartings of Victorian social class, then it becomes inevitable that he too will run aground.

Where Landow sees shipwrecks as images of crisis, in the Dickens canon shipwrecks go beyond crisis to become metaphors for the apocalyptic destruction of the past, of a life, of a society, of a relationship, of a world, of the *status quo*, or of a preconceived illusion. Dickens methodically prepares the reader for each apocalyptic moment. Meticulously he constructs his pattern of shipwreck imagery, often, as is the case in *David Copperfield* and as is the case, as well, with George Eliot's river imagery in *The Mill on the Floss*, from the very first page of the text, until at the crucial moment he employs a full-blown shipwreck (or laces some plot event so strongly with shipwreck imagery that the analogy is unmistakable) to show the total destruction of the world of the characters and of the novel. He then proceeds to attempt to salvage what can be salvaged from the apocalypse, but most often he proves a failed salvager, a mere beach-bound observer forced to collect the flotsam and jetsam of that wrecked world when it washes up on the desolate beach. The image of the shipwrecked world of Dickens' later, "dark novels" (Stevenson, 398) is a particularly modernist image which foreshadows the empty visions of later Victorian novels such as *The Mill on the Floss* and Thomas Hardy's *Jude the Obscure* as well as the twentieth-century wasteland world of T. S. Eliot.

"I was born with a caul," David, the hero of his own life, announces on the first page of his autobiography. What is interesting, however, is that he goes on to tell how his caul "was advertised for sale, in the newspapers, at the low price of fifteen guineas," because "among sea-going people" (Ch. 1) birth cauls are a good-luck charm against drowning. Thus, from page one of *David Copperfield* the shipwreck imagery is in place.

The shipwreck imagery of *David Copperfield* takes a number of different forms to serve a number of different purposes, all of which ultimately converge to form the texture of tone and theme which culminates in the apocalyptic shipwreck off the beach at Yarmouth. For example, throwaway references to shipwrecks and shipwreck lore surface frequently in offhand conversations. At the very beginning of the famous "Brooks of Sheffield" conversation between Murdstone and his cronies, one of the gentlemen asks, after Murdstone has introduced his soon-to-be stepson as Davy, "Davy who? . . . Jones?" (Ch. 2). Later, when David is being encouraged to study law at Doctor's Commons in London, Steerforth defines "ecclesiastical law" as "about people's wills and people's marriages, and disputes about ships and boats." David thinks that Steerforth's definition is preposterous: "Nonsense, Steerforth! . . . You don't mean to say that there is any affinity between nautical matters and ecclesiastical matters?'' (Ch. 23). This seemingly offhand comment becomes highly ironic in the light of the novel's later developments. David will, indeed, find himself right in the middle of a distressing situation involving marriages and boats.

As are many of his predecessors in the Dickens canon such as young Martin Chuzzlewit and Tom Pinch and Sol Gills and Walter Gay, David Copperfield is well versed in the literature of shipwreck at a very early age. To escape the oppressive presence of Murdstone, young David retires to "that blessed little room" where from his father's books "Roderick Random, Peregrine Pickle, Humphrey Clinker, Tom Jones, the Vicar of Wakefield, Don Quixote, Gil Blas, and Robinson Crusoe, came out, a glorious host, to keep me company.'' He goes on to describe how "I had a greedy relish for a few volumes of Voyages and Travels . . . the perfect realization of Captain Somebody, of the Royal British Navy, in danger of being beset by savages, and resolved to sell his life at a great price'' (Ch. 4).

The imagery of shipwreck, however, serves a more serious purpose when it begins to function prefiguratively in reference to Steerforth's ultimate fate. As David and Steerforth approach the Peggotty houseboat for the first time, Steerforth remarks on the setting: "Dismal enough in the dark . . . and the sea roars as if it were hungry for us'' (Ch. 21). Later that same evening, "Steerforth told a story of a dismal shipwreck (which arose out of his talk with Mr.Peggotty) as if he saw it all before him—and little Em'ly's eyes were fastened on him all the time, as if she saw it too'' (Ch. 21). This passage carries the irony of prefiguration one step further than it usually goes. Both Steerforth and Em'ly are actually seeing their own fates, the shipwrecks of their lives in future time. The irony of prefiguration is generally not understood by either character or reader until after the prefigured event has occurred, but in this case the tone is so ominous that the characters and the readers are apprised of the connection between shipwrecks and their futures. David the narrator warned his readers of the irony of prefiguration earlier when he cryptically intruded into his narrative with this ominous flash forward: "would it have been better for little Em'ly to have had the waters close above her head that morning in my sight . . .'' (Ch. 3).

These three different functions of shipwreck reference in *David Copperfield*—offhand conversational reference, familiarity with shipwreck literature, ironic prefiguration of shipwreck disaster—are, however, only secondary functions of the shipwreck imagery of the novel. The primary function of that shipwreck imagery prior to the ultimate apocalypse is as the controlling metaphor which defines the Yarmouth houseboat world of the Peggottys. The Peggotty houseboat sits on "the dull waste" (Ch. 3) between the sea and the river at Yarmouth. As David is introduced to the various members of the household, Mr. Peggotty regales him with the past history of the place and its former inhabitants, a number of whom are "Drowndead" (Ch. 3). Perhaps David should have kept his "caul" instead of selling it. Perhaps if he had, he might have been more successful in rescuing his loved ones from the fate of being "Drowndead."

What the Peggotty's have managed is the ramshackle construction of a positive alternative world in the midst of the wasteland world of Victorian life. They have moored a fragile bark in the destructive element. That positive world, however, is vulnerable from the moment David first comes on board: "I'm afraid of the sea," little Em'ly tells David, "I have seen it tear a boat as big as our house all to pieces" (Ch. 3). In *David Copperfield*, Dickens employs different metaphors for the different worlds of the novel much as he did to underline the oppositions between the Fagin world and the Brownlow world in *Oliver Twist*. The Yarmouth world of the Peggottys is a fragile world existing always under the threat of shipwreck whereas the world of the city and David's illusory romantic life with Dora is a world of fairy tale enchantment. As David lies in bed in the houseboat, "instead of thinking that the sea might rise in the night and float the boat away, I thought of the sea that had risen, since I last heard those sounds, and drowned my happy home" (Ch. 10). When David, after Em'ly has eloped with Steerforth, asks "Will you desert the old boat, Mr. Peggotty?" that worthy answers in almost exactly the same shipwreck terms which David used earlier in reference to his first home. "My station, Mas'r Davy," he returned, "ain't there no longer; and if ever a boat foundered, since there was darkness on the face of the deep, that one's gone down. But no, sir, no; I doen't mean as it should be deserted" (Ch. 32).

All of these associative images of shipwreck define the fragility of the familial Peggotty world in the exploitative sea of Victorian life which makes drifting castaways of every individual. All of those different shipwreck analogies converge in the final apocalyptic event which defines the novel's central theme of the individual's isolation and utter helplessness in the maelstrom of a destructive world gone mad. The storm, the shipwreck, the rescue attempts, the powerlessness of the onlookers not only comprise one of Dickens' most memorable *tour-de-force* action scenes, but also offer an elaborate metaphor for man's struggle to survive, to contribute morally, to affirm existence in the face of an unnatural, anti-existential world whose power dooms him ultimately to fail. It is a sisyphean scene of struggle, rebellion against a malevolent nature and ultimate, ever predictable, defeat. It is also one of the finest examples in the Dickens canon of the working of the alchemic imagination, the transfiguration of common knowledge into social myth.

The shipwreck apocalypse begins:

> I now approach an event in my life, so indelible, so awful, so bound by an infinite variety of ties to all that has preceded it, in these pages, that, from the beginning of my narrative, I have seen it growing larger and larger as I advanced, like a great tower in the plain, and throwing its fore-cast shadow even on the incidents of my childish days."[3]

(Ch. 55)

Thus David, the narrator, and Dickens, the meta-narrator within David the narrator, begin the shipwreck apocalypse of *David Copperfield*. That opening passage is one of those instances sprinkled throughout his fiction in which Dickens either loses control or intentionally intrudes to explain what he has been doing throughout the construction of his self-reflexive text. That passage is David (and Dickens) forcibly clasping the reader by the lapels and barking into his face, "Here it comes! Pay close attention!"

For David, the up-coming shipwreck is "an event in my life . . . so awful" that it throws a "shadow over my childish days." But for Dickens it is the culmination of the structuring of his text, "indelible . . . bound by an infinite variety of ties to all that has preceded it, in these pages . . . from the beginning of my narrative." For David it is a culminating event in a life, but for Dickens it is the climax of a text, a word construct, "these pages." As meta-fictionist, he defines the upcoming shipwreck as a rhetorical event, not a human event. It is a language apocalypse prepared for "from the beginning of my narrative" and "growing larger and larger as I advanced" and meticulously "fore-cast" throughout the writer's rhetorical construction of his text.

Thus begins Dickens' most memorable shipwreck narrative in a most uncharacteristic manner. The attention is deliberately diverted from the introduction of the shipwreck as event and directed toward Dickens' self-reflexive consciousness of the shipwreck as culmination of the rhetorical structure of his text. In doing this, Dickens is making sure that his readers are aware of the text/sub-text nature of David's narrative. *David Copperfield* is a novel about navigating and surviving the shoals of Victorian life, but it is also a novel about charting the voyage through a sea of words and the perils the writer must face before reaching the safe harbor of white at "The End" of his voyage. The very length and uncharacteristically parenthetical nature of that introductory passage underlines the clear distinction Dickens is making between David's interests in the upcoming scene and Dickens' interests in it as a culmination of his stylistic image patterning and word structuring. For David the text is an attempt to justify himself as "the hero of my own life," (Ch. 1), but, as this cunningly chosen moment of self-reflexive intrusion shows, the sub-text is Dickens' own attempt to justify the writer's art as equally heroic. For Dickens the meta-narrator, the ability to create a compelling and meaningful text out of a sea of words is heroic, not in a Carlylean sense of the writer as hero, but in the Dickensian sense of imaginative alchemy as heroism.

To Dickens the meta-fictionist's credit, he, after this initial single paragraph of sub-text intrusion, immediately relinquishes the stage to his primary text narrator, but the layered identity of this crucial scene has been established. From this sub-text intrusive opening, the scene moves back into David's voice. The reader, however, has been alerted to listen to what the waves are saying beneath the surface of that primary text voice. For example, the shipwreck is described by David as a lasting "association between it and a stormy wind, or the lightest mention of a sea-shore, as strong as any of which my mind is conscious. As plainly as I behold what happened, I will try to write it down." As the evidence of his whole canon demonstrates, the fact and the symbolic possibility of shipwreck is certainly an "association . . . as strong as any of which" Dickens the novelist's "mind is conscious." The strength of that association surfaces in all the outlets of his writing from the journalism to the novels. But Dickens' interest is that of an alchemic writer, not merely the chronicler that David claims to be when he says "as plainly as I behold what happened, I will try to write it down." Dickens' shipwreck association becomes an elaborate trope throughout his whole canon, an ongoing representation of his vision of man's relationship to the turbulent and treacherous Victorian world. But that shipwreck association also forms an elaborate trope within this most graphic of Dickens' shipwreck scenes.

Throughout this shipwreck scene, beginning with his sub-text intrusive opening, Dickens forms an elaborate imagery of apocalypse, of the storm at sea and the wrecking of the ship, and the sea's destruction of human life as representative of the manner in which the Victorian social process has plunged human values into depths of darkness, has ripped asunder Victorian moral life. While this apocalyptic shipwreck is occurring, the writer can only stand upon the beach and describe the destruction. This shipwreck scene in *David Copperfield* is, on the level of his metafictional sub-text, a grudging admission of the writer's relative helplessness in the face of the terrible problems in his society, in the face of the rapidly deteriorating "Condition of England." From this point on in his canon, Dickens will portray in increasingly desolate terms the manner in which the Victorian social process batters and drowns the better nature, the best intentions, the romantic dreams of the individual. In the shipwreck scene of *David Copperfield* Dickens presents his first and most violent (as well as most passionately constructed) of a series of apocalyptic nightmares imaging the fragility and moral desolation of Victorian society.

The oft-repeated word in Dickens' violent description of the sea off Yarmouth is the adjective "great." In the sub-text intrusive opening of the scene, the impending shipwreck is an event which the text is moving toward "like a great tower in a plain." When David actually confronts the storm, the wind is rising with "an extraordinary great sound" and "it blew great guns" tearing "great sheets of lead" off of the church tower and plucking "great trees . . . out of the earth." The storm is acknowledged by all to be "the greatest ever known to blow upon that coast" and brings upon the world "a great darkness." The storm batters the foundered ship with "great waves" and the misery and desolation of the people on shore forced to watch helplessly as this violent destruction takes place is expressed first by "a great cry" and then by "another great cry of pity from the beach." Finally, Ham and Steerforth are "beaten to death by the great wave" and Dickens' first major, exterior world, apocalypse is complete.

This repeated magnification of the power of a mad nature as well as the magnification of human misery and helplessness in the face of that power signals Dickens' heightened consciousness. This pivotal point in his writing career and in this most introspective and self-reflexive of all his books, illustrates the breaking up of his world, the shipwreck of the light, humorous, sentimental, and hopeful world of Pickwick, the Brownlows, Tom Pinch, and even Little Nell. In the novels of his youth, apocalypse had taken the form of individual failures, individual deaths, individual betrayals and suicides and temptations, but in *David Copperfield* Dickens finds in his imagery of shipwreck a trope for superseding small personal desolations and representing the apocalyptic desolation of the whole Victorian world.

Aside from this repeated rhetoric of magnification, the shipwreck scene develops an elaborate language of apocalypse to describe the breaking up of both David's and Dickens' world. This language pattern develops throughout the shipwreck passage in terms of three imagistic motifs: first, the descent into the void of the underworld; second, nature going utterly mad and thus reshaping itself; and third, the abstract (as opposed to the quite realistic aspect of the first two motifs) image, inserted by David the writer standing helpless on the shore of the whole event, of a dark tower looming over his life.

When the storm first breaks upon David in the coach traveling to Yarmouth, the clouds have "depths below them to the bottom of the deepest hollows in the earth, through which the wild moon seemed to plunge headlong." The waves offshore rise "above the rolling abyss . . . as if the least would engulf the town." The biggest waves seem "to scoop out deep caves in the beach, as if its purpose were to undermine the earth." Some violent waves "dashed themselves to pieces before they reached the land, every fragment of the late whole seemed possessed . . . rushing to be gathered to the composition of another monster." The storm, the raging sea, the terrible dilemma of the sailors, the terrible frustration of those watching from the shore is imaged as a descent into a hallucinatory, shape-shifting underworld, into a "black void."

The second motif, that of nature gone mad in the throes of apocalypse, represents the world as losing its shape and re-forming into other monsters and grotesque shapes. The waves "plunge headlong, as if in a dread disturbance of the laws of nature" and "every shape tumultuously rolled on, as soon as made, to change its shape and place and beat another shape and place away . . . the clouds fell fast and thick; I seemed to see a rending and upheaving of all nature." This shape-shifting demolition of all of nature and its laws mirrors the confusion and turmoil in David's mind as he observes the shipwreck of his world. "I had lost the clear arrangement of time and distance," David admits. "Something within me, faintly answering to the storm without, tossed up the depths of my memory and made a tumult of them." The storm's rending and upheaval of the natural world is directly equated with the upheaval of David's unconscious mind. Figuratively and psychologically, David is caught in the undertow and dashed in the surf of the shipwreck of the world of the Peggottys just as Ham and Steerforth are battered and killed by the storm's real waves.

The third motif which makes up the language of apocalypse in this passage belongs to the self-reflexive sub-text which was introduced in the opening paragraph of the chapter. That motif, of looming dark towers, begins with the doubled narrator's characterization of the real shipwreck and the writing of the shipwreck scene as "growing larger and larger as I advanced like a great tower in a plain." The same monstrous waves which created the "abyss," the "black void," and rended and reshaped the natural world in the first two apocalyptic motifs are, in this third abstract motif, "like glimpses of another shore with towers and buildings." As the sea pounds itself into grotesque shape after shape, this "ideal shore on the horizon, with its towers and buildings, rose and fell."

The "tower in the plain," the towers on that "ideal shore," are images intrusively inserted by Dickens the sub-text writer. Sentimentally, from his position of frustrated helplessness as mere observer and recorder of the shipwreck of Victorian life, he stands on the shore watching the world pound itself apart and longs to pass through that metaphoric turmoil to a safer world on the other side where the tower seems to offer shelter. But the sub-text narrator quickly realizes that his metaphoric ideal world is but a fluttering mirage compared to the reality of storm and shipwreck. The sub-text narrator returns to the "dark gloom of my solitary chamber," moves inside to escape the buffeting of the real world and, entering the world of dreams, reaches his tower on the other side of the raging sea. But that tower offers no solace to the shipwrecked wordman. Idealized sentimentality in the context of the apocalyptic shipwreck of Victorian society is immediately rejected by the writer's unconscious. Fleeing from "the black void" of the storm, the wordman falls "off a tower and down a precipice—into the depths of sleep." The apocalyptic descent into the abyss of the real external world cannot be avoided by flight into any seemingly secure and safe inner world of the imagination. The same "depths" wait for the writer within himself. Though only an observer, he is still a participant in the inevitable shipwreck of his society.

This elaborate construct of a language of apocalypse in the shipwreck scene culminates in a return to a succession of sublime words of magnification and disbelief. Near the end of the passage, the storm becomes "infinitely more terrific," the waves beat each other to pieces "in interminable hosts," and the whole world is thrown into "unspeakable confusion" by "a violence quite inconceivable." It is a language of sublimity consciously employed in series to magnify the apocalyptic destructiveness of the storm. What is happening to the world in this shipwreck scene, both the Yarmouth world of David and the Victorian world of the sub-text intrusive Dickens, has overreached the normal articulative power of words. Thus, the sub-text observer/writer is frustrated in yet another way. The apocalyptic desolation of his world has gone so far with such violence that he can no longer even describe it, much less do anything about it; he simply hasn't powerful enough words at his disposal and he must resort to words of indeterminate magnification, meaningless words such as "infinitely," "unspeakable," and "inconceivable."

But the sub-text narrator is not alone in his utter helplessness. In the real shipwreck of the primary text, the waves rolling over the foundering ship "carried men, spars, casks, planks, bulwarks, heaps of such toys, into the boiling surge." Caught in the shipwreck of Victorian life, the writer, all men, are but "toys" helpless in the grip of the dehumanized, materialistic surge.

The shipwreck scene from *David Copperfield* ends with the whole community standing upon the shore watching the ship go down:

> I found bewailing women whose husbands were away in herring or oyster boats, which there was too much reason to think might have foundered before they could run in anywhere for safety. Grizzled old sailors were among the people, shaking their heads, as they looked from water to sky, and muttering to one another; ship-owners, excited and uneasy; children, huddling together, and peering into older faces; even stout mariners, disturbed and anxious, leveling their glasses at the sea from behind places of shelter, as if they were surveying an enemy.

The whole community, from the "bewailing women" to the "old sailors" to "ship-owners" to "children" to "stout mariners," is out to bear witness to this shipwreck, to join David the narrator and Dickens the meta-narrator as they stand helplessly on the shore observing the apocalypse. All segments of society, every gender and generation is represented. This tableau of the shipwreck scene is perfect for the articulation of the point that Dickens, with his doubled narrator, is intent upon making. The whole community, all of Yarmouth society, stands and watches as the world falls apart before its eyes. The whole community, including especially the writer, stand helpless on the shore as their world deconstructs.

In *Bleak House* the same type of sub-text intrusive scene occurs when Poor Jo dies. In that novel, the sub-text intrusive meta-narrator lets out an apocalyptic howl that can be heard to the top of the steeple of St. Paul's:

> Dead, Your Majesty. Dead, my lords and gentlemen. Dead, Right Reverends and Wrong Reverends of every order. Dead, men and women, born with heavenly compassion in your hearts. And dying thus around us every day.
>
> (Ch. 47)

In both *David Copperfield* and *Bleak House*, when the moment arrives when the sub-text narrator, the author himself feeling the frustration of his own helplessness, must speak out in his own intrusive voice about the deconstruction of the world which he has been trying so hard to order, the whole community bears witness to both the apocalypse and the writer's frustrated helplessness (which the community must share) in the face of that apocalypse.

The role of David in the shipwreck scene is the role of the writer in relation to the events of history, the role of a bystander on the shore forced to watch

as the sea of life pounds all around, the role of trying to order the chaos of
nature and salvage some hope from that chaos. In *David Copperfield*, there
is little hope to be salvaged. At the end of that shipwreck scene, the Peggotty
family's boathouse (like the House of Dombey and the two houses of *Bleak
House*) is directly compared to the shipwreck which has occurred offshore:

> But, he led me to the shore. And on that part of it where she and I had looked
> for shells, two children—on that part of it where some lighter fragments of the
> old boat, blown down last night, had been scattered by the wind—among the
> ruins of the home he had wronged—I saw him lying with his head upon his
> arm, as I had often seen him lie at school!

David's past, David's home, David's friend, all have been wrecked and cast
back up on the shore in fragments which cannot be re ordered, given new
life. For both David the narrator and Dickens the meta-narrator all that remains
is post-apocalyptic desolation.

"I went away from England," David writes of his life after shipwreck,
"not knowing, even then, how great the shock was that I had to bear. . . .
As a man upon a field of battle will receive a mortal hurt, and scarcely know
that he is struck, so I, when I was left alone with my undisciplined heart, had
no conception of the wound with which it had to strive" (Ch. 58). David
wanders Europe in a state of shock like Byron's Childe Harold, but gradually
the "desolate feeling with which I went abroad, deepened and widened
hourly." This feeling of post-apocalyptic desolation begins as "a heavy share
of loss and sorrow" but by "imperceptible degrees, it became a hopeless
consciousness of all that I had lost—love, friendship, interest; of all that had
been shattered—my first trust, my first affection, the whole airy castle of my
life; of all that remained—a ruined blank and waste, lying wide around me,
unbroken, to the dark horizon" (Ch. 58). After the shipwreck of his world,
David is marooned in a hopeless, dark wasteland where, if he wanders around
a while, he will probably meet characters out of the poetry of Matthew Arnold
and T. S. Eliot.

V. THE SHIPWRECK OF INDUSTRIAL REVOLUTION AND POLITICAL REVOLUTION: *HARD TIMES* AND *A TALE OF TWO CITIES*

Every novel in the Dickens canon which follows this apocalyptic shipwreck
in *David Copperfield* builds toward a similar apocalyptic event. In *Bleak
House*, Lady Dedlock will be cast adrift, with Inspector Bucket and Esther
Summerson trying to salvage her. In *Hard Times*, the imagery of shipwreck

takes a different, more abstract, apocalyptic turn. W. W. Watt describes the style of *Hard Times* as Dickens' employment of a "symbolic shorthand" (Watt, xxxii).

The major "symbolic shorthand" of *Hard Times* is a hard, metallic imagery of machines and the dehumanization into machines of so many of the characters in the novel. However, working in parallel with this mid-century Victorian imagery of the Industrial Revolution is an eighteenth-century imagery of shipwreck. The same imagistic parallelism occurs in *Dombey and Son* where the controlling imagery of shipwreck is paralleled by the imagery of the acquisitive and destructive, ultimately apocalyptic, railway which gobbles up land and buildings and, finally, men. For Dickens, the modern analog to his favorite shipwreck imagery is the imagery of the dehumanizing shipwreck of English life which the Industrial Revolution is causing. That shipwreck is best represented by machines, the most prominent of which and the most available to Dickens' alchemic imagination was the railway train.

But the shipwreck imagery is perhaps a clearer example of Dickens' quicker-hitting, more instantly expressive shorthand style in *Hard Times*. Images of shipwreck are employed in a much less elaborate and calculated fashion than they are, for example, in *Dombey and Son* and *David Copperfield*. They function as an isolated simile or metaphor which, however, serves a dualistic symbolic purpose. On one level, shipwreck similes describe the psychic dislocation and loss occasioned by the loveless marriage of Louisa Gradgrind and Bounderby coupled with Louisa's adulterous attraction to James Harthouse. On another level, however, that same shipwreck simile images the apocalyptic desolation of Thomas Gradgrind Senior's philosophic vision of the Victorian world.

Thus, in *Hard Times*, the shipwreck imagery is not a controlling motif, prepared for from the very beginning, as it is in *David Copperfield*. Instead, it functions as a crucial metaphor at a climactic moment. Louisa Gradgrind, as was little Em'ly, has been seduced by a slick urban drifter like Steerforth. Harthouse has the same type of two syllable symbolic name as Steerforth and is also a yachtsman. Almost by reflex, Dickens represents the breakup of Louisa's world by turning to the shipwreck metaphor that appeared in so many of his earlier novels.

While these isolated shipwreck similes function on dual levels, the level of moral plot and the level of philosophic theme, they also consistently fulfill three ascending sub-functions. First, characters such as James Harthouse, in both their physical and moral existences, are defined through the use of shipwreck images. Second, shipwreck similes define the relationship of one character to another; for example, Harthouse to Louisa Gradgrind. Thirdly, shipwreck similes and metaphors expand and define the world of the novel in which these characters live and act.[4]

Shipwreck images serve as a commentary upon the relationship between James Harthouse and Louisa Gradgrind. These images generally appear at the end of a passage which describes the physical and/or moral makeup of a character or they appear as a kind of marginal iteration taking the form of an appropriately placed running headline.

After Harthouse has insinuated himself into the Bounderby household and "established a confidence" with Louisa, the narrator pauses briefly to describe him:

> . . . he had not, even now, any earnest wickedness of purpose in him. Publicly and privately, it were much better for the age in which he lived, that he and the legion of whom he was one were designedly bad, than indifferent and purposeless. It is the drifting icebergs setting with any current anywhere, that wreck the ships.
>
> (2.8)

The description's culminating metaphor sets Harthouse's character. He is an aimless, "drifting" man who reads a few blue books in order to gain the patronage of the "hard facts" men of the Gradgrind school. He is a man who projects a smooth and placid surface personality, but who is, beneath the surface, a completely impersonal opportunist. The image, however, also foreshadows the serious danger of his relationship with Louisa. Finally, this image shows Harthouse as an emblem of the moral shipwreck of the age; an age in which men indifferently follow their own inclinations no matter what harm their actions might cause to the lives of other people.

The proof of Dickens' conscious use of the imagery of shipwreck as an indicator of the result of the extramarital love relationship between Harthouse and Louisa can be found in the running headlines Dickens appended to Chapter 12 of Book Two of *Hard Times*. On the night of her meeting with Harthouse during her husband's absence, a meeting witnessed by Mrs. Sparsit, Louisa flees through a driving storm to her father. As she sinks in his arms, she begs him to save her, and the scene ends with Thomas Gradgrind looking at "the pride of his heart and the triumph of his system, lying, an insensible heap, at his feet" (2.12). The running headline that Dickens appended to this page of *Hard Times*, "Shipwrecked," refers to the condition of both father and daughter. Louisa, because of her love for Harthouse, a love which can bring her nothing but ruin, has been cast adrift in the world. She can't return to a husband she despises nor can she accept an immoral relationship with the man she loves. "She has suffered the wreck of her whole life upon a rock" (3.1).

For Thomas Gradgrind, the broken and insensible heap which lies before him symbolizes the shipwreck of his whole philosophy of life. In this pivotal scene, the shipwreck metaphor which images Louisa's personal dislocation and desolation also images the apocalyptic desolation of her father's intellectually constructed and rationally navigable world. The other running headline that appears in this chapter, the "Great Failure of the House of Gradgrind," is reminiscent of the failure of another great house, the house of Dombey, which also failed because of a shipwreck caused by the obstinacy and insensitivity of its proprietor, its Captain. That running headline is also prefigurative of the apocalyptic fall of the House of Clennam in *Little Dorrit*. In all three cases, the houses that fall, the worlds that are shipwrecked, are steered on to the rocks because their Captains are navigating by maps drawn from social illusions and dehumanizing philosophies which lack the lighthouses of compassion, imagination, and love.

Ironically, the shipwrecks which occur in *Dombey and Son, Hard Times*, and *Little Dorrit*, the apocalyptic breaking up of their flawed worlds, prove to be the ultimate salvation for both captain and crew (excepting, of course, the fanatic Mrs. Clennam, who goes down with her ship as does Captain Ahab in *Moby Dick*). Only after the great houses of Dombey and Gradgrind have fallen can these two men realize the error of their similarly fanatic philosophies of life, and through that realization, in both cases accomplished by a loving but rejected daughter, open themselves for the first time to love. Dickens shows Louisa at the moment of personal shipwreck and her father at the moment of the shipwreck of his philosophic world, but those moments of shipwreck also prove to be the first step in the process of their salvation.

The concentrated metaphorical explosion of shipwreck imagery at this crucial moment in *Hard Times* is much in keeping with the extreme differentness of conception and style of *Hard Times* from the three longer novels—*Dombey and Son, David Copperfield, Bleak House*—which immediately precede it in the Dickens canon. Shipwreck imagery as isolated metaphor representing the apocalyptic desolation of the lives and worlds of Harthouse, Louisa and Thomas Gradgrind Senior is not, however, introduced completely unannounced at this crucial scene. Early in the novel Louisa and Sissy Jupe talk about their problems with "statistics" which form the basic subject matter of McChoakumchild's curriculum and are the cornerstone of Thomas Gradgrind's blue-book philosophy of life and society:

"Statistics," said Louisa.

"Yes, Miss Louisa—they always remind me of stutterings, and that's another of my mistakes—of accidents upon the sea. And I find (Mr. M'Choakumchild said) that in a given time a hundred thousand persons went to sea on long voyages, and only five hundred of them were drowned or burnt to death. What is the percentage? And I said, Miss," here Sissy fairly sobbed as confessing with extreme contrition to her greatest error; "I said it was nothing."

"Nothing, Sissy?"

"Nothing, Miss—to the relations and friends of the people who were killed. . . ."

(3.9)

In light of the sudden accretion of shipwreck images around the moment of the "Great Failure of the House of Gradgrind" later, the early association of statistics to shipwrecks becomes highly ironic. The reef upon which Gradgrind's philosophy of life runs aground is the jagged pile of cold numbers, blue books, and statistical abstractions toward which he constantly steers. In Sissy's mind, statistics and shipwrecks go together but mean nothing because statistics cannot take into account the human suffering caused by a shipwreck. That is why the house of Gradgrind, like the house of Atreus, the house of Dombey, and the house of Sutpen, is doomed to wreck because it fails to navigate by the heart as well as the head.

At the beginning of another earlier scene, a similar confrontation in which Louisa announces to her father her decision to marry Bounderby, the imagery of shipwreck metaphorically sets the situation. Louisa, facing her father, "sat looking at him fixedly" and "was impelled to throw herself upon his breast, and give him the pent-up confidences of her heart." But Thomas Gradgrind is utterly oblivious to the emotional uncertainty and terror which his daughter feels at the prospect of this marriage. Gradgrind sees nothing because

to see it he must have overleaped at a bound the artificial barriers he had for many years been erecting, between himself and all those subtle essences of humanity which will elude the utmost cunning of algebra until the last trumpet ever to be sounded shall blow even algebra to wreck.

(1.25)

In this zany mixed metaphor, the "last trumpet" becomes a wind which blows that sturdy ship "algebra to wreck." This zany metaphor, however, rather clearly prefigures the crucial confrontation scene at the end of the novel when the shipwreck imagery bursts out. It predicts that Gradgrind will never be capable of understanding or establishing any relationship with his daughter until his whole algebraic vision of the world has been wrecked.

This early confrontation ends with Louisa realizing that her father is not capable of seeing into the turmoil of her heart; "and the moment shot away into the plumbless depths of the past to mingle with all the lost opportunities that are drowned there" (1.15). Louisa's hope that her father might understand and tell her not to marry Bounderby is drowned in Gradgrind's indifference and the course is set for the rocks upon which both daughter's and father's lives will be wrecked.

The third participant in the shipwreck of the "Great House of Gradgrind," James Harthouse (though he is at one time described as the iceberg upon which the family wrecks), is also a hopeless victim of the metaphorical shipwreck just as Steerforth was the victim of the real shipwreck off Yarmouth in *David Copperfield*. When Louisa flees to her father and collapses "Ship-wrecked" as the running headline characterizes the scene, she is not only rejecting her husband, Bounderby, but also her would-be adulterous lover, Harthouse. When Harthouse receives the news of this rejection, he reacts metaphorically with a description of the state of his own shipwreck. "The drowning man catches at the straw," Harthouse pleads, "I cling to the belief that there is yet hope that I am not condemned to perpetual exile from that lady's presence" (3.2). Harthouse, like Steerforth, is not the malevolent moustachioed villain of Victorian melodrama, but merely an aimless, careless (in his morality) man like the "drifting icebergs . . . that wreck the ships" as he is described earlier in the novel. When Louisa rejects him as well as Bounderby, he becomes a "drowning man" clinging to a spar adrift in the vast emptiness of the Victorian social world.

In *Hard Times* the shipwreck imagery is used in a different manner for different purposes. No longer is it a controlling symbolic pattern in both the language and the plot action of the novel as was its function in both *Dombey and Son* and *David Copperfield*. In *Hard Times* the imagery of apocalyptic shipwreck is employed in two ways, as isolated simile/metaphor and as marginal running headline, for two similar purposes: first, to figuratively emphasize moments of apocalyptic desolation for both the characters and the world of the novel and, second, to give visual emphasis in the margins of those pages upon which those scenes of personal and philosophic apocalypse appear. On the stage of *Hard Times* the imagery of shipwreck plays a supporting role, only coming on at crucial moments in the play to deliver its isolated apocalyptic lines which give metaphoric emphasis to the event.

In *A Tale of Two Cities*, however, Dickens' imagery of shipwreck moves back to center stage mainly because *A Tale of Two Cities* is set in an eighteenth-century past where the imagery of ships is much more appropriate than the mechanistic imagery of the Industrial Revolution. George P. Landow in *Images of Crisis* asserts: "With the French Revolution, perhaps the central event of modern history, the imagination of Europe, now politicized in an entirely new way, had changed forever" (23). In noting the use of images of storm and shipwreck to analogize revolution in novels such as George Eliot's *Felix Holt*, Elizabeth Gasksill's *North and South* and, of course, Dickens' *A Tale of Two Cities*, Landow scolds that "participants in the French Revolution, and not nineteenth-century authors, invented this representation of the masses as a raging ocean that sweeps all before it" (114).

Landow's disinterest in the metaphorical applications of images of shipwreck in these novels is understandable because he is not interested in shipwreck as metaphor but is interested in shipwreck as myth. For Landow, when "certain basic structures function as cultural codes that communicate culturally relevant information, one can begin to construct an archaeology of imagination" (15). Landow is interested in unearthing the origins of shipwreck imagery with a focus upon Christian mythology whereas the Dickens critic avoids archaeology for the study of the alchemy of imagination. Nowhere in Dickens' canon is the alchemy of imagination more powerfully at work upon the metaphor of shipwreck than in *A Tale of Two Cities*.

In keeping with the gravity of its subject matter, the French Revolution, *A Tale of Two Cities* moves the shipwreck metaphor back to center stage from its supporting role as an off-stage voice functioning as part of the "symbolic shorthand" of *Hard Times*. In *A Tale of Two Cities* the shipwreck imagery never takes objective form as it does in the very real shipwrecks of *Dombey and Son* and *David Copperfield*, nor does it burst out at crucial times with off-stage crescendoes of analogic metaphor as in *Hard Times*. Rather, the shipwreck imagery in *A Tale of Two Cities* functions as pure metaphor, an image pattern shaping itself in the mind of an omniscient narrator intent upon describing the apocalypse of revolution. As the omniscient narrator's principal analogic tool, the shipwreck metaphor functions in the same two ways that it functioned in *David Copperfield*: first, as a metaphoric pattern of ominous prefiguration of storm and impending shipwreck as the central characters are magnetically "Drawn to the Loadstone Rock" as the title of Book 2, Chapter 24 of *A Tale of Two Cities* augurs; and second, as pure metaphor (as opposed to the objective metaphor of event in *David Copperfield*) of the apocalypse of revolution.

In other words, the French Revolution becomes the event over which the apocalyptic metaphor of shipwreck is laid as it was sin the objective shipwreck scene in *David Copperfield* and in the simultaneous emotional shipwrecks of daughter and father in *Hard Times*. In *A Tale of Two Cities*, the metaphor of apocalypse has moved out of the microcosmic existential realm into a macrocosmic political realm. The shipwreck metaphor embodies the actual destruction of a world, not a personal family world, but a whole nation, a whole society, a way of life.

The imagery of shipwreck as apocalypse in *A Tale of Two Cities* gathers force in Book 2, Chapter 21 as the French Revolution begins with the storming of the Bastille. The chapter opens with echoes "afar off and scarcely audible" to the Manette household in their quiet house in London. But they are "advancing echoes" occasioning frightening thoughts in the minds of Lucie Manette which "swelled her eyes, and broke like waves" (2.21).[5] The echoes in the chapter opening are the messages of Lucie's husband's past history which form the reefs upon which her family life will run aground while attempting to navigate the storm of the French Revolution. But Lucie is not alone facing the threat of shipwreck. Sydney Carton is "like a boat towed astern" in the great steamship Stryver's wake and because "the boat so favored is usually in a rough plight, and mostly under water, so, Sydney had a swamped life of it." Thus, as the Revolution hovers over their lives, both Lucie Manette and Sydney Carton are already beleagurered and taking on water. Already vulnerable, when the storm of Revolution hits, they will be among the first engulfed.

As the Revolution begins it is described "as of a great storm in France with a dreadful sea rising." When the bloodthirsty residents of the St. Antoine district mount their attack, they are "a whirlpool of boiling waters" that like "the living sea rose, wave on wave, depth on depth, and overflowed the city . . . the sea raging and thundering on its new beach." At the drawbridge to the Bastille, "the raging storm" and "the raging sea," the sea of people caught in the storm of Revolution, takes possession of a single man: "suddenly the sea rose immeasurably wider and higher, and swept DeFarge of the wine-shop over the lowered drawbridge. . . . So resistless was the force of the ocean bearing him on," that he was like a shipwrecked mariner "struggling in the surf at the South Sea."

The metaphor is multi-leveled, holographic. It begins as a storm representing the abstract political concept "Revolution" which blows like a high wind over France, stirring up the waters and giving them force. That abstract metaphorical storm then becomes an objective physical sea of people aroused by that concept into a raging maelstrom. Thus, the metaphor of apocalypse begins with an idea, gives that idea objective physical form, then proceeds to show how that idea brings about the shipwreck of society, the apocalypse out of which a new world must be salvaged. As this chapter proceeds, the idea of Revolution, the storm, is forgotten and only "the living ocean," "the raging flood . . . surging and tossing" remains. The abstract political idea only serves to stir up the angry waves of violence which, once aroused, become a "sea of black and threatening waters, and of destructive upheaving of wave against wave, whose depths were yet unfathomed," a "remorseless sea," an "ocean of forces" so violent that "never did sea roll which bore more memorable wrecks with it." Thus, the central apocalyptic event of the novel, the objective scene of violent Revolution, like the central apocalyptic event of *David Copperfield*, the objective event of a real shipwreck, takes the form of a wind, a storm, arousing the sea which then destroys the previously secure world.

As was the case with Dickens' "symbolic shorthand" in *Hard Times*, at this crucial juncture in the middle of *A Tale of Two Cities* Dickens makes offstage metaphorical statements by means of his chapter and book titles (as he did with his running headlines in *Hard Times*). With Book 2, Chapters 22 and 24, and with the title of Book 3, Dickens' chapter titling manifests a different strategy. All of the chapter titles of Book 1 are nouns preceded by the article "the" denoting the central object of the chapter. All of the chapter titles in Book 2 preceding Chapter 21 (wherein the Revolution begins) are words or phrases objectively descriptive of either the time ("Five Years Later," "Nine Days"), the person ("Monseigneur in Town," "The Honest Tradesman"), or the action ("Congratulatory," "Knitting") of that particular chapter. However, suddenly, at Chapter 22, the titling becomes metaphorical and the metaphor which Dickens chooses is that of an angry sea and an impending shipwreck. Chapter 22 is titled "The Sea Still Rises" which is appropriate because it continues the violent action of Chapter 21 wherein the Revolution began and the raging sea metaphor for the Revolution was introduced. Chapter 24 is also titled metaphorically, but the metaphor has changed as has the time and the omniscient narrator's focus.

Chapter 24 is titled "Drawn to the Loadstone Rock" and begins:

> In such risings of fires and risings of sea, the firm earth shaken by the rushes of an angry ocean which had now no ebb, but was always on the flow, higher and higher, to the terror and wonder of the beholders on the shore—three years of tempest were consumed.
>
> (2.24)

The Revolution has been underway for three years, but for the first time since the apocalyptic metaphor of revolution was introduced three chapters earlier the omniscient narrator shifts focus from the violent events taking place on that raging sea to the "beholders on the shore," to those who, like David Copperfield helplessly watching the shipwreck off Yarmouth, will be greatly affected by this shipwreck of revolution even though they are not on board when it occurs.

The mythic, magnetic title of this chapter, "Drawn to the Loadstone Rock," clearly defines the shipwreck situation of all those characters in the novel who may think themselves safe from the storm and the rising sea of the Revolution, but who nevertheless will be drawn magnetically into its destructive power. Charles Darnay, safe in England, observing the storm of the Revolution from a far shore, is one of those who, like Ham observing the plight of the ship-wrecked mariners in *David Copperfield*, cannot simply look on helplessly from the shore as David did:

> Yes. Like the mariner in the old story, the winds and streams had driven him within the influence of the Loadstone Rock, and it was drawing him to itself, and he must go. Everything that arose before his mind drifted him on, faster and faster, more and more steadily, to the terrible attraction. . . .
> Yes. The Loadstone Rock was drawing him, and he must sail on, until he struck. He knew of no rock; he saw hardly any danger.
>
> (2.24)

Whereas the shipwreck metaphor first embodied the growth of a political idea and the death by drowning of that idea in chaotic, apocalyptic action, here in this last chapter of Book 2 the narrator abandons the macrocosmic overview for the microcosmic focus upon the individual characters whose fragile bark is forced to put off from the safety of the distant shore due to the intervention of a mythic fate. In other words, the shipwreck metaphor no longer represents either a political idea or a violent action, but rather it represents sone of those "cultural codes" or myths which Landow finds the most comforting way of handling shipwreck imagery. Charles (and Lucie, her father, Jenny Crocker, Miss Pross and, of course, Carton) are drawn into the shipwreck of the Revolution as ancient mariners were drawn magnetically, inevitably, to the Loadstone Rock. Whereas in *David Copperfield* Dickens gave Ham a choice as to whether or not he should attempt to rescue Steerforth, Dickens gives Darnay little choice, representing his action, as does George Eliot the action of Maggie Tulliver in *The Mill on the Floss*, as deterministically fated. The whole microcosmic action of *A Tale of Two Cities* is represented as a mythic shipwreck just waiting to happen.

Thus, the macrocosmic world of the French Revolution, a world of political idea and mob action, is imaged as a storm and a raging sea which shipwrecks a whole society while the microcosmic world of the novel is imaged as a doomed ship caught in the mythic, magnetic pull of that Revolution. The title of Book 3, then "The Track of the Storm," ends this complex storm/sea/Loadstone Rock/shipwreck metaphor and turns the novel's focus back upon the political idea of Revolution which earlier had been drowned when the human sea rose out of control. In the crucial center of his novel, Dickens employs the imagery of storm and shipwreck to differentiate between his macrocosmic and microcosmic themes. However, this shipwreck imagery is by no means an intrusion or dramatic assertion for effect as it was in *Hard Times*. The importance of the imagery of shipwreck has been prefigured from the very beginning of the novel.

In fact, throughout the novel, both before this centrally located apocalypse—the storming of the Bastille—and after the Revolution calms to pseudo-legal violence, the shipwreck imagery is always present but functioning in a less apocalyptic manner. Before the storming of the Bastille, the shipwreck imagery, like the river and flood imagery in *The Mill on the Floss*, functions as a prefigurative fate. As in George Eliot's novel, the threat of shipwreck looms over the whole of *A Tale of Two Cities* always directing the reader, as it did in *David Copperfield*, toward the apocalyptic event. That event may be a metaphorical shipwreck of society, as in *A Tale of Two Cities*, or an objective shipwreck, as in *David Copperfield*. When, in each Dickens novel during the latter half of his career, the apocalyptic event occurs, the shipwreck imagery intensifies with elaborate symbolic implication. After the central apocalypse of the storming of the Bastille in *A Tale of Two Cities*, the imagery of shipwreck becomes a vortex which represents the helplessness of the characters who are caught in the pull of its centrifugal force. It is the same sort of vortex which sinks the *Pequod* in Melville's *Moby Dick* and spits out that lone survivor, Ismael. In *A Tale of Two Cities*, the shipwreck of the Revolution draws Lucie Manette and Charles Darnay into its vortex but, like Ismael, they too are spared. Like David Copperfield on the beach at Yarmouth, and Coleridge's Ancient Mariner, they too survive to tell the tale and to live with their own ineffectuality in the face of the shipwreck of their world.

As is the case in both *David Copperfield* and *The Mill on the Floss*, the controlling imagery of *A Tale of Two Cities* is present from the very beginning of the novel. As the Dover Mail struggles up Shooter's Hill, the mist "made its slow way through the air in ripples that visibly followed and overspread one another, as the waves of an unwholesome sea might do" (1.2). Jarvis Lorry and Jerry Cruncher survive the "eddying mist" (1.2) on the Dover road but, when they reach the beach at the end of their journey, it is "a desert of heaps of sea and stones tumbling wildly about, and the sea did what it liked, and what it liked was destruction'' (1.4). Thus, the threat of shipwreck is prefigured in the early objective landscape of the novel, but it is also prefigured in the abstract metaphoric language of the omniscient narrator. For example, Doctor Manette, sleeping, is described as yielding "to the calm that must follow all storms—emblem to humanity, of the rest and silence into which the storm called Life must hush at last" (1.6). Here, the imagery of storm and shipwreck is aligned with mythic metaphor for the first time and hints at the manner in which the macrocosmic significance of the storm and shipwreck metaphor will develop later when the apocalypse of the storming of the Bastille occurs. As is the macrocosmic significance of the storm and shipwreck metaphor prefigured, so also is the microcosmic. The Manette household in London is described as "a very harbour from the raging streets . . . a tranquil bark in such an anchorage" (1.6). But soon this safe harbour will no longer provide shelter from the raging streets of Paris and their "tranquil bark" will be inexorably drawn to the Loadstone Rock and wrecked on the shoals of the Revolution.

After the violent shipwreck of the storming of the Bastille, the Manette family—Dr. Manette, Lucie, Charles, Miss Pross, Jerry Cruncher—become shipwrecked mariners adrift in the terror and desolation of the Revolution. Caught in the vortex of the Revolution, Dr. Manette and Mr. Lorry view the giant grindstone from the window of their lodging and what they see is "the vision of a drowning man, or of any human creature at any very great pass" (3.2). Finally, the novel moves into the interior space of the prison and the submission of Sydney Carton to the flood of history which has pulled him into the very center of its vortex. At the moment of Carton's death, Dickens chooses a shipwreck image to represent this final, small, microcosmic apocalypse:

> The murmuring of many voices, the upturning of many faces, the pressisng
> on of many footsteps in the outskirts of the crowd, so that it swells forward in
> a mass, like one great heave of water, all flashes away. Twenty three. (3.15)

Carton is the only member of the shipwrecked crew of the microcosmic world to perish in the storm of Revolution. All the other members of the Manette household survive the shipwreck, make it back to the safe "harbour" from whence they originally sailed their "tranquil bark." But they are changed, marked, as Miss Pross's loss of hearing best illustrates. They have survived the Loadstone Rock by luck and a benevolent faith, not by any power or strength of their own. Like David Copperfield helplessly watching from the beach, they have survived the apocalyptic shipwreck of their world but they have also realized how ineffectual they truly are in a world gone mad and breaking apart.

VI. SHIPWRECKS, LIGHTHOUSES, RESCUES: *OUR MUTUAL FRIEND*

Dickens' last completed novel, *Our Mutual Friend*, begins in a boat and proceeds immediately to the story of a man overboard, presumed drowned. Can shipwreck be far behind? Like the shipwreck scene in *David Copperfield*, like the symbolic shipwreck of the Gradgrind philosophy in *Hard Times*, like the violent metaphorical shipwreck of the French Revolution in *A Tale of Two Cities*, *Our Mutual Friend* also builds to an apocalyptic resolution of the personal dilemma of at least two of its central characters, Lizzie Hexam and Eugene Wrayburn. Actually, *Our Mutual Friend* begins where *David Copperfield* ends—that is, with the drowned man washing up on the beach—but, to steal a thematic phrase from *A Tale of Two Cities*, *Our Mutual Friend* is really about that man and a number of others being "Recalled to life" (title of Book 1). Whereas Steerforth could not be saved in *David Copperfield* and David could only stand helplessly on the beach accepting his friend's death, in *A Tale of Two Cities* (partially) and *Our Mutual Friend* (wholly yet qualified) that resurrection is once again possible. Thus, *Our Mutual Friend* begins with a man overboard and ends on water with a shipwrecked mariner who, like Steerforth, has harbored ungentlemanly designs on a working-class girl, floating helplessly on the current and being rescued by an intrepid boatman who succeeds in resuscitating the victim. It is a very different outcome from that of the apocalyptic shipwreck of *David Copperfield*.

Near the end of *Our Mutual Friend*, Eugene Wrayburn, while walking near the river at night in the contemplation of his potentially exploitative relationship with Lizzie Hexam, is suddenly attacked, beaten insensible and knocked into the river to drown. It is an apocalyptic breaking open of the world, the sky, both in the unexpected suddenness of the attack and the language in which the attack is described. The attack occurs "in one instant, with a dreadful crash" and "the reflected night turned crooked, flames shot jaggedly across the air, and the moon and stars came bursting from the sky" (4.6). In this final Dickens apocalypse, all creation is torn asunder in an explosion of flame and light. Luckily, however, Lizzie is nearby and, commandeering a handy boat, rescues Eugene, who is floating helplessly in the river.

Once again, as Eugene fights for his life after his attack and rescue, Dickens chooses to express this apocalyptic resolution in the language of shipwreck. As Eugene lies in bed fighting for his life, his struggle is the "frequent rising of a drowning man from the deep, to sink again" who, even in the course of "rising from the deep would disappear the sooner for fighting with the water, so he in his desperate struggle went down again" (4.10). As Stein in Joseph Conrad's *Lord Jim* will later advise, "in the destructive element immerse" (Ch. 20), so does Eugene face this sink or swim situation in *Our Mutual Friend*. As Eugene starts to slip away, he seems to be "quietly yielding to the attraction of the loadstone rock of Eternity" (4.11), an echo of a similar shipwreck situation in *A Tale of Two Cities*. Finally, the culminating image of this whole scene of apocalypse, rescue and salvage is quite typically and predictably Dickensian. When Eugene finally awakens, the "utter helplessness of the wreck of him that lay cast ashore here now alarmed her, but he himself appeared a little more hopeful" (4.11). In the end, Dickens always seems to return to his imagery of shipwreck as analogy for worlds apocalyptically broken up.

However, the major shipwreck imagery in *Our Mutual Friend* is not this familiar dark imagery of apocalypse, but rather the more optimistic imagery of that which can save the ships from running aground and breaking up on the rocks, the protective imagery of lighthouses. In setting the editorial policy and in the actual editing and writing of essays in *Household Words, The Household Narrative of Current Events*, and *All the Year Round*, Dickens had, during the seventeen years prior to the composition of *Our Mutual Friend*, become an active and outspoken polemicist for the building of additional lighthouses on the treacherous English coastline. The lighthouse as base metal for the imaginative alchemy of his novelistic pen would be readily available to a writer whose journalistic pen had spent so much time upon it.

Early in *Our Mutual Friend*, the two young lawyers, Mortimer Lightwood and Eugene Wrayburn, sup alone in the middle of London winter and discuss the boredom of their lives:

> "The wind sounds up here," quoth Eugene, stirring the fire, "as if we were keeping a lighthouse. I wish we were."
> "Don't you think it would bore us?" Lightwood asked.
> "Not more than any other place. And there would be no Circuit to go. . . . If we were on an isolated rock in a stormy sea," said Eugene. "Lady Tippins couldn't put off to visit us, or, better still, might put off and get swamped. People couldn't ask one to wedding breakfasts. There would be no precedents to hammer at, except the plain-sailing Precedent of keeping the light up. It would be exciting to look out for wrecks."
>
> (1.12)

Eugene, in his fanciful lighthouse wish which immediately metamorphoses into a social metaphor, expresses four separate dissatisfactions with Victorian society from which he desires to be protected as a lighthouse protects ships from danger. First, he longs for isolation from the hypocritical buffeting of the London social "Circuit" as represented by Lady Tippins. Second, he longs for the "plain-sailing" and simplicity of the lighthouse-keeper's life, a life uncomplicated by the irresponsible and hypocritical role-playing of London social life. Third, he longs to take responsibility for something, make some sort of meaningful contribution to society. Finally, he feels it "would be exciting to look out for wrecks."

Eugene is one of the most ennui-afflicted characters in all of British literature and his mere anticipation of excitement is almost a major character upheaval. Interestingly enough, his idea of the excitement of "looking out for wrecks" is what places him in a partially protective, though admittedly ambiguous, relationship with Lizzie Hexam after her father drowns and her brother jumps ship leaving her cast adrift and being drawn to the "Headstone" rock. For Lizzie, Eugene becomes the lighthouse keeper who, despite the great sexual power he as a gentleman holds over her, keeps the light up and steers her away from the shoals of exploitation both by Headstone and by himself. In other words, he lives up to his "plain-sailing" responsibility as lighthouse-keeper and rescues her from the metaphoric sexual shipwreck which too often drowns young working class women in the "stormy sea" of London life. Ironically, in time, Lizzie will rescue Eugene from the physical shipwreck of Headstone's apocalyptic assault at the end of the novel.

What Mortimer Lightwood cannot understand is how Eugene, who constantly complains about the boredom of English life, could long for such an alternative:

> "Why, it was but now that you were dwelling on the advantages of a monotony of two."
> "In a lighthouse. Do me the justice to remember the condition. In a lighthouse."
>
> (1.12)

For Eugene, the lighthouse offers a different, more meaningful monotony, a chosen monotony, which involves a clear-cut responsibility to society as opposed to the ambiguity, irresponsibility and unchosen reality of his non-existent law career. Later in *Our Mutual Friend*, the tension between Eugene's lighthouse-keeper's protective responsibility toward the drifting Lizzie and Eugene's gentleman's sexual attraction toward the vulnerable Lizzie momentarily causes him to let the light burn low. Old Riah describes this lapse in the lighthouse-keeper's attention to "plain sailing" in an expressive image:

> "Sir, it was only natural that she should incline towards him, for he had many and great advantages. But he was not of her station, and to marry her was not in his mind. Perils were closing round her, and the circle was fast darkening. . . ."
>
> (3.1)

Riah perceives how Eugene has allowed his own sense of responsibility to Lizzie to burn low and how Lizzie as a consequence is about to run aground on the shoals of the Victorian double standard.

Following Old Riah's advice to flee the darkening "circle" of Wrayburn's protection, Lizzie anchors in calmer waters, yet misses the attraction of Wrayburn's light.

> "It was late upon a wretched night," said Lizzie, "when his eyes first looked at me in my old river-side home, very different from this. His eyes may never look at me again. I would rather that they never did; I hope that they never may. But I would not have the light of them taken out of my life for anything life can give me."
>
> (3.9)

The shipwreck and lighthouse imagery, however, is not reserved only for the definition of the relationship of Eugene Wrayburn and Lizzie Hexam in *Our Mutual Friend*. In employing lighthouse imagery to comment upon the plight of Betty Higden, Dickens raises this motif of shipwreck and rescue to the level of Christian religious iconography, which George Landow argues is its most typical function in English literature and art. For Betty Higden the lighthouse imagery serves as a beacon of Christian salvation. As Betty flees the shipwreck of the Poor House, "all the Light that shone on Betty Higden lay beyond Death" (3.8). Suddenly, the light that has guided the other castaway souls of *Our Mutual Friend* has been elevated to the upper case. Set adrift, Betty struggles past the "gentlefolks and their children inside those fine houses" and "the humbler houses in the little street, the inner firelight shining on the panes as the outer twilight darkened" (3.8). Finally, on the verge of death with "a bright fire in her eyes," she sits by the river and sees the lighthouse-like path of "the lighted windows, both in their reality and their reflection in the water" and that water-reflected beam of light "brought to her mind the foot of the Cross, and she committed herself to Him who died upon it" (3.8). For Betty, the lighthouse transfigures into the Cross and Christ becomes the lighthouse keeper who protects her from the shipwreck of the Poor Laws and guides her across the bar into the safe harbor on the other side of "Death." Here, near the end of his writing career, Dickens' alchemic imagination gives the lighthouse imagery two distinct metaphoric forms. In the case of its imaging of the relationship of Eugene and Lizzie it carries an existential, moral signification, a secular signification of personal and social responsibility. In the case of Betty Higden, however, the lighthouse imagery carries a religious, mythic signification of a higher protection, a higher rescue from the Victorian dilemma of spiritual shipwreck.

However, one other interpretation of Dickens' turning to the imagery of lighthouses and lighthouse-keepers in his last completed novel is worth exploring. In *David Copperfield* he had presented a quite negative and frustrated image of the writer's role in Victorian society as that of a helpless onlooker on the shore. In *Our Mutual Friend* the image of the writer as lighthouse keeper is certainly qualified yet also more positive than the powerless watcher from the shore of *David Copperfield*. The writer as lighthouse keeper is still alone, isolated from the "stormy sea" of Victorian life, but he is no longer powerless. His light can illuminate and warn off from the dangers of Victorian life the ships (his readers) which must navigate those treacherous seas. Near the end of his career, he sees the writer as necessary and, to steal a term from Sartre and Camus, *engagé*, responsible for keeping up the light so that others can see.

Other characters in *Our Mutual Friend* also experience the dilemma of either spiritual or physical shipwreck. The Lammles, like two false Sirens, lure each other onto the rocks of a moneyless marriage. In an ironic echo of both Steerforth's final rest in *David Copperfield* and the situation of the lovers in Matthew Arnold's poem "Dover Beach," the Lammles find themselves washed up and marooned on a desolate beach: "The tide is low, and seems to have thrown them together high on the bare shore. A gull comes sweeping by their heads and flouts them. . . . A taunting roar comes from the sea and the far-out rollers mount upon one another, to look at the entrapped imposters, and to join in impish and exultant gambols" (I, x).

While the Lammles's shipwreck is merely metaphorical, Rogue Riderhood is physically run over by a huge steamer driving downstream in the fog toward the sea. It is a much more ethereal, impersonal shipwreck than those which occurred in *David Copperfield* and *Great Expectations*. The scene takes place in a ghostly fog and the steamer is characterized as a mechanical monster more akin to the railway train which runs down Carker in *Dombey and Son* than the sailing ship upon which Steerforth perishes. The shipwreck is described in much different, more violent, certainly less romantic terms than

Dickens' earlier apocalyptic shipwrecks. The passage, however, is somewhat similar to the shipwreck litany that Walter Gay and old Sol Gills recite in *Dombey and Son*, but the tone of the recitation by this waterside community is totally different. To these people the shipwreck is not romantic or unusual, it is destructive, intentional, impersonal, and demonic. The outraged voices of the community penetrate the scene as they go about the act of rescue:

> A cry for the lifebuoy passed from mouth to mouth. It was impossible to make out what was going on upon the river, for every boat had put off, sculled into the fog and was lost to view at a boat's length. Nothing was clear but that the unpopular steamer was assailed with reproaches on all sides. She was the Murderer, bound for Gallows Bay; she was the Manslaughterer, bound for Penal Settlement; her captain ought to be tried for his life; her crew ran down men in rowboats with a relish; she mashed up Thames lightermen with her paddles; she always was, and she always would be, wreaking destruction upon somebody or something, after the manner of her kind. The whole bulk of the fog teemed with such taunts, uttered in tones of universal hoarseness. All the while the steamer's lights moved spectrally a very little, as she lay-to, waiting the upshot of whatever accident had happened.
>
> (3.2)

This uncharacteristic Dickens shipwreck is not an act of God or an unfortunate collision of circumstance with the aroused elements of air, water, and submerged stone. Rather, this shipwreck is described as a premeditated crime, a post-Industrial Revolution act of mechanical aggression, an intentionally malicious wreaking of destruction. The world has changed and so has Dickens's perception of the nature of shipwreck, the nature of society, and the possibilities for protection and rescue from the "stormy sea" of Victorian life.

Despite the atypicality of Dickens' use of the metaphor of shipwreck in *Our Mutual Friend*, it is somehow appropriate that in one of the final shipwreck allusions of his career he returns to his favorite shipwreck narrative, *Robinson Crusoe*. *Our Mutual Friend* begins with a dinner at the Veneerings and Dickens returns to their "bran' new" board for another dinner party at the end. When Mortimer Lightwood sits down at the Veneering dining table, he no longer can avoid that rapacious gossip, Lady Tippins:

> "Long banished Robinson Crusoe," says the charmer, exchanging salutations, "how did you leave the Island?"
>
> "Thank you," says Lightwood. "It made no complaint of being in pain anywhere."
>
> "Say, how did you leave the savages," asks Lady Tippins.
>
> "They were becoming civilized when I left Juan Fernandez," says Lightwood. "At least they were eating one another, which looked like it."

"Tormentor. . . . You know what I mean, and you trifle with my impatience. Tell me something, immediately, about the married pair. You were at the wedding. . . . How was the bride dressed? In rowing costume?"

Mortimer looks gloomy and declines to answer.

"I hope she steered herself, skiffed herself, paddled herself, larboarded and starboarded herself, or whatever the technical term may be, to the ceremony?"

"However she got to it, she graced it," says Mortimer.

Lady Tippins with a skittish little scream, attracts the general attention. "Graced it! Take care of me if I faint, Veneering. He means to tell us that a horrid female waterman is graceful!"

"Pardon me, I mean to tell you nothing, Lady Tippins," replies Lightwood.

(4."Chapter the Last")

Throughout this whole exchange, like Robinson Crusoe the shipwrecked mariner returned from his desert island to supposed civilization, Mortimer is realizing that the true savagery, the true cannibalism, lies in the gossip of supposedly civilized "Society."

Disdaining "Society," affirming the better post-shipwreck life which Eugene and Lizzie have built for themselves on their desert island of love, Mortimer refuses to participate in the savagery of Lady Tippins's "gossip-mongering." Refusing to converse with the "Voice of Society," as Lady Tippins christens this gathering of gossips, is a moral decisison on Mortimer's part and he finds an unexpected ally in the innocuous Twemlow. Thus, the final word in *Our Mutual Friend* is the rejection of supposedly civilized "Society" by this intrepid Robinson Crusoe and his man Friday (Twemlow) and a return to the post-shipwreck world of rebirth of Eugene and Lizzie.

VII. DICKENS'S METAPHOR FOR HIS AGE

Throughout his canon, Dickens uses the reality and the metaphoricality of shipwreck in a myriad of ways. In *Barnaby Rudge* and *A Tale of Two Cities* he uses a shipwreck metaphor as symbol of violent social upheaval and of the vortical entrapment of the individual in that social upheaval. In *Hard Times* the imagery of shipwreck serves as a commentary upon the psychic dislocation and foundering of the central characters. In the case of the Lammles in *Our Mutual Friend*, the imagery of shipwreck becomes a comic expression of their fatal navigational error in marrying.

But most importantly, from *Dombey and Son* on, the imagery of shipwreck serves as the major symbolic component in the recurrent building of each Dickens novel to an apocalyptic resolution. In *Dombey and Son* all of the litany-like recitation of eighteenth-century shipwreck lore and the metaphoric representation of the sinking of the great merchant House of Dombey prefigures the post-Industrial Revolution version of a shipwreck apocalypse, the pulverizing of Carker by the railroad train. In *David Copperfield* a real, fully described shipwreck is the apocalyptic event upon which all of the action and relationships in the novel turn. *Bleak House* is the narrative of a whole series of failed salvage operations. All of the characters are ships lost in the fog trying to avoid running aground and perishing. Only a few of those castaway mariners survive. *Hard Times* builds to the bi-level moral shipwreck of both Louisa Gradgrind and the Gradgrind philosophy which her father had launched with such high hopes. Physical violence characterizes the shipwreck apocalypses of *A Tale of Two Cities* and *Our Mutual Friend*. In the maelstrom of the French Revolution and in the personal attack of Bradley Headstone upon Eugene Wrayburn, Dickens images the social class struggle of Victorian life as an apocalypic shipwreck which must be survived if any change to a more enlightened society is to occur.

At the most crucial moments in his novels, when moral action, human relationships, or social decisions need to be resolved, the danger and potential negative consequences of those actions, relationships, or decisions are most often couched either in real scenes of shipwreck or in a metaphoric language of shipwreck.[6] As each novel moves toward its apocalyptic resolution, Dickens's alchemic imagination is repeatedly fueled by the imagery of shipwreck. That imagery is perhaps the most appropriate representation of the cautionary nature of Dickens' vision of Victorian society. There is a tentative duality about shipwreck as a novelist's way of imaging his world. In a way, as Lionel Stevenson characterizes the "dark novels" of the latter half of the canon, Dickens is a doomsayer, a frustrated chronicler of a society on the rocks, a sinking society struggling to stay afloat in the violent vortex of apocalypse. Yet, in his constant reshaping of this shipwreck imagery of apocalypse in the successive later works of his canon, Dickens comes to emphasize the marvelous powers and instincts for survival and rescue from the turbulent sea of Victorian life. Dickens, in the final analysis, is a writer whose alchemic imagination found a metaphor for his age, that of a generation of shipwrecked mariners, quite similar to Albert Camus' eloquent metaphor for the struggle of mid-twentieth-century man, the myth of Sisyphus.

NOTES

1. Since all of the novels of Charles Dickens are cited and/or quoted from in the

course of this essay, all quotations will be noted parenthetically within the text by Book Number (when applicable) and/or by Chapter Number so that any edition of Dickens' novels may be consulted.

2. Other critics have circled and briefly touched upon the subjects and issues concerning both Victorian culture and the novels of Charles Dickens which are raised in this essay. Garrett Stewart discusses the motif of drowning in *The Old Curiosity Shop, Dombey and Son,* and *A Tale of Two Cities.* Martin Postle talks of the eighteenth-century affinities for ships of both Dickens and J.M.W. Turner. E. Pearlman takes a Freudian pass at the novel which I approach from the viewpoint of metafictional self-reflexivity and social consciousness. G. W. Kennedy also deals, in a more limited context, with Dickens' use of his favorite shipwreck narrative. Peter I. DeRose also discusses the sea imagery in *David Copperfield.* Janet Larson analyzes the Dickensian style in much more depth than is attempted in this essay with the emphasis upon its use as metaphoric language in *Little Dorrit.* This essay looks at the structural movement of Dickens's plots, characters, and imagery toward consistent apocalyptic resolutions. All of these sources have noted similar preoccupations with the sea, shipwrecks, and apocalyptic resolutions of Dickens's alchemic imagination.

3. All of the following references to the shipwreck scene in *David Copperfield* are, unless otherwise noted, from Chapter 55.

4. Recast, the argument of the following three and one-half paragraphs originally appeared in my essay, "*Hard Times*: A Dickens Fable of Personal Salvation."

5. All quotes in this paragraph and the two paragraphs which follow are taken from Book 2, Chapter 21.

6. If the traumatic event of the Staplehurst train wreck hadn't occurred so late in his life (1865), perhaps train wrecks or lethal train accidents like that in *Dombey and Son* might have been a more prominent metaphorical choice. Dickens, however, by more than just the evidence of this essay, was much more comfortable with late eighteenth- and early nineteenth-century images than with post-Industrial Revolution images such as the railway in *Dombey and Son* and the machines in *Hard Times.*

WORKS CITED

Altick, Richard. *The English Common Reader.* Chicago, Ill.: University of Chicago Press, 1957.

Beeman, M. M. *Lloyd's of London: An Outline.* Kingswood, Surrey: Windmill Press, 1937.

Broodbank, Sir Joseph. *History of the Port of London.* 2 vols. London: Daniel O'Connor, 1921.

Conrad, Joseph. *Lord Jim.* Ed. Thomas Moser. New York: Norton, 1968.

DeRose, Peter I. "The Symbolic Sea of *David Copperfield.*" *Proceedings of Conferences of College Teachers English of Texas* 41 (1976): 44–57.

Dickens, Charles. *The Pickwick Papers.* The Oxford Illustrated Dickens. Oxford: Oxford University Press, 1956.

―――――. *Barnaby Rudge. The Oxford Ilustrated Dickens*. Oxford: Oxford University Press, 1956.

―――――. *Bleak House. The Oxford Illustrated Dickens*. Oxford: Oxford University Press, 1956.

―――――. *David Copperfield. The Clarendon Dickens*. Ed. Nina Burgis. Clarendon Press, 1981.

―――――. *Dombey and Son. The Clarendon Dickens*. Ed. Alan Horsman. Oxford: Clarendon Press, 1974.

―――――. *Hard Times. The Oxford Illustrated Dickens*. Oxford: Oxford University Press, 1956.

―――――. *Household Words: A Weekly Journal, 1850–1859, Conducted by Charles Dickens*. London: Bradley and Evans.

―――――. *Martin Chuzzlewit. The Clarendon Dickens*. Ed. Margaret Caldwell. Oxford: Clarendon Press, 1982.

―――――. *Nicholas Nickleby. The Oxford Illustrated Dickens*. Oxford: Oxford University Press, 1956.

―――――. *The Old Curiosity Shop. The Oxford Illustrated Dickens*. Oxford: Oxford University Press, 1956.

―――――. *Oliver Twist. The Clarendon Dickens*. Ed. Kathleen Tillotson. Clarendon Press, 1966.

―――――. *Our Mutual Friend. The Clarendon Dickens*. Ed. E. Salter Davies. Oxford: Clarendon Press, 1952.

―――――. *A Tale of Two Cities. The Oxford Illustrated Dickens*. Oxford: Oxford University Press, 1956.

Fowles, John. *Shipwrecks*. Boston: Little, Brown, 1975.

Huntress, Keith, ed. *Narratives of Shipwrecks and Disasters, 1586–1860*. Ames: Iowa State University Press, 1974.

Hyde, Francis E. *Liverpool and The Mersey: The Growth of a Port, 1700–1970*. Newton Abbot, England: David & Charles, 1971.

Kennedy, G. W. "The Uses of Solitude: Dickens and *Robinson Crusoe.*" *Victorian Newsletter* 52 (Fall 1977): 25–30.

Landow, George P. *Images of Crisis: Literary Iconography*. London: Routledge & Kegan Paul, 1982.

Larson, Janet. "Apocalyptic Style in *Little Dorrit.*" *Dickens Quarterly* 1:2 (1984): 41–49.

Palmer, William J. "*Hard Times*: A Dickens Fable of Personal Salvation." *Dalhousie Review* 52:1 (1972): 67–77.

Pearlman, E. "David Copperfield Dreams of Drowning." *American Imago* 28 (1971): 391–403. Rpt. in *The Practice of Psychoanalytic Criticism*. Ed. Leonard Tennenbaum. Detroit, Mich.: Wayne State University Press, 1976.

Postle, Martin. "Dickens and *The Fighting Temeraire*." *Dickensian* 81 (1985): 95–102.

Spark, Muriel. *The Prime of Miss Jean Brodie*. New York: Dell, 1961.

Stevenson, Lionel. "Dickens's Dark Novels." *Sewanee Review* 51 (1943): 398–409.

Stewart, Garrett. "The Secret Life of Death in Dickens." *Dickens Studies Annual* 11 (1983): 177–207.

Thornton, R. H. *British Shipping*. Cambridge: Cambridge University Press, 1959.

Watt, W. W., ed. "Introduction." *Hard Times*. New York: Holt, 1958.

Zimmerman, Erich W. *Ocean Shipping*. New York: Prentice-Hall, 1923.

Dickens and Opera

Robert Bledsoe

> "I certainly, sir," returned Mrs. Sparsit, with a dignity
> serenely mournful, "'was familiar with the Italian Opera at
> a very early age."
>
> *Hard Times*, Chapter 7

I

Throughout Dickens' novels there are numerous allusisons to music.[1] Dickens
frequently draws on musical imagery to express moods of happiness,
reconciliation, and tranquility. Nature, kettles, and crickets all sing soo-
thingly, fountains play liquid music, noble hearts evoke love by touching
harmonious chords of memory, and rough urban sounds soften into the gentle
music of enchanted cities.

In addition to containing many allusions to music, his works reflect his
fascination—or obsession—with the theater (see, *inter alia*, Garis and Axton).
Therefore it would seem natural for Dickens to be greatly interested in the
art that combines music and drama—opera. The purpose of this paper is to
consider the significance of opera in Dickens' life and thought. The subject
divides itself into four main parts: (1) Dickens' known reactions to operatic
performances he attended in London, Paris, and elsewhere; (2) the nature of
the articles and stories about opera that appeared in *Household Words*; (3)
the connection between narrative themes in some operas and those in his
novels; and (4) his modified editorial policy towards articles about opera as
illustrated by Henry Fothergill Chorley's writings for *All the Year Round*. The
evidence suggests that a longstanding assumption, succinctly expressed by
J. B. van Amerongen (73)—that for opera Dickens "entertained and expressed
undisguised dislike if not contempt"—is erroneous.

As a young man, Dickens went to operas and occasionally recorded his reaction to the singing and acting. In this period, the 1830s, he seems to have attended mostly opera in English, generally, though not exclusively, performed at Covent Garden or Drury Lane. In 1834 he wrote to F. C. Beard that he had been to the Lyceum to see an English opera, *The Mountain Sylph*.[2] Through his sister Fanny he met the composer John Hullah, and in December, 1836, their attempt at English opera, *The Villager Coquettes*, was performed at the St. James Theatre with moderate success.[3]

In April, 1841, Dickens accepted Miss Coutts's offer of her box at Drury Lane, where a visiting German company was performing *Fidelio* (Pilgrim *Letters*, 2:265). On November 24, 1841 he wrote Miss Coutts that his "domestic peace is so disturbed by rumours of [English soprano] Adelaide Kemble . . . that I can never hope for peace of mind until I have carried Mrs. Dickens to Covent Garden Theatre. If, to this end, you can let me have your box any night next week, you will eternally oblige me . . ." (Pilgrim *Letters*, 2:431). The same soprano inspired him four days later to invite Daniel Maclise to dine "at *half past four*, as preparation for the classic Addle Head (Pilgrim *Letters*, 2:433).[4] Probably he went to Drury Lane again in October, 1843, for an English version of *La Favorita*, the popular fourth act of which he termed "natural, simple, and affecting." (Kathleen Tillotson and Nina Burgis note that the *Examiner*'s review of this performance is "unmistakably in Dickens's style" [81].)

In *Pictures from Italy*, Dickens tells us that he attended one act of *Norma* at the theater in Carrara and also saw an unspecified comic opera.[5] He also mentions the "second-rate opera company" that was at the Carlo Felice operahouse there (*Pictures from Italy*, "Genoa and its Neighbourhood"). While he was staying in Genoa he wrote to Emile de La Rue on May 24, 1845, that he would see him that night at the opera (Pilgrim *Letters*, 4:314).

Back in London, during the forties he increasingly attended performances at Her Majesty's Theatre in the Haymarket. It was expensive—the *Harmonicon*, England's leading musical magazine in the 1830s, noted that a box cost well over three hundred pounds per season (11 [1833]:66). And performances there had long been regarded as fashionable, unlike those at Covent Garden, Drury Lane, or the Lyceum. To it, pronounced *The New Monthly Magazine* in 1834, came "the aristocracies of rank, wealth, and taste" (40 [April 1834]:499). After 1847, the theater in the Haymarket fought the new Royal Italian Opera Company just starting up at Covent Garden, a rivalry occasionally alluded to in *Household Words*. From that time, Dickens went frequently to both houses, seeing the standard operas of the time, among them

Bellini's *Norma* and *Pirata*, Donizetti's *La Favorita, La Fille du Régiment, Lucrezia Borgia*, and Meyerbeer's *Le Prophète*. In 1852 he wrote Cerjat that the company at Covent Garden was "wonderfully fine" (Pilgrim *Letters*, 6:670)

Dickens may have gone to these operas simply to pass time. On some occasions, however, he clearly became engrossed in the music drama. For example, in 1844 he was impressed by a performance of *Il Pirata* at the Théâtre Italien in Paris. He wrote to Forster that

> [t]he passion and fire of a scene between her [Giulia Grisi], Mario, and Fornasari was as good and great as it is possible for anything operatic to be. They drew on one another, the two men—not like stage-players, but like Macready himself: and she, rushing in between them; now clinging to this one, now to that, now making a sheath for their naked swords with her arms, now tearing her hair in distraction as they broke away from her and plunged again at each other; was prodigious.
>
> (Pilgrim *Letters*, 4:238–39

At this time the principal singers who performed in Paris at the Théâtre Italien in the winter performed in London at Her Majesty's Theatre from Easter to midsummer. Thus, Dickens saw Grisi at Her Majesty's and, later, Covent Garden, as well as at the Opéra. It was also probably around this time that the manager of Her Majesty's, Benjamin Lumley, who made a point of knowing the well-connected, is first mentioned in Dickens's letters. On December 1, 1846, Dickens dined with Lumley in Paris, and the conversation turned to the threat to Lumley's theater that might be posed by the establishment of a rival company being formed at Covent Garden to perform with some of Lumley's own disgruntled stars, chief among them Grisi and Mario, whose performances Dickens had so admired. Though Lumley claimed to feel that their loss would be good riddance, since they were demanding and generally troublesome, Dickens wrote to T. J. Thomson that he believed Lumley to be really "hugely afeared of the opposition opera" (Pilgrim *Letters*, 4: 672).

And in a few months, Lumley had to fight the newly-formed Covent Garden company in earnest. His main weapon was the English debut of Jenny Lind, who sang only at Her Majesty's for three seasons, her last seasons before retiring from opera, subsequently performing only in recitals and oratorios. Dickens seems to have been caught up in Lindomania. He and Macready called on her May 5, 1847, the day after her debut, and on May 26, 1847, Dickens wrote to Miss Coutts, apologizing that he could not accept her invitation since he was going to Macready's "to meet Jenny Lind, who is

almost the greatest genius, to my thinking, that the world has ever produced''
(Pilgrim *Letters*, 5:72). On June 3, 1847, Dickens, his wife Catherine, her
sister Georgina, and Dr. John Elliotson went to Her Majesty's to hear Lind
sing in Donizetti's *La Fille du Régiment* (performed as *La Figlia del Reg-
gimento*) and Dickens wrote Lumley the next day complaining vehemently
about the rudeness of the theater's box door keeper (Pilgrim *Letters*, 5:78–79).

On April 26, 1849, Dickens invited John Leech to join him at Catherine
Hayes's debut in *Lucia di Lammermoor* at Covent Garden, adding that they
had "a box at the other house, and can run over and hear Jenny [as Amina
in *La Sonnambula*] if we be in the mind" (Pilgrim *Letters*, 5:522). A similar
last minute invitation to go to the opera was extended to Frank Stone on July
3, 1849: "We have a loin of mutton at ½ past 5 today and are going to see
Lucrezia Borgia, afterwards. Will you come to the Mutton *and* the Opera?
(Pilgrim *Letters*, 5: 563).

Edgar Johnson tells us that Dickens and Miss Coutts went to see Donizetti's
Lucrezia Borgia at Covent Garden in 1855 (2:800), and that "[f]rom the time
of his residence in Paris in 1855, and perhaps even from that of his earlier
stay in 1846, he enjoyed the opera there. . . ." (2:1130). It was during this
period, too, that, according to Forster, Dickens saw and enjoyed Auber's new
piece, *Manon Lescaut*. He called it

> most charming. Delightful music, an excellent story, immense stage tact, capital
> stage tact, capital scenic arrangements, and the most delightful prima donna
> ever seen or heard, in the person of Marie Cabel. . . . She sings a laughing
> song in it which was received with madness. . . .[6]
>
> (2:167)

Thus, in the decade preceding Dickens' editorship of *Household Words*,
we know he attended many performances of operas and responded to some
of those performances with enthusiasm for the performers and for the dramatic
possibilities of music drama. With Dickens' own opera-going in mind, it is
instructive to look at how opera played a part in the editorial decisions he
made for his journal *Household Words* during the 1850s.

II

Anne Lohrli notes that Dickens included occasional pieces about music and
musicians in *Household Words*.[7] Not many of these treat opera, but an examination of several of those that do suggests that they divide themselves

roughly, but not arbitrarily, into two groups: a relatively large group dealing only incidentally with opera, and a smaller group, particularly (and not surprisingly) pieces by George Augustus Sala, in which references to opera presume on the reader's part a fair degree of familiarity with and interest in operatic concerns ("I suppose there was never a more assiduous playgoer than Charles Dickens. . . . I am passionately fond of the opera; but I don't like the play" [Sala 1:131]).

The group of articles dealing incidentally with opera shows how operatic allusions fit into the journal's goal of being both *dulce* and *utile*. In "Music in Humble Life" (1:161–64), George Hogarth, Dickens' father-in-law, points out that "the Muse . . . is taking up with the humble and needy, and leaves nothing better to her aristocratic friends than their much-loved Italian Opera." Hogarth gives the credit for this accomplishment to Hullah's pioneering work with music education in the 1840s. It is interesting that Hogarth wrote about the middle-class muse, since he would have been an appropriate choice for an article on the muse's "aristocratic friends" at the opera house, given his previous publications and work as music critic on the *Daily News* and elsewhere.[8] That Hogarth's only contribution to *Household Words* is on "humble music" presumably reflects Dickens' intention that the journal should appeal to the common reader.[9]

Allusions to opera come into George Dodd's "Music Measure" (7: 297–301) merely because many of the tunes played by mechanical music machines (the music box, the barrel organ, and the Apollonicon) were operatic: themes from the overtures to *Tell*, *Le Prophète*, *Figaro*, *Zauberflöte*, *Freischütz*, and so forth. Rosina's aria from Rossini's *Barbiere* is mentioned because M. Debain's new invention, the *piano-mécanique*, grinds it out "bran new" (300).

Grenville Murray's reason for describing the Pera Theatre, an attraction for soldiers in the Crimean war (10:570–72), is to point out that young men who are unimportant back home can represent themselves in such provincial locations as being "highly connected" (572). As backdrop to these social maneuvers, "an English autumnal prima donna is tearing one of Verdi's operas into shreds, and screaming in a manner which is inconceivably ear-piercing" (571).[10]

Percy Fitzgerald, in "They Order This Matter Better in France" (15: 193–96), writes about the French claque at the Opéra and the Opéra comique, citing Berlioz's journalism as one of his sources.[11] But the article, with its focus on the "claqueur element" in every French opera house, is not really about opera but about theatrical audiences and, more centrally, about social differences between the English and the French. "Such is a description of the way they order things in France; whether better or otherwise, may seem doubtful enough," concludes the narrator, unsentimentally (196).

Fitzgerald's vignette, "The Datchley Philharmonic" (16:213–16), suggests what kind of specific operatic allusions Dickens considered most acceptable—that is, most widely comprehensible to his readers—in his sketch of the first concert put on by the best musicians of "Datchly." Provincial up-to-the-minute opinion, represented by Belmore Jones, favors "the modern romantic school, and was for a step in the Verdi direction. In short, nothing less than a revival in its entirety of the famous Troubadour of that master" (214). Still something of a novelty, *Trovatore* had been given its first English production in May of 1855; but an opera by Verdi is an idea too radical for Mrs. G. Malkyn, the local prima donna—"a person of much consideration, and having funded and other moneys" (214). Consequently she wins the struggle to present scenes from Bellini's *Norma*, widely known and frequently performed in England since 1833. Fitzgerald's concern is to caricature the provincial star of dubious talent who always gets her way (her rationalization for why she insists on slower tempi than the conductor wants is that she sings the role like her great predecessors, Pasta, Malibran, and the still active Grisi). The organizers claim that the concert is successful, but Mrs. G. Malkyn's second performance is met with "marked" public apathy (216), resulting in the discontinuation of public-spirited attempts to elevate the operatic taste of Datchley's citizenry.[12]

Fitzgerald's other piece touching on opera is less sketch than short story. The central character of "Going for a Song" (18: 569–72) is again a provincial singer, but one markedly more pathetic than the rich Mrs. Malkyn. Mademoiselle Amélie Piquette was the "first woman and leading voice whenever the light operas of Auber Adolphe Adam were played" at the Théâtre Impérial (569).[13] When her voice cracks she descends to "semi-dramatic readings" at private parties and ends up trying to make money in Turkey, where the Sultan finds her voice so bad that he commands her to shup up or be thrown into the Bosphorus. The grim little story then is abruptly terminated with the sentence: "Why pursue the sad chronicle further?" (572).[14]

By way of contrast to these articles and stories where opera is mentioned only incidentally, Dickens printed two pieces by George Augustus Henry Sala within the space of a month which assume a readership keenly interested in stories and gossip about musical performers: "The Musical World" (9: 561–67), and "Music in Paving Stones" (10: 37–43).[15] In the first, Sala sets out to analyze the three divisions of the musical world: the fashionable, the middle-class, and the country. In fact, however, it is only the first two that concern him: the fashionable, that is, the operatic, and the middle-class, or the world of music retailing at "Messrs. Octave and Piccolo's establishment" on Regent Street. His comments on fashionable opera center on the nature of the new opera company, The Royal Italian Opera, which, under the musical direction of Michael Costa, had been formed recently (1847) to give seasons at Covent Garden, in rivalry with the established, decades-old site of Italian opera at Her Majesty's Theatre in the Haymarket, where for many years Costa had conducted, before his defection to the new house. In 1853 the older company at Her Majesty's had, temporarily, folded: Grand Opera was to be experienced only at Covent Garden. To the Victorian theatergoing audience, Covent Garden for so long had been firmly established as home of "legitimate" theater that, for some, it was hard to accept it as the city's principal opera house. Sala's piece reflects that feeling:

> The Grand Opera exists no more. I know there is an establishment in the vicinity of Covent Garden [i.e. The Royal Italian Opera]. . . . But I cannot call it THE Opera. It can never be more to me than Covent Garden Theatre—the conquered, but never to be the naturalised domain of Italian music. . . . [T]he indignant voices of Colman, Sheridan, Kenny, and O'Keefe, seem to be crying to Bellini and Donizetti, Meyerbeer and Mozart, "What do ye here?"
>
> (561, 562)

In the ongoing war between the two companies, Sala sides nostalgically with those who wanted a return to the palmy days of Her Majesty's: "The opera should, and can only be in Haymarket, over against palatial Pall-Mall. Come back then, Mr. Costa, whom I honor, to those cari luoghi" (562).[16]

The other half of Sala's article deals with the odd people one encounters in that "great Bourse or High Change of the Ars Musica," the music store of Octave and Piccolo. The operatic element of this piece centers on theophrastian portraits of foreigners currently and formerly prominent in English musical circles: the former "king of tenors," Teodor Gaddi, now a "shabby, broken-down old beggarman" (565), and Polpetti, the reigning monarch who will make millions off of English audiences before going home to spend everything in Italy. The English are touchy on this point, Sala notes, while defending him:

> Do not let us be too hard upon the "confounded foreigners" who come here to sell their crotchets and quavers for as much gold as they will fetch. Only consider how many million pounds sterling a year we make by spinning shirts and welding iron for the confounded foreigners; how many millions of golden pennies our travelling countrymen turn by cutting canals, and making railroads,

steamers, suspension bridges, in lands where we ourselves are but "confounded foreigners."

(566)

Sala continues his theme of describing the business side of operatic music in his next article "Music and Paving Stones," comprised of thumbnail characterizations of types to be met on the paving stones of Regent Street, in the vicinity of "Octave and Piccolo's music warehouse" (37): among others, the great German basso "Bompazek," the glamorous contralto "Madame Lesbia Perigord," and the genial old musical amateur who once wrote an opera about Hector and Andromache ("or some equally dreary and equally classical subject" [43]).

For all their differences, the articles published in *Household Words* share many common assumptions which show its editorial point of view towards operatic subjects. They contain operatic information, stereotypes, and clichés that can be considered widespread among Dickens' reading public, and they assume that Opera is mainly of interest to the Fashionable, not to ordinary people. Not surprisingly, too, there is the assumption that opera *houses* may be interesting, but more for the things they—in common with all theaters—tell us about social interactions in general than for the music dramas which take place in them.

Indeed, perhaps the most interestingly written of all the "operatic" pieces in *Household Words* is "Theatrical Ashes" (13 [22 March 1856]), a meditation on the great Covent Garden fire of 1856. Coming so soon after Sala's call for a return to the good old days at Her Majesty's, the burning seemed to signal (incorrectly, as it turned out) that the recently started company would have to give up. Its author, Albert Richard Smith, laments the "really miserable end of a such a splendid building:"

> If it was fated to be burnt down, the fire should have burst out—provided all could have got away—in the last scene of le Prophète, with Mario singing the drinking song, surrounded by his beautiful bacchantes, as the flames began to lap and twine about the gilded doors and costly draperies of the palace of Munster.

(218)

Instead of such an appropriate end, however, the opera house burned (fortunately with no loss of life) towards the end of an evening when it had been leased for a ball. Smith muses wistfully on his many memories of the house. These are, most poignantly, mainly of Covent Garden as it was to the author's childish imagination—a legitimate theater, not an opera house. Memories of

King Lear, Paul Clifford, and *Comus*, of performances like Fanny Kemble's Juliet, and of children's pantomimes like *Aladdin* and *Beauty and the Beast* move him most. Nevertheless, as the most fitting memorial to the house, he imagines an operatic allegory in the form of a statue representing staples of the current operatic repertory:

> I would have a souvenir of the late theatre also in the market-place. It should have a fountain, the basin supported by Norma, Don Giovanni, Dulcamara, Valentine, Maffeo Orsini, and Fides; and on top I would have a statue, suggested by the antique, of Mario sitting amongst the ruins of Covent Garden.[17]
>
> (220)

III

The casual approach to opera reflected in Dickens' own opera-going and in his editing of *Household Words* changed in the early 1860s into something altogether more interesting. The immediate cause of this change was the reaction Dickens had to two operas which he saw in Paris: one a revival of a classic, Gluck's *Orphée*, the other a recent opera by Gounod, *Faust*. A secondary reason for the change was probably Dickens' growing friendship with the minor novelist and major music critic, Henry Fothergill Chorley, whose operatic tastes almost certainly influenced Dickens' during the 1860s.[18]

Both *Orphée* and *Faust* deal with loss, and both with resurrection: Eurydice's physical resurrection in *Orphée* and Marguerite's spiritual resurrection in *Faust*. Both operas moved him profoundly. Gluck's *Orphée* (performed in the version by Berlioz) is based on a version of the myth of Orpheus in which Orpheus brings his wife Eurydice back from Hades and, thanks to the timely intervention of Amor, a *dea ex machina*, lives with her happily ever after.

In order to understand Dickens' response to *Orphée*, we must remind ourselves how many characters in his novels are related to themes of coming back from the dead, resurrection, and being born again—some of the best known being the Reverend Stiggins in *Pickwick*, Scrooge in *Christmas Carol*, the resurrection men in *Tale of Two Cities*, and, in *Our Mutual Friend*, Nicodemus Boffin, the man to whom Jesus explained the necessity of being born again spiritually, and John Harmon. All are concerned with being "born again" (Welsh, esp. 196–212, and Sanders). For Dickens music was almost always associated with memory as an artistic analogue of natural supernaturalism. And memory is a miracle, a resurrection of the past, just as in *Sartor*

Resartus. This important connection between music and memory in Dickens' works is present from first to last. Mr. Pickwick, for example, exhibits the association in a comically confused manner:

> Yielding by degrees to the influence of the exciting liquid [punch], rendered more so by the heat, Mr. Pickwick expressed a strong desire to recollect a song which he had heard in his infancy, and the attempt proving abortive, sought to stimulate his memory with more glasses of punch, which appeared to have quite a contrary effect.

(Ch. 19)

More sententiously, at any rate more Wordsworthianly, the narrator of *Oliver Twist* remarks that "a strain of gentle music . . . will sometimes call up sudden dim remembrances of scenes that never were, in this life" (Ch. 30). For David in *David Copperfield*, Agnes "touched the chords of my memory so softly and harmoniously, that not one jarred within me; I could listen to the sorrowful, distant music, and desire to shrink from nothing it awoke" (Ch. 60). The voice of Little Dorrit ministers through music to Arthur Clennam, who,

> listening to the voice as it read to him, heard in it all that great Nature was doing, heard in it all the soothing songs she sings to man . . . [I]n the tones of the voice that read to him, there were memories of an old feeling of such things, and echoes of every merciful and loving whisper that had ever stolen to him in this life[19]

(2.34)

Toward the end of *Our Mutual Friend* the music of nature can be heard at Plashwater Weir Mill Lock (though not by Rogue Riderhood): "The voice of the falling water, like the voices of the sea and the wind, were as an outer memory to a contemplative listener" (4.1). There is also the organ-playing of Tom Pinch in *Martin Chuzzlewit* and John Jasper in *The Mystery of Edwin Drood*, the duet of the kettle and the cricket in *The Cricket on the Hearth*[20]—the list goes on and on.

These and many similar passages all contribute to Dickens' evocation of the connections among music, time, and memory (Cerny 49–50, 86, and Ford). Indeed, Dickens spoke of the specific connection between music and resurrection in a speech he made to the Royal Society of Musicians in 1860. "Ladies and gentlemen," he said, "these may appear to you vagrant ideas, but music is suggestive of all the fancies. You know it can give back the dead" (Fielding, 297).

In Gluck's *Orphée*, music gives back the dead quite literally. Therefore Dickens was predisposed to find a music drama about Orpheus's rescue of

Eurydice interesting. The appearance of the celebrated Pauline Viardot-Garcia as Orpheus added to the interest and to Dickens' appreciation of the perform- ance, not only because her performance had been so highly praised by Berlioz and by Turgenev, but also because Viardot had long been highly praised by H. F. Chorley in the columns of the *Athenaeum*. In November, 1862, Dickens wrote to Forster:

> Last night I saw Madame Viardot do Gluck's Orphée. It is a most extraordinary performance—pathetic in the highest degree, and full of quite sublime acting. Though it is unapproachably fine from first to last, the beginning of it, at the tomb of Eurydice, is a thing that I cannot remember at this moment of writing, without emotion. It is the finest presentation of grief that I can imagine. And when she has received hope from the Gods, and encouragement to go into the other world and seek Eurydice, Viardot's manner of taking the relinquished lyre from the tomb and becoming radiant again, is most noble. Also she recognizes Eurydice's touch, when at length the hand is put in hers from behind, like a most transcendant [sic] genius. And when, yielding to Eurydice's entreaties she has turned round and slain her with a look, her despair over the body is grand in the extreme. It is worth a journey to Paris to see, for there is no such Art to be otherwise looked upon. Her husband stumbled over me by mere chance, and took me to her dressing-room. Nothing could have happened better as a genuine homage to the performance, for I was disfigured with crying.
>
> (Nonesuch *Letters*, 3.322)

Dickens' respect for Viardot was no passing fancy. Praise for her artistry later appeared in at least three different articles in *All the Year Round*: "Shake- speare Music" (March 28, 1863), "German Opera and its Makers" (part 2, July 15, 1865), and "Music About Music" (July 22, 1865).[21] And, while the emphasis in his letter to Forster is on Viardot's powers as an actress, it is likely that he was just as susceptible to the opera's theme of loss and new life as he was to the power of Viardot's performance.

A few months after seeing *Orphée* Dickens was also greatly moved by the operatic version of the first part of Goethe's *Faust*, as adapted by Jules Barbier and Michel Carré and set to music by Charles Gounod. Marguerite's spiritual rebirth is shown onstage in the last scene when she dies: Mephistopheles pronounces her condemned, but a choir of angels, responding that she is saved, takes her to heaven, forgiven. Thus, like *Orphée*, *Faust* joins music, memory, and spiritual resurrection (salvation). As with *Orphée*, there is evi- dence in Dickens' letters for the powerful impact *Faust* had on him. On February 19, 1863, writing after his return to London about his experiences in Paris, he told Macready that Viardot was "most splendid" in Orphée, and then explained how Gounod's opera, like Gluck's, moved him to tears:

An opera of Faust, a very sad and noble rendering of that sad and noble story. Stage management remarkable for some admirable, and really poetical, effects of light. In the more striking situations, Mephistopheles surrounded by an infernal red atmosphere of his own. Marguerite by a pale blue mournful light. The two never blending. After Marguerite has taken the jewels placed in her way in the garden, a weird evening draws on, and the bloom fades from the flowers, and the leaves of the trees droop and lose their fresh green, and mournful shadows overhang her chamber window, which was innocently bright and gay at first. I couldn't bear it, and gave in completely.

(Nonesuch *Letters*, 3.342–43)

Another reason for finding *Faust* so moving in addition to its treatment of the theme of resurrection was the opera's treatment of the unhappy liaison between Faust and Marguerite which culminated in Marguerite's murder of her illegitimate child. Edgar Johnson is surely right in suggesting that Dickens was reminded of his own "guilty love" (2:1008). Such an implication seems present in his letter to Macready, and is even more strongly suggested in the letter he wrote to Georgina before returning from Paris on February 1, one day after he saw the opera:

[Faust] is a splendid work, in which that noble and sad story is most nobly and sadly rendered; and it perfectly delighted me. But I think it requires too much of the audience, to do for a London Opera House. The composer must be a very remarkable man indeed. Some management of light throughout the story is also very poetical and fine. We had Carvalho's box [Carvalho was the manager of the Théâtre Lyrique]. I could hardly bear the thing; it affected me so, and sounded in my ears so like a mournful echo of things that lie in my own heart.

(Edgar and Eleanor Johnson, 339)

Dickens' final comment (in the manuscript of this letter now in the collection of the Huntington Library) reinforces the probability that Dickens saw his own situation with Ellen Ternan sadly mirrored in *Faust*: "But, as a certain Frenchman said 'No weakness, Danton!' So I leave off."[22]

Dickens was soon glad to find himself proven wrong in his belief that *Faust* was too demanding for an English audience. His friend Chorley had been urging in the pages of the *Athenaeum* that it be presented in London ever since he had enthusiastically reviewed its Paris premiere in 1859. In the summer of 1863, only a few months after Dickens saw it in Paris, the opera was performed in London at Her Majesty's Theatre, under the management of James Henry ["Colonel"] Mapleson. Chorley found the production "most admirable."[23] Luigi Arditi, the opera's conductor, recorded in his memoirs that *Faust* was so popular in Chorley's English version that the "early winter season" at Her Majesty's "was exclusively confined to the one work" (112).[24]

Privately Chorley shared with Dickens an intensely personal happiness at the opera's success. Dickens wrote Georgina on June 18, 1863 that Chorley was made

> so happy by the success of Faust . . . that it is quite impossible to understand what he means. When he told me what his feelings were, he drew a dial in the air, and punched with his forefinger all the twelve hours in it. Then he said "*You* understand" and I said (with deep feeling) "I do."[25]

A personal bond existed between Dickens and these two operas for several reasons: his artistic interest in themes of resurrection; his personal interest in a singer, Viardot; his close friendship with that singer's English supporter, the music critic Chorley; and, not least, his realization that music drama could touch in his own heart the powerful, painful, but liberating chords of memory about which he so frequently wrote.

In the last five years of his life, Dickens seems to have attended performances less frequently. At the same time he privately acknowledged that he felt a far greater susceptibility to the emotional power of music drama than he did in the 1840s when he somewhat grudgingly conceded that Giulia Grisi's acting could be mentioned in the same breath as Macready's. An example of this deeper sensibility is seen in the letter he wrote Viardot from Gad's Hill on August 16, 1865, responding to a letter from her in which she expressed concern on hearing of his involvement in the Staplehurst railway disaster:

> I take the opportunity of Chorley's coming near you, to thank you for your kind and affectionate letter received after my escape from that terrible accident. It gave me the greatest pleasure to be remembered to one whom I so heartily admire, and whose genius I so fervently recognise. . . .
>
> Will you tell Chorley how I can best send you a book next October. It will be "Our Mutual Friend" which I am now finishing with great pains, and which I hope will interest you, half as much as it interests me!
>
> My kindest regard [sic] to your good husband, and to the young ladies, whether they remember me or no. I have not been to the opera these four years, missing you. When you were in the Prophete, I went perpetually. And if you were to do Orphée, in London, I believe I should go every night.
>
> (Waddington, 67)

IV

Perhaps Dickens' own increased susceptibility to the emotional power of music drama made him more receptive to printing articles about it in his journal. Certainly the articles relating to opera which he printed in *All the Year Round* during the mid 1860s are far more detailed than those in *Household Words* during the 1850s. Moreover, they presume an audience interested in following contemporary operatic productions, not just in England but also on the Continent.

One article in *All the Year Round*, possibly by Percy Fitzgerald,[26] does employ the same kind of casual tone towards opera that was so common in *Household Words*: "The Opera at Rome" (November 17, 1860:129–33). Nine columns long, the article is mostly about the theater itself ("Much like Old Drury in size and general bearings, but painted in a dull, a sad-coloured stone, which gives it a cheerless and almost penitential character," 130) and about the audience (the "ducal banker," the "magnificos of the municipality," and the policemen who assist the censors, 131). Only a few sentences at the end are about the performance (Verdi's *Simon Boccanegra*).[27] The writer for *All the Year Round* finds nothing much to praise about the opera or the performance (at Boccanegra's death, "interior voices, typical of stomachic suffering, seem to proceed also from the bassoons and bass instruments" 133)—with the exception of Coletti himself: "to magnificent Coletti, dramatic artist unrivalled, save by his brother Ronconi, all homage!" (133).

Another article, "Amina and the Mill Wheel" (June 29, 1861: 320–23), is a timely piece, occasioned by the successful debut in 1861 at Covent Garden of Adelina Patti as Amina in Bellini's *La Sonnambula*, a debut which "has stirred up the tired town" (323). It takes the form of armchair reminiscences about several great singers who took the role on the London stage before Patti: Malibran ("Never has opera-queen singing English ever transported her subjects as she did" 321), Persiani (all in all, "the best" 321), Adelaide Kemble (competent, but Amina was "the least admirable among the few parts played by her during her bright and brief career on the English opera stage" 322), Jenny Lind (the "type" of Amina, but not so good as Persiani in the final rondo 322), Viardot ("remarkable," but more for acting than for "beauty of tone" 322), Sontag (who came to the role too late in her career), and Alboni (who was wrong for the role in both "voice and figure" 323). Like the articles in *Household Words*, this piece treats opera as a pleasant entertainment; unlike them, it is detailed and concerned not only with the performance but with the music of the opera.

"Amina and the Mill Wheel," according to the *All the Year Round* Office Letter-book, is by Henry Fothergill Chorley (Oppenlander, 252). Naturally, given Chorley's vast knowledge of opera, the piece draws on a greater depth of experience and presupposes a greater degree of interest in its audience than the earlier operatic pieces in *Household Words*. Nevertheless, in its chattiness, and in its emphasis on performance and performer, the article has some things in common with the relatively superficial articles that Dickens had published in the earlier journal.

More important are two long articles which differ strikingly in tone and purpose from the articles discussed so far: (1) "German Opera and its Makers" in three parts (July 8, 1865: 573–76, July 15, 1865: 583–87; and July 22, 1865: 607–11); and (2) "Depths and Heights of Modern Opera" (October 9, 1869: 450–54). These articles are intensely concerned with opera as art, not simply popular entertainment. Their publication in Dickens' family magazine suggests that Dickens had come to view opera as a subject worth serious didactic treatment, and *All the Year Round* as an appropriate outlet for such discussions.

The articles treat the issue that was increasingly assuming a position of importance in European musical life: nationalism—the relative significance and merits of the Italian, French, and German traditions. Both articles maintain that, contrary to general English opinion, the real home of nineteenth-century music drama is France. Accordingly, they denounce the German "music of the future," most particularly Wagnerian opera, because it threatens the continued healthy development of opera. As the titles indicate, the subject matter of the articles is quite varied; both, however, discuss the "music of the future" controversy which was beginning so thoroughly to shake nineteenth-century European thought. The intellectual tenor of the articles reflects a consistent point of view, and internal evidence suggests that they are probably by a single hand, Chorley's.

Before either of these operatic articles appeared, Dickens had already published in *All the Year Round* an article in which Chorley denounces the music of the future, lumping together Schumann, Liszt, and Wagner as part of the same unwholesome phenomenon. In it, Chorley criticizes the so-called re-generation of German music currently being discussed in continental intellectual circles. He notes sarcastically that the Germans consider it "new and noble to represent music as something which music never was and never will be—an expression of political feelings . . . of a defiant and exclusive nationality, frowning at one country, scowling at another, sneering at a third, ignoring a fourth" ("Old, New, and No Music," October 22, 1864: 261).[28] Beethoven was the source of much of the problem, since his music, though "sublime," set an example of "mischief" to succeeding generations of "idle dreamers and theorists" (261), particularly in his final works; but the main blame for the false "regeneration" is Wagner's, whose talent and promise has deteriorated from the mildly interesting *Flying Dutchman* and *Tannhaüser* to the deplorable *Lohengrin* and the "insolent" theorizing of *Oper und Drama* (263).

Dickens wrote Wills about this article: "I've gone through the No. carefully, and have been down upon Chorley's paper in particular, which was 'a little bit' too personal. It is all right now, and good, and them's my sentiments too of The Music of the Future" (Nonesuch *Letters*, 3:339).[29] Thus, instead of supporting Edgar Johnson's statement that "there is no indication that [Dickens] ever heard of Wagner" (2:1130), the publication policy of *All the Year Round* shows that Dickens was very much aware of, and determined to combat, the growing influence of the music of the future.[30]

The first of the operatic articles, "German Opera and Its Makers," is an elaborate, three-part, quasi-encyclopedic epitome of the history of German opera from the early eighteenth century to the present. One of its major points is to stress the importance of the *French* school for the development of music drama: ". . . we are now only reluctantly waking up to the fact that to the Grand Opéra of Paris . . . all Europe has been greatly indebted for the formation of dramatic as distinguished from musical opera" (573). The article concludes that German opera, despite its distinguished history, has reached a dead end:

> The nightmares imposed on a helpless and astray public by Herr Wagner, may be "left alone in their glory"—for the moment at least. What manner of influence they have had, was to be heard last autumn in the horrible music of the Carlsruhe Festival, described in these columns. We imagine it to be already decaying.[31]
>
> (July 22, 1865: 611)

The second of the operatic articles, "Depths and Heights of Modern Opera," criticizes two specific performances of operas whose styles are worlds apart, and whose common trait is that both are worthless: Offenbach's *La Grande Duchesse de Gérolstein* in Paris, and Wagner's *Rheingold* in Munich. Offenbach's opera, analyzed and denounced in the first section of the article, represents the "depths" of modern opera—opera "in the mire," as the subtitle has it—because the music is "trite and colourless" (451). "Lower in the setting of burlesque and in offence to delicacy, stage music can hardly sink" (451). The concluding section of the article, "In the Mist," takes up the Wagner question in detail.[32] Printing such a detailed analysis represented a commitment on Dickens' part to fight the music of the future, an endorsement of his comment on an earlier article of Chorley's: "them's my sentiments, too." Europe, according to Chorley, needs Gounod to give it another *Faust* or *Mireille* in order to stop the growing public interest in Wagner's music (450).

When "Depths and Heights of Modern Opera" was published in 1869, London opera-goers had not yet seen a production of any of Wagner's operas—the first, "L'Ollandese Dannato" (*Der Fliegende Holländer*), was presented at Drury Lane under the joint management of Mapleson and Gye on July 23, 1870, twenty seven years after its first performance in Dresden.[33]

Chorley made a trip to Munich in order to see *Rheingold* and report to his English readers that Wagner's acceptance by a "band of enthusiasts" is a wonder for "the Annals of Charlatanry" ("Depths and Heights," 451). Wagner has come a long way since the "not altogether irrational Rienzi" (451), an opera in which Wagner showed some talent. Today the "case" of Wagner "is one not of principles in art carried out, but of the same utterly annulled: not of progress, but of destruction" (452). The diatribe continues: Wagner's vocal phrases "can only strike the ear as so much cacophonous jargon" (452), and "[e]ven the most credulous of Herr Wagner's partisans become tepid, vague, apologetic, and scarcely intelligible, if they are called on to defend or explain Herr Wagner's text" (452). The scenery adds to the "dull absurdities":

> There is a final effect of a rainbow, not greatly larger than a canal bridge, which keeps close to the earth for the convenience of the dramatis personae, who are intended to mount upwards on it. . . . Add to these wonders mists that come and go on the open landscape without any apparent rhyme or reason, clouds, darkness, sunbursts, all so many hackneyed effects dear to our children and "groundlings" at Christmas time; and some idea may be formed of the shows to exhibit which the music has been bent and broken. The congregation declare that the utter want of success which attended the rehearsal was owing to the stupidity of the Munich machinists and painters. Yet these till now have borne a deservedly high character throughout Germany; and the stage of the Bavarian capital is one notoriously convenient for any purposes of change or effects of space.
>
> (453)

The relation between the staging of *Das Rheingold* and that of an English Christmas pantomime is stressed as preparation for an analogously reasoned denunciation of the music as being interesting only insofar as it is derivative:

> The absence of melody is, of course, in accordance with Herr Wagner's avowed contempt for everything that shall please the ear. This being the condition of matters, it is not wonderful that a common four-bar phrase of upward progression, repeated some thirty times or more in the prelude, should please, and (to be just) its effect at representing the ceaseless flow of water, is picturesque

and happy. The river nymphs are next announced by a phrase borrowed from Mendelssohn's overture to Melusine. There is a pompous entry for the principal bass voice, there is an effect of nine-eight rhythm, borrowed from Meyerbeer's scene in the cloisters of Saint Rosalie (Robert [*Robert le Diable*]); and these are all the phrases that can be retained by those who do not believe in what has been described by the transcendentalists, as "concealed melody."

(453)

The failure of the performance thus must be attributed directly to the work itself, not to an unsatisfactory production:

It will not avail to plead that it is ungenerous or unjust to judge from a rehearsal; when, as in the case of Das Rheingold, such rehearsal was tantamount in correctness and spirit to any first performance ever attended by European critic.

(453)

Though further rehearsals were called off, guests were not so much disappointed as relieved to be "spared another dismal evening, to be spent in wonder—at the mouse brought forth by the mountain, at the pigmy production of the self-styled Musician of the Future" (454).

Dickens attended many operas for over twenty years, and did so because he enjoyed them. At first it seems that he responded to the casually entertaining aspects of fashionable Italian operas performed at Her Majesty's and Covent Garden, an interest apparently reflected in the number of articles in *Household Words* which allusively (and superficially) treat opera as casual entertainment. He later became more susceptible to the power of drama set to music than his reactions to his early opera-going would suggest. We know he respected the opinions of his close friend, Henry Chorley, one of the century's leading writers about opera in England. We know, too, the intensity of his reactions to a performer like Viardot, to operas in which he saw themes that were analogous to themes in his own writing, and to experiences in his own life: *Orphée* and *Faust*.

That the French tradition of music drama was so vigorously defended, and the German music of the future so energetically attacked in *All the Year Round*, may seem at first glance surprising. But in opera, Dickens's tastes were like Chorley's. To Chorley's expressions of antipathy toward the music of the future, Dickens echoed, "them's my sentiments, too."[34]

NOTES

1. Several general works provide information about Dickens and music (esp. Light-

wood, Cudworth, Ruff, Auerbach). A series of articles in the *Dickensian* in the 1930s by J.W.T. Ley is thorough and useful. Differing from the preceding in its emphasis on the critical significance of music in Dickens, with particular reference to *The Mystery of Edwin Drood* is Jean-Louis Cupers's "Approches musicales de Charles Dickens." Future work needs to take into account recent work on the relation between music and literature as discussed by Steven Paul Scher in his chapter in *Interrelations of Literature* (225–50). See also Scher's anthology, *Literature und Musik*.

2. September 1834. The opera, by John Barnett, was accompanied by a farce, *The Dead Guest (The Letters of Charles Dickens,* Pilgrim Edition 1:40). Subsequent references to Dickens' letters before 1852 are to this edition. Later references are to Dexter's Nonesuch edition.

3. Edgar Johnson, *Tragedy and Triumph* 1:153–54. Hullah noted that "notwithstanding the various opinions expressed as well on the book as on the music, [it] was a success, and that of a very decided kind. It was played in London abuut sixty successive nights, and afterwards in Edinburgh . . ." (16). Dickens' description of his agony at seeing his sister win a prize at the Royal Academy of Music during his "hard experiences in boyhood" (Forster, Chapter 2) is well known. Forster adds that Dickens always felt "extreme enjoyment in witnessing the exercise of her talents [and] the utmost pride in every success obtained by them." For more information on Fanny see Carlton. Much later John Hullah's method for teaching singing to large classes was the subject of occasional comment in *Household Words*.

4. In December, however, he wrote Henry Burnett (husband of his sister Fanny) that the soprano Adelaide Kemble "is much talked about—I think her desperately unpleasant—almost repulsive." Pilgrim *Letters,* 2:497.

5. The chorus was made up of labourers in the marble quarries who "acquitted themselves very well; unlike the common people of Italy generally, who . . . sing vilely out of tune." "To Rome by Pisa and Siena," *Pictures from Italy.*

6. Johnson notes that Dickens "liked Auber's *Masaniello* and *Fra Diavolo*" (*Tragedy and Triumph* 2: 1130).

7. Lohrli emphasizes the importance which articles of "social import" held in the general editorial policy. Of course, discussions of music in general played a larger part in the journal's editorial social consciousness than those of opera in particular (4).

   Dickens' concern for wholesome entertainment for the working classes, for example, can be seen in George Dodd's "Music in Poor Neighbourhoods" (12:137–41), the point of which is that music in public houses encourages people to drink less, not more. This style of public-interest writing is still more vividly represented by Sala's "Sunday Music" which appeared the following month (12:261–64), defending outdoor bands playing on Sunday afternoons because they provide "innocent amusement for the tens of thousands of overworked humanity" (261) and "some relief for the toiling many" (264)—themes which call to mind some of Dickens' earliest social concerns as expressed in *Sunday Under Three Heads* (1836). Subsequent attributions from *Household Words* are taken from Lohrli's compilation.

8. Hogarth (1783–1870) wrote music criticism for *The Daily News* from 1846 to 1866, and also for *The Illustrated London News*. For an impression of Hogarth the journalist late in life see Bennett 10–11. Hogarth's wife, Georgina, was the daughter of George Thomson, influential in Scottish music because of his pub-

lication of six volumes of national airs (between 1793 and 1841) with accompaniments commissioned from such important contemporary composers as Haydn, Weber, and Beethoven. Shortly after the article in *Household Words*, a new edition of his *Memoirs of the Musical Drama* 2 vols. (London: Bentley, 1838) appeared, with substantial additions bringing it up to date, under a new title: *Memoirs of the Opera in Italy, France, Germany, and England* (1851).

9. The appeal of music (not of opera) to the common man is frequently discussed in *Household Words*. The author of "London Musical Clubs" (3:179–81) describes an evening singing old catches and canons, concluding with reflections on efforts "worthily made" in the last few years—Jullien's cheap concerts as well as Hullah's schools—to make music popular with the middle class. The office book's attribution of this piece is to H. Cole who, according to Lohrli (231) "may be Henry (later Sir Henry) Cole, 1808–1882." The subject of Hullah's classes is resumed in a short story by H. O. Pearson, "The Humble Confessions of a Tenor" (15:283–85), cast in the form of the "autobiography" of a tenor in one of Hullah's singing classes in a "suburban village" of London (285) who can't reach G, but who wins the hand of Miss Sophia Lute, a soprano in the same class. Their wedding breakfast is attended by "the whole Hullah class" (285). The romantic, pseudo-musical moral is: "What can I recommend better to the inhabitants of small towns and villages in general, than a Hullah singing class [?]" (285).

10. A reader of English music criticism in the 1840s and 1850s might attribute the woman's screaming to Verdi's inability to write for the voice rather than to the soprano's inadequacy. See Budden 1:33–35, and Bledsoe, "Henry Fothergill Chorley and the Reception of Verdi's Early Operas in England," 650.

11. Berlioz was well known to the English musical public. His opera, *Benvenuto Cellini*, was performed at Covent Garden in 1853. In the summer of 1855 he conducted a series of concerts in London with the New Philharmonic. Moreover, his musical journalism was frequently cited by British critics during the 1850s. See Ganz, passim.

12. Most of the concert is devoted to the compositions of the local organist, Mendelssohn Jackson.

13. The reason for conflating the names of two composers, Daniel Auber and Adolphe Adam, is not clear. Perhaps it is merely an authorial or printer's slip for "Auber *or* Adolphe Adam."

14. Fitzgerald's final (non-operatic) musical piece for *Household Words* was "Out of Tune" (19:396–403). It peeps "stereoscopically" at the "little cathedral town of Ivysburg" so that its readers (those who "fancy exceedingly small interiors in the Dutch manner" [396]) can learn of the struggles between the new Dean and his organist, on the one hand, and the disappointed Reverend Maydew and the old organist Mr. Twingles, on the other.

15. A third musical article (with no direct bearing on opera) appeared about the same time: "A Little More Harmony" (10:1–5), also by Sala, is a description of a "Grand Morning Concert" at the "Nineveh Rooms, Arrow-head Street, Cuneiform Square" where wives of eminent men ("peeresses, bishopesses, judgesses, bankeresses, baronetesses, stock-brokeresses, and merchant-princesses" [3]) join "a great many foreigners . . . who come with free admissions" (3) to hear musical morceaux, principally those played by the currently fashionable, and notably mercenary, harpist, Panslavisco (4–5).

16. Opposite sentiments about the relative attractions of the two houses were ener-

getically maintained by several critics, most notably Henry Fothergill Chorley, who gloated over the same situation that *Household Words* deplored:

> The "old house," then, was fairly beaten out of the field by the new one. And, after all that had been whispered, and asserted, and published in print, the Italian Opera in Covent Garden had entirely superseded the house in the Haymarket, with all its traditional Fashion. . . . But there was no questioning the fact that, long before 1853 set in, the tide, fashionable and unfashionable, had turned to Covent Garden to hear great musical performances—and that in 1853 "the dear old house" [Her Majesty's] was closed.

(Chorley 2: 194, 195)

Chorley's views were of no consequence to Dickens' editorial policies during the mid-1850s. Neither of the two contributions identified by Lohrli as written by Chorley for *Household Words* was on a musical subject: "The Brown Hat" (1: 133–35) and "Poetry in the Bye-Ways" (1: 151–53).

There were, however, other writers for *Household Words* who, like Chorley, did not share Sala's nostalgia for Her Majesty's Theatre. Grenville Murray, for example, cited the new company at Covent Garden as a standard against which to compare some continental houses unfavorably, reporting from Naples in "The Roving Englishman: Beautiful Naples" (7:302–05) that the San Carlo no longer stands comparison with Covent Garden as it used to do. . . . All the recognized singing celebrities of Europe are elsewhere; some with Mr. Gye at Covent Garden, some in Paris, more at St. Petersburgh, and a few in Vienna. If you carry the remembrance of the singing, scenery, and decorations, the general *mise en scène* of Covent Garden, with you to Naples, you will find a woeful falling off.

(304)

17. The operas alluded to are Bellini's *Norma*, Mozart's *Don Giovanni*, Donizetti's *L'Elisir d'Amore* (Dulcamara), Meyerbeer's *Les Huguenots* (Valentine), Donizetti's *Lucrezia Borgia* (Orsini), and Meyerbeer's *Le Prophète* (Fidès). The final Household Word on the burning was a piece by John Hollingshead about the rebuilding of the opera house, "A Phantom Theatre," (17: 484–86).

18. Chorley's friendship with Dickens receives only passing mention in Forster and Johnson, but Kaplan notes that Chorley's "desperate search for affection made him always loyal, sometimes, sweet, and occasionally generous" (491). For more information about their relationship, see Hewlett (2:227–41), Grubb, Bledsoe ("Dickens and Chorley"), and Tomlin. Chorley's literary criticism for the *Athenaeum* is discussed in Marchand, esp. 183–93.

19. Jerome Beaty uses this passage as a counterargument to criticism which maintains that Dickens' later novels are "darker" (236).

20. "[T]he kettle and the Cricket, at one and the same moment, and by some power of amalgamation best known to themselves, sent, each, his fireside song of comfort streaming into a ray of the candle" ("Chirp the First"). Marlow's article links this image with memory as an "expressive symbol."

21. My attention was called to these articles by Patrick Waddington's "Dickens, Pauline Viardot, Turgenev: A Study in Mutual Admiration" (72, n. 70).

22. Quoted by permission of the trustees of the Huntington Library, San Marino, California.

23. Chorley had been one of the first English critics to praise Gounod's music in the early 1850s. When he first met Gounod in March, 1850, Chorley recorded in his diary: "It was a great pleasure to me in Paris to add to my list of sensations Gounod, of whom the world will one day hear as *the* composer, or else H.F.C. is much mistaken" (Hewlett 2:94). After the success of *Faust* at the Théâtre Lyrique in Paris in March, 1859, Chorley reviewed it enthusiastically for the *Athenaeum*, reminding his readers that he had long ago called attention to Gounod's merits (March 26, 1859:427–28). The opera had been presented in Canterbury Hall in London in May, 1860, to a relatively small audience, but that performance was not a full production. The first real English production (sung in Italian) was Mapleson's at Her Majesty's (*Athenaeum* June 20, 1863: 816–17). Chorley wrote of his

> pleasure in a success which has outdone all expectations, and which has silenced for ever those who have sneered at M. Gounod as a man whose productions in no respect justified the pretensions and professions of his admirers,—among whom we were the earliest.
>
> (817)

The successful English translation of the opera—which Chorley himself had written in 1859 (as he noted in his "gossip" feature in the *Athenaeum* January 9, 1864: 60)—was first produced in January, 1864.

24. Chorley did not review the performance for the *Athenaeum*, presumably to avoid a conflict of interest. The reviewer is identified in the marked copy of the *Athenaeum* now kept at City University, London, as P. Wright. Wright noted (of "Even Bravest Heart May Swell," Valentine's cavatina in the second act, soon to become one of the best known parts of the opera) that "[t]he new song, taken from the second theme of the Introduction, with an episodical second part, is about as happy as are usually such *quasi-impromptu* movements, and owes its effect to the exquisite finish and feeling of the singer" January 30, 1864: 163). Attribution cited by permission of City University, London.

25. Ms, Huntington Library, quoted by permission.

26. Attribution from Oppenlander, 268. I give below my reasons for attributing to Chorley three articles which Oppenlander leaves unattributed.

27. The author reserves his praise for the baritone Coletti, well known to London audiences in the 1840s. This was the same performer Carlyle had discussed in his notorious diatribe, "The Opera," published in the *Keepsake* (1842), and whom Carlyle exempted, to a degree, from his general censure of audience and performers:

> One singer in particular, called Coletti or some such name, seemed to me, by the cast of his face, by the tones of his voice, by his general bearing, so far as I could read it, to be a man of deep and ardent sensibilities, of delicate intuitions, just sympathies; originally an almost poetic soul, or man of genius, as we term it; stamped by Nature as capable of far other work than squalling here, like a blind Samson, to make the Philistines sport!

28. The article appeared in two parts, October 22, 1864; 260–64, and November 5, 1864: 294–300. It is discussed at greater length in my article, "Dickens and Chorley," 159–61.

29. October 8, 1864. Oppenlander (253) attributes the article to Chorley on the basis of this comment.

30. In another article about music, not specifically about opera, "Music About Music" in two parts (*All the Year Round,* March 9, 1867:256–59; March 16, 1865: 280–82), the author refers to "the reign of Decay, began by Schumann, and continued by the usurpation of Delirium, under Herr Wagner's sceptre" (281). That this article too may by Chorley's is suggested by its praise for Viardot's Orphée (March 9, 1867:257); its praise for the setting of "the 'Orpheus' song" (March 16, 1867: 282) [i.e. Shakespeare's lyric from *Henry VIII,* "Orpheus with his lute"] by Arthur Sullivan, a friend of Chorley's; and its praise for Henrietta Sontag's performance in Auber's setting of Scribe's libretto "L'Ambassadrice" (281), also praised by Chorley in his *Athenaeum* columns.

31. This reference to the article on the Carlsruhe Festival (i.e. to "Old, New, and No Music") is one reason to believe that Chorley was its author. Three others are: (1) the congruence of the comments about the importance of French opera with Chorley's opinions as consistently expressed in the weekly columns of the *Athenaeum* since the 1830s; (2) the reference to the Orphée of "that matchless artist among modern singers:—Madame Viardot" (July 15, 1865: 583); (3) the following reference to Mendelssohn:

> It was among his many unfulfilled plans, cut short by early death, to write an opera based on Shakespeare's Winter's Tale; and, in a letter on the subject which exists, besides due regard to the interest of Hermione and Perdita, an anxious wish is expressed that Autolycus shall be well seen after.
>
> (July 8, 1865: 575)

The librettist of Mendelssohn's projected opera based on Shakespeare's *Winter's Tale* was to have been Chorley himself, who, as its recipient, would be in a position to refer to an unpublished letter "which exists." The letter may no longer exist, but several letters from Chorley to Mendelssohn about the possibility of collaborating on *A Winter's Tale* are in the "Green Books" now in the Bodleian Library, Oxford.

32. I assume this article was written by Chorley for the following reason: Chorley reported in a signed article (having retired from the journal's staff the year before, he no longer wrote anonymously) in the *Athenaeum* (September 11, 1869: 347–48) on the "full dress stage rehearsal" of *Das Rheingold* at Munich (347). His sentiments are exactly the same as those expressed in *All the Year Round,* down to spotting the resemblances to Mendelssoshn's Melusine overture and to Meyerbeer's *Robert le Diable,* discussed below ("coolly appropriated by the unblushing insulter of Judaism in music!" 348). The report prompted a response from Walter Bache defending Wagner (*Athenaeum* September 18, 1869: 378), the substance of which was in turn attacked by Chorley in the issue of September 25, 1869: 410–11.

33. Chorley's successor as the music reviewer for the *Athenaeum* was C. L. Gruneisen, whose review of *Fliegende Holländer* was largely favorable: "The Music of the Future is still an open question in this country. If Wagner will produce another 'Fliegende Holländer' there would be unanimity in musical Europe, and his return to the legitimate school of the lyric drama would be heartily welcomed" (July 30, 1870: 154; attribution from marked copy at City University, cited by permission). The Dutchman of the production, Charles Santley, recalled in his memoirs that "Wagner . . . failed to attract the public. We only played it two

or three nights, and to very poor houses'' (285). But J.W. Davison, the reviewer for the *Times*, remembered the occasions as ''a distinct success'' (291).

34. For research subsidies used in the preparation of this article the author would like to thank the Division of Fellowships and Seminars, National Endowment for the Humanities, and the Graduate College of the University of Texas at El Paso. Some of the material in Section III was presented at a conference on Dickens and the Theater in March, 1986, at the University of Texas at Austin.

WORKS CITED

Amerongen, J.B. van. *The Actor in Dickens*. 1926; rpt. New York: Benjamin Blom, 1969.

Arditi, Luigi. *My Reminiscences*. New York: Dodd, Mead, 1896.

Auerbach, Emily. ''The Musicians of Charles Dickens.'' *Sphinx* 4 (1984): 149–65.

Axton, William F. *Circle of Fire*. Lexington: University Press of Kentucky, 1966.

Beaty, Jerome. ''The 'Soothing Songs' of Little Dorrit: New Light on Dickens's Darkness.'' *Nineteenth Century Literary Perspectives: Essays in Honor of Lionel Stevenson*. Ed. Clyde de L. Ryals. Durham: Duke University Press, 1974.

Bennett, Joseph. *Forty Years of Music 1865–1905*. London: Methuen, 1908.

Bledsoe, Robert. ''Dickens and Chorley.'' *Dickensian* 75 (1979): 155–66.

—————. ''Henry Fothergill Chorley and the Reception of Verdi's Early Operas in England.'' *Victorian Studies* 28 (1985): 631–55.

Budden, Julian. *The Operas of Verdi*. 3 vols. New York: Oxford University Press, 1973–81.

Carleton, William J. ''Fanny Dickens: Pianist and Vocalist.'' *Dickensian* 53 (1957): 133–43.

Cerny, Lothar. *Erinnerung bei Dickens*. Amsterdam: Verlag B. R. Grüner, 1975.

Chorley, Henry F. *Thirty Years' Musical Recollections*. 2 vols. 1862; rpt. New York: Da Capo, 1984.

Cudworth, Charles. ''Dickens and Music.'' *Musical Times* 111 (June 1970): 588–90.

Cupers, Jean-Louis. ''Approches musicales de Charles Dickens.'' *Littérature et Musique*. Ed. Raphaël Célis. Bruxelles: Facultés universitaires Saint-Louis, 1982). 15–56.

Davison, J. W. *From Mendelssohn to Wagner, Being the Memoirs of J. W. Davison*. Ed. Henry Davison. London: Wm. Reeves, 1912.

Dickens, Charles, ed. *Household Words* (1850–1859). 19 vols. London: Bradbury & Evans, 1850–59.

—————. *The Letters of Charles Dickens*. Ed. Walter Dexter. 3 vols. Bloomsbury: Nonesuch, 1938.

————. *The Letters of Charles Dickens* [1837–1852]. Eds. Madeline House, Graham Storey, and others. Pilgrim edition. 6 vols. Oxford: Clarendon Press, 1965–88.

Fielding, K. J. *The Speeches of Charles Dickens*. Oxford: Clarendon, 1960.

Ford, George. "Dickens and the Voices of Time." *Dickens Centennial Essays*. Ed. Ada Nisbet and Blake Nevius. Berkeley: University of California Press, 1971. 41–66.

Forster, John. *The Life of Charles Dickens*. 2 vols. London: Dent, 1969.

Ganz, A. W. *Berlioz in London*. 1950; rpt. New York: Da Capo, 1981.

Garis, Robert. *The Dickens Theatre*. Oxford: Clarendon, 1965.

Grubb, Gerald. "Dickens and Chorley." *Dickensian* 52 (1956): 100–09.

Hewlett, Henry T. *Henry Fothergill Chorley: Autobiography, Memoirs, and Letters*. 2 vols. London: Richard Bentley, 1873.

Hogarth, George. *Memoirs of the Opera in Italy, France, Germany, and England*. 2 vols. 1851; rpt. New York: Da Capo, 1972.

[Hullah, Frances]. *Life of John Hullah, LL.D. by his wife*. London: Longmans, 1886.

Johnson, Edgar and Eleanor. *The Dickens Theatrical Reader*. Boston: Little, Brown, 1964.

Johnson, Edgar. *Charles Dickens: His Tragedy and Triumph*. 2 vols. New York: Simon and Schuster, 1952.

Kaplan, Fred. *Dickens: A Biography*. New York: Morrow, 1988.

Lightwood, James. T. *Charles Dickens and Music*. London: Charles H. Kelley, 1912.

Lohrli, Anne. *Household Words: A Weekly Journal 1850–1859 Conducted by Charles Dickens: Table of Contents, List of Contributors and their Contributions, based on the Household Words Office Book*. Toronto: University of Toronto Press, 1973.

Marlow, James E. "Memory, Romance, and the Expressive Symbol in Dickens." *Nineteenth Century Fiction* 30 (1974): 20–32.

Marchand, Leslie. *The Athenaeum: A Mirror of Victorian Culture*. Chapel Hill: University of North Carolina Press, 1941.

Oppenlander, Ella Ann. *Dickens'* ALL THE YEAR ROUND*: Descriptive Index and Contributor List*. Troy, NY: Whiston, 1984.

Ruff, Lillian M. "How Musical Was Charles Dickens?" *Dickensian* 68 (1972): 31–42.

Sala, George Augustus. *Things I Have Seen and People I Have Known*. 2 vols. London: Cassell, 1894.

Sanders, Andrew. *Charles Dickens: Resurrectionist*. New York: St. Martin's, 1982.

Santley, Charles. *Student and Singer*. London: Edward Arnold, 1892.

Scher, Steven Paul. "Literature and Music." in *Interrelations of Literature*. Ed. Jean-Pierre Barricelli and Joseph Gibaldi. New York: MLA, 1982. 225–50.

——————. *Literatur und Musik*. Berlin: Erich Schmidt Verlag, 1984.

Tillotson, Kathleen and Nina Burgis. "Dickens at Drury Lane." *Dickensian* 65 (1969): 81–83.

Tomlin, E.M.W. "Charles Dickens and Henry Fothergill Chorley." *Études Anglaises* 32 (1979) 434–48.

Waddington, Patrick. "Dickens, Pauline Viardot, Turgenev: A Study in Mutual Admiration." *New Zealand Slavonic Journal* 1 (1974): 55–73.

Welsh, Alexander. *The City of Dickens*. Oxford: Clarendon Press, 1971.

Dickens and Unitarianism

John P. Frazee

The subject of Dickens' involvement with Unitarianism has received scant attention from scholars since John Forster, Dickens' friend and first biographer—and himself a Unitarian—offered what has come to be the standard account not only of that involvement but also of the development of Dickens' religious views generally. According to Forster, Dickens took sittings for himself and his family in the Unitarian chapel in Little Portland Street (in 1843) and formed a long-lasting friendship with its minister, Edward Tagart. But "after two or three years" Dickens stopped attending. Thereafter he entered "those trying regions of reflection which most men of thought and all men of genius pass through" (1: 282). Forster claimed credit for helping Dickens through his period of religious doubt by calling his attention to Stanley's *Life of Dr. Arnold*, implying that Dickens found in Arnold's Broad Church sentiments the way out of his religious crisis. Describing Dickens's mature religious views, Forster claimed that "Upon essential points, he had never any sympathy so strong as with the leading doctrines of the Church of England; to these, as time went on, he found himself able to accommodate all minor differences" (1: 336).

Forster's account presents problems. The only evidence he offers of Dickens's religious struggles is a dream Dickens had while in Italy. In the dream a spirit bearing some indefinite relationship to the dead Mary Hogarth informed Dickens that the Catholic religion was the true one for him. The dream is certainly open to interpretations other than Forster's. Dickens' modern biographer, Edgar Johnson, for example, sees it as a manifestation of the creative restlessness that regularly overcame Dickens as he began a new piece of writing: he was struggling with the opening pages of *The Chimes* at the time and mentions his difficulties in the same letter in which he recounts to

Forster the contents of his dream (1: 518). A less sober eye might, like Scrooge, attribute the dream to a bit of underdone potato—especially in light of Dickens' settled dislike of Catholicism. The dream's meaning is uncertain at best, and one must wonder at Forster's decision to offer it as evidence of Dickens' spiritual state while withholding those "other evidences" to which he alludes in the *Life*. Equally troubling is Forster's decision to offer his description of Dickens' mature religious views without proof. Thus, unless one believes that Forster's long friendship with Dickens gives his account unimpeachable authority, the *Life* provides a rather shaky foundation on which to base an understanding of Dickens' religious views.

Unfortunately, most modern scholars do rely on Forster's account, modifying it only in small ways. J. M. Connell argues, for example, that Dickens' reconciliation with the Church was "far from complete" in later life, but he accepts "Forster's word for it" that in his later years Dickens should be "reckoned a Churchman again" (234). Noel Peyrouton labels Dickens' involvement with Unitarianism "a flirtation" based more on his regard for Tagart than on his acceptance of the doctrines of Unitarianism (104). Echoing Forster, Peyrouton concludes that in the end Dickens' views were those of a liberal Anglican. Like Peyrouton, Archibald Coolidge follows Forster in dismissing Dickens' involvement with Unitarianism as of no lasting importance and, with Forster, points to the importance of the *Life of Arnold*. As evidence that Dickens broke with Unitarianism, Coolidge identifies the denomination with "the excesses of informal religious and moralistic fervour" that Dickens attacked in *Pickwick Papers, The Old Curiosity Shop, Barnaby Rudge*, and *Bleak House* (57–58). This identification, however, is based on a serious misunderstanding of the nature of Unitarianism, which was not characterized by the "excesses" Coolidge describes.

In his *Dickens and Religion*, Dennis Walder devotes several pages to a survey of the biographical evidence of Dickens' religious beliefs. Walder recognizes the shortcomings of Forster's account—noting, for example, that Forster "offers precious few" evidences of Dickens' religious turmoil in the late 1840s (11). He speculates that Dickens' religious views may have been shaped by his friendships with men who shared "a liberal, Romantic religion," a possibility Forster does not consider (14). But despite his reservations, in all essentials Walder's survey follows Forster. He concludes that Dickens' attitudes toward religion can best be described by examining the novels Dickens wrote, the project that makes up the bulk of his book. Walder's examination, however, yields nothing incompatible with Forster's account.

Among modern scholars only Edgar Johnson takes a position substantially different from Forster's. Johnson contends that in adult life Dickens inclined toward Unitarianism. Unfortunately, he makes this point about a matter of considerable biographical importance almost in passing, with no attempt to document it (2: 1133). On the matter of Dickens' religious beliefs, then, Johnson's account, like Forster's, rests more on his authority as biographer than on any evidence he offers.

The tendency to rely on Forster as an authoritative source of information about Dickens' religion may be due in part to the fact that Dickens himself rarely offered direct expressions of his religious beliefs in his fiction, his public speeches, or even in his correspondence. He had a lifelong distaste for doctrinal controversy, arguably *the* leading trait of his religion. His distaste is evident in a letter to the reverend R. H. Davies, written in 1856: "I discountenance all obtrusive professions of and tradings in religion, as one of the main causes why real Christianity has been retarded in this world" (Nonesuch *Letters*, 2: 818). Eight years later, writing to W. F. de Cerjat, a Swiss businessman whom he met in Lausanne in 1863 and with whom he shared some of his most extensive discussions of religious issues, Dickens asserted that "the Church's hand is at its own throat" because of the doctrinal wranglings of the various parties: "Here, more Popery, there, more Methodism—many forms of consignment to eternal damnation as there are articles, and all in one forever quarreling body . . . these things cannot last" (Nonesuch *Letters*, 3: 402).

Dickens' distaste for doctrinal controversy governed the raising of his children, a point he emphasized in a valedictory letter to his son Henry: "You know that you have never been hampered with religious forms of restraint, and that *with mere unmeaning forms I have no sympathy"* (Nonesuch *Letters* 3: 673; emphasis added). So important was this point for Dickens that in his will he took a posthumous opportunity to counsel his children "to guide themselves by the teaching of the New Testament in its broad spirit, and to *put no faith in any man's narrow construction of its letter here or there"* (Forster, 2: 422,; emphasis added).

Despite his distaste for doctrinal controversy and the absence of a formal statement of his religious beliefs, Dickens was by no means indifferent to religion. He could be drawn into discussions of particular religious issues by correspondents with whom he agreed—or more often by those with whom he disagreed. These discussions are scattered throughout Dickens' correspondence, testifying to his lifelong engagement with religion in its inclusive sense. His correspondence is thus a valuable resource for understanding Dickens' religion.

Another important—but generally undervalued—resource is Dickens' retelling of the New Testament, written for his own children in 1846 and published in 1934 as *The Life of Our Lord*. I consider *The Life of our Lord* to be a much more reliable indicator of Dickens' beliefs than do most scholars. Peyrouton discounts it because Dickens wrote *The Life* for the limited understanding of his children, and

> any *easy* version of the Gospels . . . is most likely to have a quality identifiable
> as 'consistently Unitarian' and . . . such is not inconsistent with or contradictory
> to what a Broad Churchman of Dickens's temperament and predilection would
> entertain as proper for the young child's initiation into the Christian philosophy.
>   (111)

Walder similarly argues that to call *The Life* a Unitarian work is "to read into it a theological significance hardly applicable, unless this simply means having a moral emphasis," and that "in teaching his children, Dickens chose not to dwell on the supernatural element of Christianity . . ." (13). Dickens's letters show, however, that he credited children with at least the *intuitive* capacity to understand the implications of, for example, the doctrine of innate depravity.[1] Moreover, it should be noted that Dickens wrote *The Life* during the period of his supposed religious crisis. And finally, *The Life of Our Lord* is, as I will demonstrate, entirely compatible with other statements Dickens made to adults. It must be considered theologically significant.

In addition to relying too uncritically on Forster and underestimating the theological significance of *The Life of Our Lord*, scholars have heretofore considered the question of Dickens' relation to Unitarianism with an inadequate or mistaken understanding of the doctrines and history of Unitarianism. Accordingly, I propose to consider the question afresh, beginning with a brief description of the three most important strains of Unitarianism in England in the nineteenth century. Then I will focus more narrowly on a comparison of Dickens' religious views with those of the two Unitarians who most influenced his decision to join the Unitarian church: William Ellery Channing, the eminent American Unitarian with whom Dickens became acquainted during his visit to America in 1841–2; and Edward Tagart, the minister of the Unitarian chapel in Little Portland Street, which Dickens joined in 1843 after hearing Tagart preach a memorial sermon on Channing. From this approach will emerge a clearer and more complete picture of the degree of Dickens' sympathy with Unitarian doctrines as well as whether his views changed, as Forster claimed, after his official association with the denomination.

I

The roots of English Unitarianism can be traced back at least to the decades before the Restoration, when rejection of the doctrine of the Trinity, the defining tenet of Unitarianism, caused controversy within the Church of England (Webb, "Unitarian Background" 4).[2] While the Toleration Act of 1689 made non-Anglican worship legal, denial of the Trinity remained a punishable offense until 1813. Despite that prohibition, however, Unitarianism as a denomination came into being in 1774 when an openly Unitarian chapel was established in Essex Street.

Thus, at the time Dickens took sittings in the Little Portland Street Chapel, English Unitarianism as a denomination was less than seventy years old—or only thirty if one dates its inception from the year when professing its leading doctrine was made legal. Despite (or perhaps because of) its relative youth, Unitarianism in the 1840s found itself in the midst of an intra-denominational struggle that eventually reshaped the denomination. Participants in that struggle aligned themselves either with the old school, associated with the work of Joseph Priestley, or with the new school, led by James Martineau.

Joseph Priestley, known today primarily as a scientist and as the discoverer of oxygen, was equally or better known by his contemporaries for his political radicalism and for the series of treatises he published during the 1770s that stimulated and directed the evolution of English Unitarianism out of English Presbyterianism.

Imbued with the rationalism characteristic of his era, and unrestrained by the desire for comprehension that dictated moderation to the Presbyterians, Priestley added several new tenets to the anti-Trinitarianism that was the essence of Unitarianism. His reading of the Scriptures led him beyond the Arian view of Christ, common among English anti-Trinitarians, to a Socinian view. Whereas Arians believed that Jesus was subordinate to God but pre-existent and divine, Socinians like Priestley insisted on "the *proper humanity of Christ*" as "essential to natural and revealed religion" (iv).

Priestley arrived at his humanitarian view of Christ as a logical consequence of his thoroughgoing materialist philosophy, which allowed him to dismiss the concept of the separation of the body from the soul—and beyond that the pre-existence of the spirit—on which both Arian and Orthodox Christologies depended.[3] Moreover, he argued movingly that the lesson Jesus was sent to teach about the perfectibility of man and the promise of eternal life would have been vitiated were he anything but human:

There appears to me to be a most evident propriety that a person who acted so

important a part with respect to mankind, as Christ did, who was sent to be our
instructor and example, and especially who came to ascertain the great doctrine
of a *resurrection from the dead*, should be, with respect to his *nature*, the very
same that we ourselves are; that he might exhibit before us an example of proper
human virtue, and especially that he might die as we ourselves die, and his
resurrection be the resurrection of a *man like ourselves*; . . . and thereby give
us the greater reason to hope, that because *Christ lives we shall live also.*
                                                                                                              (325–26)

While he insisted on the simple humanity of Jesus, Priestley relied on his
miraculous birth, on those biblical accounts of the miracles performed by
Jesus that could withstand rational scrutiny, and especially on his resurrection
as evidence of the divinity of Christ's *mission* (Webb, "Unitarian Background" 12).

By joining his own materialist philosophy and the associationist psychology
of David Hartley, Priestley also contributed to English Unitarianism the doctrine of philosophic necessity, which he called *necessarianism*. Priestley contended that all behavior, physical and moral, arises from motives and
responses which are material in their essence. There are no innate faculties;
there is no innate moral sense. If motives and the environment remain the
same, behavior remains the same. If they are altered, behavior alters. Priestley
argued that "every human volition is subject to certain fixed laws, and that
the pretended *self-determining power* is altogether imaginary and impossible"
(356). Priestley's necessarianism, in other words, dispensed with the concept
of free will.

Because he believed in a benevolent God who "disposes of all things, even
to their minutest circumstances, and always for the best of purposes" (Willey,
179), Priestley's necessarianism was progressive and optimistic: "all evil is
ultimately subservient to good, and . . . it is the intention of Providence
finally to exterminate all evil." This deterministic view implied neither fa-
talism nor passivity, for Priestley went on to say that "we may, and ought,
as his own children, to act like God, exerting ourselves, by every means in
our power, to remove the distresses of our fellow creatures" (Webb, "Unitarian Background" 12). Late in his life Priestley extended his necessarian
conception to include a belief in *universal restoration*, the doctrine that ultimately all men will be saved.

Following attacks on his home and laboratory in 1791, Priestley emigrated
to the United States in 1794 (Webb, "Unitarian Background" 13). But his
work was carried on by his followers (especially Theophilus Lindsay, minister
of the chapel in Essex Street, and Thomas Belsham, an important systematizer

of Priestley's ideas). By the 1820s Priestleyan Unitarianism was well established in England.

Because Priestleyan Unitarianism so thoroughly reflected the spirit of the age in which it evolved, it was vulnerable to the changing cultural and intellectual climate of the first half of the nineteenth century. The rise of romanticism made the cool Priestleyan rationalism unappealing, while advances in science and the advent of higher criticism called into question the reliance on the Bible, and especially the evidence of the miracles. So, beginning in the 1830s and continuing in various forms for three decades thereafter, Priestleyan Unitarianism came under attack from a new generation of Unitarians. Their leader was James Martineau, the brother of Harriet Martineau.

Martineau launched his attack in a review of *The Life and Works of Dr. Priestley*, which appeared in the *Monthly Repository*, the leading Unitarian journal of the day, in 1833. Martineau questioned Priestley's faith ''in the devotional influences of truth,'' with its emphasis on the critical and philosophical to the neglect of the emotional and social aspects of religion:

> Unitarianism, we think, must discover more variety in its resources, must avail itself of more flexibility of appeal, must wield in turn its critical, its philosophical, its social, its poetical, its devotional powers, before it gain its destined ascendancy over the mind of Christendom.
>
> ("Life" 14)

Martineau characterized Priestley as having a ''mediocrity of sensibility'' and a ''want of perception of the beautiful,'' faults which led him, for example, to see ''vastly too much philosophy, and vastly too little poetry, in the Scriptures'' ("Life" 27; 41). In short, to Martineau's tastes Priestley was not romantic enough. How far this romantic reaction against Priestleyan rationalism took the denomination is suggested by a statement offered in 1851 by the Rev. John Hamilton Thom, Martineau's ally. Thom stated flatly that ''Our path to God lies not through the reasoning powers. . . . The moral God, the Father of Spirits, is spiritually discerned'' (Webb, ''John Hamilton Thom'' 228).

Because their faith relied more on spiritual discernment than scriptural evidence, the new school had no need for the miracles. Looking back in 1876, Martineau observed that the appeal to miracles had grown ''out of keeping with the feeling of the time,'' and that abandoning them as the foundation of faith had allowed Unitarians of the new school to maintain their faith against the corrosive power of higher criticism:

Miracles had already lost all special religious value, before they fell under critical doubt: and as, on declaring themselves incredible, they had already become indifferent, they could pass innocently away, and leave the disciple's allegiance precisely where it had long rested.''

(Introduction 37)

The new school was generally repelled by Priestley's necessarianism, with its mechanistic explanation of morality and elimination of the concept of free will. In Martineau's view, Priestley's necessarianism excluded ''any moral element from the Divine administration'' (''Memoirs and Papers'' 115). Moreover, it reduced God to ''the ultimate-happiness maker, by no means fastidious in his application of means, but secure of producing the end'' (Short, 255).

In addition to these important differences on points of theology and philosophy, Martineau strongly opposed the effort, associated with the Priestleyan old school, to define and spread Unitarianism. In the 1850s Martineau resisted the use of the name ''Unitarian'' because it identified the church with a doctrine and thereby would ''check the spontaneous course of gradual change'' in religious beliefs (''Unitarian Position'' 376). So strong was his desire for a comprehensive church that in 1886, in ''A Way Out of the Trinitarian Controversy,'' Martineau even tried to erase the principal difference between Unitarianism and Trinitarianism by arguing that their different conceptions of the godhead were more apparent than real.

The development of Martineau's religious thought was influenced by William Ellery Channing, whose views constitute the third strain of Unitarianism available to Dickens in the 1840s. American Unitarianism was, as Conrad Wright has suggested, ''of indigenous origin, largely independent in its earliest stages of similar tendencies in English thought'' (6). Priestley's influence, central to the evolution of English Unitarianism, was much less important in America; like many religious liberals in Boston, the center of Unitarianism in America, Channing admired Priestley the man but rejected many of Priestley's ideas.[4]

Channing did, however, share Priestley's strong opposition to the doctrine of the Trinity. Whereas Martineau (more than forty years after the death of Channing) attempted to reconcile the Unitarian with the Trinitarian position, Channing (in sermons like ''Christianity a Rational Religion'') explicitly and frequently attacked the doctrine of the Trinity as unscriptural and irrational.

Channing shared with Priestley, too, a belief in the authenticity and significance of the miracles. In his ''Evidences of Christianity'' Channing argued eloquently for the historical importance of the Christian miracles:

[Christianity's] truth was attested by miracles. Its first teachers proved themselves the ministers of God by supernatural works. They did what man cannot do, what bore the impress of a divine power, and what thus sealed the divinity of their mission. A religion so attested must be true.

(210)

And as Priestley did, Channing attached special importance to Christ's resurrection, which he described in "Unitarian Christianity" as "that signal event . . . which powerfully bore witness to his divine mission, and brought down to men's senses a future life" (378).

Channing forcefully rejected materialism and necessarianism because these doctrines "make God the only power in the universe and rob man of his dignity" ("Introductory Remarks" 5). And whereas Priestley's philosophy led him to regard the concept of free will as an illusion, Channing shared with Martineau the belief that free will was essential to Christianity:

This attribute of free agency, through which an intelligent being is strictly and properly a cause, an agent, an originator of moral good or moral evil, and not a mere machine, determined by outward influences, or by a secret, yet resistless efficiency of God, which virtually makes him the author and sole author of all human actions . . . this moral freedom seems to us the noblest object of philosophical investigation. . . . It is the ground of responsibility, the fountain of moral feeling . . . it is the chief tie between the soul and its Creator."

("Remarks on Milton" 512)

On the question of the divinity of Jesus, Channing probably shared the views of most other New England Unitarians, who were Arians.[5] However, the theological distinction between the Socinian and Arian views, so important to Priestley, was much less so to Channing:

Others are more interested in studying Christianity under different aspects. Not a few attach supreme importance to the right decision of the question, "what rank Jesus holds in the Universe,—whether he be God, archangel, or man?" . . . I ask to approach his pure spirit, to learn his thoughts, feelings, emotions, principles, purposes. I ask to comprehend more and more of that love, which was so calm, yet so intense, within his heart. I ask to comprehend that expanded philanthropy which embraced a world . . . that spiritual philanthropy, which looked with constant and infinite concern on the soul of man, which felt for his sins far more than for his pains, which reverenced him as immortal, and thirsted to exalt him to immortal excellence. These are the *mysteries* of theology which I am most anxious to explore. To understand Christ's rank, I should esteem a privilege; yet I may know this, and be no better and happier for the truth. But to discern the beauty, loveliness, harmony, and grandeur of his mind, this is a knowledge which cannot but exert a creative and purifying power on everyone who can attain to it.

("Jesus Christ" 996)

In his emphasis on *feeling* the character of Jesus rather than *knowing* his rank and on Jesus' philanthropic example, Channing anticipated the new school of Martineau.

Channing also shared Martineau's distaste for the kind of aggressive theological controversy that characterized Priestleyan Unitarianism. Martineau quoted with evident approval the following statement by Channing:

> I have little or no interest in Unitarians as a sect. I have hardly anything to do with them. I can endure no sectarian bonds. With Dr. Priestley, a good and great man, who had most to do in producing the Unitarian movement, I have less sympathy than with many of the orthodox.
>
> ("Memoirs of Channing" 119)

And in "Spiritual Freedom" Channing exhorted his audience to

> remember that those who differ in word or speculation may agree in heart; that the spirit of Christianity, though mixed and encumbered with error, is still divine; and that sects which assign different ranks to Jesus Christ may still adore that godlike virtue which constituted him the glorious representative of his Father.
>
> (181)

While Dickens's letters contain no references to James Martineau or other important figures in the new school, his associations with old-school and American Unitarians are easily established. As already noted, Dickens met Channing, the leader of American Unitarians, on his American visit in 1842, and his admiration for Channing unquestionably contributed to Dickens' decision to join the Unitarians.[6] He also had ready access to Channing's works, the one-volume edition of which (published in England in 1840) was in Dickens's library at the time of his death (Stonehouse, 19).

His admiration for Channing also brought Dickens into contact with old-school Unitarianism when he attended a memorial service for Channing at the Unitarian Chapel in Little Portland Street. There he met—and began his long friendship with—Edward Tagart, minister of the Chapel and a principal figure in the Priestleyan old school.[7] Thus, at the outset of his involvement with Unitarianism, Dickens found himself personally associated with important representatives of two of the three strains of Unitarian doctrine. Comparing their views to Dickens' will allow us to take the measure of Dickens' Unitarian beliefs.

II

This comparison should begin with the defining doctrine of Unitarianism, the belief in "the strict and proper Unity of God." In his sermon, "The Rise and Progress of Unitarian Christianity" (1833), Edward Tagart formulated the doctrine in the following way:

> Whilst other churches, to use the language of the Articles, are dedicated to "three persons in the unity of the Godhead, of one substance, power and eternity, the Father, the Son, and the Holy Ghost"—"to us," in the language of the Apostle Paul, "there is One God, the Father, and one Mediator between God and man, the man Christ Jesus."[8]
>
> (10)

A debate about such an issue as the Trinity is probably too arcane to have engaged Dickens deeply. His writings are silent on the topic, unless he would have included it among those "obtrusive professions of and tradings in religion" which he considered to be "one of the main causes why real Christianity has been retarded in this world." He was, however, echoing here the sentiments of many Unitarians, especially of the old school, who believed that the spread of Christianity was retarded because the doctrine of the Trinity defied common sense (Webb, "Unitarian Background" 11).

On the question of the humanity of Christ, the best source of Dickens' views is *The Life of Our Lord*. As a Unitarian of the old school would, Dickens stressed Christ's humanity. In his recounting of the miracles performed by Christ, for example, Dickens attributed them to God and treated Christ as a distinctly separate and human agent who served, in the words of St. Paul that were so important to Unitarians, as a "Mediator between God and man": "God had given Jesus Christ the power to do such wonders [i.e., the miracles]; and he did them, that people might know he was not a common man, and might believe what he taught them, and also believe that God had sent him" (862). Dickens' emphasis on the significance of the miracles was also consistent with the view of both Priestley and Channing: miracles were one-time exceptions to the prevailing natural laws to demonstrate not Christ's divinity but his divine mission.

In a letter to de Cerjat in 1864, some fifteen years after he finished *The Life of Our Lord* (and long after his supposed religious crisis and return to the Established Church), Dickens made plain his continuing belief in the signal importance of a recognition of the humanity of Christ as the cornerstone of Christianity: "The church that is to have its part in the coming time must be a more Christian one, with a stronger hold upon the mantle of our Saviour, *as he walked and talked upon the earth"* (Nonesuch *Letters*, 3: 402; emphasis added). Here, as in *The Life*, Dickens's language reflects the Unitarian position on Christ's humanity.

Just as they differed with the Established Church (as well as with other dissenting denominations that Dickens attacked in his novels) over the doctrine of the Trinity and the divinity of Christ, Unitarians also differed emphatically with these groups over the prevailing doctrines of Original Sin and the innate depravity of man. Edward Tagart described the Unitarian position in the following way:

> Whilst, by other professing Christians, the nature of man is viewed as wholly sinful and inclined only to evil, and "therefore deserving God's wrath and damnation," to us it appears that the nature of man, though imperfect, is, on the whole good, and designed for good—that sin can only consist in actual transgression; and we reject, as unscriptural and irrational, the imputation of Adam's guilt to his posterity.
>
> ("Rise" 11)

It is suggestive of the affinity between this point of Unitarian doctrine and Dickens' practice in his novels, at least as perceived by unsympathetic critics, that an unfavorable review in the *Rambler* (a liberal Catholic periodical) could, as late as 1862, describe as a failing in his work Dickens's belief in what amounts to a Unitarian view of sin: "Nothing can be more indefinite or more human than his religion. He loves his neighbor for his neighbor's sake, and knows nothing of sin when it is not a crime" (Collins, 437). The (wholly unintended) echo of Tagart—and behind him Priestley—in this criticism is almost uncanny.

In his sermon "Unitarian Christianity," William Ellery Channing pointed out that the orthodox doctrine of innate depravity becomes most troubling when applied to children:

> Now we object to the systems of religion which prevail among us. . . . According to [Orthodoxy's] old and genuine form, it teaches that God brings us into life wholly depraved, so that under the innocent features of our childhood is hidden a nature averse to all good and propense to all evil, a nature which exposes us to God's displeasure and wrath, even before we have acquired power to understand our duties or to reflect upon our actions. . . . Now, according to the plainest principles of morality, we maintain that a natural constitution of the mind, unfailingly disposing it to evil, and to evil alone, would absolve it from guilt; that to give existence under this condition would argue unspeakable cruelty; and that to punish the sin of this unhappily constituted child with endless ruin would be a wrong unparalleled by the most merciless despotism.
>
> (377)

Dickens took a position identical to Channing's in a letter to the children's author Mrs. Godfrey in 1839, several years before his official association with Unitarianism began:

> I do most decidedly object, and have a most invincible and powerful repugnance to that frequent reference to the Almighty in small matters, which so many excellent persons consider necessary in the education of children. I think it monstrous to hold the source of inconceivable mercy and goodness perpetually up to them as an avenging and wrathful God who—making them in His wisdom children before they are men and women—is to punish them awfully for every little venial offence which is almost a necessary part of that stage of life. I object decidedly to endeavouring to impress them with a fear of death, before they can be rationally supposed to become accountable creatures, and so great a horror do I feel at the thought of imbuing with strict doctrines those who have just reflection enough to know that if God be as rigid and just as they are told He is, their fathers and mothers and three fourths of their relations and friends must be doomed to Eternal Perdition, and if I were left to choose between the two evils I would far rather that my children acquired their first principles of religion from a contemplation of nature and all the goodness and beneficence of the Great Being Who created it, than I would suffer them with such a strict construction ever to open a Bible or a Prayer Book, or enter a place of Worship. I do declare to you my dear Madam, that I daily see such evil and misery springing up from this fatal mistake, that whenever I see the slightest approach to it, I cannot in my conscience let go by [sic] without my most solemn protest.
>
> (Pilgrim *Letters*, 1: 568)

For orthodox Christians the pain of the doctrine of innate depravity was eased by the doctrines of atonement and grace. In "Unitarian Christianity" Channing described—and rejected—these doctrines in the following:

> This system also teaches that God selects from this corrupt mass a number to be saved, and plucks them, by a special influence, from the common ruin; that the rest of mankind, though left without that special grace which their conversion requires, are commanded to repent, under the penalty of aggravated woe; and that forgiveness is promised them on terms which their very constitution infallibly disposes them to reject, and in rejecting which they awfully enhance the punishments of hell. These proffers of forgiveness and exhortations of amendment, to beings born under a blighting curse, fill our minds with a horror which we want words to express.
>
> (377)

In writing *The Life of Our Lord* Dickens manifested his desire to instill in his own children a belief in the "inconceivable mercy and goodness" of God, in the fundamental goodness of man, and in a concept of salvation antithetical to the Calvinist doctrine that Unitarians, especially of the old school, deplored. In his analysis of the parable of the workers in the vineyard, for example, Dickens emphasized both God's mercy and man's capacity (and duty) to do good:

Our Saviour meant to teach them by this, that people who have done good all their lives long, will go to Heaven after they are dead. But that people who have been wicked, because of their being miserable, or not having parents and friends to take care of them when young, and who are truly sorry for it, however late in their lives, and pray God to forgive them, will be forgiven and will go to Heaven too.

(872)

Dickens's extra-biblical explanation of the reasons for wickedness strikes me as basic reading for any critic of his fiction, but for present purposes it is enough to notice his emphases on the fundamental goodness of man and the forgiveness assured to man by God through honest repentance. His position is perfectly compatible with that of the Unitarians, leaning perhaps toward the necessarianism of Priestley in its optimism.

As several of his comments cited above suggest, Dickens believed that the Old Testament was a document whose utility was past and that efforts to reconcile the Old Testament with the New or (worse) to apply the lessons of the Old Testament directly created only confusion and conflict. Dickens always preferred the New Testament and, it appears, would have willingly dispensed with the Old Testament as any basis for religious faith. *The Life of Our Lord* may again be cited as evidence of Dickens' position. He worked on his "children's New Testament" (Pilgrim *Letters*, 4: 573), a work he never intended to publish, in the midst of pressing professional and philanthropic obligations: he was writing about the ragged schools—founded, incidentally, by a Unitarian; he was helping Miss Coutts with her charitable activities; and he was struggling to get both *The Chimes* and *Dombey and Son* under way. The project was clearly important to him; perhaps it was in some sense recreational or restorative. In any case the circumstances of the composition of *The Life* underline the importance for Dickens of the New Testament. Late in his life Dickens reminded his son Henry of his effort to "render the New Testament intelligible to you and lovable [sic] by you when you were a mere baby" and impressed upon the nineteen-year-old boy "the priceless value of the New Testament, and the study of that book as *the one unfailing guide in life*" (Nonesuch *Letters*, 3: 673–74; emphasis added).

Several other explicit statements of the importance of the New Testament to Dickens may be found in his letters. In the letter to the Rev. R. H. Davies mentioned above (dated 24 December 1856) Dickens said, "There cannot be many men, I believe, who have a more humble veneration for the New Testament, or a more profound conviction of its all-sufficiency, than I have" (Nonesuch *Letters*, 2: 818). Two years later Dickens was even more emphatic: "Half the misery and hypocrisy of the Christian world arises (as I take it) from a stubborn determination to refuse the New Testament as a sufficient guide in itself, and to force the Old Testament into alliance with it—whereof comes all manner of camel-swallowing and of gnat-straining'' (Nonesuch *Letters*, 3: 79). In what may have been his last letter Dickens stressed (somewhat defensively) his strong affection for the New Testament:

> I have always striven to express veneration for the life and lessons of Our Saviour; because I feel it; and because I rewrote that history for my children—every one of whom knew it from having it repeated to them—long before they could read, and almost as soon as they could speak. But I have never made proclamation of this from the house tops.
>
> (Nonesuch *Letters* 3: 784)

And finally, in his will Dickens exhorted his children "to try to guide themselves by the teaching of the New Testament."

Dickens's lifelong belief in the centrality and sufficiency of the New Testament was an important tenet of Unitarianism as well. As Channing described it,

> Our religion, we believe, lies chiefly in the New Testament. The dispensation of Moses, compared with that of Jesus, we consider as adapted to the childhood of the human race, a preparation for a nobler system, and chiefly useful now as serving to confirm and illustrate Christian Scriptures. Jesus Christ is the only master of Christians, and whatever he taught, either during his personal ministry or by his inspired Apostles, we regard as of divine authority and profess to make the rule of our lives.
>
> ("Unitarian Christianity" 367)

In a letter to de Cerjat in 1863 Dickens, too, endorsed the idea that the Old Testament was a document belonging to the "childhood of the human race," as Channing phrased it. Interestingly, though, this idea, expressed by Channing in 1819, had by 1863 become current among the so-called "Broad Church" Anglicans, including Bishops Colenso and Jowett, whom Dickens defended against de Cerjat's objections in the following remarks:

> [C]ertain parts of the Old Testament have done their intended function in the education of the world *as it was*; but . . . mankind, like the individual man, is designed by the Almighty to have an infancy and a maturity, and . . . as it advances, the machinery of its education must advance too.
>
> (Nonesuch *Letters*, 3: 352)

Removed from the context of Dickens' own earlier remarks and of the doctrines of Unitarianism, these comments might seem to support Forster's argument that Dickens was an Anglican of the Dean Stanley (Broad Church) variety. In their proper context, however, they reflect Dickens's continuing belief in a position long associated with the Unitarians.

Another position long associated with the Unitarians was their reliance on the power of human reason to resolve religious questions. Old-school Unitarians especially were often criticized for exalting reason above faith because of their hard-headed historical and scientific examination of sacred texts and their rejection of doctrines that could not be justified logically. Tagart alluded to this common criticism of Unitarianism in the sermon on Channing that attracted Dickens to the Little Portland Street Chapel and its minister. Despite his allegiance with the old school, Tagart nevertheless praised Channing for his "rescue" of the Unitarianism

> from the charge of coldness and insensibility, by an evidence of warmth, and vigour, and enthusiasm, which carried refutation with it; by a demonstration of a spirit of power and love; by a combination of argument with feeling, in the same way as other writers combine argument with wit, so close as to render it impossible to separate and distinguish either without destroying both.
>
> ("Tribute" 13)

Later in the sermon he praised Channing for stressing the harmony between reason and religion and thereby making this distinctive feature of Unitarianism acceptable: "His bright and convincing representations of the harmony between reason and religion . . . have given to our views an interest unfelt before, have inspired a confidence in their worth and power" (20-21).

If Tagart's eulogy or the friendship Dickens formed with Channing during his American visit earlier in the year moved Dickens to read his copy of Channing's collected sermons, he would have encountered a stirring defense of reason in "Christianity a Rational Religion":

> Christianity is a rational religion. Were it not so, I should be ashamed to profess it. I am aware that it is the fashion with some to decry reason, and to set up revelation as an opposite authority. This error, though countenanced by good men, and honestly maintained for the defense of the Christian cause, ought to be earnestly withstood; for it virtually surrenders our religion into the hands of the unbeliever. It saps the foundation to strengthen the building. It places our religion in hostility to human nature, and gives to its adversaries the credit of vindicating the rights and noblest powers of the mind.
>
> (233)

Channing is almost endlessly quotable as a Unitarian polemicist, but perhaps this small addition from the same sermon will suffice to show how powerfully Channing advocated this doctrine so distasteful to Unitarianism's opponents:

The development of [our rational nature] is the end of our being. Revelation is but a means, and is designed to concur with nature, providence, and God's spirit, in carrying forward reason to its perfection. . . . If I could not be a Christian without ceasing to be rational, I should not hesitate as to my choice. . . . I ought not to sacrifice to any religion that reason which lifts me above the brute and constitutes me a man. . . . Christianity wages no war with reason, but is one with it, and is given to be its helper and friend."

(233)

Dickens was not a systematic thinker, and we should be surprised, I think, to find the author of *Hard Times* championing any cold or technical notion of reason. But then Channing's is not a cold or technical notion, either. When Channing and Dickens use the term or concept, both mean something like "common sense," the phrase Dickens himself used in the letter he wrote to his American friend C. C. Felton announcing his affiliation with Unitarianism: "Disgusted with our Established Church, and its Puseyisms, and daily outrages on common sense and humanity, I have carried into effect an old idea of mine, and joined the Unitarians" (Pilgrim *Letters*, 3: 455). More than a decade later, in the letter to de Cerjat mentioned above, Dickens emphasized the importance for religion of "not gradually shock[ing] and los[ing] the more thoughtful and logical of human minds" by insisting on positions that defy common sense. And later on in the same letter he marvelled at those "successors of the men who protested against human judgment being set aside," successors who now "call names and argue nothing" (Nonesuch *Letters*, 3: 351–52).

Consistent with Dickens' belief in the exercise of common sense in religious matters is his belief in the importance of religious toleration and preserving the right to exercise "human judgment" on religious issues. As late as 1864 (in another letter to de Cerjat) Dickens was still chiding the Protestant establishment for its intolerance:

[T]he idea of the Protestant establishment, in the face of its own history, seeking to trample out *discussison and private judgment*, is an enormity so cool, that I wonder the Right Reverends, Very Reverends, and all other Reverends, who commit it, can look in one another's faces without laughing, as the old soothsayers did. Perhaps they can't and don't.

(Nonesuch *Letters*, 3: 402; emphasis added)

Dickens here echoed the sentiments expressed by Edward Tagart in his "The Rise and Progress of Unitarian Christianity" some three decades before. In this sermon Tagart reminded his audience of the leaders of the Reformation

who renounced the infallibility of the Pope, but maintained their own. They claimed a right to differ from the church, but would not allow others to differ from themselves. The principles of religious liberty were by no means understood. The right of private judgment was not conceded. The duty of persecution was maintained; and the iron hand of religious bigotry fell with all its weight upon the unhappy persons who ventured to express doubt whether the doctrine of the Trinity were true.

("Rise" 18)

That Dickens admired the Unitarian position on toleration is clear. In the 1843 letter to Felton he explicitly cited their practice of "Charity and Toleration" as one of the denomination's attractions for him. He was also clearly—if wryly—conscious of the "iron hand of bigotry" that might fall on him if his membership in a denomination so far removed from the religious mainstream became known: "The Tories will love me better than ever, if this gets wind. My children shall return the compliment, please God!" (Pilgrim *Letters*, 3: 456).

The other quality that attracted Dickens to the Unitarians, as he indicated in his letter to Felton, was the denomination's emphasis on the union of faith with action. His admiration for Channing may have been founded in part on Channing's efforts to abolish slavery in America. Tagart's memorial sermon warmly praises Channing's efforts in this regard. In England, Unitarians were intimately involved in efforts to achieve reform, as Dickens knew first hand. His friend William Johnson Fox was a Unitarian minister who edited the *Monthly Repository*, a periodical that began as a Unitarian journal and evolved under his editorship into a journal that "led the way in the advocacy of reforms that took the long years of the nineteenth century to complete" (Mineka 44).

Dickens own practice of "good works" requires no documentation. But its foundation in his religious beliefs should be noted. For Dickens, doing good works was not just a means to gain Heaven: "people who have done good all their lives long, will go to Heaven after they are dead" (*The Life of Our Lord* 872). It as the essence of Christianity itself: "Remember!—It is Christianity TO DO GOOD always—even to those who do evil to us" (*The Life of Our Lord* 891). This belief in doing good, so central to Dickens' character as a public man and an artist, was central to the character of Unitarianism as well. It helped draw Dickens to Unitarianism in the first place. At the beginning of his official involvement with Unitarianism he said approvingly of them that they "*would* do something for human improvement" (Pilgrim *Letters*, 3: 455). In this respect, as in so many others, Dickens found Unitarianism coinciding with his own beliefs.

III

Many of the greatest Unitarians were, to use Edward Tagart's term "self-converted": "One by one, without communication with each other,—by the light of their own enquiries and convictions,—they have been led to the adoption and profession of Unitarian principles" ("Rise" 24). By just such gradual and intuitive means, I believe, Dickens came to the Unitarian church in 1843. Joining the Unitarians was not an impulse based merely on his attraction to Edward Tagart, as Peyrouton contends, but was, as Dickens himself said, an "old idea." Nor was his involvement a mere "flirtation," as Peyrouton argues. As this survey of Dickens' comments on religious issues, comments spanning his mature life, makes clear, Dickens' religious views changed in no essential way from the years before his official association with Unitarianism, through those years, and on to the very end of his life. Moreover, as this comparison of his views with those of the leading Unitarians with whom he was acquainted demonstrates, Dickens' religious beliefs were from first to last compatible with the leading doctrines of Unitarianism, especially as formulated by Unitarians of the old school and given eloquent expression by Channing.

In arguing that Dickens was a Unitarian on his pulses both before and after his official association with the Little Portland Street Chapel, I must reject the standard view that Dickens moved toward Broad Church Anglicanism sometime during the 1840s. This view is based, I believe, on an imperfect understanding of the relationship between Unitarianism as a dissenting denomination and the Broad Church movement within the Established Church. The Broad Church movement was in fact partially a response to the challenge to the Established Church posed by Unitarianism. The clergymen who came to be identified with the Broad Church movement met the Unitarian challenge by adopting, sometimes in spite of themselves, many positions traditionally identified with Unitarianism. F. D. Maurice, who in 1853 published his *Theological Essays*, illustrates the point dramatically. Although the *Essays* were an explicit attempt by this son of a Unitarian minister to answer the challenges posed by Unitarianism, Maurice found himself virtually espousing Unitarian doctrines before his attempt finally devolved into a theological muddle.[9]

Another was Dean Stanley himself, whose religious views Forster claimed to have influenced Dickens' own. In October of 1872 *The Unitarian and Universalist Missionary* gleefully printed the heading "Dean Stanley at the Unitarian Position" in its "Notes of Progress" column. The substance of the accompanying article consisted of extracts from and commentary on a sermon recently delivered by Stanley, a sermon the column's author characterized as "clear[ing] away the corruptions of orthodoxy" and "settl[ing] down by the side of the cautious Unitarians":

> Accordingly, like Unitarians, [Stanley] places the centre of truth respecting Christianity with Jesus. He called up the lawyer who asked Jesus the question "What shall I do to inherit Eternal life?" and, of course, the Dean did not find reason to show that Jesus demanded belief in the Athanasian Creed, or the Five Points of Calvinism. He said:—"The lawyer knew what he was about. He did not ask, What am I to think, or What am I to say? or What am I to feel? but What am I to do? He knew something of the great doctrine everywhere proclaimed in the Bible, 'He that doeth righteousness is righteous.' He was only perplexed by wishing to know how he should do what was right. This principle, too, our Lord recognised. He sanctioned the principle that to do is the great thing." This is enough to justify the heading of this paragraph. For Unitarians have stood on that foundation a long time; and we feel some pleasure in finding an eminent clergyman of the Church of England in this respect with us.
>
> ("Dean Stanley" 135)

The theological convergence of Unitarianism and the Broad Church, resisted by men like Maurice, accomodated urbanely by men like Stanley, and celebrated by the Unitarians—this convergence would have allowed Dickens, playing the country squire late in his life, to attend an Anglican church occasionally without having to submit to "the daily outrages on common sense and humanity" that characterized the Church for him twenty-five years earlier. The key point—missed by all commentators—is that the Established Church changed, not Dickens.[10]

IV

A final question remains: Why would Forster, himself a Unitarian, not acknowledge Dickens' Unitarian sympathies? The answer, I believe, lies in Forster's conception of his duty as biographer. We know that Forster took pains to preserve Dickens' status as a national monument, even at the expense of the truth. As James A. Davies, Forster's biographer, notes:

> Forster edited and falsified documents to stress the lively, sparkling side of Dickens, removed vulgarisms or the cutting response, and suppressed socially damaging facts such as Dickens' dandyism, the extent to which his family sponged on him, his antagonism towards the established church, and the depth of his pessimism about the condition of England.
>
> (251)

Forster's treatment of Dickens' religious beliefs fits the pattern Davies describes. Without doing great violence to the truth, he could choose to identify Dickens with a wing of the Established Church represented by no less respectable a figure than Dean Stanley. Or he could risk tarnishing his friend's reputation by presenting the "socially damaging fact" of his sympathy with a by no means thriving or entirely respectable dissenting denomination —remember Dickens' rueful comment on the likely Tory reaction to his joining the Unitarians.[11] Understandably, Forster preferred to dismiss Dickens' involvement with Unitarianism with a Podsnapian wave of his arm. In doing so he was behaving no worse than other nineteenth-century biographers of prominent Unitarians had. The historian R. V. Holt observes that

> as late as the nineteenth century, biographers often felt that to have been a Unitarian was a stain on the reputation of the subject of their biography and in characteristic fashion strove to conceal this stain. So that what began as persecution and persisted as prejudice now survives as ignorance.
>
> (14)

Interestingly, this concealment extended even to Joseph Priestley himself!

Free of the prejudice that must have influenced Forster's account and possessing a better understanding of the denomination that coincided in so many respects with Dickens' expressed views, we can now correct the false impression created protectively by Forster and perpetuated too readily by subsequent scholars. And we can begin to reconsider Dickens' fiction in light of his lifelong Unitarian sympathies.[12]

NOTES

1. See, for example, Dickens' letter to Mrs. Godfrey, in Pilgrim *Letters*, 1: 568, quoted below.
2. This summary relies heavily on Webb and Short.
3. For a convenient summary of materialist philosophy, see Willey, 173–77.
4. "Next to Lardner, the most laborious advocate of Christianity against the attacks of infidels, in our own day, was Priestley; and whatever we may think of some of his opinions, we believe that none of his opposers ever questioned the importance of his vindications of our common faith" (Channing, "Objections" 407).

   Daniel Walker Howe observes that

   > The distinction between Priestley's Unitarianism and that of the Harvard moralists [like Channing] was particularly important; it went well beyond Arian-Socinian Christological differences. Priestley was a philosophical materialist, a determinist, and caustic critic of the Scottish common sense

philosophy admired at Harvard. . . . Henry Ware, Jr., perhaps the most
generous of the Harvard moralists, edited *Views of Christian Truth, Piety,
and Morality* (Cambridge, 1834), a selection of Priestley's least controversial
writings, on the grounds that the man had never enjoyed a fair hearing in
New England; but even Ware was careful to disavow Priestley's "obnox-
ious" intellectual "errors" in his preface.

(317 n. 16)

5. According to Wright, "Arianism continued to be the commonest form of Unitarianism in New England until well into the nineteenth century" (210). Martineau
   also labeled Channing an Arian ("Memoirs of Channing" 117). 6. In the sentence immediately prior to the one in which Dickens announced that he had joined
   the Unitarians, Dickens asked his correspondent, C. C. Felton, for news of the
   Channing family, presumably wanting to know how the family was faring in the
   months after Channing's death (Pilgrim *Letters*, 3: 453–54).
7. Webb describes him as a "captain on the Priestleyan side" ("Unitarian Background" n. 23). Dickens also knew William Johnson Fox, a Unitarian minister
   of the old school who had turned away from the denomination, becoming a
   journalist and editor of the *Monthly Repository*.
8. The quotation from St. Paul is from 1 Timothy 2.5.
9. The following specimen from *Theological Essays* will illustrate the tangled
   logic—and prose—that characterized Maurice's effort:

   I do think that our theories of Inspiration, however little they accord with
   Unitarian notions, have a semi-Unitarian character; that they are derived
   from that unbelief in the Holy Ghost which is latent in us all, but which was
   developed and embodied in the Unitarianism of the last century. I have not
   been able to conceal this opinion in the present case or in other cases. I
   have not tried to conceal it; for I am persuaded that we must go further from
   Unitarianism, if we would embrace Unitarians; that we shall never know
   them as brothers, till we bring out our own faith more fully, and disengage
   it from some of the elements of distrust which we, in imitation of them,
   have allowed to mingle with it. Especially do I look forward to this result,
   however distant and improbable it may seem, from a full assertion of that
   portion of our creed which refers to the Person of the Comforter. I do see
   in that, such a bond of loving fellowship for all men—such a breaking down
   of sect-barriers—that I long to speak of it even if it be with the most
   stammering tongue, to those who have been divided from us. I have not
   entered upon that subject here.

   (242–43)

10. Only Walder even addresses the issue, commenting that "it would be difficult
    to say whether Dickens was turning toward Broad Church ideas or whether they
    were turning towards him" (176). But he seems not to have understood the
    implication of his comment. For an account of the complex ways that Unitarianism
    was at first influenced by Latitudinarian Anglicanism only to influence the de-
    velopment of the Broad Church in its turn, see Wigmore-Beddoes.
11. Unitarianism had not prospered in the decades after Dickens' comment to Felton
    in 1842. The struggle between the old and new schools persisted, with the new
    school of Martineau gradually gaining ground. The new school's desire to abandon

the Unitarian name cannot have helped the denominational cause. Nor did the fact, already mentioned, that other denominations were becoming more liberal. According to a column in *The Unitarian and Universalist Missionary*, the total number of Unitarian congregations in 1872 was 356, compared with 332 in 1865. The anonymous author who provided these statistics commented: "These figures certainly show little or no increase above that arising from the national increase of population, which is about one *per cent. per annum.*"

12. The first draft of this essay was written during a National Endowment for the Humanities Summer Seminar for College Teachers, directed in avuncular fashion by Professor George Ford at the University of Rochester in 1984. I am grateful to the NEH and to Professor Ford for their support of my work. I also want to thank The University of Texas of the Permian Basin, which provided a grant in 1985 that allowed me to do additional research. Professor R. K. Webb, of the University of Maryland, Baltimore County, read the penultimate draft of this essay with sympathy and insight and offered many valuable suggestions for improvement. My Summer Seminar colleague, Professor Michael Kearns, not only listened patiently to the original presentation on which this essay is based but joined the faculty at UT Permian Basin in time to read the final draft, helping me to spot and untie some knotty prose. Any remaining errors of fact or interpretation or infelicities of style are, alas, my own.

WORKS CITED

Chadwick, Owen. *The Victorian Church.* 2 vols. London: Adam & Charles Black, 1966.

Channing, W. E. "Christianity a Rational Religion." *Works.* 233–46.

—————. "Evidences of Christianity." *Works.* 188–220.

—————. "Introductory Remarks." *Works.* 1–11.

—————. "Jesus Christ the Brother, Friend, and Saviour." *Works.* 992–1000.

—————. "Objections to Unitarian Christianity Considered." *Works.* 401–08.

—————. "Remarks on the Character and Writings of Milton." *Works.* 496–521.

—————. "Spiritual Freedom." *Works.* 172–88.

—————. "Unitarian Christianity." *Works.* 367–84.

—————. *The Works of William Ellery Channing, D.D.* Boston, 1891. Collins, Phillip, ed. *Dickens: The Critical Heritage.* New York: Barnes & Noble, 1971.

Coolidge, Archibald. "Dickens and Latitudinarian Christianity," *Dickensian* 59 (1963): 57–60.

Connell, J. M. "The Religion of Charles Dickens," *Hibbert Journal* 36.2 (1938): 225–34.

Davies, J. H. *John Forster: A Literary Life.* Leicester: Leicester University Press, 1983.

"Dean Stanley at the Unitarian Position." *Unitarian and Universalist Missionary.* 1.10 (Oct. 1872): 135.

Dickens, Charles. *The Letters of Charles Dickens.* Ed. Walter Dexter. Nonesuch Edition 3 vols. London: Nonesuch Press, 1938.

——————. *The Letters of Charles Dickens.* Ed. Madeline House, et al. Pilgrim Edition 6 vols. Oxford: Clarendon Press, 1965–88.

——————. *The Life of Our Lord.* Vol. 1 of *The Nonesuch Edition of the Works of Charles Dickens.* 38 vols. London: Nonesuch Press, 1938.

Forster, John. *The Life of Charles Dickens.* 2 vols. New York: E. P. Dutton, 1948.

Holt, R. V. *The Unitarian Contribution to Social Progress in England.* 2nd ed. rev. London: Lindsay Press, 1952.

Howe, Daniel Walker. *The Unitarian Conscience: Harvard Moral Philosophy, 1805–1861.* Cambridge, Mass.: Harvard University Press, 1970.

Johnson, Edgar. *Charles Dickens: His Tragedy and Triumph.* 2 vols. New York: Simon & Schuster, 1952.

Martineau, James. *Essays, Reviews, and Addresses.* 3 vols. London: 1890.

——————. Introductory Chapter. *A Retrospect of the Religious Life of England.* By John James Tayler. 2nd ed. London, 1876. 3–42.

——————. "The Life and Works of Dr. Priestley." *Essays* 1: 1–42.

——————. "Memoirs and Papers of Dr. Channing." *Essays* 1: 81–148.

——————. "The Unitarian Position." *Essays* 2: 371–80.

——————. "A Way Out of the Trinitarian Controversy." *Essays* 2: 525–38.

Maurice, F. D. *Theological Essays.* 1853. rpt. London: James Clarke, 1957.

Mineka, Francis. *The Dissidence of Dissent: The Monthly Repository, 1806–38.* Chapel Hill: University of North Carolina Press, 1944.

Peyrouton, N. C. *The Life of Our Lord*: Some Notes of Explication." *Dickensian* 59 (1963): 102–12.

Priestley, Joseph. *Disquisitions Relating to Matter and Spirit.* London, 1777; rpt. New York: Arno Press, 1975.

Short, H. L. "Presbyterianism under a New Name." *The English Presbyterians: From Elizabethan Puritanism to Modern Unitarianism.* C. Gordon Bolam, et al. Boston: Beacon Press, 1968. 219–86.

Stonehouse, J. H., ed. *Catalogue of the Library of Charles Dickens.* London: Piccadilly Fountain Press, 1935.

Tagart, Edward. "The Rise and Progress of Unitarian Christianity." London, 1833.

——————. "A Tribute to the Memory of the Rev. William Ellery Channing, D.D." London, 1842.

Thom, J.H. *St.Paul's Epistles to the Corinthians. . . .* London, 1851.

"Unitarian Statistics." *The Unitarian and Universalist Missionary*. 1.3 (March 1872): 41.

Walder, Dennis. *Dickens and Religion*. London: Allen & Unwin, 1981.

Webb, R. K. "John Hamilton Thom: Intellect and Conscience." *The View from the Pulpit: Victorian Ministers and Society*. Ed. P. T. Phillips. Toronto: Macmillan of Canada, 1978. 211–43.

—————. "The Unitarian Background." *Truth, Liberty, Religion: Essays Celebrating Two Hundred Years of Manchester College*. Ed. Barbara Smith. Oxford: Manchester College, 1986. 2–30.

Wigmore-Beddoes, D. G. "How the Unitarian Movement Paid Its Debt to Anglicanism." *Transactions of the Unitarian Historical Society*. 13.2 (Oct. 1964): 69–79.

Willey, Basil. *The Eighteenth Century Background*. New York: Columbia University Press, 1940.

Wright, Conrad. *The Beginnings of Unitarianism in America*. Boston: Starr King Press, 1955.

Comic Subversion and *Hard Times*

Grahame Smith

In a recent issue of *Dickens Studies Annual*, Nicholas Coles makes the case, with what one hopes is definitive brilliance, for seeing fiction and other modes of writing as totally opposed forms of discourse.[1] Coles's specific case is the politics of *Hard Times* and his argument centers on the "fallacy in the procedure of reading the politics of the novels through Dickens' speeches and journalism [which] is that it ignores crucial differences between those forms of discourse; fiction and journalism use different modes of presentation, which reflect differing imaginative activities, and differing purposes and occasions for writing." (145–46). In drawing attention to the opposing viewpoints of *Hard Times* and *Household Words* Coles contributes to a case that one would like to believe is now as near to proof as anything in literary study can be, that the attempt to use the novels, letters, speeches, journalism,and personal opinions as interchangable counters in the creation of a monolithic structure called "Dickens" is as theoretically limited as it is practically uninteresting.

Many years ago I drew attention to a discrepancy in Dickens' attitudes towards the Ragged Schools in life and in art (Smith, *Dickens, Money and Society* 216–18). The letters in which he expresses his determination to help Miss Coutts in her financing of such projects is ample proof of his belief in the practical efficiency of such efforts: the cure may be almost as bad as the disease but anything is better than leaving the situation untouched. In *Our Mutual Friend*, however, a different order of judgment is embodied, an imaginative response which must be true to its intellectual and emotional sense that, judged at the level of art, such philanthropic activities are damaging socially as well as personally. The only result of failing to respect this form of the distinction between life and art is confusion. And this misunderstanding is always liable to privilege what Dickens "really" thought in his attempts

at "consecutive reasoning" (the phrase is Keats's, of course) at the expense
of what are for some the more complex, because more deeply thought out
and felt, responses of art. Returning to Coles's subject, politics, in relation
to Dickens in general, one relevant emphasis is the frequently suggested move
from early radicalism to more conservative positions in Dickens' social
thought. According to this view, one consistent theme that emerges in the
later letters is a hardening of the political arteries which manifests itself in
Dickens' support for harsh punishment for criminals and such episodes as his
mounting of a private prosecution against a girl swearing in the street. There
is, of course, something deeply comforting about this move from youthful
folly (well, idealism) to a maturely realistic grasp of the nature of the world
we live in. Did not Wordsworth and Coleridge take the same route, a path
that would almost certainly have been followed by Keats, Shelley, and Byron
if they had only lived long enough?

But what justification is there for privileging one thread of a complex life
in this manner? The letter-writing Dickens and the Dickens of the novels may
be very different in this respect. The Dickens for whom the trial of Magwitch,
in his penultimate completed novel, is a matter of "civic gewgaws and monsters" and its gallery of onlookers "a large theatrical audience" (*Great Expectations* 56), can hardly be seen as conservative. But my purpose is not to
rehabilitate Dickens' radicalism in opposition to critical denigrations of it.
That would be to succumb to the temptation of monolithic interpretation
merely from the other side. What I think is more interesting is to dissolve
these large categories in a recognition of the fact that the life and the work
form a grid pattern, a complex crossing and recrossing of threads, any one
of which might be unpicked and held up in triumph as constituting the key
to the understanding of a single text or of the whole life.

I have already suggested a distinction between the Dickens of the letters
and the Dickens of the novels, a separation which has been developed in film
theory to deal with some of the problems which arise in the area of cinematic
authorship. Film theorists quite happily refer to Howard Hawks and "Howard
Hawks." Howard Hawks without quotation marks represents the real man
who, amongst other things, was a film director. "Howard Hawks" stands
for the sign system inscribed on the surface of the visual and aural text, a
sign system within which it may be possible to discern the recurrence of
certain patterns, obsessions, visual motifs, and so on. Dickens lends himself
to a particularly complex version of this treatment: Dickenses abound, as it
were. Even the letter writer is not a single entity, but a correspondent who
appears in different guises depending on whether he is writing to his wife or

Maria Winter, to the conservative Miss Coutts or the radical Douglas Jerrold, to Wilkie Collins or John Forster.

As an auteur Dickens is even more complex, his genius intersected by myriad lines of force. From a strictly literary point of view we might disentangle Shakespeare, the Bible, the eighteenth-century novel, and Romantic poetry. This high-art aspect of his work is modified by the popular; above all, by stage melodrama. Dickens as visionary and as "special correspondent for posterity" (Bagehot, 394) exist sometimes cheek by jowl. Serial publication feeds in its own strands of authorship; public opinion in general is both a constraint and something to be challenged: Dickens may tone down the horrors of slum life in the decriptive passages of *Oliver Twist*, but he insists always on giving a special value to his illegitimates, the products of loving passion rather than lawful sheets. Specifically, the complaints of the real-life dwarf who suggested the Miss Mowcher of *David Copperfield*, and the contribution of Bulwer-Lytton to the ending of *Great Expectations*, represent additions to authorship of real significance. Nor should the carte blanche offered to John Foster to shape monthly and weekly parts to their optimum size be forgotten.

Since film theory has appropriated the quotation mark, the Dickens I am presenting here might be denoted by italics: *Dickens!* Such a construct is composed of pressures, influences, and forces of every possible kind; a maelstrom of politics, religion, social criticism, literature, the theater, Christmas, foreign travel, amateur theatricals, education, crime, long walks, and heaven knows what else. This is clearly the deconstructionist's version of "here is God's plenty," but for lesser mortals the choices may seem a trifle daunting. The idiocy of generalization notwithstanding, one feels some urge towards summary. My italicized Dickens may represent a kind of shorthand for an immense range of references, but it is in practice impossible to hold all of this in mind simultaneously in teaching, writing, or even thinking about him, and so formulae such as "Yes, Dickens is a radical," "No, he's not," "Well, sometimes he is and sometimes he isn't" seem unavoidable.

One route out of this impasse is that of David Lodge's scholar-critic, Maurice Zapp, who thinks of writing about a literary text from every possible angle, an operation which would invade and, ultimately, annihilate the writer's space, to use a Zappian term, but this is only a complete version of the single master thread move. My own suggestion centers on the inescapable fact that Dickens began as a comic writer, developed as a comic writer, and remained a comic writer to his dying day. This momentous discovery may, I'm aware, appear as a very stale crust for critical gums to mumble on, but I want to insist on it if only because it is possible to plough through acres of writing on Dickens without turning over a single hint that he is operating in a comic mode. Like David Copperfield's love for Dora, Dickens is so steeped in comedy that it would be possible to wring him out and use the surplus to create half-a-dozen other comic writers. Critical avoidance of Dickensian comedy is all the more surprising if we acknowledge that it is inseparable from his way of seeing the world, the medium in which all aspects of his work live and have their being. If Dickens' themes, obsessions, subject matter, image patterns, and so on are figure, then comedy is the ground against which they stand out not separably, as it were, but colored, however lightly, around the edges.

Comedies would, if there were world enough and time, be the only truly appropriate term to use in relation to such a protean mass of material. But this is not the place to describe, much less analyze, the huge range of Dickensian humor: farce, satire, wit, comic pathos and tenderness, black humor, surreal transpositions of language, and the rest. However, one bias in this comic vision has not, I think, been sufficiently foregrounded, that contained in Mark Tapley's reply to Martin Chuzzlewit's reference to his feelings: "I'm thankful," says Mark, "that I can't say from my own experience what the feelings of a gentleman may be" (Chapter 15). It would be quite foreign to my purpose to erect this little joke in passing into a thematic center in Dickens' work. But what I do believe is that it is an example of a mood or atmosphere or tone that is never far from the surface of his novels and is liable to pop up in the most unexpected circumstances. On the other hand, it is far from being merely an obsessive tic, a spasm of uncontrolled because uncontrollable laughter. I shall comment later on its wilder manifestations, but my stress for the moment falls on its place in an attempt to understand, at the imaginative level, the complexities of living in his own period. For example, it is quite clear that Dickens' reaction to the gentlemanly ideal of his own day is a very complex one. It has sometimes been taken to be central to his moral scheme, the counterpointing of Joe Gargery and Pip being an obvious example of Dickens' treatment of the implied clash between the true and the false gentleman. This might be seen as the respectable face, as it were, of the preoccupation; other aspects do not fit quite so tidily into the image of a thematically responsible author.

Dickens' artistic success in this area was perhaps made possible by a crucial aspect of his own experience, the constant shifts in his social position during his earlier life. The move from being the much-loved product of a lower middle-class family to working boy and the climb upwards via school, clerking, reporting, journalism and, finally, creative writing were enough to impress on anyone the complexities of the English class system. The affronts to gentility afforded by butchers loudly demanding payment at the foot of the stairs, agonizing visits to the pawnbroker and fears that his murky past would be uncovered left scars on Dickens' psyche which a lifetime was not long enough to heal. These hurts to the boyish and adolescent self were only compounded, of course, by the reactions of the Beadnell parents to his love for their daughter, a rejection on class and economic grounds which he was by then old enough to understand in all its ramifications. As Dickens himself acknowledged these were all aspects of the forces that had helped to make him what he was and he was not more inclined than Magwitch to try to ''bend the past out of its eternal shape'' (Chapter 56). One fruit of this experience can be seen in the force of the encounters between Bradley Headstone and Eugene Wrayburn in *Our Mutual Friend* where the ineradicable sense of inferiority of the self-made man and the effortless savoir-faire of the Oxbridge, public-school product is presented with a masterly command of nuance and gesture. The fact is, of course, that Dickens himself was both self-made man *and* gentleman.

But what kind of gentleman was Dickens? A host of details from the life reinforce the sense that he did not fit easily into the recognized categories of his period. That exuberant hair and those rather too colourful waistcoats might have suggested to some that he was a nouveau riche upstart and vulgarian. One variation on this social distaste was the dismay of George Henry Lewes at the absence of books from Dickens' establishment, the response of an intellectual who expected to possess his own library rather than consume books with the devouring energy of genius in the Reading Room of the British Museum. Again, Dickens' appearance and personal manner, at least in his earlier years, might have led to his being bracketed with Bohemians of the Count D'Orsay variety, except for his evident commitment to the domestic life.

It is clear that Dickens came to formulate some thought-out positions in the process of adjusting to wealth and upward social mobility. His refusal to put his servants into livery on the grounds that payment of wages did not amount to personal ownership is a clear enough example. And the savagery of some of the letters generated by his involvement with the Administrative Reform Association in the mid-1850s testifies to a profound disillusion with social institutions and mores. However, a disproportionate degree of attention has been given to this kind of thing because it fits neatly into our modern sense of the writer-intellectual conscientiously taking up his considered positions on the large questions of the day. What this emphasis fails to register is an element of sheer wildness in Dickens, that almost demonic energy that exhausted male house guests on twenty-mile walks and ruined the dresses of unfortunate girls by dragging them into the sea. The mental equivalent of this hobbledehoydom is revealed at its most glaring in the infamous dummy books (shades of Gatsby) in the Tavistock House library:

> *Five Minutes in China*, 3 vols., *Forty Winks at the Pyramids*, 2 vols. . . . *A Carpenter's Bench of Bishops, Kant's Eminent Humbugs*. . . . *Hansard's Guide to Refreshing Sleep*. . . . *Malthus's Nursery Songs*. . . . *The Wisdom of Our Ancestors*, vol. 1 Ignorance 2 Superstition 3 The Block 4 The Stake 5 The Rack 6 Dirt 7 Disease. Alongside this bulky work [in Edgar Johnson's words] was "*The Virtues of Our Ancestors*, a single volume so narrow that the title had to be printed sideways".
>
> (Johnson, 2:750)

This is the side of Dickens which revels in Count Smorltork and Lord Mutonhead and which defines the word "aristocratic" as "when lords break off door-knockers to beat policemen, and play at coaches with other people's money (*Nicholas Nickleby* Chapter 15).

How *can* serious people like us take this kind of thing seriously? Sniggering distaste from the gentlemen scholars and icy aloofness from the critic as intellectual are clearly discernible patterns in the massive volume of responses to Dickens,[2] but for an active celebration of this aspect of his life and art we have to go back to Chesterton's joyful respect for his vulgarity and populism. Awkward as it may be for the modern sensibility, however, this is a Dickens we ignore at our peril because the man who delights, in an early letter, in the prospect of doing the "nobs",[3] as he calls them, by publishing the same material in two outlets, so securing extra payment for himself, is revealing an attitude of mind that will remain a constant in his work.

What I am attempting here is the foregrounding of one image out of the multitude that compose Dickens' work. His vision of the thronging streets of the metropolis has been seen often enough as the appropriate setting of a maimed humanity, eccentric at best, at its worst alienated to madness. But another kind of warfare is conducted on these streets, one prompted by the sight of a top hat or a condescending glance, a warfare which individualizes, however fleetingly, the anonymous crowd for whom derision is an unconscious political response to oppression and its accompanying slighting of the self. The lower orders cheeking their betters, the cab driver's insolent rejection of a meager tip, the contemptuous whistle of a street arab, the delighted response to middle-class discomfiture—these form a comic ground against which even the more somber figure of the later novels must be placed.

Dickens' comic commitment to such moments is undeviating, I think, some secret pleasure imparting at least one thread of consistency to his work no matter at how low (in every sense of the word) a level. These irrepressible outbursts of laughter constitute a noise which interferes with more soberly responsible thematic strategies and deflates pretension whenever it dares raise its head. The noise, in the other sense, that I am seeking to evoke here is the sound of that laughter heard in Bleeding Heart Yard after Panks has shorn the Patriarch of his Samson-like locks with those all-too Freudian shears. Awestruck by the enormity of his daring, Panks makes off, "pursued by nothing" but that sound, "rippling through the air and making it ring again" (*Little Dorrit* 2.32). For an extended example of the demolition of genteel pretensions we could do no better than turn to Dickens' penultimate completed novel, and the discomfiture of Pip by Trabbs's boy.

It might seem, however, that of all the novels *Hard Times* would be most resistant to an approach by way of comic subversion. Leavis's reading is one of unremitting seriousness and for other critics, as Coles points out, Dickens is in a conceptual muddle in *Hard Times* and so, by implication, lacks control of the full range of artistic effects that are deployed so brilliantly in, say, *Bleak House*. But that deep prejudice in favor of the low and vulgar (which extended to serial publication itself, of course)[4] is as evident in *Hard Times* as elsewhere. The vehicle of Mrs. Sparsit's destruction is verbal cleverness, but the impulse behind this witty deflation is the street arab's delight in discomfiting the nobs, above all in her total physical and personal humiliation at the end. Her unmasking, and Bounderby's, before a crowd of gleefully interested bystanders is the kind of urban comedy in which Dickens delighted from *Sketches by Boz* on.

The presence of the circus in a work of "serious" polemical intent has clearly embarrassed many critics. It seems revealing that Leavis, for example, sanitizes the horse-riding of that atmosphere of gin-soaked moral laxity and rowdyism which are clearly aspects of the total impression Dickens wishes to make. But, as so often, it is the great contemporary, Forster, who strikes the right note in referring to contemporaries' dislike of Dickens' "playful" handling of a notion of the day in *Hard Times*.[5]

It is tempting to take up "playful" in its post-modernist sense and subject *Hard Times* to the rigours of a deconstructionist reading. There are certainly gaps enough in this text: the nature of Stephen's promise to Rachael to avoid union action and the novel's presentation of trades unionism, given Dickens' known views of such matters in life. These problems are perhaps soluble, however, in traditional terms. Textual scholarship reveals the presence of an omitted section of manuscript which goes some way to explaining Stephen's choice and Coles is surely right in arguing that what "is wrong with the union from the point of view of *Hard Times* is . . . that it crushes the life of the individual" (168). Individuality, and the mystery of individuality, if not the thematic center of the book, is at least a motif that runs continuously through it.

But the novel is playful in other senses too. Far from being insecure in setting the book outside London and in dabbling in political and philosophical ideas that are outside his range, I believe that Dickens is totally in command here, seizing a practical opportunity and exploiting its artistic potential to the full. The genesis of *Hard Times* is deeply revealing of Dickens in his dual function as popular and creative genius, for the writing of the novel did, of course, involve an element of practical necessity. *Household Words'* function as entertainment and instruction was central to Dickens' social outlook, but there was no conflict between this humanizing role of cherishing "that light of fancy which is inherent in the human breast" (Preliminary Word) and the economic return he insisted on from all his professional activities. And so when it became clear, early in 1854, that *Household Words'* profits and circulation were declining, it was decided by Dickens and his associates (again the implications for authorship in the non-personal sense are obvious) that only he could save the day by producing a novel in weekly parts, although he had not intended to write another novel for at least a year after the creative effort of *Bleak House.*

This response to market forces and intense practicality might suggest that *Hard Times* was taken on in a spirit of mechanical pot-boiling, but once embarked on a creative project Dickens showed an amazing ability to tap the deepest sources of his imagination. We know that he was constantly pre-occupied by such issues as the place of the imagination in a scientific-technological age, education in its widest sense, and the meaning for individual human lives of vast industrial changes in society. Under the pressure of a practical necessity these concerns fused into an imaginative statement of permanent interest, a fusion made possible by another example of Dickens' ability to turn commercial pressures to aesthetic advantage.

Although he complained so bitterly of the spatial constraints of weekly publication, Dickens made use of this in the same spirit of artistic experiment which prompted the brilliantly contrasted narrative structure of *Bleak House,* with one half of its story being told in the first person by the youthful Esther

Summerson while the other half is recounted with apparent impartiality by the witty, sardonic, but also humane third-person narrator (Smith, *Bleak House* Section 2). What Dickens seems to have done in *Hard Times* is to seize the opportunity presented by the novel's method of publication to push his tendency towards allegory and a non-realistic presentation of human and social truth to an extreme point. That this was a conscious process is suggested by the letter of protest he wrote to a journalist, Peter Cunningham, who had suggested that Dickens' visit to Preston to gather material for his *Household Words* article "On Strike" was the novel's source. Dickens replied that the book's "title was many weeks old, and chapters of the story were written, before I went to Preston or thought about the present strike." More important, he goes on to say that Cunningham's claim "localizes . . . a story which has a direct purpose in reference to working people all over England"[6] which suggests that a quality of symbolic representativeness was central to Dickens's artistic vision in *Hard Times*.

Although the novel has never been without its admirers—John Ruskin and, later, George Bernard Shaw were early advocates of its truth and power—it was, and has remained, one of the less popular of Dickens' works, although a significant shift of opinion followed its full-scale rehabilitation as the greatest of Dickens' novels by F. R. Leavis in 1948. The very qualities which made the novel appear untypical to many readers—its lack of the exuberant wealth of detail that seems central to Dickens' art, for example—were the source of Leavis's admiration. Leavis's reading of *Hard Times* is persuasive and of lasting importance in the history of the book's reception but, as with any thought-out literary response, it is colored by Leavis's general critical position. His concern with the formal properties of works of literature is combined with rigorous moral and social criticism of human life and this results in a view of the novel that may make it appear solemn, as opposed to serious.

There is no question that Dickens was in deadly earnest in his critique of what he saw as some of the central cruelties and follies of his society. But despite the pressures exerted on him by the brevity of weekly publication, *Hard Times* is far from lacking the tone of his other work. There is an exuberance of spirit, if not of detail, in his satire of a world dominated by a pervasive concept of utility; and fun, too, as in the absurd confrontation between Bounderby and the circus performers. Although the novel's brevity would make the structural complexity of *Bleak House* out of place, *Hard Times* shares some of that novel's brilliance at the level of the detail of its language, and this amplitude, albeit within constraints, is echoed in the novel's thematic concerns, which are richer than is suggested by Leavis's rigorously unified scheme of interpretation.

The number of targets being aimed at here is very large. The fairly sympathetic view of industrialism taken in *Bleak House*, at least in the person of Mr Rouncewell the ironmaster, is modified in *Hard Times* into a comprehensive anatomy of its ills despite the book's acknowledgment that the products of Coketown minister to the comforts of life. The external evils of the factory system, its reduction of Coketown to a productivity machine rather than a center of civilized life, and its pollution of the environment are all vividly sketched. At the human level, its boring repetitiveness is seen as producing a crushing monotony in the lives of men and women who become only ''hands'' in an almost literal sense. The notion of human impoverishment is present also in the novel's treatment of education at both the formal level and within the family. For some radical critics the obvious positive contrast to the evils of Coketown would have been the trades union movement but this, too, is subjected to critical scrutiny, above all in the relation of the individual worker to the organization through the story of Stephen Blackpool. Opposed to all of these is the circus, a haven of fun, spontaneity, varied and demanding physical skills, and sexual freedom (this last point is clearly hinted at in the description of the circus people as an extended family or commune). Around these thematic centers Dickens finds room for attacks on the British class system in Mrs Sparsit, Parliament via Harthouse, and the cult of the self-made man in Bounderby. A more personal note is perhaps struck by the episodes dealing with Stephen's hopeless attempt to divorce his dipsomaniac partner where Dickens' generalized hatred of the social divisiveness of one law for the rich and another for the poor is possibly intensified by the dissatisfaction with his own marriage which was to end in separation from his wife in 1858.

This polemical richness cannot be reduced to a single unifying theme, but an engagement with conceptions of what is truly useful in the enhancement of worthwhile living is a recurrent pattern in many, if not most, of the novel's episodes. This keynote is struck by the title of Chapter 1, ''The One Thing Needful,'' a reference to Luke 10.14. When Jesus arrives at the house of Martha she busies herself with the chores necessitated by the visit. She complains that her sister, Mary, is doing nothing to help in sitting and listening to Jesus, but he replies ''Martha, Martha, thou are careful and troubled about many things. But one thing is needful: and Mary hath chosen that good part''. The one thing needful for the Gradgrind system is, of course, facts, facts acquired through a never-ending grind of mechanical mental activity. For

Jesus, and for the novel, there is a kind of inactivity which focuses on what is most important in human life, the acquisition of wisdom and the giving of love.

The obliquity of this thematic contribution through a biblical allusion is another sign of Dickens' status as a popular genius. He delights in such great commonplaces whether in the Bible, Shakespeare, literature in general, or in the ability of the common language to focus wisdom in proverbs and sayings. He takes particular pleasure in reanimating such clichés as ''an Englishman's home is his castle,'' with Wemmick, and ''as the crow flies,'' with Mr. Tulkinghorn. But this indirection is of more general interest. One sign of Dickens' inexhaustible fertility is the way in which the novels can be seen, with enlightening clarity, through the spectacles of recent critical theory. *Hard Times* may not be a deconstructed work, but it does leave the reader to do a good deal of construction. The novel's brevity seems to have occasioned in Dickens an almost experimental fervor, a determination to push his tendencies towards objectification to an extreme point and this ''fascination with what's difficult'' leads Dickens into that subversive playfulness which I am arguing is central to his genius. But despite his Joycean exuberance of language and openness of form, Dickens has too much respect for his audience, and for his commercial prospects, to allow his work to drift into incomprehensible ambiguities. And the levels of which he was by now the master allowed him to have his cake and eat it in this area. Suspense, melodrama, fun, and sentiment are deployed, quite without cynicism, in a manner that gripped the huge audience while Dickens satisfied his own private concerns as an artist with a playfulness that might best be described as a kind of teasing.

The highly self-conscious reader is teased by the extreme objectivity of the novel's form, its lack of generalizing statements of intention, to construct his own version of its meaning. For Nicholas Coles, ''*Hard Times* is the Dickens novel which readers have least known what to do with, and about which there has been least agreement as to how it requires to be read'' (173). This general relationship of novel to audience is reinforced by a pervasive tone at the local level, a consistent pulling of the reader's leg, as in this little explosion occasioned by a narrative reference to Peter Piper: ''If the greedy little Gradgrinds grasped at more than this, what was it, for gracious goodness sake, that the greedy little Gradgrinds grasped at!''(1.3).

Characters too are teased and not simply the Gradgrinds and Bounderbys. The wall-eyed and lisping Sleary is the butt of much humor, but a more surprising example is Stephen Blackpool, who one would have thought would have been immune to such treatment. But on the first occasion when he calls on Mr. Bounderby, for example, we find the following: "Stephen made a bow. Not a servile one—these hands will never do that! Lord bless you, Sir, you'll never catch them at that, if they have been with you twenty years!—and, as a complimentary toilet for Mrs. Sparsit, tucked his neckerchief ends into his waistcoat" (1.11). I shall return later to the opening of this paragraph, but for the moment it is Stephen's "complimentary toilet" that seizes the attention. The combination of tenderness and comedy in such a characteristic example of Dickens' style is almost impossible to analyze. The gesture is the working man's equivalent of the gentleman's lifting his hat to the lady and while the action does nothing to impair Stephen's dignity, its verbal expression is undeniably comic in its gentle mockery of the character.

But this teasing comic subversion is frequently far from tender, its often abrasive quality well represented by the lines immediately preceding Stephen's gesture of courtesy to Mrs. Sparsit: "Stephen made a bow. Not a servile one—these hands will never do that! Lord bless you, Sir, you'll never catch them at that, if they have been with you twenty years!" This example of free indirect speech introduces one of the novel's most successfully subversive devices, a linguistic pattern which Dickens deploys with consummate ease. The transition from neutral narrative description ("Stephen made a bow") to the explosive contempt of Bounderby and his ilk is achieved with seamless mastery, as in this more extended example:

> Then came Mr. Gradgrind and Mr. Bounderby, the two gentlemen at this present moment walking through Coketown, and both eminently practical, who could, on occasion, furnish more tabular statements derived from their own personal experience, and illustrated by cases they had known and seen, from which it clearly appeared—in short, it was the only clear thing in the case—that these same people were a bad lot altogether, gentlemen; that do what you would for them they were never thankful for it, gentlemen; that they were restless, gentlemen; that they never knew what they wanted; that they lived upon the best, and bought fresh butter; and insisted on Mocha coffee, and rejected all but prime parts of meat, and yet were eternally dissatisfied and unmanageable.
>
> (1.5)

This does surely pull the reader up in a teasing, if exhilarating, manner. What on earth is going on, one might well ask: one moment we are strolling the streets of Coketown with these gentlemen, the next . . . ? This movement into the tone and vocabulary of hectoring public speeches is funny, of course, once its initial surprise has been assimilated, but it does also operate on a more subtle level. The absorption of the language of the world of "telegrams and anger"[7] into the novel's narrative has the effect of condemning Gradgrind and Bounderby from the inside, as it were, the verbal equivalent of giving them enough rope with which to hang themselves. Standing condemned out of their down mouths, their exposure is accomplished far more effectively than through authorial statement, if only because the judgment passed on them is partly the reader's through his participation in grasping the force of what Dickens is up to.

This dual effect of subversion through reader involvement is maintained by other verbal patterns of great richness. Relevant here is David Lodge's well-known analysis of the novel's use of fairy-tale elements (159–63). The Giant Bounderby and Mrs. Sparsit as the Bank Fairy are wonderfully amusing, although the mill as a Fairy Palace strikes a more sinister note of ironic inversion. The subversive intention does, however, remain unmistakable in all manifestations of the pattern. In Coles's words, by making "the dominant forces of his time into ludicrous versions of the Giant and Ogre of a children's story, transposing them into a mode of existence which is anathema to them . . . Dickens is able to overpower them, to do in fiction what he could never do in the public market-place of opinions" (172). My final example of comic subversion is a pattern related to the fairy-tale but less well known, I think, another splendid embodiment of Dickens' ability to take off from the realistic level into the realm of fantasy, metaphor, and linguistic virtuosity.

As with Shakespeare's Hotspur, for Dickens it is an "easy leap" to take up the hint suggested by the title of Chapter 6 in Book 1, "Sleary's Horse-manship", to deploy a beautifully worked out little pattern of imagery in the course of a few pages. Since Sleary's troupe is essentially a "Horse-riding" it is entirely appropriate that it should put up at the "Pegasus's Arms," a joke which may have had its genesis in the world of popular entertainment which Dickens knew so intimately as well as in the realm of learning of which he is sometimes supposed to have been so ignorant. As Paul Schlicke points out " 'Pegasus' was a name inevitably linked with the equestrian circus; Ducrow had a favourite steed of this name, and there was a statue of the mythical winged horse atop Hughes's Royal Circus" (161). The notion of Mr. Sleary being associated with poetic inspiration is a delight which clearly also operates as a signal of deeper intentions with regard to the role of the circus in the novel's artistic economy. The conceit is continued by way of W.E.B. Childers as a "most remarkable sort of Centaur" and Kidderminster as "Cupid" and reaches its climax in the only extended description of the company as a whole which the novel has space for or which, perhaps, Dickens needs:

Meanwhile, the various members of Sleary's company gradually gathered together from the upper regions, where they were quartered, and, from standing about, talking in low voices to one another and to Mr. Childers, gradually insinuated themselves and him into the room. There were two or three handsome young women among them, with their two or three husbands, and their two or three mothers, and their eight or nine little children, who did the fairy business when required. The father of one of the families was in the habit of balancing the father of another of the families on the top of a great pole; the father of a third family often made a pyramid of both those fathers, with Master Kidderminster for the apex, and himself for the base; all the fathers could dance upon rolling casks, stand upon bottles, catch knives and balls, twirl hand-basins, ride upon anything, jump over everything, and stick at nothing. All the mothers could (and did) dance upon the slack wire and the tight-rope, and perform rapid acts on bare-backed steeds; none of them were at all particular in respect of showing their legs; and one of them, alone in a Greek chariot, drove six in hand into every town they came to. They all assumed to be mighty rakish and knowing, they were not very tidy in their private dresses, they were not at all orderly in their domestic arrangements, and the combined literature of the whole company would have produced but a poor letter on any subject. Yet there was a remarkable gentleness and childishness about these people, a special inaptitude for any kind of sharp practice, and an untiring readiness to help and pity one another, deserving often of as much respect, and always of as much generous construction, as the every-day virtues of any class of people in the world.

(1.6)

Much attention has been lavished on this often quoted passage: the individuality of the circus people and their mastery of a range of complex physical skills (as opposed to the stultifying monotony of the Hands' lives), their kindness and family feeling. Less commented on is the stress on what the Victorians might have called their irregularity. These ladies who drive "a Greek chariot" are not "at all particular in respect of showing their legs" and the reference to "two or three handsome young women . . . with their two or three husbands, and their two or three mothers, and their eight or nine little children" creates an unmistakable aura of slightly indiscriminate sexual activity, an impression reinforced (however comically) by Cupid and the Centaur. Is there any reason to believe, as far as the latter are concerned, that Dickens is not exploiting its traditional symbol of energy, especially of a sexual nature, or that he had not seen them, as did Keats, at their most ferociously vital on the Elgin Marbles in the British Museum?

The effects at work here are rich indeed. The comic aspects of the circus people are intensified by their association with the mysterious beauty of a mythical past while simultaneously, with the paradox of art, their role as entertainers is dignified so that it can bear something of the weight of symbolic and thematic importance necessary for Dickens' imaginative purposes. On a more general level, comic subversion is also operating. Fairy-tale and classical imagery combine to create a fictional universal parallel to the "real" world of the utilitarians, itself a fiction as created in the pages of *Hard Times*, which subverts these pseudo-Benthamites not in direct statement but through imaginative creation, a mode of perception and understanding whose validity they deny. The best, perhaps the only, answer to the proposition that there is no real difference between push-pin and poetry is not to attempt to argue the point, but to create poetry.

Gradgrind and Bounderby, those deniers of myth, fairy-tale, and imagination in all its guises are hopelessly entrapped in having their positions undermined by a fiction of which they are a part (they are, after all, imaginative creations), a fiction not of the polemical, Harriet Martineau-like variety to which they might accord a limited validity, but one which 2oyfully celebrates the mystery of life in an artisry which is no less mysterious in its ultimate sources and power.

Possibly the greatest mystery of all is Dickens' ability to fuse differing levels of his work into a satisfying whole. It would be absurd to argue that only the classically educated could grasp the centaur reference; on the other hand, it is fair to assume that it was missed by the majority of his contemporary readers. But for them ample compensation was provided in the form of humor, sentiment and action. What is most striking about all of this, and a sure sign of the popular genius, is the complete absence of anything patronizing in Dickens' manipulation of these levels. Another dimension of what might be called his respect for both his audience and his own artistry is the fact that Dickens introduces a new tone into the presentation of the urban poor in English literature: the Stephen Blackpool episode to which I referred earlier is a case in point and a fine early, extended example is the treatment of the Kenwigs family in *Nicholas Nickleby*. Dickens may be savage with his Barnacles and his Bounderbys, but a mockery without humiliation and a tenderness without sentimentality is reserved for the humble poor.

My final example of the fusion of levels bears directly on the theme of comic subversion as it operates in *Hard Times*. It is surely the most wonderful joke to create such fact-freaks as Gradgrind and Bounderby and then subvert them within the context of an imaginative fiction. And the joke is both sophisticated, delicious even, in its entangling of, say, Mrs. Sparsit in the gossamer webs of fairy-tale imagery, and broadly farcical, cruel even, in its reduction of Tom Gradgrind to a level of "disgraceful grotesqueness" in his "comic livery" (3.7). This is an art which is truly vulgar, of and for the people, but all the people and not simply one segment at the expense of the others.

NOTES

1. "The Politics of *Hard Times*" 15 (1986).
2. I am thinking of the tone adopted towards Dickens, in such celebrated works of criticism as John Hollaway's essay on *Hard Times* in *Dickens and the Twentieth Century*, and John Carey's *The Violent Effigy*.
3. To John Macrone, 3 August 1836 (Pilgrim *Letters*, 1:160).
4. See Dickens' preface to the Cheap Edition of *The Pickwick Papers*.
5. Unsigned review in the *Examiner*, 9 September 1854: 568–69.
6. Quoted in Norton Critical edition of *Hard Times* (275).
7. The phrase is, of course, from E. M. Forster's *Howard's End*.

WORKS CITED

Bagehot, Walter. *Dickens: The Critical Heritage*. Ed. Philip Collins. London: Routledge & Kegan Paul, 1971.

Coles, Nicholas. "The Politics of *Hard Times*: Dickens the Novelist versus Dickens the Reformer." *Dickens Studies Annual* 15 (1986): 145–179.

Dickens, Charles. *Hard Times*. Ed. George Ford and Sylvère Monod. Norton Critical edition. New York and London: Norton, 1966.

—————. *The Letters of Charles Dickens*. Eds. Madeline House and Graham Storey. Pilgrim Edition. Oxford: Clarendon, 1965.

Ford, George, and Sylvère Monod, eds. *Dickens and the Twentieth Century*. London: Routledge & Kegan Paul, 1962.

Holloway, John. "*Hard Times*: a History and a Criticism" in *Dickens and the Twentieth Century*. Eds. John Gross and Gabriel Pearson. London: Routledge & Kegan Paul, 1962. 159–74.

Leavis, F. R. *The Great Tradition: George Eliot, Henry James, Joseph Conrad*. New York: G. W. Stewart, 1948.

Lodge, David. *The Language of Fiction*. London: Routledge & Kegan Paul, 1966.

Schlicke, Paul. *Dickens and Popular Entertainment*. London: Allen & Unwin, 1985.

Smith, Grahame. *Bleak House*. Studies in English Literature, No. 54. London: Edward Arnold, 1974.

—————. *Dickens, Money and Society*. Berkeley and Los Angeles: University of California Press, 1968.

Writing as a Woman:
Dickens, Hard Times, and Feminine Discourses

Jean Ferguson Carr

In his 1872 retrospective essay on Dickens, George Henry Lewes presents Dickens as an exemplary figure whose career has upset the balance between popular taste and critical judgment.[1] The essay depends on what seems initially an aesthetic opposition between show and Art, between "fanciful flight" and Literature, but these critical terms also demark class and gender boundaries that preserve the dominant literary culture. Dickens becomes "the showman beating on the drum," who appeals to the "savage" not the "educated eye," to "readers to whom all the refinements of Art and Literature are as meaningless hieroglyphs." He works in "delf, not in porcelain," mass producing inexpensive pleasure for the undiscerning reader, but is found wanting by the "cultivated" reader of "fastidious" taste. The essay attempts to contain Dickens' impact by identifying him as lower-class, uneducated, and aligned with feminine discourses, but it also suggests the difficulty of accounting for Dickens' influence and the importance of investigating the "sources of that power." Despite Lewes's isolation of Dickens as a "novelty" or as a madman, he concedes that he "impressed a new direction on popular writing, and modified the Literature of his age, in its spirit no less than in its form" (143).

Dickens' admirers, following John Forster, have responded to the essay as mistaken and insulting.[2] As John Gross wrote, the essay "still has the power to irritate," with its innuendo about hallucinations and lower-class vulgarity, and its casual anecdotes about the author's inadequate library.[3] Lewes's class bias and his narrow definition of education have undermined the influence of his critique of Dickens for modern readers, but his subtle positioning of Dickens in relation to women writers and his articulation of the categories by which novels will be judged has been more durable. When, for example, Gordon Haight concludes that "Dickens was a man of emotion, sentimental throughout; Lewes was a man of intellect, philosophical and scientific" (167), he is echoing the gender-based oppositions of Lewes's argument.

The essay on Dickens is part of the broader attempt begun by Lewes in the 1840s to serve as arbiter of the emergent literary class and of its premier form, the novel. Like Lewes's 1852 essay "The Lady Novelists," it seeks to position those literary newcomers who threaten the status and boundaries of nineteenth-century literary territory, to control the impact of a broader-based literacy and of women's emergence into more public spheres.[4] The critique of Dickens depends on polarities that usually mark gender differences in nineteenth-century criticism, as, for example, the difference between feeling and thinking, between observing details and formulating generalizations. "Dickens sees and feels," Lewes intones,

> but the logic of feeling seems the only logic he can manage. Thought is strangely absent from his works. . . . [K]eenly as he observes the objects before him, he never connects his observations into a general expression, never seems interested in general relations of things.
>
> (151)

Lewes makes still more explicit his identification of Dickens with this secondary realm of women's writing in this backhanded compliment:

> With a fine felicity of instinct he seized upon situations having an irresistible hold over the domestic affections and ordinary sympathies. He spoke in the mother-tongue of the heart, and was always sure of ready listeners.
>
> (146–47)

Dickens is thus identified with the feminine, as instinctual and fortunate, as seizing rather than analyzing, as interested in "domestic affections and ordinary sympathies." He "painted nothing ideal, heroic," Lewes explains. "The world of thought and passion lay beyond his horizon" (147)

Lewes evokes many of the same oppositions when instructing Charlotte Brontë on the "proper" realm for women writers, when cataloguing the "lady novelists" of the day, or when marking the novel as the particular "department" of women, the form that values "*finesse* of detail, . . . pathos and sentiment."[5] His acknowledgment that Dickens is "always sure of ready listeners" rehearses a charge often made against nineteenth-century women

writers, that the financial success and popularity of their work, its very at-
tentiveness to audience concerns, marks it as "anti-" or "sub-literary,"
concerned with sales not posterity. Dickens thus joins the company of writers
like Fanny Fern and Mary Elizabeth Braddon who, as one critic put it,
discovered: "a profitable market among the half-educated, . . . giving the
undiscriminating what they wanted to read."[6] The use of a category like the
"subliterary" works to regulate the effects of the novel as a newly-positioned
literary discourse that challenges the cultural hegemony of upper-class men
of letters.

In July 1845, Dickens described the aim and rhetorical stance of a proposed
journal, *The Cricket*: "I would at once sit down upon their very hobs; and
take a personal and confidential position with them."[7] In 1850, he finally
established a periodical to fulfill the role of domestic comrade, that aspired
"to live in the Household affections, and to be numbered among the Household thoughts, of our readers."[8] In establishing a journal to be "familiar in
their mouths as Household Words" (as the motto read), Dickens was making
use of a feminine guise, privileging the intimate, private, and informal qualities usually associated with women over the social, public, and authoritative
powers usually associated with men. But he was also disrupting the conventional wisdom that sharply divided the domestic and public spheres, for his
journal insisted on the interpenetration of these realms.[9]

This gesture of cultural cross-dressing is part of a recurring exploration by
Dickens in the 1850s of the discourses usually identified as feminine.[10] Michael Slater has argued that in the decade 1847 to 1857 Dickens was "apparently preoccupied with women as the insulted and injured of mid-Victorian
England," and that the novels in this period feature more women characters
in more prominent positions than do other of his novels. But he also sees
Dickens as "voicing no general condemnation of prevailing patriarchal beliefs
and attitudes."[11] I do not find it surprising that Dickens did not "voice" a
"general condemnation" of the ideology within which he wrote. What I want
to investigate is why his interest hovers at the edge of articulation, why it
goes so far and then retreats, or goes so far and then is silent. Why is Dickens
simultaneously empathetic with oppressed women and insistent on the constraints and stereotypes that restrict them? What does his practice suggest
about how women are rendered silent in Victorian culture and novels, how
their perspective is undermined or preempted? To use Pierre Macherey's
terms, such issues become part of what is "unvoiced," "unspoken" both in
the novels and in Dickens' public postures.[12] The issue is not so much, then,
whether Dickens crafted complex psychological women characters along the

lines of George Eliot or Charlotte Brontë, but how women are positioned in the powerful discourses of the novels as in contemporary social practices. In Dickens' novels, the notion of "writing as a woman" is problematic, as opposed to the confident assumptions Lewes makes of what it means "to write as women," of what the "real office" is that women "have to perform," of the "genuine female experience."[13] Dickens' experimentation suggests that much is unknown, even to the women who "experience" their lives and desires, that there is no ready language for what women wish to "write." Although Dickens himself certainly does not articulate a program of women's liberation, and indeed deploys many cultural tropes that restrict women as "relative creatures," his novels often make the "commonsense" notions of Lewes untenable.[14]

The proliferation of child-wives in his novels and his portrait of Esther Summerson's strained narrative have often been cited by critics as signs of Dickens' preference for coy, idealized, and subservient women. His advocacy of the domestic values of hearth and home has similarly been dismissed as a sign of a peculiar weakness, a bourgeois sentimentality aimed at pleasing or appeasing his readers. Along with his taste for melodrama and Christmas morality, such quirks are explained away as a cultural disguise the master assumed to protect his more radical designs. The more critically acceptable Dickens provides cynical and witty analysis of cultural conventions and hypocrisies from a disengaged position. In other words, Dickens is valued as a prototype of the (male) modern artist as rebel and cultural critic; he is embarrassing in his assumption of what we label (female) "Victorian" values. Like Lewes, then, we perpetuate the stigma of writing as a woman, associating feminine discourse with a lack of analysis and rigor, with pandering to "cheap" tastes. And we resist identifying Dickens with either its problems or its effects.

When Dickens' experimentation with "writing as a woman" is examined within this contest for literary territory and power, it involves more than merely being a woman writer or adopting a feminine persona.[15] By aligning himself with terms and oppositions usually associated with women (for example, fancy vs. reason or fact, the personal vs. the institutional), Dickens, in effect, explores how his own position as a writer of fiction is marked off as suspect or inferior.[16] He experiments with writing that traverses opposed realms and deploys narrative tropes that mark breaks in discursive power—stuttering, deception, metaphor, eccentricity, strain of voice or prose, interruptions. In this context, for example, Dickens' insistence on a linkage between "romance" and familiar things is more than a personal credo or a rehearsal of a romantic ethos.[17] The preference in *Hard Times* of the devalued term "fancy" over the more culturally respectable term "imagination" locates his argument in a contemporary ideological contest, rather than as a repetition of an earlier aesthetic debate. The problematic position of women characters and writers functions as a figure of Dickens' own position in a culture suspicious of fancy and wary of claims to "domestic" power. Deflecting the unease of his position onto women as an oppressed class allows Dickens to be more extreme and critical than he could if he were evaluating his own position directly.[18]

I would like to focus on what has usually been cited as a negative portrait of women, the failure to create a strong, likable heroine or a credible mother figure in *Hard Times* (1854). The novel itself is an instance of the conditions of feminine discourse, written not in any expansive artistic mode, but under the urgency of periodical publishing, as a project his printers hoped would attract readers to *Household Words*. Dickens disliked the conditions of weekly publication and deplored as "CRUSHING" the consequent lack of "elbow-room" and "open places in perspective."[19] But the process must have underscored the constraints embedded in the social and material production of discourse. Indeed much of the novel explores what cannot be said or explained, what cannot be portrayed. The women of this fictional world in particular are restricted by and to their social positions, defined within narrow ideological bounds that afford little relief. The characters do not operate primarily in personal relationships to each other, nor do they "forget" their social positioning, or the polarities that operate in Coketown. They are constructed in oppositions, as women and men, mothers and daughters, middle-class thinkers and lower-class workers. The usual cultural positions for women remain curiously unpopulated, incomplete, present but not functioning as they ought. This schematic underdevelopment need not be explained away as a technological effect of the novel's weekly form, or as a style of abstraction.[20] The ideological and technical constraints also create the possibility for Dickens to write as if from within the realm that Lewes marks off for women writers—a realm of fancy, romance, ordinary events, and mass production; a realm that remains apart from what fastidious or learned readers will value.

The novel is constrained from the beginning by the powerful social discourse of the Gradgrind system, which exists in the novel as what Bakhtin called "the word of the fathers." Bakhtin argues that such a word need not be repeated or reinforced or even made persuasive, but has "its authority already fused to it":

The authoritative word demands that we acknowledge it, that we make it our own; it binds us, quite independent of any power it might have to persuade us internally; we encounter it with its authority already fused to it. . . . It is, so to speak, the word of the fathers. Its authority was already *acknowledged* in the past. It is a *prior* discourse. It is therefore not a question of choosing it from among other possible discourses that are its equal.[21]

Against such a word, opposition or argument is already preempted, made secondary or unhearable. Unlike the opposing terms of "wonder" and "fancy," which require constant justification in the novel, the simplest reference to "fact" evokes the authority of learning and scientific knowledge. The effect of such an authority is to make all private exchanges in the book dependent on arguments that cannot be imagined within the novel's authorized categories, so that the characters speak a kind of shadow dialogue.

The effect of this social construction is especially destructive to the transparent figure who serves as the heroine's mother. In a more self-consciously "feminist" novel, Mrs. Gradgrind might be expected to suggest the alternative to patriarchal discourses. In *Hard Times*, the mother is comically ineffectual and trivial, represented not as a person but as an object, as a "feminine dormouse" (102), and a "bundle of shawls" (59). Yet she is not even a particularly satisfactory object. Her central representation, repeated three times, is as a "faint transparency" that is "presented" to its audience in various unimpressive attitudes:[22]

Mrs Gradgrind, weakly smiling and giving no other sign of vitality, looked (as she always did) like an indifferently executed transparency of a small female figure, without enough light behind it.

(60)

A transparency is an art form popularized by the dioramas in which a translucent image painted on cloth is made visible by backlighting.[23] Its fragility and potential for varying production make the transparency a felicitous medium to suggest Mrs. Gradgrind's ambivalent positioning. The failure of the transparency renders her almost invisible in the novel, making her neither a pleasing image nor one that is easily readable. But the particularity of the image insists on a producer as well as a product, raising the issue of what painter "executes" her so indifferently, what producer withholds the light that might have made her more substantial, in other words, why she has been neglected as a cultural formation. Vaguely discernible through the translucent object, the producer remains a shadowy, unnamed, prior force, whom we know by traces and effects. At Mrs. Gradgrind's death, for example, we are told of an effect, but not of a cause—"the light that had always been feeble and dim behind the weak transparency, went out'' (226). And the physical depiction of her as recumbent, ''stunned by some weighty piece of fact tumbling on her'' (59; see also 60, 62, 137) leaves unnamed the force that stuns her with its weight and carelessness. We are left with an authorless piece of evidence, a ''piece of fact''; but in *Hard Times* ''fact'' is easily traced back to the Gradgrind system. When we are told that finding herself alone with Gradgrind and Mr. Bounderby is ''sufficient to stun this admirable lady again, without collision between herself and any other fact'' (62), we know what constitutes her as an object of its gaze. It is under her husband's ''wintry'' eye that Mrs. Gradgrind becomes ''torpid again'' (102); under Sissy Jupe's care or even in Louisa's presence, she can be ''rendered almost energetic'' (94). Both fact and its proponents are equally capable of rendering Mrs. Gradgrind nonexistent, a product of a careless fancy: ''So, she once more died away, and nobody minded her'' (62).

Mrs. Gradgrind has been so slighted as a ''subject'' that she is surprised when Louisa asks about her: ''You want to hear of me, my dear? That's something new, I am sure, when anybody wants to hear of me'' (224). And the outcome of such a lifetime of being constituted by others is that she cannot even claim to feel her own pain; when Louisa asks after her health, she answers with what the narrator calls ''this strange speech'': ''I think there's a pain somewhere in the room . . . , but I couldn't positively say that I have got it'' (224). She is certainly slighted by Dickens, appearing in only five of the novel's thirty-seven chapters, and then usually in the final pages or paragraphs. Even her introduction seems almost an afterthought, located not in the chapter with Mr. Gradgrind, the children, or even the house (ch. 3), but in a parenthetical position as audience for Mr. Bounderby (ch. 4).[24] But if Dickens is cavalier about her presence, he strongly marks her absence from that nineteenth-century site for Mother, as idealized figure in her children's memories or in their imaginative dreams of virtue.[25] Mrs. Gradgrind's expected place as her children's earliest memory has been usurped by the father who appears as a ''dry Ogre chalking ghastly white figures'' on a ''large black board'' (54). Louisa's return ''home'' for her mother's death evokes none of the ''dreams of childhood—its airy fables'' and ''impossible adornments'' that Dickens describes as ''the best influences of old home''; such dreams are only evoked as a lengthy litany of what her mother has *not* provided for her child (223).

Mrs. Gradgrind does not offer a counter position—covert or otherwise—to the world of fact and ashes. She cannot overtly defy her husband, nor can she save herself from her daughter's scorn. Her advice to Louisa reflects this helplessness, and its incomprehension of the accepted referents makes her ridiculous in her child's eyes: "Go and be somethingological directly," she says (61), and "turn all your ological studies to good account" (137). When she is dying, Mrs. Gradgrind tries to express her loss—of something and of words with which to articulate it—to her daughter:

> But there is something—not an Ology at all—that your father has missed, or forgotten, Louisa. I don't know what it is. . . . I shall never get its name now. But your father may. It makes me restless. I want to write to him, to find out for God's sake, what it is. Give me a pen, give me a pen.
>
> (225)

To the transparent Mrs. Gradgrind, all authoritative knowledge must come from the father, yet she worries that he has missed or forgotten something. She does not imagine herself finding or naming it, but remembers it as unsaid. The outcome of this "insight" is invisible to the patriarchal eye; it disappears as "figures of wonderful no-meaning she began to trace upon her wrappers" (225–26). When Louisa tries to fashion a meaning of her mother's words, her aim is to "link such faint and broken sounds into any chain of connexion" (225), in other words, to translate her mother into the Gradgrind discourse. Mrs. Gradgrind emerges "from the shadow" and takes "upon her the dread solemnity of the sages and patriarchs" (226)—she "hears the last of it"—only by dying, not as a living speaker addressing her daughter knowingly and directly. She remains stubbornly unincorporated by the novel's powerful discourses, a no-meaning that can be neither heard nor reformed.

But the mother is ridiculous, rather than tragic, only within the father's terms of judgment—terms which a society divided into opposites cannot unimagine or unspeak, and against which the lower-class opposition of fancy and heart will have little impact. The mother's very imprecision undercuts the authority of the father's discourses, making them a lesson imperfectly learned and badly recited. The novel cannot construct an imagined alternate culture, in which Mrs. Gradgrind would "discover" the language to define the "something missing," in which "ological" would not be required as an ending that validates an object's existence. Instead it unfolds the boundaries and effects of such a system. Louisa learns painfully that Mrs. Gradgrind's point-of-view has been confined to its position of "no-meaning" (225) by concerted efforts by her father and his system of definition. Towards the end of the novel, Louisa reverses the charge of "no-meaning" and demands that her father justify instead what his "meaning" has produced: "Where are the graces of my soul? Where are the sentiments of my heart? What have you

done, O father, what have you done, with the garden that should have bloomed
once, in this great wilderness here!'' (239). In this confrontation, Louisa
recognizes the contest her father has suppressed and her mother has barely
suggested, a contest for how to determine the shape and value of the social
realms:

> I have grown up, battling every inch of my way. . . . What I have learned has
> left me doubting, misbelieving, despising, regretting, what I have not learned;
> and my dismal resource has been to think that life would soon go by, and that
> nothing in it could be worth the pain and trouble of a contest.
>
> (240–41)

The novel presents several scenes between Louisa and her father in which
this authority is examined and questioned, scenes which pointedly exclude
Mrs. Gradgrind, as someone whose objections or interests are irrelevant. The
chapter ''Father and Daughter'' opens with an oblique questioning of the
absolute value of such authority (131–32), but only once the ''business'' is
resolved does Gradgrind suggest, ''now, let us go and find your mother''
(137). Yet the exploration of Gradgrind's power makes an obscure and un-
acknowledged connection between his power and her mother's ''death'' from
the novel. By what seems a frivolous word-game on the part of the narrator,
Gradgrind's governmental blue books (the emblem of his power) are associated with an infamous wife-killer: ''Although Mr Gradgrind did not take
after Blue Beard, his room was quite a blue chamber in its abundance of blue
books'' (131). The narrator denies that this ''error'' has any meaning, thus
resisting the implication that Gradgrind's intellectual system of power has
something to do with the oppressed status of his wife. The blue books are
accorded the power of fact, which is to prove ''usually anything you like,''
but the narrator's flight of fancy is not to prove anything. It refers, not to the
authoritative realms of statistics and science, but to fairy-tales; it is not a
''fact'' derived from texts, but is ''something missing,'' an association produced by the unconscious. It remains, at best, as a kind of insider's joke, in
which readers can remember that its ''power'' derives from texts with which
Dickens was aligned, both in general (fiction and fairy tale), and explicitly
(Blue Beard is the basis for Dickens' Captain Murderer, whose tale he published in 1860 as one of his ''Nurse's Stories'').[26]

The reference to the wife-killer, Blue Beard, who charms all with his show
of courtesy and devotion before devouring his wives in the privacy of their
home, is an ''error'' that suggests the gap between public and private, between
acknowledged power and covert violence. Like the marginalized tensions

created by Mrs. Gradgrind throughout the novel, this slip of the pen provokes despite its claim to marginality. The error is allowed to stand, thereby suggesting what would otherwise be too bizarre to consider. It reminds us that Gradgrind has been a social "wife-killer," obliterating his wife's role as mother to her daughter and keeping her from fuller participation in the daughter's narrative. He has "formed his daughter on his own model" (168), and she is known to all as "Tom Gradgrind's daughter" (143). He has isolated Louisa in his masculine realm, depriving her of any of the usual female resources with which to oppose his power; as Tom mentions with devastating casualness, Louisa "used to complain to me that she had nothing to fall back upon, that girls usually fall back upon" (168). The reference to Blue Beard reminds us that Gradgrind's realm is *not* absolute except by force and mystification, that his "charmed apartment" depends on the exclusion of a more powerful, more resistant "other." The rest of the chapter teases out the possibilities that his power can be questioned. Through a series of fanciful images—that make the narrator not an unworthy companion of Mrs. Gradgrind—the absolute value of his authority is obliquely undermined. Gradgrind is presented as needing to enforce his positions with military might, relying on his books as an "army constantly strengthening by the arrival of new recruits." His solutions persist because they are isolated within a necromancer's circle, protected from critique or even outside knowledge. From his enclosed, abstracted fortress, he orders the world as if "the astronomer within should arrange the starry universe solely by pen, ink and paper, . . . could settle all their destinies on a slate, and wipe out all their tears with one dirty little bit of sponge" (131–32). All these questions about Gradgrind's power are delivered as amusing details, as arguments the novelist is not able to give serious articulation. Yet the details attack not the effect of Gradgrind's power, as Louisa does with hopeless inertia, but the claim to power, its genealogy and maintenance.

It is not surprising that Louisa and her mother, and even Dickens, cannot find words for what is missing from their lives, words having been usurped as the tools of the Gradgrind system, defined and delimited by male authority. Mrs. Gradgrind does not articulate an opposition, nor does the novel openly pursue the traces of her petulant complaints. *She* remains unaware that her headaches and worries are symptoms of a cultural dissatisfaction, although she knows that her head began "to split" as soon as she was married (137). She complains to Louisa about the trouble that comes from speaking—"You must remember, my dear, that whenever I have said anything, on any subject, I have never heard the last of it; and consequently, that I have long left off saying anything'' (225), but the ideological implications of these remarks are shortcircuited by the personal contexts in which she declines to speak. These scenes do not transform Mrs. Gradgrind into a covert rebel, but represent her as willful and self-absorbed, betraying Sissy and Louisa by her silence and diverting attention from their more pressing needs.

In fact, Mrs. Gradgrind seems to exist primarily as the cautionary exemplum of the Gradgrind system, having been married for the ''purity'' of being as free from nonsense ''as any human being not arrived at the perfection of an absolute idiot, ever was'' (62). She proves her usefulness to the system, admirably serving as the negative against which the father seems more caring, more responsive than he seems in isolation. Her mother seems unsympathetic to Louisa's discontent, worrying over it as ''one of those subjects I shall never hear the last of'' (138). And she serves as the agent who reinscribes the ideological positions of the Gradgrind system, who insists on reality being defined as what is kept ''in cabinets'' or about which one can ''attend lectures'' (61). Louisa is scolded for running off to look at the forbidden circus by her mother, not by the father whose prohibition it is and who has caught her in the crime. The hapless Mrs. Gradgrind ''whimpers'' to her daughter; ''I wonder at you. I declare you're enough to make one regret ever having had a family at all. I have a great mind to say I wish I hadn't. *Then* what would you have done, I should like to know'' (61). Yet in this pathetic effort to enforce her husband's laws, Mrs. Gradgrind has unknowingly allied herself with her child's rebellion. Her words give her away: she has ''wondered'' (a crime against reason), she has ''regretted'' (a crime against fact), and she has ''wished'' (a crime against her husband). Dickens notes that ''Mr. Gradgrind did not seem favourably impressed by these cogent remarks.'' Yet what seems initially a silly, self-indulgent speech has deflected the father's wrath from his daughter and has suggested the terms for opposition—wonder, regret, desire.

Hard Times appears to authorize an oppositional discourse of fancy, which is lisped by the circus-master Sleary and represented in Sissy Jupe, the substitute mother whom Gradgrind praises as the ''good fairy in his house'' who can ''effect'' what 10,000 pounds cannot (294). Gradgrind's approval, and the conventionality of Sissy's depiction as a house fairy, devalues her status as an opposition figure. Indeed Sissy rarely speaks in opposition, or at all. Her power is cited by men like Harthouse and Gradgrind, and by the narrator. Unlike Mrs. Gradgrind, Sissy cannot be mocked for ''cogent remarks,'' but simply *looks* at Louisa ''in wonder, in pity, in sorrow, in doubt, in a multitude of emotions'' (138). Her effect is largely due to the novelty of her discourse, a novelty produced by her status as an outsider who does not understand the conventions of the system. "Possessed of no facts" (49), girl number twenty does not recognize that "fancy" is a significant term, but uses it unthinkingly. She silences the cynical Harthouse by presenting "something in which he was so inexperienced, and against which he knew any of his usual weapons would fall so powerless; that not a word could he rally to his relief." Sissy insists on her words to Harthouse remaining a "secret" and relies on a "child-like ingenuousness" to sway her listener. And what Harthouse notices is her "most confiding eyes" and her "most earnest (though so quiet)" voice (252–57). Sissy's "wonder" is powerful only as long as she does not "speak" it in her own right, but presents it in her disengaged role as go-between. Her "power" depends on "her entire forgetfulness of herself in her earnest quiet holding to the object" (253)—depends, in other words, on a strenuous denial of herself as a contestant for power. The narrator comments that "if she had shown, or felt the slightest trace of any sensitiveness to his ridicule or astonishment, or any remonstrance he might offer; he would have carried it against her at this point" (255).

Sissy's discourse derives its power, not from any essential woman's knowledge that Louisa and her mother could share, but from her experience as a working-class child who knows counter examples and a different word than "fact." Louisa acquires from Sissy not the power to be "a mother—lovingly watchful of her children" but to be "learned in childish lore; thinking no innocent and pretty fancy ever to be despised" (313). The opposition Sissy seems to represent—of imagination, emotion, questioning of patriarchal discourses—stands like the circus-master's fancy, a fantastic dream that amuses children but does not displace Gradgrindian fact. It has no ability to construct a shared feminine discourse that can alter the rigid polarities of fact and fancy, meaning and no-meaning. When Louisa tries to inquire about such forbidden topics as love, she is on her own, pursuing a "strong, wild, wandering interest peculiar to her; an interest gone astray like a banished creature, and hiding in solitary places" (98).

In her dramatic confrontation with her father (238–42), Louisa tries to construct a realm outside the powerful sway of reason and logic. Yet she can imagine this realm only as the "immaterial part of my life," marking it as that which has no material existence or is irrelevant. She thereby perpetuates the construction of her world as absolute in its polarities—as world that is either material or immaterial, fact or fancy, reason or nonsense.[27] To use Bakhtin's terms, she remains "bound" to "the authoritative word" in its totality; she cannot "divide it up," or "play with the context framing it" or "play with its borders" (Bakhtin, 343). She suggests she might have come closer to a desired end "if I had been stone blind; if I had groped my way by my sense of touch, and had been free, while I knew the shapes and surfaces of things, to exercise my fancy somewhat, in regard to them" (240). Passionate as this scene is, Louisa's specific argument shows the difficulty of evading the power of patriarchal discourse; she can only "prove" the worth of an oppositional realm by the tools she has learned from her father. Her vision remains defined as "no-meaning," as existing only in opposition to what persists as "meaning." Louisa tries to imagine a realm "defying all the calculations ever made by man, and no more known to his arithmetic than his Creator is," but ends up describing herself as "a million times wiser, happier." Like her mother, her power lies in speaking the father's word imperfectly, making her father's statistical practices meaningless by her exaggerated application. Like her mother, Louisa's complaints refer only to "something" missing; there are no words for what might be gained. The Gradgrind system is too powerful to allow Louisa or her mother to break away or to communicate very well with each other. All they can do, in their separate ways and unbeknownst to each other, is to disrupt the functioning of the father's word, and to indicate a lack, an incompleteness.

The schematic quality of *Hard Times* indicates a broader lack or incompleteness in the authoritative discourses of Dickens' social and literary world. Like Louisa and Mrs. Gradgrind, Dickens must articulate his valuing of "fancy" and his concern about crossing proscribed boundaries in language devalued by the patriarchal discourses of reason and fact. That Lewes sees him as hallucinating a world no wise man would recognize indicates the disturbing effect of this crossing of boundaries. Both Lewes and Dickens identify the disturbance as somehow connected with women, seeing women as touched by issues that more successfully acculturated males do not notice. Lewes saw much of Dickens' power—and what made him a disturbing novelist—as the ability to represent something that could not otherwise be acknowledged. "What seems preposterous, impossible to us," he wrote in 1872, "seemed to him simple fact of observation" (Lewes, 145). Writing as a woman places Dickens in a position to observe what seems "preposterous, impossible."

At the same time, of course, for a powerful male novelist like Dickens, the position of outsider is exaggerated. Dickens can be seen as exploiting the exclusion and material oppression of women and the poor when they serve as analogies for his own more temperate marginality as a lower-middle class writer of fiction in a literary culture that preferred educated reason over experienced fancy. For male writers like Dickens and Trollope, writing "as a woman" brought literary respect and considerable financial return, whereas a writer like Charlotte Brontë was censured for her unwomanly productions and underpaid by her publisher.[28] Unlike women who transgress the boundaries of the literary establishment, Dickens could signal his difference as significant rather than ridiculous. Unlike the poor with whom he was so closely identified, Dickens had access to the means of publication; he had the influence and position to pressure contemporary methods of production and dissemination of literary and social discourse. Such was his influence as spokesman of social discontent, that women writers of the nineteenth century, in both England and America, had to come to terms with his boundaries and codes, with his literary conventions for observing the social world and its institutions. Writers like Mary Elizabeth Braddon, Elizabeth Gaskell, Elizabeth Stuart Phelps, and Rebecca Harding Davis both quote and revise his portrayal of women's writing and social position. Their attempts to write as women are circumscribed within Dickens' example and within the audience that he so powerfully swayed.

This assessment of Dickens' sympathetic identification with feminine discourses in the 1850s returns to the intertwined, ideological interests involved in any attempt to write "as a woman," in any project that *assumes* the position of an outsider, of an other. Dickens' experimentation with excluded positions of women and the poor provided him with a way of disrupting the status quo of the literary establishment. But, ironically, his experimentation also helped him capitalize on his status as an outsider in that literary realm. The inarticulate masses became, in effect, his constituency and his subject matter, supporting his powerful position within the literary and social establishment as arbiter of how to write about cultural exclusion. Dickens' growing influence as an editor and public spokesman for the literary world make his representations of women's writing dominate the literary scene. His example carves out a possible space for women writers in his culture, but it also takes over that space as its own. His assumed position as outsider complicates assumptions about gender difference in writing and problematizes what Lewes so confidently called "genuine female experience." It disrupts and forces out into the open the literary establishment's defensive cultural narratives, and, in the process, constructs its own protective practices and standards. In writing as a woman, in speaking for a silenced group, Dickens both makes possible and makes complicated a challenge to "the father's word" by those who use "the mother-tongue."

NOTES

1. "Dickens in Relation to Criticism," *Fortnightly Review* 17 (1872): 141–54. Lewes had written in *The Leader* in 1852 about *Bleak House* and had engaged with Dickens in a debate about the scientific basis for spontaneous combustion. For an early summary of the relationship between the two, see Gordon S. Haight, "Dickens and Lewes," *PMLA* 71 (1956): 166–79.

2. See Forster's rebuttal of Lewes's essay in *The Life of Charles Dickens* (1872–1874), ed. A. J. Hoppé, 2 vols. (1927; London: Dent, 1966), II, 267–79. Forster argued: "When the characters in a play are puppets, and the audiences of the theatre fools or children, no wise man forfeits his wisdom by proceeding to admit that . . . through his puppets, he spoke 'in the mother-tongue of the heart' " (2.270). See also the excellent discussion of Lewes's essay by George H. Ford, in *Dickens and His Readers: Aspects of Novel-Criticism Since 1836* (1955; rpt. New York: W. W. Norton, 1965), pp. 149–54, which focuses on Lewes's concern about "realism" and his derogation of Dickens' imagination. Ford describes the essay as "an extremely sophisticated piece of irony" (151) and as "the most effective attack on Dickens ever written" (154). "Like the walrus and the carpenter," he concludes, "Lewes weeps over the oysters he is consuming, and he assures his victim and his audience that it is all for the best" (154).

3. *The Rise and Fall of the Man of Letters* (London: Macmillan, 1969) 73. Gross discusses Lewes's career as writer and editor of periodicals but does not mention his influence on any women writers except George Eliot. For other discussions of Lewes's influence as a critic, see Monika Brown, "George Henry Lewes," *DLB 55: Victorian Prose Writers before 1867*, ed. William B. Thesing (Detroit, Mich.: Gale Research, 1987), 128–41; Harold Orel, *Victorian Literary Critics* (New York: St. Martin's Press, 1984), pp. 5–30; Edgar W. Hirshberg, *George Henry Lewes* (New York: Twayne, 1970); Alice R. Kaminsky, "George Eliot, George Henry Lewes, and the Novel," *PMLA* 70 (1955): 997–1013; Morris Greenhut, "George Henry Lewes as a Critic of the Novel," *Studies in Philology* 45 (1948): 491–511.

4. In "The Principles of Success in Literature," a six-part essay appearing "by the editor" of the new *Fortnightly Review* in 1865, Lewes discussed the "profession" of literature, and the necessity to protect it from the "incompetent aspirants, without seriousness of aim, without the faculties demanded by their work," those who "follow Literature simply because they see no other opening for their incompetence; just as forlorn widows and ignorant old maids thrown suddenly on their own resources open a school" (1 [1865]: 86). As he did of his letters and reviews of Brontë, Lewes saw this essay as furnishing "nothing more than help and encouragement" (86). Lewes's defense of literature is generous in comparison to the vituperative review of *A Tale of Two Cities* by James Fitzjames Stephen, who blamed Dickens for "infect[ing] the literature of his country with a disease" and promoting instead an "incurable vulgarity of mind and of taste, and intolerable arrogance of temper." He charged him with a "complete disregard of the rules of literary composition" and a lack of "intellectual excellence" or concern for "the higher pleasures" of fiction (*Saturday Review* 8, 17 December 1859: 741–43).

5. "The Lady Novelists," *Westminster Review* 58 (1852): 72. See also "The Principles of Success in Literature," and his reviews of Brontë's *Jane Eyre, Shirley*, and *Villette*. Only Brontë's side of their correspondence seems to have survived,

but her letters to Lewes and to her friend W. S. Williams discuss what Lewes wrote to her; see Clement Shorter, *The Brontës: Life and Letters*, 2 vols. (1908; rpt. New York: Haskell House, 1969). In a letter to her "mentor" (Nov. 6, 1847), Brontë recites the terms of Lewes's advice, his warning to "beware of melodrama," his exhortion to "adhere to the real," and describes her early adherence to such "principles": "I restrained imagination, eschewed romance, repressed excitement, . . . sought to produce something which should be soft, grave, and true." But she also questions the authority of his views: "when [imagination] is eloquent, and speaks rapidly and urgently in our ear, are we not to write to her dictation?" (1. 365–66). In her letter of Jan. 12, 1848, following Lewes's review of *Jane Eyre*, Brontë writes, "If I ever *do* write another book, I think I will have nothing of what you call 'melodrama'; I *think* so, but I am not sure" (1. 386). Brontë was furious at Lewes's published "discovery" that she was a woman, especially after she had requested that he avoid the issue. She wrote to him on Jan. 19, 1850: "after I had said earnestly that I wished critics would judge me as an *author*, not as a woman, you so roughly—I even thought so cruelly—handled the question of sex" (2. 106). I am indebted to Margaret L. Shaw's discussion of Lewes's effect on Charlotte Brontë and his efforts to consolidate the emerging category of the "man of letters" (PhD dissertation, Univ. of Pittsburgh, 1988). See also Franklin Gary, "Charlotte Brontë and George Henry Lewes," *PMLA* 51 (1936): 518–42.

6. Jay B. Hubbell, *Who Are the Major American Writers?* (U of North Carolina P, 1972) p. 79. Hubbell was specifically discussing the "decline" of literature in the 1870s in America. In the 1872 essay Lewes argued that unknowledgeable readers "were at once laid hold of by the reproduction of their own feelings, their own experiences, their own prejudices" (151).

7. Letter to John Forster, *The Letters of Charles Dickens*, ed. Madeline House and Graham Storey, The Pilgrim Edition, Vol. 4 (Oxford: Clarendon Press, 1965–88): 328.

8. Charles Dickens, "Preliminary Word," *Household Words* 1 (March 1850): 1.

9. For the details of Dickens' periodical experimentation, see Anne Lohrli, ed., *Household Words* (Toronto: University of Toronto Press, 1973), and Harry Stone, ed. *Charles Dickens' Uncollected Writings from Household Words*, 2 vols. (Bloomington: Indiana University Press, 1968).

10. In "Critical Cross-Dressing: Male Feminists and the Woman of the Year," *Raritan* 3(1983): 130–49, Elaine Showalter considers whether the fashion in the 1980s to address the "woman question" is a disguised form of "power play": "Is male feminism a form of critical cross-dressing, . . . or is it the result of a genuine shift in critical, cultural, and sexual paradigms . . . ?" (131, 134).

11. *Dickens and Women* (Stanford, Calif.: Stanford University Press, 1983), pp. 243–44. In her essay, "Writing in a 'Womanly' Way and the Double Vision of *Bleak House*," *Dickens Quarterly*, IV, 1 (1987): 3–15, Suzanne Graver makes a compelling argument for Dickens' "masculine stake" in discerning contemporary gender relations, in representing the value and authority of women's knowledge. Although she argues for Dickens' "remarkably insightful portrait of a woman experiencing her knowing self as not-knowing" (10), she also charges him with using "Esther's obliqueness not to subvert Victorian womanly ideals but to celebrate a dutifully willed acceptance of them" (4).

12. *A Theory of Literary Production*, trans. Geoffrey Wall (1966; London: Routledge & Kegan Paul, 1978); see especially pp. 82–89.

13. "The Lady Novelists" (1852), p. 72.
14. The phrase "relative creatures" is from Sarah Stickney Ellis's influential advice book, *The Women of England* (London, 1838; rpt. Philadelphia: Herman Hooker, 1841) p. 100. See Dianne Sadoff's discussions of women characters in *Monsters of Affection: Dickens, Eliot and Bronte on Fatherhood* (Baltimore, Md.: Johns Hopkins University Press, 1982), pp. 58–64. See also Anne Robinson Taylor's discussion of Esther, "The Author as Female Child," in *Male Novelists and Their Female Voices: Literary Masquerades* (Troy, N.Y.: Whitson Publishing Co., 1981), pp. 121–56.
15. See Peggy Kamuf, "Writing like a Woman," in *Women and Language in Literature and Society*, ed. Sally McConnell-Ginet, Ruth Borker, and Nelly Furman (New York: Praeger, 1980), pp. 284–99, for an argument against an essentialist "female writing" (as proposed in Patricia Spacks' *The Female Imagination*, 1972) and her warning about seeing literature as "expressions, simple and direct, of individual experience" (286).
16. In "Patriarchy Against Itself—The Young Manhood of Wallace Stevens," *Critical Inquiry* 13 (Summer 1987): 742–86, Frank Lentricchia discusses Stevens's sense of poetry as a "lady-like" habit, his "feminization of the literary life" and his "struggle to overcome this feminization" which his culture equated with "the trivialization of literature and the literary impulse" (751). He argues for "the cultural powerlessness of poetry in a society that masculinized the economic while it feminized the literary" (766).
17. In *Bleak House* (1852), for example, his preface proposes to explore "the romantic side of familiar things," and the opening number of *Household Words* insists "that in all familiar things, even in those which are repellent on the surface, there is Romance enough, if we will find it out" (1 [1850]: 1).
18. For an analysis of Dickens' habit of deflecting self-critique, see Jean Ferguson Carr, "Dickens and Autobiography: A Wild Beast and his Keeper," *ELH* 52 (1985): 447–69. See also Carr, "The Polemics of Incomprehension: Mother and Daughter in *Pride and Prejudice*," in *Traditions and the Talents of Women*, ed. Florence Howe (Champaign, Ill.: University of Illinois Press, 1989).
19. Letter to John Forster, [February 1854], *The Letters of Charles Dickens*, ed. Walter Dexter, vol. 2 (London: Nonesuch Press, 1937–38): 543. To Mrs. Richard Watson, Nov. 1, 1854, he wrote that he felt " 'used up' after Hard Times" and that "the compression and close condensation necessary for that disjointed form of publication gave me perpetual trouble" (2. 602). See his letter to Miss Coutts, Jan. 23, 1854 (2. 537) for a description of his printers' urging to write the novel. In *Dickens' Working Notes for his Novels* (Chicago, Ill.: University of Chicago Press, 1987), Harry Stone discusses Dickens' efforts to accommodate his working procedures to the constraints of weekly serialization (p. 249), and the plans show his calculations for the unfamiliar size of a weekly part (pp. 251–53).
20. See, for example, David Craig's discussion of the novel's "simplifying mode," in his introduction to *Hard Times: For These Times* (New York: Penguin, 1969), p. 28. All following page references are to the Penguin edition.
21. M. M. Bakhtin, *The Dialogic Imagination*, ed. Michael Holquist, trans. Caryl Emerson and Michael Holquist (Austin and London: University of Texas Press, 1981), p. 342.
22. See also 137, 224. This passage is one of the few references to Mrs. Gradgrind in Dickens's working plans for the novel (Stone, 253): "Mrs Gradgrind—badly done transparency, without enough light behind."

23. In *The Shows of London* (Cambridge, Mass.: Harvard University Press, 1978), Richard D. Altick defines transparencies as "pictures made with translucent paints on materials like calico, linen, or oiled paper and lighted from behind in the manner of stained glass" (p. 95) and discusses their popularity in the Chinese shadow and magic-lantern shows of the 1770s (p. 119) and in the dioramas of the 1820s on (pp. 169–70). In Daguerre's "double-effect" technique, transparencies were painted on both sides, their appearance transformed by the amount and angle of light shown through the image (pp. 169–70). Transparencies, or lithophanes as they were sometimes called, could also be small porcelain figures held against a light.

24. Dickens changed his mind about its positioning, marking in his working plans its postponement from ch. 3 (*"No not yet"*) to ch. 4 (*"Now, Mrs. Gradgrind"* (Stone, p. 253).

25. His working plans indicate an early decision about whether to make it "Mrs Gradgrind—or Miss? Wife or sister? *Wife*" (Stone, p. 253). In *Dickens at Work* (London: Methuen, 1957), John Butt and Kathleen Tillotson argue that the choice of "wife" over "sister" emphasizes "more powerfully" the absolute influence of Gradgrind over his children. (p. 206).

26. Reprinted in *Charles Dickens: Selected Short Fiction*, ed. Deborah A. Thomas (New York: Penguin, 1976), pp. 218–29. The naive narrator of the tale assumes Captain Murderer "must have been an offshoot of the Blue Beard family, but I had no suspicion of the consanguinity in those times." Like Gradgrind, Captain Murderer's "warning name would seem to have awakened no general prejudice against him, for he was admitted into the best society and possessed immense wealth" (p. 221). And, like Gradgrind, much of his power comes from being the determiner of meanings and names.

27. Several of Dickens' initial titles in his working plans for the novel reflect this insistence on polarity: "Hard heads and soft hearts," "Heads and Tales," and "Black and White" (Stone, p. 251).

28. See Margot Peters's discussion of the inequity of publishers' payments, in *Unquiet Soul: A Biography of Charlotte Brontë* (1975; rpt. New York: Atheneum, 1986), pp. 355–56. Brontë received the same unsatisfying sum of £500 for her third novel *Villette* as she had for the first two, as compared to Thackeray's £4200 for *The Virginians* or the £1000 Dickens could command for a short story. Peters quotes George Gissing's telling comment about author-publisher relations:

> A big, blusterous, genial brute of a Trollope could very fairly hold his own, and exact at all events an acceptable share in the profits of his work. A shrewd and vigorous man of business such as Dickens . . . could do even better. . . . But pray, what of Charlotte Brontë? Think of that grey, pinched life, . . . which would have been so brightened had [she] received but . . . one-third of what in the same space of time, the publisher gained by her books.
> (355–56)

Change and the Changeling
in *Dombey and Son*

Gerhard Joseph

In Chapter 29 of *Dombey and Son*, Dombey's sister Mrs. Chick is on the
verge of telling Lucretia Tox that Dombey, for whom they both have had
rather different marital expectations, is about to take Edith Granger to wife.
In a gesture of preparatory delicacy, Mrs. Chick coughs.

> "My dear Louisa must be careful of that cough," remarked Miss Tox.
> "It is nothing," returned Mrs. Chick. "It's merely change of weather. We
> must expect change."
> "Of weather?" asked Miss Tox, in her simplicity.
> "Of everything," returned Mrs. Chick. "Of course we must. It's a world
> of change. Anyone would surprise me very much, Lucretia, and would greatly
> alter my opinion of their understanding, if they attempted to contradict or evade
> what is so perfectly evident. Change!" exclaimed Mrs. Chick, with severe
> philosophy. Why, my gracious me, what is there that does not change! even
> the silkworm, who I am sure might be supposed not to trouble itself about such
> subjects, changes into all sorts of unexpected things continually."[1]

It is indeed a world of change, as we might all readily admit (or not?), and
as *Dombey and Son* would seem to demonstrate on a massive scale as well
as in such comic local touches as the foregoing exchange. For as Steven
Marcus argues in a discussion that is the starting point for my argument,
change in all departments of personal and cultural behavior is the chief subject
of the novel.[2] In one of the several ways *Dombey* has been seen as a "swing"
novel in Dickens' career, it is the first of his works to convey its thematic
material through the operation of a fairly well-controlled symbolic system,
the opposition of the railroad and the sea. To be sure, that opposition is an
intermittent thing: it does not yet have the concentrating power of, say, the
fog and the mire in *Bleak House*, the prison in *Little Dorrit*, or the river and

the dustmounds in *Our Mutual Friend*. But it does serve to pose the outermost question of the novel, the issue of whether change or immutability is the fundamental principle of existence, of whether "temporariness" or "permanancy" carries all before it, as Susan Nipper puts the matter within another local context early in the novel (Ch. 3).

The question takes us back philosophically at least as far as the pre-Socratics—to a Parmenides who insisted that nothing ever changes and to a Heraclitus who countered with the notion that nothing ever stays the same. But to stay with the Victorian contemporaries of Dickens, that ancient opposition was explored conventionally enough by a Catholic poet like Gerard Manley Hopkins throughout his work (but especially in "That Nature is a Heraclitian Fire"), by a Tennyson who insisted that the pendant poems to stand at the beginning of his Complete Works be "Nothing Will Die" and "All Things Will Die," and by a Matthew Arnold who in "Dover Beach" uses the ebb and flow of the seawave to the same figural effect as Dickens. Broadly speaking and to spell out the obvious, the ocean waves that speak to Paul Dombey as he is dying and to Florence thereafter establish the mystery of cosmic repetition as one of Dickens' themes. Its centrality is confirmed by the fact that Dickens had "Phiz" portray those waves in the frontispiece for the entire novel, an illustration of Paul and Florence seated together upon a couch while the waves of that cosmic ocean well up about them.

I will have something to say about the railroad as an emblem of radical change that Dickens pits against the ever-recurring seawave shortly, but I would like for the moment to stay with the issue of recurrence as it applies to Dickens' creation of character. For, to return to the conversation between Mrs. Chick and Miss Tox cited above, in reply to Mrs. Chick's assertion that "it's a world of change," one might wish to say that one of the things that never changes is Mrs. Chick herself. An insensitive, self-important advocate of the dying Mrs. Dombey's "making an effort," of rousing oneself, in the novel's opening chapter, she enunciates that same empty homily, gives voice to the same verbal tic at the novel's close. In such repetitive, not to say obsessive behavior, she may serve as an illustration of what has long been encapsulated in the phrase "a Dickens character," what E. M. Forster defined as a Dickensian characterological "flatness" based upon a single unchanging principle of behavior or speech.

This is not to say that Forster's flat/round opposition does not allow for a certain amount of leakage and is not by now merely a jumping-off point for a more nuanced sense of the matter. Thus, even the early Dickens creates characters with a certain amount of weight and complexity—and, indeed, characters who undergo profound moral change. But their transformation is of the sort that has usually been attributed to Dombey—a wholesale change, a radical conversion of the heart. (Thus, Chapter 59, "Retribution," the chapter in which that "change" in Paul Dombey occurs, stresses the word and the concept again and again.) To the extent that Dickensian character transformation does involve such sudden conversion, it has its source in melodrama. And, if we are to follow Peter Brooks's recent discussion of melodrama as a secular outgrowth of Judeo-Christian spiritual autobiography,[3] we can see that such change echoes a Biblical conversion pattern—say, the inspired, lightning-like turn of an earlier Paul who, like Paul Dombey, fell from a horse. (I am tempted into asserting the analogy suggested by the name, if only because Paul Dombey's fall from his horse seems an isolated event that has no apparent plot function, although admittedly Dombey's fall does not lead immediately to his conversion as did the accident that befell Saul of Tarsus.)

That is, in thinking about the issue of Dickensian "flatness" and its relation to change, one is well advised to interweave Forster's generalization with that of another classic statement from twentieth-century Dickens critcism, Edmund Wilson's notion of "The Two Scrooges," the thesis of his 1938 landmark essay.[4] While the overnight transformation of Scrooge in *A Christmas Carol* is said to demonstrate the phenomenon of change in the early Dickens in its purest form, Wilson reenforces the example of Scrooge with a discussion of Dombey's precipitous turn from pride at novel's end. "The world of the early Dickens," says Wilson,

> is organized according to a dualism. . . . there are bad people and there are good people, there are comics and there are characters played straight. The only [moral] complexity of which Dickens is capable is to make one of his noxious characters become wholesome, one of his clowns turn into a serious person. The most conspicuous example of this process is the reform of Mr. Dombey, who, as Taine says, "turns into the best of fathers and spoils a fine novel." (58)

Still, the issue of change is more complex than that. Even in these days of structuralism and post-structuralism's "linguistic turn," most of us still probably read novels because of an abiding interest in human personality. But the abstraction "character," while a natural enough isolation of a given "aspect" of the novel, distorts the whole for the sake of an instrumental concentration on the part, ignores the full textual pattern of *Dombey* through the focus upon a single element. A consideration of "change" in character ought surely to be read in the light of other kinds of transformation the novel charts.

Raymond Williams's introduction to the Penguin edition describes with admirable concision the various social, political, and economic changes racking English society in the 1840s, changes reflected in the novels of the decade such as *Dombey*. The very fact that this novel first appeared in book form in 1848, the year that various political revolutions were sweeping over the Continent—ones that England somehow managed to avoid, focuses the whole issue of the *pace* of historical change. That was at any rate a subject dear to the hearts of nineteenth-century historians such as Carlyle, Macaulay, and T. H. Greene. If violent, radical change was the Continental model, the gradualism of the English revolution in the seventeenth century and the Reform Bill era in the nineteenth served as a counter-model in which the English Whig historian—and the novelist-historian—could take pride. (In their very different ways Dickens' *A Tale of Two Cities* and George Eliot's *Middlemarch* may be read as demonstrations of such pride.)

Whatever its expression in human character, that radical transformation was perceived by Dickens to be both a reality and a further threat in the 1840s may be gathered from *Dombey*'s most famous image of external change, the coming of the railroad and its ravishment of the English landscape, of the area of London's Camden town known as Staggs's Gardens, the home of the Toodles family:

> The first shock of a great earthquake had, just at that period, rent the whole neighborhood to its centre. Traces of its course were visible on every side. Houses were knocked down; streets broken through and stopped; deep pits and trenches dug in the ground; enormous heaps of earth and clay thrown up; buildings that were undermined and shaking, propped by great beams of wood. Here, a chaos of carts, overthrown and jumbled together, lay topsy-turvy at the bottom of a steep unnatural hill; there, confused treasures of iron soaked and rusted in something that had accidentally become a pond. . . . Hot springs and fiery eruptions, the usual attendants upon earthquakes, lent their contributions of confusion to the scene. Boiling water hissed and heaved within dilapidated walls; whence, also, the glare and roar of flames came issuing forth; and mounds of ashes blocked up rights of way, and wholly changed the law and custom of the neighbourhood.
>
> (120-21)

So much for the rhetorically orchestrated, extended, two-page description as it appears in Chapter 6. When next the reader is in the vicinity of the Toodles residence, in Chapter 15, there is not a trace of the former landscape—or of Staggs's Gardens which has made way for the railroad: "There was no such

place as Staggs's Gardens. It had vanished from the earth. . . . [It] had been
cut up root and branch. Oh woe the day,'' the Dickensian narrator moralizes,
''when not a 'rood of English ground'—laid out in Staggs's Gardens—is
secure'' (289–90).

Because of the bravura treatment accorded the radical change in Staggs's
Gardens and because of the symbolic portentousness of the railroad in the
novel as a whole, the passages quoted above have occasioned a good deal
of critical comment. But while the privileging of these particular ''linguistic
moments'' as a synecdoche for the idea of social change in the novel as a
whole makes a certain sense, one might just as readily single out other less
apocalyptic descriptions of landscape alteration to come up with a rather
different impression of change.

To get to Captain Cuttle's lodgings on the brink of a canal by the India
Docks in Chapter 9, for instance, the meticulously charted gradations of the
change from land to water is what the Dickensian narrator gives us (179). Or
better yet, if we are looking for a slowly changing landscape to pit against
the ''root and branch'' upheaval of Staggs's Gardens by the industrial machine, the description of Harriet Carker's cottage in Northern London will
serve:

> The neighbourhood in which [the house] stands has as little of the country to
> recommend it, as it has of the town. It is neither of the town nor country. The
> former, like the giant in his travelling boots, has made a stride and passed it,
> and has set his brick-and-mortar heel a long way in advance; but the intermediate
> space between the giant's feet, as yet, is only blighted country, and not yet
> town; and, here among a few tall chimneys belching smoke all day and night,
> and among the brick-fields and the lanes where turf is cut, and where the fences
> tumble down, and where the dusty nettles grow, and where a scrap or two of
> hedge may yet be seen, and where the bird-catcher still comes occasionally,
> though he swears every time to come no more—this . . . home is to be found.
> (555)

My point is that the sense of personal and social, interior and exterior
transformation that *Dombey* presents is not necessarily epitomized by the
earthquake metaphor associated with Staggs's Gardens, for the novel contains
counter-images of gradualism that are just as significant. In such oscillation,
the novel exemplifies a debate about the nature of change that cut across all
departments of Victorian life but that was most clearly focused in discussions
of geological change—and of the significance of earthquakes in particular.

Scientists were divided into two diametrically opposed schools, ''catastrophists'' who held that the present form of the earth was the result of violent
catastrophes, such as earthquakes, volcanoes, and floods, and ''uniformitar-

ians'' who believed that it was rather formed by slower processes working over a longer period of time. The uniformitarian view was initially formulated by James Hutton, a Scot, in 1785, and it might well have triumphed rather easily over its rival, championed by the German, Abraham Gottlob Werner. But the intercession of the French Revolution—surely, said Burke, the most momentous event the world has ever known—followed by the earth-shaking Napoleonic wars, reenforced a catastrophist sense of the matter, confirming an ancient sense that it was by violent convulsions that change, at least in the political sphere, was wrought. If so, why not also in all realms—personal, cultural, and natural? And so, though Hutton's theory had been supported for a while by the gradualism of Lamarck, in 1812, on the very eve of that "world-earthquake, Waterloo," Georges Cuvier, a comparative anatomist, published his *Discours sur les revolutions de la surface du globe*, which, along with the work of his English disciple, William Buckland, served largely to make England and France remain adherents of catastrophism for the next twenty years. It was only with the publication of Lyell's *Principles of Geology* in 1833 that this view came gradually to be displaced and the uniformitarian hypothesis substituted, a transformation signalled in the political realm by the passage of the First Reform Bill.[5]

It is in light of this debate that one can best discriminate among literary figures and their concepts of change in the nineteenth century. Both with respect to change within the individual psyche and within the larger social body, writers of the century can be very roughly divided into catastrophists and uniformitarians. Thus, on the basis both of his description of his spiritual conversion in *Sartor Resartus* and of his account of a cataclysmic French Revolution, Thomas Carlyle would seem to provide us with a preeminent example of the catastrophist frame of mind, while John Henry Newman in his painstakingly spelled out movement from Evangelicalism to Roman Catholicism—and the abstract "grammar of assent" that he distilled therefrom—may serve as paradigm of literary uniformitarianism. Generally speaking, as A. Dwight Culler has suggested in his study of Tennyson in light of the debate, to move from the Romantic "visionary" imagination to its less fevered Victorian counterpart is to move, with many exceptions and qualifications to be sure, from literary catastrophism to literary uniformitarianism.

And where does Dickens, or more precisely, *Dombey and Son* stand with respect to this overriding Victorian opposition? As a disciple of Carlyle on the evidence of several key works (say, *Hard Times* and *A Tale of Two Cities*), Dickens might be expected to convey something like a Carlylian sense of precipitous social change. And, as we have seen, the earthquake-like transformation of Staggs's Gardens does indeed present an image of social change of a pretty sweeping, catastrophist sort. But as we have also seen, other less obtrusive descriptions of the landscape insist upon uniformitarianism—or at least upon a sense of change that is less abrupt than has sometimes been attributed to the novel.

The issue with respect to personal change is just as debatable: in citing E. M. Forster on Dickensian "flatness" and Edmund Wilson's "two Scrooges" thesis in support of the idea of sudden conversion, I have been provisionally implying that Dickens accepted a characterological version of catastrophism, that he conveyed the idea that when characters change they do so like Staggs's Gardens, with the radicality and totality that we associate with the effects of an earthquake.

In final exemplification of that hypothesis, let me concentrate upon the moment of change in Dombey, the turning point of the relation between Florence and her father in Chapter 59 ("Retribution"). Trapped within a despairing isolation, wandering about his ransacked mansion, Dombey is moving toward madness and suicide. His son has died, his manager has betrayed him, his wife has deserted him into what he assumes to be adultery, his fortune has disintegrated, his House and all his dynastic plans are in utter ruin. Florence alone "had never changed to him—nor" he suddenly realizes, "had he ever changed to her." Then his thoughts break up, he becomes incoherent. Finally, his mind collapses totally; he looks into the mirror and sees not himself but a horrific other, something that he thinks of as an "it." And as he is about to kill himself, Florence steps forth bathed in a shaft of light—at which moment he looks into the glass and sees his human reflection once more. She has restored him to himself, but as a radically altered being.

One might of course object that in abstracting and cropping this scene, I am indulging in a special pleading to support a catastrophist argument—and that, instead, the breakup of Dombey has been developing all along, that the death of his son, his humiliation by Edith and Carker, and the flight of Florence are but way stations in a carefully calibrated subversion of Dombey's pride, and that the moment I have concentrated on above, the moment of final disintegration, just *seems* precipitous. "Ground, long undermined," says the narrator of Dombey's sudden breakup," will often fall down in a moment; what was undermined here in so many ways, weakened, and crumbled, little by little, more and more, as the hand moved on the dial" (938). That is of course the thrust of the uniformitarian response to the catastrophist argument concerning "earthquakes" on all natural and cultural levels of existence—though to be geologically accurate one ought to talk about the gradual shifting of tectonic plates rather than, as Dickens does, the undermining of ground.

What, then, might a gradualist account of Dombey's change leading up to the climactic mirror conversion scene look like? While that account must include what we would today call sudden "traumas," various catastrophist quakes like the death of young Paul and the paralytic stroke of Mrs. Skewton, various subsidiary "thunderbolts," to allude to the title of the chapter detailing Edith's flight with Carker, it is Dombey's change toward the unchanging Florence, "the still point of the changing world" (Marcus, 351), upon which one must finally concentrate. That alteration in Dombey involves nothing less than the giving up of a life-long misogyny, whose initial economic expression disguises something more elemental. For Dombey's prizing of the son and dismissal of the daughter would seem to be essentially economic in nature: that is, by patriarchal custom it is through the son that the father affirms his identity and extends his power over the future—Dombey's ship on which Walter Gay is thought to have gone down, the *Son and Heir*, says it all. The proverbial combination, which has about it the same redundancy as the empty simulacrum "Dombey and Son" the father hopes to fill, asserts with a proud but false confidence the male sense that control must pass through the paternal line. Woman, of course has a role in the production of such an heir but a subservient one; once the son is actually born, she has essentially a "nursing" function.

A nursing function: Steven Marcus has an odd, highly tangential footnote in his chapter on *Dombey and Son* (312). In suggesting that Dickens named his heroine Florence Dombey after the Italian city, Marcus says that he bases part of his argument on a statement by Cecil Woodham-Smith, Florence Nightingale's biographer, that until people began naming daughters after her, the name Florence was very rare. And, according to Woodham-Smith, Florence Nightingale was herself so named because she had been born in Florence. For my purposes, such a serendipitous conjunction of naming impulses generates the linkage of two apparently unrelated lines of thought; (1) the Victorian professionalization of nursing by Florence Nightingale gave that ancient womanly calling both an added dignity and, as recent feminst students of Nightingale have suggested, a new vantage of attack upon patriarchal control; and (2), insofar as it thematizes the threat of the nurse both as a class and as a psychic force, *Dombey and Son* prepares for the feminist revolutionary potential of Nightingale.

With the death of the first Mrs. Dombey after Paul's birth, Dombey must of course procure a nurse. The Polly Toodles that he engages is an insult to his pride primarily on class grounds, and his insistence that she change her name to "Richards" and abandon her family represents an attempt to insulate himself and his son from the contamination of the lower orders. Still, no amount of insulation will protect him from "the thought of being dependent for the very first step towards the accomplishment of his soul's desire, on a hired serving-woman who would be to the child, for the time, all that even *his* alliance could have made his own wife" (67). In her surrogacy, the nurse, because she has not been willed by the father, because she has not been specifically chosen for a Dombey alliance, represents a bitter defeat at the very outset of the Dombey and Son project.

But there is worse yet: Dombey fears that a great temptation has been placed in the nurse's way: "Her infant son was a boy too. Now, would it be possible for her to change them?" And should such a substitution occur, would he, should he discover it later in life, be able "to pluck away the result of so many years of usage, confidence, and belief, from the imposter, and endow a stranger with it" (71)?

Most Victorians knew what a true changeling was: a substitute for an infant whom the fairies had kidnapped. In its place they left either a starving imp or an aged, useless member of the elfin tribe. If the changeling took the form of a child, it had an old face, a small or wizened body, and was often infirm. And middle-class Victorian saw changelings all around them—in the newspapers and journals they read, in the studies of the collectors and theorists of the emerging discipline known as "folklore," and in popular and mainstream literature. They wondered, for instance, over the violent passions and demonic energies of which the Brontës wrote—about that "gypsy brat," Heathcliff, that "imp of Satan" whose changeling soul tormented both himself and those around him; about Jane Eyre, who when rejecting Edward Rochester's early advances, is angrily accused of being not *his* Jane but a changeling. As for Dickens, the dwarfish Quilp of *The Old Curiosity Shop* with his large head, yellow skin, and high squeaky voice and that ancient-faced "weird changeling to whom the years are nothing," the "elfin Smallweed, christened" Bart in *Bleak House*—such characters bore the authentic impress of the other-worldly creature.[6]

It has by now been thoroughly established in specialized scholarship that Dickens was the preeminent nineteenth-century example of the novelist who assimilated the world of fairy and fairy tale into the realistic novel, and his adaptation of the fairy changeling is a further instance of such assimilation. For though the changeling fear passes from the elder Dombey's thoughts almost immediately, young Paul does have something preternatural about

him; he does have the "old, old face" (151) and the melancholy temperament
of the fairy changeling, especially at Brighton and the closer he moves towards
death:

> He was childish and sportive enough at times, and not of a sullen disposition;
> but he had a strange, old-fashioned, thoughtful way, at other times, of sitting
> brooding in his miniature armchair, when he looked (and talked) like one of
> those terrible little Beings in the Fairy tales, who, at a hundred and fifty or two
> hundred years of age, fantastically represent the children for whom they have
> been substituted.
>
> (151)

But, of course, it is not a fairy that Dombey fears will steal his son but
rather a nurse. The belief in fairy changelings was essentially a lower-class
phenomenon and was especially associated with the Irish poor. I would thus
suggest that the fear of the substituting powers of the nurse or governess is
the "realistic," upper and middle-class version of the despised "Irish,"
lower-class superstition concerning the child stolen by the fairies. The real
fear at the heart of the middle-class version of the myth, embodied in
Dombey's momentary terror, is the possibility that in relying on the nurturing
powers of an outsider in class and family, one is in danger of losing one's
identity as projected through the child. The substituting or corrupting nurse
has frequently been a subject of English, especially Anglo-Irish, comedy—from
Maria Edgeworth's gentleman in her "Essay on Irish Bulls" who says of a
woman he sees, "I hate that woman, for she changed me at nurse," to the
ultimate Victorian sendup of that venerable theme, Miss Prism's famous
blunder at Victoria Station in *The Importance of Being Earnest*. But it is a
deadly serious subject, as *Dombey and Son* demonstrates.

The very title of the novel suggests that all human beings within Dombey's
purview are to be malleable to his will, to the "firm" that in that very name
captures a cash-nexus steeliness which shall control all. And if economic
exchange is the inflexible law that governs the intercourse between men and
men, that is even truer of the relation between men and women. For in a
male barter system that characterizes Victorian life, women are the primary
tokens of exchange and are therefore all—wife, sister, nurse—eminently
substitutable for one another. But the nurse or governess, though apparently
the least of such tokens, is the most threatening of the three precisely because
while not *of* the family she is within it, an exogamous "threshold figure"
existing between "within the family" and "outside the family." [7] Therefore,
if contagion from without is to enter, she is the most likely to be the carrier,
and the fear that she will substitute one of her own children for the "son and

heir'' is a consequent threat of absolutely primal force. (In this context, Dombey's insistence that Polly Toodles change her name to ''Richards'' is intended to insulate his dynastic project on three fronts: as a bare surname, it depersonalizes the nurse; as a more dignified name than Toodles, it decontaminates her class origins and a Sleary-like lack of ''seriousness''; and as a man's name, it works to efface her existence as a woman.) Even when Paul has died Dombey cannot forgive Polly Toodles for her emotional theft of what he had determined to be exclusively his:

> . . . everyone set up some claim or other to a share in his dead boy, and was a bidder against him! Could he ever forget how that woman had wept over his pillow, and called him her own child! or how he, waking from his sleep, had asked for her, and had raised himself in his bed and brightened when she came in.
>
> (353)

But Dombey has a subtle enough revenge upon the Toodles clan for the imagined theft of his child, for he in turn steals their first-born child. That is, in seeing to it that Polly's oldest son Rob is sent to be educated by the Charity Grinders, Dombey in his turn initiates a comparable loss to the Toodles family, a process of the corruption of the Toodles son (in a comic register, to be sure) that is only alleviated at novel's end.

One might at this point object that there is something disproportionate in my concentration upon Dombey's fear of Polly Toodles, a passing thought of his that occupies merely an early moment within a massive narrative. But that moment inaugurates the major action of the novel, the substitution of the child by the ''good'' or the ''bad'' nurse. For the largest structure of the novel does indeed involve a change in Dombey whereby the simulacrum ''Dombey and Son'' becomes ''Dombey and Daughter after all,'' as Miss Tox would have it (941); that structure does chart a ''stealing of the son'' and his replacement by the daughter in a cautionary tale about male identity which would, to its profound regret, try to repress the power of the feminine within. And in her successful intrigues to throw Florence into the company of Paul and of Dombey himself at the very outset of the action, the ''good'' nurse Polly Toodles initiates a graduated process of substitution.

For the nurse or governess, precisely because she is salaried (and Dombey stresses the economic quality of Polly's link to the family), is the primary intervening force in an apparently non-monetary Oedipal circuit; she is the economic hole in the familial cell which first allows larger socio-economic questions to intrude. Indeed, psychoanalysis itself, according to Jane Gallop's

Lacanian view of the nurse, "can and ought to be the place of symbolic inscription of the governess" or nurse. Because she is like the analyst a *paid* intruder into the family (and Freud came to insist upon the importance of the patient's payment), the sense of a welcome replacement she generates in the child is that child's earliest model of the transference available to the analysand in the psychoanalytic situation. Such transference may serve to release her or him from the dominance of the parent (male or female)—that Lacanian phallic "other," the subject who sets him or herself up as the authority "who presumes to know" (Gallop, 144–46).

Of course, the Victorian governess or nurse is a highly ambivalent maternal rescuer, as the alternative benign and malign readings of the governess's protectiveness in Henry James's "Turn of the Screw" demonstrate in exemplary fashion. As for Dickens, his "Nurse's Stories" of the terrifying Captain Murderer suggests the sadistic workings upon the child's imagination of which he deems the nurse (and tradition of the nurse) capable. And in *Dombey and Son* the good nurses Polly Toodles and Susan Nipper are more than matched by the various bad nurses, the maternal witches who destroy or attempt to steal children.

The most overt early parallel to Polly Toodles is "Good Mrs. Brown," who steals Florence from the London streets while Polly is trying to save Rob the Charitable Grinder, her child "stolen" by Dombey, from being beaten up. The full significance of that bad nurse's theft only becomes clear retrospectively, much later in the novel, when we see the relationship between Good Mrs. Brown—now identified as Mrs. Marwood (in a novel full of such name changes to emblematize the floating nature of identity that the substitution impulse generates) and her daughter Alice. Only then do we surmise that Mrs. Brown/Marwood had stolen Florence, made her put on Alice's old cloak, and cut her hair in a perverse attempt to reclaim a daughter that *she* had lost. "If I hadn't once had a gal of my own . . . that was proud of her hair," Mrs. Brown says to Florence as she relents in her cutting, "I'd have had every lock of it, She's far away, she's far away! Oho! Oho" (131). It is as a direct result of this incident that young Paul Dombey loses his "second mother" (142), suffers his "Second Deprivation," the title of the chapter in which the incident occurs and which ends with the dismissal of Polly Toodles. Naturally, the nurse is fired by Dombey not for having lost the worthless daughter but for the corruption of the prized son, for "taking my son—my son . . . into haunts and into society which are not to be thought of without a shudder" (142).

The generous "second mother," Polly Toodles, thus serves as a benign surrogate against which the carefully paralleled bad biological mothers, Mrs. Marwood for Alice and Mrs. Skewton for Edith Granger, who send their daughters into prostitution on different levels of society, are measured and found wanting. In like fashion, Walter Gay's loving substitute fathers, his uncle Sol Gills and Captain Cuttle, serve to underline the narcissistic deficiencies of Dombey, the novel's most important bad biological father (though conceivably one of the reasons Rob the Grinder goes bad is the relative passivity of *his* father). What the novel gives us in this character configuration is a series of variations on what Freud called the "family romance," the child's need to fantasize idealized parents as substitutes for the natural ones who have in one way or another abandoned him. (I pass by the biographical implications of this pattern, except to note that Dombey, the bad natural father, is redeemable, whereas the narrative does not "forgive" either Edith's or Alice's mother, just two of the biological mothers in Dickens' novels upon whom he is particularly hard. For as he said of his own mother with respect to his youthful abandonment in Warren's blacking factory, for which he seems to have forgiven his father at least in part, "I never afterwards forgot, I shall never forget, I never can forget, that my mother was warm for my being sent back."[8]

Freud's family romance, in this novel the child's substitution of the loving nurse for the abandoning mother and the loving uncle for the absent father, may thus be seen as a psychic inversion of the parent's changeling fear. Unlike the parent who fears an exchange of children, the child who has been "deserted" or "changed" at birth welcomes a rescuing replacement of parents. For as the Swiss psychoanalyst Alice Miller has put the matter in a consideration of parental narcissism relevant to *Dombey and Son*, the child always needs some defense against the controlling parent—the elder Dombey, Mrs. Skewton, and Mrs. Marwood, those didactic caricatures of a primary narcissism that drives all of us who are less than saints.

In *The Drama of the Gifted Child*, Miller describes a situation shared by many highly productive men and women who in the midst of their lives fall into deep depression. These patients, she observes, have generally been reared by parents who are emotionally insecure whatever their patina of self-assurance, and whose own narcissistic needs prompt them to value the child not for "herself alone" (to echo Yeats) but rather as extensions of themselves, as objects whose attentive admiration and strict responsiveness are intended to provide the parent with a perpetually self-flattering "mirror."[9] The girl or boy who grows up in such a situation (generally an only or an oldest child) bears the primary burden of providing the self-reflection the parent requires.

But the child's alternative pathological responses to such a soul-wrenching demand, *either* the death-seeking docility of young Paul Dombey or the angry rebelliousness of an Edith Granger or Alice Marwood, is self-defeating.

In the passivity of John and the rebelliousness of James Carker to Dombey's economic control, we see the "brotherhood" of the same inverted responses, one that links the familial servitude of child to parent to the later economic servitude of employee to employer. And thus we can also see why James Carker, the bought manager, and Edith Dombey, the bought wife, enraged rebels against a paralleled economic and familial "management," are natural, if uneasy, allies. Whether the novel's primary critique is Freudian or Marxist, whether it intimates that the exploitation endemic to the familial or the capitalist exchange system is more essential, strikes me as a chicken-and-egg pseudo-question, since the two forms of exploitation are always already mutually implicated.

With respect to the family, at any rate, the potential release from the deadly bind that Miller describes, to the extent that the parent can contribute to it, would seem to involve a forced transformation of that parent's "mirrored framework" (Miller, 35). Whether such a transformation is a linear "advance" or merely a cyclical regress to origins is the novel's most significant version of the change/immutability opposition with which I began.

Let me return to the climactic "mirror scene" of Chapter 59, which I have already paraphrased, but now as the final stage of a graduated process rather than as the precipitous moment of earthquake-like change. For in light of Miller's critique of the parental need for self-reflection, it seems appropriate that the annihilation of Dombey's ego happen before a mirror. It is only when such an emptying out has occurred that Dombey can truly abandon his dream of sole authorship and ownership, his dynastic "Dombey and Son" enterprise that would exclude a dependency upon woman, upon the "nurse" in all her forms. Only such a relinquishment of the "son," such a total humbling of patriarchal desire, will allow a "daughter" to appear at last. And such a final embrace of the sexual other, a recognition that identity requires the dependence upon gender alterity, rescues the self from death through the intercession of a daughter, making the glass give back an image of the resurrected self.

The certainty that Dombey and Son is "Dombey and Daughter after all" is thus the changeling theme's final turn of the screw. To the extent that the parent expects the child to be a mirror, the child who refuses that need even minimally may well strike the disappointed parent as a changeling, and the more intense the expectation, the more "fantastic" the changeling's representation of the parentally-imagined "true" self. The son born to Dombey, the "old, old" child who evaded the mirroring function that Dombey required, was thus not a changeling presented to the father by the fairies, nor by the nurse, but rather by the mad extremity of paternal desire itself. In the demand for a perfectly replicating child, the parent paradoxically enough seeks a self-sufficiency that will not require a mirror, a self that will obviate the need for representation. But when Dombey confronts that psychic opacity, it presents itself as a hideous ungendered neutrality, as an "it" in the glass. For the human need for the mirror's gaze to define the self is a constant, as is the consequent drive for mirroring substitutions, for primarily maternal representations.

The novel, to the degree that it focuses on Dombey's need, describes the fading unto death of the same-sex changeling mirror; the confrontation of a terrible blank wherein no recognizable human representation is available; and the nick-of-time rescue of the father reduced to abandoned child "after all" (another version of the Dickens orphan) by what he has been fleeing from the start—the comforting gaze of the last of the novel's "second mothers" as Polly Toodles had been the first—the true maternal child, one of Dickens' oxymoronic "little mothers."[10] For this Florence, who prefigures a more famous Victorian Florence outside of fiction, now becomes the father's supportive nurse in his old age. Like Lear's Cordelia, she has moved from a "nothing" at the beginning of the action to being all at the close. ("Whoever is to be really free and happy . . ." says Freud, "must have overcome his deference for women and come to terms with the idea of incest with mother or sister"[11]—and *Dombey and Son* would suggest, with daughter.) For in his total dependency upon Florence, Dombey embraces the mother he has attempted to exclude in all her guises from his paternal and patriarchal project. In tracking these changing forms of the "second mother" with whom we all, women as well as men, must make do, the novel affirms the inevitability of substitution, of mirroring, of "fantastic" representation; and it affirms the changeling fear as the systole and the family romance as the answering diastole of the heart's desire.

To return, finally, to the issue of whether the catastrophist sense which dominated my earlier discussion of change in *Dombey and Son* or the gradualist sense which dominated the later is more characteristically Dickensian: "Ground long undermined will often fall down in a moment," says the narrator of Dombey's change. As recent theorists have reminded us, whenever we get the establishment of a structural opposition such as self and other, subject and object, presence and absence, further meditation will usually show how the two terms inhabit each other. The "long undermining" of Dombey's pride and the "fall in a moment" are precisely such differential signs that provide limits for each other's definition. I hope it does not strike the reader as too outrageous an evasion, as too exasperating a shaggy-dog ending to a long argument that, at least as far as *Dombey and Son* is concerned, the catastrophist/ uninformitarian dialectic about the nature of change teases us out of thought in some such way.

NOTES

1. *Dombey and Son* (London: Penguin, 1970) 489–90, ed. Peter Fairclough with an introduction by Raymond Williams. All *Dombey* references are to this edition and will be cited parenthetically.
2. "The Changing World," in *Dickens: From Pickwick to Dombey* (New York: Basic Books, 1965), pp. 293–357.
3. *The Melodramatic Imagination: Balzac, Henry James, Melodrama, and the Mode of Excess* (New York: Columbia University Press, 1984).
4. "Dickens: The Two Scrooges," in *Eight Essays* (New York: Anchor Books, 1954), pp. 11–91; rpt. from *The Triple Thinkers* (New York: Oxford University Press, 1938).
5. My summary is substantially indebted to A. Dwight Culler's account of the debate in "The Poetry of Apocalypse," *The Poetry of Tennyson* (New Haven, Conn.: Yale University Press, 1977), pp. 14–28. For more recent surveys of the catastrophist/uniformitarian opposition, climaxing in Darwin's uniformitarian incorporation of catastrophist progressivism, see Gillian Beer, *Darwin's Plots: Evolutionary Narrative in Darwin, Geroge Eliot, and Nineteenth-Century Fiction* (London: Routledge and Kegan Paul, 1983) and George Levine, *Darwin and the Novelists: Patterns of Science in Victorian Fiction* (Cambridge, Mass.: Harvard University Press, 1988).
6. The foregoing paragraph is substantially indebted to an as yet unpublished paper by Carole Silver, " 'The Child That Went With The Fairies': The Victorians and the Changeling," presented at the CUNY Conference on Victorian Popular Culture, May 1987. Harry Stone's discussion of *Dombey and Son*, in *Dickens and the Invisible World: Fairy Tales, Fantasy, Novel–Making* (Bloomington: Indiana University Press, 1979), alludes to the changeling motif in passing.
7. Jane Gallop, *The Daughter's Seduction: Feminism and Psychoanalysis* (Ithaca, N.Y.: Cornell University Press, 1982), p. 146.
8. Quoted in John Forster, *The Life of Charles Dickens*, ed. A. J. Hoppe. 2 vols. (London: Dent, 1966) 1·32.
9. *The Drama of the Gifted Child* (New York: Basic Books, 1981), p. 35. I follow the application of Miller's thesis to *Dombey and Son* in part from an unpublished paper by Elizabeth Tenenbaum, "The Illusion and Reality of Power in *Dombey and Son*," given at a CUNY Victorian Seminar in 1987.
10. As John O. Jordan has, however, suggested to me in private conversation, Florence has her limitations as a "mother," is finally something of a "bad nurse" to Edith: while she advises Edith to confess and ask forgiveness of Dombey, she does not make a like request of Dombey with respect to a sinned against Edith.
11. Sigmund Freud, "The Most Prevalent Form of Degradation in Erotic Life,"

Collected Papers of Sigmund Freud, trans. Joan Rivière. Vol. IV (New York: Basic Books, 1959), 211.

Embodying *Dombey*:
Whole and in Part

Robert Newsom

One of the great pleasures to be had from Dickens' work derives from the apparent paradox of its imaginative diversity on the one hand and its intense coherence on the other. *Bleak House* is for me the paradigmatic novel in this regard and offers, I think, the best example of a work that is various, divided, and at odds with itself and at the same time almost insanely all of a piece. Its variousness is evident not only in the usual rich panorama of Victorian life that Dickens presents, but in such things for example as the narrative's being itself divided between two very different beings who inhabit incompatible worlds—one an omniscient and therefore magical being and the other a character within the story. Its variousness is evident too in the psychological divisions within the first-person narrator herself (she is forever talking to herself and treating herself as though she were somebody else), and it is evident in the pervasive air of mystery that leads countless characters and the reader to ask, in the words of the novel's most famous question, "What connexion can there be . . .?" between one mysterious happening and the next (Ch 16, 197).[1] Its coherence is evident not only in a plot that resolves all mysteries and ties up all loose ends, but in such things for example as the fact that almost every element in the novel can be seen as forwarding a demonstration of the good Victorian maxim that "Charity Begins at Home." It is evident also (as I have argued elsewhere) in Dickens' unity of formal strategy, his dwelling throughout the novel, as he announces in the Preface, "on the romantic side of familiar things" (4) so that the whole novel can be read as an extended gloss on that phrase, an attempt to generate and explore exhaustively all the ways in which one might play with the tension between the familiar and unfamiliar.

Bleak House is also useful in providing an example of the paradox of variety versus coherence in Dickens' work because it seems peculiarly self-conscious on this score. The tension between romantic and familiar is itself a version of the tension between the various and coherent, for the experience of the "romantic" is the experience of a world that is perpetually novel or different, while the experience of the "familiar" is the experience of a world that continually resembles nothing so much as itself. Chapter twenty-five of the novel presents in small a comic version of the dilemma between ways of seeing the world as either various or coherent that several of the novel's most important characters share along with the reader. It takes us first into the head of the law stationer Mr. Snagsby, for whom life has come to make no sense at all, but to be rather a series of continual and unpleasant, even frightening surprises; and then it takes us into the very different head of Mrs. Snagsby, who, in the words of the chapter's title, "sees it all": unlike her mystified husband, she suffers from no doubts but believes she has discovered the master key that unlocks all mysteries, the explanation that makes everything fall into place. Resembling Mr. and Mrs. Snagsby by turns, the reader perpetually is made to feel either that the novel makes no sense or that it makes oppressively coherent sense, that not only *is* there connection between apparently unconnected events, but that indeed everything in the novel is connected with everything else.

Of course, Mrs. Snagsby's explanation turns out to be wrong, and the reader is made to wait several hundred pages for the correct solution to the various mysteries and puzzles in which her husband has unwittingly found himself involved. But unlike a conventional mystery story's mystery, the mysteries of *Bleak House* do not all resolve themselves with perfect neatness (and Mrs. Snagsby's error is only one among many mistaken interpretations or deductions made by the novel's characters). The novel in fact famously ends with an incomplete sentence and the words "even supposing—" followed by nothing more decisive than a dash. "Supposing what?" we are led to ask, but the novel gives us no more help than to sit patiently before us, waiting for another reading. If the novel's mysteries *were* all solved (or indeed soluble), there would of course be no lasting paradox and play between what I have been calling variousness and coherence. What saves the novel from the sort of paranoid interpreting I have practiced upon it (which follows the novel's own example of establishing connections everywhere) is that it seems as endless in its coherences as in its variety. That is, there seems to be an almost endless supply of things we can identify in the novel as its "real" subjects, master themes, centers, origins, or whatever we choose to call them.

I begin this discussion of *Dombey and Son* by discussing a later novel not only because *Bleak House* presents a clearer example of the play of variety and coherence than does *Dombey and Son,* but also because *Bleak House* shows us structures and concerns that *Dombey and Son* is only tending towards. Perhaps most importantly, the self-consciousness of the later novel about the play of the romantic and the familiar is consistent with its taking the form of a mystery (actually there are two main mysteries) and with its posing fundamental epistemological questions about the limits of knowledge, whereas there is very little if any mystery in *Dombey and Son*—there are no detectives—and very little worry about what can or can't be known.

It is clear from the very first page of the novel that Dombey's pride is of the sort that inevitably goes before a fall; no real suspense develops even about the means that will bring him down; and there are no real surprises.[1] (After all, if the end really is assured, can it matter so very much what the means are?) If the anxiety of *Bleak House* generated by the play of variousness and coherence has to do with knowledge, the analogous anxiety in *Dombey and Son* is expressed in much more fundamental terms; rather than questioning the coherence of anything so slippery as knowledge or understanding, it expresses its worries in terms of the physical. *Bleak House* worries that things make no sense, *Dombey and Son* worries more primitively that they will fall apart. This issue is expressed already in the novel's title and the family's name—"Dombey" is an anagram of "embody," one of whose meanings is to bring parts together into an organized whole.[2] And the novel's full title, appearing on the original wrappers and the engraved title page of the first edition, elaborates the question: "Dealings with the Firm of Dombey and Son, Wholesale, Retail and for Exportation." The distinction between dealing goods wholesale and retail has of course to do with whether they are sold as a whole lot or divided into individual parts or pieces. The word "retail" in fact comes from the French *retailler,* meaning "to cut again." The last element in the series, "exportation," is undoubtedly meaningful too. Since the only way something could be exported from Great Britain in the nineteenth century was to go out to sea, and since going to sea in this novel is associated with dying, we may say that the title announces interests not only in embodiment and dismemberment, but in disembodiment too.

In a classic essay, Julian Moynahan sees in the novel a struggle between firmness and wetness. Dombey is the head of a "firm," and he and it embody firmness, he in the literal firmness of his rigid, inflexible face and body. Opposed to him are Florence, forever dissolving into tears, and the sea, representing not just death, but the fluidity of nature, and therefore mortality and immortality and the powerful changefulness of things against which Dombey has set his proud and obstinate wilfulness.[3] The significance of wetness is real, but what also needs to be stressed is the loss of wholeness entailed in dissolving or melting. For there is a good deal of going to pieces in the novel, not all of which involves dissolving in tears. The most obvious example is of course Carker's horrible dismemberment and mangling by the train. He is

> beaten down, caught up, and whirled away upon a jagged mill, that spun him round and round, and struck him limb from limb, and licked his stream of life up with its fiery heat, and cast his mutilated fragments in the air.
> When [Mr. Dombey, who has witnessed the death] . . . recovered from a swoon, he saw them bringing from a distance something covered, that lay heavy and still, upon a board, between four men, and saw that others drove some dogs away that sniffed upon the road, and soaked his blood up, with a train of ashes.[4]
>
> (Ch. 55, 875)

It is as violent a death as any in Dickens, but it is by no means the only violence in the novel. In spite of the domesticity of the novel's concerns and scene, this is in fact one of Dickens' *most* violent novels, in imagery if not always in deed, and its violence often takes the form of taking things apart. Carker's mangling is simply an especially notable instance of much real and imaginary smashing. The Dombey ship the *Son and Heir* is smashed to bits with all hands except Walter lost, and when news of the disaster reaches England, as the title of Chapter thirty-two puts it, "The Wooden Midshipman goes to Pieces." The ruin of the Dombey firm is also described as a "tremendous smash" (Ch. 58, 910). Much of the violence done to people in the novel does not actually tear them apart, but it is strong stuff nonetheless. The blow that Dombey deals his daughter just after he has discovered his wife's apparent elopement with Carker is perhaps even more shocking than Carker's death because it is Dombey's answer to her reaching out to him with open arms in love and sympathy, and its psychological effects are far more hurtful than the bruise it leaves upon her breast; they too are described in terms of a murderous tearing apart of the body, ironically the idealized image Florence has maintained of Dombey himself:

> she looked at him, and a cry of desolation issued from her heart. For as she looked, she saw him murdering that fond idea to which she had held in spite of him. She saw his cruelty, neglect, and hatred dominant above it, and stamping it down. She saw she had no father upon earth. . . .
>
> (Ch. 47, 757)

She had seen the murder done. In the last lingering natural aspect in which she had cherished him through so much, he had been torn out of her heart, defaced, and slain. . . . If her fond heart could have held his image after that, it must have broken; but it could not; and the void was filled with a wild dread that fled from all confronting with its shattered fragments. . . .

(Ch. 49, 779)

Dombey's real blow dealt against his daughter is but an echo of the blow he wants to deal his wife:

he tore out of the room, and out of the house, with a frantic idea of finding her yet . . . and beating all trace of beauty out of the triumphant face with his bare hand.

(Ch. 47, 756)

When old Mrs. Brown throttles Rob the Grinder to get news of Carker's whereabouts out of him, her daughter urges her on:

"Well done, mother. Tear him to pieces!"
"What, young woman! blubbered Rob; "are you against me too? What have I been and done? What am I to be tore to pieces for, I should like to know? . . . Call yourselves females, too!" said the frightened and afflicted Grinder, with his coat-cuff at his eye. "I'm surprised at you! Where's your feminine tenderness?"

(Ch. 52, 826)

The violence here is edging towards the comic—Rob is obviously not in real danger—and much of the novel's violence is comic and merely imaginary, but it is extreme nonetheless:

"By the Lord, Sir," cried the Major, bursting into speech at the sight of the waiter, who was come to announce breakfast, "it's an extraordinary thing to me that no one can have the honour and happiness of shooting all such beggars through the head without being brought to book for it. But here's an arm for Mrs. Granger if she'll do J. B. the honour to accept it.

(Ch. 27, 462)

The violence here is gratuitous, since the waiter has in fact only done his job, and in such a context the idea of bursting into speech and offering an arm becomes positively grisly. The novel, indeed, often calls attention to polite gestures as though merely pieces of bodies were involved, and Mrs. Skewton, as the novel's chief representative of bodily decay, naturally is frequently singled out for such treatment. She gives "Mr. Dombey her hand; which Mr. Dombey, not exactly knowing what to do with, dropped" (Ch. 27, 471).

Much of the violence imagined by characters in *Dombey and Son* is directed against themselves. Rob the Grinder bemoans his father's low opinion of him thus:

> Nobody thinks half so bad of me as my own father does. What an unnatural thing! I wish somebody'd take and chop my head off. Father wouldn't mind doing it, I believe, and I'd much rather he did that than t'other [—that is, speak ill of him].
>
> (Ch. 38, 621)

Threats are often made against oneself as a demonstration of sincerity or loyalty. Thus Rob again, this time to Carker:

> "And if you ever find me out, Sir, doing anything against your wishes, I give you leave to kill me."
> "You dog!" said Mr. Carker, leaning back in his chair, and smiling at him serenely. "That's nothing to what I'd do to you, if you tried to deceive me."
>
> (Ch. 42, 678)

Rob's loyalty (like Carker's) is nonexistent, but truer hearts make equally violent threats against themselves. Captain Cuttle is so convinced that Florence's broken heart can only be mended by Walter's true love that he would sooner "have these here blue arms and legs chopped off" than stand in the way of her emigration with Walter (Ch. 56, 880). Inasmuch as the Captain has already lost a hand, he knows whereof he speaks. Upon first hearing that he has a probably successful rival for Florence's affections in the person of Walter, Toots confides to Captain Cuttle that his isn't a selfish love and he only wishes her happiness.

> "It's the sort of thing with me, Captain Gills, that if I could be run over—or—or trampled upon—or—or thrown off a very high place—or anything of that sort—for Miss Dombey's sake, it would be the most delightful thing that could happen to me."
>
> (Ch. 32, 546–47)

Susan Nipper is no less vehement in her loyalty to Florence. When she finally protests Dombey's treatment of his daughter to his face, she declares that Florence is

> the blessedest and dearest angel . . . that ever drew the breath of life, the more that I was torn to pieces Sir the more I'd say it though I may not be a Fox's Martyr.
>
> (Ch. 44, 703)

Part of the comedy of these last two examples comes about because they deny the real consequences of being torn apart or smashed. Toots asserts that the experience that must end all experience will be most delightful, and Susan asserts that it will somehow fortify her powers of speech.

A more sinister denial of death and falling apart is played out by Mrs. Skewton and the Major, who together and more perhaps than any other characters in the novel focus our attention on the body and questions about its integrity. Mrs. Skewton embodies decay. She is a sort of living mummy who disintegrates into ashes every night only to be revivified every day in her guise as Cleopatra (Ch. 27, 474–75). But even during the day she presents a ghoulish enough spectacle, so much so that Florence doesn't quite know how to kiss her. "Florence was timidly stooping to pick out a place in the white part of Mrs. Skewton's face, when that lady presented her ear, and relieved her of her difficulty" (Ch. 30, 505). When paralysis inevitably strikes her down,

> they took her to pieces in very shame, and put the little of her that was real on a bed. Doctors were sent for, and soon came. Powerful remedies were resorted to; opinions given that she would rally from this shock, but would not survive another; and there she lay speechless, and staring at the ceiling, for days.
>
> (Ch. 37, 613)

In fact she does rally, and becomes well enough to repeat the ritual of falling "to pieces as usual" so that she can be "put away in bed" (Ch. 40, 661). But her recovery is grim indeed because when her consciousness does return, it too is in pieces and makes a hash of memory and of language. She confuses Edith's first and second husbands, cutting up their names and then grafting the pieces onto one another, so that Dombey is sometimes called "Domber," sometimes "Grangeby" (Ch. 40, 657).

> "Your wife's mother is on the move, Sir," says the Major to Dombey.
> "I fear," returned Mr. Dombey, with much philosophy, "that Mrs. Skewton is shaken."
> "Shaken, Dombey!" said the Major. "''Smashed!''
>
> (Ch. 40, 660–61)

Mrs. Skewton dies, as it were, bit by bit. She is appropriately terrified by a vision of a piece of a body, a "stone arm"

> —part of a figure of some tomb, she says— . . . raised to strike her. At last it falls; and then a dumb old woman lies upon the bed, and she is crooked and shrunk up, and half of her is dead.
>
> (Ch. 41, 672–73)

The Major is of course also prone to stroke and exhibits symptoms that are violently apoplectic. Unlike Mrs. Skewton, he is threatened not by dying bit by bit, but exploding, although that too involves a going to pieces. He is

> a wooden-featured, blue-faced Major, with his eyes starting out of his head, in whom Miss Tox recognised, as she herself expressed it, something . . . truly military. . . .
>
> Major Bagstock had arrived at what is called in polite literature, the grand meridian of life, and was proceeding on his journey down-hill with hardly any throat, and a very rigid pair of jaw-bones, and long-flapped elephantine ears, and his eyes and complexion in the state of artificial excitement already mentioned. . . .
>
> It may be doubted whether there ever was a more entirely selfish person at heart; or at stomach is perhaps a better expression, seeing that he was more decidedly endowed with that latter organ than the former.
>
> (Ch. 7, 143–44, 145)

The Major's feeding is particularly revolting and particularly ominous. He is described after one meal as in such a state of repletion that "essence of savoury pie [is] oozing out at the corners of his eyes, and devilled grill and kidneys [are] tightening his cravat" (Ch. 20, 349–50). It is almost as though he is turning himself inside out or at least leaking at the seams.[5]

What I wish to emphasize in all of these examples is not just the violence nor the preoccupation with death that accompanies it, but rather the particular anxiety about going to pieces or being torn to pieces. There are of course plenty of other places in Dickens' fiction where violence and death are thematized, but *Dombey and Son* is, I think, unique in its emphasis.[6] In *Our Mutual Friend*, for example, there is a continual grisly playing with death and with bodies and even pieces of bodies (see Hutter), but with quite a different effect. For in the later novel, as Catherine Gallagher has demonstrated, nothing really dies, and no pieces (of bodies or indeed of anything else) are really lost. Far from being a novel portraying a modern urban wasteland, *Our Mutual Friend* portrays a world in which there is no waste, because everything cast off is reclaimed, and death itself is sometimes seen as positively refreshing. (Recall Jenny Wren's famous injunction to "Come up and be dead!") Moreover, the line between living and dead is continually blurred, and several characters wander back and forth between this world and the next. But in *Dombey and Son*, death throughout is final and involves an irreversible disembodiment. ("Doom" and "tomb" resonate in its title, as many readers have noticed.)[7] Death is emphatically "the *unknown* sea that rolls round all the world" (Ch. 1, 60), and once one has gone to pieces there doesn't seem to be any hope of being restored to wholeness. The finality of death is underscored by the image of ashes, which is strewn through the novel—we have seen it already of course in the ashes that are used to soak up Carker's blood and in reference to Cleopatra; ashes are used also to connect death with the railway and to describe the "flinty opposition" between Dombey and his second wife, which makes "their marriage way a train of ashes" (Ch. 47, 736). But we are reminded of ashes too in what we might expect to be a more hopeful description, that of little Paul's funeral:

> All of him that is dead, they lay there, near the perishable substance of his mother. It is well. Their ashes lie where Florence in her walks . . . may pass them any day.
>
> (Ch. 18, 311–12)

Going to pieces of course signifies more than dying. It also signifies a giving in to life and powerful feeling, for to fear death, as we all know, means to fear life. Julian Moynahan, Steven Marcus, and F. R. Leavis have all dealt in turn with Dombey's fear of feeling, the death in him of feeling, and his hatred of feeling. Moynahan connects Dombey's problems with Wilhelm Reich's theory of character. Reich was an early disciple of Freud who broke with his mentor when he found Freud backing away from his early belief that every neurosis entailed an actual damming up of libido. The radical younger analyst held in *Character Analysis* (his most important work, still widely read) that every repression entailed not only a mental, but a somatic component in the form of defenses sustained in the body itself, habitual and literal ways of holding feelings in that constitute in Reich's phrase, "character armor," and he held that repressed material could be unlocked as well or better by analytic work done upon the patient's body as upon the patient's talk. Though Moynahan does not note it, the narrator in fact refers to Dombey's "cold hard armour of pride" at the very beginning of the great chapter "Domestic Relations" (Ch. 40, 647). Steven Marcus, in what continues to be the best single work on *Dombey*, does note the armor along with Dombey's alienation from his own body and goes on to characterize Dombey as "impotent" (338–339, 356). Though there can be no doubt about Dombey's emotional inflexibility and defensiveness, and though it is certainly hard to imagine in him a good lover, nonetheless it seems to me that Moynahan and Marcus both overlook something that Dickens has been at pains to point out. Reichian character defenses, like Freudian defenses, are unconscious and, when they interfere with our ability to love or to work, are signs of illness. But Dombey is not unconscious of what he is doing with his body. To use his sister's favorite formulation, he is forever making an "effort" and, as the Preface reminds us, his nature is engaged in a "perpetual struggle with itself. . . . A sense of his injustice is within him, all along." He is not unfeeling or unconscious of feeling, but at war with his feelings. Significantly, he does quite a bit of crying himself in the course of the novel, but he cries alone, and only for his son and himself. Dombey's pride is above all things a wilful pride, which is why it is not evidence of disease, but of sin. He is not cured, but punished (the chapter of his downfall is called "Retribution"), made to relent, and then forgiven. Moynahan, following the Reichian argument, writes that, in the scene in which Dombey observes his daughter while he is apparently napping under a handkerchief (Ch. 35, 585–88), his "brief change . . . is described as a melting. Clearly, he is afraid that if he once lets go he will be dissolved or drowned in a sea of feeling" (124). But this is simply untrue. There isn't even any fluid imagery in the scene. Rather, Dombey is said simply to "soften" towards Florence as her image "became blended with [that of] the child he had loved" (Ch. 35, 587).[8]

As for impotence, obviously Dombey cannot be technically impotent, having fathered two children. He is, no doubt, lousy as a lover, but it is clear that his attraction to Edith has a powerful sexual basis. The point of Dombey's trip to Brighton is to remove him from the scene of his grief, not to hunt up a new wife. On the contrary, until Dombey meets Edith and her mother, he had planned not to do any socializing at all. Although Edith and Dombey significantly have in common the loss of a small loved son as well as an unhealthy and insolent pride, their respective prides are said to be quite different, and they never to our knowledge confide in one another about the loss of their children. Much more is made of Edith's beauty, especially through the medium of the Major's randy military brand of bawdiness:

> "If Joe Bagstock were a younger man, there's not a woman in the world whom he'd prefer for Mrs. Bagstock to that woman. By George, Sir! said the Major, "she's superb!"
> "Do you mean the daughter?" inquired Mr. Dombey.
> "Is Joey B. a turnip, Dombey," said the Major, that he should mean the mother?"

Edith (who is often assumed to be frigid—with no more reason than Dombey is assumed to be impotent) regards herself as having quite literally prostituted herself in marrying Dombey. It is hard to imagine her feeling such guilt (as she expresses most forcibly to Florence in the chapter called "Relenting" [Ch. 61]), were her marital duties merely ceremonial and decorative. In fact, the only marital relations one *can* imagine her as having are sensual—no matter how ultimately unsatisfying to both parties. There is no hint that they are to be reproductive, for nothing suggests that Dombey intends to try and produce another son, even though at just under thirty Edith is well within child-bearing age (Ch. 21, 365). The shame she feels before Carker is the shame she feels before his recognition that there is no love between Edith and her husband and that she has therefore merely sold herself for sex. Her elopement with Carker and its sham infidelity are meant to punish both Carker, by unmasking his sensuality and hypocrisy before the world, and her husband, by dishonoring him and exposing the lovelessness of their marriage before the world. When Dombey refuses to admit the prostitution and sham entailed in his marriage, Edith effectively broadcasts them at large.

What then *is* Dombey's problem if it isn't a neurotic flight from feeling? An obvious direction in which to look is towards the novel's larger social interests. Most readers have taken Dombey quite seriously as a critical portrait of economic, bourgeois man. Marcus says little Paul dies of middle-class culture, although he recognizes too that the novel simultaneously defends that culture, and he writes that in *Dombey and Son* "all emotions become class emotions" (329, 342). Even Leavis works rather hard at portraying Mr. Dombey as an earlier version of Mr. Gradgrind, imbued with the "particular spirit of class" depending on "the new money-power" (7). But in spite of the wonderful exchange between Dombey and son on the question "what's money?" (Ch. 8, 152), it may be argued that this novel is actually only secondarily interested in the kind of critique of business or of political economy detailed with far greater explicitness in *Hard Times* and perhaps even in *A Christmas Carol*. Far from this being the "business" novel that Dickens himself termed it, *Dombey and Son* says remarkably little about business. We know more about the operations of Toots's tailors Burgess & Co. than we do either of Dombey and Son or Solomon Gills's instrument shop, which of course doesn't transact any business at all in the whole course of the novel.[9]

Dombey's pride is more fundamental and more dangerous a sin than the more usual, and profitable, vice of the businessman—mere greed. As Andrew Sanders reminds us, pride is the deadliest sin, and the very first pages of the novel make clear why:[10]

[The three words "Dombey and Son"] conveyed the one idea of Mr. Dombey's life. The earth was made for Dombey and Son to trade in, and the sun and the moon were made to give them light. Rivers and seas were formed to float their ships; rainbows gave them promise of fair weather; winds blew for or against their enterprises; stars and planets circled in their orbits, to preserve inviolate a system of which they were the centre. Common abbreviations took new meaning in his eyes and had sole reference to them. A. D. had no concern with anno Domini, but stood for anno Dombei—and Son.

(Ch. 1, 50)

As he is elsewhere described, by the Major, "Dombey is as proud . . . as Lucifer" (Ch. 26, 449), and indeed his pride is equivalent to Lucifer's in that it puts itself in the place that only God can occupy. He is whole in the sense of being a totality, although like God, Dombey has parts that paradoxically do not diminish the wholeness of the whole. It is of course not a trinity that Dombey embodies. Instead it is an unholy and unwholesome chain of twins. Dombey assumes himself to be all-powerful and therefore self-sufficient; or rather, he assumes an eternal and self-sustaining sequence of identical Dombeys and Sons (he is himself at least three generations distant from the origins of the firm; perhaps significantly, the exact remove isn't specified). To admit dependence upon anyone is a humiliation, but to admit dependence upon women for the very continuation of the sequence involves an especially humiliating negation of self-sufficiency. As many readers have noted, Dombey is, at first, almost willing to let little Paul die before hiring a wet-nurse; a bit later he will magisterially assert his self-sufficiency and wholeness: "I am enough for him [Paul] . . . and all in all" (Ch. 5, 103). That this sense of wholeness and self-sufficiency really is at the center of Dombey becomes clear in the moment of his asking for forgiveness before his daughter: "Oh my God, forgive me, for I need it very much!" (Ch. 59, 940).[11]

Women are feared because they are both necessary and different and therefore remind Dombey that he not only *is not* all there is, but that his immortality—the continuation of an endless series of identical Dombeys and Sons—is dependent on that quite different other. He can only tolerate wives who, like his first, are broken in spirit and content to be treated like pieces of furniture or who, like his second, mask their difference by themselves assuming a pride as great and impenetrable as his.

This is not to say Dombey is without redeeming features. For one thing, and it is something often lost sight of, he is intensely honorable. When the firm does fail at last, Dombey insists on putting everything he owns into paying off its debts, and, as Cousin Feenix, says, "His pride shows well in this" (Ch. 58, 914). But the ideals of autonomy and integrity that he upholds are, nevertheless, generally discredited and are seen to be inseparable from his alienation and woodenness. He excludes what his daughter embodies, what the novel, along with its characters, repeatedly calls "heart"—as for example in the title of the important chapter twenty-four, "The Study of a Loving Heart" (about Florence), or comically and ironically in Mrs. Skewton's hideous parody of a romantic ideology of "heart":

> "What I want," drawled Mrs. Skewton, pinching her shrivelled throat, "is heart." It was frightfully true in one sense, if not in that in which she used the phrase. "What I want is frankness, confidence, less conventionality, and freer play of soul. We are so dreadfully artificial."
> We were, indeed.
>
> (Ch. 21, 363)

Heart represents much more than simply a capacity for feeling, although it certainly depends upon such a capacity. Most importantly, it represents a capacity for feeling for others, an acceptance of affectional dependence on others, the humility that such dependence involves, and—Mrs.Skewton is quite right—the frank expression of the feeling even when it goes against convention. In being thus humble, it is the perfect opposite of pride, although it is not without its own sense of honor. Where Dombey's honor involves loyalty to self, however, "heart" involves loyalty to others.

We might almost say that Dombey's pride amounts to little more than *machismo*—he takes it for granted that he shall have to fight a duel with Carker (Ch. 51, 812)—while Florence's "heart" represents traditional female sympathy and submissiveness. But the example of Mrs. Skewton is only one among many that demonstrates that heartlessness is by no means a male prerogative. Alice's mother and Mrs. Chick provide further evidence of heartlessness. Plenty of the novel's males, on the other hand,—especially the group who gather around the Wooden Midshipman, notably Walter, Captain Cuttle, and Toots, are obviously and amply endowed with "heart." What I am suggesting is that in *Dombey and Son* Dickens is intentionally (whether or not consciously is another question) undermining conventional expectations about the behavior of men and women. This is an idea that has been raised only to be dismissed by Nina Auerbach in her essay on the novel. She writes:

> The separation between the sexes that prevails in *Dombey and Son* reminds us over and over that "they are nothing alike" [this is a quotation from Ruskin's *Sesame and Lilies*]; but certain bizarre and equivocal mutations lead to a suggestion of what we now call an androgynous vision. . . .
>
> (119)

To say that there is a prevailing separation between the sexes seems to me to confuse Dombeyism with the novel's critique of Dombeyism. Surely the separation that Dombey enforces forms a crucial part of the pride that must have a fall, and surely the rest of the novel is replete with counterexamples of men and women who not only do not enforce such a separation, but who in their own behavior blur conventionally masculine and feminine qualities. To refer to these as "bizarre . . . mutations" seems not only to confuse Dombey with the novel, but positively to embrace Dombeyism. Captain Cuttle may not be the first person one thinks of as the model androgyne, but the care he lavishes upon Florence in her flight from her father is as tender as could be. He is so moved by her plight "that he fairly overflowed with compassion and gentleness" (Ch. 48, 762). Leaving her to rest he kisses her hand "with the chivalry of any old knight-errant," but then walks "on tip-toe out of the room" (Ch. 48, 765)—hardly a knightly move. Later when preparing her dinner he is described as a cook of "extraordinary skill" (Ch. 49, 773). Perhaps significantly, he is named after an odd mollusk that wears its shell on the *inside* of its body.

Walter, who is no less chivalric than the Captain, is also no less delicate. When we first meet him, he is described as Dombey's complete opposite: "The boy, with his open face, and flowing hair, and sparkling eyes, panting with pleasure and excitement, was wonderfully opposed to Mr. Dombey, as he sat confronting him in his library chair" (Ch. 6, 139). Upon his return to find Florence under the Midshipman's protection, it is he who insists that she have a proper chaperon. When Florence confronts him with the constrained manner he has borne towards her, he is so mindful of her difficult situation that it is left to her to make the move and the proposal.

More interesting, undoubtedly, are the instances of the blurring of masculine and feminine afforded by the two marriages outside of Florence and Walter's that are held up as examplary: the Toodles's and the Toots's. In both cases there is a striking mutuality of authority. Dombey turns to Mr. Toodles to verify the terms of his contract with Polly, but Toodles's laconic reply is simply "Polly heerd it. . . . It's all right." And the point is underscored:

> "As you appear to leave everything to her," said Mr. Dombey, frustrated in his intention of impressing his views still more distinctly on the husband, as the stronger character, "I suppose it is of no use my saying anything to you."
> "Not a bit," said Toodle. "Polly heered it. *She's* awake, Sir."
>
> (Ch. 2, 69-70)

Toots' marriage to "the Nipper" similarly inverts the masculine pride of Dombeyism in several ways. Toots always defers to Susan's judgment. As he says, "If ever the Rights of Women . . . are properly attended to, it will be through her powerful intellect" (Ch. 60, 946), and one of his greatest delights in his marriage is the succession of girls that Susan bears. "The oftener we can repeat that most extraordinary woman," he exclaims, ". . . the better!" (Ch. 62, 972).

I do not mean to deny that there is at the same time plenty in this novel to make a modern reader cringe, and especially things having to do with questions of sex and of class. We might wish both Toodles and Toots to be intellectually a little more powerful, and we might wish Polly and her husband to be a little less humble. I really *do* wish that Susan had not met Florence on her return in her old servant's dress. But even as we cringe we ought to appreciate the point. The kind of learning that Toodles and Toots lack—think of the Charitable Grinders and Dr. Blimber's—is better left unlearned; the reddening with which Polly says "she hoped she knew her place" (Ch. 2, 68) isn't a humble blush, but an angry flush; and the Susan who puts on her old dress for Florence is thereby asserting that she's the same woman who, among all the characters in the novel, is the first of only two to go before Mr. Dombey and, fact to face, stick it to him. (The other, of course, is Edith.)

The novel pretty clearly *is* too deeply equivocal about middle-class culture to be, in the great revolutionary year of 1848, revolutionary. But if—like every Dickens novel—it cannot imagine political solutions, it is nonetheless radical in its analysis. If it apparently accepts many of what we might call the divisions of behavior between the sexes, it at the same time wants to ungender them, to free them from the constraint of being the exclusive property of one sex or the other. The novel likes some manly men and womanly women, but it also likes many manly women and womanly men, and it even hates some manly men and manly women as well as some womanly men. What it really hates is toughness—"Joey B. . . . [is] hard-hearted, Sir, is Joe—he's tough, Sir, tough" (Ch. 7, 145)—and what it really likes is heart, and to its credit it doesn't have a theory explaining in which sexes those qualities do or ought to reside. In short, when it comes to gender, this novel likes to mix it up with a freedom that is not only remarkable in its own period, but that would be remarkable even in an age working much harder and more self-consciously to be free. Not to see this is to fall into the trap of Dombeyism, a trap not only that some tough male critics have fallen into (or perhaps have never gotten out of), but that some tough female ones have fallen into as well.[12]

Mrs. Skewton, we have seen, correctly includes "less conventionality" among the qualities of "heart," and if the novel in practice undoes many of the conventions that surround gender, it also offers a theory of convention, or custom, or habit, significantly through the medium of another eventual partner in what we are to take as an exemplary marriage: that is, the rather curious figure of Mr. Morfin, who is forever ruminating about habit, and whose name suggests a habit of an especially powerful and dangerous kind. (Morphine had been around for thirty-five years.) Mr. Morfin speaks—repeatedly, even habitually—against habit. As he says to Harriet Carker, who will inspire him to give up his own "sorrowful habit" of bachelorhood (Ch. 58, 917):

> In short, we are so d—d business-like. . . . We go on taking everything for granted . . . until whatever we do, good, bad, or indifferent, we do from habit. Habit is all I shall have to report, when I am called upon to plead to my conscience, on my death-bed. "Habit," says I; "I was deaf, dumb, blind, and paralytic, to a million things, from habit." "Very business-like indeed Mr. What's-your-name," says Conscience, "but it won't do here!"[13]
>
> (Ch. 33, 559–60)

The thought here anticipates ideas that will powerfully inform Dickens's next several projects.[14] But perhaps the reason it is relegated not only to a minor, but to an otherwise insipid character in *Dombey and Son* is that it isn't after all terribly well integrated into the imagination of *this* novel. It sounds as though we might have here an explanation of what's wrong with Dombey and with business, and in fact Morfin's theorizing about habit does have resonance with concerns shared by the narrator and several characters. The words "habit" and "custom" especially come up a lot, and there is a good deal of play with their various senses. A "habit" may of course signify clothing, like Rob the Grinder's charitable and horrible "habit," which includes "strong leather small-clothes" that lead his mother to want to see him "before he gets used to 'em" (Ch. 5, 119). By the same logic that connects these senses of "habit," the words "custom" and "costume" are related—are cognate, that is—and Dickens also plays with the business senses of "custom" in an exchange between Walter and Captain Cuttle concerning old Sol. Walter remarks that Sol is old:

> ". . . and besides, his life is a life of custom—"
> "Steady, Wal'r! Of a want of custom?" said the Captain. . . .
> "Too true," returned Walter, "but I meant a life of habit, Captain Cuttle—that sort of custom."[15]
>
> (Ch. 15, 280)

In the scene of Paul's death with its final explanation of "the old fashion," the connections are established yet again:

The old, old fashion! The fashion that came in with our first garments, and will
last unchanged until our race has run its course. . . . The old, old fashion—Death!
(Ch. 16, 197)

Clothes, we are reminded, are the sign of the Fall. They come into existence
at the same moment that death does and at the same moment that the very
possibility of change and therefore of ''fashion''—that is, of doing things
either the same way or differently—comes into being.

The narrator attends to the habits of several characters and is plainly fascinated by the questions of character and identity that all the senses of habit
raise: The Captain we are told, in a description that connects him with the
wooden midshipman, ''was one of those timber-looking men, suits of oak
as well as hearts, whom it is almost impossible for the liveliest imagination
to separate from any part of their dress, however insignificant'' (Ch. 9, 179).
He has the habit of biting his hook as though it were still a hand supplied
with nails (Ch. 15, 283), raising the interesting possibility that he is a nail-
biter who couldn't give up the habit even when he gave up the nails, much
as Mrs. Skewton habitually assumes the pose of Cleopatra even after the looks
that would justify it are long gone (Ch. 21, 362). Habit also raises the question
with which this discussion began: the play of variety and coherence, for to
be a creature of habit is to be coherent at the expense of being able to change;
it is to have a clear identity and therefore unity, but it is also to be a prisoner
of that identity and incapable of growth.

It is clear, however, that Dombey's problem is not a matter of mere habit:
this is the point of the narrator's insisting that he is involved in a constant
struggle with himself and that he is quite conscious of the wrongs he is
committing. He does not exclude Florence because he's simply in the habit
of not thinking about her; his exclusion of her involves rather an active and
changing response to her, based first upon what he observes of her relations
with Paul and second upon her relations with Edith, so that indifference and
neglect are transformed into jealousy and then hatred and rage. As we have
already seen in considering the Reichian argument, Dombey isn't the habit-
uated prisoner of disease, unconsciously compelled to repeat himself, but the
willing author of his monomaniacal and evil project.

The word ''author'' is of course purposeful. Several critics have seen
parallels between Dickens and Dombey, the first I am aware of being Steven
Marcus (see esp. pp. 346 and following). In a very astute essay, Gabriel
Pearson extensively develops the parallel and suggests that Dickens in creating
Dombey is creating himself as a wilful and self-conscious literary architect.
Both Marcus and Pearson emphasize Dickens as the good (that is, ruthless)

businessman in writing *Dombey and Son*. But of course Dickens authors the *whole* book, which includes Dombey's punishment and all the characters who oppose him. The success of *Dombey and Son* the book depends upon the failure of Dombey and Son the firm. Dombey really is afraid of going to pieces and the world of the novel really justifies him in that fear. Dickens, who shares those fears, is, however, by virtue of being the author and therefore the providential omnipotence at the center of things, in a position to be both more philosophical and more playful.

In a famous letter to Forster, Dickens announces his plan for the novel, which happens to be also the first for which he wrote number plans.[16] The letter amply testifies to Dickens' concern about preserving unity throughout the course of a novel written and published in parts. It is the longest, most sustained, explicit, and itself unified discussion by Dickens of the plan of any of his novels and for that reason marks not so much the critical moment in Dickens' career that many scholars have assumed it to be—the moment in which early Dickens is supposed to give way to late, the moment when he is supposed to turn from being a great entertainer to being a "serious" novelist—but in fact a *unique* moment. Dickens' letter is longer, more explicit, and more unified than his accounts of any other of his novels, it may be argued, because this novel *is* more obviously unified or all of a piece than any of his others.[17]

We have already noted that its plot is almost entirely without detection and without suspense, and this has the effect of making its unity therefore unusually apparent. Its plot presents an almost classically tragic progression up until Florence's rescue of her father: specifically, it has strong resemblances to the most wonderfully lean and clear plot of Dickens' master, the plot of Shakespeare's *King Lear*, as Kathleen Tillotson was first to note (170) and as Alexander Welsh has most recently and fully argued. In his obsession with the continuity of the family name, Dombey in fact behaves much more like Shakespeare's king than a Victorian businessman. Like Lear too, in his pride he rejects a loving daughter and receives the natural (as opposed to providential) punishment of being stripped of everything by those he foolishly trusts and surrounds himself with, so that he is left more alone even than Lear, in just as ruined a state within as without, and almost as mad. His plea at last for God's forgiveness with its rending admission—"I need it very much"—perhaps recalls Lear's equally rending plea—"O reason not the need." In both cases insolently proud old men are punished by being forced to recognize that they are not all in all, and not the indivisible center of things.[18]

In his letter to Forster describing the plan of the novel, Dickens falls back on one of the most conventional of images to represent an organic unity by likening his plot to a tree ("So I mean to carry the story on," he writes, "through all the branches and offshoots . . . that come up. . . .").[19] But the novel makes clear something that the letter has forgotten. On the very first page of the novel, Dickens reverts with entirely opposite effect to the image of a tree to describe Dombey and his son:

> On the brow of Dombey, Time and his brother Care had set some marks, as on a tree that was to come down in good time. . . . while the countenance of Son was crossed with a thousand little creases, which the same deceitful Time would take delight in smoothing out and wearing away with the flat part of his scythe, as a preparation of the surface for his deeper operations.
>
> (Ch. 1, 49)

An alert reader, one might think, could be prepared here not only for the clearly announced chopping down of Mr. Dombey, but for the more subtly suggested mowing down of little Paul as well. But in any case, it is clear here that trees are for chopping down, and the novel's coherence indeed incorporates that fact. If *Dombey and Son* embodies Dickens' successful and self-conscious attempt "to make an effort," as Mrs. Chick would say, his willful attempt to create a unified and firm artistic (and commercial) whole, it is no wonder that the project should at the same time express deep fears about going to pieces. Fortunately for Dickens and for us, however, it is also his wisdom in spite of those fears to understand at some level, and unlike his protagonist, their inevitable vanity. We could otherwise have had a very wooden novel indeed.

NOTES

1. For example, it is already clear to any reader by Number 2 that little Paul is going to die, as John Butt and Kathleen Tillotson note in *Dickens at Work* (100).
2. Steven Marcus noted the anagram in a Columbia graduate seminar almost twenty years ago.
3. To my mind, the best discussion of the role of change in the novel is Marcus's.
4. For convenience, I quote the text of the Penguin edition, ed. Peter Fairclough, and refer parenthetically to both chapter and page numbers.
5. It is a very curious irony that this character, faced with instantaneous and awful death from the first instant we are introduced to him, does not die. It is another curious irony that he succeeds, at least for the duration of the novel, in the supposedly not only unwholesome but impossible project of resisting change. Unlike Dombey, unlike Mrs. Skewton, unlike even the constant Miss Tox and Florence, he is at the end of the novel precisely what he was at the beginning.

He has apparently not aged as much as a minute in the dozen or so years the novel covers. The notion of Bagstock's leaking at the seams might recall Cuttle's description of Bunsby as "a man as has had his head broke from infancy up'ards, and has got a new opinion into it at every seam as has been opened" (Ch. 39, 640). It also prefigures Dombey's imagining suicide and his own blood leaking out of him, across the room, and under the door into the hall outside (Ch. 59, 938-39).

6. One of the best general overviews of violence in Dickens is given by John Carey in *Here Comes Dickens: The Imagination of a Novelist*, which in England appeared under the more appropriate title *The Violent Effigy*. Carey, however, makes little if any attempt to differentiate Dickens' interest in violence as it manifests itself progressively throughout his career or in individual novels, and he is not much interested in how actual violence done in the novels is transformed into violent imagery.

7. There also seems to be in the name Paul Dombey an echo of the *dome* of St. Paul's, the cathedral which of course dominates the City of London. Perhaps there is intended an ironic contrast between the effectively godless Mr. Dombey and not only the cathedral, but also the Saint after whom he is named and who is for Protestantism the most important interpreter of the teachings of Christ.

8. Moynahan chooses as one of his epigraphs an early passage (Ch. 3, 83) in which Dombey recalls the scene at his first wife's deathbed:

> He could not forget that he had no part in it. That at the bottom of its clear depths of tenderness and truth, lay those two figures clasped in each other's arms, while he stood on the bank above them, looking down a mere spectator—not a sharer with them—quite shut out.

Moynahan writes that this shows "with great precision" Dombey's fear of dissolving in feeling because it reveals the first Mrs. Dombey and Florence "drowned at the bottom of a body of water" (124). But I don't see any reason to suppose that the image is one of drowning or that there is anything fearful in it, even to Dombey. The water in question would seem rather here to be the proverbial well of truth that Dickens often refers to, as in the first chapter of *Bleak House* with its description of Chancery and the little "well" of solicitors at the bottom of which it would be vain to look for truth (6). The passage seems therefore rather to emphasize Dombey's loneliness and having shut himself out from the truth of (admittedly fluid) feeling.

9. The name "Burgess" is in fact cognate with "bourgeois." That this business should be a tailor's perhaps also connects with the novel's concerns about being cut up: "tailor" and "retail" are also cognate.

10. Sanders (95) seems to be quite right in taking the explicit religiosity of the novel seriously. Although Dickens flirted with Unitarianism at one point and generally was vague in his attachments to doctrine, much in *Dombey and Son* points to a deep belief in the soul's immortality and, conversely, damnation of some kind for the irremediably wicked. Perhaps it is the very orthodoxy of Dickens's religious feeling in this novel that produces so much clearer a sense of the boundary between life and death, between this world and the next, than we find in *Our Mutual Friend*.

11. Lynda Zwinger (438) takes Dombey to task first for not asking forgiveness of Florence directly and second for not offering a full confession enumerating the

wrongs he has done her. But this is to mistake a plea for divine general foregiveness with confession. Following the orthodox Christian logic of the novel, it is quite right that Dombey should seek God's forgiveness first and that his central recognition should be his acknowledgement of that need.

12. Auerbach, for example, is as disgusted by all the melting at the end of the novel as is Moynahan. She describes Dombey at the end as "faded" and "enfeebled," "weeping on his granddaughter at the seashore" (128). But in fact there is no evidence of fading or enfeeblement; he is minding two small children on the beach and keeping up with them, and as for his crying, surely only the unredeemed Mr. Dombey or the Major or Mrs. Chick would see in that a sign of weakness. Of course, it is hardly fair for men to deny women the right to want to be tough and to be Dombeys; but it seems to me that Dickens truly does imagine a more radical questioning of the psychology of gender than Auerbach and many other writers give him credit for.

13. J. Hillis Miller (145) was the first to notice this interesting speech.

14. The manifesto that Dickens writes for the first number of *Household Words* makes it clear that a central function of the periodical will be to open readers' eyes to wonders of the natural and manmade worlds that our habitual ways of seeing blind us to. Much of the exploration of memory in *David Copperfield* has a similar motive, and Dickens's dwelling "on the romantic side of familiar things" in *Bleak House* clearly develops the same project, as does the argument for our need of Fancy in *Hard Times*.

15. Earlier, Sol has delivered the following speech, in which the connections between custom, costume, and business also are made:

> "You see, Walter," he said, "in truth this business is merely a habit with me. I am so accustomed to the habit that I could hardly live if I relinquished it: but there's nothing doing, nothing doing. When that uniform was worn," pointing out towards the little Midshipman, "then indeed, fortunes were to be made, and were made. But competition, competition—new invention, new invention—alteration, alteration—the world's gone past me. I hardly know where I am myself; much less where my customers are." (93; ch. 4)

16. Forster's letter is in Book 6, ch. 2 of *The Life of Charles Dickens* 2: 20–21). It is extensively quoted, and one of the fullest reprintings is in the Introduction to the Clarendon edition, edited by Alan Horsman (xiv–xv). That edition also includes a transcription of the number plans as Appendix B.

17. Marcus (296) writes that *Dombey and Son* "is not just a massive novel, but a monolithic one as well: all its parts seem to move together when they move at all." *Little Dorrit* would be my candidate for Dickens's next most unified work, and that novel notably resembles *Dombey and Son*—both are about failures of business and the falls of houses. The latter would more strikingly resemble the former did it not reverse its protagonists' genders relative to *Dombey and Son*. But Mrs. Clenham's wilful rigidity surely is heir to Dombey's.

18. Of course the punishments differ: in Shakespeare's play, Lear and his constantly loving daughter die (although in the stage version regularly produced until 1823, Cordelia *does* breathe and she and her father live happily on [Bradley, 197], much as do the reconciled Dombey and Florence). *Lear* is also like *Dombey* in being about a man going to pieces in several ways: it involves the king's foolish

hope of preserving identity and authority in spite of his attempt to separate himself from his kingship and his foolish attempt to divide up his kingdom.

19. In the same letter, Dickens uses a less hackneyed image to describe the novel, the image of a soup. "This is what cooks call 'the stock of the soup.' All kinds of things will be added to it, of course" (Forster, 2: 20). A soup of course suggests a much less structured or coherent whole than does a tree. Indeed, it suggests an epitome of variousness. The word "stock" is interesting not only for its commercial resonances and the echo of it in the Major's name (and the sense of "stock" suggested by "the Bagstock *breed*"), but also because its derivation takes us back to wood and trees. It is cognate with "stick" and derives in fact from the Old English for "tree trunk." So it mediates nicely between Moynahan's opposites of firmness and wetness.

WORKS CITED

Auerbach, Nina. "Romantic Imprisonment: A Daughter After All." *Romantic Imprisonment: Women and Other Glorified Outcasts*. (New York: Columbia University Press, 1985), 107–29.

Bradley, A. C. *Shakespearean Tragedy: Hamlet, Othello, King Lear, Macbeth*. 1904; rpt. Cleveland: Meridian Books, 1955.

Butt, John, and Kathleen Tillotson. *Dickens at Work*. London: Methuen, 1957.

Carey, John. *Here Comes Dickens: The Imagination of a Novelist*. New York: Schocken Books, 1974.

Dickens, Charles. *Bleak House*. Ed. George Ford and Sylvère Monod. New York: Norton, 1977.

—————. *Dombey and Son*. The Clarendon Dickens. Ed. Alan Horsman. Oxford: Clarendon Press, 1974.

—————. *Dombey and Son*. Ed. Peter Fairclough. Harmondsworth: Penguin Books, 1970.

Forster, John. *The Life of Charles Dickens*. Ed. A. J. Hoppé. 2 vols. London: J. M. Dent, 1966.

Gallagher, Catherine. "The Bio-Economics of *Our Mutual Friend*." The Dickens Universe. University of California, Santa Cruz, August 1986.

Hutter, Albert O. "Dismemberment and Articulation in *Our Mutual Friend*." *Dickens Studies Annual* 11 (1983): 135–75.

Leavis, F. R. "The First Major Novel: *Dombey and Son*. F. R. and Q. D. Leavis. *Dickens the Novelist*. (London: Chatto & Windus, 1970). pp. 1–30.

Marcus, Steven. "The Changing World." *Dickens: from Pickwick to Dombey*. New York: Basic Books, 1965. pp. 293–357.

Miller, J. Hillis. *Charles Dickens: The World of his Novels*. 1958. Bloomington: Indiana University Press, 1969.

Moynahan, Julian. "Dealings with the Firm of Dombey and Son: Firmness versus Wetness." *Dickens and the Twentieth Century.* Ed. John Gross and Gabriel Pearson. (Toronto: University of Toronto Press, 1962), pp. 121–31.

Newsom, Robert. *Dickens on the Romantic Side of Familiar Things: Bleak House and the Novel Tradition.* New York: Columbia University Press, 1977.

Pearson, Gabriel. "Towards a Reading of *Dombey and Son.*" *The Modern English Novel: The Reader, the Writer, and the Work.* Ed. Gabriel. Josipovici. (London: Open Books.) pp. 54–76.

Reich, Wilhelm. *Character Analysis.* Trans. Theordore P. Wolfe. New York: Farrar, Straus & Giroux, 1949.

Sanders, Andrew. *Charles Dickens: Resurrectionist.* New York: St. Martin's Press, 1982.

Tillotson, Kathleen. *Novels of the Eighteen-Forties.* Oxford: Clarendon Press, 1954.

Welsh, Alexander. "Dombey as King Lear." in *From Copywright to Copperfield: The Identity of Dickens.* (Cambridge, Mass.: Harvard Univserity Press, 1987), pp. 87–103.

Zwinger, Lynda. "Fear of the Father: Dombey and Daughter." *Nineteenth-Century Fiction* 39 (1985): 420–40.

The Blighted Tree and the Book of Fate: Female Models of Storytelling in *Little Dorrit*

Nancy Aycock Metz

Though Arthur Clennam does not tell his story in the first person, his fixation on the generative experiences of childhood and on the role of memory in redeeming time make *Little Dorrit* a fictional memoir in all but form. It is, as Janet Larson has called it, "a profoundly autobiographical novel, written at a time of intensified self-questioning and vocational crisis." K. J. Fielding, locating *Little Dorrit*'s central strand of meaning in the "return to the scene of an unhappy and even wronged childhood to find freedom and fulfillment" finds the novel "as saturated with a sense of past Time as *Copperfield*." For R. Rupert Roopnaraine, the circular pattern embedded in the language and structure of the novel underscores these same preoccupations; *Little Dorrit* is "very much a novel of memory, of time past, and of inexorable recurrence."[1] Thoroughly self-conscious, Clennam regularly broods on his past, employing, for the purpose, a rich figurative vocabulary grounded in his own thoughtful absorption in the problematic narrative life has become for him. However glum his reminiscences, they emerge from certain positive assumptions about the value of remembering. Clennam believes that his history is unique, that circumstances and people have shaped his destiny in discoverable ways, that he has a coherent story to fashion, if only for himself.

In Dickens' fiction, these assumptions receive their most assured dramatization in the autobiographical storytelling of David Copperfield. They take us back to Dickens' earlier expressed confidence in his ability to discover

221

"how all of these things have worked together to make of me what I am," and to David's ultimately secure consciousness of origins, development, and fulfillment. As Avrom Fleishman has shown, David's complex narrative synthetically merges the nostalgic, the realistic, and the mystical to present the story of a life imbued with significance from the beginning, which becomes, over time, a self-conscious—and conspicuously successful—quest. The writing of his story as a connected narrative is both validation and reward for David, "the achievement of an inner discipline, the sense of self-knowledge in the control of his chosen medium, the quiet assertion of a slowly realized and always gentle, but ultimately well-assured identity, the unexpressed conviction that a man, within limits, may become the hero of his own story."[2]

As intensely preoccupied as *Little Dorrit* is with this same business of ordering the past, of getting one's life story straight, it is also, to an unusual degree, beset with doubts about the process and its likely ends. Beneath the dominant text of the novel, controlled by Clennam's perspective, runs a set of assumptions quietly subversive of conventional autobiography and, by extension, of fiction itself: that time is radically *dis*continuous, that the amplitude and contradictions of life will always elude the formal constraints of narrative, that pasts cannot, in any fully meaningful way, be reconstructed, any more than futures can be foretold.

Chapter 24 occupies a peculiar position in this ongoing dialectic. With Clennam's story now well known to the reader, Dickens turns its matter over to Flora and Amy—two of the women who, in Larson's terms, "serve as mediators for his relation with himself and the universe."[3] The "Fortune Telling" chapter explicitly counterpoints their two relatively compact narratives against a background that implicitly includes Clennam's own more attenuated tale of love and loss. The stories told here are not the only frame tales in the novel—not even, perhaps, the most complex or interesting from certain points of view. Janice Carlisle has pointed out that Dickens' use of the first person in the memorandum book he began keeping six months before he started composing *Little Dorrit* "suggests that he was increasingly anxious to let his characters present themselves in their own voices," and indeed the voices of this novel do speak with rare distinctiveness and autonomy.[4] Consider Miss Wade's anomalous "History of a Self-Tormentor," a remarkable experiment in self-concealing language, or Amy's letters from Italy, by contrast so apparently transparent, yet composing on closer scrutiny a written account of her impressions that William Burgan and others have shown to be rhetorically sophisticated.[5] But within this extended framework of self-presentation, "Fortune Telling's" internal tales merit special attention.

While the chapter appears to stall the forward movement of the plot, circling back over familiar history in a pair of amusing and sentimental oral histories, in retrospect it is seen to be structurally pivotal. The chapter sets in motion the detective work that will ultimately catapult the Dorrit family from "Poverty" to "Riches," and it plants the seed of misunderstanding that will keep Amy and Arthur at a confused arm's length until the novel's dramatic climax. More importantly, from the point of view of *Little Dorrit*'s concern with autobiography, its two contrasting stories, fashioned from overlapping cores of experience, allow Dickens some interesting play with the methods of narrative; they open up questions of form, value, and authority in storytelling. And what emerges from this heightened exercise in telling and listening is considerably more than the difference in "slant" or point of view one might predict. Instead of the same kernel story relayed with differing protagonists, emphases, and resolutions, the chapter explores two patterns of perception—themselves at odds—as they further contrast to Clennam's distinctively structured autobiographical musings. Whatever else is going on here, it seems clear that Dickens is playing with notions of storytelling that he associates specifically with gender differences. These "feminine" ways of seeing, remembering, and telling, modelled formally for us in Flora's and Amy's juxtaposed confessions, play an important part in the conflicting autobiographical impulses of *Little Dorrit*.

After Clennam's first meeting with Flora, Dickens fixes his hero's attitudes towards his own history in a remarkable metaphor. Clennam sits before a dying fire and ponders, not just the past, but the process of trying to reach it. "To review his life was like descending a green tree in fruit and flower, and seeing all the branches drop off, one by one, as he came down towards them" (158).[6] No David, who can call up childhood events palpably before him, Clennam complains often of the barrenness of his early years ("No childhood; no youth . . . "), of retrospectives composed of blank spaces ("the gloomy vista . . . So long, so bare, so blank"), and of imagination grasping empty air (157). But he keeps climbing down that blighted tree, because, like Dickens's other self-conscious autobiographers, Clennam believes that memory makes meaning, that past and present link causally, and that recovery of childhood is the only way to eventual health. His urge to come to terms with the past, to clear up its mysteries and make reparations, to close it off and so restrict its capacity to harm, motivates most of his actions in the plot. In pursuit of these goals, Clennam returns home, befriends Amy, attempts to re-open the Dorrit case.

But the process is fraught with contradictions from the beginning, as the absurdity of the original metaphor—experienced but not analyzed by Clennam—suggests. What a curious metaphor it is, and how difficult to visualize! With the impossible logic of a dream, Clennam pictures himself stranded, about to fall, with rotten limbs collapsing under the mere influence of his approach and bare trunk below. His sense that past experiences have ben diseased in themselves and that they have supplanted healthier growth is vividly realized in this daydream, but more palpable than any specific image is the physical sensation of falling, of footholds altogether missing in a perilous descent. Clennam laments here not just the past that *was,* but the past that *never was;* on some level he conceives of himself as having mysteriously leapt the gap to become what he is, of having skipped childhood—or misplaced it—to be formed over a dizzying void. In this he participates in the larger psychological atmosphere of *Little Dorrit,* where past selves routinely "vanish" without a trace, to be inadequately memorialized in souvenirs, inscriptions, and portraits—where not only death, but the normal process of aging or of circumstantial change can leave one terrifyingly stranded across a gulf of identity, without a secure sense of roots or progress.

The extent to which these conditions define the limits of self-knowledge for the novel's characters and frustrate their quest for coherence and mutual understanding is unique in Dickens. As characters move from one class or marital state to another, as their dreams are exploded or fulfilled, a part of themselves simply perishes out of remembrance. Change entails irrevocable loss; each transition apes the great one to a degree sometimes absurd, often tragic. Fanny, "having formally wound up her single life and arranged her worldly affairs" (588), prepares for marriage as she would for imminent death. Flora, calling up her romantic past, behaves "like a mummer at her own funeral." Clennam feels his younger self expire with Minnie's confession of love for Gowan. The past is a haunting reality in *Little Dorrit.* Amy's sorrowful acknowledgement that "no space in the life of a man could overcome that quarter of a century behind prison bars" (463) resonates with a truth applicable to other human prisons as well. But here there are none of *Copperfield*'s summonable (and thus exorcisable) "phantoms." "Reviewed," the past recedes, only to re-appear, the unwelcome guest at the feast, when the conscious striving to reach or escape it is momentarily relaxed.

According to Roopnaraine, "Of all the characters in this novel, Clennam is the only one who constantly orients his life backward into the past" (63). The most intellectual of these variously dislocated characters, he is also singularly unsuccessful in locating some philosophical standing ground with his history. His twenty-year exile, radically severing young adulthood from middle age, exacerbates certain alienating habits of mind he has anyway. There has been for him no process of subtle revision, no ongoing fiction of identity within which memory re-organizes and re-interprets experience against a shifting background of present needs and understandings. Rather, in a much more fundamental way than Flora does, he dwells on the past as a set of isolated tableaux—his mother's Bible readings, his confinement in the "dragon" closet, his parents' quarrels—and his endless recapitulations of these scenes brings him no closer to actualizing himself in the present.[7] If for David memory powerfully integrates experience, carrying it forward in surges that both subsume and redefine self, for Clennam remembering is more often a faculty apart, the curator of a past kept "in its old sacred place" (143). Yet Clennam believes as fervently as David does in some meaningful sequence and pattern of events accessible by memory and imagination. The unresolved tension between this belief—that the roots of self can be systematically discovered to follow the laws of organic development—and his emotional experience of lack, discontinuity, and fragmentation—are fittingly summed up in the metaphor of Clennam's thwarted descent from a tree blighted by his very approach.

When Clennam looks to the future, the same desire to believe in some intrinsic design in the order and arrangement of events shapes his speculations. If the present moment has been the culmination of a pattern visible only in retrospect, so today's events, and tomorrow's, work invisibly toward resolution. As he leaves Hampton Court, troubled by his conversation with Mrs. Gowan, Clennam wonders what the future holds for himself, Henry Gowan, and Pet Meagles: "Where are we driving, he and I, I wonder, on the darker road of life? How will it be with us, and with her, in the obscure distance?" Here the language figures the future as a destination that will give coherence and closure to the journey, revealing a purpose implicit from the beginning but requiring perspective to apprehend. The concept of perspective is invoked repeatedly as Clennam imagines how his story will end. Perhaps the "unbarring hand of death" will release Amy's father, allowing him to be "such a friend to her as he wished to be, by altering her whole manner of life." Were such a script to be enacted in fact, the unhappy, abused child who still lives in the adult Clennam could wring meaning from suffering, becoming the liberal father he never possessed. "He regarded her, in that perspective, as his adopted daughter, his poor child of the Marshalsea hushed to rest" (183).

Or perhaps his past has been preparing him for some final act of unselfish devotion, a redeeming gesture of sacrificial love that will ennoble despair even as it closes off hope. Dickens, reading Clennam's thoughts and projecting them onto the landscape after Pet Meagles's confession, seems to suggest some such line of thinking: "They came out of the avenue next moment, arm-in-arm as they had entered it; and the trees seemed to close up behind them in the darkness, like their own perspective of the past." Here "perspective" carries a technical sense that is submerged in the first quoted passage. The arching, intersecting trees close off the scene in familiar iconography. Clennam's life becomes one of those Pre-Raphaelite paintings Dickens so scorned, its details ordered to illumine some radiant moment of awareness or expectation.

For Clennam, this way of envisioning his story is independent of circumstances; it is a habit of perception deeply ingrained in consciousness. Long after the memory of Pet Meagles has ceased to trouble him, he will compose another resolution to his narrative, this time with Little Dorrit at its center, in nearly identical terms:

> Looking back upon his own poor story, she was its vanishing point. Everything in its perspective led to her innocent figure. He had travelled thousands of miles towards it; previous unquiet hopes and doubts had worked themselves out before it; it was the centre of the interest of his life; it was the termination of everything that was good and pleasant in it; beyond there was nothing but mere waste, and darkened sky.
>
> (714)

Critics have generally accepted at face value Clennam's way of conceiving Amy here, and to a certain extent Dickens clearly invites them to do so.[8] Yet whatever authority is conveyed to this image-making by its placement as the culmination of Clennam's prison meditations is qualified by what we now know of his previous reveries—all arranged with studied manipulation of perspectives and forms—all dissolved under the remote, inscrutable sovereignty of time. Indeed, the language of the passage, with its confident aesthetics—its "perspective," "vanishing point," "centre," and "termination"—itself dissolves under a closer scrutiny. According to Janet Larson:

> This ironic optical illusion, coquetting with time and space, with presence and absence, is a strangely unstable iconographic arrangement—shifting from the personal "she" to the impersonal "it," undecided in its direction of movement . . . ambivalent in its attitude toward a "vanishing point," that is at once "centre" and the "termination" of everything. . . . this enigmatic vision confesses the picture's own incredibility by trying to banish the figure it has also put at the center.[9]
>
> ("The Arts . . ., 167)

Like the metaphor of the blighted tree, the image of Amy as the redeeming end of Clennam's "poor story" is carefully worked out, yet in the end completely impossible. Its elements recede into contradiction and paradox the nearer we approach them, the more we attempt to invest them with determining meaning.

Indeed, as Dickens' long narrative ultimately makes clear, it is the configuration of Clennam's time-ordering daydreams, as much as any resolutions they individually enact, that addresses the novel's consistent focus on the methods and value of autobiography. Both the preoccupation and the forms in which it is expressed in Clennam's reveries are necessarily entangled with questions of gender. As Diane Sadoff (drawing on Roland Barthes) has written, "The story of a life, even the life of a public institution like Chancery or the Circumlocution Office, is a tale of origins and ends, of purposes, motivations, consequences, outcomes, genealogies, fatherhood." In more than this generic sense, Clennam allies himself to the pursuit of what Sadoff calls "narrative teleology." His personal story can be read psychoanalytically as an attempt "to seek the figure of the father, to write the paternal metaphor, and to acquire paternal authority."[10] Thus, Clennam's daydreams bespeak his willed trust that causality works itself out against an evolutionary time scheme, that meaning emerges from the structure imposed on details, that events tend toward some final revelation of design, freezing and enclosing the flow of time. The intensity, frustration, and sheer persistence of his autobiographical quest result, in part, from his unconscious attempt to make the facts of experience mesh with these assumptions—assumptions which are periodically rendered doubtful and incomplete by their rhetorical contexts.

Chapter 24 creates one of these corrective contexts. Here Flora, following up on her promise to Clennam to assist Little Dorrit, summons her to Casby's house and supplies her with breakfast, needlework, and a highly colored, loosely strung account of her youthful romance with Clennam. Flora's "Fortune-Telling," with its vague hints of some future reconciliation, is followed by the introduction of Pancks in his new role as "gypsy" and by Amy's fairy tale forecasting of her own future to Maggie, later on in her prison garret. Significantly, Clennam is present in this chapter not as the fashioner of narratives, but as their subject. In a neat reversal, the artificer of daydreams is now "fictionalized" himself, and the women who represent for him the "beginning" and the "end" of his own story speak, for the first time, in their own voices. To be sure, these voices—heard at the margins of Clennam's text, enclosed within Dickens's own fictional transmutation of anguished boyhood—possess necessarily a limited and provisional autonomy. In one sense, it might be said of them what Nancy K. Miller says of certain heroines of eighteenth-century feminocentric texts—that they are "masculine representation[s] of female desire produced ultimately for an audience not of women but of men."[11] But if scatterbrained Flora and reticent, self-denying Amy represent unsatisfactory, predictable "images" of women, they also embody certain well-defined structures of thought and feeling antithetical to the dominant, decidedly masculine storytelling mode of the novel. From their respective angles of vision, they each undo "narrative teleology," unravelling or etherealizing plot and creating in the process a revolutionary perspective for narrative, outside the framework of origins, consequences, or outcomes.

The opposition they represent is not a simple one. The stories these women tell could themselves scarcely be more different. Flora's is all detail; Amy's, purest abstraction. Flora is the corpulent romance queen in her drama of love denied; Amy a ghostly figure in a vague allegory of mind rather than heart. Flora's story is expansive, hypnotic, effusive; Amy's, stripped down and distanced. Despite their outward differences, however, each story bears the inscription of what Helene Cixous has called a "decipherable libidinal femininity," that is, an outlook characterized by some combinations of the following traits: a closeness to the body's needs and rhythms; an embracing of risks and of openness; a toleration for spaces and intervals, even at the expense of symmetry; a respect for otherness that opposes the instinct for appropriation or territoriality.[12] The concept of a distinctive "libidinal femininity" within an enclosing masculine text may provide a useful point of reference for examining the tales Amy and Flora create—for locating the sources of their peculiar dissonances and power to reshape context and meaning.

Flora's story narrates the history of her courtship with Arthur Clennam, the intervention of their parents to prevent the engagement, Flora's marriage to Mr. F, his death, and the reappearance of Clennam on the scene years later. But to summarize her in this way is of course to leave out absolutely everything of interest, everything certainly that distinguishes her account from what Clennam has already revealed. To begin with, the time scheme of her narrative shares nothing with any previous version of these events we have heard. In her reference to "old times forever fled," she mocks Clennam's obsessively retrospective stance, but as Janet Larson has pointed out, her true angle of vision is "transhistorical"; "she calls each moment into being on her own terms" (*Dickens and the Broken Scripture*, 255). Clennam's metaphor of climbing down a tree to retrieve the past could never be applied to Flora, in whom past and present are thoroughly interfused. Indeed, the more involved in her storytelling she becomes, the more she approaches "full mermaid condition," a metaphor which aptly suggests the fluid and inchoate nature of her time sense. For Flora, storytelling is a process not of retrieval and reinterpretation, but of letting go. Thus her narratives remain capable of surprising herself and her listeners. Once the living stream of memory, association, and fancy has been released, who can fully predict what will wash to the surface? Certain broad themes persist, but no conscious attempt on Flora's part to extract a meaning from her narrative accounts for what is most memorable in it—the pickled salmon that made her father sick at the wedding breakfast, the glass coach that broke down twice on the way to the ceremony, leaving Mr. F's Aunt to be brought home in a rush-bottomed chair, "like the fifth of November," the proposal on a donkey in Tunbridge Wells.

Details rule in Flora's narrative, intruding themselves persistently in defiance of the laws of grammar, the principles of causation, and the conventions of narrative. These details conceal no intrinsic structure; they subvert order, in fact, as the following representative passage demonstrates:

> I will draw a veil over that dreamy life, Mr. F was in good spirits his appetite was good he liked the cookery he considered the wine weak but palatable and all was well, we returned to the immediate neighbourhood of Number Thirty Little Gosling Street London Docks and settled down, ere we had yet fully detected the housemaid in selling the feathers out of the spare bed Gout flying upwards soared with Mr. F to another sphere.
>
> (278)

Here, the equal importance given to the weakness of the wine, the housemaid selling feathers out of the spare bed, and the death of Mr. F, suggests that this is a story which is, figuratively speaking, going nowhere. Indeed, though Clennam remains fearful of Flora's designs on him, he misreads her badly even to apply the concept of design to her improvised dramas. For, in Flora's story, the details never add up; they defiantly go their own way.[13] Against Clennam's hopeful belief that somewhere down the road—from some as yet unreached "perspective," at the end of a vista or the turn of a path—the organization of things and the meaning encoded therein will suddenly become visible, Dickens posits Flora's love affair with mysterious and romantic possibility, with the glorious state of "might-be" communicated in word, look, and gesture. As generous as Flora is with language, as imaginatively diffuse and profuse, she yet never once scripts an ending. When closure is inferred, she pulls back immediately: "It's as well to leave that alone now, for I couldn't undertake to say after all, but it doesn't signify lie down a little!"

(279). When she sums up her account of herself to Amy in a gloriously high-flown rhetorical question ("Ask me not if I love him still or if he loves me or what the end is to be or when"), we should take her, literally, at her word, for in the fiction born of Flora's freewheeling self-expression, the one consistent message seems to be that *"anything can happen."*

Through Clennam, Dickens presents a tale of flawed adolescent love, in which the memory of pain predominates over the whimsy achieved by virtue of distance and time. Dickens expects his readers to respond seriously and sympathetically to Clennam's version of the shared love story. For the most part, he exploits the comic possibilities in Flora's effusions. But as William Myers has pointed out, Flora is more than a comic formula. She comes "generously alive" at the wedding of Amy and Arthur," breaking out of her fixed identity "as a challenge to . . . fellow-characters and the reader alike."[14] Actually, the process Myers describes begins much earlier. One need only compare Flora to that other Dickensian romantic, the lugubrious Mr. Moddle—with his stale variations on the theme of "Another"—to see how "generously alive" Flora has been all along. The "challenge" she represents—even in her most ludicrous flights of fancy—accounts for the profoundly unsettling effect her presence has on the reader, the guilty laughter and the pity made disconcertingly amusing. Conceived in the author's disappointment and spite over his unresolved love for Maria Beadnell, Flora succeeds in exacting her own sympathy, acceptance, and even revenge.

The story she tells, with its dark hints about "watchful eyes," and "fatal reasons," lovers destined to "pine asunder" and haunted by memories of "bliss" belongs to a tradition which has changed very little in the last century. The assumptions on which these formulas are based are culturally derived. According to Janet Batsleer,

> In the western capitalist world . . . falling in love is considered one of the most precious, unique and intimate of life's experiences. Yet countless thousands of stories retell that experience in the most conventional and formulaic way imaginable. In fact, the uniqueness of the experience is itself one of the common conventions, the formulas of the genre. This only happens to you once in a lifetime, the stories tell us over and over again.[15]

Flora's one story, retold in endless permutations, recapitulated and embellished often within a single telling, perfectly embodies the characteristic paradox between form and desire in conventional romance. Like the drugstore novels of today, the romance Flora fabricates functions as both narcotic and weapon in a world over which she has otherwise little power. "Romance comforts women, affirms their value, offers to resolve in imagination conflicts

that remain unresolved in reality'' (Batsleer, 104). As more than one critic
has pointed out, Flora's story is the verbal equivalent of the brandy she takes
with her tea; its very breakdowns in sense and logical sequence testify to its
function as rhythmic intoxication.[16]

Indeed, Flora sorely needs her intervals of relief and escape. Far more than
for the often self-pitying Clennam, hers ''is a barren story, with no variety
in it, and is all told in the first page'' (ms. cancellation, 20). The most casual
descriptions of the ''Patriarch,'' ''fast asleep, with his philanthropic mouth
open, under a yellow pocket-handkerchief in the dining room'' speak worlds
of the life to which Clennam's departure has relegated Flora. Though our
sympathy is overtly directed to Clennam's disappointment at the shattering
of his youthful illusions, in interesting ways, Flora's own hurt, boredom, and
repression subversively rewrite the simple satire Dickens began by creating.
As Elaine Showalter has shown, Mr. F's aunt's baffling, seemingly unmotivated hatred voices the bitterness and rage beneath Flora's aggressive good
nature.[17] And in her storytelling to Amy, Flora finds another voice, in its own
way, equally liberating.

If Flora drugs herself with words, the language she employs has also a
curious power to re-order reality. As Casby's daughter and Clennam's one-
time lover, Flora is shut out in her ''air-tight'' house from the worlds of travel
and work. About the former she questions Clennam with a closeness matched
only by the demonstrable lack of context for her remarks, and she is never
more ludicrously out of place in Clennam's eyes than in her raid upon the
Works, where she and Mr. F's aunt constitute thoroughly ''unnatural appar-
itions.'' How different is the world she creates as ''novelist''—not just in its
lady's magazine exaltation of romantic love—but in its smallest props and
details. In her account, furnishings and servants, illnesses and eatables—pint
bottles, wings of fowl, bits of ham and asparagus—fill every spare space,
and in their cumulative force finally swamp the plot, refusing ultimately to
be ''background'' at all. Here, too, Flora enacts a fundamental—and revolutionary—tenet of romance, for ''if in the standard accounts, women rarely
appear as actors upon the public stage of history,'' ''the romantic novelist
reinstates women and reverses the account.'' ''Here the history that men have
made becomes the backdrop and women the protagonists in a drama of quite
different significance'' (Batsleer, 95).

What disturbs Clennam (and by implication Dickens) is that Flora's ''dramas'' blur the line between fantasy and reality; they seem pathetic and neurotic
at the same time that they are comic.[18] Certainly there is no gainsaying the
thorough eccentricity, the sheer dottiness of Flora's verbal performances. But

neither is Clennam necessarily the best judge of the state of mind from which they proceed. Flora's effusions threaten Clennam in ways he himself does not fully understand. In her own person, she embodies the suspicion, terrible to contemplate for someone of Clennam's temperament—that memory itself, that most sacred and potent of Dickensian faculties, may prove in the crisis deceptive and unreliable.

Early in the novel, his father's watch and coded message ("Do Not Forget") establish inflexible conditions for Clennam's rebirth out of inherited anxiety and depression. As Jerome Beaty has pointed out, Clennam "must learn the truth of his own past before his life can resume healthy growth (233). But as his interactions with Flora dramatize, the failure to learn the past's "truth" may have complex origins. Clennam is prone to blame his lack of "will" and spirit, character flaws theoretically correctible through self-discipline and right thinking.

But what if the problem lies in the mind's reconstruction of the past, in dim consciousness itself? The shock of seeing Flora has not, after all, been the shock of seeing her changed, but of really *seeing* her for the first time. Though he persists in locating the source of his disillusionment in Flora, Clennam, who "heartily wished he could have found the Flora that had been, or that never had been" (148) at least suspects through her physical presence a deeply disquieting truth about his own most firmly held assumptions—about the sources of knowledge and redeeming power in human relationships. As for Flora, she is sometimes capable of surprising even Clennam with her shrewdness, her thorough grounding, even in midflight, in the way hearts and minds really work. "I know I am not what you expected," she tells Clennam simply. "I know that very well."

Against the pain of such knowledge and in the pure love of performance, Flora exercises her art. But unlike Clennam, who time after time demands textual closure from experience larger and less controllable than any text can be, Flora's intoxicated role-playing masks a more sober awareness of narrative as fabrication. Experience has taught her that dreams and life differ radically—will never converge—and that life unmediated by fancy can be a pretty depressing business. Thus she is never more than a long run-on sentence away from some tacit acknowledgement that the game is just a game.

Whereas Clennam is shocked to discover that the Flora he thought he loved never was, Flora knows, when she chooses to know, that Clennam is a character she has invented. Her characteristic way of describing Mr. F to Amy ("worthy man but not poetical manly prose but not romance") underscores her role as an active creator and manipulator of texts rather than their victim. Her rhetorical patterns are funny precisely because they continually rupture the illusions they create, call attention to their own artifice, halt their own momentum. As F. R. Leavis has commented, they "are also poetic in a strong way, and register, in their imaginative freedom and energy, much vivid perception and an artist's grasp of the real" (242). Absurd, but with the deeper logic of metaphor, Flora's language is functionally "self-pleasuring" (Larson, *Dickens* 254); it hymns the infinite elasticity and adaptability of life and the saving power of "comforts" to assuage pain. As she tells Amy, "such is life my dear and yet we do not break but bend, pray make a good breakfast while I go in with the tray" (276).

In chapter 24, Flora tells her story to a silent, subdued Amy, troubled by Flora's hints that Clennam might still cling to his old love. Flora's story thus directly motivates Amy's, and in a way the two narratives share the same masterplot as well. They each work out in fiction the question Amy articulates for Maggie, of what to do with "the shadow of Some one who had gone by long before; of Some one who had gone on far away quite out of reach, never never to come back" (285). It should be said at once that this underlying plot betrays its male authorship and in a rather obvious way functions to soothe Dickens' wounded vanity by re-writing painful episodes from his personal past. Amy's version of the story especially, with its memory of the hero as a cherished hidden "treasure," belongs to myths about womanhood that have arisen from the dominant patriarchal culture within which many of Dickens' more conventional attitudes were shaped. Some see Amy herself as a perfectly flat representation of this culture's values. As a "portrait of a mature woman," Kathleen Woodward has written, Amy is "unconvincing and boring" (142). With other similarly dutiful and passive female characters, she betrays Dickens as "not so much the recorder of Victorian womanhood as the dupe or the exploiter of its ideal."[19]

The woman whose diminutive name gives this novel its title is a good deal harder to sell to modern audiences than the more substantial, less well-behaved Flora. Her qualities of gentleness, modesty, humility, empathy, compassion, tenderness, nurturance, sensitivity, and unselfishness have been shown to constitute a perilous and limiting ideal for women. But it has always seemed to me that with Amy no less than with Flora, Dickens' insights outran his more limited intentions. As her "Tale of the Princess" makes abundantly clear, sanctification for Little Dorrit—as a Spirit of Love or Truth, as an Angel of Death, or even (as Clennam calls her in a rare moment of insight) as a "kind of domesticated fairy"—exacts its cost in silence and concealment, in the loss of any "story" to tell.[20] Whereas Flora glories in the "confidential," from the beginning of their relationship, Amy holds back. Aware that to be completely silent would be an ungenerous return for tendered intimacies, Amy offers a confidence of her own. But the secret she tells Flora (regarding her residence in the Marshalsea) is a calculated barter. Clearly it is *not* the one closest to her heart, and the story she tells is chiefly notable for its omissions: "she condensed the narrative of her life into a few scanty words about herself and a glowing eulogy upon her father" (279). Though her more sustained venture into narrative takes place over a week later, this early exchange with Flora appropriately frames a tale whose surface transparency belies a fierce commitment to concealment and diversion.

Indeed the very telling of the tale is a diversionary tactic; the promise of a story rids Amy of Maggie's presence and indirectly of Clennam's too, as Maggie delivers the message below stairs that her mistress is unwell. It purchases for her an hour's communion with the only audience she does not in some way fear, and it accounts, in part, for the peculiar form Amy's narrative assumes. In the interval between her private musings and the formal recapitulation of them in story form, nearly everything of narrative interest has been censored out. From her confusion of hurt, self-doubt, and unreturned love, Amy emerges with a pristine allegory, so spare and emotionally neutral as to seem thoroughly anticlimactic in paraphrase. Her story involves a "tiny woman" who lives alone and a clairvoyant Princess who, in a single look, perceives the shadow the little woman keeps hidden in "a very secret place." The story ends with the Princess's discovery that the tiny woman has died and that the shadow she so carefully hid from scrutiny "had sunk quietly into her own grave" (286).

About the broad meaning of the allegory, critics have been in substantial agreement. Mary Ann Kelly sees it as a way for Little Dorrit to "distance her ambivalent feelings, to invest something intangible and unmanageable with some comprehensibility, and to construct a model which can provide for her a sense of order, purpose, and duty." According to Barbara Hardy, the "Tale of the Princess" "has been the story of Little Dorrit herself, uttered, like Jagger's "poor dreams," reticently in release and relief." Others have speculated on the tale's striking metaphors—its succession of chinese boxes within the last of which is discovered only the image of insubstantiality. Amy's locked shutters and doors, her "very secret place" connect her "with the shadow world of secrets, repression, and fantasy," according to Elaine Showalter. With no bold attempt to discover whether she will turn out to be the "hero" of her own life, Amy's timid verbalization conceals its autobiographical nature, briefly permitting a space where desire can be enjoyed and rhetorically contained. Her disguised autobiography goes over the head of the retarded Maggie to parable for the novel's larger audience the tale-teller's profound self-division. "With its Doppelganger motif, this fiction enables Amy to flirt with despair and hope, entertaining alternate versions of her destiny''; it "allows her to peep at her 'Shadow' of love.''[21]

Viewed thus in the context of Dickens' extended characterization of Amy, her story opens out to a legible—though still ambiguous—reading of her outlook shortly after the first meeting with Flora. But unlike the self-contained "History of a Self-Tormentor,'' Amy's narrative is only decipherable in the light of all that supports it. In itself, it is barely there. This fact is the more striking given the privileged form in which Dickens has Amy frame her story, for the "Tale of the Princess'' is surely one of the most anomalous fairy tales in the rich Dickensian tradition of spirits and magical play. Harry Stone has summarized in detail the special characteristics, motifs, and archetypes with which such literature is normally associated in Dickens' imagination:

> The happy endings, the fairy godmothers, the beautiful princesses (whether appreciated or neglected), the unblemished princes, the dazzling transformations, the blissful sanctuaries, the redeeming tasks, the perfecting quests, the benign disguises, the fortunate coincidences, the propitious signs, the responsive environment, the fulfilled wishes—all are allied to that amiable fairy-tale realm of bright hopes, unfading summers, and limitless possibilities.[22]

The larger novel of which Amy's tale is a small part turns on a particularly sophisticated use of these same mythic elements. Mr. Dorrit's sudden accession to riches is one of those "dazzling transformations'' which owe their power and resonance to childhood reading, as Dickens himself makes amply clear when he has Ferdinand Barnacle tell Lord Decimus, regarding the Dorrit case, "the Fairy came out of the bank and gave him his fortune'' (547).

By contrast, how pallid is Amy's attempt in the same genre. Amy's "fine'' king, supplied vaguely with "plenty of everything,'' fills his role as fictional royalty in the thinnest, most perfunctory way imaginable. Here, no sense of the marvelous irradiates detail; no fairy-tale perspective transforms the everyday into the visionary. Amy's story does not amaze, and it does not follow either of the paths of development one might expect from its Cinderella premise. Here there is no wish-fulfilling happy ending in which a gallant Clennam renounces his mother, his class status, and his former love to marry the prison waif, and there is no martyred Amy either, sacrificing herself on the altar of Clennam's well-being. Properly speaking, Clennam is not even in this story, except as a thoroughly internalized Shadow, a particularly worrisome part of Amy's consciousness. Magic, to use common Dickensian paradigms, has nothing to do with liberation from enchantment, imprisonment, or disguise, with Sleeping Beauties, Ugly Ducklings, or Children in the Wood.

Still, to the extent that the story has a center of energy, magic is its source. The supernatural power she gives to her Princess is the single most important piece of information the narrative conveys, revealing Amy's deepest, though still unexpressed desire. This power is not at all what one might expect. Amy's Princess does not grant wishes or preside over metamorphoses; she does not save the tiny woman from harm or supply her with protective talismans. She does not "do" anything; she simply "knows." Amy's princess understood her lessons before her masters taught them to her" (284), and she is able to read the tiny woman in the same instantaneous leap of precognition. In effect, magic gives to Little Dorrit as storyteller the power to structure a world where looks supplant the need for language, where conversation automatically becomes redundant and questions need neither be asked nor answered. To this unusual condition of things is owing the faint absurdity, the air of tautology in the story's dialogue and plot progression: "You keep watch over this, every day?" the Princess asks the tiny woman, "Remind my why." The form of the story, thus, communicates an important source of the conflict and self-division Amy feels, one that has little to do with love, returned or otherwise. It articulates her profound wish to be *understood* and that in some non-verbal, *a priori* way. Curiously, the narrative fantasizes a condition where storytelling itself would be necessary, where confessions could be telegraphed rather than committed to words and structures.

No wonder, then, that this fable is mere vehicle, without narrative interest or color. Though it appears on the surface more ordered and conventional than Flora's verbal outpourings, it may be read in fact as a kind of anti-narrative. In a real sense, the story begins and ends with a single, penetrating gaze; everything else is arbitrary. The story can easily accommodate Maggie's interjected modifications. The Princess can be a "reg'lar one," the King can have "Hospitals with lots of Chicking," because none of these plot elements matter in the least. Moreover, the story fails to develop. We don't even know how old the tiny woman is when she dies, and Maggie's very proper questions about such basic storytelling matters get shrugged off revealingly. Most strikingly, meaning fails to emerge from relationships. The Princess is an embodied power, scarcely human—the "wonder of the world." Between her and the protagonist there is confidence wholly without intimacy or even sympathy; the Princess scarcely grieves when the tiny woman dies, and her lack of feeling is presented unsentimentally. About the meaning of events to the only character left alive at story's end, the narrator says almost nothing.

Janet Larson claims that the Princess, "faithfully following the tiny woman's life to its predicted end, discovers that her vaunted 'power of knowing secrets' comes to much less than expected," that it consists instead of "a rather more modest capacity for hearing pain confessed." But however plausible such an inference might be, there is no evidence that the Princess herself "discovers" this truth, or even that Amy has been thinking in these terms. Where we might expect closure, we are given only a rather flat restatement of the obvious: "and then she knew that the tiny woman had told her the truth" (286). This story, which begins in solitude and silence, ends that way too. Since nothing is resolved along the way, since there is no outcome in the conventional sense, the conclusion must be signalled externally in Amy's "That's all, Maggy."[23]

Amy's one formal story fails from sheer lifelessness; its subtext reveals a tale-teller wary of approaching too closely the materials from which, conventionally, narratives have been fashioned. But though she is nearly inarticulate in this long novel, Amy is nevertheless central to its imaginative outlook, defining a way of seeing and an attitude toward experience that run counter to the symmetrical elements in *Little Dorrit*'s plot and theme. The kind of story she *might* tell had she language and inclination can only be inferred from what we know about her characteristic angle of vision, but its influence is nevertheless felt in indirect ways.

Michael Hollington's discussion of Amy seems to me to get closest to her symbolic function.[24] Against Clennam's "traumatized fixation on the past," impeding "forward action and progress," Amy stands as the novel's chief embodiment of present commitment. Her "eschewal of false and premature millennia" in favor of what can be known and done now to ease visible suffering aligns her with the creative forces in the novel against the Merdle's, Mrs. Clennam, and even, to an extent, against the hero himself.[25] Of this imaginative outlook, the fine needlework which is Amy's trademark is the perfect emblem, embodying her pleasure in labor as a continuous process, willingly undertaken a single small stitch at a time. The value of such work arises out of its homeliness and practicality, its beauty, and the presentation of self and time it represents. Flora, who misunderstands much, knows how to appreciate such gifts. Hearing from Clennam's lips the news about the Dorrit's fortune, she vows that the dress over which her friend has patiently worked "shall never be finished by anybody else but shall be laid by as for a keepsake just as it is" (404).

Unlike those characters who constrict the past to the dimensions of one life, one question to be answered, one outcome to be anticipated, Amy's decentered openness to experience makes the world a larger place. Outside the locked Marshalsea gates, at the window overlooking the prison yard, on the balcony in Venice, Amy characteristically fronts moving panoramas of scenery and people, herself a stationary separate figure receptive to variety and amplitude even in their more threatening forms. For her the shape of impressions never resolves itself into a glimpsed horizon, a foreclosed "perspective"; her sense of the profound otherness of experience precludes any purely subjective reading of sensory data. In Italy the scale and terrific age of all she encounters sets her musing on more philosophical themes: "One of my frequent thoughts is this," she writes to Clennam, "Old as these cities are, their age itself is hardly so curious, to my reflections, as that they should have been in their places all through those days when I did not even know of the existence of more than two or three of them, and when I scarcely knew of anything outside our walls" (537). Hollington comments: "Little Dorrit is here countering the idealist perceptual notions of Rigaud and many other characters by recognizing the separate existence of other phenomena, independent in time and space of herself as a necessary perceiving object. She feels life going on before and after and outside herself" (111).

I believe that Dickens found Little Dorrit's way of seeing and responding to experience profoundly suggestive, but more than a little frightening in its implications for fiction. Thus it is fitting that the "text" with which he ultimately associates Amy is both playfully and portentously conceived. Just as Clennam is identified with the tree of blighted memories, Dickens connects Amy to the "Book of Fate," St. George's three registers of birth, death, and marriage. In the final chapter of the novel, the verger, who had taken her in on her night of houseless wandering, makes this connection explicit:

> This young lady is one of our curiosities, and has come now to the third volume of our Registers. Her birth is in what I call the first volume; she lay asleep on this very floor, with her pretty head on what I call the second volume; and she's now awriting her little name as a bride, in what I call the third volume.
>
> (801)

The passage, with its heavy symbolic weighting and its clever play with books and reading, makes an obvious claim on the reader's attention, but the precise nature of this claim is difficult to assess. Janice Carlisle has usefully called attention to the parody involved in Dickens' "final self-conscious reference to his own literary forms." For her, "the functionary's concern for his three volumes is a witty allusion to the form of publication that was the major rival of Dickens' twenty-number serials'' (195). But it seems to me that the parody is aimed at a target much closer to home. In St. George's Register, Dickens imagines with considerable whimsy and some real foreboding the indeterminate fiction Little Dorrit has become carried to absurd extremes. Viewed analogically as "fiction," the registers stand at a distant remove from Clennam's notion of narrative as memory organized to reveal design. They give printed form to a world that is completely without closure, a condition of things that Amy, "her head resting on that sealed book of Fate, untroubled by its mysterious blank leaves" (171), accepts with perfect serenity. It does not dismay her that life revises constantly the volumes on which her brief biography is inscribed or that, in the process, her story is shorn of its uniqueness and plot interest. To the extent that her narrative has the kind of theme Clennam always seeks in his own imaginative projections, it is the theme of all fiction—life itself—and hence hardly a "story" at all. The appeal of "fiction" so conceived must reside outside teleological paradigms, in a realm of silence and possibilities at once creative and fearful. St. George's Registers are more compelling for the questions they raise than for the answers they supply. The sexton understands well their unique claims as literature: "What makes these books interesting to most people is—not who's in 'em, but who isn't—who's coming, you know, and when" (171).

These are questions that *Little Dorrit* as a novel does not, cannot, answer. But the posing of such questions redefines the context of the novel's conclusion and transposes Amy's earlier silences into a different key. When Arthur and Amy "come into" the registers as man and wife in the final chapter of the novel, the finality of that act and its authority to resolve the complex skein of the plot are by implication diminished and qualified. Their two signatures, we have been reminded, are surrounded by blanks vaster, more compelling, more eloquent than the modest offset against the unknown that even one perfect marriage can effect. For his two protagonists Dickens articulates, finally, a future as flat and cliched as anything Amy might have put into her own flimsy narrative—simply, "They passed along in sunshine and in shade" (802).

Thus the novel's celebrated open ending echoes the narrative conventions of its most conspicuously unsuccessful storyteller, and the novel which begins as Clennam's quest for origins and fulfillment ends as . . . something else. "In every human being," writes Helene Cixous, "there is a complex relationship between different libidinal economies which would be passive and active, constantly binding and unbinding themselves, exchanging, spending and retaining'' (Conley, 131). Something of the effects of this peculiar dynamic may be discerned in *Little Dorrit,* where Flora's and Amy's ''fortune telling,'' enfolded within Clennam's ''barren story,'' fashioned out of Dickens's unresolved memories and desires, set in motion frictions among narratives that richly complicate the novel's autobiographical stance.[25]

NOTES

1. Janet Larson, ''The Arts in These Latter Days: Carlylean Prophecy in *Little Dorrit,*'' *Dickens Studies Annual* 8 (1979): 140; K. J. Fielding, ''Dickens and the Past: The Novelist of Memory,'' in *Experience in the Novel,* ed. Roy Harvey Pearce (New York: Columbia University Press, 1968), 124, 129; R. Rupert Roopnaraine, ''Time and the Circle in *Little Dorrit,*'' *Dickens Studies Annual* 3 (1974): 60.
2. See Fielding, 112–23, for a fuller discussion of these ideas; Avrom Fleishman, *Figures of Autobiography* (Berkeley: University of California Press, 1983), pp. 202–04; Jerome H. Buckley, ''The Identity of David Copperfield,'' in *Victorian Literature and Society,* ed. James Kincaid and Albert Kuhn, (Columbus: Ohio State University Press, 1984), p. 237.
3. Janet Larson, *Dickens and the Broken Scripture* (Athens: University of Georgia Press, 1985), p. 219.
4. Janice Carlisle, ''*Little Dorrit:* Necessary Fictions,'' *Studies in the Novel* 7 (Summer 1975): 198.
5. For Miss Wade's ambiguous ''history,'' see Kathleen Woodward, ''Passivity and Passion in *Little Dorrit,*'' *Dickensian* 71 (September 1975): 140–48; for Amy's letters, see William Burgan, ''Little Dorrit in Italy,'' *Nineteenth-Century Fiction* 29 (March 1975): 393–411.
6. All references to *Little Dorrit* are taken from the Clarendon edition edited by Harvey Peter Sucksmith (Oxford: Clarendon Press, 1971).
7. ''Memory for Flora is not that magical chemistry which dissolves the space between past and present. The past remains out there, a fixed set of frozen experiences . . . '' Roopnaraine, 67.
8. See for example, Janice Carlisle, ''It is true of the novel as a whole, as it is true of what Clennam calls his ''poor story,'' that Little Dorrit is ''its vanishing point'' (203).
9. See also Richard Stang, ''*Little Dorrit:* A World in Reverse,'' in *Dickens the Craftsman,* ed. Robert Partlow (Carbondale: Southern Illinois Press, 1970): 156–64.
10. Dianne F. Sadoff, ''Storytelling and the Figure of the Father in *Little Dorrit,*'' *PMLA* 95 (March 1980): 234, 235.
11. Nancy K. Miller, *The Heroine's Text: Readings in the French and English Novel, 1722–1782* (New York: Columbia University Press, 1980), p. 150.
12. Verena Andermot Conley, ''Appendix: An Exchange with Helene Cixous,'' in *Helene Cixous: Writing the Feminine* (Lincoln and London: University of Nebraska Press, 1971), p. 133.
13. See Cixous's comments on how the feminine libidinal economy manifests itself in literary texts: ''You will have literary texts that tolerate all kinds of freedom—unlike the more classical texts—which are not texts that delimit themselves,

are not texts of territory with neat borders, with chapters, with beginnings and endings etc., and which will be a little disquieting because you do not feel the arrest, the edge'' (Conley, 137).

14. William Myers, "The Radicalism of Little Dorrit," in *Literature and Politics in the Nineteenth Century*, ed. John Lucas (London: Methuen, 1971), p. 88.

15. Janet Batsleer, Tony Davies, Rebecca O'Rourke, and Chris Weedon, *Rewriting English: Cultural Politics of Gender and Class* (London and New York: Methuen, 1985), p. 86.

16. See, for example, F. R. Leavis, "Dickens and Blake: 'Little Dorrit,' " in *Dickens the Novelist* (London: Chatto & Windus, 1970), p. 242.

17. Elaine Showalter, "Guilt, Authority, and the Shadows of *Little Dorrit*," *Nineteenth-Century Fiction* 34 (June 1979): 36–39.

18. See Jerome Beaty, "The 'Soothing Songs' of *Little Dorrit:* New Light on Dickens's Darkness," in *Nineteenty-Century Literary Perspectives: Essays in Honor of Lionel Stevenson*, ed. Clyde de L. Ryals (Durham, N.C.: Duke University Press, 1974), pp. 227–28. Beaty emphasizes Flora's "unconscious parody of coyness and girlishness." "Flora ludicrously and pathetically sets Arthur 'free' from their one-time engagement."

19. Andrew Sinclair, *The Better Half: The Emancipation of the American Woman* (New York: Harper & Row, 1956), p. 93; quoted in Nina Auerbach, *Romantic Imprisonment* (New York: Columbia University Press, 1986) p. 107. Auerbach provides helpful data on the critics' changing perception of Dickens's female characters.

20. On Amy as a Spirit of Love or Truth, see Alexander Welsh, *The City of Dickens,* (London: Oxford University Press, 1971), pp. 141–228.

21. Mary Ann Kelly, "Imagination, Fantasy, and Memory in *Little Dorrit*," *Dickens Studies Newletter* 13 (June 1982): 48; Barbara Hardy, "Dickens' Storytellers," *Dickensian* 69 (1973): 77; Showalter, 29; Larson, *Dickens*, 237. Julia Swindells's reading of the tale in *Victorian Writing and Working Women: the Other Side of Silence* (Minneapolis: University of Minnesota Press, 1985) is less sensitive to context and sublety: "What she feels called upon to justify, significantly enough, is being a single woman—living alone" (p. 87).

22. Harry Stone, *Dickens and the Invisible World* (Bloomington and London: Indiana University Press, 1979), p. 39.

23. Larson, *Dickens* 245: "The story's conclusion has only the sense of an ending with Amy's 'That's all, Maggie,' and leaves the reader 'staring and ruminating.' But I find no support for Larson's claim about "the princess' continued life *to tell the tale*" (my emphasis, 237). As far as we know, both shadow and story "were at rest together" when Amy stops speaking to shade her face from the sunset.

24. Michael Hollington, "Time in *Little Dorrit*" in *The English Novel in the Nineteenth Century*, ed. George Goodin (Urbana: University of Illinois Press, 1972), pp. 109–25.

25. I would like to thank Virginia Fowler, Janet Larson, and Ruth Salvaggio for their helpful comments on earlier drafts of this essay.

Domestic Fictions: Feminine Deference and Maternal Shadow Labor in Dickens' *Little Dorrit*

Sarah Winter

In his essay on Dickens' *Little Dorrit* (1855–57), Lionel Trilling argues that in this novel "the desire for money is subordinated to the desire for deference."[1] In Victorian society rituals of deference—a wife's deferring to her husband's wishes, a child's deferring to adult discipline and expectations, or a servant's deferring to a master's or mistress's orders—played an important role in the maintenance of gender and class hierarchies. The crucible of hierarchical relationships and of the deferential strategies for acting out and coping with them is the Victorian "Home"—domestic hierarchies, materially and spiritually supported by feminine domestic labor, perpetuate the bonds which construct patriarchal society as one big "Family" where everyone has his or her appointed place. The desire for deference Trilling describes is most dramatically fulfilled by Little Dorrit herself, the novel's exemplary performer of social deference and domestic labor. Yet Little Dorrit's deference and domestic labor serve far more numerous and ambivalent purposes in the novel than simply to support her imprisoned father and "fallen family".[2] In fact, I will be arguing that while Little Dorrit embodies and carries out Dickens' novelistic project of reform, her deference also defers this project, so that Dickens's social criticism becomes another "circumlocution." Although Dickens wants his readers to follow Little Dorrit's example of serving others, he also demonstrates how desirable and comforting it is *to be served*, even how serving others ultimately serves one's own best interests.

243

Dickens claims that Little Dorrit is "inspired to be something . . . different and laborious, for the sake of the rest" (111). What is different about Little Dorrit and her work? Her difference for Arthur lies both in her special treatment by his mother, and also in her double life, the secret of which he learns when he visits her at home in the Marshalsea prison. Little Dorrit is both the breadwinner and the housewife in the Dorrits' nineteenth-century single-parent household: she both works outside the prison—keeping the location of her home secret from her employers—and she also works at home, where she must conceal both her outside work and the necessity for it from her father: "over and above her other daily cares, the Child of the Marshalsea had always upon her the care of preserving the genteel fiction that they were all idle beggars together" (114). Thus she takes upon herself not only the physical labor of housework and let[ting] herself out" (93), but also the "emotions work" of maintaining her family's illusions of "gentility" within the prison. Little Dorrit's most important "difference," then, is her refusal to make any difference: her unobtrusive domestic labor purposely obscures the contrasts between "genteel" life inside and outside the prison.

I take the term "emotions work" from Arlie Russel Hochschild's *The Managed Heart,* an impressive study of the exploitation by modern capital of the worker's emotions in service-sector jobs.[3] Hochschild defines "emotions work" or "emotion management" as labor which "requires one to induce or suppress feeling in order to sustain the outward countenance that produces the proper state of mind in others" (7). Hochschild also explains that even acts of emotion management which seem only to serve an individual's personal interests are actually formulated within a context of socially defined "feeling rules":

> Acts of emotion management are not simply private acts; they are used in exchanges under the guidance of feeling rules. Feeling rules are standards used in emotional conversation to determine what is rightly owed and owing in the currency of feeling. Through them, we tell what is "due" in each relation, each role.
>
> (18)

Following this economic concept of emotion payment and emotional indebtedness, we could extend Trilling's observation about *Little Dorrit* to say that deference becomes the most desired source of "wealth" and status in the novel. The deference of the "Collegians" can make the indebted Mr. Dorrit (at least in his own mind) into a beneficent patriarch—he may not be rich, but he can still afford to be "magnanimous" (274). Later in the novel, Mr.

Dorrit needs to receive deference from innkeepers and servants in order to confirm the social value of his long-deferred wealth. Most instrumental to the maintenance of his "genteel" patriarchal fiction, however, is Little Dorrit's emotion work. In Dickens' novel, feminine domestic labor and emotion management provide the deferential capital needed to "liberate" the emotional debtor from the "prisons" of diminished patriarchal power and fallen families.

Hochschild believes that women have traditionally made more use of emotion management than men, principally because:

> women in general have far less independent access to money, power, authority or status in society, [and therefore,] lacking other resources, women make a resource out of feeling and offer it to men as a gift in return for the more material resources they lack.
>
> (163)

Hochschild goes on to explain that women have been obliged to make the best of the limited leverage these emotional resources have offered, both in personal relationships and in society at large; they do not passively allow their emotions to run their lives, nor secretly manipulate those around them, but rather "adapt feeling to a need or purpose at hand, and they do it so that it *seems* to express a passive state of agreement" (167). Thus women perform an almost invisible labor of emotional accommodation, which may improve their situation without, however, radically redistributing power:

> The emotion work of enhancing the status and well-being of others is a form of what Ivan Illich has called "shadow labor," an unseen effort, which, like housework, does not quite count as labor but is nevertheless crucial to getting other things done. . . . In fact, of course, when we redefine "adaptability" and "cooperativeness" as a form of shadow labor, we are pointing to a hidden cost *for which some recompense is due. . . .*[4]
>
> (167, 70; my emphasis added)

Dickens does not ignore the emotional debts which Little Dorrit's shadow labor creates, but rather spends a great deal of narrative time and anxiety attempting to repay her.

Little Dorrit's emotion management is directed both inward and outward; she simultaneously manages both her own feelings and desires and attempts to satisfy the desires of others. She represents her management of her own desires in the story of the "tiny woman" and the "Princess" (341–43). Her fictional account of the tiny woman's love for a man whom she cannot have (presumably Arthur) is embedded in a larger fantasy of a perfect father-daughter family, that of the powerful and rich King and his daughter the Princess. If Little Dorrit's father had been a "King," (a real Patriarch, instead of the father of the Marshalsea), then she might have been the Princess, and her management of her desires would have been as unproblematic as their fulfillment. Little Dorrit imagines that if she were the Princess, she would already know everything that the "masters" of the world had to "teach," and thus she would never need to perform the deferential shadow labor of the "tiny" domestic worker. Instead, she would be able to ride out in her carriage and *openly* practice an omniscient charity. Little Dorrit's fantasy of feminine wisdom and altruistic power, however, depends on the model of the aristocratic, patriarchal family: in order for her to be a Princess her father must first be a King. Moreover, Little Dorrit's Princess-role neither frees her to desire, nor to fulfill her desires, but rather takes her beyond desire to a removed and beneficent curiosity. The Princess is Little Dorrit's ideal precisely because she *does not need to control her desires*. The tiny woman's predicament demonstrates that performing emotion management *creates* desire, even if only for a "shadow." Members of the ideal, aristocratic family are charitable and wise, but the "head" of a "fallen" family must defer and control the hidden and painful desires constantly generated by her shadow labor.

Little Dorrit's perfect application of Victorian feeling rules seems to have more in common with the Princess's wisdom than with the tiny woman's self-denial, yet her story-telling reveals that even she cannot live up to the Victorian code of feminine emotional self-control and lack of self-interested desire. Little Dorrit's deference, therefore, as well as her fictions about herself, also allow her to manage and diminish her desires so that they make no demands upon their already lost objects: "nobody missed it, . . . nobody was the worse for it" (342). Seen through the tiny woman's eyes, Little Dorrit's emotion work has a double purpose: by devoting herself to other people's desires she can both try to forget her own, and also spare others the pain of having to "treasure" a shadow. Although the tiny woman is "proud" of her beloved shadow, Little Dorrit can only cry and attempt to resign herself to prospects from which even her imagination cannot remove the "inescapable brand" of her domestic prison (337–38). Fortunately, however, her deference and selfless service will not be in vain, even though she seems unaware that her very stance of laboring on while suppressing her love will ultimately earn her its object.

Little Dorrit's outward-directed emotion management functions to keep secrets and preserve illusions. Little Dorrit is the object of desires for a deference which, because of her "difference"—her ideal character—she can guarantee as genuine. When her father, and later Arthur, look into "her earnest face" and "clear true eyes" (433), they need not suffer the slightest doubt or fear that there is anything but authentic loyalty and love behind her deference. In her mediation of other characters' desires, Little Dorrit becomes the standard against which all emotional or domestic behavior is measured, so that any character who desires love, or deference, or even power, in some sense "borrows" from Little Dorrit's emotional capital, and thus ends up indebted to her. Because she is the novel's ideal and source of its emotional-economic legitimacy and solvency, (she guarantees that Dickens's novel, and his moral message, will pay off in the end), Little Dorrit becomes the implied third term in every relationship. As Arthur finally realizes, she is the "vanishing point" of his own story: "Every thing in its perspective led to her innocent figure" (801).

Little Dorrit's mediations in the novel bring her both between men and between women.[5] Her deference and emotion management "erase" the incestuous content of her relationships with her father and Arthur, so that no matter how maternally, conjugally or filially she behaves toward them, she can maintain her status as innocent child, rather than woman.[6] Little Dorrit comes between her father and the standards of the outside world, helping him to believe that the Father of the Marshalsea receives from his fellow prisoners the deference due to a true patriarch. At the end of the novel, Little Dorrit's devotion also inspires Arthur to accept the position she has engineered for him with the help of Mr. Meagles and Daniel Doyce. Thus Little Dorrit uses her prodigious (and painfully won) skill at emotion management to serve the men she loves: she succeeds in reinstating them in positions of conventional (if diminished) masculine authority, despite their failures.

If Little Dorrit is Dickens' exemplary "managed heart," then Miss Wade is her negative double or shadow, "an unsubduable nature" (62): "I am self-contained and self-reliant; your opinion is nothing to me; I have no interest in you, care nothing for you, and see and hear you with indifference" (62). Miss Wade is a former domestic worker (a governess) who, unlike Little Dorrit, refuses to perform shadow labor or put up with what she sees as the "fool's" role of maintaining domestic fictions by giving or accepting deference: "If I could have been habitually imposed upon, instead of habitually discerning the truth, I might have lived as smoothly as most fools do" (725). Although Dickens calls Mr. Dorrit's patriarchal delusions "self-imposition" (276), he also implies that Little Dorrit is actually responsible for her father's state: "[her] love alone had saved him to be even what he was" (276). Thus

Miss Wade seems to voice Dickens' ambivalence about Little Dorrit's emotion management: according to Miss Wade's discernment, deference supports a system of "swollen patronage and selfishness calling themselves kindness, protection, benevolence, and other fine names" (734). Miss Wade's much resented category of "[l]ittle images of grown people" (726) clearly includes Little Dorrit.

Even though Dickens presents Miss Wade as a woman whose grievances are in some sense justified by her illegitimate birth and resulting lack of social status, he finally judges her and decides her fate in the novel according to the standards set by Little Dorrit. Miss Wade's "unhappy temper" (727) is her own fault after all—Dickens entitles her autobiographical letter to Arthur, "The History of a *Self-Tormenter*" (725). Thus Miss Wade's discernment of the truth and her indictment of social hypocrisy, despite Dickens' own similar criticisms, finally are shown to result merely from her bad attitude. Miss Wade's fate demonstrates what seems to be the novel's message of domestic accommodation: in order to achieve and maintain a reasonably "happy" temper, one must learn to accept the imposition of domestic fictions. Miss Wade also threatens the patriarchal family by her attempt to reproduce herself and her desires through Tattycoram. However, as Mr. Meagles warns her, in Dickens' world such a feminine desire for self-reproduction, along with its erotic component, is a perversion: "If it should happen that you are a woman, who, from whatever cause, has a perverted delight in making a sister-woman as wretched as she is (I am old enough to have heard of such), I warn her against you, and I warn you against yourself" (379). Mr. Meagles is also quick to dispel the last attractions of such a sisterhood by pointing to Little Dorrit as a positive example for Tattycoram:

> "You see that young lady who was here just now—that little, quiet, fragile figure passing along there, Tatty? Look. The people stand out of the way to let her go by. The men—see the poor, shabby fellows—pull off their hats to her quite politely. . . . I have heard tell, Tattycoram, that her young life has been one of active resignation, goodness, and noble service. Shall I tell you what I consider those eyes of hers . . . to have always looked at, to get that expression?"
> "Yes, if you please, sir."
> "Duty, Tattycoram."
>
> (881)

Here Tattycoram learns part of the secret about how Little Dorrit is repaid for her deferential emotion work: it is a simple exchange—when you give deference you get deference back. Thus Dickens represents a kind of utopia of perfectly managed hearts, within the prison. Yet this ideal of reciprocal deference obscures the very nature of the deferential relationship—an exchange between two people of *unequal* status. Tattycoram receives this egalitarian domestic fiction as a fringe benefit of her domestic labor, in addition to her "wages" of duty (another word for shadow labor), which she promises to count perpetually, even up to "five and twenty thousand" (880).

Therefore, Little Dorrit's emotion management and her status as feminine ideal in the novel reveal a further function of her domestic labor and deference: coming between, and *separating*, women. Little Dorrit's mediation does not enable women to work together and create empowering bonds through common experience. Rather, Dickens uses Little Dorrit's "ideal" example to encourage women *to work alone at home,* and to hope for the same kind of "success" she achieves at the end of the novel through emotional accommodation and shadow labor in service of the patriarchal family. In the world of Dickens' novel, no political movements or class or gender consciousness-raising are possible, because men and women are encouraged to think of their own familial and personal experiences as unique and unrelated to the situations of others, even though the novel's plot should bind together all the individual characters' stories. The much put-upon and "squeezed" Bleeding Hearts also fail to live up to the metaphorical connotations of their nickname: they neither revolt, nor even "torment themselves" over their poverty and unemployment, but rather, symptomatically, they build "Happy Cottages" (630). Even the proletariat is satisfied with the facades of domestic fictions.

In the end, the novel's exemplary "managed heart," Little Dorrit, does receive her heart's desire: marriage to Arthur. Little Dorrit's desire is fulfilled precisely because she simultaneously denies and nurtures it through shadow labor, like the precious but precarious resource it is. Little Dorrit's service ultimately wins her the love and domestic happiness, if not the disinterested mastery, she desired. Finally, then, Dickens' novel proposes complementary strategies to its female and male readers: *Little Dorrit* promises women that if they practice self-management and dedicate themselves to the service of the patriarchal family they, like Little Dorrit, will ultimately get what they want, while it counsels its males readers to control their desires, and, more importantly, to accept and make use of feminine domestic labor and emotion management.

Before she proposes marriage to Arthur (828), Little Dorrit comes into possession of a secret whose revelation could explode his already unstable domestic fiction: she knows the true meaning of the mysterious inscription in Arthur's father's watch, "Do Not Forget" (406). Rigaud's theft of the box with the family documents forces the domestic ''Nemesis'' to reveal her own theft and false position in the Clennam household: Mrs. Clennam is not Arthur's real mother and she has withheld the fortune that should have belonged to Little Dorrit, the niece of Arthur's real mother's patron. Mrs. Clennam has not only assumed the rights and privileges of maternity, but she also attempts the ultimate usurpation of paternal authority—she makes her own will into the will of God. According to Jeremiah Flintwinch, however, she has only succeeded in becoming God's dark shadow: ''I call you a female Lucifer in appetite for power!'' (851). Despite Jeremiah's harangue, Mrs. Clennam does not seem to fear *divine* judgment. Yet she rises from her chair ''as if a dead woman had risen'' (853), when Rigaud threatens to reveal her false maternity to Arthur, and she asks Little Dorrit to keep the truth from him until after she is dead: ''Let me never feel, while I am still alive, that I die before his face, and utterly perish away from him, like one consumed by lightning and swallowed by an earthquake'' (860). Although Little Dorrit promises not to tell Arthur the truth, Mrs. Clennam's apocalyptic nightmare of domestic punishment still comes true: the Clennam house collapses, and Mrs. Clennam becomes a living ''statue'' (863). Dickens implies that this latter state was a logical possible development of her ''rigid'' and ''Bumptious'' character (851), yet Mrs. Clennam's final silence and paralysis are in fact ''enforced upon her'' (863). Who is the ''enforcer'' here?

In her discussion of Mrs. Clennam as an ''emasculating'' mother, Elaine Showalter connects her to the image of the mother in Freud's ''Medusa's Head'' essay; she concludes that '[i]n Clennam's world, . . . adult women are potentially entrapping, engulfing, and sexually omnivorous.''[7] While I agree that for Arthur Mrs. Clennam functions as a maternal ''Gorgon,'' I also believe that she meets her own Nemesis in Little Dorrit herself. Little Dorrit is also a ''Medusa,'': the petrifying power of her role as feminine ideal effectively paralyzes any woman who fails to live up to her standard. Yet Little Dorrit's ''enforcement'' of Victorian gender roles within the novel does not make her an unambiguously powerful nor oppressive figure—she neither ''castrates,'' nor tyrannizes, nor manipulates, in fact, as we have seen in the story of the tiny woman, she too must defer her own desires. Rather, Little Dorrit is the ''vanishing point'' of the novel's enforcement of patriarchy—her shadow labor covers patriarchy's tracks. She is also the ideal ''Sphinx'' who never asks Oedipus the riddle of origins, and thus spares him the knowledge of his father's *and mother's* true names.

Little Dorrit's role as vanishing point in his own story also causes Arthur a great deal of distress and guilt during his feverish days and nights of self-torment in the Marshalsea prison:

> None of us clearly know to whom or to what we are indebted in this wise, until some marked stop in the whirling wheel of life brings the right perception with it. . . . It came to Clennam in his adversity, strongly and tenderly. . . . "If I, a man, with a man's advantages and means and energies, had slighted the whisper in my heart, that if my father had erred, it was my first duty to conceal the fault and to repair it, what youthful figure with tender feet going almost bare on the damp ground, with spare hands ever working, . . . would have stood before me to put me to shame? Little Dorrit's." . . . Always, Little Dorrit. Until it seemed to him as if he met the reward of having wandered away from her, and suffered anything to pass between him and his remembrance of her virtues.
>
> (787)

Arthur is in prison not only for bankruptcy, but also for his emotional debt to Little Dorrit. This passage seems to me exemplary of the function and consequences of Little Dorrit's shadow labor and emotion management in the novel. All Dickens' readers should ideally come to this "right perception" of the Little Dorrits in their lives, and should feel to some extent "put to shame." Arthur makes Little Dorrit his inspiration in his search for his father's fault; her emotion management of Mr. Dorrit teaches Arthur to create domestic fictions in order to "conceal" paternal weaknesses. Moreover, Little Dorrit's suppression of Arthur's real mother's identity and his parents' adultery allows Arthur finally to repay his debt to her by marrying her: if he had known that Mrs. Clennam had deprived Little Dorrit of her fortune, Arthur's guilt would probably have made marriage to her a virtual emotional bankruptcy, distressing to his masculinity. Dickens never tells us what Arthur believes about the fall of his house and his mother's final paralysis; presumably marriage to Little Dorrit also dissolves his obligation to find out the truth about his origins—he has a new domestic fiction to keep him "happy."

By marrying Little Dorrit, however, Arthur also, unknowingly, makes some reparation for that paternal fault to his real mother, with whom Little Dorrit has been associated since her first appearance in the novel. According to Affery, a "shadowy figure of a girl" has been haunting the Clennam house: "Who else rustles about it, making signals by dropping dust so softly? Who else comes and goes, and marks the walls with long crooked touches when we are all a-bed?' " (854). These nocturnal activities are shadow labor beyond the grave, the haunting of a martyred mother to whom "some recompense" *is still due.* Although Dickens later discredits Affery's interpretation of these mysterious phenomena (863), he does not deny that the house collapses under the pressure of maternal secrets, almost as if it had been sucked into the vacuum left by Mrs. Clennam's revelations, despite Little Dorrit's prompt cover-up. When the Clennam house falls following the limited identification of Arthur's real mother, (the reader never learns her name, nor the contents of her "mad" letters), it crushes and buries not only the domestic blackmailer and wife-killer, Rigaud, but also the shadow of a repressed, guilt-producing maternity.

Little Dorrit, the novel's universal emotion banker, takes on Arthur's emotional debts to his real mother, and Mrs. Clennam's debts to Arthur and to herself, and then burns the "IOUs" in the fire (893). By burning the lost codicil, Little Dorrit once again chooses to keep family secrets and to preserve domestic fictions. Thus Little Dorrit is also the novel's ideal emotional creditor and Mother—she extends a limitless credit of domestic devotion and of "forgiving and forgetting" (881), and she never asks for repayment. With Little Dorrit in charge of emotional indebtedness, no debtor should have to face his or her domestic prison.

In fact, the only characters in the novel who do end up paying their emotional debts dearly, are two women who only become indebted because they refuse to extend or to accept unlimited emotional credit. Dickens describes Mrs. Clennam as a merciless judge of emotional "defaulters": "Forgive us our debts as we forgive our debtors was a prayer too poor in spirit for her" (86). Miss Wade refuses to take credit for not having any improper intentions toward the friend of her fiance, and she interprets her future mother-in-law's advice as the condescension of an employer: "Her other servants would probably be grateful for good characters, but I wanted none" (773). Thus these negative doubles of Dickens' heroine become the "petrified" objects of the resentment—"an inward protest and feeling of antagonism" (134)—which Little Dorrit's infinite emotional credit provokes.

Dickens also repays Little Dorrit by *not paying her back*. All the negative and violent feelings generated by the "impositions" of her emotion management and shadow labor are redirected at her own shadows, Mrs. Clennam and Miss Wade. Dickens attempts a partial resolution of this ambivalent attitude toward guilt-producing maternal devotion by illuminating (as on the title page of the 1857 edition of the novel) the ideal figure of the "Little Mother." He reminds his readers not to forget *her,* but his warning also applies to Little Dorrit's threatening, abused doubles, laboring almost unnoticed in the domestic shadows.

Little Dorrit, the novel, also carries out Dickens' project of emotion management through its own domestic fiction. Despite Dickens' criticism of hypocritical "Patriarchs" and aristocratic, family-run bureaucracies like the Circumlocution Office, he finally falls back on the patriarchal model of marriage, supported by feminine domestic labor and deferential emotion work. If something does go wrong with the Family, individuals like Mrs. Clennam and Miss Wade, and even Mr. Dorrit, will be the guilty parties, and not the patriarchal family structure itself. Thus *Little Dorrit* proposes a "practical"[8] alternative to the "self-torment" of rebellion or of constant dwelling-upon the faults of those with whom one is forced to live: Dickens' readers should create and take comfort in domestic fictions like Arthur's and Little Dorrit's marriage, "a modest life of usefulness and happiness" (895).[9] Little Dorrit even promises readers concerned with the duration of her emotional credit that she will "lovingly close [their] eyes on the Marshalsea and all its blighted fruits" (895). *Little Dorrit*'s offer of maternal devotion and forgiveness may not change "Society," but hopefully it will reform a few emotional debtors.

As for the prison, in all its connotations, Dickens seems finally to reject Miss Wade's revolutionary impulses once again: "If I had been shut up in any place to pine and suffer, I should always hate that place and want to burn it down, or raze it to the ground" (61). Instead, the novel concludes in favor of Mr. Meagles's "practical" and charitable speculation: "I dare say a prisoner begins to relent towards his prison after he is let out" (60). If anyone is ever "let out" of prison in Dickens' world, then she or he might no longer need to call it home.

NOTES

I am indebted to the following people for invaluable advice and encouragement: Jann Matlock, D. A. Miller, Christine Froula, Deborah White, Cassandra Cleghorn, Shawn Rosenheim, Hilary Schor, and Helene Moglen and John O. Jordan of the "Dickens, Women, and Victorian Culture" conference.

1. Lionel Trilling, "Little Dorrit," in *The Opposing Self* (New York: Harcourt Brace Jovanovich, 1950), p. 51.
2. Charles Dickens, *Little Dorrit* (New York: Penguin Books, 1967) 112. Subsequent references to the novel are to this edition and are cited parenthetically in the text by page number.
3. (Berkeley: University of California Press, 1983) 7. Subsequent references are cited parenthetically in the text by page number.
4. My use of Illich's term "shadow labor" follows Hochschild's limited use; I intend "shadow labor" to represent metaphorically (following the novel's own representations) the capital yet repressed status of feminine and maternal domestic labor, and the economy of "diminished" desire, (a desire whose expression or fulfillment in the real world seems impossible, but which is nevertheless—or

correspondingly—powerful and "treasured," like the tiny woman's desire for the "shadow"), which underlies Little Dorrit's emotion management. For critiques of the sexism in Illich's constructions of gender see Gloria Bowles, et al. "Beyond the Backlash: A Feminist Critique of Ivan Illich's Theory of Gender" *Feminist Issues* 3 (Spring 1983): 3–43.

5. I am indebted to Eve Kosofsky Sedgwick's *Between Men: English Literature and Male Homosocial Desire* (New York: Columbia University Press, 1985) for her analysis of male homosocial bonding, which challenged me to question more closely the position of a female mediator like Little Dorrit.

6. Only the prostitute, who at first confuses the identities of Maggy and her Little Mother, reminds Little Dorrit that there are some domestic and social "falls" that her deferential shadow labor cannot redeem or clean up (218). This "woman" (as Dickens euphemistically [?] calls her) sees something in Little Dorrit's eyes that Arthur and Mr. Dorrit cannot see, perhaps a glimmer of the tiny woman's desires. Little Dorrit's sexuality cannot be entirely idealized away, although it seems that only a "woman" can see Little Dorrit's own vulnerability to a fall.

7. Elaine Showalter, "Guilt, Authority and the Shadows of *Little Dorrit*," *Nineteenth-Century Fiction* 34 (June 1979): 39.

8. The Meagles's seemingly idiosyncratic use of the word "practical"—which in their vocabulary seems to mean "charitable," or "kind" or "sentimental"—also demonstrates the usefulness of service in Dickens's novel: it is "practical" for the Meagles to be kind to Tattycoram because in return she will be loyal to them. Their practicality also extends to employing attractive female domestics: "why not have something pretty to look at, if you have anything at all?" (241).

9. Dickens also identifies Little Dorrit's marriage as a passage out of the "death" of her sexually ambiguous earlier life:

> this young lady is one of our curiosities, and has now come to the third volume of our Registers. Her birth is in what I call the first volume; she lay asleep, on this very floor, with her pretty head on what I call the second volume; and she's now a-writing her little name as a bride in what I call the third volume.

(894)

The second volume is the burial register (219); Little Dorrit's rite of passage takes her from birth, to death, to marriage, as if her shadow labor finds its eternal life in the roles of wife and mother.

The Encapsulated Romantic: John Harmon and the Boundaries of Victorian Soliloquy

Carol Hanbery MacKay

Tyger Tyger burning bright,
In the forests of the night;
What immortal hand or eye,
Could frame thy fearful symmetry?

William Blake, ''The Tyger''

At the center of Charles Dickens' *Our Mutual Friend* (1864–1865), the character John Harmon engages in a protracted soliloquy in which he argues whether or not he should reclaim his real name and resume his social identity. Readers and critics alike have found this exposition problematic, usually seeing its length and form as implausible and awkward.[1] Yet somehow this problematic soliloquy works: to expose the complex interrelationships of the plot, to establish Harmon's parallels with other characters, and to explore the concept of identity. I submit that the problematic nature of this soliloquy inheres more in its yoking together of Romantic and Victorian elements than in its length or narrative range.[2] More specifically, Harmon's soliloquy demonstrates how some of the aesthetic, formal, and psychological elements of Romanticism can be contained or encapsulated by a Victorian emphasis on social concerns.[3] Furthermore, what accounts for this soliloquy's problematic nature also explains its success within the overall narrative: encapsulation creates an additional tension between the two sets of elements that enhances them both, thereby stretching the soliloquy's form and extending its power.

Periodicity criticism has its pitfalls, but for purposes of this discussion the pertinent elements raised by Harmon's soliloquy may be visualized as forming

255

a spectrum, one end of which may be designated as primarily Romantic, the other as primarily Victorian.[4] As the image of a spectrum implies, some of these elements seem to cluster as polar opposites; others reflect differing stances that do not necessarily imply binary opposition. Instances of some qualities even lie close to one another on the imaginary spectrum. Thus, although a degree of schematization is inevitably suggested by the figure of a spectrum, these qualities should be interpreted as fluid, rather than as mutually exclusive.

To schematize, then: Romantic qualities tend to inhere in the quest for its own sake; the individual symbolically containing society; isolation; self-negation; the exotic, made specific by drugs, distortions of perception, and heightened awarenesses; circular structure; spatial orientation; timelessness or circular time; a confrontation with death consolidating identity; ambivalent and transcendent rhetoric; transcendence, which is spiritual, abstract; melancholia; tension set up by opposing forces; "centripetal" vision, that is, meaning invested in particulars, especially primal images; and an interest in oneness and the absence of boundaries. Distinctive Victorian qualities inhere to a large degree in the goal ending the quest; society symbolically containing the individual; public personae; projection and role-playing; the quotidian; parallel structure; temporal orientation; parallel time schemes, characterized by alternatives and the conditional; identity socially defined; ironic and sentimental rhetoric; rationalization; earnestness; resolution, which is both material and practical; "centrifugal" vision, namely, meaning projected in parallels, conditionals, the tendency to domesticate everything, to form boundaries; and an interest in rules, roles, and games.

As for the very definition of soliloquy, it already suggests an appropriate Romantic forum: it is a solitary talking to oneself.[5] Byronic isolation is as basic to Romanticism as is the soliloquist's self-division and propensity to self-debate. In this respect, Byron's *Manfred* provides us with an interesting case in point. Self-conscious and acutely analytical, Manfred dramatizes self-division through his numerous soliloquies, finally acknowledging, "[I] was my own destroyer, and will be / My own hereafter."[6] Equally of interest in this respect is that Satan, whom Manfred is here echoing, is the only character in *Paradise Lost* who soliloquizes ("The mind is its own place, and itself / Can make a Heav'n of Hell, a Hell of Heav'n" [Bk. 1, ll. 254–55]; "Which way I fly is Hell; myself am Hell" [Bk. 4, l. 75]. In fact, Milton's invocations in *Paradise Lost* seem to be prototypes for much Romantic soliloquizing. At the same time, Manfred's essential isolation manifests itself not only in his soliloquies but in monologues which show him speaking more to himself than to others. Again, Byron's indebtedness to Milton becomes apparent. As Louis Martz observes, *Paradise Regained* is essentially an extended meditation in which Satan is only the objectification of Christ's temptations, resistance to which enables him to discover his true nature as the son of God.[7]

In a similar vein, David Perkins reads *Manfred* as "an extended soliloquy, for the purpose of psychological revelation, in which the 'characters' are openly conceived as expressions of inner debate and the varying moods within Manfred himself."[8] Further underscoring this problematic drama's underlying dialectic are the Abbot's words, which emphasize Manfred's choice as between pride and penitence and recognize the "awful chaos" of his opposing forces:

> Light and darkness—
> And mind and dust—and passions and pure thoughts
> Mixed, and contending without end or order,—
> All dormant or destructive.
>
> (3.2.164–67)

Moreover, the play also introduces the concept of self-division in terms of separation from a loved one who seems like a part or double of one's self. Manfred speaks of his youthful love for Astarte as a time when they "had one heart, / And loved each other as we should not love" (2.2.26–27). Separated from Astarte by her death, as Heathcliff will be separated from his Cathy, Manfred indeed has no one but himself with whom he can truly commune.

Yet soliloquy is equally appropriate to the Victorian era, not only in the melodramatist's reliance on it as a stage convention but in the novelist's practice of depicting characters as engaging in solitary problem-solving strategies that help them shape identity and adjust their social roles.[9] Charlotte Brontë's *Jane Eyre*, for example, can be read as a series of self-debates in which Jane works out the dialectic of her self-worth and eventually tests that sense of self in the social arena. Likewise, William Makepeace Thackeray's *Vanity Fair* provides a key to character through soliloquy: Becky Sharp, old Osborne, and even honest William Dobbin reveal in soliloquy how rationalization has determined self-image. (The same point could of course be made about many of Robert Browning's dramatic monologists.) George Eliot also recognizes and exploits the value of soliloquy. Although she refrains from the "unrealistic" notion of having isolated characters expound at length, she often has her heroines exclaim aloud in soliloquy at moments of insight or decision-making—their solutions turning into resolutions that will allow their new inner harmony to affect the outer world.[10]

In this context, John Harmon's long soliloquy is both unique and paradigmatic. It could be called paradigmatic of the whole "genre" of soliloquy because his narrative encompasses the full range of the soliloquist's possible scenarios: Harmon is strikingly divided from himself by his new social identity; he confronts his own mortality ("before my eyes in its most appalling shape") and is tempted to choose death; he rationalizes his behavior in terms of a balance sheet that shows the greater good of his remaining dead to the world; and he finally resolves on a course of action that tests his inner strength.[11] Yet the very monumentality of this soliloquy also underscores its uniqueness and points to it as an intriguing example of Romantic Victorianism. In this light, John Harmon's soliloquy takes on the dimensions of an epic quest, a Romantic quest for imaginative freedom modified by a Victorian's "socializing vision."

In effect, this unique form takes the romance quest through the life-and-death wasteland of self-isolation towards an identity revitalized, because it is community-shared.[12] Walter L. Reed argues that "panoramic novelists such as Dickens, Balzac, and to some extent Dostoyevsky subject the single, extrasocial personality of the Romantic hero to a pluralistic, socializing vision."[13] This is not to deny the socio-political implications in the Romantic vision, however. Bradford K. Mudge has recently pointed out that for William Wordsworth and *The Prelude* "crisis is a political and social given that the poet learns to manipulate for the sake of his poem and—more important—for his own peace of mind."[14] But the Romantic's manipulation of the social order primarily for his own ends points up a crucial distinction between the Victorian and Romantic visions of society. The Victorian tends to see the individual as contained within society, rhetorically seeking significance in the external, social order. In contrast, the Romantic sees society within the individual, rhetorically finding significance within the self or particular images. Essentially, the Victorian "centrifugal" bias contrasts with the Romantic "centripetal" vision. Hence the logic of self-division easily leads to the Romantic's view of society as symbolic of the self.

At this point, then, let us establish the specific parameters of the quest that Harmon evokes. He recalls and relives how he has assumed several different guises since he disposed of his own identity through the convenience of his supposed drowning. Now Harmon confronts his true self and asks the crucial question: should he come back to life—in effect, resurrect himself—or should he bury his old self under his current disguise forever? He sums up the two alternatives and finds his decision self-apparent:

> Dead, I have found the true friends of my lifetime still as true[,] as tender and as faithful as when I was alive, and making my memory an incentive to good actions done in my name. Dead, I have found them when they might have slighted my name, and passed greedily over my grave to ease and wealth, lingering by the way, like single-hearted children, to recall their love for me when I was a poor frightened child. Dead, I have heard from the woman who would have been my wife if I had lived, the revolting truth that I should have purchased her, caring nothing for me, as a Sultan buys a slave.[15]
>
> (429)

So "dead" John Harmon resolves to stay, and he carefully projects his future course as John Rokesmith, finally declaring, "And now it is all thought out, from the beginning to the end, and my mind is easier" (430).

The soliloquy proceeds through three distinct stages, in which Harmon progressively recreates his sense of space, time, and morality. Paradoxically, it also moves from the past into the future while simultaneously returning full circle—as does *The Prelude* in its own fashion. In this respect, the soliloquy's structure also resembles the dialectical spiral that M.H. Abrams sees as characterizing Wordsworth's "Tintern Abbey," Percy Bysshe Shelley's "Ode to the West Wind," and Samuel Coleridge's conversation poems.[16] The implications of self-creation almost demand this multilayered effect: they call for Harmon to enter another realm through a new level of rhetoric that is both timeless and of his time. This self who narrates himself employs his own language, a rhetoric that partakes of both Romantic and Victorian elements.

Echoes of Romanticism resound throughout Harmon's soliloquy. In his confrontation with nothingness—"there was no such thing as I" (426)—he struggles with the primal forces of life, death, ego, and identity, recalling William Blake's *Urizen:*

> Dark, revolving in silent activity:
> Unseen in tormenting passions;
> An activity unknown and horrible,
> A self-contemplating shadow . . .
> (Ch. 1, 18–21)

Or the protagonist of Byron's "Lara":

> He stood a stranger in this breathing world,
> An erring spirit from another hurl'd;
> A thing of dark imaginings . . .
> (Canto 1, 315–17)

Here are Harmon's words:

> It is a sensation not experienced by many mortals . . . to be looking into a churchyard on a wild windy night, and to feel that I no more hold a place among the living than these dead do, and even to know that I lie buried somewhere else, as they lie buried here. Nothing uses me to it. A spirit that was once a man could hardly feel stranger or lonelier, going unrecognized among mankind, than I feel.
>
> (422)

Compare the mood and setting of Wordsworth's sonnet, ''Composed among the Ruins of a Castle in North Wales'':

> Through shattered galleries, 'mid roofless halls,
> Wandering with timid footsteps oft betrayed,
> The Stranger sighs . . .
>
> (1–3)

Or Coleridge's ''A Lover's Complaint to his Mistress'':

> The dubious light sad glimmers o'er the sky:
> 'Tis silence all. By lonely anguish torn,
> With wandering feet to gloomy groves I fly . . .
>
> (1–3)

Compare, too, the Romantic's aggressive despair in John Keats's *Endymion:*

> Long in misery
> I wasted, ere in one extremest fit
> I plung'd for life or death.
>
> (Bk. 3, 378–80

And finally, take note of the similar tone evoked by Shelley's lines ''On Harriet Shelley'':

> The cold earth slept below,
> Above the cold sky shone;
> And all around, with a chilling sound,
> From caves of ice and fields of snow,
> The breath of night like death did flow
> Beneath the sinking moon.
>
> (1–6)

Harmon's status as one of the ''living dead'' accords him the kind of perspective found in Coleridge's ''The Rime of the Ancient Mariner,'' which suggests that he should define himself. Yet Harmon's talent for role-playing throws into doubt the whole question of the integrated self.[17] In succession, his soliloquy uncovers a long series of separate identities: John Harmon ("divided in my mind"); an unnamed seaman (who disembarks with Radfoot); Radfoot himself (as the dead "Harmon"); Julius Handford (who helps to identify the body as Harmon's); John Rokesmith (Mr. Boffin's secretary and the Wilfers' lodger—"our mutual friend"); and a disguised seaman (who questions Pleasant Riderhood about "the scene of my death"). Self-divided and fragmented, Harmon epitomizes the self-tortured Romantic spirit who, like the protagonist of Keats's *Endymion* or Shelley's "Alastor," can find relief only in transcendence. Indeed, death remains attractive to Harmon even though he rejects it on the level of basic survival: "John Harmon, struggle for your life," he apostrophizes in the black water (426). Yet he concludes his soliloquy by agreeing in the name of Rokesmith to bury the identity of Harmon. The chapter itself concludes on the following note:

> And so busy had [Rokesmith] been all night, piling and piling weights upon weights of earth above John Harmon's grave, that by that time John Harmon lay buried under a whole Alpine range; and still the Sexton Rokesmith accumulated mountains over him, lightening his labour with the dirge, 'Cover him, crush him, keep him down'."
>
> (435)

But despite his affinities with the Romantic outlook, Harmon has a distinctly Victorian cast. His ultimate decision to "stay dead" turns an existential Romantic crisis into a matter of Victorian role-playing. Rather than an expansive soul soliloquizing on the slopes of the Jungfrau or a Prometheus eternally tortured by the gods, Harmon is a relatively passive protagonist whose crisis has been induced by the corrupt forces of an urban society and whose goal revolves around a social identity. While Manfred dramatizes a full range of emotions, finally feeling the complete despair of his predicament, Harmon retains a Victorian degree of emotional control. Harmon may act out feelings of despair, but lacking the Romantic's overweening pride, he remains rational and capable of surrendering one sense of himself to a more viable social role. In one respect, neither hero is actually engaging in self-debate, for each seems to enter the scene with his mind essentially made up. Yet whereas Manfred reveals multiple sides to his character, Harmon primarily assumes a variety of different disguises that serve his practical purpose. And finally, Manfred's struggle proves to be a fatal affair, while Harmon stays alive in Rokesmith—his integrity still intact.

Even at its most Romantic, Harmon's soliloquy must hold back to some degree. Thus, the "strangeness" Harmon speaks of is not amplified by a torrent of exotic imagery. It is merely cited as an aspect of the experience. Similarly, while one has the sense of boundaries, rules, and self-identity as being suspended in the first half of the soliloquy, Harmon lacks the full-blown Romantic's urge to transcendence. The conflated Victorian-Romantic vision may suggest, but not fully evoke, infinitude.

What would a "pure" Victorian version of Harmon's story be like? Dickens himself provides us an example in Chapter 2, "The Man from Somewhere." The story of the man we later know as John Harmon is told in a self-parodic, hyper-Victorian way, in which the basic factors of Victorianism are carried to an extreme. Firstly, the tale that we hear in Chapter 2 is surrounded by narrative and formal frames (1.253–59). We are kept completely outside the tale. In an ironically evoked social setting at the Veneerings's, Mortimer Lightwood reluctantly tells this story of "the man from Somewhere." Thus, the rendition is enacted for entirely formal reasons; we find here none of the internal thrust of Harmon's personal need in his soliloquy. And, initially at least, poor Harmon has neither a name nor a spatial location: in fact, he is also referred to as "the man from Nowhere." In contrast to the emotional focus on Harmon's struggle, we hear the partygoers' constant interruptions and attempts at wit, in a parody of Victorian irony. The primal imagery of Romanticism is reduced to "Dust"—that is, urban refuse—from which the family's wealth comes. Finally, death emphatically ends this version of the story, as Lightwood receives a note and announces, "Man's drowned!"

There is no cyclical rebirth in this Victorian world. Dickens further distances us from this extremely encapsulated version through structural parallels. We cannot help but recall Gaffer Hexam's vocation—fishing for corpses—from Chapter 1, "On the Look Out," and the appearance of a real-life note to end the divertissement at the party is another reminder of the Victorian awareness of structures of meaning, as well as a parody of melodramatic coincidence. The narrator speculates that Lightwood might have been moved by something in this story—and this oblique, conditional reference to the world of personal, emotional involvement is the sole germ of Romanticism encased within Dickens's self-mocking Victorian husk.

To return to the arena of the soliloquy, what remains true to the Romantic spirit in Harmon are the tensions between opposing forces that inform his character and that further acknowledge the Romantic-Victorian dialectic.[18] The soliloquy inverts Dickens' customary ironic rhetoric, the tendency to draw comic distinctions between the narrator and reader on the one hand and the fictional characters on the other. Harmon all but takes over as narrator, and his vision finds problematical boundaries within himself and his experience. In Romantic terms, Lawrence Frank recognizes in Harmon "the story of the quintessential romantic self," a self who "journeys between the poles of psychic fragmentation and of psychic paralysis" (28). For Donald Stone, a Romantic tension exists in *Our Mutual Friend* between "Byronic willfulness" and "Wordsworthian quiescence," which, "in the end . . . seem like alternative forms of the same Dickensian death wish" (260). Keats himself seemed to embody an extremely rich dichotomy between the egotistical sublime and negative capability, which already shows him moving from the Romantic to the Victorian paradigm of identity.[19] This split also suggests the contrast between Carlyle's active hero and Scott's passive one. Of course, Carlyle himself stands poised at the threshold of Romantic Victorianism, and in *Sartor Resartus* he recounts his protagonist's psychic journey from "the centre of indifference" to "the everlasting yea" (Bk. 2, Chs. 8–9)—a journey that resembles Harmon's own. These very extremes point to the basic Romantic-Victorian contrast between spiritual and social concerns, which Harmon epitomizes in his rebirth and attention to duty.

On the other hand, what seems particularly Victorian about Harmon's soliloquy begins with its encapsulation: hemmed in by a labyrinthine urban environment, caught up in the entanglements that competition for social position and wealth engender, Harmon hardly resembles a poet pouring out his heart in the wilderness. Here it is worth noting Marcus Stone's illustration for this chapter. Entitled "More Dead Than Alive," the etching depicts the event from the past that Harmon is currently narrating: a half-drowned form is crawling onto the shore, the rain almost sweeping away our view of the waterfront backdrop (see accompanying illustration).[20] Stone effectively incorporates primeval elements into the urban scene, but the man-made backdrop is the more menacing: it looms large, surrounding Harmon, threatening to engulf him once Nature has had her way with him. As he tries to retrace his steps on the night of his attempted murder, he can recall only bits and pieces of an urban landscape—"And I have nothing else in my mind but a wall, a dark doorway, a flight of stairs, and a room" (421)—recreating the sequence of his encapsulation. If this soliloquist is ever to reintegrate his identity, he will have to find his place in this urban environment and in the social hierarchy that supports it: his brand of Romantic-Victorian rhetoric may catapult him through self-creation, but without mutuality he cannot sustain that new identity.[21]

With typical Victorian persistence, Harmon pursues his goal of determining his social identity. Ordering himself to "think it out," he reviews his past and projects two possible futures. By this point in the soliloquy, Harmon displays his predominantly Victorian mode. Rhetorically and semantically, he employs parallelism to posit or project solutions. (Earlier, the more Romantic Harmon internalized images and embedded his linguistic structures.) Harmon takes each step cautiously yet surely, repeatedly confirming to himself, "Now, stop, and so far think it out, John Harmon. Is that so? That is exactly so" (423). Moreover, despite the fact that he is apparently renouncing his father's entangling inheritance, Harmon calmly and objectively recognizes how money helped him conceal his identity and assisted him in his plans for "proving" Bella Wilfer's character. Finally, in an impressive *tour de force,* as if he were a lawyer standing apart from himself and dispassionately presenting two opposing arguments, he sums up his alternatives and concludes, "John Harmon shall come back no more" (430). The consummate Victorian is, after all, a manipulator of rules, a master of games, a self-conscious role-player.[22] In making this decision, however, Harmon is acting out of a sense of social responsibility toward himself and others, for among other concerns, he is compelled "to repair the wrong" of Gaffer Hexam's having been falsely accused of murdering him: "In that intent"—as in all such respects—"John Rokesmith will persevere, as his duty is" (428).

Romantic and Victorian elements thus combine in this soliloquy to create an almost self-contained narrative of spiritual challenge and moral accomplishment. If we also recognize the elemental imagery of water, disguise, circularity, and identity, then we might begin to read the soliloquy as a quest indeed. In fact, the quest motif's language of myth prompted Edgar Johnson to proclaim, "*Our Mutual Friend* is *The Waste Land* of Dickens' work."[23] Harmon draws us into his narrative partly because it challenges him and us to decipher his journey's circularity: " 'This is like what I have read in narratives of escape from prison,' said he, 'where the track of fugitives in the night always seems to take the shape of the great round world, on which they wander; as if it were a secret law' " (422). Conflation of Romantic and Victorian elements is often embodied in images. The reference to a narrative—occurring as it does within a narrative—displays the ironic, Victorian mentality which consciously manipulates contained structures of meaning. There is further irony in the escaped prisoners' entrapment in the larger world. At the same time, the urge to transcend, the endless quest, and the circular form reflect the Romantic impetus. This hero must now descend into the hellish underworld of his own past, with its fragmented sense of space and time, before he can solve the mystery of his own identity, undergo rebirth,

More Dead Than Alive

and project solutions for himself and others. Whereas more mundane soliloquists use rhetorical self-division to provoke themselves to uncover answers close to the surface, Harmon's profound division from his previous identity encourages the kind of self-questioning that produces a virtual rebirth.

As Albert Hutter has noted, "The central images of this novel—separation, dismemberment, and alienation—are contained within Harmon's story. In turn, through the development of Harmon's character . . . these motifs are reversed into the patterns of detecting, articulating, and resurrecting."[24] For our purposes, Hutter's comments highlight the essential function of Harmon's epic soliloquy for the transformation of the devalued into the valorized triad. I would argue that the devalued concepts are largely spatial in nature. While "separation," "dismemberment," and "alienation" happen or exist in time, the crucial image, feeling, or connotation is spatial. In contrast, the second triad evokes a more temporal sense. "Detecting," "articulating," and "resurrecting" are processes or events more than states or sudden actions (that is, virtually timeless). Although he does not make this point, perhaps Hutter's intuitive perception of this distinction led him to nominalize the three "timeless" elements, while expressing the second three as verbals. If we accept this distinction, we can perceive the necessity of combining "spatial" Romantic with "temporal" Victorian rhetoric. In order to transform the devalued into the valorized, a rhetorical or conceptual bridge between the spatial and the temporal must occur. This transformation is precisely what Dickens accomplishes by harmonizing Romantic and Victorian rhetorics.

Harmon's soliloquy occurs almost exactly at midpoint in the novel—in the last chapter of the ninth number. The serial novelist—writing in a temporal, linear frame—suddenly comes up against the experience of Romantic chaos and dispersal. Even Dickens' number plan shows, not the Victorian ironist considering his character from the outside, but the Romantic adventurer, ready to destroy existing constructs for the sake of the quest into the unknown. The note reads, "Bury John Harmon under mounds and mounds! Crush him! Cover him! Keep him down!"[25] But, working his way through this morass, the serial novelist begins to impose a Victorian sense of order, as he recognizes in this text a central microcosm of the whole. Thus, we can imagine Dickens initially casting off his Victorian garb to indulge the free Romantic in him, but then coming to terms with his larger task, something he had only sketched out. Once again, we see Dickens' relationship to his work in conflation and resolution.

This central position of Harmon's soliloquy recalls a famous Romantic monologue that also occurs at midpoint in its overall narrative—the Creature's extended and uninterrupted recitation to his maker in Mary Shelley's *Frankenstein*. Although the novel's other narratives attempt to contain and control the quality of monstrosity, the Creature's formal discourse is itself already highly controlled, almost a parody of Victorian rhetoric. Like Harmon's soliloquy, the monologue of the Creature stretches form to its limits, and both employ a mixture of rhetorical expansiveness and hyper-linguistic self-control. In both novels, the themes of the quest, isolation, relation to community, and the *Doppelgänger* also appear. Yet a primary difference surfaces when we note that, for Harmon, the creation of self is merely figurative. In fact, we would probably not expect a literal creation—such as we discover in *Frankenstein*—to appear in a typical Victorian work. Nonetheless, the need to contain the threatening forces of created selves is much the same in both texts. Note, for instance, the layers of formal and rhetorical enclosure in both sequences. Oddly, the creative pressure of the literal creation of a self in *Frankenstein* requires an exceptionally indirect, intellectual, and controlled rhetorical envelope (in Mary Shelley's words, "Invention . . . does not consist in creating out of void, but out of chaos"),[26] while Harmon's figurative self-creation may indulge itself in primal—what for heuristic purposes I am calling "Romantic"—rhetoric.

In the first half of Harmon's soliloquy, Romantic elements—especially Romantic isolation and self-isolation—predominate. Harmon knows what it is like to have passed beyond life's boundaries. Looking into a graveyard, he announces, "A spirit that was once a man could hardly feel stranger or lonelier, going unrecognized among mankind, than I feel" (422). Harmon's isolation from his own past recalls the recurrent elegiac tone in Romantic literature, as in Wordsworth's "Ode: Intimations of Immortality" or Coleridge's sense of lost poetic power. The sense of lost identity brings to mind John Clare's "I only know I am, that's all."[27] The emphatic strangeness of the experience suggests a quasi-Romantic evocation of the exotic. As he tries to piece together his past, Harmon virtually relives it in all its pain, gradually re-establishing the sense of space and time that has been blocked from his conscious memory: "Now, I pass to sick and deranged impressions; they are so strong, that I rely upon them; but there are spaces between them that I know nothing about, and they are not pervaded by any idea of time" (425). The derangement of the senses is a distinctly Romantic motif, particularly as it is evinced by Coleridge ("Kubla Khan") and Thomas De Quincy (*Confessions of an English Opium-Eater*). Recalling this state of semi-consciousness, Harmon acknowledges the attractions of death and the urge toward transcendence:

I heard a noise of blows, and thought it was a wood-cutter cutting down a tree. I could not have said that my name was John Harmon—I could not have thought it—I didn't know it—but when I heard the blows, I thought of the wood-cutter and his axe, and had some dead idea that I was lying in a forest.[28]

(426)

Negation holds sway—"there was no such thing as I"—and it is only a basic instinct for physical survival that causes Harmon to save himself from drowning at the last moment. Once again, we need not look far to find Romantic Thanatos—for example, in Keats's "half in love with easeful Death" ("Ode to a Nightingale", 52) or Coleridge's Ancient Mariner. The Romantics share with Harmon a fundamental ambivalence about life and death.

For the Romantic, the goal of the quest is less significant than the quest itself, but for the Victorian that goal becomes all-important. Typically, the problematic form of Romantic quests reveals the primacy of process over solution.[29] For example, Keats's *Endymion* is diffuse and remains unfinished, while *The Fall of Hyperion,* even more a fragment, is admittedly Miltonic, its inversions drawing attention to imitative form. Taken as an extended preliminary to *The Reclose, The Prelude* discloses the importance of growth and process.[30] As for the Ancient Mariner, his quest is endless, and the poem itself invokes a complex archaic apparatus with its self-reflexive commentary. And Blake's *Milton* is more than just problematic in form—as prophecy it imaginatively rewrites the past and becomes enamoured of its own recreated stages. Revealing his Romantic roots, Queen Victoria's own Poet Laureate, Alfred Tennyson, gives us a curious mixture of Romantic Victorianism in two of his poems about a classic quest, "Ulysses" and "The Lotus Eaters." In the former, the speaker evinces despair about obligatory work and returns to a Romantic spirit in his final self-exhortation, "To strive, to seek, to find, and not to yield" (l. 70), while in the latter the soporific state of the mariners compares unfavorably with the hero's drive to return to home and duty.

Thus, the self-directive to "think it all out" to a clearcut solution in the second half of Harmon's soliloquy points up the Victorian emphasis on control and order taking precedence. Harmon transforms the Romantic's energy to effect his own rebirth into a programmatic retailoring—a far cry from the phoenix's mystical creation of "organic filaments" for the retailoring of Carlyle's tailor (*SR*, Bk. 3, Chs. 5–7). The transitions are subtle—the soliloquy does not obviously divide in half or make an abrupt switch from Romantic to Victorian rhetoric—but the change is nonetheless complete by the soliloquy's end. At this point, Harmon delivers seven strong reasons why he should not return to society under his real name, each reason carrying the weight of his moral conviction (429). To this accounting, he adds the three-fold summation of his greater value to both the Boffins and Bella if he can remain "dead." But what of the fair maiden? It is not Bella but peace of mind which is Harmon's prize—a goal he will insure, however, by proposing to her as Rokesmith, proving "beyond all question" that she will not accept him for his own sake (430).

Garrett Stewart provides us with yet another principle for recognizing this soliloquy as roughly divided into Romantic and Victorian halves. Based on Harmon's attitude and relation to death that division becomes more apparent. As Stewart observes, "The Romantic self never knew what it was to exist without exploring from the inside out what it might be not to exist."[31] During the first half of the soliloquy, Harmon recreates in his imagination the circumstances that led to his near-death and confronts them as "fanciful" (422), yet significant. These circumstances serve to make him feel the experience of being among the living-dead. In this state of mind, he pursues the memory of his near-drowning and his self-apostrophe to save himself. Now we see the Victorian mind at work. In Stewart's terms, "The post-Romantic self in fiction is likely to yield itself to definition at the point of death." Harmon needs to recall the actual threat of death to catapult himself to self-definition and decision-making. In this respect, he repeatedly acknowledges that the identity of John Harmon as dead has yielded him a better result than if he were admitted among the living: "If the dead could know, or do know, how the living use them, who among the hosts of dead had found a more disinterested fidelity than I?" (429). The attempted murder thrusts the Victorian Harmon to the point of death and return, giving him in fact the Romantic's self-induced speculative experience.

To give Bella her due, her role in the soliloquy and in the novel as a whole serves as further commentary on issues raised by the soliloquy's divided nature. The soliloquist Harmon gives Bella little credit for recognizing his true worth, but at least he admits that she realized truly the "shocking mockery" (429) that would have resulted from their enforced marriage. In contrast, the married John Rokesmith treats his wife like a child, putting her in the doll's house she says she does not wish to inhabit (4.5.746), and Dickens' own sentimental rhetoric reduces the more complex portrait of the first half of the novel to an encomium on "The Complete British Housewife" (749).[32] But as Stone's illustrations reflect the two Bellas in the two halves of the novel, what they reveal is the continuity of Dickens' sexism.[33] Romantic sexism depicts her as haughty and mysterious but still a cipher; Victorian sexism treats her as doting and subservient, not worthy of knowing the truth about her husband's identity until she has been thoroughly—and unrealistically—tested.[34] The soliloquy ends with a very Victorian resolution—Harmon will propose to Bella in the name of Rokesmith—but in another respect, this conclusion remains open-ended and uncertain, reflecting the Romantic mode. These aspects of the soliloquy further comment on the structure of the novel and Dickens' use of the marriage convention to conclude his fiction. If Victorian closure repeatedly depends on the apparent finality of marriage, Dickens has nonetheless given us the comparative grounds for reading into it some of his buried ambivalence.[35]

In most stage adaptations of *Our Mutual Friend,* this key soliloquy is conspicuously absent. In many of these adaptations, the novel has been reduced to a romance-comedy plot, and Harmon, as sole hero in this plotline, reveals his identity in the initial exposition or in a very Victorian public announcement.[36] Modern readers may find the romance-comedy aspects of Harmon predictable and boring in the first place, especially in comparison with the more problematic and emotionally charged characters of Eugene Wrayburn and Bradley Headstone. At the same time, however, we must recall that Dickens invests Harmon and his soliloquy with the weight not only of the plotline but of the story's key imagery and its pattern of development. From its inception, the novel grew out of the Harmon character. Writing to John Forster sometime in 1861, Dickens declared, ''I think a man, young and perhaps eccentric, feigning to be dead, and *being* dead to all intents and purposes external to himself, and for years retaining the singular view of life and character so imparted, would be a good leading incident for a story.''[37] Dickens went on to energize his protagonist with the novel's epic central soliloquy, to empower him as master of competing rhetorics.

But despite the dramatic potential of having Harmon reenact his life-and-death struggle, there remains something about this soliloquy that makes it seem even too stagey for the stage. In this sense, Harmon's soliloquy recalls the ''closet dramas'' of Coleridge, Wordsworth, Byron, Keats, and Shelley. Problematic in form, these plays demanded more than either the stage of the period or dramatic convention could offer. In fact, Byron reported that he purposefully made *Manfred* ''quite impossible for the stage, for which my intercourse with Drury Lane has given me the greatest contempt'' (Perkins, 810). Likewise, Harmon's soliloquy is both too extended and too internalized for easy adaptation.

Yet in the context of narrative, where unspoken language is allowed rhetorical free play, Dickens manages to turn the problematic form of such a soliloquy to good account. We can see a similar case in *A Tale of Two Cities,* which concludes with Sydney Carton's famous unspoken words, "It is a far, far better thing I do than I have ever done; it is a far, far better rest I go to than I have ever known."[38] What both these soliloquies have in common is competing rhetorics. In Carton's soliloquy, it is the tension between the rhetoric of isolation and the rhetoric of transcendence that both expresses and resolves Dickens' perception of the separation of human minds. Carton's isolation combines with his willed self-transcendence to evoke a very Romantic image and desire—the urge to cross boundaries of time and consciousness. Equally, the parallel structures reflect the Victorian author's technique of effecting that movement through the mechanism of controlled rhetoric. Elsewhere in his canon, Dickens reserves his use of soliloquy for occasional self-apostrophe. For him, there is nothing between brief expressions of self-address and the large-scale tensions that inform the more problematic soliloquy.

Besides creating time-bound tensions between their opposing forces, the Romantic and Victorian elements in Harmon's soliloquy also invoke its more timeless features. In fact, its very mixture of elements already suggests that this soliloquy transcends particular time. In addition to Romantic and Victorian qualities, we can recognize references that draw from a spectrum of archaic to Modernist symbols. Frank, for example, sees archaic ritual in the mode of repetition, recalling Mircea Eliade's *The Myth of the Eternal Return* (Frank, 245). Granting the Modernist propensity to draw upon such mythology, we can also look ahead through the urban quest and the theme of death by water to see T. S. Eliot's *The Waste Land* and the Modernist search for order in circularity.[39] Of course, Modernism has specific roots in both Romanticism and Victorianism. Steven Connor (152–58), Albert Hutter (161–63), and Michael Wheeler (104) have all pointed out Modernist elements in *Our Mutual Friend* that specifically pertain to Harmon's soliloquy. Recognizing that Dickens prefigured and influenced the Moderns, these accounts also point to Modernism's characteristic shifting of rules and identities—which recombines the Romantic desire to transcend rules and the Victorian's tendency to be bound by them. Such range recommends that we acknowledge the archetypal nature of this soliloquy and the means by which the Romantic and Victorian impulses reflect prototypical experience.

Interestingly enough, much of this soliloquy's archetypal imagery focuses on the concept of the *Doppelgänger,* which has particular import for both the Romantic and Victorian *Weltanschauungen.* In this respect, the double can reflect both Romantic fragmentation and the Victorian urge to integration: not only is Harmon mirrored in shadow characters like Eugene Wrayburn, Rogue

Riderhood, and Bradley Headstone, but he contains doubles *within* himself, providing a challenge to—and the grounds for—possible reintegration.[40] For both the Romantic and the Victorian, the double is psychologically disturbing and rhetorically problematic. Both share a desire to circumvent the double: the Romantic, by denying spatial separation of the double through its sub-division into multiple sub-characters; the Victorian, by asserting the temporal separation of the double through transformation—that is, the character manages to pre-empt the double. This is not to say that the circumvention is always successful, but rather that each age reveals a characteristic method for easing this discomfort.

In *Manfred,* for example, the double loses some of its disturbing potency through multiplication. The figures who populate this internalized ''closet'' drama are understood to be contained within Manfred, illustrating the Romantic denial of spatial separateness; they are merely sub-characters, not potentially equal to him, as an archetypal double would be. On the other hand, Robert Louis Stevenson's *The Strange Case of Dr. Jekyll and Mr. Hyde* epitomizes the Victorian solution to the problem of the double: we now see a complete temporal separation of protagonist and double. In this case the disturbing existence of an equally powerful double in a separate space at the same time is eliminated. As we might expect, Harmon moves from a relatively Romantic multiple, internalized division to the more Victorian temporal, external transformation. Initially, even his psychological faculties seem sub-divided, while later, his struggle rhetorically subsumes a series of three possible fates: drowning, near-drowning, and marrying. The disturbing doubles—namely, Headstone, Riderhood, and Wrayburn—actually experience variations on the same three fates that Harmon preempts in his epic soliloquy. (Sometimes, in fact, the double counters the effort to preempt. Wrayburn, for example, remains a disturbing figure at novel's end, having himself undergone a reversal—a transformation from Victorian to Romantic.)

Drawing on the complexes that constitute the Romantic and the Victorian worldviews, Harmon as soliloquist achieves his quest as neither a pure Romantic nor a Victorian could do. At the threshold of Romantic Victorianism, Harmon partakes of both purviews yet operates beyond them, utilizing the tensions that exist between them. Like any outsider, he is liberated by his exclusion, retreating from and returning to boundary lines at will. What finally empowers this problematic soliloquy is not so much its timeless scope as its encapsulation of one opposing force by another. The Romantic's typical effort to exceed formal boundaries gains strength here from fighting against its social as well as its formal layer of encapsulation. Paradoxically, Harmon is even more isolated by his urban encapsulation than a Romantic such as Manfred, whose cosmic predicament still permits the invocation of spirits and dialogue with fellow wanderers. Though the novel's resolution eventually puts Harmon and Bella in a Victorian bower of domestic bliss, Harmon achieves a resolution on his own terms from his self-generated quest as an encapsulated Romantic.

NOTES

1. Garrett Stewart, for instance, refers to it as "a long and improbable monologue" in *Dickens and the Trials of Imagination* (Cambridge, Mass.: Harvard University Press, 1974), p. 192; Steven Connnor cites the fact that other critics have found it "mechanical and flat" in *Charles Dickens* (Oxford: Basil Blackwell, 1985), p. 156; and Michael Wheeler calls it "unconvincing" in *English Fiction of the Victorian Period 1830–1890* (London: Longman, 1985), p. 103.

2. Other critics who examine the interplay of Romantic and Victorian elements in *Our Mutual Friend* include Donald Stone and Lawrence Frank, although Frank's final reading of the novel almost turns Dickens into a pure Romantic. See Stone, *The Romantic Impulse in Victorian Fiction* (Cambridge, Mass.: Harvard University Press, 1980), and Frank, *Charles Dickens and the Romantic Self* (Lincoln: University of Nebraska Press, 1984). Stewart devotes an entire chapter—"The Golden Bower of *Our Mutual Friend*"—to a discussion of the Blakean elements associated with Jenny Wren's Romantic vision. He also cites the comment by J. Hillis Miller: "the history of nineteenth-century fiction can be seen in part as the history of its internalization for individual characters of that Romantic experience previously restricted to the extraordinary imagination of the gifted poet." See *Imagination*, p. 207.

3. For an accounting of how the Victorian novel served as a serious social critique, see Raymond Williams, *Culture and Society, 1780–1950* (New York: Columbia University Press, 1958). In general, the shift to public personae in the Victorian period is supported by the work of Michel Foucault, *The History of Sexuality,* Vol. 1: *An Introduction,* trans. Robert Hurley (New York: Pantheon, 1978). More recently, and with specific attention to Dickens (but not *Our Mutual Friend*), Dirk den Hartog has argued that Romanticism can be viewed as an adversary subculture within Victorian culture—in effect offering a subversive perspective. See his *Dickens and Romantic Psychology: The Self in Time in Nineteenth-Century Literature* (London: Macmillan, 1987).

4. If, for instance, periodicity issues did not particularly illuminate my argument, I might very well have designated the extremes of the spectrum as metaphysical and psychological (or possibly realistic). Nonetheless, I believe that my study of Harmon's soliloquy and several recent forums have demonstrated a revitalized critical insight stemming from juxtaposing readings of Romantic and Victorian texts. The 1985 conference on "The Romantic/Victorian Threshold," cosponsored by the City University of New York and the Browning Institute, and the 1986 special session on periodization at the annual conference of the Modern Language Association constitute two such examples. I am grateful to the organizers and participants of these forums for their comments and suggestions on earlier versions of this study, and I wish in particular to thank Gerhard Joseph, Donald Stone,

Marshall Brown, Andrew Cooper, Bradford K. Mudge, and Walter L. Reed for their engaged criticism.

5. Coined by St. Augustine, *soliloquium* refers to solitary speech that may in practice merge into prayer or an internal series of thoughts. See *Confessions*, trans. E. B. Pusey (London: Dent, 1907), Bk. 11, sec. 7, par. 14.

6. George Gordon, Lord Byron, *Manfred*, in *Byron's Poetry*, ed. Frank D. McConnell (New York: Norton, 1978), Act 3, sc. 4, 11. 139–40. Further citations to this edition will appear in parentheses in the body of the text.

7. Louis Martz, *Poet of Exile: A Study of Milton's Poetry* (New Haven, Conn.: Yale University Press, 1980), pp. 250–68 generally.

8. David Perkins, ed., *English Romantic Writers* (New York: Harcourt, Brace and World, 1967), p. 810.

9. See my book, *Soliloquy in Nineteenth-Century Fiction* (London: Macmillan, and Totowa, N. J.: Barnes & Noble, 1987), in which I argue this thesis; I am grateful to Macmillan for permission to reproduce here elements of the book's argument. In addition to the novels cited in this essay, I also study the soliloquies in *Villette*, *Wuthering Heights*, *Pendennis*, *Romola*, and *Middlemarch*.

10. On the question of realism and the natural model of soliloquy what he calls "self-talk"—see Erving Goffman, *Forms of Talk* (Philadelphia: University of Pennsylvania Press, 1981), esp. pp. 78–123.

11. Charles Dickens, *Our Mutual Friend*, ed. Stephen Gill (Harmondsworth: Penguin Books, 1971), Bk. 2, Ch. 13, 421–30. Further citations to this edition will appear in parentheses in the body of the text. The soliloquy constitutes most of the chapter entitled "A Solo and a Duet"—the "single most important chapter" in the novel, according to Masao Miyoshi. See Miyoshi, *The Divided Self: A Perspective on the Literature of the Victorians* (New York: New York University Press, and London: University of London Press, 1969), p. 272. For a summary of the soliloquist's likely scenarios charted as stages of self-division, transcendence, rationalization, and projection, see Figure 2.1 in *Soliloquy in Nineteenth-Century Fiction* (41).

12. For a study of the romance "genre" with specific reference to *Our Mutual Friend*, see Tracy Seeley Flood's unpublished paper, "Dickens and Romance: More Than (a) Fancy," delivered to The Dickens Project conference on "Victorian Writers: Work, Women, and Worship," University of California at Riverside, 21 February 1987. Flood's comparative investigation breaks down periodicity considerations and permits a reading of Modernist romance. I, too, think such a reading is possible to accomplish for *Our Mutual Friend*.

13. Reed, *Meditations on the Hero: A Study of the Romantic Hero in Nineteenth-Century Fiction* (New Haven, Conn.: Yale University Press, 1974), p. 29.

14. Mudge, "'Song of Myself': Crisis and Selection in *The Prelude*," *Texas Studies in Literature and Language* 27 (1985): 1–24. Mudge further observes that "Wordsworth's spiritual liberation, his 'freedom in himself' [*Prelude* 14.131], is above all a liberation from the political responsibilities which hampered his poetic vision in books 7–11" (20). To turn the screw once more, we would do well to note Humphrey House's revisionist reading of Dickens, in which he questions some of the long-held premises about the novelist's social vision. See *The Dickens World*, 2nd ed. (London: Oxford University Press, 1942).

15. Here we can recognize reverberations of Wordsworth's "We Are Seven" (lines 65–69), in which a little girl is depicted as unable to accept the deaths of her brother and sister:

"But they are dead; those two are dead!
Their spirits are in heaven!"
'Twas throwing words away; for still
The little Maid would have her will,
And said, "Nay, we are seven!"

Michael Cotsell further observes that Dickens particularly admired this poem. See *The Companion to Our Mutual Friend* (London: Allen & Unwin, 1986), p. 182.

16. M. H. Abrams, "Structure and Style in the Great Romantic Lyric," in *From Sensibility to Romanticism: Essays Presented to Frederick A. Pottle*, ed. Frederick W. Hilles and Harold Bloom (London: Oxford University Press, 1965); rpt. Harold Bloom, ed., *Romanticism and Consciousness* (New York: W.W. Norton, 1970), pp. 201–29. Of course, Abrams leaves out the counterevidence of Byron's irony and Keats's "negative capability."

17. Robert Langbaum studies the rise and decline of the Romantic self's vitality in *The Mysteries of Identity: A Theme in Modern Literature* (Chicago: University of Chicago Press, 1977). See especially his first two chapters, "Wordsworth: The Self as Process" and "Arnold: Waning Energy." Other examinations specifically look to the French Revolution as a major source of Romantic disillusionment, which could be linked to Romantic self-division and fragmentation.

18. For John Kucich, "Dickens's apparent dualism, rather than being a symptom of unresolved conflict, can be recognized as a coherent strategy of representation." In a study chiefly citing *Our Mutual Friend*, Kucich further observes, "To define repression . . . as a tropological code suggests, among other things, that psychic states in Dickens are themselves only the product of linguistic manipulations, which belie the unmediated, monadlike structure of the self usually associated with ego psychology and its depth/surface model of desire and repression." See "Repression and Representation in Dickens's General Economy," *Nineteenth-Century Fiction* 38 (1983): 62–77; esp. 64–65. On the other hand, since this study of Harmon's soliloquy deals with his story as narrated by himself—represented as manipulated and mediated by his own language, so to speak—it is still appropriate for us to discuss character psychology in his case.

19. Keats first refers to the concept of *"Negative Capability"* in his letter of 22 December 1817 to his brothers George and Tom: "that is when man is capable of being in uncertainties, Mysteries, doubts, without any irritable reaching after fact & reason." See *The Letters of John Keats*, ed. Maurice Buxton Forman, 4th ed. (London: Oxford University Press, 1952), p. 71. Walter Jackson Bate discusses the concept at length in *Negative Capability: The Intuitive Approach in Keats* (Cambridge, Mass.: Harvard University Press, 1939).

20. See the first edition (London: Chapman & Hall, 1865), Vol. 1, opposite p. 280. Stone's original watercolor sketch, housed in the Berg Collection of the New York Public Library, depicts a figure that looks rather ape-like, as if he is rising from some primeval swamp.

21. For another reading that argues that identity consists in mutuality, see Vera Dellwardt's unpublished paper, "The Articulation of Identity in *Our Mutual Friend*," delivered to The Dickens Project Conference on "Dickens, His Contemporaries, and Heirs," University of California at Santa Barbara, 2 February 1985. J. Hillis Miller argues both for and against self-creation in the novel: having noted that it is impossible "to create out of nothing a new self," he goes on to

acknowledge Harmon's regenerative powers and the role of transcendence. See *Charles Dickens: The World of His Novels* (Cambridge, Mass.: Harvard University Press, 1958), pp. 279–327.

22. For a discussion of masks and games in the novel, see John M. Robson, "*Our Mutual Friend:* A Rhetorical Approach to the First Number," *Dickens Studies Annual* 3 (1974) esp. 210–13.

23. See Edgar Johnson, *Charles Dickens: His Tragedy and Triumph*, 2 vols. (New York: Simon & Schuster, 1952), 1: 1043. At that time, Johnson did not know that T. S. Eliot had intended to use a line from the novel as his title: "He do the Police in different voices." Note, too, that Astarte shared with Manfred "The quest of hidden knowledge, and a mind/ To comprehend the Universe" (2.2.110–11).

24. Albert D. Hutter, "Dismemberment and Articulation in *Our Mutual Friend*," *Dickens Studies Annual* 11 (1983): 158.

25. Ernest Boll reproduces the number plans (which are bound with the manuscript, now housed at the Pierpont Morgan Library) at the end of his article, "The Plotting of *Our Mutual Friend*," *Modern Philology* 42 (1944): 96–122. They have also been reproduced by Cotsell, *The Companion to Our Mutual Friend*, and by Harry Stone, ed., *Dickens' Working Notes for His Novels* (Chicago, Ill.: University of Chicago Press, 1986).

26. Mary Shelley, "Author's Introduction," *Frankenstein; Or, The Modern Prometheus*, ed. Maurice Hindle (1831; Harmondsworth: Penguin, 1985), p. 54. The example of *Frankenstein* raises the question of whether or not my spectrum might also be framed in terms of poetic and prose soliloquies. As I have been arguing, *Frankenstein* is already a "mixed bag," one that crosses many boundary lines and refuses easy categorization, but, ultimately, I think that the differences between the Creature's and Harmon's soliloquies significant point up periodicity distinctions.

27. "I Feel I Am," *Poems of John Clare's Madness*, ed. Geoffrey Grigson (London: Routledge & Kegan Paul, 1949), line 14.

28. Stewart sees in Harmon's struggle for life "images of the typical Dickensian fever" and observes, "[T]he mystery itself turns on a typical displacement of identity, what the psychologists of the Doppelgänger would call an autoscopic phenomenon" (*Imagination*, pp. 192–93). Although this sense of separation does occur for Harmon in the image of himself as a felled tree, it is not always so clearcut, for "the figure like myself [who was] assailed" could also be Radfoot, his near but denied double. By compounding his doubles and making them doubly ambiguous, Dickens further blurs his Romantic-Victorian boundaries.

29. German Romanticism was also very much concerned with process. We can go back earlier than Hegel to Lessing to find the contention that the search for identity is more joyous than the attainment of it.

30. Jonathon Arac has recently argued that Wordsworth concentrates on "the frustration of the goal" more than the goal itself. See "Bounding Lines: *The Prelude* and Critical Revision," *Boundary* 2 (1979): 31–48.

31. Stewart, "The Secret Life of Death in Dickens," *Dickens Studies Annual* 11 (1983): 179.

32. Two studies which bemoan this shift include Ruth Bernard Yeazell, "Podsnappery, Sexuality, and the English Novel," *Critical Inquiry* 9 (1982): 339–57, and Kucich, "Dickens' Fantastic Rhetoric: The Semantics of Reality and Unreality in *Our Mutual Friend*," *Dickens Studies Annual* 14 (1985): 167–89.

33. As we know, Dickens worked closely with his illustrators, always letting them know his intentions. His letters and memoranda to Stone are on file in the Morgan Library. His remarks for "Miss Riderhood at Home" reveal his attention to detail: "I would like John's false beard and whiskers in the leaving-shop to be more ragged and shaggy."

34. For an alternative reading of this testing process, see Edwin Eigner's unpublished paper, "Shakespeare, Dickens, and the Morality of the Pious Fraud," delivered to The Dickens Universe Consortium on 8 August 1986; this argument also appears in his book, *The Dickens Pantomime* (Berkeley: University of California Press, 1989).

35. For a reading of how the marriage-ending in Dickens can be equated with death, see Alexander Welsh, *The City of Dickens* (Oxford: Clarendon Press, 1971), p. 219.

36. According to H. Philip Bolton, *Our Mutual Friend* exists in forty-one dramatizations. See his *Dickens Dramatized* (London: Mansell, 1986). I have examined three of these versions, none of which includes Harmon's soliloquy: Henry Brougham Farnie, *The Golden Dustman* (first played at Sadler's Wells, London, 16 June 1866; Ms. at Harry Ransom Humanities Research Center, University of Texas at Austin); Harriette R. Shattuck, *Our Mutual Friend: A Comedy, in Four Acts* (Boston: Walter H. Baker, [1879]); and I[sabelle] M. Pagan, *Mr. Boffin's Secretary: A Comedy in Four Acts* (London: J.M. Dent, 1902).

37. *The Letters of Charles Dickens*, ed. Walter Dexter (London: Nonesuch Press, 1938), 3:271. One of the titles that Dickens considered for his novel was "Rokesmith's Forge."

38. Charles Dickens, *A Tale of Two Cities*, ed. George Woodcock (Harmondsmith: Penguin, 1970) Bk. 3, Ch. 15, p. 404. For an amplification of some of my following remarks, see MacKay, "The Rhetoric of Soliloquy in *The French Revolution* and *A Tale of Two Cities*," *Dickens Studies Annual* 12 (1983): 197–207.

39. Stewart sums up the death-by-water motif on p. 248, n.12 of *Imagination*. He further develops this theme in "The Secret Life of Death in Dickens," pp. 177–207, and in his more recent book, *Death Sentences: Styles of Dying in British Fiction* (Cambridge, Mass.: Harvard University Press, 1984).

40. With special regard to this novel, Robert Newsom notes how doubles can blur boundaries of the self. See Newsom, "' To Scatter Dust': Fancy and Authenticity in *Our Mutual Friend*," *Dickens Studies Annual* 8 (1980): 54.

Faith's Incubus: The Influence of Sir Walter Scott's Folklore on "Young Goodman Brown"

Barbara Fass Leavy

This essay proposes to analyze the influence of Sir Walter Scott on Nathaniel Hawthorne's controversial short story, "Young Goodman Brown." Not Scott the novelist, acknowledged by Hawthorne critics to be the American author's favorite writer: parallels between Scott's and Hawthorne's fiction have been drawn.[1] Nor Scott the poet, although Julian Hawthorne's claim that his father had early in his life aspired to write poetry and had regularly read Scott's verse to his children (1: 103) has not to my knowledge inspired any scholarship on the subject.[2] Rather, the following discussion will focus on Scott the folklorist, whose essay on the "Fairies of Popular Superstition," used to introduce the ballad of "Tamlane" in the *Minstrelsy of the Scottish Border*[3] as well as related subjects in the *Letters on Witchcraft and Demonology* appear to have had a profound effect on Hawthorne's story. In both of Scott's works he would have found the argument that Calvinist theology had transformed folklore into demonology, rendering the harmless fairy king and his revels diabolical. In addition, in Scott's essay on the fairies Hawthorne could have read almost the entire text of the Auchinleck version of the medieval poem *Sir Orfeo*, which Scott included among the works related to "Tamlane." I will argue that in the story of Goodman and Faith Brown, Hawthorne works out his own version of the Orpheus and Eurydice myth, sustaining Scott's premise that Puritanism committed crimes not only against the human spirit but folklore and literature themselves.

That "Young Goodman Brown" is particularly saturated with folklore has long been recognized, although scholarship on the subject is in some ways too vague and in others too narrowly defined. The vagueness results from the difficulty in identifying specific sources for Hawthorne's folklore.[4] The narrowness results from the tendency to follow the nineteenth-century American search for native themes and forms: Neil Doubleday has claimed that "Hawthorne's treatment of New England witchcraft is an American Gothic that deserves separate consideration, an answer to the demand for the use of distinctively American materials" (253). Daniel Hoffman, who has written an excellent analysis of "Young Goodman Brown," is another example of a critic reluctant to go outside America to study folklore's "shaping role" in Hawthorne's fiction (p. x).[5] Thus what Bernard Cohen has defined as a "large gap in Hawthorne scholarship," the author's "knowledge and use of legends" (95),[6] remains open because it is tacitly assumed that a nineteenth-century American writer who drew on folklore drew only or mainly on that indigenous to America. Thus the paradoxical situation exists that on one hand it is generally acknowledged that Scott was Hawthorne's favorite writer, while, on the other hand, the renowned British romantic folklorist is overlooked as a potential source for Hawthorne's folklore.

This study of "Young Goodman Brown" and the relationship between its specifically New England locale and the European folklore depicted in Scott's narratives of mortals captured by the otherworld will differ from most criticism of "Young Goodman Brown" in making Goody rather than Goodman Brown the focus of interest. Faith's dream and her plea to her husband that he not leave her vulnerable to its visitation acquire added significance from Scott's essay on the fairies. The matter of narrative emphasis acquires even more complexity from folklore. Is the wife stolen (literally and/or figuratively) by the otherworld, or the husband who fails to rescue her the main character in the story groups to which "Young Goodman Brown" appears to belong? Is it Orpheus or Eurydice who can claim to be the protagonist of the renowned myth and related folklore—or do they share the focus of interest? The ballad of "Tamlane" is particularly telling on this point, as will be seen, and Hawthorne seems to have picked up its implications. In any event, if Faith rather than her husband dominates this essay, it is because folklore grants her a more significant role than she seems usually to play.[7]

I.

The world's folklore is replete with stories of mortals abducted by supernatural folk and carried to the otherworld, and such tales are as ambiguous and seductive as those magic realms in which the humans find themselves. In his *Ministrelsy*, Scott not only recounts several instances of wives spirited away from their husbands, but expresses a keen awareness that most fail to rescue their wives from the otherworld. He also provides a theoretical framework to help account for such failure, explaining how the fairies became thought of as demons (particularly after the Reformation):

> The fulminations of the church were . . . early directed against those who consulted or consorted with the Fairies; and, according to the inquisitorial logic, the innocuous choristers of Oberon and Titania were, without remorse, confounded with the sable inhabitants of the orthodox Gehennim; while the rings, which marked their revels, were assimilated to the blasted sward on which the witches held their infernal sabbath.[8]
>
> (2:146)

Such passages link the introduction to "Tamlane" to Scott's *Letters on Witchcraft and Demonology*, which, as will be seen, virtually describes (and may be a source for) the landscape which Goodman Brown traverses in his fateful journey into the forest.

Despite Scott's division of fairy lore into categories that, for example, distinguish popular narratives from Renaissance romances that treat fairy themes, what emerges from his classifications are the common threads that unite various fictions. Thus he would have instructed Hawthorne on a point argued in recent years by the folklorist Richard Dorson: "By its very nature the study of folklore requires an international breadth of vision . . . One extended family of water goblins unites the Japanese kappa with the Scottish kelpie" (1). In establishing such family relationships, Scott also would have made it possible for Hawthorne to synthesize the diverse influences of an environment that may have been chauvinistically American in its emphasis, with an education that still encouraged a wider scope, including classical mythology and European literature. It may have been because of Scott that Hawthorne could compare the Auchinleck version of *Sir Orfeo* with the classical versions of Orpheus's quest, could recognize in the medieval poem a mixture of folklore, classical mythology, and demonology that has occupied medievalists to this day.[9] And it was probably because of Scott that Hawthorne would have recognized that America provided a unique physical and social environment for the story of the wife who strays into an otherworld from which her husband cannot or will not retrieve her.

It is Faith's dream that supplies one of the most striking parallels between "Young Goodman Brown" and *Sir Orfeo*. As Scott summarizes the latter, "Heurodis dreams that she is accosted by the King of Fairies . . . She relates her dream to her husband, who resolves to accompany her [to fairyland] and attempt her rescue'' (2:138–39). Goody Brown too informs her husband that she has suffered a fearful dream and he ruminates on it soon thereafter: '' 'Poor little Faith' thought he, for his heart smote him. 'What a wretch am I, to leave her on such an errand! She talks of dreams, too. Methought, as she spoke, there was trouble in her face, as if a dream had warned her what work is to be done to-night' '' (75).[10]

But, unlike Orfeo, Goodman Brown pays little heed to his wife's dream. True, Faith has been much vaguer than her counterpart in *Sir Orfeo:* where Heurodis prophesies for her husband the dangers that await her, Faith is merely suggestive: "A lone woman is troubled with such dreams and such thoughts, that she's afeard of herself, sometimes" (74). Each wife has appealed—directly or indirectly—to her husband for protection, Faith's appeal couched in the suggestive language critics have not failed to heed in exploring the sexual themes in the tale. She asks him to "sleep in [his] own bed" that night, and implores, "Pray tarry with me this night, dear husband, of all nights in the year" (74). Be that as it may, both Orfeo (initially) and Goodman Brown (ultimately) fail the wives who depend upon their protection. If Hawthorne is merely allusive where the *Orfeo* poet is precise, it is because he is often deliberately ambiguous where other authors are explicit. In addition, what is thematically significant in Hawthorne's story is that he has redefined that failure on the husband's part to which Scott's essay draws explicit attention. Whereas many husbands cannot muster the strength necessary to retrieve their wives from the otherworld, Brown symbolically fails his wife by believing first, that she has gone there, and, second, that she has done so because of her own sinful will.[11]

Despite this apparent difference—which is only apparent, because folklore suggests that indeed the man's failure is essentially a psychological one and, therefore, Brown bears close comparison to the husbands of other narratives—the dreams of Heurodis and Faith establish a crucial connection between Hawthorne's story and *Orfeo*. Scott's influence on Hawthorne points to that large body of folklore concerning the demon figure of the incubus who lies behind the dreams of Heurodis and, quite possibly, Faith. Recognizing Scott's influence will not only illuminate the folklore but highlight the dream-world of Faith, and make plausible the argument that, according to the lore and literature with which Scott and Hawthorne were familiar, the allusions of Faith to her troubling dreams are consistent with her presence at a witches' sabbath, whether in reality or only in her husband's mind.

To place ''Young Goodman Brown'' in a landscape created for Hawthorne in large part by Scott is paradoxically to be confronted with an apparent difference between the writers over the question of whether America possessed a unique tradition concerning the supernatural. Yet within this difference is an important clue to Scott's influence on Hawthorne and the way in which the British writer would have influenced the American's way of interpreting the folklore to which both "Tamlane" and "Young Goodman Brown" belong. According to Scott's position, Calvinist theology had a profound effect on popular superstitions. In contrast, Hawthorne contended that New England lacked a genuine sense of the supernatural. In the end, however, both authors make the same point: that in their time the magic as well as the profound symbolism potentialized by the supernatural had not only been undermined but virtually destroyed.

Hawthorne's most extensive statement on this subject can be found in his 1847 review of John Greenleaf Whittier's *The Supernaturalism of New England,* in which he had objected to the way in which America had debased the supernatural in its preoccupation with materialism. The emphasis on common realism had caused a ghost to "so [mingle] with daily life, that we scarcely perceive him to be a ghost at all. If he indeed comes from the spiritual world, it is because he has been ejected with disgrace on account of the essential and inveterate earthiness of his substance" (Whittier, 132). There is, maintains Hawthorne, no special New England supernaturalism, by which he means that his part of the country has made no positive contribution to the folklore it inherited from Europe. It is his language and imagery, strikingly similar to that of Scott's contrary view (both quoted below), that reveal how years after the publication of "Young Goodman Brown," Hawthorne remained preoccupied with its themes and setting, both of which appear to be firmly attached in his mind to the entire subject of folklore.

In disclaiming that there is anything unique about New England supernaturalism, Hawthorne writes:

> The contrary is rather remarkably the fact; the forest-life of the first settlers, and their intercourse with the Indians, have really engrafted nothing upon the mythology which they brought with them from England—at least, we know of nothing. . . . We should naturally look for something duskier and grander in the ghostly legends of a wild country, than could be expected in a state of society where even dreams are covered with the dust of old conventionalisms. But, if there be any peculiarity, it is, that our superstitions have a more sordid, grimy, and material aspect, than they bore in the clime from which they were transplanted. (Whittier, 131)

What Hawthorne proposes to look for, Scott would have claimed to have found. He agrees with Hawthorne insofar as he recognizes in the New England landscape a perfect setting for old superstitions to flourish. Scott disagreed only in the importance he places upon this feature as adding its special touch to the American treatment of folk material. He writes that the Calvinists brought with them "the same zeal for religion and strict morality which everywhere distinguished them."

> Unfortunately, they were not wise according to their zeal, but entertained a proneness to believe in supernatural and direct personal intercourse between the devil and his vassals, an error to which, as we have endeavored to show, their brethren in Europe had from the beginning been peculiarly subject. *In a country imperfectly cultivated, and where the partially improved spots were embosomed in inaccessible forests, inhabited by numerous tribes of savages, it was natural that a disposition to superstition should rather gain than lose ground, and that to other dangers and horrors with which they were surrounded, the colonists should have added fears of the devil,* not merely as the Evil Principle tempting human nature to sin, and thus endangering our salvation, but as combined with sorcerers and witches to inflict death and torture upon children and others.[12]
>
> (*Letters* 222; emphasis added.)

Scott's mixture of an imperfectly cultivated landscape, fear of Indians, and fear of the devil is precisely what Goodman Brown experiences when he first enters the forest in his rendezvous with evil:

> the traveller knows not who may be concealed by the innumerable trunks and the thick boughs overhead; so that, with lonely footsteps, he may yet be passing through an unseen multitude. "There may be a devilish Indian behind every tree," said Goodman Brown to himself; and he glanced fearfully behind him, as he added, "What if the devil himself should be at my very elbow!"
>
> (75)

To move from "Young Goodman Brown" back to Scott's writings and forward again to Hawthorne's review of Whittier is to recognize that Hawthorne objected to more than a coarse materialism which defeated the imaginative apprehension of the supernatural. The very uniqueness which Scott pointed to in the New England temperament was the quality from which Hawthorne recoiled, the dour Puritanism that blighted the lives of so many of his characters, and his way of recoiling was not to repudiate New England demonology so much as to deny any claims for uniqueness. Insofar as intercourse with the wildnerness and with Indians led to nothing more than an association of these tribes with the devil's followers, to that extent American belief undermined the sources of folklore themselves. For it is the very transformation of folklore into demonology, a process that Scott had attributed to the Protestant reformers in his introduction to "Tamlane," that helps feed Hawthorne's conception of "Young Goodman Brown." And in his understanding of how native themes interacted with traditional beliefs, Hawthorne found in Scott a basic mentor.

With the help of Scott's introduction to "Tamlane," "Young Goodman Brown" can be placed within the frame of some widely distributed groups of folktales, most involving a figure to whom the general name "demon lover" can be assigned. It was, again, one of Scott's purposes to show the connections among the fairy king of popular lore, the Pluto of ancient antiquity, the Oberon of Shakespeare's play, and the devil worshipped at witches' sabbaths. The ballad of "Tamlane" is itself a good starting point for looking at what Hawthorne could make of these connections.

Janet, according to the poem, becomes pregnant by a "wee wee man," an elf who will soon prove to be a mortal captive in fairyland, thrall to the Queen of the Fairies and possessed of magic powers while living the supernatural life. But the time has come when Tamlane must be offered up by the fairies as their tithe to hell. To avoid this permanent damnation, he turns for help to the mother of his child. In saving him, Janet also achieves her own freedom from evil, for in each other's love they will find release—or so the ballad implies—from the deviant impulses that made them susceptible to diabolical seduction in the first place. And so Janet reclaims Tamlane by holding fast to him as he turns in her arms to an adder, a burning faggot, a red-hot iron, a toad, an eel, and, finally, in a progression that renders him increasingly harmless, a dove, a swan, and a naked man, reborn to the real world:

> They shaped him in her arms at last,
> A mother-naked man:
> She wrapt him in her green mantle,
> And saw her true love wan!
> (2:204)

There are some unusual features to this story also important in "Young Goodman Brown." First, in most tales of humans taken by the fairies and in need of rescue, it is usually either the man or the woman who is in trouble. However reciprocal the help on some symbolic level, it is rarely found in the narrative itself. In "Tamlane," as in "Young Goodman Brown," both man and woman, independently, become prey to the supernatural realm. In Hawthorne's story it is a devil who, ironically, reveals to them their mutual need: "Depending upon one another's hearts, ye had still hoped, that virtue were not all a dream. Now are ye undeceived'' (88). And in the scene that follows, their diabolical ''communion'' is marked by just the opposite of what such affinity implies, for the results of their welcome ''to the communion of [their] race'' is their separateness, their alienation from each other:

> The husband cast one look at his pale wife, and Faith at him. What polluted wretches would the next glance shew them to each other, shuddering alike at what they disclosed and what they saw.
> ''Faith! Faith!'' cried the husband. ''Look up to Heaven, and resist the Wicked One.''

(88)

But in this exhortation to his wife, there is no gesture on Brown's part towards her. Not all critics, of course, would agree that Faith was in need of her husband's help, for many have insisted that it is only the perverted fancy of her wayward husband that has placed her at the unholy rite. It is he who has projected upon her what Frederick Crews has designated his own ''nastiness'' (102). But to argue this is to ignore Faith's own earlier plea to her husband that if he leaves her alone that night, he also leaves her vulnerable to fearful influences and, despite any ambiguity created by Hawthorne's suggestion that Goodman Brown's experiences in the forest may be but a dream, Faith's dream is not only real but alarms her. The only hope for this couple is in their mutual love and support. Goodman Brown's alienation from his wife, however, leaves his bride to find her help, if she can, without any aid from him.

Brown's failure leads to another aspect of the Tamlane pattern also important in ''Young Goodman Brown.'' Tamlane specifically appeals to Janet for release from fairyland. While she literally holds on to him, he symbolically clings to her, and any who follow Crews in finding a maternal theme in Brown's relationship to Faith will be struck by Tamlane's transformation in Janet's arms to a ''mother-naked man,'' wrapped in ''her green mantle.'' Similarly, Goodman Brown undertakes his excursion into the forest with the confident assumption that Faith will provide ultimate safety from whatever he encounters there, that he, too, can hold on to her: ''Well; she's a blessed angel on earth; and after this one night, I'll cling to her skirts and follow her to Heaven'' (75).

That Janet and Faith provide the help needed for their men's redemption is, of course, nothing new in the world of folklore. Many a young woman's courage and fidelity releases some hero from enchantment or from the beast form sorcery has compelled him to assume. Folktales similarly tell of women who, victims of enchantment, seek the resourcefulness of some hero to rescue them from the fairies, or to release them from some loathsome shape. There are, indeed, female Tamlanes who turn to frightful beasts and shapes in the arms of their lovers, who cannot be redeemed unless these men can overcome their revulsion and hold them fast or bestow on them the disenchanting kiss(es).[13] A comparison of what would appear to be complementary folklore patterns, however, reveals that women usually succeed in saving their men, whereas failure on the man's part is as common in such tales as it is in those narratives that form variants of the Orpheus myth. Too often the man cannot overcome the anxiety or the horror he experiences as he attempts to rescue his mate.

This folk motif adds a compelling dimension to Goodman Brown's misogyny at the end of the story and to what can be assumed to be its devastating effects on his wife Faith, especially if his emotional neglect of her leaves her the victim of evil powers she had already hinted at. Edward Jayne has noted that the "way Faith is left behind, waving from her doorway, offers complex symbolization which explains his final abandonment of her on moral grounds at the story's end" (104). Her frightful dreamworld can be projected onto the forest in which witches assemble to worship the fairy folk now deemed devils. And so the voice Brown hears in the forest and suspects is his wife's is described in such a way as to combine in its tone and imagery Faith's temptation, her need for help, and the desertion that foreshadows the conclusion of Hawthorne's tale: "There was one voice, of a young woman, uttering lamentations, yet with an uncertain sorrow, and entreating for some favor, which, perhaps, it would grieve her to obtain. And all the unseen multitude, both saints and sinners seemed to encourage her onward" (82).

Again, Scott was particularly aware of the difference between success and failure in the human attempt to retrieve a mate from the alien otherworld. He commments on *Sir Orfeo,* a work in which, he says, "Gothic mythology [had been] engrafted on the fables of Greece" (2:138), describing how the minstrel had so charmed the fairy king that the latter had surrendered Heurodis, the married pair now returning safely to Winchester, where the king resumed his duties with his wife safely beside him. Scott deems this ending "less pathetic indeed, but more pleasing, than that of the classical story" (2:144). What lends the classical version its pathos, as Hawthorne, an excellent Latin scholar at Bowdoin, was certain to have understood, was more than Orpheus's inability to heed the injunction that in their journey back to the world he was not to look back at his wife. Virgil had also allowed Eurydice a lament that is both a mournful cry over her perpetual imprisonment in the world of shades and a reproach to her husband.[14]

Eurydice's lament makes it possible to link the classical myth to a tradition recorded by Scott, who prefaces the brief story by again revealing his keen awareness that some mortals fail to rescue their spouses from the otherworld: "The catastrophe of *Tamlane* terminated more successfully than that of other attempts, which tradition still records" (2:180). The account that follows deserves quoting in full, for, despite some obvious differences, its setting, main narrative line, as well as its imagery bear a striking resemblance to "Young Goodman Brown":

> The wife of a farmer in Lothian had been carried off by the Fairies, and, during the year of probation, repeatedly appeared on Sunday, in the midst of her children, combing their hair. On one of these occasions she was accosted by her husband; when she related to him the unfortunate event which had separated them, instructed him by what means he might win her, and exhorted him to exert all his courage, since her temporal and eternal happiness depended on the success of his attempt. The farmer, who ardently loved his wife, set out on Hallowe'en, and, in the midst of a plot of furze, waited impatiently for the procession of the Fairies. At the ringing of the Fairy bridles, and the wild unearthly sound which accompanied the calvacade, his heart failed him, and he suffered the ghostly train to pass by without interruption. When the last had rode past, the whole troop vanished, with loud shouts of laughter and exultation; among which he plainly discovered the voice of his wife, lamenting that he had lost her forever.
>
> (2:180–81)

In contrast to the aristocrat Orfeo, the Lothian farmer is an ordinary man who could easily lend himself to the psychological portrait of Goodman Brown. The analogy that would have interested Scott is that of the farmer's wife's dwelling with the fairies and Faith's participation in a witches' sabbath. That such an analogy is plausible is, again, part of Scott's purpose in writing his introduction to "Tamlane," since he attacks the Reformers' equation of fairyland with the devil's domain. Indeed, *Sir Orfeo* is followed in Scott's essay by the section in which the writer turns his attention to how the Christians had transformed the fairies into demons, and to the intensification of the moral revulsion against them which occurred after the Reformation, when countless so-called witches were executed for no more serious charge than consorting with what Scott insists on calling the fairies. Following this discussion, Scott turns to stories of the fairies of the British Isles, and his accounts reveal his belief that such lore has been tainted by demonology. Among the stories he relates is that of the farmer of Lothian.

Once the story pattern characterized by the Orpheus myth is combined with demonology, then the basis for the husband's failure is not some error or failure of will alone, but the kind of moral revulsion experienced by Goodman Brown. A story from Iceland, not (to my knowledge) familiar to Scott or to Hawthorne, spells out the psychological mechanism that both authors were likely to have recognized as operating in the farmer of Lothian. William A. Craigie tells how a farmer's daughter was carried off by elves and how her father sought for her with the help of a priest:

> he saw one woman, who had a face of bluish colour, with a white cross on her forehead. The priest asked him how he liked the one with the cross. "Not well," said he. "Yet this woman is your daughter," said the priest, "and I shall get her, if you wish, but she has now become like a troll from living with these folk." The man said that he did not wish it.
>
> (151)

Katharine Briggs has commented on this story that it "was love that had failed here rather than courage, but presumably the girl had eaten fairy food and would return to them without her soul. The cross on her forehead, however, would seem to show that her baptism had still some power to protect her" (112). That she might still be saved makes all the more terrifying her father's rejection of her (probably on more grounds than Briggs suggests), and implies the triumph of evil. In the story of the Lothian farmer, the supernatural folk react to the husband's paralysis of will with triumph: "the whole troop vanished, with loud shouts of laughter and exultation."

Similarly, when Goodman Brown virtually repudiates Faith by assuming that the pink ribbon he sees is a sign of her guilt, the woods resound with demonic merriment,

> while, sometimes, the wind tolled like a distant church bell, and sometimes gave a broad roar around the traveller, as if all Nature were laughing him to scorn. But he was himself the chief horror of the scene, and shrank not from its other horrors. "Ha! ha! ha!" roared Goodman Brown when the wind laughed at him. "Let us hear which will laugh loudest!"
>
> (83)

As for the farmer's wife, whose voice is heard "lamenting that he had lost her forever," it has already been noted that Goodman Brown had heard a woman's voice "uttering lamentations," and already argued that this scene foreshadows the end of the story. The final grief of Faith is, of course, never heard in the tale, for her husband's revulsion towards her would make him deaf to it.

One reader of this essay has reminded me that Faith is not only an unloved wife, but a mother and a survivor to the end of "Young Goodman Brown." That this is so suggests the insight Hawthorne brought to folklore, recognizing as a concommitant to the typical weakness of the male folklore character a strength on the part of the female character. If—to draw on related folk-lore—Brown remains a psychological "frog," it is not because Faith cannot bestow the redeeming kiss. Nonetheless, Faith is deprived of the loving husband and father implied in the disenchanted Tamlanes of folk narratives.

Hawthorne was well aware that in these stories men often fail their wives out of moral and psychological cowardice. In his review of Whittier's *Supernaturalism of New England,* he singles out for praise the ballad "New Wife and the Old," in which a bridegroom is haunted by a demon in the form of his first, dead wife, so that his new marriage is blighted. In three stanzas of the ballad, the wife's purity is compared to the husband's guilty horror. It is the contrast between the possibility of connubial comfort and the man's fearful alienation from his wife that must have impressed itself on Hawthorne, for he had already used such images in "Young Goodman Brown" and in his sketch, "The Haunted Mind."

> Broken words of cheer he saith,
> But his dark lip quivereth,
> And as o'er the Past he thinketh,
> From his young wife's arms he shrinketh;
> Can those soft arms round him lie,
> Underneath his dead wife's eye.
>
> She her fair young head can rest
> Soothed and child-like on his breast,
> And in trustful innocence
> Draw new strength and courage thence;
> He, the proud man, feels within
> But the *cowardice* of Sin!
>
> She can murmur in her thought
> Simple prayers her mother taught,
> And His blessed angels call,
> Whose great love is over all;
> He, alone, in prayerless pride,
> Meets the dark Past at her side!
> (Whittier, 70–71; emphasis added)

When Brown hesitates briefly before commencing his journey in the forest, he thinks of returning to his wife and the bed she had implored him not to leave her alone in: "And what calm sleep would be his that very night, which was to have been spent so wickedly, but so purely and sweetly now, in the arms of Faith!'' (80–81). Brown, however, is completely self-centered in his musings; it is only his own plight that concerns him, and there is no consideration that in leaving Faith he has helped to destroy the very innocence upon which he feels dependent.

Insofar as Goodman Brown can be found in the company of those husbands (and fathers and sometimes brothers) who fail to retrieve their womenfolk from the otherworld, and Faith among the wives who willingly or unwillingly find themselves in its power, ''Young Goodman Brown'' can be classified with at least two groups of folktales. One of these involves what the folklorists label the ''Man on a Quest for his Lost Wife'' (Type 400); the other, ''The Danced-out Shoes,'' tells of a princess's ''nightly visit to the supernatural being'' (Type 306).[15] What these two types have in common is the sojourn of the female in the otherworld, often to join a demon lover, and the travels to this land of the hero who wishes, but often fails, to retrieve her for his world.

It can, of course, be argued that Goodman Brown is not searching for Faith, that his own evil purposes draw him to the forest, and that until he finds what he thinks is evidence of her presence there, he has no idea that he has ''lost'' her to Satan's crew. But Hawthorne is purposely vague about Goodman Brown's specific errand that fateful night, so that while it is true that there is no quest for his stolen wife, neither is his sojourn so clearly spelled out as to work directly against such a motif. Critics have found Hawthorne's purposeful vagueness on this point thematically significant. Crews, for example, argues that a ''causal connection appears to subsist between Brown's mysterious rendezvous with the Devil and his flight from his wife's embraces'' (100). He is not the only one to assert that the couple has been symbolically separated from the beginning of the tale: Michael Colacurcio has claimed that what ''determines Brown's practical belief in Faith and in all 'other' goodness is the subconscious effort of his own dark (if ambivalent) reasons for being in the forest, reinforced no doubt by the violence of his blasphemous nihilism'' (288). For Robert Cochran it is not Brown's nihilism but his idealism that effectively costs him his wife, his ''belief that his Faith was 'a blessed angel on earth,' '' an idea ''not only hopelessly naive, but hopelessly demanding'' (154). Crews believes that Brown has unconsciously transformed Faith into an idealized mother, nurturing a ''transparently filial desire to 'cling to her skirts and follow her to heaven.' A bridegroom with such notions is well prepared for an appointment with the Devil'' (105–06). And perhaps he was well prepared to discover his wife has one as well. What such interpretations have in common is the assumption that the marital relationship in "Young Goodman Brown" will be defined *after* the groom's mysterious sojourn, and that what exists before is a couple alienated from each other even if neither fully comprehends how or why. Faith's fears on that night may have to do with an uneasiness rising to consciousness that her husband is withdrawing from her. Brown chides her: "What, my sweet, pretty wife, dost thou doubt me already, and we but three months married!" (74).

The objection may also be raised that Faith has, in fact, begged her husband to stay with her and that he is, in fact, fleeing her, not searching for her. Such a contradiction is, however, very much a part of the structure of Type 400 tales. For many of the stories in this group, it is not necessary that the wife wishes to leave her husband, but only that, through some error on his part, he has lost her. Among the motifs common in such tales are those concerning the breaking of some taboo upon which the marriage rests (Type 400 tales reverse the genders in the Cupid-Psyche pattern), so that it is a reluctant wife who leaves her husband and forces him to embark on a quest to win her back, often from a former lover whose demon status is comparable to the devils worshipped at witches' sabbaths. In the most profound sense—one that Hawthorne would have recognized—Brown has indeed broken a taboo in leaving his wife behind for what may have been some last wicked fling forbidden to all pious men, but even more so to married ones. So long as Brown pushes his wife away from him, to that extent is the couple separated and the journey into the forest not so different from deliberate quests for wives lost to demon forces in comparable tales.

The parallels between "Young Goodman Brown" and *Sir Orfeo* suggest that Hawthorne had a precedent for his conception. Because the medieval poem can be traced to classical mythology, critics assume that Orfeo's long sojourn in the forest involves a search *for* Heurodis. But this is not necessarily the case.[16] A grief-stricken, maddened Orfeo lives the life of a wild man in the woods until, one day, he has a chance meeting with the fairy host and thereby discovers the whereabout of his wife. Scott underscores the chance nature of Orfeo's discovery, in consequence of which Orfeo "pursues the hawking damsels. . . . They enter a rock, the king continues the pursuit, and arrives at Fairy-Land" (2: 142). Scott's final comment has to do with the parallels between "this romantic legend" and "popular tradition," for the Land of the Fairies is "placed in the wilderness" (2: 144–45). In short, in both *Sir Orfeo* and "Young Goodman Brown," the husbands are sojourning in the forest, neither experiencing any thought of meeting his wife there until the accidental meeting reveals her presence and each enters the domain of the otherworld. In one instance the meeting will result in the wife's rescue; in the other, in her symbolic abandonment. Again, it should be evident by now that folklore stresses the psychological dimension of the husband's response to his wife, and in the context of popular narratives, whether Faith is actually present at a sabbath or whether she only appears so as the result of the devil's deceit (that is, in her husband's perverted fancy) does not so much demand critical resolution as a recognition of how Hawthorne was able to exploit folklore to create this ambiguity.

Insofar as Faith is even imagined to be at the witches' revels, "Young Goodman Brown" can also be placed in the folktale group concerning the young woman whose nightly journeys to the otherworld arouse the suspicion of her family, who arrange to have her followed and thereby discover the secret of her regular absences. In this widespread story type there is a variety that comes from India (Type 306A) in which a wife leaves her husband each evening, ostensibly to return to her parents' home, in reality to join a demon king and spend the night at his revels. Though the Indian variants probably had no direct influence on Hawthorne, they form a connection between two folklore patterns that interact in "Young Goodman Brown." On the one side is the Orpheus story; in the Indian tales, the husband who seeks his lost wife uses his musical skills to convince the ruler of the otherworld to relinquish her. On the other is a common tenet in European witchcraft lore, that wives left their husbands sleeping unawares while they attended witches' sabbaths, wooden effigies sometimes left in their stead in the event that the spouse should awaken.[17]

The fantasies of such women, of course, are erotic in nature, but only a few critics of "Young Goodman Brown" have appreciated that Faith's plea to her husband to remain in their bed the night of his journey speaks to her sensuality. Such overt eroticism being frowned upon in her society, there is a virtual split between Faith the innocent wife and Faith as her husband's sexual partner. As Roy R. Male has written, in "the town daylight . . . Faith is simple and innocuous." But "Faith and her pink ribbon, so pure in the sunlight, are fiendish at night. There is just a faint suggestion of the transition at sunset, when Faith whispers softly to Brown, 'tarry with me' " (77). To confuse the innocent and the fiendish, as the Reformers—according to Scott—confuse the fairies with devils, is, however, to create in Faith a reverse Duessa, depicting as foul what less sin-ridden and less superstitious folk would perceive as fair.[18] But whereas in much folklore the deviant women who sought in forbidden realms the pleasures offered there could be redeemed by strong and persistent men who followed them in order to bring them back to the virtuous life, those men obsessed with evil rejected the sinner, at best through a dour misogyny such as Brown's, at worst by deliberately leaving them in the demonic realm or by destroying them at the gallows or the stake.

As James Lynch has noted, Hawthorne uses folklore surrounding the devil for his own psychological ends in fiction (113). Faith is indeed a flesh-and-blood woman, not an angel, and insofar as fallen man and woman are not perfect and need each other's love and support, that far Faith depends on the protection of her husband as a bulwark against her own potential waywardness. If Brown fails her, she will be more vulnerable to the kind of supernatural lover she may have hinted at in her plea that he remain that night in their bed instead of setting off without her. Included in the catalog of such lovers in Scott's introduction to "Tamlane"—the Plutos, the Oberons, the generalized fairy kings of popular lore—is the incubus, the demon whose way of stealing women for the otherworld is to be present in their dreams, turning their erotic fantasies into the nightmares to which the name of this demonic invader was also attached.

II

The incubus is, I suggest, the source and subject of Faith's dream. The term "incubus" applies to two sets of beliefs, sometimes but not always combined: "Incubus was for centuries the popular term for a nightmare: it meant a demon or fiend who seduced women at night during their sleep" (Liddon and Hawkins, 58). Both the nightmare and the sexual union derive from beliefs prevalent in the Puritan culture of "Young Goodman Brown." G. L. Kittredge analyzes the demon lovers termed incubi in his *Witchcraft in Old and New England* but omits from his discussion the relationship of the incubus to a particular variety of bad dream: the nightmare. The connection of folk beliefs concerning demon lovers with dream experience involves much theorizing and controversy over the nature of dreams themselves. "Incubus" denotes a particular kind of nightmare in which the sleeper experiences a crushing weight on his or her body and the feeling of suffocation. The source of the oppression thus victimizes the sleeper and is often conceived of as a human-appearing demon (sometimes ugly, sometimes beautiful) or even an animal.[19] Several treatises on the incubus/nightmare appeared in the early nineteenth century, and many explanations—from physiological to what would now be called psychological—were offered to account for the terrifying dream.[20]

Scott's *Letters on Witchcraft and Demonology* (1830) reflect the then current beliefs, although in the first of them he uses another term for incubus when he describes

> the disorder called Ephialtes, or nightmare, or indeed any other external impression upon our organs in sleep, which the patient's morbid imagination may introduce into the dream preceding the swoon. In the nightmare an oppression and suffocation is felt, and our fancy instantly conjures up a spectre to be on our bosom.
>
> (28)

He presents an extensive account of how one nightmare hag plagued her victim. But in the introduction to ''Tamlane,'' the incubus appears as a variety of demon lover. Scott quotes from Dunbar to describe ''Pluto that elricke incubus / In cloke of grene, his court suit in sable'' (2: 138); and from a collection of Scottish poems to depict the ''King of Pharie and his court, with the Elf Queen'' and ''many elfish incubus'' (2: 180). The latter passage immediately precedes the story of the farmer of Lothian, conceivably reinforcing any connection Hawthorne might make between incubus lore and the theme of the husband who fails to retrieve his wife from the otherworld.

From other reading, Hawthorne would have learned more about the incubus, both as nightmare demon and as demon lover. Both Byron in ''The Vision of Judgment'' and Milton in *Paradise Lost* write of Asmodeus, who, in the Apocryphal Book of Tobit destroys seven husbands of Sara, until, according to Milton, the odor of fish ''drove him, though enamor'd from the Spouse / Of Tobit's Son'' (IV, 170–71). Byron specifically refers to Asmodeus as an incubus (Stanza LXXXV). In Milton, Hawthorne would read that the purpose of the demon's attention was the moral degradation of the victim, to whom he could appear in the form of man or woman to lead the mortal to sin. And in Shakespeare's *Romeo and Juliet,* Hawthorne would find the incubus portrayed in its androgynous form as demon lover and suffocating nightmare, who tormented horses as well as humans:

> This is the hag, when maids lie on their backs,
> That presses them and learns them first to bear,
> Making them women of good carriage.
>
> (1. 4, 88–94)

These literary images would parallel the treatment of the incubus in Cotton Mather's *Wonders of the Invisible World*. That devils tempt man everywhere to sin, especially in those places where sensuous pleasures are available, and that beds are a location where men are particularly vulnerable to temptation is a point of doctrine for Mather, who writes that the "Devil makes his Witches to dream strange things of themselves and others, which are not so" (279). There were certain women "that imagined they rode upon Beasts in the Night, and that they had *Diana* and *Herodius* in company" with them. "Satan transforms himself into the likeness of divers Persons, and deludes the Souls that are his Captives with Dreams and Fancies" (279). Such women are converted by the devil and, in turn, torment men in the manner of the nightmare hag. According to Mather, one John Louder testified that after a quarrel with Bridget Bishop, he went to bed, and "did awake in the Night by Moonlight, and did see clearly the likeness of this Woman grievously oppressing him; in which miserable condition she held him, unable to help himself, till near Day" (135), and Bernard Peache similarly swore that Susan Martin had taken hold of his feet, and "drawing his Body up into an Heap, she lay upon him near Two Hours; in all which time he could neither speak nor stir" (141).

There are some differences to be noted between Scott's treatment of this material and its treatment by Mather and Hawthorne. Scott's depiction of the nightmare hag in his first *Letter* on witchcraft omits all of the erotic connotations save those associated with the very name of "Ephialtes," even though popular superstition concerning the incubus as demon lover involved lurid descriptions of sexual relations between humans and devils. Perhaps some reticence constrained Scott. In the description of the New England landscape, on which, I have argued, Hawthorne probably drew for his setting of "Young Goodman Brown," Scott remarks on the "direct personal intercourse between the devil and his vessels," and lest it should be thought that his term is but a neutral one depicting contact, tells of the "Evil Principle tempting human nature to sin" (*Letters* 222). Nonetheless, Scott begins with a naturalistic explanation for the nightmare, the physical sensation of being crushed, and describes how the fancy provides the source of the oppression. Some physicians in the nineteenth century, such as John Waller in his *Treatise on the Incubus or Night-Mare* (1816), followed in the path of Chaucer's Pertelote in prescribing physics or advising on changes in diet to avoid the nightmare dream. Scott emphasizes psychology more than does Waller as he links physical symptoms to the dreamer's imagination, but his skepticism perhaps places him more squarely in the rationalists' camp than in the realm inhabited by Mather and Hawthorne.

Hawthorne anticipates theories of the nightmare dream that were to be articulated much later in Ernest Jones's treatise on the incubus, *Nightmares,*

Witches, and Demons, influenced by Freud's theories of repression. In some of Hawthorne's tales and sketches the fiend is a projection outward of the usually well-hidden feelings and desires of the dreamer: that which is usually buried emerges during those times and places Mather had already described as making man particularly prone to sin. In "The Haunted Mind" (1835) Hawthorne describes, if he does not actually name, repression:

> In the depths of every heart, there is a tomb and a dungeon, though the lights, the music, and revelry above may cause us to forget their existence, and the buried ones, or prisoners whom they hide. But sometimes, and oftenest at midnight, those dark receptacles are flung wide open.
>
> (*Tales* 201–02)

It is at this time that the dreamer is rendered vulnerable to the fiends within and, as a consequence, without:

> Well for the wakeful one, if riotously miserable, a fiercer tribe do not surround him, the devils of a guilty heart, that beholds its hell within itself. What if Remorse should assume features of an injured friend? *What if the fiend should come in women's garments, with a pale beauty among sin and desolation, and lie down by your side?* What if he should stand at your bed's foot, in the likeness of a corpse, with a blood stain upon the shroud? Sufficient without such guilt, is this *nightmare* of the soul; this *heavy, heavy* sinking of the spirits; this wintry gloom about the heart; this indistinct horror of the mind, blending itself with the darkness of the chamber.
>
> (*Tales* 202–03; emphasis added.)

Faith's imploring of her husband that he remain with her to dispel the effects of her bad dreams, or prevent the visitations that will plague her thoughts without him at her side, renders "The Haunted Mind" particularly suggestive. For in this sketch can be found not only the concept of the nightmare as an erotic experience and, in its heaviness, an emotionally suffocating one, but the counter idea that the dreamer might be protected by a spouse who represents a more innocent, sanctioned relationship:

> As your head falls back upon the pillow, you think—in a whisper be it spoken—how pleasant in these night solitudes, would be the rise and fall of a softer breathing than your own, the slight pressure of a tenderer bosom, the quiet throb of a purer heart, imparting its peacefulness to your troubled one, as if the fond sleeper were involving you in her dream.
>
> (*Tales* 203)

Given the belief that the incubus visitation crushed the tortured sleeper, it can hardly be mere chance that Hawthorne writes of the "slight pressure of a tenderer bosom,'' of the supportive, protective spouse. Ironically, Brown's last-minute thought that he might be home with his wife, enjoying the "calm sleep [that] would be his that very night, which was to have been spent so wickedly, but so purely and sweetly now, in the arms of Faith,'' negates the hopefulness of "The Haunted Mind,'' for not he but Faith is the spouse troubled by the fearful dreams. His initial departure, despite her entreaties, foreshadows his failure to help her, and hence her inability to help him.

Little has been said in the critical literature about Faith's dream and little importance has been attributed to it. Usually it is dismissed by interpreters of the story as a mere presentiment concerning her husband's sojourn on that regrettable night and its dire effects. Even in Rita Gollin's book devoted entirely to Hawthorne's interest in dreams, there is only a glance at Faith's with the suggestion that the husband and wife may be experiencing a shared dream (124). Those critics who do pay attention to the overtly erotic invitation Faith extends Goodman Brown as she asks him to tarry with her that night use their arguments only to emphasize the sexual content of Hawthorne's theme, to identify the nature of the human sin that overcomes the bridegroom who leaves his wife to her fearful thoughts. That is, Goodman Brown's not Faith's sexuality is at issue. That her thoughts may be sexual in nature and that Faith may be asking her husband to protect her against forbidden desires by substituting a sanctioned love for one that comes unbidden, provoking guilt and fear, has not been part of even those discussions of "Young Goodman Brown'' that have explored the sexual source of Brown's sin. But a consideration of Faith's dream as one characterized by the incubus helps to make sense out of the rest of the story, whether or not Goodman Brown's experience is real or but a dream, and whether or not as a dream it is one shared by his wife. For Faith may have a demon lover who plagues her and from whom only her husband's loving presence in their bed can protect her. And so Faith continues to live with and bear children to a husband whose heart is closed against her, serving his bodily needs without any spiritual communion between them, abandoned to her own desires and the invasive demons that would serve them.

Hawthorne understood that dreams and fancies were the externalizations of desires ordinarily repressed, and women wailing for their demon lovers in dreams or in a wilderness inhabited by devils were familiar to him from the folklore and literature he knew. The psychological understanding he brought to such lore would allow him to conceive that a demon in Faith's dream and a demon in the forest are ultimately the same, and the distinction between dream and reality in "Young Goodman Brown'' may not be as crucial as some of the criticism would have it. There is little question that Goodman Brown would answer in a strongly affirmative fashion the question posed in "Fancy's Show Box" (1837), which Hawthorne wrote two years after "Young Goodman Brown": could the soul be stained by guilty desires unacted as by guilty deeds? And the very context for this question suggests that the incubus was no stranger to Hawthorne: "In the solitude of a midnight chamber, or in a desert, afar from men, or in a church, while the body is kneeling, the soul may pollute itself even with those crimes, which we are accustomed to deem altogether carnal" (*Tales* 450).

III

The sojourn of Goodman Brown into the forest has been compared to other psychological journeys in nineteenth and twentieth-century literature, journeys into the self that make Hawthorne's story his own *Heart of Darkness*.[21] In the framework supplied by folklore, Goodman Brown's sojourn also takes its place among tales concerning the search for the erring or lost wife. Hawthorne's sources in Scott's essay on the "Fairies of Popular Superstition" make it possible to read Goodman Brown as a peculiarly American Orpheus, whose failure with regard to his wife, played out in a psychological realm, leaves Faith in as lamentable a state as Virgil's Eurydice.

The lengthy excerpts from the Auchinleck *Sir Orfeo* provide an intermediary between "Young Goodman Brown" and the classical myth. Scott in fact refers to *Orfeo and Heurodis*, "in which the story of Orpheus and Eurydice is transformed into a beautiful romantic tale of faery" (2: 138). The protagonist of both Hawthorne's story and the medieval poem is told by his wife that she has experienced a fearful dream. In one instance, Heurodis specifically relates that she will be spirited away to the otherworld. In the other, Faith merely alludes to the nature of her dream so as to invoke in an informed reader the lore of the incubus who, according to Scott, corresponds to the figure who kidnaps Heurodis. Both husbands wander in a forest, neither on a specific quest that has been defined for the reader. And each discovers or thinks he discovers his wife among the inhabitants of another world.

There are additional parallels. In *Sir Orfeo* the King of the Fairies is accompanied by a large host, hunters and armed nights, these in turn accompanied by revelers:

> And otherwhile he seighe other thing;
> Knightis and leuedis com daunceing,

> In queynt attir gisely,
> Queyete pas and softlie:
> Tabours and trumpes gede hem bi,
> And al maner menstraci.

(2: 141)

Similarly, Goodman Brown observes the diabolical scene from his hiding place before he becomes part of it:

> Once, the listener fancied that he could distinguish the accents of town's-people of his own, men and women, both pious and ungodly, many of whom he had met at the communion-table, and had seen others rioting at the tavern.

(82)

In both works, a rock features prominently in the landscape providing passage to the world inhabited by these people. Scott had paid particular attention to the entrance to fairyland: "They enter a rock, the king continues the pursuit, and arrives at Fairy-Land," and later, the "entrance to the Land of Faery is placed in the wilderness" (2: 142, 145). In Hawthorne's story, Goodman Brown prepares to join the unholy company:

> At one extremity of an open space, hemmed in by the dark wall of the forest, arose a rock, bearing some rude, natural resemblance either to an altar or a pulpit, and surrounded by four blazing pines, their tops aflame, their stems untouched, like candles at an evening meeting.

(84)

Later, the "four blazing pines threw up a loftier flame, the obscurely discovered shapes and visages of horror on the smoke wreaths above the impious assembly. At the same time the fire on the rock shot redly forth and formed a glowing arch above its base . . . " (86). What Scott had merely pointed to as the wilderness entrance to the otherworld has become for Hawthorne a sign of the horror to be found there.

Like *Sir Orfeo*, Hawthorne's tale contains vivid images of horror. Orfeo finds folk who seem dead but in reality are not, who have bodily wounds, or lie stupified by madness. Some are maimed and have no arms, others seem inseparable from their arms—that is, weapons—some strangle as they eat, or drown in water, or shrivel with fire:

> Wives ther lay on childe bedde;
> Some ded, and sum awedde;
> And wonder fele ther lay besides,
> Right as thai slepe her under tides;

Eche was thus in this warld y-nome,
With fairi thider y-come.

(2: 142)

As he listens to the devil presiding over the unholy sabbath, Goodman Brown can envision a comparably gruesome scene:

This night it shall be granted you to know . . . secret deeds; how hoary-bearded elders of the church have whispered wanton words to the young maids of their households; how many a woman, eager for widow's weeds, has given her husband a drink at bed-time, and let him sleep his last sleep in her bosom; how beardless youths have made haste to inherit their father's wealth; and how fair damsels—blush not, sweet ones!—have dug little graves in the garden, and bidden me, the sole guest, to an infant's funeral. By the sympathy of your human hearts for sin, ye shall scent out all the places—whether in church, bed-chamber, street, field, or forest—where crime has been committed, and shall exult to behold the whole earth one stain of guilt, one mighty blood spot."

(87)

Such parallels between "Young Goodman Brown" and *Sir Orfeo* do not, of course, establish an automatic connection with the classical Orpheus story. But Hawthorne would have been encouraged to link Celtic with classical mythology as branches of a single family, particularly by the introduction to "Tamlane" in which Scott relates the fairies of popular superstition to the characters from ancient myth: it has already been apparent that Pluto takes his place among the various demon lovers who prey on women. Hugo McPherson, in his study of Hawthorne's use of classical mythology in *The Tanglewood Tales*, argues that Hawthorne, turning for help to Charles Anthon's *Classical Dictionary*, had greatly abbreviated Anthon's account of the Argonauts, adding supplementary information on a few of the heroes (104). Anthon's entry on "Orpheus" contains many themes to be found in "Young Goodman Brown" and in *Sir Orfeo*. Even if it cannot be proven that Hawthorne looked at Anthon before writing his short story in 1835, the entry in the 1833 edition of the dictionary has enough in common with Hawthorne's use of the Orpheus and Eurydice myth in "Young Goodman Brown" to make it worth taking into account for a consideration of how Hawthorne conceived of Orpheus himself.

Anthon ties the myth of Orpheus and Eurydice to the religious system known as Orphism, and the struggle between it and the rites of Bacchus are presented as classical versions of the conflict in "Young Goodman Brown":

the system of Orpheus, though subsequently so far altered and distorted as to become in some measure identified with that of Bacchus, would seem originally to have been directly at variance with it. A contest thereupon ensues between their respective votaries, and the followers of Orpheus are compelled to succumb. They betake themselves to the woods in order to practise there in security the rites to which they are attached. But the celebration of the orgies, the scene of which was invariably laid in woods and on mountains, lays open the place of their retreat to the followers of Bacchus, and the system of Orpheus is prostrated. In the language of poetry, Aristaeus pursues Eurydice . . . into the woods, where the serpent (the system of Bacchus) occasions her death. . . . The meaning of the legend evidently is, that, afflicted at the overthrow of the favourite system which [Orpheus] had promulgated, and the consequent gross corruption of the times, he endeavored to reclaim men from the sensual indulgences to which they had become attached, by holding up to their view the terrors of future punishment in another world.

(1076)

Despite the importance of Orpheus to *The Tanglewood Tales*, Hawthorne did not include in it the story of Orpheus and Eurydice. Only Orpheus the singer, the poet on the Argo, is portrayed, for it was his song that made things happen, that inspired the heroes of the legendary journey to courageous action. Indeed, "The Golden Fleece," and the entire *Tanglewood Tales*, conclude with an image of Orpheus's song that tells how Jason, after winning the coveted prize, comes back to the ship:

With one bound, he leaped aboard. At sight of the glorious radiance of the Golden Fleece, the nine-and-forty heroes gave a mighty shout; and Orpheus, striking his harp, sang a song of triumph, to the cadence of which the galley flew over the water, homeward bound, as if careening along with wings!

(*Tales* 1469)

The reduction of Jason to the pronoun "he" emphasizes the figure of the poet-hero who emerges in importance precisely because his name is the only one mentioned in the concluding paragraph. Here Hawthorne implies his own identification with those nineteenth-century writers, like Carlyle, Emerson, Dickens, and Arnold, who searched for an art whose beauty was not merely an end in itself but moved men to action. Successful art was act as well as word, or the word that became alive as act.

The Orpheus who had quested for his Eurydice was instead a failure, as Scott had reminded his readers in the introduction to "Tamlane." As such Orpheus joined other failures in folklore and literature, including Goodman Brown, his defeat inconsistent with the all-important poet-hero of the Argo. Such inconsistency may account for Hawthorne's omission from *The Tanglewood Tales* of the renowned and affective myth. But a study of the folklore surrounding "Young Goodman Brown" raises some provocative questions about whether Hawthorne's omission is itself analogous to Orpheus's failure to bring his wife back from the otherworld, about whether Hawthorne's possible conception of himself as Orpheus caused him to identify himself with Goodman Brown as well.[22] There is in the folklore with which this essay has been concerned as well as in the criticism surrounding Hawthorne and Scott reason to argue for such an identification.

Some years ago, Philip Rahv described a conflict upon which he believed rested the "whole tone and meaning of Hawthorne's work," the split between the Puritan and the nineteenth-century man of appetite and perspective, the former of whom "did not so easily pacify and curb the latter as is generally assumed" (26). According to Rahv, Hawthorne's conflict is reflected in the literary character Rahv calls the "Dark Lady of Salem" who appears as Beatrice in "Rappaccini's Daughter," Hester in *The Scarlet Letter*, Xenobia in *The Blithedale Romance*, and Miriam in *The Marble Faun*. "Hawthorne's description of her," writes Rahv,

> is wonderfully expressive in the fulness of its sensual imaginings. He is in-genious in devising occasions for celebrating her beauty, and conversely, for denigrating, albeit in equivocal language, her blonde rival—the dovelike vir-ginal, snow-white maiden of New England. But the two women stand to each other in the relation of the damned to the saved, so that inevitably the dark lady comes to a bad end while the blonde is awarded all the prizes—husband, love, and absolute exemption from moral guilt.
>
> (30)

According to U. C. Knoepflmacher, this polarity can also be found in Scott, the pairing of the dark Rebecca and the fair Rowena of *Ivanhoe* a paradigm for the rebellious undercurrents in a "counterworld" of Victorian fiction, which exists "beneath the moralism and the collective ethic of love invoked by most Victorian novelists to protect themselves and their readers from impulses antagonistic to society" (352). This counterworld is "asocial and amoral, unbound by the restraints of the socialized superego" (352). Through Rebecca, whose "superiority to her blonde rival" (355) is imme-diately sensed by Brian de Bois-Gilbert, Scott "manages both to entertain and to deny the allurements of 'spheres' in which men and women may move free from restraint and contradiction" (356). The influence of Scott's polarities appear to be widespread in nineteenth-century English literature, and his specific influence on Hawthorne's dark ladies indirectly supported when Knoepflmacher notes that in a George Eliot novel, a character talks of wishing to avenge "the *neglected dark-haired heroines of Scott's romances*" (354; emphasis added). In short, Knoepflmacher's study suggests that the Victorian counterworld is not only a separate sphere but a veritable otherworld comparable to the magic realms of folklore, which often have "dark ladies" presiding over them.

In folklore, "dark ladies" appear in the guises of demon women and ferocious goddesses who pose a threat to the men who are attracted to them, but also fear them and are frequently destroyed by them. According to Robert Graves, the gentle and pathetic Eurydice can be counted among them. He traces Orpheus's dead bride to the serpent-grasping ruler of the Underworld," to whom male human sacrifices were offered, "their death being apparently caused by viper's venom." Hence Eurydice's death by snakebite, argues Graves, is a rationalization of an older story, necessitated by the transformation of this fearsome female figure into an innocent heroine (I, 128, n. 33.1). Graves's interpretation of classical myth is not shared by all scholars, but his view does bear comparison to the work of John Friedman and Richard Bernheimer, who have found a connection between Heurodis in *Sir Orfeo* and the demonic figure of Herodias, or Eurydice as interpreted in the Middle Ages, both scholars explaining why Heurodis is a likely candidate for abduction to the otherworld (Cotton Mather's association of the nightmare demon with Herodias can be recalled here). Graves's argument is also sustained by a recent French study in which Eurydice is associated with Melusine, the wife of Count Raymond of Lusignan, who took the shape of a serpent one day each week (Markale, 150–52). If her husband respected her privacy on that day, if he did not spy on her and discover her reptilian nature—in other words, the "darkness" beneath her fair exterior—she would be saved. But, in the words of Scott's *Minstrelsy*, "the prying husband broke the conditions of their union," and hardly had Melusine "discovered the indiscreet intruder, than, transforming herself into a dragon, she departed with a loud yell of lamentation, and was never again visible to mortal eyes" (2: 119).[23]

Scott appears to have drawn on the Melusine story in *The Bride of Lammermoor*. His treatment of the French legend is consistent with his theories about folklore and demonology and also consistent with Hawthorne's treatment of similar themes in "Young Goodman Brown." In the novel, a local legend surrounding a mermaid fountain symbolizes the relationship between Lucy and Ravenswood and foreshadows the debacle that overcomes them. Baron Raymond of Ravenswood meets at the fountain a beautiful young lady (perhaps more figuratively than literally called a Naiad), and he continues to meet her under her condition that they only meet on Friday and that they will part as soon as a nearby chapel bell tolled the hour of vespers. When Raymond tells a hermit about his liaisons, the latter invokes works of demonology such as the *Malleus Maleficarum* to convince the at first resistant lover that his lady is a fiend. The hermit contrives to delay the church bells, and when the nymph discovers that she had been betrayed, she bids her lover farewell and plunges into the fountain's well. Scott has wrought signficant changes in the Melusine legend. The French fairy assumes her reptilian form one day a week, and Scott's Naiad meets her lover once each week. But whereas the serpentine shape is an outward sign of the sin for which Melusine is being punished, the tryst in Scott's novel is far from sinful. Thus, whereas Count Raymond of Lusignan discovers the truth about his wife, Baron Raymond of Ravenswood is caught in a terrible error. For he learns that the hermit is mistaken when he tells Raymond that he will discover his beloved's true form. Scott specifically says that after the allotted hour had passed, ''no change took place upon the nymph's outward form'' (*Bride* 57).[24] Only in the hermit's mind is she a loathsome creature, just as Faith becomes loathsome in the mind of a husband too well influenced by the clergy who followed in the steps of the notorious demonologists.

Can Faith be added to the numerous so-called dark ladies that Hawthorne would have known from folklore, from literature based on it, and specifically from Scott?[25] The latter often used folklore to illustrate theories of demonology that had to have had a strong impact on Hawthorne. But can a parallel be constructed between Goodman Brown's rejection of his wife and Hawthorne's omission of Eurydice from *The Tanglewood Tales?* Again, like Eurydice, whom some consider to have her origins in demonic women traditionally associated with a satanic ruler of the underworld, Faith seems in her words to her husband as he leaves her to imply at least a potentially similar relationship to the incubus. For those who, like Rahv, attribute the fates of the dark ladies of Salem to conflicts within Hawthorne, or who, like Knoepflmacher, believe that the descendants of Scott's Rebecca point to a counterworld which many nineteenth-century writers could neither assent to nor wholly negate, a comparison of Hawthorne the writer to Goodman Brown-Orpheus would hold. There are in nineteenth-century literature many characters whose plights symbolize those of the conflicted artist, and it is conceivable that Young Goodman Brown can be placed on the list of them.

NOTES

1. See Koskenlinna and Grant.
2. I disagree with Koskenlinna's contention that a consideration of Scott's poetry as it affected a writer who worked in a different gentre would have complicated

her study without any compensatory gain in understanding the relationship between Hawthorne and Scott (v–vi).

3. Van Pelt mentions Scott's *Minstrelsy* as one of Hawthorne's folklore sources (15). Today scholars are aware that John Leyden had more of a role in the *Minstrelsy* in general and the introduction to "Tamlane" in particular than Scott acknowledges. Hawthorne, however, would have assumed he was reading Scott and so my study will follow his assumption. Interested readers can refer to Dobie.

4. Van Pelt describes the difficulty in locating exact sources (6).

5. Although Hoffman insists that an understanding of folklore is essential for understanding much American literature, he narrows his focus to witchcraft in analyzing "Young Goodman Brown."

6. For other discussions of Hawthorne and folklore (of which there are few) see Leisey, Winslow, and Hoffman's introduction.

7. Shriver and Jayne focus on Goody Brown.

8. I chose this early edition because it was one that Hawthorne could have known. For factual information about Hawthorne's reading of Scott see the appendix to Lathrop's book and Kesselring's monograph.

9. Bliss was apparently unaware of Scott's inclusion of *Sir Orfeo* in the *Minstrelsy*, for he did not list it among other places it could be found in the early nineteenth century (x–xi).

10. Citations from "Young Goodman Brown" are to *Mosses from an Old Manse*.

11. Whether or not Hawthorne intends us to think that Faith was actually present at the witches' sabbath has occupied many Hawthorne critics. My interpretation of the folklore is such that psychological and real events merge in the narratives Hawthorne would have known, and therefore I find no need to take a stand on this point.

12. According to the *Salem Athenaeum*, Hawthorne or some member of his family borrowed Scott's *Letters on Witchcraft* in 1836, a year after the composition of "Young Goodman Brown" (Lathrop, 343). Given Hawthorne's interest in both the author and his subject, however, it is unlikely that Hawthorne waited six years after its publication to read Scott's book.

13. For a survey of just one such folktale pattern, that of the *fier baiser* (fearful kiss), see Schofield.

14. For a discussion that focuses on Orpheus's failure and Eurydice's lament, see Anderson.

15. These are the classifications of Aarne and Thompson.

16. See Murphy on the virtual elimination of the quest motif in *Sir Orfeo* (20).

17. This piece of accepted doctrine among the witchhunters is an important element in the history of witchcraft. Francesco Guazzo, Nicolas Remy, and Reginald Scot were among those who debated the matter. For a discussion of the degree of reasonableness and rabidity among the witchcraft commentators, see Shumaker.

18. It is curious that Leibowitz, who studies *The Faerie Queene* as a source for "Young Goodman Brown," discusses Una as a significant influence on Hawthorne's story but says nothing of Duessa. But a recognition of how complex a character Faith is makes the wider influence of Spenser's work more apparent, particularly in light of Scott's linking of medieval and renaissance romance to a folk tradition.

19. Robbins is an excellent source for information about the incubus; for a discussion of the incubus in literature, see Kiessling.

20. Frequently cited in studies is Waller's book. If Hawthorne's boast about having

read everything published during the previous century were true, he may very well have read Waller, who does not, however, take a psychological approach to the nightmare.

21. See Cook; and Walcutt's chapter on "Young Goodman Brown."

22. Critics have long found it interesting that in his early writing days, Hawthorne assumed the pen-name of Oberon. According to Scott's folklore, this would connect him as well to malevolent versions of the fairy king. The world's folklore, however, provides evidence that the demon lover who kidnaps a mortal woman, and the husband or lover who descends to the otherworld to get her back have much in common. It is consistent with the dialectical tendencies of nineteenth-century thought that Hawthorne might identify with both Oberon and with Orpheus. Dauber has said of Hawthorne's use of Oberon in "The Devil in Manuscript" that this work is a psychomachia, "Hawthorne's ego in motion. It is the translation of a divided self into narrative" (57).

23. Melusine's "lamentation" as described in Scott evokes the imagery of "Young Goodman Brown," where Brown hears what he suspects is Faith's voice "uttering lamentations" (82). I have written at length elsewhere about the Melusine legend: see Fass. Since this essay on Hawthorne was first written, Mitchell's book on Scott and medieval romance has appeared; Mitchell alludes to the Melusine story in *The Bride of Lamermoor* and notes the significance of the name *Raymond* (119). In the *Minstrelsy*, however, Melusine's husband is referred to as Guy de Lusignan (2: 118). Mitchell discusses which versions of the story Scott might have known (27), without, however, mentioning Paracelsus, an important source because Paracelsus's interpretation of the Melusine story influenced nineteenth-century writers' interpretation of the romance. (See n. 24 below.)

24. Scott would have found precedent for his conception of Melusine in Paracelsus's treatise on the nature spirits (see Fass 32–33). With regard to the influence of this treatise on Scott, see Parsons (158, 163, 164). Bensick argues for the influence on Hawthorne of Paracelsus (59–62).

25. Cohen suggests grounds for such a connection when he compares Faith to Eve, and Faith's dream to Eve's ("Paradise" 285). The nymph who is misperceived by her husband to be a demon is the subject of one of the early nineteenth-century's most popular works of fiction, Friedrich de la Motte Fouque's *Undine*, also influenced by Paracelsus's work (see Fass 46–57). According to Parsons (159), the German novella inspired Scott's White Lady of Avenel, a character in *The Monastery*. It is thus likely that Hawthorne knew his Undine directly and via Scott.

WORKS CITED

Aarne, A. A., and Stith Thompson. *The Types of the Folktale*. 2nd ed. rev. Helsinki: Suomalainen Tiedeakatemia, 1961.

Anderson, W. S. "The Orpheus of Virgil and Ovid: *flebile nescio quid*." in *Orpheus: The Metamorphoses of a Myth*. Ed. John Warden. Toronto: University of Toronto Press, 1982. pp. 25–50.

Anthon, Charles. *Bibliotheca Classica of J. Lempriere: Enlarged, Remodelled, and Extensively Improved*. 2 vols. New York: Carvill, 1833.

Bensick, Carol M. *La Nouvelle Beatrice: Renaissance and Romance in "Rappaccini's Daughter."* New Brunswick, N.J.: Rutgers University Press, 1985.

Bernheimer, Richard. *Wild Men in the Middle Ages: A Study in Art, Sentiment, and Demonology.* Cambridge, Mass.: Harvard University Press, 1952.

Bliss, A. J., ed. *Sir Orfeo.* Oxford: Clarendon Press, 1966.

Briggs, Katharine. *The Vanishing People: Fairy Lore and Legends.* New York: Pantheon, 1978.

Cochran, Robert W. "Reply to Thomas E. Connolly." *College English* 24 (1962): 153–54.

Cohen, Bernard. "Hawthorne and Legends." *Hoosier Folklore* 7 (1948): 94–95.

————. "*Paradise Lost* and 'Young Goodman Brown.' " *Essex Institute Historical Collections* 44 (1958): 282–96.

Colacurcio, Michael J. "Visible Sanctity and Specter Evidence: The Moral World of Hawthorne's 'Young Goodman Brown.' " *Essex Institute Historical Collections* 110 (1974): 259–99.

Cook, Reginald. "The Forest of Goodman Brown's Night: A Reading of Hawthorne's 'Young Goodman Brown.' " *New England Quarterly* 43 (1970): 473–81.

Craigie, William A. *Scandinavian Folk-lore: Illustrations of the Traditional Beliefs of the Northern Peoples.* 1896. Rpt. Detroit: Singing Tree Press, 1970.

Crews, Frederick C. *The Sins of the Fathers: Hawthorne's Psychological Themes.* New York: Oxford University Press, 1966.

Dauber, Kenneth. *Rediscovering Hawthorne.* Princeton, N.J.: Princeton University Press, 1977.

Dobie, M. R. "The Development of Scott's 'Minstrelsy': An Attempt at a Reconstruction." *Edinburgh Bibliographical Society Transactions* 2 (1940): 65–87.

Dorson, Richard. *Folklore Research Around the World: A North American Point of View.* Bloomington: Indiana University Press, 1961.

Doubleday, Neil F. "Hawthorne's Use of Three Gothic Patterns." *College English* 7 (1946): 250–62.

Fass [Leavy], Barbara. *La Belle Dame sans Merci and the Aesthetics of Romanticism.* Detroit, Mich.: Wayne State University Press, 1974.

Friedman, John B. "Eurydice, Heurodis, and the Noon-Day Demon." *Speculum* 41 (1966): 22–29.

————. *Orpheus in the Middle Ages.* Cambridge, Mass.: Harvard University Press, 1970.

Gollin, Rita K. *Nathaniel Hawthorne and the Truth of Dreams.* Baton Rouge: Louisiana State University Press, 1979.

Grant, Douglas. "Sir Walter Scott and Nathaniel Hawthorne." *University of Leeds Review* 8 (1962): 35–41.

Graves, Robert. *The Greek Myths*. 2 vols. Baltimore: Penguin Books, 1964.

Hawthorne, Julian. *Nathaniel Hawthorne and his Wife: A Biography*. 1884; Hamden, Conn.: Archon Books, 1968.

Hawthorne, Nathaniel. *Tales and Sketches*. New York: Library of America, 1982.

———. "Young Goodman Brown." *Mosses from an Old Manse*. Ohio State University Press, 1974.

Hoffman, Daniel G. *Form and Fable in American Fiction*. New York: Oxford University Press, 1961.

Jayne, Edward. "Pray Tarry With Me Young Goodman Brown." *Literature and Psychology* 29 (1979): 100–13.

Kesselring, Marion L. *Hawthorne's Reading, 1818–50*. New York: The New York Public Library, 1949.

Kiessling, Nicholas K. *The Incubus in English Literature: Provenance and Progeny*. Pullman: Washington State University Press, 1977.

Kittredge, G. L. *Witchcraft in Old and New England*. Cambridge, Mass.: Harvard University Press, 1929.

Knoepflmacher, U. C. "The Counterworld of Victorian Fiction and *The Woman in White*." in *The Worlds of Victorian Fiction*. Ed. Jerome H. Buckley. Cambridge, Mass.: Harvard University Press, 1975. 351–69.

Koskenlinna, Hazel M. "Sir Walter Scott and Nathaniel Hawthorne: Parallels and Divergences." Diss. University of Wisconsin, 1968.

Lathrop, George Parsons. *A Study of Hawthorne*. 1876; rpt. New York: AMS Press, 1969.

Leibowitz, Herbert A. "Hawthorne and Spenser: Two Sources." *American Literature* 30 (1959): 459–66.

Leisey, Ernest E. "Folklore in American Literature." *College English* 8 (1946): 122–29.

Liddon, S. C., and D. R. Hawkins. "Sex and Nightmares." *Medical Aspects of Human Sexuality*. Jan. 1972: 58–65.

Lynch, James J. "The Devil in the Writings of Irving, Hawthorne, and Poe." *New York Folklore Quarterly* 8 (1952): 111–31.

Male, Roy R. *Hawthorne's Tragic Vision*. New York: Norton, 1964.

Markale, Jean. *Melusine: ou l'androgyne*. Paris: Editions Retz, 1983.

Mather, Cotton. *The Wonders of the Invisible World: The Trials of the Witches*. Amherst, Wisc.: Amherst Press, 1862.

McPherson, Hugo. *Hawthorne as Myth-Maker: A Study in Imagination*. Toronto: University of Toronto Press, 1969.

Mitchell, Jerome. *Scott, Chaucer, and Medieval Romance: A Study in Sir Walter*

Scott's Indebtedness to the Literature of the Middle Ages. Lexington: University Press of Kentucky, 1987.

Murphy, Christina J. "Sir Orfeo: The Self and the Nature of Art." *University of Mississippi Studies in English* 13 (1972): 19–30.

Parsons, Coleman. *Witchcraft and Demonology in Scott's Fiction: With Chapters on the Supernatural in Scottish Literature.* Edinburgh: Oliver & Boyd, 1964.

Rahv, Phillip. "The Dark Lady of Salem." *Essays on Literature and Politics: 1932–1972.* Ed. Arabel J. Porter and Andrew J. Dvosin. Boston: Houghton Mifflin Co., 1978. pp. 25–42.

Robbins, Rossell Hope. *The Encyclopedia of Witchcraft and Demonology.* New York: Crown Publishers, 1959.

Schofield, William Henry. *Studies on the Libeaus Desconus.* Boston: Ginn & Co., 1895.

Scott, Sir Walter. *The Bride of Lammermoor.* London: Dent (Everyman's Library), 1966.

—————. "The Fairies of Popular Superstition," *Minstrelsy of the Scottish Border.* 5th ed. 3 vols. Edinburgh: Longman, 1821.

—————. *Letters on Witchcraft and Demonology.* New York: Gordon Press, 1974.

Shriver, M. M. "Young Goody Brown." *Études anglaises* 30 (1977): 407–19.

Shumaker, Wayne. *The Occult Sciences in the Renaissance: A Study in Intellectual Patterns.* Berkeley: University of California Press, 1972.

Van Pelt, Rachel E. S. "Folklore in the Tales of Nathaniel Hawthorne." Diss. University of Illinois, 1962.

Walcutt, Charles Child. *Man's Changing Mask: Modes and Methods of Characterization in Fiction.* Minneapolis: University of Minnesota Press, 1966.

Waller, John. *A Treatise on the Incubus or Night-Mare: Disturbed Sleep, Terrific Dreams, and Nocturnal Visions. With the Means of Removing These Distressing Complaints.* London: Cox, 1816.

Whittier, John Greenleaf. *The Supernaturalism of New England.* Ed. Edward Wagenknecht. Norman: University of Oklahoma Press, 1969.

Winslow, David J. "Hawthorne's Folklore and the Folklorists." *Southern Folklore Quarterly* 34 (1970): 34–70.

Novels by Eminent Hands:
Sincerest Flattery from
the Author of Vanity Fair

Juliet McMaster

"Imitation is the sincerest form of flattery" is at best an arguable aphorism, especially when it comes to parody. It would take more than the usual allowance of *sang froid* for Henry James to receive Thurber's "The Beast in the Dingle," for instance, with a modest bow, or for Richardson to read "Shamela" as though it were a laudatory review. And yet the degree of attention paid by the parodist to the work parodied—far greater than that paid to a book under review by a reviewer, for instance—implies a dedication, even a devotion, beyond the ordinary. Jane Austen wrote *Northanger Abbey*, it is often supposed, as a parody of the Gothic novel in general, and *The Mysteries of Udolpho* in particular. And yet within *Northanger Abbey* itself appears an unqualified advertisement: the enlightened parodist Henry Tilney declares, "The person, be it gentleman or lady, who has not pleasure in a good novel, must be intolerably stupid. I have read all Mrs. Radcliffe's works, and most of them with great pleasure. 'The Mysteries of Udolpho,' when I had once begun it, I could not put it down" (Ch. 14). *Northanger Abbey*, a parody by a great novelist of a relatively minor one, is probably the largest single reason for the enduring fame of *Udolpho*. Did the grand genre of melodrama suffer by the Crummles sections of *Nicholas Nickleby*? Probably it was given a new lease of life.

Thackeray's parodies of his contemporaries in *Novels by Eminent Hands*[1] have the characteristics of the best parody: they are both devastating take-offs of the worst characteristics of Bulwer, Disraeli, Mrs. Gore, Lever and the rest, *and* tributes, more or less heartfelt, to works that are in different degrees seminal for Thackeray's own best work. He apparently wrote without malice: "They will all be good natured," he claimed (*Letters* 2. 270). But the "fun," as he tuned his fine ear and filed his ventriloquist's tongue to imitation, becomes barbed, and it is easy to see how the subjects would writhe under his parodist's pen. The rebuttals were often bitter, and form on their own an acidic chapter in literary history.

But they were not all that happened to him. Meanwhile his own operations had been deeply affected by the concentrated attention—such as that required by an act of mimicry—that he had paid to his contemporaries' texts. As the parodies, even when he is most fully immersed in his borrowed identity, smack of Thackeray, so thereafter, even when he is most himself, his own writing has fleeting flavors of Mrs. Gore, of Disraeli, of Charles Lever. Julia Kristeva has made us aware "Every text builds itself as a mosaic of quotations, every text is an absorption and transformation of another text."[2] But if intertextuality is a condition of all literature, it is more particularly present in overt parody, and, I would claim, in Thackeray's fiction. "Thackeray was above all things receptive," as Chesterton characterized him. And to explore the interaction of his subjects' texts with his parodies, and then with his own "independent" work, is to discover much about his creative processes. As *Coningsby* becomes "Codlingsby," for instance, and then the devices, images, phrases, and tones further modulate to inform *Vanity Fair, Pendennis* and the rest, we have a visible and demonstrable example of texts as intermingling, a process that blesseth him that gives and him that takes.

Thackeray's parodies, we know, were a preparation for his major work. *Punch's Prize Novelists,* the original title for *Novels by Eminent Hands,* ran in *Punch* from April to September of 1847, overlapping with early numbers of *Vanity Fair.* The first of them, the pastiche of Bulwer-Lytton, was written in January, the month in which *Vanity Fair* began its serial run. The parodies, in which Thackeray was so clearly reacting from the unrealistic excesses, in language and content, of his contemporaries, by a negative process defined his own commitment to realism. So much has been accepted, though not fully demonstrated.[3] But the process as I see it is more complex, and involves not only reaction but absorption and imitation. Just as the parodees (to coin a temporarily useful though ungraceful term) were not the same after undergoing the process of being parodied, but adapted or reacted—ruefully accepted or angrily lashed out against his burlesque—so the parodist too was changed, and learned and absorbed where he had also mocked.

I had the chance to observe this process from doing a particular job. I have been annotating *Novels by Eminent Hands* for the annotations volume of the new edition of Thackeray's works (soon to begin emerging from Garland Press).[4] The annotator, I have come to believe, is one of the unsung heroes of the academic profession. Though usually regarded, like Johnson's lexicographer, as "a harmless drudge," the annotator, I will claim, like the parodist, gathers a unique intimacy with the work under study. One sees it from the inside, in its nitty gritty detail; and one comes, for all the dangers of pedantry that haunt the occupation, very close to the creative process. It is from this angle that I have approached Thackeray's parodies, and also the works they burlesque—for in annotating parody one inevitably takes on the originals too. I am necessarily discussing not only *Novels by Eminent Hands*, but *Eugene Aram, Coningsby, Lords and Liveries, Charles O'Malley* and so on; and beyond all of them, an important aspect of intertextuality in Thackeray's major work.

The seven "novels by eminent hands" parody the fiction of Bulwer-Lytton, Disraeli, Mrs. Gore, G.P.R. James, Charles Lever, "Jeames" (Thackeray's own pseudonym), and James Fenimore Cooper. The usual length is three chapters, or three weeks' worth in *Punch*, though "Codlingsby," the parody of Disraeli, has four chapters, and "The Stars and Stripes," the parody of Cooper, only two. There is at least one illustration per chapter, executed by Thackeray himself, and placed with care in relation to his own text and the layout on the *Punch* page. So far as one can generalize about a set of pastiches that are carefully individualized, Thackeray's major target is various kinds of inflation and distortion. With considerable gusto, he sets about out-Heroding Herod: further distending Bulwer's windy rhetoric; capping Disraeli's brand of international snobbery by bringing monarchs to pay court to the fabulously wealthy Sidonia figure; adding impossible gymnastic stunts to the muscular feats of Lever's military hero; and outdoing Cooper in a flourish of backwoods American chauvinism. The unstated positive values that emerge from all these negative examples are for a low mimetic narrative conveyed in an honest, level discourse: by the time we have ruled out all these false departures, we are left, in fact, with a Novel Without a Hero—the novel that Thackeray was writing concurrently with the parodies. In *Vanity Fair* itself, of course, the left hand of the parodist occasionally invades what the right hand of the realistic novelist is writing. In a long passage in Number 2 (for February 1847), which Thackeray deleted from later editions, he includes brief parodic versions of his action, according to which Amelia Sedley and her suitor are treated first in the Newgate style of Harrison Ainsworth and then after the manner of the Silver Fork school of Mrs. Gore.

Several of Thackeray's parodees are historical novelists; and Thackeray gleefully attacks them for bad history, and for other kinds of inaccuracy. One of the recurring jokes in the set of parodies is the deliberate error. The reader may take nothing on faith: when he reads of "the coasts of Rutland and merry Leicestershire" (172), he needs to know that Rutland and Leicestershire are inland counties, and have no coastlines. A reference to "the memorable 26th of June 1782" should raise a similar suspicion. The date referred to, the day of the famous and inexplicable sinking of the *Royal George,* with 900 souls aboard, was not so memorable after all, being August 29th, not June 26th. In "George de Barnwell" the narrator alerts the reader that he may encounter "some trifling inaccuracies" in a following account of a meeting of eighteenth-century wits. The chapter title, "Button's in Pall Mall," contains the first error, since Button's was in Russell Street in Covent Garden, not Pall Mall. In what follows the reader is bombarded with a colorful array of historical impossibilities, while Swift and Pope are flung together with Johnson and Savage as though they were exact contemporaries, and all are thrust into the post-Waterloo London of "Regent Street" and "Wellington Street." These are jokes for the cognoscenti, and the annotator can be in her element.

As with history, so with geography. "Barbazure," the parody of G.P.R. James, is set in France, "upon one of those balmy evenings of November which are only known in the valleys of Languedoc and among the mountains of Alsace." Again, the alert reader, if not already secure on the topography of France, needs to read with an atlas to hand, as Languedoc is in the south-west while Alsace is in the north-east. In the journeys that follow he is shunted to and fro across the map of France like a shuttlecock. The hero of this tale, a knight returning from the crusades, gives this pocket history of his experiences:

> "I stood by Richard of England at the gates of Ascalon, and drew the spear from sainted King Louis in the tents of Damietta . . . well-a-day! since thy beard grew, boy, (and marry 'tis yet a thin one), I have broken a lance with Solyman at Rhodes, and smoked a chibouque with Saladin at Acre."
>
> (128)

With an encyclopedia to hand one can demonstrate that this experience must have been protracted over some four centuries; the young listener's beard must indeed have been some time a-growing.

To spend this kind of energy in attacking his parodees for bad history and geography (and some of the deliberate errors have a delectable wit about them) argues an intense concern for accuracy. And Thackeray's own serious works do show a sustained concern for getting things right. He was not an antiquarian as Scott was, but he had a way of absorbing and reproducing the *feel* of a past age. As Thackeray cheerfully attacks Bulwer, James, and Cooper for their slapdash and pretentious parade of historicity, he is himself feeling his way towards the kind of period saturation that informs *Henry Esmond*. So far the parodies of unhistorical novels give him an impulse toward his own best work. They are the negative examples by which he defines his own purposes. But, as Chesterton memorably said of Thackeray, "Whenever he sneers it is at his own potential self."[5] And the Thackeray who assaulted the inaccuracies of his contemporaries was ready enough to cry *mea culpa* about inaccuracies of his own; "As sure as I read a page of my own composition, I find a fault or two, half a dozen. Jones is called Brown. Brown, who is dead, is brought to life . . . " and so on.[6] John Sutherland, in his study of *Thackeray at Work*, considers a kind of inspired carelessness to be one of Thackeray's great creative assets.[7] So his parodies of egregious errors in his parodies prepare us for his major works both as negative examples that show what the best work will not be like, and as models that a mere contemporary cannot but follow in humility and gratitude.

Another general characteristic of the parodies is their extraordinary sensitivity to language. Thackeray can hit off, in syntax and vocabulary, the particular magniloquence of Bulwer, with his flourish of capitalized abstracts, the linguistic pomposity of Disraeli, the bumbling prolixity of James. Some notes on vocabulary must suffice as an example of a general linguistic sophistication. Without benefit of the *OED,* Thackeray had a feel for the semantic history of a word. This becomes easily demonstrable when Johnson, the great lexicographer, is present as a character. In "George de Barnwell" we are told in passing that the waiter is "removing a plate of that exquisite dish, the muffin, (then newly invented)" (91). The reader is at once alerted to some dubious history, social and linguistic. Neither the word "muffin" nor the thing was yet in genteel use in the early part of the eighteenth century. (Thackeray jokes about this humble confection again in *The Rose and the Ring,* set "ten or twenty thousand years ago," where the distracted King Valoroso "leaves his august muffins untasted.") But presently Johnson is coining an aphorism with a deliciously Thackerayan ring to it. "The muffin we desire to-day would little benefit us tomorrow" (91). The word "muffin," of course, doesn't appear in Johnson's own dictionary. And "springald," for a young spark, which Savage uses in conversation with Johnson, is a word which Scott revived as an archaism, but which Johnson had firmly listed as obsolete. Thackeray had similarly revelled in Johnsonism in the first number of *Vanity Fair,* in which Miss Pinkerton, Johnson's devoted fan, is shown using such words as ''billet'' (for a note or brief letter), a word which Johnson lists as current but the *OED* shows as archaic by the turn of the century.

Thackeray has a fine ear, too, for jargon, and for the specialized lingo by which a novelist attempts to assume the role of expert. These lingos are different for each novelist. For James we have the technical terminology of chivalry. The mounted hero of ''Barbazure'' appears

> in the fullest trappings of feudal war. The arblast, the mangonel, the demi-culverin and the cuissart of the period glittered upon the neck and chest of the war-steed; while the rider, with chamfron and catapult, with ban and arrière-ban, morion and tumbril, battle-axe and rifflard, and the other appurtenances of ancient chivalry, rode stately on his steel-clad charger, himself a tower of steel.
>
> (128)

Thackeray not only exaggerates James's penchant for mediaeval terminology (in one of his novels, *Philip Augustus* of 1831, James had provided a long explanatory note on armour, along with profuse description); but in the process he creates a wildly comic picture for the reader who can follow. The horse wears parts of a man's armor, and is weighed down besides with a crossbow, a cannon, and a device for hurling rocks; while it is the man who wears the horse's frontlet. The specialized vocabulary of heraldry, which provides the ''azure'' of Barbazure's name, likewise takes on a life of its own. Barbazure's ''well-known cognizance'' is ''the sinople couchant or'' (130). ''Sinople'' is a rather recherché term, even among students of heraldry—a variant of the adjective ''vert'' or green. But here it has been transmogrified into a kind of animal, a gold one, that we are to visualize as posed in the couchant or crouching position. Words, loosed from their referents, become self-determining and creative, and we enter the realm of the inspired verbal nonsense that produces such charming monsters as the Rocking-horse-fly and the Bread-and-butter-fly in *Alice Through the Looking Glass.*

Thackeray seems to have an elastic vocabulary, and to be tirelessly limber in his adaptations. In the military parody, ''Phil Fogarty,'' he gabbles the technical terminology of fortification, still with egregious planted errors; in ''The Stars and Stripes'' he goes nautical, and characters betake themselves ''to splice the taffrail,'' while a fierce company of boarders has ''made their lodgement on the . . . binnacle'' (173). One could wish for an illustration of such a feat.

Sometimes the errors come so thick and fast that it is hard to tell whether they reflect the attitude of the severe satirist exasperated by the inaccuracies of novelists who set themselves up as experts, or of a genial layman who simply looks up the words and dumps them in, with the breezy "Whatever!" familiar among today's students.

Then there are the pictures. As always, Thackeray's illustrations are an integral part of the text: sometimes they are even built in as part of the grammar of his sentence, as in "Crinoline," where a section ends with the words "they were struck all of a heap by seeing—" and the immediately following illustration provides the object of the verb. The placement of each illustration is crucial,[8] and Thackeray clearly insisted on a suitable layout for his work on the *Punch* page. The dénouement of "Barbazure" is an execution. At the foot of the *Punch* page we see the public executioner with sword poised to decapitate the lovely heroine; and the breathless viewer must turn the page to find out that the executioner, her lover in disguise, actually chops off the head of the dastardly Barbazure instead (Figure 1). The double-frame sequence, with the carefully planned layout, marks a step on the way to the motion picture and the animated cartoon.

For the annotator the illustrations provide a challenge, for they include as many topical references as the copy, but without the words to look them up by. Louis Philippe, Talleyrand, Joachim Murat, and others must be recognized and identified, and likewise statues in Hyde Park and other topical or topographical references. My chief discovery about the illustrations, I think, is that they include a set of caricatures of the authors parodied. This is clearest in the case of Disraeli, who was already a familiar face to readers of *Punch*. A caricature by Richard Doyle ran within a month of "Codlingsby" (12 June 1847, 239), where Disraeli appears as the Jewish superman, Rafael Mendoza, in the same top hat and ringlets (Figure 2). In a review of *Coningsby* Thackeray had written that in Sidonia Disraeli "paints his own portrait . . . in the most splendid fashion" (6. 507), so the visual equivalence of Disraeli/Sidonia/Mendoza is to be expected. One recognizable caricature alerted me to the possibility that there might be more—though it is harder to find contemporary likenesses of such figures as Mrs. Gore and G.P.R. James, and the cases are occasionally disputable. But I think James, who sported a moustache (unusual in the 1840s, as in the age of chivalry) can be recognized in the person of the dashing Philibert in the initial illustration for "Barbazure" (Figure 3). The big eyes and tapering pretty face of the heroine Amethyst in "Lords and Liveries," who appears in an opera box, likewise belong to Mrs. Gore, the fashionable lady novelist, who moved in the best society (Figure 4). George de Barnwell has the same prominent nose and heavy eyebrows as Bulwer-Lytton (Figure 5), whom Thackeray had caricatured on other occasions.[9] In "Crinoline," the self-parody, Thackeray provides a Frenchified but perfectly recognizable self-portrait as the Parisian journalist, Jools de Chacabac (Figure 6). The round face, button nose and spectacles are a kind of visual shorthand that readers of *Punch* were already familiar with. And Thackeray had recently provided his readers with another self-portrait, the famous one in Number 3 of *Vanity Fair* (104).[10]

One notable use to which Thackeray put his illustrations was as a visible cross-reference to the author of *Vanity Fair*. The most crucial year of Thackeray's career was 1847, when he rocketted from relative obscurity to a place at the top of the tree alongside Dickens (*Letters* 2. 333). It was of course *Vanity Fair* that did it. In his ongoing and officially anonymous work for *Punch,* Thackeray was willing to tip the wink to his audience that here they were in contact with the author of a great success. The yellow cover for the monthly part-issues of *Vanity Fair* bore the famous picture of "the moralist, who is holding forth on the cover" (95), a fool in fool's cap. And in the initial illustration for "Phil Fogarty" (Ch. 2), the dishevelled hero in a nightshirt casts a shadow of a fool's cap on the wall (Figure 7). The mermaid on Romané's helmet in "Barbazure" (Figure 8), surely a rather gratuitous ornament for the purpose, is another piece of self-referentiality. Thackeray recurrently refers to Becky Sharp as a siren and a mermaid, and in Number 7 for July, the month in which "Barbazure" likewise emerged, Becky had discoursed on her useful skill in swimming, and was depicted in an illustration as a seductive damsel luring George Osborne towards the rocks (*VF* 298). During the course of the months in which *Punch's Prize Novelists* and *Vanity Fair* were running simultaneously, Thackeray had changed from a David who challenged the Goliaths of the literary world into a Goliath himself. And his pictures show some cheerful celebration of the fact.

He couldn't always maintain the cheerfulness, however. July of 1847 finds him, in a letter to his mother, lamenting his changed relations with his contemporaries:

> Jerrold hates me, Ainsworth hates me, Dickens mistrusts me, Forster says I am false as hell, and Bulwer curses me—he is the only one who has any reason—yes the others have a good one too as times go. I was the most popular man in the craft until within abt. 12 months—and behold I've begun to succeed. It makes me very sad at heart though, this envy and meanness—in the great sages & teachers of the world. Am I envious and mean too I wonder?
>
> (*Letters* 2. 308)

He attributes the changed attitude of his peers to his success with *Vanity Fair,* when probably the emerging parodies had just as much to do with it. He had

The man (who knew his trade) advanced at once, and poised himself to deliver his blow : and, making his flashing sword sing in the air, with one irresistible, rapid stroke, it sheared clean off the head of

the furious, the blood-thirsty, the implacable BARON DE BARBAZURE!

1. The paired illustrations for the climax of ''Barbazure.''

2. Variations on Disraeli: in profile, by Count D'Orsay (1834), in top hat, by Richard Doyle in *Punch* (1847), and (right) by Thackeray as "Rafael Mendoza."

3. An 1846 portrait of G.P.R. James, and Thackeray's "cavalier."

4. A contemporary likeness of Catherine Gore, and Thackeray's "Amethyst."

5. Thackeray's "George du Barnwell" and an engraving of Bulwer.

6. Thackeray's self-portraits, as the narrator of *Vanity Fair*, and as "Jools de Chacabac."

7. Phil Fogarty casts the shadow of "the moralist who is holding forth on the cover" of *Vanity Fair*.

8. "Especially the one on the white horse": Thackeray's opening illustration for "Barbazure." Note the mermaid on the helmet.

9. Thackeray's caricature of Louis Philippe, with his "old wig, curling at the top like a rotten old pear," in allusion to the famous cartoon by Charles Philippon.

10. Napoleon as rendered by Phiz in *Charles O'Malley* and by Thackeray in *Vanity Fair* (May 1847) and ''Phil Fogarty'' (August, 1847).

hoped to keep them "all good natured," but then it is easier for a parodist to feel good-natured than for his subjects. Dickens, who must have wondered when his turn was coming, had reason—"a good one too as times go"—for mistrusting this cheerful and deadly satirist in the nest, as Thackeray seems to know in his heart of hearts.

Bulwer (now Bulwer-Lytton), he admits, has the best reason for his enmity. "George de Barnwell" is one more round in the sport of "Bulwer-baiting" that Thackeray had indulged in since his work for *Fraser's Magazine*. In *Catherine* (1839–40) he had already attacked the Newgate novels, and Bulwer's in particular, for their championship of the criminal, and it was easy for him to begin his new series with some more of the same. His moral objection remains as before, that to elicit sympathy for rogues is to confuse virtue with vice. In *Catherine* the narrator had argued,

> We say, let your rogues in novels act like rogues, and your honest men like honest men; don't let us having any juggling and thimble-rigging with virtue and vice, so that, at the end of three volumes, the bewildered reader shall not know which is which.
>
> (3. 31)

In "George de Barnwell" he pursues the same argument, though with much more sophistication. His "hero" (taken not from the Newgate Calendar but from Lillo's play) is an apprentice who murders his uncle and benefactor. Like Eugene Aram, he aspires to be a scholar, and he holds forth in magniloquent terms to justify his action:

> "And wherefore, Sir, should I have sorrow . . . for ridding the world of a sordid worm; of a man whose very soul was dross, and who never had a feeling for the Truthful and the Beautiful? . . . "Dog," I said to the trembling slave, "tell me where thy Gold is. *Thou* hast no use for it. I can spend it in relieving the Poverty on which thou tramplest; in aiding Science, which thou knowest not; in uplifting Art, to which thou art blind." . . . But he spake not, and I slew him."
>
> (8. 97)

To this passage Thackeray, as editor of his own parody, attaches a note in which he accuses his other self of "gross plagiarism" of *Eugene Aram,* and quotes the original: "I had destroyed a man noxious to the world! With the wealth by which he afflicted society, I have been the means of blessing many" (Book 5, Chapter 7). As Gordon Ray has shown, this devastating parallel was too much for Bulwer-Lytton, who excised the offending passage, and some other morally dubious ranting, from later editions of *Eugene Aram* (*Uses*

393). Here is the first demonstrable instance of Thackeray's parodies as affecting the work of his subjects.

For the reader who knows all of Thackeray's novels, as the contemporary readers of *Punch* could not, there is a certain irony in Thackeray's sustained attack on the muddled morality of the Newgate novel. The same author who attacks Bulwer-Lytton for confusing vice and virtue is after all the creator of Becky Sharp and Beatrix Esmond; and *Vanity Fair* itself, which chronicles the fortunes of a spritely and attractive woman who may be a murderess, is included in modern treatments of the Newgate novel.[11] His contemporary, William Roscoe, was later to be severe on Thackeray for the very fault for which he attacked Bulwer: "We do maintain that there is a sin against good taste and right moral influence in mingling too intimately real vice and the ridiculous; they may be alternated, but not mixed, still less chemically combined after Mr. Thackeray's fashion."[12] It becomes doubtful whether Thackeray is most notable for reacting against or for using the pattern of the Newgate novel. (There is a similar ambiguity in the personal relation of the two men. Bulwer's biographers have argued that Thackeray's recurring attacks were motivated less by disapproval than by envy of a social status and literary success that Thackeray wished he could achieve himself.)[13]

In certain ways "George de Barnwell" reads like a homogenized blend of the parodist with the parodee. The middle section is a scene in which the hero is present with the wits of the eighteenth century, Savage and Johnson, Addison and Steele, Pope and Swift. He matches wits with them—improves on Pope's translation of Homer, caps verses with Swift, and writes a paper for the *Spectator* that beats Steele's best—and wins a chorus of praise. The scene mocks similar episodes in Bulwer's *Devereux* in which, for instance, the title character shines in badinage with St. John and Swift, "two of the most extraordinary men of the age" (Book II, chapter 7). But the passage reads less like a parody of *Devereux* than a trial run for *Henry Esmond*. In spite of, or because of, his reaction from Bulwer, Thackeray introduces his hero to Swift, Addison and Steele, and makes him write a paper for the *Spectator* that can't be distinguished from the real thing. (A later hero, Harry Warrington in *The Virginians,* encounters Johnson and Richardson.) And Esmond, like George de Barnwell, receives an accolade of praise from the wits he associates with, and finds that geniuses are but men after all.

The prefatory passage on "Noonday in Chepe" likewise has a familiar ring for the Thackerayan.

'Twas noonday in Chepe. High Tide in the mighty River City!—its banks

wellnigh overflowing with the myriad-waved Stream of Man! The toppling
wains, bearing the produce of a thousand marts; the gilded equipage . . . [and
so on, through coach, carriage and cart.] The dauntless street urchins, as they
gaily threaded the Labyrinth of Life, enjoyed the perplexities and quarrels of
the scene, and exacerbated the already furious combatants by their poignant
infantile satire. And the Philosopher, as he regarded the hot strife and struggle
of these Candidates in the race for Gold, thought with a sigh of the Truthful
and the Beautiful, and walked on, melancholy and serene.

(85)

The inflated language belongs to the parody of Bulwerese. But the substance
of the vision is familiar:

As the Manager of the Performance sits before the curtain on the boards, and
looks into the Fair, a feeling of profound melancholy comes over him in his
survey of the bustling place. . . . Yes, this is VANITY FAIR; not a moral place
certainly; nor a merry one, though very noisy.

(*VF* 1)

Although *Vanity Fair* was well under way by the time "George de Barnwell"
began its three-week run, the preface, "Before the Curtain," had yet to be
written, as it appeared as part of the last double number for July, 1848. It
sounds as though the melancholy "Philosopher" who looks on at the "Labyrinth of Life" in the parody of Bulwer is near kin to the melancholy "Manager of the Performance," "a man with a reflective turn of mind," who
contemplates the spectacle of Vanity Fair. In both cases Thackeray provides
a verbal genre painting of the Field full of Folk, with an emphasis on the
response of the spectator, and some of the same details appear in both compositions. The "yokels looking up at the tinselled dancers" of *Vanity Fair,*
for instance, are a more vivid and less verbally weighted version of the
"rustics" in "George de Barnwell": "The glittering panes behind which
Birmingham had glazed its simulated silver, induced rustics to pause" (*GB,*
85). It is perhaps not surprising that Thackeray shines through his parody
even when he is ostensibly writing as Bulwer-Lytton. But what is happening,
it seems to me, is that Thackeray is learning how to be Thackeray in the
process.

In spite of having the most reason of all the parodees, by Thackeray's own
admission, to bear a grudge, Bulwer-Lytton did not take any published revenge
on Thackeray. It remained for his biographer, Michael Sadleir, to take up the
cudgels on his behalf nearly a century later, when he pillories Thackeray for
his "sycophancy, cruelty and treachery" (252). But Disraeli harbored a
grudge for "Codlingsby" that lasted beyond Thackeray's death: in 1880 he

included a hostile caricature of Thackeray as the novelist St. Barbe in *Endymion*. St. Barbe is "jealous of everybody and everything" (Ch. 82); his conversation consists of "sarcastic paradoxes duly blended with fulsome flattery" (Ch. 34); he is ready to go down on his knees to anyone who wears a star and ribbon (Ch. 33); and he writes novels in which "he has quizzed all his friends" (Ch. 20). Disraeli, apparently, did not take kindly to being parodied.

"Codlingsby" follows the events and characters in *Coningsby* much more closely than "George de Barnwell" follows *Eugene Aram,* with the reproduction of the two main characters Coningsby and Sidonia as Codlingsby and Rafael Mendoza, with parallel scenes set in London, the university, and the mansions of the rich. "I said we should meet again," the mysterious Sidonia tells Coningsby (4. Ch. 11); "I told you we should meet again where you would little expect me," Raphael tells Codlingsby (99): the parallels are this close.

Thackeray is regrettably not free of the antisemitism that pursued Disraeli through the early part of his political career, when he was jocularly called the "Jew d'esprit" and greeted on the hustings with shouts of "Shylock" and "old clothes!" But Thackeray reacts to the same kind of inflated language and self-aggrandizing imagery that he objected to in Bulwer. According to Sidonia everybody who is anybody is of the Hebrew race, including the Jesuits, French marshals, and heads of state (Ch. 15). So Thackeray shows Rafael Mendoza holding court in his palace behind the old-clothes shop, with ministers from several nations dancing attendance, and an "old man," splendidly recognizable from the illustration (perhaps Thackeray's best political cartoon—see Figure 9) as Louis Philippe, King of the French, consulting him about the manifold troubles that were about to lead to his downfall in the following year. "His Majesty," says Rafael, "is one of *us*" (113).

Disraeli had written in all seriousness of his heroine,

the beauty of the countenance was not the beauty of the Saxons. It was a radiant face, one of those that seem to have been touched in their cradle by a sunbeam. . . . Her eye, too, was the rare eye of Aquitaine; soft and long, with lashes drooping over the cheek, dark as her clustering ringlets. (*Coningsby* 4. Ch. 4)

Thackeray couldn't resist parodying such purple passagery, and launches into a purple passage of his own, a gleeful gilding of the lily:

Her hair had that deep glowing tinge in it which has been the delight of all painters, and which, therefore, the vulgar sneer at. It was of burning auburn. Meandering over her fairest shoulders in twenty thousand minute ringlets, it hung to her waist and below it. A light blue fillet clasped with a diamond aigrette (valued at two hundred thousand tomauns . . .) with a simple bird of paradise, formed her headgear.

(109)

Sidonia's fabulous wealth and the luxuries of the rich and titled provide Thackeray with further opportunity for exuberant hyperbole; indeed in some ways *Coningsby,* if read after ''Codlingsby,'' reads as a parody of itself:

He traversed saloon after saloon hung with rare tapestry and the gorgeous products of foreign looms; filled with choice pictures and creations of curious art. . . . Coningsby alternately gazed up at ceilings glowing with colour and with gold, and down upon carpets bright with the fancies and vivid with the tints of Aubusson and Axminster.

(1. Ch. 4)

And thus ''Codlingsby'':

The carpet was of white velvet—(laid over several webs of Aubusson, Ispahan and Axminster, so that your foot gave no more sound as it trod upon the yielding plain than the shadow did which followed you)—of white velvet, painted with flowers, arabesques, and classic figures, by Sir William Ross, J.M.W. Turner, R.A., Mrs. Mee, and Paul Delaroche. The edges were wrought with seed-pearls, and fringed with Valenciennes lace and bullion.

(108)

One can see the parodist rolling up his sleeves to go one better: if *he* invokes the great carpet-making towns of Aubusson and Axminster, (he seems to mutter), I'll throw in Ispahan too. If he shows art as subservient to the fashionable taste for display, I will cast a handful of miscellaneous painters underfoot. Like the ''simple bird of paradise'' that crowns the chaste Miriam's coiffure, the ''bullion'' (gold viewed as grossly detached from its romantic and aesthetic connotations) provides a grand climax (or bathos) of vulgarity.

Thackeray viewed Disraeli as an outrageous name-dropper; and he used his joke of the deliberate error to suggest that Disraeli gets the names all wrong. In the scene set in Cambridge during Eights week he drops a series of clangers that a university man would never be guilty of. He utterly confuses the places, colleges, and customs of Oxford and Cambridge, and produces a series of references that are split between the two: ''the Hoop Inn, opposite Brazennose,'' ''a dashing young sizar at Exeter,'' and ''from Carfax to Trumpington Street.'' It would be enough to make a university man's hair stand on end.

So much for reaction. But of course Thackeray developed his own concerns too. He revived the mélange of universities in *Pendennis,* where Pen attends "the University of Oxbridge"—thus giving a term to the language now indispensable to British journalists and sociologists, and meriting an entry of almost half a column in the supplement to the *OED.* The less common "Camford" is also his invention. There are other carry-overs between "Codlingsby" and the major work, as Thackeray defines his own purposes and refines his images. Miriam's crassly commercial gesture of lighting a Codlingsby's chibouk with a thousand-pound note has its subtler variant in the previous number of *Vanity Fair,* where George Osborne had lighted his cigar with Amelia's love-letter (140). In "Codlingsby" Thackeray re-arranged the straightforward chronology of *Coningsby* by starting *in medias res* and then filling in the background with a flashback to the hero's younger days—a manipulation of chronology that was to become his standard procedure. The elaborate description of fashionable décor (for which he had an artist's eye), often authenticated by passing references to artists and brand names, was to appear frequently in his novels: a generosity of allusion that draws in a whole culture as the scene of his particular action was increasingly to be his mode.

But to be profitably imitated as well as parodied would not propitiate Disraeli, as we see from *Endymion,* written when he was politically and artistically secure, and the Earl of Beaconsfield to boot. Having been caricatured and parodied by Thackeray, Disraeli is like the cabinet minister in his own novel, cautious of St. Barbe, and hoping fervently "that both the literary and the graphic representations of himself in 'Scaramouch' [that is, *Punch*] might possibly for the future be mitigated" (*Endymion* Ch. 34). For his part, Thackeray might reply in the person of the burly bargeman who gives Codlingsby a black eye: "I likes wopping a lord!" (104).

Catherine Gore is a woman novelist who is due for reassessment.[14] But the entry on her in *The Oxford Companion to English Literature,* even as updated by Margaret Drabble in 1980, still spends almost a quarter of its space on the fact that her novels were parodied by Thackeray. The same is true for the entry on G.P.R. James. Thackeray's parodies, that is, like Jane Austen's of the Gothic novel, would seem to have enlarged their reputations, for this century at least, rather than damaged them. They are remembered for his parodies of them.

" 'Lords and Liveries,' by the authoress of 'Duke and Dejeuners,' 'Hearts and Diamonds,' 'Marchionesses and Milliners,' etc. etc." is a take-off of Mrs. Gore's penchant for titles with titles in them, such as *Memoirs of a Peeress* (1837), *Cecil a Peer* (1841) and *Peers and Parvenus* (1846), the novel most specifically parodied here. It is typical of Thackeray to focus on the class contrast—it gives him a chance to introduce the character beloved in his fiction (because no man is a hero to his valet), the footman, a "Jeames." *Peers and Parvenus* follows the parallel histories of a scion of the nobility and a child of the rural working class. It is probable that the impulse to write parody of the Silver Fork and the Newgate style of novel was the original seed of *Punch's Prize Novelists,* for that was what Thackeray had begun in Number 2 of *Vanity Fair* for February, before the *Punch* parodies began their run. After his fragments of parody the narrator proceeds,

> Thus you see, ladies, how this story *might* have been written, if the author had but a mind; for, to tell the truth, he is just as familiar with Newgate as with the palaces of our revered aristocracy, and has seen the outside of both. But as I don't understand the language or manners of the Rookery, nor that polyglot conversation which, according to our fashionable novelists, is spoken by the leaders of *ton*; we must, if you please, preserve our middle course modestly, amidst these scenes and personages with which we are most familiar.
>
> (*VF* 884)

Having steered between the Scylla of Low life and the Charybdis of High life, the novelist of *Vanity Fair* settles for an "appeal to the middle classes" (*VF* 104). But it seems he had needed to steer that course in order to find his true direction. And the fragments of parody that he set aside in *Vanity Fair* he took up again to complete in *Punch's Prize Novelists.*

The fragment on the Silver Fork novel had begun,

> Or suppose we adopted the genteel rose-water style. The Marquis of Osborne has just despatched his *petit tigre* with a *billet-doux* to the Lady Amelia.
> The dear creature has received it from the hands of her *femme de chambre*, Mademoiselle Anastasie.
>
> (*VF* 882)

Of the forty-one words here, three are titles, and six are in a foreign language. The proportion is roughly maintained in "Lords and Liveries," which is peppered with titles and scraps of French, German, Italian, and Latin. It is a charming enough tale of how the *blasé* Earl of Bagnigge rouses himself from his *ennui,* for the sake of a bet, to win the hand of the beautiful Amethyst Pimlico, ward of the Duchess of Fitzbattleaxe, by disguising himself as a footman. Of course it all happens in the highest reaches of languid and fashionable society:

> "Tell me about this girl, Franklin Fox" [says the titled hero].

"In the first place, she has five hundred thousand acres, in a ring fence, in Norfolk; a county in Scotland, a castle in Wales, a villa at Richmond, a corner house in Belgrave Square, and eighty thousand a year in the three per cents."

"*Après?*" said Bagnigge, still yawning.

(116–17)

Thackeray gets his mileage out of the foreign phrases. Though some are simply colorless and gratuitous, a mere snobbish signal that a speaker has been put through his paces on the grand tour, in some he permits himself nonsensical flourishes like the monster "Sinople." Such is the gourmet confection, "*suprême de cochon en torticolis à la Piffard,*" or "stiff-necked pig in a rich sauce à la Glutton," a sufficiently memorable dish.

A feature of Mrs. Gore's novels is the indulgence in what we now call brand-name fashion. She scatters her pages with references to the Harrod'ses and Tiffanys of the day, to the extent that a commentator in *The Westminster Review* humorously suggested she might be taking commissions:

A book like *Pin Money* [1831] is, in fact, a sort of London Directory. . . . We are not sure the authoress of this work has made any bargain with her tradespeople; but we are very certain she might. . . . None of the persons commemorated would hesitate to give a popular authoress the run of the shop, for the sake of being down in her list.

(Oct. 1831, 433–44)

Thackeray picks up this habit, and makes the most of it. His "young dandies" dawdle after the opera, "smoking their full-flavoured Cubas (from Hudson's)" (114)—Hudson's of Oxford street being tobacconists to the royal family. A flurry of such references sends the annotator scurrying all over the map of nineteenth-century London. But then so do the other works of Thackeray; an ear attuned to the nuances of class and fashion makes him a reliable chronicler of the fine shades of gentility in an address, in a hotel, or a place to eat ices or buy jewelry.

Mrs. Gore, while choosing characters from among the breathtakingly rich and titled, nevertheless has her own vein of moralizing about the ultimate worthlessness of worldly pursuits. Of George Joddrell, the wealthy heir to a peerage in *Peers and Parvenus,* the narrator sighs, "But while thus indulging in excesses beyond his scope of enjoyment, the pampared child was far from happy" (Ch. 3). Thackeray is quick to pounce on this shallow moralizing: "with all this splendour, this worship, this beauty; with these cheers following her, and these crowds at her feet, was Amethyst happy? Ah, no! It is not under the necklace the most brilliant that Briggs and Rumble can supply . . . that the heart is most at ease" (119). The parodist shares with his reader the amused perception that though Mrs. Gore in moral vein denounces worldliness, she certainly gives it the full treatment before rejecting it. But of course the same accusation has been levelled at Thackeray himself. And even in the cheerful pastiche, ''was Amethyst happy? Ah, no!'' we can hear an intimation of a more solemn and enduring tone:

> Ah! *Vanitas Vanitatum!* Which of us is happy in this world? Which of us has his desire? or, having it, is satisfied?
>
> (*VF* 878)

If Thackeray is the best parodist of the Silver Fork novel, he was also a practitioner. And as *Vanity Fair* has been claimed as a Newgate novel, it has also been called ''the culmination of the fashionable novel.''[15]

''Barbazure,'' like ''Lords and Liveries,'' is an affectionate rather than a barbed parody, though poor George Paine Rainsford James, who took himself seriously as a historian and clung to his sinecure as Historiographer Royal, may have been rueful about the wild anachronisms and other inaccuracies attributed to him.[16] But perhaps he felt they were only signs of Thackeray's bad history, not his own. For James at the time was the bigger figure, though Thackeray was in the process of changing all that.

For his parody of James, Thackeray did not fasten on a single identifiable novel from among the three or four dozen extant at the time, but chose to consider them as a mélange about an endlessly elastic period. Like *Richelieu* (1829), James's first and definitive novel, the story is explicitly set in the seventeenth century; but presently we are back among the crusades, and shuttling between Richard and Sulayman in their different centuries, with a suggestion that the tone of undifferentiated archaism and olde-worldiness is common to all James's books, on whatever period. In keeping with this comfortable far-away-and-long-ago mood, Thackeray makes the fairy tale of ''Blue Beard'' the ''history'' that his ''G.P.R. Jeames'' is narrating. The tale was a favorite with Thackeray, to which he returned often. For with an insane wife incarcerated in a private asylum, he had reason to identify with a man who concealed guilty matrimonial secrets.[17] And he indulges in his usual macabre joking on the subject, investing the uxoricide with a tender sensibility:

> in the midst of all his power and splendour there was a domestic grief which deeply afflicted the princely Barbazure. His lovely ladies died one after the other. No sooner was he married than he was a widower; in the course of eighteen years no less than nine bereavements had befallen the chieftain.
>
> (131)

The tale is in fact stamped all over with Thackerayan trademarks. Fatima, eager to become Lady Barbazure the tenth, jilts her impoverished early suitor Romané very much as Agnes Twysden jilts the hero of *Philip* for a better match, and similarly makes a merit of it.

> My former engagements . . . I look upon as childish follies;—my affections are fixed where my dear parents graft them—on the noble, the princely, the polite Barbazure. 'Tis true he is not comely in feature, but the chaste and well-bred female knows how to despise the fleeting charms of form. . . . That he has been married is likewise certain—but ah, my mother! who knows not that he must be a good and tender husband, who, nine times wedded, owns that he cannot be happy without another partner?
>
> (133)

The lady Fatima, in fact, connives in the system of Society, and sacrifices love to interest, as the girls in *The Newcomes,* Thackeray's most sustained attack on the Marriage à la Mode theme, accept the world's values as their creed. "I believe in elder sons, and a house in the town, and a house in the country," they chant (14. 596).

James aspired to follow in the footsteps of Scott, and Thackeray too was steeped in Scott, particularly *Ivanhoe.* Allusion to *Ivanhoe* is almost a tic with Thackeray, and he could play endless variations on the game. In the "Proposals for a Continuation of *Ivanhoe,*" which he wrote for *Fraser's Magazine* in 1846, (subsequently elaborated as the Christmas book, *Rebecca and Rowena* of 1850), he had satisfied his sense of romance by getting rid of the goody-goody Saxon Rowena so that Ivanhoe could marry the fiery Jewess Rebecca instead. The ticklish question of religion is solved by having Rebecca convert to Christianity. In "Codlingsby," in a passage of jocular self-referentiality, Thackeray allows Rafael Mendoza to retell this story as part of his own family history. According to his revision, predictably, the religions difference is resolved differently.

> An ancestress of ours made a *mésalliance* in the reign of your King John. Her name was Rebecca, daughter of Isaac of York, and she married . . . Sir Wilfrid of Ivanhoe, then a widower by the demise of his first lady, Rowena. The match was deemed a cruel insult amongst our people; but Wilfrid conformed, and was a Rabbi of some note at the synagogue.
>
> (110)

In "Barbazure" the *Ivanhoe* game is still going on. While Scott's Ivanhoe had faced his foe, Sir Brian de Bois-Guilbert, as "The Disinherited Knight," Romané calls himself "The Jilted Knight." And the villain holds forth in terms almost identical.

Have you confessed yourself, brother? [asks Sir Brian] . . . then take your place in the lists, and look your last upon the sun; for this night thou shalt sleep in paradise.

(Ivanhoe Ch. 8)

So Scott; and thus Thackeray:

"Hast thou confessed, Sir Knight?" roared the Barbazure; "take thy ground, and look to thyself; for by Heaven thy last hour has come!"

(135)

Thackeray's passage is very close, without being identical: it is clearly not a quotation, which he would need to look up, but a loose repetition from memory, arguing a knowledge of *Ivanhoe* which at points is almost verbatim. The same text was still percolating through that highly absorbent creative consciousness of his when he chose to call his speciously attractive heroine of *Vanity Fair* "Rebecca."

Nowadays it is difficult to read Mrs. Gore or G.P.R. James except through Thackeray's parodies of them. Their texts are inevitably colored—heightened, and perhaps distorted—by Thackeray's rendering, for he has made us re-perceive them, as Jane Austen made us re-perceive *Udolpho*. What is more, he even made James re-perceive himself. Thackeray, with his "two cavaliers," once and for all identified the invariable James formula of beginning a novel with one or more figures on horseback. In a biography called *The Solitary Horseman* James's biographer has catalogued all the cavaliers in the many novels, and shown that though they appear in most of the novels before Thackeray's parody, they are suppressed in all the later ones (Ellis, 257). James himself humorously complained of having had to renounce "the two solitary horsemen—one upon a white horse—which, by one mode or another, have found their way into . . . the books I have written. . . . To say the truth, I do not know why I should wish to get rid of my two horsemen, especially the one on the white horse" (*The Fate,* 1851; Ellis, 258). But a study of his pre-Thackeray equestrian openings produces no prominent white horses. What James is remembering, it seems, is not his own texts, but Thackeray's parody of them—or, more precisely, Thackeray's illustration, which sets the hero Romané firmly on a white charger (see Figure 3 above). When Thackeray parodied something, it's not the same any more, even to its own author.

"Phil Fogarty, a tale of the Fighting Onety-oneth, by Harry Rollicker," is a parody of Charles Lever's *Charles O'Malley, the Irish Dragoon* (1841), by "Harry Lorrequer." Even to announce this fact is to glimpse already the complex relation whereby the work parodied also becomes a model to be imitated. The protagonist of Lever's first novel, *Harry Lorrequer* (1839), goes on to become the "editor" of the subsequent novel *Charles O'Malley*, just as Pendennis of *Pendennis* goes on to become the editor of *The Newcomes* and *Philip*. *Charles O'Malley* seems to have been the basic and essential Lever novel for Thackeray: he had used it as a model before, for instance in the duel scene in *Barry Lyndon* (1844).[18]

His parody is more than usually pointed and lively. *O'Malley* is filled with rollicking action from page to page, and the sometimes violent mishaps of the characters are greeted with bursts of laughter on all sides. So too in "Phil Fogarty," where Thackeray shows quite a turn for macabre humor of his own. "Ha! there goes poor Jack Delamere's head off!" comments a doctor in the thick of battle. "The ball chose a soft one, anyhow. Come here, Tim, till I mend your leg. Your wife has need only knit one half as many stockings next year" (141). Lever habitually scattered his pages with drinking songs, so Thackeray includes one too. One prominent word in his song, "howl," moves to a new text to become the name of Elias Howle, the malicious satirist recognizable as Thackeray in Lever's *Roland Cashel* of 1850: "a publisher's man of all-work, ready for every thing, from statistics to satire, and equally prepared to expound prophesy, or write squibs for 'Punch' . . . His head was capacious, but not remarkable for what phrenologists call moral development" (Ch. 22).[19] Nobody seems to have ventured to try counter-parody; when Disraeli and Lever were moved to riposte, they turned to more personal attacks.

The action of "Phil Fogarty" follows *Charles O'Malley* as closely as "Codlingsby" follows *Coningsby*. O'Malley, of the 14th Dragoons, is wounded during his peninsula campaigns, sojourns after his capture among the French, meets Napoleon and many other dignitaries of the Napoleonic era, and escapes in time to participate, on the right side, in Waterloo. Likewise Phil Fogarty; although his adventures as recorded here stop short of Waterloo. Thackeray had other uses for the Waterloo section of *Charles O'Malley*.

He read the novel, clearly, with great care, at least once before *Barry Lyndon*, and again, it seems, when he was preparing to write his parody. Phil has O'Malley's breezy courage and *sang froid*, and the adventures are packed in breathlessly short space in both. The heroes' affairs of honor must be fitted into a tight schedule of other commitments. "Can you make it before eleven, Phil?" asked Eugène Beauharnais, his second. "The Emperor reviews the troops in the Bois de Boulogne at that hour, and we might fight there handy before the review." "Done!" says Phil (150). And in the actual encounters, handled vividly but tersely, Phil is a true reincarnation of O'Malley. "My eye glanced toward my opponent," records O'Malley, "I raised my pistol and fired. My hat turned half round on my head, and Bodkin fell motionless on the earth" (Ch. 59). Phil has a similarly close call:

> I felt a whizz past my left ear, and putting up my hand there, found a large piece of my whiskers gone; whereas at the same moment, and shrieking a horrible malediction, my adversary reeled and fell.
> *"Mon Dieu, il est mort!"* cried Ney.
> *"Pas du tout,"* said Beauharnais. *"Ecoute; il jure toujours."*
>
> (151)

The great heroes of the Napoleonic wars, Wellington, Pickford, Soult, Murat, Messina, and Napoleon himself, are conscripted to dance attendance on the wild Irish lad, who takes it all in his stride. On the day of Waterloo, O'Malley contrives to be at hand as prisoner when Napoleon discusses strategy with Soult, and then to escape and report to Wellington in time to save the day.[20] Phil also has his endearing moments of intimacy with the great Emperor, who condescends to unbend before the young Irishman, addressing him affectionately, we hear, and "pinching my ear confidentially, as his way was" (148). Certain liberties are taken with the august person of the Emperor in both stories: a brother officer of O'Malley's accidentally plays at leap-frog over Napoleon's back—a feat improved on by Phil Fogarty, who jumps right over Napoleon, horse and all, on his Irish hunter Bugaboo. Phiz, the illustrator of *Charles O'Malley,* provided two illustrations in which Napoleon appears. Thackeray improves on this figure too, by getting recognizable caricatures of Napoleon into three of his illustrations. His hand was in, after all. The Emperor was figuring in the chapter initials for *Vanity Fair* too (see Figure 10). It is clear that Thackeray was steeped in Napoleonic history at the time. He not only introduces the famous names into his text as characters, but produces recognizable likenesses of them in his pictures—for instance of Napoleon's brother-in-law Joachim Murat, of Josephine and Talleyrand.

"We do not claim to rank among the military novelists. Our place is with the non-combatants" (*VF* 361). That decision, clearly a reaction from Lever, who had improbably placed his military hero at the very elbows of Napoleon and Wellington, produced the most brilliant and original of all the many treatments of Waterloo. The fact that we are left with "The Girl I Left Behind Me"—with Becky and Amelia, and the panic-stricken civilian, Jos Sedley—while the guns of the great convulsion of nations boom in the distance, memorably concentrates the drama and brings it home. Thackeray has found himself as a great novelist, once and for all, and he has done it partly by departing from the practice of the second-rate novelist, Charles Lever. But while he strikes out his new and original course, he simultaneously follows where Lever has led. *Charles O'Malley*, and not any historical treatment, I would suggest, is Thackeray's major single source for the great Waterloo number. (It must be remembered that "Phil Fogarty" ran in *Punch* during August of 1847; and number 9 of *Vanity Fair*, the Waterloo number, emerged in September.)

Even for the action among the non-combatants Lever has furnished dramatized hints, though clearly he and Thackeray both worked with historical sources too. O'Malley, with orders to carry dispatches out of Brussels, is forced to ride "a tall, scraggy-looking mule," because as his servant tells him "there isn't a horse to be had for love or money in the town" (Ch. 117). We know how Thackeray elaborated horses, love and money in Becky's transactions with Lady Bareacres and Jos Sedley. But it is when we come to the climax of the battle, the two magnificent paragraphs in which Thackeray does turn his attention to the military action, that his debt to Lever is most apparent. The Tillotsons have identified Thackeray's major historical source as G. R. Gleig's *Story of the Battle of Waterloo* of 1847.[21] He had asked Murray, the publisher, for an early copy of it (*Letters* 2. 294), and provided a footnote reference to it in Number 8 for August, the pre-Waterloo number. But Gleig's account of the climax of the battle, though it furnishes some facts, supplies no major images or phrases that reach Thackeray's poetic rendering of the ascent of the Imperial Guard up the Hill of St. Jean, where the English had maintained their defensive position all day. For those he recalled Lever instead. Everyone remembers Thackeray's description of the "final onset" of the French.

> It came at last: the columns of the Imperial Guard marched up the hill of St. Jean, at length and at once to sweep the English from the height which they had maintained all day, and spite of all . . .
>
> (*VF*, 405)

But rather than quote the whole familiar passage, I will extract the salient phrases that recall *Charles O'Malley:*

Charles O'Malley, Chapter 120	*Vanity Fair,* Chapter 32
Prussian cannon thundered . . . artillery thundered	unscared by the thunder of artillery
the dark columns of the Guard had now commenced their ascent	the columns of the Imperial Guard marched up the hill

the dark ranks of the Guard	the dark rolling column
Already they gained the crest of the hill	It seemed almost to crest the eminence
the leading files waver; they fall back	it began to wave and falter
the Guards [English] rushed upon the leading divisions	Then at last the English troops rushed

That Napoleon ordered out his Imperial Guard as his last resort, and that they marched up to encounter the British at the top of St. Jean, these are historical facts available to both novelists. But the cadence that renders this manoeuvre as climactic, and the insistent images of the forces of the Imperial Guard as a single complex entity, "columns," "dark" columns, breasting the crest of a hill—these tropes belong to a poetic realization of historical fact, and they are what Thackeray shares with Lever.

In both novels the Waterloo chapter is a climax to a personal drama as well as a national one. In *Charles O'Malley* the hero's rival in love, Captain Hammersley, is shot down as the battle closes, and the chapter ends with the image of "his blood-stained corpse . . . his breast shattered with balls, and bathed in gore" (Ch. 120). Thackeray's climax to the Waterloo number, justly famous for its economy and restraint, also closes with the image of the body of the hero's rival in love: "Darkness came down on the field and city: and Amelia was praying for George, who was lying on his face, dead, with a bullet through his heart" (*VF* 406).

I am not trying to prove, of course, that Thackeray ripped off Lever. His audience, for one thing, was much more familiar with *Charles O'Malley* than we are today, and besides had just been treated to Thackeray's parody of it; so that we are dealing with deliberate and recognizable allusion rather than plagiarism. Thackeray's great text has outlasted what it alludes to; but as we recover the allusion we can discover the process of reaction and imitation, and the subtle independence of one text and another. It is by reacting from Lever that Thackeray strikes out his memorably creative invention of staying with the non-combatants; then, momentarily, on Lever's own military subject Thackeray strikes recognizably the same notes; but even in the echoes we are reminded of the differences; for these two comparable deaths of comparable figures at the end of renderings of the same historic battle occur at the end of *Charles O'Malley*, but only as the middle of *Vanity Fair:* the whole shape thereby definitively diverges, and *Vanity Fair* makes its own particular music.

Vanity Fair is the most distinctively Thackerayan of all Thackeray's works. And yet it grows out of his absorption in other texts, an absorption that was also expressed as parody.

The last two parodies in the series represent some falling-off, and Thackeray did not choose to reprint them in the *Miscellanies*. The series must have drawn fire from some big guns, for *Punch* refused to run a parody of Dickens (alas!), and the series petered out. Nonetheless, "Crinoline" and "The Stars and Stripes" have their moments.

It is typical of Thackeray that he should include a self-parody in the series. The parodist, to adapt his address in *Vanity Fair,* "professes to wear . . . only the very same long-eared livery" in which his parodees are arrayed (95). "Crinoline" is Thackeray's take-off of himself. He writes in his old familiar *Punch* guise, as the ill-spelling footman, Jeames; and his protagonist is another incarnation of himself, this time as a Frenchman, Jools de Chacabac, who is the London correspondent for the Paris *Oriflamme* (as Thackeray had been Paris correspondent for the *London Constitutional* as a young man). This situation of narrator and protagonist as the worldly and greenhorn aspects of the writer has its interest, for Thackeray was to use it again, with considerable subtlety, in *Philip*. Here the worldly-wise Pendennis, Thackeray's cynical self, expounds the experience of the turbulent young Philip Firmin, who was the penny-a-liner in Paris of the 'thirties, like young Thackeray and Chacabac. As a binge of self-referentiality, "Crinoline" also shows an amusing awareness of his own habit of "redoubling," or going backwards in the chronological sequence of his fiction in order to make the second scene account for the first.[22] Each chapter of "Crinoline" backs up on itself, so that the reader begins to despair of ever getting anywhere. And the reader is right. The tale ends with the intimation of yet another back-tracking: "But how had these two young Erows become equainted with the noble Marcus [Marquis]?—That is a mistry we must elucydate in a futur vollam" (166). The future volume is not forthcoming. Evidently Thackeray already knew of the procrastinating tendency which, in *The Virginians,* made him take twenty-three months to get to the incident that had been depicted all along on the monthly cover.

"Stars and Stripes" is a bifurcated narrative, and provides a parody of James Fenimore Cooper's leather-stocking tales, particularly *The Last of the Mohicans,* in the first chapter, and of his nautical tales, particularly *The Pilot,* in the second. In order to satirize Cooper's doctrine of the noble savage, Thackeray brings two simple Americans, Ben Franklin and Tatua (Chief of the Nose-ring Indians, and a dead ringer for Chingachgook) to the court of

Louis XVI and Marie Antoinette at Versailles. Franklin whittles a stick in the royal presence; and the doomed representatives of an effete civilization recognize the moral authority of the noble chieftain: "The gigantic Indian . . . stood undaunted before the First Magistrate of the French nation: again the feeble monarch quailed before the terrible simplicity of the glance of the denizen of the primaeval forests" (168). Thackeray savors the grim historical irony of Louis's support of the American revolutionaries, who, as history was to show, furnished a model for the French revolution after them. Marie Antoinette indulges in some fashionable primitivism—"They have the refinement of the Old World, with all the simple elegance of the New," she says of her uncouth guests (167). But the shadow of the guillotine overspreads the domestic royal circle. Tatua's blanket is decorated with scalps—"the black, the grey, the auburn, the golden ringlet of beauty, . . . the snowy tress of extreme old age, the flaxen down of infancy" (168)—and he has condescended to accept a peacock's feather from the Princess of Lamballe as a further decoration. Now this unfortunate lady, the friend of Marie Antoinette, makes it into the encyclopedias by virtue of the fact that when she was killed by the revolutionary mob a few years later, her head was displayed on a pike under the Queen's window. The peacock feather, a gift to one savage by one who will die at the hands of others, is a grim emblem of vanity and mortality.

Thackeray's Cooper, for all his sturdy republicanism, can be detected in the act of snobbery. A passage in *The Pilot* perhaps gave the snob-detector his point of departure for the parody. The heroic Pilot, or John Paul Jones, keeps a gift and letter from Marie Antoinette as precious relics: "That the royal and lovely Antoinette has deigned to repay my services with . . . her gracious approbation is not the least of my boasts. . . . Her life is beyond all reproach, . . . and it has been the will of Providence to place her far beyond the reach of all human misfortunes" (Ch. 14). The ironies of that passage—the worship of royalty by a republican, and the attribution of a godlike immunity to one who was soon to be subject to the guillotine—may well have provided the idea for the scene in Versailles in the presence of "the lovely Antoinette" herself (167).

But though his take-off of Cooper is pointed and amusing, it is not like "Codlingsby" or "Phil Fogarty," which resemble their originals even while mocking them. "The Stars and Stripes" does not *feel* like Cooper. Thackeray and Cooper remain too far apart in their world views and their fictional purposes to make an inspiring blend. As usual Thackeray could learn and absorb what he had read with the detached and barbed absorption of the parodist. In Cooper's chronicles of Leatherstocking, wandering forwards and backwards in chronological sequence from novel to novel, we have perhaps a model for the chronicles of Esmonds and Warringtons of *Pendennis, Henry Esmond,* and *The Virginians.* But with this parody there is less of the cultural seepage that I have been talking about, less of the exchange of fictional strategy and commingling of reputations that happened in England when a big novelist in the same pool parodied and imitated his contemporaries, and provoked defences and reprisals. Cooper of Cooperstown, safe across the Atlantic, was relatively impervious. Thackeray's parody was mere English water, so to speak, off an American duck's back. And whereas critical studies of the other novelists parodied in the series routinely mention Thackeray's pastiche, and the justice or malice thereof, most critics of Cooper seem to be serenely ignorant of the existence of "Stars and Stripes."

In his respectful act of mimicry in *Novels by Eminent Hands* Thackeray was discovering not only How Not To Do It, but also how to do it. As the writers he parodies are affected and changed by his parodies, so this memorably receptive novelist absorbs and improves on what he mocks. Huckleberry Finn, we remember, objects to the kind of meal in which "everything is cooked by itself," and prefers a more homogeneous mix: "In a barrel of odds and ends, it is different; things get mixed up, and the juice kind of swaps around, and things go better" (Ch. 1). It's as good a metaphor as any for intertextuality, and especially for the process that we see at work as Thackeray mingles with Mrs. Gore, Lever, and the others, and the ingredients modulate and blend together, becoming eventually those richly redolent dishes, *Vanity Fair* and the other great delectable novels.

NOTES

1. First published as *Punch's Prize Novelists* in *Punch,* 1847, but partly reprinted in the *Miscellanies* in 1856 as *Novels by Eminent Hands,* the title by which the set of parodies is best known. My text for all quotations from Thackeray's works is *The Oxford Thackeray,* ed. George Saintsbury, 17 vols. (London: Oxford University Press, 1908). The parodies appear in volume 8. For correspondence, I cite from *The Letters and Private Papers of William Makepeace Thackeray,* ed. Gordon N. Ray, 4 vols. (London: Oxford University Press, 1945–46).

2. *Séméotike: Recherches pour une Sémanalyse* (Paris: Éditions du Seuil, 1969), p. 146. I use the translation of Jeanine Parisier Plottel in her "Introduction," *Intertextuality: New Perspectives in Criticism,* ed. Jeanine Parisier Plottel and Hanna Charney, *New York Literary Forum* II (1978), p. xiv.

3. James H. Wheatley argues "how central to all of Thackeray's career the act of parody is." *Patterns in Thackeray's Fiction* (Cambridge, Mass.: MIT Press, 1969), p. 6. Gordon N. Ray notes briefly how in both *Vanity Fair* and *Novels*

by Eminent Hands Thackeray "announced his break with the conventions of contemporary fiction," and brought to bear "at once the sixteen-inch guns of his great novel and the forty-millimeter artillery of his magazine parodies." *Thackeray: The Uses of Adversity: 1811–1846* (London: Oxford University Press, 1955), p. 389. Robert A. Colby has further explored some of Thackeray's debts to the novelists he parodied, noting the similarity of the plot of *The Virginians* to G.P.R. James's *Henry Masterton*, and the "unlike likeness" between *Henry Esmond* and Bulwer's *Devereux*. *Thackeray's Canvass of Humanity: An Author and his Public* (Columbus: Ohio State University Press, 1979), pp. 394, 328.

4. The edition, under the general editorship of Peter L. Shillingsburg, will begin publication with the *Vanity Fair* and *Henry Esmond* volumes. The annotations will appear in a separate volume under the editorship of Edgar F. Harden.

5. Introduction to *The Book of Snobs* (London, 1911), ix.

6. "De Finibus," *Roundabout Papers,* 17, 593.

7. See for instance his chapter on "The Virtues of Carelessness," *Thackeray at Work* (London: Athlone Press, 1974), pp. 56–73.

8. Joan Stevens has demonstrated how crucial is the placing of Thackeray's illustrations, for instance in "Thackeray's *Vanity Fair,*" *Review of English Literature* 6 (1965): 19–38, and "A Fairy Tale Mishandled: *The Rose and the Ring,*" *AUMLA* 23 (1965): 5–23.

9. For reference to a caricature that caused a quarrel between Bulwer-Lytton, Dickens, and Forster on one side, and Thackeray on the other, see *Letters,* II, 296n, and the account by Gordon Ray in *Thackeray: The Age of Wisdom: 1847–1863* (London: Oxford University Press, 1958) pp. 135–36.

10. It is likely, though more disputable, that Thackeray intends the substantial figure of Lanty Clancy (p. 147) for Charles Lever, who was fat from his boyhood; and that the burly Tom Coxswain (p. 171), who is fat where his original Tom Coffin was lank and lean, could be the by then portly James Fenimore Cooper. But Thackeray had not met Cooper, and it is difficult to discover the currency of published likenesses of him.

11. Keith Hollingsworth, *The Newgate Novel* (Detroit: Wayne State University Press, 1963), p. 212 ff.

12. "W.M. Thackeray, Artist and Moralist," in *Poems and Essays* (London: Chapman and Hall, 1860), II, 300. I touched on this subject in *Thackeray: The Major Novels* (Toronto: University of Toronto Pres, 1971), p. 89.

13. See Michael Sadleir, *Bulwer: A Panorama. Edward and Rosina, 1803–1836* (London: Constable, 1931), p. 252, and Allan Conrad Christensen, *Edward Bulwer-Lytton: The Fiction of New Regions* (Athens: University of Georgia Press, 1976), 227–28.

14. An appreciative treatment of her and her work is included in Alison Adburgham's *Silver Fork Society: Fashionable Life and Literature from 1814 to 1840* (London: Constable, 1983).

15. Matthew Whiting Rosa, *The Silver-Fork School* (New York: Columbia University Press, 1936), p. 206.

16. See S.M. Ellis, *The Solitary Horseman: The Life and Adventures of G.P.R. James* (Kensington: Cayme Press, 1927), pp. 70, 77–79.

17. See my " 'Bluebeard at Breakfast': An Unpublished Thackeray Manuscript," *Dickens Studies Annual* 8 (1980): 197–230.

18. In both novels the wild young Irish protagonist impetuously challenges the more experienced military man, shoots him down, and must flee the country at the

outset of his adventurous career. In both cases the victim turns out not to be seriously injured after all.

19. See Ray's account of their relation, *Letters,* I, cxlvii and II, 451n.
20. Thackeray had already objected to this kind of implausibility in *Barry Lyndon:* "These persons (I mean the romance-writers), if they take a drummer or a dustman for a hero, somehow manage to bring him into contact with the greatest lords and most notorious personages of the empire" (6. 70).
21. See Geoffrey and Kathleen Tillotson's Introduction to their edition of *Vanity Fair* (London: Methuen, 1963), pp. xxix ff.
22. This characteristic of Thackeray's writing was first memorably explored by John A. Lester in "Thackeray's Narrative Technique," *PMLA* 69 (1954): 392–409.

William Thackeray's Fiction and Caroline Norton's Biography: Narrative Matrix of Feminist Legal Reform

Micael M. Clarke

> So, God bless the Special Jury! pride and joy of English
> ground,
> And the happy land of England, where true justice does
> abound!
> British jurymen and husbands, let us hail this verdict proper:
> If a British wife offends you, Britons, you've a right to
> whop her.
> Though you promised to protect her, though you promised
> to defend her,
> You are welcome to neglect her: to the devil you may send
> her:
> You may strike her, curse, abuse her; so declares our law
> renowned;
> And if after this you lose her,—why, you're paid two
> hundred pound.
> (Thackeray, "Damages, Two Hundred Pounds," 1850)

William Makepeace Thackeray and Caroline Norton both wrote for *Fraser's* magazine early in their careers, and they were friends at least as early as 1845. Each has been studied in his or her own sphere—Thackeray as one of the great Victorian novelists, and Norton as a feminist reformer of laws relating to child custody, divorce, and married women's property. When the two are studied together, however, a significant pattern emerges which has not yet received the critical attention it deserves. A number of incidents in Thackeray's fiction correspond closely to simmilar events in Norton's life, indicating that she is probably the "original" of several of Thackeray's characters. And his novels are informed by some remarkably liberal views regarding the nineteenth-century women's movement. Thackeray's friendship with Norton may have convinced him that her story, made more eloquent perhaps by her charm and intelligence, exemplified the injustices under which women lived.

The three Thackerayan characters who resemble Caroline Norton are Lady Lyndon in *Barry Lyndon,* Becky Sharp in *Vanity Fair,* and Clara Pulleyn Newcome in *The Newcomes.* All three are associated with the very issues of adultery, child custody, married woman's property, and divorce that characterized Norton's historic struggles. Thackeray presents the three as quite different personalities who receive different degrees of approval: Lady Lyndon is a foolish but otherwise innocent victim; Becky is a highly ambiguous figure as to either sexual guilt or authorial approval; and Clara is without doubt guilty of adultery, but nonetheless an object of sympathy. Their connection with Norton is hinted at by certain key details of their stories, by the timing of Thackeray's historically allusive novels, and by the fact that they all, despite their differences, allow Thackery to raise and resolve the very issues Norton represented. No other woman bears quite so many resemblances to these characters, was so key a figure in reforming the laws, and was at the same time so good a friend to Thackeray as Caroline Norton.

Thackeray and Norton probably met when both were contributors to *Fraser's Magazine;* Norton began contributing to the journal in 1831 or 1832 (Perkins, 38; Acland, 44–48), Thackeray, at least by 1835 (Gulliver, 67). Both came from upper-class backgrounds, both had been driven into journalism by financial need, and both were to be separated from their spouses, Norton in 1836 due to marital difficulties, Thackeray in 1842 because his wife was mentally ill.

Thackeray's letters and diaries provide some glimpses of their relationship: in 1845, Norton arranged for Thackeray to dine with Lord Melbourne, who thought he was a clergyman; in 1847, Thackeray wrote to thank Norton for a book, to apologize for making impertinent remarks about her appearance in his "Grumble about the *Christmas Books,*" and to promise a visit (Ray, *Letters* 2. 229; 263–65). In the same year, Jane Brookfield advised her husband against accepting an offer to share a house with certain friends, warning him against the effect that such company would have on his reputation as a minister, and significantly (jealously perhaps, for she enjoyed Thackeray's admiration herself) pairing Norton's name with Thackeray's: "Cannot you call up visions of cosy little Sunday dinners with *Mrs. Norton*, Mr. Thackery, & Mr. and Mrs. Wigan?'' (Ray, *Wisdom* 74–75)

Thackeray's diary records a remark made shortly after March 10, 1847, by ''C.N.,'' presumably Norton, which is very much in the spirit of *Vanity Fair*:

> I tried in vain to convince the fine folks at W. Fox's that revolution was upon us: that we were wicked in our scorn of the people—they all thought there was poverty and discontent to be sure, but that they were pretty good in themselves; that powder and liveries were very decent & proper though certainly absurd—the footmen themselves would not give them up C.N. said.

And in 1848, Thackeray attended a party at the Duke of Devonshire's with Norton, ''she sitting bodkin in her own brougham, and indeed there are very few more beautiful bodkins in the world'' (Ray, *Letters* 2. 373 n. 93). Lionel Stevenson maintains that Norton ''pushed'' Thackeray in his career as writer by introducing him to influential people (156), and states that Thackeray was still seeing her as late as 1861.

Existing evidence leads to the conclusion that Thackeray's relationship with Norton was a friendship—spiced perhaps with a feeling of mutual attraction—but neither a love affair nor a sexual relationship. Both had other, deep emotional involvements at various times, Norton with Sidney Herbert, and Thackeray with Jane Brookfield, and although Norton delighted in being unconventional, she was interested in society, not seduction. And Thackeray's letters and diaries indicate that for him, a sexual relationship would have ended the friendship.

However, Norton was a witty, beautiful, intelligent, and elegant woman whose dinners must have been delightful to the often lonely, restless, and sometimes cash-strapped Thackeray. Lady Eastlake's description best sums up the style of Norton's charm in terms which evoke Becky Sharp and indicate why Thackeray would enjoy her company:

> She is a beautiful and gifted woman: her talents are of the highest order, and she has carefully cultivated them—has read deeply, has a fine memory, and wit only to be found in a Sheridan. No one can compare with her in teling a story—so pointed, so happy, and so easy; but she is rather a professed story teller. . . . [S]he is a perpetual actress, consummately studying and playing her part, and that always the attempt to fascinate—she cares not whom.
> (Acland, 208–09)

Norton's satirical remarks against the sacred icons of nineteenth-century England must have struck a responsive chord in Thackeray's own nature. And so it would not be surprising, even without certain other influences such as his wife's insanity and Jane Brookfield's unhappy marriage, if Thackeray, captivated by this Becky Sharp with a heart, became an advocate for the improvements in women's conditions that Norton fought for.

Caroline Norton was indeed a subject for literature. Allusions to her life and character appear in a number of works: Dickens, for example, is said to have based the trial scene in *Pickwick Papers* (1836–37) on Norton's notorious "criminal conversation" trial (Acland, 90). Norton also inspired Benjamin Disraeli's Lady Montfort in *Endymion* (1881), a novel about the political influence of women in which Thackeray appears as a radical writer always complaining about "Gushy's" success (Blake, 735–36). She is also the (depoliticized) heroine of Meredith's *Diana of the Crossways* (1885), in which Thackeray's spirit is evoked in the first chapter:

> A great modern writer, of clearest eye and head, now departed, capable in activity of presenting thoughtful women, thinking men, groaned over his puppetry, that he dared not animate them, flesh though they were, with the fires of positive brainstuff. He could have done it, and he is of the departed! Had he dared, he would (for he was Titan enough) have raised the Art in dignity on a level with History.
>
> (15–16)

The passage echoes Thackeray's own comment in 1856 that Norton would be a good character for a book if England were not "so awfully squeamish," and that "there might be some good fun in that forthcoming serial" if "one's hands were not tied" (Ray, *Letters* 3. 617).

Many readers will be familiar with the outline of Caroline Norton's life. In 1827 Caroline Sheridan, then nineteen, married George Norton "for practical reasons" (Acland, 22–23; Fowler, 235): her mother was a widow with seven children, and he seemed a good match in the "marriage market" that Thackeray so frequently attacks. The marriage soon fell apart. George lacked intelligence, and he was a heavy drinker, and sometimes violent. But Caroline was not to be intimidated, and she did her share to aggravate their mutual hostilities. She complained about George to family and friends, she wrote about her unhappiness in the dedication of a book, and she socialized with, and flirted with, other women's husbands. She even supported the Whigs while her husband tried to make a political career as a Tory.

Beginning in about 1830, William Lamb, Lord Melbourne, then Home Secretary and a powerful Whig who was also to be Prime Minister, became a daily visitor to Caroline Norton's home. She even used her influence with Lord Melbourne to obtain a post for her husband which he was to enjoy as a 1,000 pounds-per-year sinecure for the rest of his life (Acland, 52–53). One is of course reminded of Becky Sharp, Rawdon Crawley, and Lord Steyne. But in 1836, impelled by some combination of jealousy, greed, and political expediency, George filed suit against Lord Melbourne for "criminal conversation" with his wife Caroline, and the marriage was irrevocably ended.

We will probably never know what Caroline's relationship with Melbourne was. At the trial, George's witnesses were so patently untrustworthy that Melbourne was acquitted by a jury which never even left the box to deliberate. Caroline's cry of "I am innocent!" rings through her writings just as Becky's similar cry haunts the conclusion of *Vanity Fair*. In neither case can we be sure of the truth. Both her biographers, Alice Marreco Acland and Jane Gray Perkins, conclude that there was no sexual relationship between Caroline and Lord Melbourne.

But the question of sexual innocence aside, Norton's situation demonstrated the powerlessness of women under the current legal system. Because she had been judged innocent in the "criminal conversation" trial, George could not divorce her (it was necessary to prove adultery to obtain either an ecclesiastical separation or a civil divorce). And because Norton, always eager for a reconciliation and fearful of losing her children, had returned to George after he had been violent and probably unfaithful, she had "condoned" his behavior in the eyes of the law. Therefore she could not divorce him. George confiscated her books, clothes, and jewelry when they separated, and had the door of their house chained against her as, by law, everything a married woman owned or earned belonged to her husband.

The Nortons's three sons, Fletcher, Brinsley, and William, were George's greatest weapon. For six years, Norton lived in constant fear, alternately placating and fighting her husband for the privilege of seeing her children. She was especially concerned about the oldest, who was in poor health, and she was tortured by not knowing where they were. At one point, she writes, the boys were sent to George's sister in Scotland, who flogged one for reading a letter from Caroline, and stripped another, tied him to a bed-post, and whipped him. Eighteen years later, Norton wrote of that period of her life:

> I learnt, too, the *Law* as to my children—that the right was with the father; that neither my innocence nor his guilt could alter it; that not even his giving them into the hands of a mistress, would give me any claim to their custody. The eldest was but six years old, the second four, the youngest two and a half when we were parted. . . .
> What I suffered on my children's account, none will ever know or measure.
> (*English Laws* 49–50)

Sadly, George's behavior was within the law. A brief review of the laws will show why. Before passage of the Marital Causes Act in 1857, divorce was a three-step procedure. It was easier for a man to obtain a divorce, not only because he controlled the family's money and possessed an income, but also because a sexual double standard was built into the law. A man could divorce his wife on the grounds of adultery alone, while a woman had to prove the husband guilty of adultery *combined with* bigmy, incest, bestiality, or desertion. To obtain a divorce, a man would first sue his wife's purported lover for "criminal conversation," as George Norton sued Lord Melbourne—an action that amounted to requesting compensation for damage to property. Next, the injured husband would go to an ecclesiastical court to obtain a decree of separation on the grounds of his wife's adultery (in the Church, divorce was not permissible). Finally, if he had succeeded in these two courts in establishing his wife's guilt, the husband could then proceed to the House of Lords to petition for a private Act of Parliament to dissolve the marriage. As Norton pointed out, this system reflected a great deal of confusion regarding whether marriage is a sacrament or a civil contract—and it often turned out in practice to be a contract for the rich and a sacrament for the poor, or a contract for the man and a sacrament for the woman. (*English Laws* 143)

What could Caroline do? She wrote years later of that time: "These boys having been the gleam of happiness in my home, it was not to be supposed I would give them up without a struggle, because it was so 'written in the bond' of English law." And so she fought the law. Caroline's campaign was conducted on two fronts. Socially, she used her influence with literary and political men to enlist supporters such as Serjeant Talfourd, who in 1836 introduced an Infant Custody bill into the House of Commons. And to gain public and political support for the bill, she wrote a pamphlet, which she published in 1837 at her own expense, entitled *Separation of Mother and Child by the Custody of Infants Considered*. It was, as Acland puts it, the "First blow in her long battle for legal reform" (103).

In August of 1838, while Talfourd's bill was being debated in the House of Commons, Norton was attacked in the *British and Foreign Review,* which called her a "she-devil" and insinuated that she was sleeping with Talfourd in order to persuade him to change the law so that she could escape punishment for her crimes. In February, 1839, *Fraser's* carried Nathaniel Ogle's long article defending Norton and advocating the Infant Custody Bill which Thackeray would surely have read, as his *Catherine,* which deals satirically with some of the same issues—sexual double standards, respectability, and unhappy marriage, child custody—was appearing in *Fraser's* at the same time.

Norton fought on with her pen, publishing a letter in two papers, and then publishing another pamphlet, *A Plain Letter to the Lord Chancellor on the Infant Custody Bill* (1839). In it, Norton begins by refuting the Bill's opponents. Some had claimed that fathers had absolute power over their children by divine right, but Norton argues that the law is willing to interfere with such "divine" right when property and inheritance are concerned, as if the law deemed property more important than the safety of mothers and children. Some had argued that the authority of the father necessarily arises out of the inferiority of women, but Norton, who never explicitly quarrels with the idea that women are inferior, argues that women's weakness is cause for the law to guard them against oppressive husbands (6–7).

The bill's opponents had argued that infant custody could encourage women to abandon their husbands, or perhaps boldly to indulge in vice once the fear of losing their children was removed. Norton responds that the real checks to dissolute behavior in women lie in other areas in which they are also at a disadvantage: loss of reputation and social isolation. And of course, Norton points out, it is sometimes the husband who mistreats and abandons his wife, and yet the law continues to give him full privileges over his children. Thus, she argues, passage of the Infant Custody Bill would not make women worse, but would make men better, for the laws, as they stood, allowed for extraordinary abuses of male privilege (20). The *Plain Letter* combines logic with emotional persuasion, and sometimes with insult, as when she writes: "To be allowed to see a little child occasionally . . . might satisfy a *father,* because at the best he does little more in his own home" (47).

Talfourd held up the Infant Custody Bill twice while Norton negotiated privately with her husband over money and custody of the children, but when those negotiations fell through, Talfourd went ahead. In the summer of 1839, the Infant Custody Bill was made law. It gave mothers of children under seven the right to petition for a custody hearing—a limited improvement, but a beginning. One issue had been partially resolved, although Caroline had yet to discover that because George had removed the children to Scotland, the new law did not apply to them.

Sadly, the youngest boy died after a fall from a horse while his mother still struggled to gain custody. George Norton did not notify her for a week. She reached her son too late, and in a letter to a friend, dated 13 September 1842, she reflected: "It may be sinful to think bitterly at such a time. . . . But it is not in the strength of human nature not to think, 'This might not have happened had I watched over them!' '' (Acland, 135) It was an incident which Thackeray was to include, with some modification, in *Barry Lyndon*.

From this time on, Caroline Norton was permitted to see the two surviving boys regularly—not because she had changed the infant custody laws, but because George, filled with remorse over William's death, was now willing to accede to some of her requests. Two issues remained, which Norton would address fifteen years later: divorce and married women's property. Actually, as Thackeray was to show, the three are inextricable: women's fears of losing their children and of poverty would cause them to forego the relief of divorce, even if it were available. Before considering that part of Caroline Norton's history, it is appropriate to compare what we have seen of her life and ideas with the uses Thackeray makes of them in his fiction.

Three novels which most clearly reflect aspects of Norton's life and character are *Barry Lyndon, Vanity Fair,* and *The Newcomes. Barry Lyndon,* published in *Fraser's* in 1844, is a fictional autobiography narrated by Barry Lyndon himself. In it, as I have argued elsewhere (Clarke), Thackeray demonstrates through ironic narrative how a mind like Barry's justifies itself in terms of accepted misogynistic values of the culture. Certain parallels indicate that the novel alludes to Norton. The most obvious parallel is that Lady Lyndon's son is killed in a riding accident at the age of nine; Norton's son had been eight when he died in 1842. Redmund Barry resembles George Norton too—both use their wives to promote their careers, both serve one term in Parliament, and both are physically abusive to their rebellious, intellectual wives. Acland describes George Norton in terms which fit Redmund Barry well:

> He was true to the spirit of his class and times in that money was more important to him than anything else—than honour, justice, or truth. Money was his obsession, and conditioned every thought and action.
>
> (65)

Thackeray also supports Norton's arguments concerning Infant Custody by demonstrating that Barry uses his wife's love for her son to bend her will to his. Norton had asked, in her 1839 *Plain Letter*:

> But the question is, on what principle the legislature should give a man this power to torment; this power to say to his wife, "You shall bear blows, you shall bear inconstancy, you shall give up property, you shall endure insults, and *yet* you shall continue to live under my roof, *or else,* I will take your children, and you shall never see them more."
>
> (46)

Thackeray drives the same point home, expanding its significance beyond the legal to the social, in a footnote written by the fictive "editor" of Barry's memoirs:

> From these curious confessions, it would appear that Mr. Lyndon maltreated his lady in every possible way; that he denied her society, bullied her into signing away her property, spent it in gambling and taverns, was openly unfaithful to her; and, when she complained, threatened to remove her children from her. Nor, indeed, is he the only husband who had done the like. . . . The world contains scores of such amiable people; and, indeed, it is because justice has not been done them that we have edited this autobiography.
>
> (Ch. 1. 2, 312)

Barry Lyndon lends imaginative life and power to Norton's arguments, and it anticipates the debate which would surround passage of the Divorce Act. Thackeray's purpose, he declares, is to do justice to the "amiable people" who so mistreat their wives, and whom the law has given absolute power, and the world thoughtless acceptance. The ultimate purpose of *Barry Lyndon* is to lay bare the unconscious assumptions which animate such men, and to demonstrate how they operate in the larger world. As in *Barry Lyndon,* so in the world, writes Thackeray: misogyny, though evil, is not recognized as such, and thus, like an essentially materialistic system of ethics or a false sense of honor, it can flourish and do inestimable harm.

Thackeray's best-known female character is Becky Sharp of *Vanity Fair* (1847–48). Becky is an ambiguous figure, a Clytemnestra who exacts revenge for the sufferings of the daughters of England (Di Battista). Becky may also represent Thackeray's doubts about Norton and her relationship with Melbourne. Perhaps because of the mystery and fascination surrounding Norton, Becky seems to call forth some of Thackeray's best writing. He even seems to delight in the uncertainty, in that Becky represents the greater truth that none of us knows our neighbor's heart, and certainly none has the right to judge:

> Her history was after all a mystery. Parties were divided about her. Some . . . said that she was a criminal; whilst others vowed that she was as innocent as a lamb, and that her odious husband was in fault. She won over a good many by bursting into tears about her boy.
>
> (2. 370)

Most readers will already have recognized certain similarities between Caroline and Becky: for example, Caroline married George at least in part for the money and title he expected to inherit, just as Becky expected that

Rawdon would inherit from Miss Crawley. Both women are witty and un-conventional, and both know "How to Live Well On Nothing A-Year," and how to deal with the law. Becky is even complimented by her creditors' lawyers "upon the brilliant way in which she did business, and [they] declared that there was no professional man who could beat her" (2. 11).

Thackeray's descriptions of Becky often recall Norton: "Becky loved so-ciety, and, indeed, could no more exist without it than an opium-eater without his dram" (2. 372). Becky was presented in court just as Norton had been. More importantly, Becky's relationship with Lord Steyne resembles Norton's with Lord Melbourne. Both men are considerably older than the women, both are powerful and wealthy, and both have had scandalous love affairs. Mel-bourne, of course, had been sued for "crim. con." before, and found guilty. And Steyne, Thackeray tells us,

> whose carriage was always at [Becky's] door, who passed hours daily in her company, and whose constant presence made the world talk about her. . . . Lord Steyne, though a nobleman of the greatest station and talents, was a man whose attentions would compromise any woman.
>
> (2. 216)

The words were as true of Melbourne as of Steyne.

Although Becky exemplifies Norton's intelligence, wit, and bold humor, and elements of her life seem to allude to Norton's, she does not entirely resemble Norton. Thackeray's greatest indictment of Becky is that she cares little for either her son or her dull but generous and loyal husband, Rawdon. Neither of these charges fits Caroline, for she loved her children—they were the true motivating passion of her work—and George was not docile like Rawdon, but aggressive and violent. These alterations make Becky Sharp a less sympathetic character than her real-life counterpart Caroline Norton.

Why would Thackeray make such changes? It seems fair to conclude that the good woman/bad woman dualism which runs through *Vanity Fair,* ironic though it may be, made such simplification necessary. However, despite such alterations, the significance of Becky's story as a reflection of Caroline's history remains: both represent women's powerlessness—good women and bad are equally liable to lose their children. Norton/Becky provided Thackeray with the most effective counterpoint to Amelia. As Acland writes:

> In the almost flamboyant effect of her personality she was very far removed from the ideal feminine type of the day. The pure, gentle, timid, docile woman—a type soon to be crystallised in the person of Amelia Sedley—held a high place then in the public imagination. It was impossible for Caroline to

model herself on the lines of such doves with folded wings. And because she
could not pretend to be an Amelia Sedley, many people thought she must be
a Becky Sharp instead.

(156–57)

By making Becky's character even less conventional than Norton's, Thackeray
made possible a more thorough critique of respectable society: in their struggles to survive on their own, both women enter that shadowy area which
safely cocooned women need not enter. But Becky's defiant wickedness
provides a more effective critique than Norton's more mixed, socially conservative character in that Becky recognizes and exploits the sham values of
Vanity Fair, while Norton never rejected them altogether.

But Thackeray's most powerful argument against this system came in a
novel, *The Newcomes,* published serially between 1853 and 1855. By then,
Thackeray and Norton had known one another for at least ten, possibly fifteen,
years. A brief survey of the rest of Norton's history demonstrates that Thackeray's novel constitutes a commentary on certain debates then raging in Parliament.

By 1853, Norton had been separated from her husband for seventeen years,
sharing custody of the two surviving boys and receiving an allowance for
him. Now she was again engaged in litigation with him—this time over money
only. In 1848, Caroline had signed an agreement with George, a contract she
thought it was, which allowed George to borrow money by using as security
Caroline's expected inheritance upon her mother's death. In return George
signed a separation agreement, allowing Caroline to live separately and promising her an allowance; it was a fraction of the 1,000 pounds a year George
was still receiving from Melbourne's "patronage" position. (Caroline also
depended for support on her brother, her uncle, and on earnings from her
writing.) However, when George learned that Caroline had been left a sum
by Melbourne, he stopped paying the allowance. The "contract" Caroline
thought he had signed now turned out to be invalid because husband and
wife, being one, could not enter into legal contract. Norton stopped paying
her bills so that her creditors would sue George, and he subpoenaed her
bankers and publishers, claiming that all Norton earned was his. He stunned
Caroline in court by publicly repeating the old accusation of a love affair with
Melbourne, using it as justification for not supporting a woman who was still
"profiting" fromm her crimes. He also claimed the copyright to her works,
which outraged Norton more than their disputes over money. "Let him claim
the copyright on THIS," she challenged in her *Letter to the Queen* (153), a
scathing attack on George and on male privilege generally. And in *English*

Laws she wrote: "I will never again write, while my copyrights are held to be Mr. Norton's; except on this single subject of the state of the Laws of Protection for Women" (73).

Concurrently, two bills were before Parliament, a Divorce Bill and a Married Woman's Property Bill. Feminists had worked for years to get these bills considered, but now they languished in committee. One would make divorce more accessible and the other would give married women legal title to their own property and earnings. Now, impelled again by personal difficulties, Norton re-entered the political arena to support the moribund bills by publishing *English Laws for Women in the Nineteenth Century* (1854) and *A Letter to the Queen on Lord Chancellor Cranworth's Marriage and Divorce Bill* (1855). Some of the claims Norton makes in these documents anticipate arguments John Stuart Mill was to use six years later: that progress was equated with removing obstacles to women's happiness, for example, or that women's oppression is similar to slavery, in that it seems natural when people are accustomed to it. But, unlike Mill, Norton wrote as a woman, and *English Laws,* especially, is a passionate autobiography as well as political document, an autobiography in which her sufferings are offered to the public in hope of finding a remedy for other women in similar situations. Norton's *Letter to the Queen,* which was shorter, less personal and less bitter, had a better reception however, and was favorably reviewed.

At the same time, Thackeray was bringing out *The Newcomes: The Memoirs of a Most Respectable Family* (1853–55). In this novel, Clara Newcome resembles Caroline Norton in several ways. First, their names are similar, and Clara signs a letter in an impassioned way reminiscent of Caroline: "the *wretched, lonely* C.N." (13. 255). Both have three children, whom they will lose if they attempt to escape their marriages. And the "crim. con." suit which Barnes brings against Clara's lover is similar to that which George had brought against Melbourne. Although the Norton-Melbourne trial had taken place some twenty years earlier, it was again topical, as Caroline fought the old battles again with George, both using the public press as their forum. Thackeray's readers could not have missed the connections.

When, after years of misery, Clara runs away with another man, Thackeray makes it clear that she was forced into an impossible choice between marriage to an insulting, violent, bully, and escape with a lover and consequent loss of property, friends, and children. Barnes sues the lover, whom Thackeray presents as a good man who could not bear to watch her suffering. Like Caroline, Clara watches helplessly as her good name is dragged through court and into the scandal-sheets. Thackeray describes the situation with angry sarcasm:

> Suppose a young creature taken out of her home, and given over to a hard master whose caresses are as insulting as his neglect; consigned to cruel usage; to weary loneliness; . . . suppose her schooled into hypocrisy by tyranny—and then, quick, let us hire an advocate to roar out to a British jury the wrongs of her injured husband, to paint the agonies of his bleeding heart. . . . Let us console that martyr, I say, with thumping damages; and as for the woman—the guilty wretch!—let us lead her out and stone her.
>
> (13. 230)

The crucial difference between the Newcomes and the Nortons is that Barnes wins, which provides Thackeray grounds on which to attack the system, and to support the Marital Causes Act then before Parliament. For example, Clara's powerlessness only serves to make Barnes, her husband, more arrogant. What Norton had argued, Thackeray demonstrates: the law did not serve to make women better, but to make men worse. *The Newcomes* is Thackeray's most direct attack on existing marriage laws, and demonstrates their injustice in a way that supports the Divorce Bill and reflects favorably on Norton, the Bill's most controversial and influential supporter.

In 1857, the Divorce Act was passed into law. It benefited women in two essential ways. It established a separate civil court, so that a special Act of Parliament was no longer required for divorce. And it expanded the grounds on which women could obtain a divorce, although a double standard remained: a husband's adultery was still not sufficient grounds for a woman to obtain divorce, while a wife's adultery was.

The 1850s were crucial years for the women's movement in England. Gradually the Victorian public was beginning to recognize the injustices of the laws and to accept legislative reforms. Thackeray's novels and Norton's political writings were a factor in that shift in public opinion. Jane Perkins's evaluation of the impact of Norton's *English Laws* also applies to Norton's story as Thackeray presents it in *The Newcomes:*

> The impression it made . . . is incalculable, coming as it did at a time when public opinion had so far outstripped the law in its judgment of the rights and wrongs of women that it was ready to be set on fire by the story of a woman who, to use her own words, ''had learned the English law piecemeal by suffering under it.''
>
> (239)

By transforming Norton's history into the emotionally powerful medium of fiction, Thackeray echoed and expanded her critique of cultural attitudes toward women. The effect he wished to have on his readers was both moral and political. Thackeray, who had studied law for a year, was now helping to change it, for a shift in the Victorian public's moral perceptions brought about by Thackeray's fiction and Norton's rhetoric underlies some of the reforms achieved in the nineteenth century by feminists. If Thackeray had not "re-invented" Norton's history as fiction, such important legal measures as Infant Custody and the Divorce Act might not have been accomplished when they were. By broadening the significance of Norton's story beyond the legal, Thackeray laid bare the social and cultural biases which made unjust laws seem natural. And by putting a legal and historical debate into novels, he enabled his readers to visualize the sufferings of women like Norton, circumventing any prejudice against her scandal-ridden past or against the feminist movement itself. He created "parables of history" out of the life story of his beautiful, brilliant, but unhappy friend, Caroline Norton.

WORKS CITED

Acland, Alice, [Marreco]. *Caroline Norton*. London: Constable, 1948.

Blake, Robert. *Disraeli*. New York: St. Martin's, 1967.

Clarke, Micael M. "Thackeray's *Barry Lyndon:* An Irony Against Misogynists." *Texas Studies in Literature and Language* 29 (1987): 261–77.

Di Battista, Maria. "The Triumph of Clytemnestra: The Charades in *Vanity Fair.*" *PMLA* 95 (1980): 827–37.

Fowler, Lois Josephs. "Norton, Caroline." *Dictionary of Literary Biography*. Ed. Ira B. Nadel and William E. Fredeman. 64 vols. to date. Detroit, Mi.: Gale Research Co., 1983. 21: 234–38.

Gulliver, Harold Strong. *Thackeray's Literary Apprenticeship*. 1934; Valdosta, GA: Norwood, 1977.

Holcombe, Lee. *Wives and Property: Reform of the Married Women's Property Law in Nineteenth-Century England*. Toronto: University of Toronto, 1983.

Horstman, Allen. *Victorian Divorce*. New York: St. Martin's, 1985.

Meredith, George. *Diana of the Crossways*. 1885. Intro by Lois Josephs Fowler. New York: Norton, 1973.

Norton, Caroline. *English Laws for Women in the Nineteenth Century*. 1854. *Selected Writings of Caroline Norton: Facsimile Reproductions*. Ed. James O. Hoge and Jane Marcus. Delmar, N. Y.: Scholars' Facsimiles & Reprints, 1978.

————. *A Letter to the Queen on Lord Chancellor Cranworth's Marriage and Divorce Bill*. 1855. In *Selected Writings*.

[Ogle, Nathaniel]. "The Custody of Infants' Bill." *Fraser's Magazine* 19 (February 1839): 205–14. [Author per *Wellesley Index*].

Perkins, Jane Gray. *The Life of Mrs. Norton*. c. 1909; rpt. London: John Murray, 1910.

Ray, Gordon N. *The Letters and Private Papers of William Makepeace Thackeray*. 4 vols. Cambridge: Harvard UP, 1946.

——————. *Thackeray: The Age of Wisdom, 1847–1863*. 1958. New York: Farrar, Straus and Giroux, 1972.

——————. *Thackeray: The Uses of Adversity, 1811–1846*. 1955. New York: Farrar, Straus and Giroux, 1972.

Shanley, Mary Lyndon. " 'One Must Ride Behind': Married Women's Rights and the Divorce Act of 1857." *Victorian Studies* 25 (1982): 355–76.

Stevenson, Lionel. *The Showman of Vanity Fair: The Life of William Makepeace Thackeray*. London: Chapman & Hall, 1947.

Thackeray, William Makepeace. "Damages, Two Hundred Pounds," in *The Ballads of Policeman X*. 1850. *The Works of William Makepeace Thackeray*. Ed. Anne T. Ritchie and Leslie Stephen. 26 vols. London: Smith, Elder, 1910–11; rpt. New York: AMS Press, 1968. 15: 277–79.

——————. Diary in the British Museum Ms. Collection.

——————. "A Grumble About the Christmas Books, by Michael Angelo Titmarsh." *Fraser's Magazine* 35 (January 1847): 111–26.

——————. *The Luck of Barry Lyndon*. 1844. Ed. Martin J. Anisman. New York: New York UP, 1970.

——————. *The Newcomes: Memoirs of a Most Respectable Family*. 1853–55. Vols. 12–13 of *Works*.

——————. *Vanity Fair: A Novel Without a Hero*. 1847–48. Vols. 1–2 of *Works*.

The Professor: Charlotte Brontë's Hysterical Text, or Realistic Narrative and the Ideology of the Subject from a Feminist Perspective

Ruth D. Johnston

The essay which follows explores the construction of sexual identity *in* representation. I argue that the realistic notion of identity as a particular temporal/spatial structuration is assumed (if modified) in the psychoanalytic account of the constitution of the subject, which means that both the theory and aesthetic practice consequently furnish a model of subjectivity that is exclusively masculine. In this context I examine Charlotte Brontë's *The Professor* as a hysterical text, by which I mean a text that interrogates the possibility of constructing a feminine subjectivity in realistic signifying practices, the narrator's biological sex in this novel serving to render the repression of the feminine explicit. In addition, I choose this novel as an exemplary hysterical text because it also makes explicit the relation (actually the complicity) of retrospective narration and geometrical perspective (that is, literary and pictorial realism), a relationship which I also explore in my definition of realism, to which I now turn.

I regard temporal structure (which includes questions of enunciation and address) to be the fundamental feature of the nineteenth-century novel.[1] Time in a realistic narrative is conceived as a continuous and consistent medium stretching to infinity, which means that the significant distinction is past vs. present. (Contrast the medieval notion of time as discontinuous and its corollary that meaning derives from the opposition between earthly time and eternity.) Realistic time is thus analogous on the one hand to the definition of space in the Renaissance perspective system and on the other to the conception of nature in Western scientific thought in the post-Renaissance era. Such art and such science belong to an empirical epistemology, which presents knowledge as a process occurring between an already-constituted subject and object and consisting in the extraction of an essence from the real object.[2]

This knowledge process depends on temporal and spatial consistency to support the empiricist/realistic notion of identity as cumulative. Any appearance of an object is understood as only partial, making it necessary to compare a whole series of views in order to detect which elements are repeated. The "sameness" that emerges from such an examination and that enables us to recognize a structure is an abstraction that constitutes the object's identity. Note further that subject and object are constituted in relation to one another insofar as successive views are compared in relation to a single, fixed viewpoint. In fact, subjectivity is a product of this system of representation.[3] However, because the knowledge operation consists in the discrimination between the real (the essence) and the inessential (the purely accidental), a distinction which already exists in the structure of the real object, both the object and process of knowledge are thought to inhere in the real object. In short, what the empiricist concept of knowledge suppresses is the notion of knowledge as production (Althusser 36–38).

In literary realism, *dis*covery of identity is actually *re*covery, for the process or temporal order to which a particular manifestation belongs can be apprehended only through the operation of memory, that is, retrospection. The identity of a person or object cannot be perceived immediately and independently but must be *recognized* through placement in the context of the whole system: memory must supply all the previous states which help to define that identity but which are not evident at present. In realistic narrative, memory operates on two levels: first, the characters' individual acts of recall, which are subordinated to/encompassed by the second level, the retrospection of the narrator. As a result, the narrative continuously superimposes two viewpoints insofar as every moment is shown as concrete, occurring in the "present" (of the characters), and simultaneously as part of a process that occurr*ed* in the narrator's past, which explains why literary realism presupposes past-tense narration.

The narrating consciousness in a realistic narrative, which determines the temporal relations among events as it records them in some unspecified future, is the analogue of the implied spectator whose vision coordinates all spatial relations within the frame in a three-dimensional painting. The location of the narrator/spectator/subject *outside* the diegesis insures the continuity of space and time as well as the validity of the system beyond the scope of the text. But the price of such uniformity is the subject's alienation from concrete existence; for the focus of this disembodied consciousness is not the particulars in themselves but their relationship. This definition of focus in turn clarifies the designation of realism as mimesis; for what is imitated is not the concrete object but the system to which it belongs. It is the perpetuation of a particular logic or organization that is at stake—retrospective narrative in the case of literature, geometrical perspective in the case of painting. Thus realism refers to a system that is self-reflexive.

It is precisely this empiricist concept of knowledge which supports realism that Lacan regards Freud as having transformed by a Copernican revolution. Lacan conceives of psychoanalysis as a theory of the subject and quite explicitly states that his notion of the subject both assumes and differs from the Cartesian subject of consciousness (*Fundamental Concepts* 44). His elaboration proceeds from a linguistic analysis of the *cogito* in which he distinguishes two levels—that of enunciation (the moment of speaking) and that of the statement. (The difference between these two levels corresponds to the distinction mentioned above between the narrator's discourse and the character's discourse in literary realism, with exceptions noted below.)

Even though the present-tense verb invites us to conflate the speaking subject (of the enunciation) and the subject in the statement or proposition, Lacan insists that the two levels of the "I think" are irreducible. His distinction makes it clear that the subject of consciousness (of empiricism) "who thinks he can accede to himself by designating himself in the statement" necessarily regards himself as an object (*Écrits* 315). In Lacan's reading, however, the *cogito* takes its place at the level of enunciation, and the subject is inscribed in the vibration between the two levels. That is, the pronoun "I" in the statement is a signifier which in linguistics is called a "shifter" because it is unstable; it refers only to a function at the moment of utterance. Since it can only "designate," not "signify," the speaking subject, that subject is therefore reduced to a "punctuality of being" (*Écrits* 298; *Fundamental Concepts* 140).

This fragility of being is pushed to the extreme in Lacan's theory and becomes the "fading" of the subject, which is bound up with its splitting: the first division involves the distinction of self and sign, which results in another division between conscious and unconscious processes in discourse (*Fundamental Concepts* 141). Consequently, Lacan re-writes Descartes's *cogito* as Freud's *"Wo es war, soll Ich werden,"* which he translates as follows:

"I am not wherever I am the plaything of my thought [that is, on the statement level, where the 'I' is taken as object of thought by the subject of consciousness]; I think of what I am where I do not think to think [the unconscious]" (*Écrits* 166).

This "fading" of the subject thus implies a disjunction between knowledge and consciousness (*Écrits* 302) insofar as the unconscious discourse (the locus of knowledge) erupts in the gaps of conscious discourse. This interference introduces a pulsative (radically discontinuous) temporal dimension into psychoanalytic epistemology: as in realism/empiricism, the Freudian subject also emerges from "where it was," but Lacan argues that the verb tense in Freud's *"Wo es war"* should not be taken as the aoristic but as "a distinct imperfect" which vascillates between "an extinction that is still glowing and a birth that is retarded," from which the subject emerges as it disappears from what is said (*Écrits* 300). Lacan calls this flickering process a dialectic but emphatically distinguishes it from Hegelian dialectic, which remains caught in the "mirage of consciousness" (*Écrits* 126).

Not only does Lacan's linguistic analysis of the *cogito* suggest a rewriting of the narrative structure that organizes literary realism, but his alignment of the Cartesian subject ("which is itself a sort of geometral point, a point of perspective" [*Fundamental Concepts* 86]) with the subject constituted in the Renaissance perspective system (which is monocular, addressed to *one* eye only) implies a re-writing of pictorial realism as well.

Lacan argues that this geometrical system is not concerned with vision *per se* but with the rationalization of space (*Fundamental Concepts* 94) in relation to which the conscious subject is reduced to a "punctiform object," a "point of vanishing" (*Fundamental Concepts* 83). This geometrical dimension suggests the following empiricist schema of pictorial mimesis: I (the conscious subject of representation reduced to the punctiform from which perspective is grasped) am presented with an image beyond which is the object itself (*Fundamental Concepts* 106).

In this schema, what is elided in the illusion of consciousness—or seeing oneself see oneself—is the function of the gaze: the organization that governs the production, necessarily unconscious, of the subject in the visible (*Fundamental Concepts* 83). Therefore, in Lacan's rewriting, it is the subject that is turned into a picture or is "photo-graphed" (that is, inscribed in the visible). Thus Lacan superimposes on the empiricist schema another that inverts it in which the gaze (or point of light) is situated outside (in the place of the "beyond" of the object above) and determines the subject through the mediation of the screen (the mask that represents the subject in the visible and is situated in the place of the image in the schema above). The screen, unlike geometrical space, is not transparent but opaque. The gaze thus presents a play of light and opacity in which, if the subject figures at all, it is only as screen (*Fundamental Concepts* 96). In other words, Lacan locates the relation of appearance and being not between the image and the object as in the empiricist schema, but between the subject and the screen or mask. Mimesis in this sense can be compared with animal mimicry, which reveals that there is no "*itself* that is behind." Rather, in mimicry there is only the *effect* of camouflage, which is "not a question of harmonizing with the background but, against a mottled background, of becoming mottled" (*Fundamental Concepts* 99). In Lacan's mimesis there is not a mastery but a subjection to the background.

Lacan's emphasis on the production of the subject in discourse is extremely important for feminist theory in general insofar as it posits sexual identity as a cultural/linguistic effect, *not* a biological/natural given. And his articulation of the question of subjectivity in relation to geometrical perspective and linguistic/fictional structures makes his work indispensable to the consideration of the operation of ideology in literary and pictorial texts. But his theory stalls precisely in accounting for the production of feminine subjectivity because of his assumption that the phallus—the "privileged signifier" of division in language—"inaugurates" the procedure in both sexes (*Écrits* 287, 288). More specifically, Lacan insists on the distinction between the penis and the phallus, even criticizing their equation as merely "an imaginary effect" that results in a crude reduction of sexual difference to a visible perception (which does not, however, prevent this "mystification" from becoming culturally normative). Nevertheless, for Lacan this "imaginary function of the phallus" becomes "the pivot of the symbolic process that completes *in both sexes* the questioning of the sex by the castration complex" (*Écrits* 198, Lacan's italics). That is to say, the symbolic process (in contrast to the imaginary process that posits one-to-one correlations between image and reality) puts sexuality *per se* in question insofar as it entails the recognition of the phallus *qua* signifier, which means a recognition that it has no *natural* referent, that its status is that of a mark: arbitrary. Henceforth two different relations to this signifier of lack—a lack in being and a lack in having—will distinguish the sexes.

The problem here is the double function of the phallus—as signifier of lack *in* both sexes and of sexual difference *between* them. Vis-à-vis the second function, what is missing from the account is an explanation of why the little girl imagines herself as castrated, or why she also equates the penis with the phallus and sees herself from a masculine perspective that is already installed at this supposedly "inaugural" moment. For clearly, this moment involves the interpretation of a sight, and elsewhere Lacan insists that the imaginary and symbolic orders are *not* sequential stages in the development of the subject but processes that operate synchronically, dialectically (*Écrits* 54, 55; also *Fundamental Concepts* 63). Yet here, Lacan treats this "imaginary effect" or "pivot" as a condition of the symbolic, an origin or given which defines difference as a *natural* perception. Applying his own terms to the account, we can say that he himself elides the gaze here, the production of difference in the visible. In so contradicting his own theory of the subject, Lacan reverts to the very empiricist/idealist ideology he is at such pains to criticize, thereby ironically completing his return to Freud by repeating the naturalization of the scene of castration in the essay "Some Psychological Consequences of the Anatomical Distinction Between the Sexes."

There Freud describes the little boy's knowledge as retrospective, hence deriving from a constructed, temporalized process:

> . . . when a little boy catches sight of a girl's genital region, he begins by showing irresolution and lack of interest; he sees nothing or disowns what he has seen, he softens it down or looks about for expedients for bringing it into line with his expectations. *It is not until later,* when some threat of castration has obtained a hold upon him, that the observation becomes important to him: *if he then recollects or repeats it,* it arouses a terrible storm of emotion in him and forces him to believe in the reality of the threat which he has hitherto laughed at.
>
> (187, italics mine)

Is this not "emotions recollected in tranquility"? That is, significance for the boy subject depends on the temporal separation of the look and the threat (castration), perception and consciousness. His understanding involves a retrospective interpretation or reading of events instead of immediate perception, much as in realistic art the visible figure is separate from its full meaning or identity.

The little girl, on the other hand, when she notices the penis of a brother or playmate "makes her judgement and her decision in a flash. She has seen it and knows that she is without it and wants to have it" (187–88).[4] In contrast comprehension for the little girl apparently coincides with perception; her knowledge is described as immediate in the sense of unmediated, unconstructed. What this "immediacy" of vision glosses over is that the little girl in this scenario (necessarily) adopts a masculine perspective. The opposition retrospective/immediate sets up an illusory difference which in no way affects the interpretation of the sight; it merely obscures the circularity of the reasoning. For in the argument the only constructed vision or perspective is defined as masculine, and the little girl is "by nature" excluded from this structure of seeing, yet she sees exactly what the little boy sees, thereby grounding his constructed vision of her supposed inferiority *in nature,* in a sensory perception.

No wonder that in re-viewing the castration scene, Luce Irigaray argues that "the gaze is at stake from the outset" (*Speculum* 47), which in her view implies that the little girl's castration does not initiate the scene; rather, the scene accomplishes her castration by closing off the possibility of a different interpretation—of difference itself. For the little girl presents "the possibility of *a nothing to see."* But instead of offering a challenge to an imaginary that privileges vision, her having nothing to see is defined "as her *having* nothing" (*Speculum* 48). In short, Irigaray questions not only why the little girl should see herself as a little boy, but also the predominance of vision over the other senses.

Notice too Irigaray's alignment of visual dominance with the imaginary, her insistence that the gaze is implicated from the "outset." In another essay she associates the subject with the imaginary:

> any theory of the subject has always been appropriated by the "masculine."
> When she submits to (such a) theory, woman fails to realize that she is
> renouncing the specificity of her own relationship to the imaginary.
>
> (*Speculum* 133)

Her argument is an indictment not of psychoanalytical theory as a whole but of its failure to investigate fully the implications of the theory, especially as regards the sexual determination of its discourse (*This Sex* 72–73). Irigaray specifically challenges Lacan's painstaking distinction between the imaginary order (which he associates with the ego or consciousness and its identifications) and the symbolic (the order of language, the unconscious, which determines the subject). Irigaray implies that the supposed difference between the two registers is illusory, that the theory does not begin to entertain the notion of heterogeneity, that it only offers more of the Same.

Her procedure entails a re-interpretation of the text that brings to the surface the complicity of the two orders "from the outset." Thus Lacan describes the effects of the mirror stage, in which the *infans* accomplishes the discrimination of discrete form, as pre-sexual: he locates the agency of the ego, "before its social determination," in a fictional direction that may approach but never coincide with the emergence of the subject (*Écrits* 2). Irigaray, on the other hand, argues that this ego is already socially determined as masculine insofar as the mirror stage marks the entry into the visible world, whose laws and values—symmetry, unity, identity—are alien and already exclusive of the feminine.

In other essays as well, Irigaray's procedure serves to reveal and to disrupt the dichotomies that serve to organize discourse in our culture, "including the one between enunciation and utterance," precisely because (and in direct contradistinction to Lacan) it makes possible the organization of the subject in that discourse in terms of yet another "onto-theo-logical" dichotomy: the subject-object relation (*This Sex* 78, 79, 80).

As we have seen, these dichotomies are crucial to Lacan's rewriting of the Cartesian *cogito;* he insists that they are operative even though the use of the shifter and the present tense verb obscure their function, and he situates his subject in the difference between the oppositional terms. Compare Irigaray's response to the question "Are you a woman?," which suggests how these dichotomies serve to reduce the idea of difference so that there is no place for the woman:

> A man's question? I don't think a woman—unless she had been assimilated to masculine . . . models—would ask me that question.
> Because "I" am not "I" [neither subject nor object, which means that quotation marks always surround the pronoun when the woman speaks], I *am* not [cannot exist in current discourse], I am not *one* [not one, coherent, identical, identifiable . . .] . As for *woman* try and find out . . . In any case, in this form, that of concept and of denomination, certainly not.
>
> (*This Sex* 120)

Irigaray also interrogates linearity in reading, which although not in itself a dichotomy, similarly imposes a hierarchical organization upon the text. A consequence of phonetic writing, linearity organizes the text to move in a single, irreversible direction (which makes it "teleological") and enforces the principle of non-contradiction by subordinating all the elements (the word, the utterance, the sentence, even the phoneme) to retroactive interpretation, which means that its temporality is that of consciousness, the very retrospection (founded upon the opposition past/present) that divides the perceptible from the intelligible (at least for the little boy in Freud's castration scenario).

To sum up, if Lacan's theory enables us to look for *what* is repressed in realistic systems of representation, namely the division/production of the subject in representation, Irigaray's interrogation of psychoanalytic theory suggests *why* that production is repressed: in order to obscure the procedures whereby difference is reduced to the masculine model.

It is in these terms that I will now attempt a re-reading of *The Professor*: to discover the narrative processes that constitute the subject and to discover how these processes render feminine subjectivity impossible.

The fact that the narrator of *The Professor*, William Crimsworth, is male is not *in itself* significant. Insofar as all of Brontë's novels are retrospective, all her narrators are designated as masculine in their relations to language and structures of knowledge, and their biological sex serves only to make these relations either explicit or implicit in the event of a shift in position. Initially, therefore, *The Professor* seems not unlike many other first-person nineteenth-century novels, aside from Brontë's, in which the doubling of mature and young perspectives of the protagonist is analogous to the more usual doubling of omniscient narrator's and protagonist's consciousnesses, for this temporal distance suffices to create an emotional distance that situates the narrator outside the fictional world in a position of control of the diegesis. In fact, this is so much the case in *The Professor*, at least on the surface, that Terry Eagleton argues that "it is really in a sense a third-person narration. Crimsworth delivers his success-story externally, judiciously, treating himself as an admirable object of his own narration" (77).

Such a description invites a comparison between Crimsworth and another male narrator who is (literally) present to himself as a third person, Henry Esmond. But what emerges from this juxtaposition is precisely that the great difference between the autobiographical narratives can be accounted for in terms of their very different temporal structures. For Esmond writes as if he had moved "outside of time." He frequently states that young Esmond felt this way or remembered such a thing to the last day or last hour of his life.[5] While it is true that by the end of his narrative Crimsworth distances himself from the action level to such an extent that the "evenings passed in that little parlor" with Frances resemble "a long string of rubies," each gem "unvaried" (218), far more frequently in the novel, especially in the two middle sections, Crimsworth is literally and figuratively near-sighted, a deficiency which threatens his control over his own story. In these instances he can be said to assume a "feminine" position in relation to language and to knowledge. It is here where Crimsworth's biological sex comes into play, raising the question of the relation between biology and representation and making explicit the manner in which realistic narrative constitutes the "feminine" only as a deficient version of the masculine.

The connection between narrative control and the temporal structure is registered at the beginning of the Belgian section when William-narrator conceives of his autobiography as a series of four pictures hanging in the cell where he keeps his records, each representing a stage of his life. The last picture, which is draped, he may choose not to reveal. (But in saying so, he reveals that he has a choice; he displays his mastery.) He does, however, describe the three unveiled paintings, and each picture has a spatial perspective that corresponds to, is a metaphor for, the temporal structure that organizes the respective portion of William's narrative. The Eton picture, for instance, "is in far perspective, receding, diminutive" (45), which means that this part of his life is viewed from the mature narrator's temporally distant perspective and as such accords with the way his early youth is verbally represented in the letter to Charles which prefaces his narrative. Not only its status as preface and as letter, but also its texture sets it apart from the subsequent narrative. Thus while several critics, Charles Burkhart among them, call William's introductory letter "Charlotte's nod to the past, the earlier epistolary style of Richardson" (51), it is most *un*-Richardsonian because it becomes an instrument for strong control over the past via retrospection and summary rather than immediacy, as well as over the reader via extreme discretion, even disdain, rather than confidentiality.

The insufficiency of temporal distance and consequent lack of mastery which are more characteristic of the middle sections of the narrative are made evident in the second picture hanging in William's cell, which represents his life at X—. It is a picture of unmitigated lack of differentiation. It shows unrelieved bleakness in "a yellow sky, sooty clouds; no sun, no azure; the verdure of the suburbs blighted and sullied—a very dreary scene" (45). This picture also lacks any spatial perspective which figuratively places this stage temporally in relation to the narrator. Whereas the figures in the Eton picture are diminutive, here the canvas itself is "huge." And there appears to be no retrospective filter through which its unmixed hues/emotional tones are recalled. Significantly, the description is merely a series of nouns and adjectives; there are no verbs here to express temporal relationships. (In contrast, William says the Eton picture "*is* in far perspective," relating it to the narrator's time level, while his childhood "*was* not all sunshine," the past tense serving to distance the events recorded in the pictorial representation.) Furthermore, besides being "huge," the canvas of the X— picture itself is said to be "dingy," "cracked and smoked" (45). Inasmuch as the canvas becomes part of the scene represented on it, the distinction between reality and its representation dissolves and along with it that between subject and object.

The third picture hanging in William's record chamber, this one of Belgium, complicates the relation of subject and object in another way by transforming the spectator into an auditor. No visual image of this landscape is provided; instead, William describes the emotions which the sound of the word "Belgium" evokes in him. The switch from the visual to the aural thus signals yet another model of retrospection, the evocation of the past as echo, which is more ephemeral and more immediate than any fixed visual representation, even one which collapses the distinction between object and image as the second picture does. Thus on the one hand, "Belgium" represents a past that is not so remote as Eton: it continues to affect the narrator emotionally, for he says, using the present tense, *"whenever uttered has* in my ear a sound, in my heart an echo, such as no other assemblage of syllables, however sweet or classic, can produce" (45, italics mine). And this sense of presence is reenforced by the use of such terms as "resurrection" and "ghosts" to designate these memories. On the other hand, insofar as the resurrection is tied to the sensation which evokes it, it defies permanent as well as definitive (pictorial or verbal) formulation, which impermanence William suggests when he laments the difficulty of articulating such emotions:

> but while I gaze on their vapoury forms, and strive to ascertain definitely their outline, the sound which wakened them dies, and they sink . . . like a wreath of mist, absorbed in the mould, recalled to urns, resealed in monuments.
>
> (45)

It is tempting to interpret this sound-picture as a model for a feminine signifying practice, not only because of William's positive response to it (in contrast to his negative attitude toward the second picture) but also because in some feminist theories feminine writing is described in terms of closeness to voice, which is a version of the supposed privileged relation between the woman and the pre-Oedipal phase. For the voice is conceived as the voice of the mother and in terms of proximity to the body, in opposition to vision, which creates distance. Hélène Cixous, for example, argues that women's privileged relation to the imaginary affords them a privileged (but not exclusive) relation to writing, which she associates with voice:

> The Voice sings from a time before law, before the Symbolic took one's breath away and reappropriated it into language under its authority of separation.
>
> (*The Newly Born Woman* 93)

Julia Kristeva furnishes an interesting counter-example: she substitutes the term *semiotic* for Lacan's imaginary and associates it with pre-Oedipal oral and anal processes whose articulation she designates the *chora*, a pulsative modality that precedes figuration and is analogous only to "vocal or kinetic rhythm'' and which interacts with the symbolic in the signifying process (24–28). Kristeva, however, refuses to associate the semiotic specifically with the feminine on the grounds that such an identification defines the feminine as essence. She thereby pinpoints the problem with any idea of feminine writing such as the one advanced by Cixous. At the same time, Kristeva's own theory can be criticized because it fails to distinguish women's oppression from that of other marginal and dissident groups, as though the male avant-garde writers whom she always cites as her examples can represent the oppression of women, Blacks, the working class, and so forth.

In this connection, Mary Ann Doane's caveat that as a challenge to the existing hierarchical power structure of the senses investment in the voice risks recuperation either as some form of essentialism or as a form of romanticism is very apropos (''Voice in the Cinema'' 48–49). And indeed, the model of retrospection offered in the third picture can be described as an evanescent revival of a Wordsworthian ''picture of the mind.'' As such it forms a sequence with the other two paintings that recapitulates in miniature the narrative tradition which Brontë inherited. The Eton picture designates a model of distant retrospection that evokes but exaggerates the narrative structures appropriated from spiritual autobiography (for example, by Defoe) to impose a providential pattern on the protagonist's experience; the picture of X— recalls Richardson's ''writing to the moment'' pushed to extreme limits. Like the other two pictures, the Wordsworthian model is also exaggerated so as to make explicit its procedures and assumptions.

For recall that Wordsworth's retrospective narratives are poems, which means that they imitate spoken rather than written discourse. (No doubt that is why we refer to the ''narrator'' as the ''speaker.'')[6] Accordingly, the poems actualize both the speaker and the instance of uttering more than other texts—specifying to a greater degree the speaker's intonation and gestures by means of meter, spacing, punctuation, typography, and particularizing the speaker's spatial and temporal location (as the realistic narrator's is not) as well as that of the person addressed (for example, the speaker's sister in ''Tintern Abbey'' as opposed to the unspecified reader of a realistic text)—all in an effort to create the illusion of presence.

But it is only an illusion, for the poet is not present, and the poem is not spoken but re-cited in accordance with written instructions furnished in the text. The illusion functions to suppress the operation of reproductive mechanisms that regulate sound (harmonize it, impose a rhythm on it, modulate the pitch) and govern its transformation into language. The reference to ''echo'' in connection with the third picture of Brontë's text, therefore, makes evident the hidden repetition to which sound is subjected in such recitation. As Irigaray observes, the echo is a re-presentation which presupposes a single speaker and depends on the intervention of neutral blanks and silences in order to permit "words and their repetition to be discriminated and separated out and framed"; in this doubling process, the hiatus divides the present from the past, which it defines "as a present which has taken place" (*Speculum* 257).

Applying this notion of echo to Wordsworth's poems (staying with "Tintern Abbey" as our exemplary model), we can say that the relation between the text or script and the speech act that it imitates, exactly duplicates the relationship *within* the poem between the speaker's memory and his past sensory perception, which he never re-captures, only re-constructs, although the poem creates the illusion of temporal continuity through superimposition—of the speaker's memory ("the picture of the mind") and a revival of that picture on the one hand; of the speaker's current relation to the past and his sister's repetition of that relation in the future on the other hand. Superimposition is a device that depends on/insures the preservation of the distinction between past, present, and future in order to create the illusion of continuity between the speaker's present and past selves; it indicates the speaker's investment in an empiricist notion of identity. Hence romanticism can be regarded as a *qualified* form of realism.

In Brontë's text, on the other hand, the proximity articulated in terms of the perspectives organizing the middle two pictures is manifested in William's narrative account of these stages of his life as *disruptions* of the retrospective temporal structure. Although the narrative is related in past tense for the most part, the present tense being reserved to designate the narrator's time zone, certain other present-tense insertions close the temporal gap between protagonist and narrator and make it difficult to distinguish the two time zones. One such disruption occurs when William-narrator portrays some of his students at Mlle. Reuter's pensionnat. Incidentally, he calls these descriptions "sketches" taken from his portfolio, and in fact pictures are used throughout the narrative to objectify his consciousness of other characters. However, because these are portraits, the perspective system is not specified as it is in the landscapes cited above. Instead, he uses scientific discourse to set them at a distance: he calls them "specimens," which he is careful to locate as to "genus" and "class." Furthermore, the descriptions follow a deductive order, moving from placement in a class or country to more specific, individual traits, most of which are selected according to the principles of the science of phrenology. Despite the use of scientific discourse, however, the first sketch, that of Aurelia Koslow, is given in present tense, which might be rationalized by locating the "sketch" in the narrator's time zone. However, even the account of her habitual behavior in class, which follows the description, is given in present tense: "The moment I enter the room, she nudges her next neighbor and indulges in a half-suppressed laugh. As I take my seat on the estrade, she fixes her eye on me . . ." (85). It is difficult to account for the present tense here except as William-narrator's failure to subordinate the past to the present, in other words his immersion or absorption into/by the past, because in the parallel sketch of the second student, Adèle Dronsart, he uses *past* tense to describe *her* habitual behavior in class: ". . . when I looked along the row of young heads, my eye generally stopped at this of Adèle's; her gaze was ever waiting for mine; and it frequently succeeded in arresting it" (86–87). It is unnecessary to discuss his sketch of the third student, Juanna Trista, except to say that it is given entirely in the past tense and therefore resists correlation with either one of the patterns established by the first two sketches.

Because the narrator's perspective is so close to the protagonist's, indeed at times collapses into it, it is especially significant that within the diegesis William-protagonist also occasionally experiences difficulties in separating the object from its representation. His response to his mother's portrait on the occasion of Edward Crimsworth's birthday party registers just such a confusion. William's lack of introduction to any of the young ladies present at the celebration thwarts his desire to dance with them. So though "tantalised,"[7] he instead seeks out his mother's picture and proceeds to relate to it in a manner that merges desire and identification, which is to say substitutes a narcissistic relationship that represents the unresolved masculine version of the Oedipus. Specifically, William recognizes that his "heart grew to the image" because it is "a softened and refined likeness" of himself. Interestingly, this Oedipal configuration is immediately balanced by the "feminine" version, for the narrator uses a simile that compares William's pleasure in looking at the portrait to that of fathers who find in their daughters' faces "their own similitude . . . flatteringly associated with softness of hue and delicacy of outline" (18).

Notice that both versions similarly align sexual difference with subject-object positions: the subject is always male (son or fathers), the object female (mother or daughters). On the other hand, a reversal in the subject/object opposition insofar as it refers to genealogy is suggested by the transposition of generations (offspring looks at parent; parents look at offspring), which not only subverts chronology but further implies, since the offspring is the image of the parent and vice-versa, that neither is the original. Moreover, insofar as the figure compares biological and artistic modes of reproduction, it also blurs the distinction between reality and its representation: the mother's *portrait* and *real* daughters are equated in that they evoke similar responses. But since the fathers and daughters are part of a simile, they exist only figuratively in contrast to the "reality" of William and his mother's picture. In Lacan's terms, the experience may therefore be said to belong to the Imaginary register. But in this imaginary, sexual difference is already operative in that feminine subjectivity is foreclosed regardless of the inversions that occur.

If the mother's portrait is a sort of mirror image because William both desires and identifies with it and so implicitly jeopardizes his subject position, when he literally looks in the mirror, he sees himself quite specifically as an object of desire. On his way to his first interview with Mlle. Reuter he says,

> I remember very well that before quitting my chamber, I held a brief debate with myself as to whether I should change my ordinary attire for something smarter. At last I concluded it would be a waste of labour. . . . And off I started, cursorily glancing sideways as I passed the toilet-table, surmounted by a looking glass: a thin, *ir*regular face I saw with sunk, dark eyes under a large, square forehead, complexion *destitute* of bloom or attraction; something young, but *not* youthful, *no object to win a lady's love, no* butt for the shafts of Cupid.
> (65, italics mine)

William is here relating to himself as women habitually relate to themselves. He is seeing himself as *someone else* would see him, while he identifies with the object. And this position occurs "at the cost of [his]self being split into two."[8] At the same time, the fact that there is a *literal* mirror in this instance and that he is *literally* (biologically) male makes explicit (1) that his designation as "feminine" is purely a construction of the process of looking and refers only to a position in relation to the image; (2) that the position is constructed in negative terms as the forfeit of subjectivity. Both these "mirror images" are, moreover, significant as analogues within the diegesis to William-narrator's project of writing his autobiography, a literary exercise that is conventionally described as looking at oneself to paint a self-portrait.

The passages above suggest a problematic relation to the symbolic order, hence to signifying systems. This dis-ease accounts for the distrust of language registered in a number of ways throughout the narrative. First, Brontë's characters use an idiom which may be described as highly formal, oratorical, or dramatic. These extremities of language suggest how the characters must strain to imbue speech with emotional tones that ordinary words lack.

The narrator as well as the protagonists finds ordinary language inadequate to articulate the feelings and attitudes he wishes to describe. Frequently he inserts self-conscious explanations about his choice of words which call attention to the process of writing. Furthermore, a tension marks the estrangement of the narrator from his language. This tension is revealed in the violent metaphors and the tendency to describe things by their opposites, that is, negatively (Kroeber 191). For instance, Chapter 19 opens with a rejection of extremes of emotion as inappropriate in a realistic representation: if novelists conscientiously studied real life, says the narrator, "they would give us fewer pictures chequered with vivid contrasts of light and shade . . ." (140). Despite this prescription, the narrator proceeds to specify what will be excluded, precisely those agonies of men "who have plunged like beasts into sensual indulgence," who then are "wrung together with pain, stamped into the churchyard sod by the inexorable hell of despair." Moreover, these agonies are not discernably less intense than the pain of "the man of regular life and rational mind," described in paragraph 2 in terms of "acute pain" which "racks him," "writhing limbs," Death which "roots up and tears violently away" what he loves. In short, extremes of emotion are presented (negatively) even as they are overtly rejected. This incomplete sublimation makes evident the contradictions that are ordinarily rationalized in the realistic text, which in turn exposes realism as a homogenizing process.

Another signal of the distrust of language consists in the use of phrenology and physiognomy, which constitutes an attempt to transform physical characteristics into fixed signs indicating inner qualities, giving access to the reality hidden beneath the surface appearance, which is seen as a disguise. Even in the classroom context, which disposes of social, economic, and class roles, outward behavior provides no clear index of true motives. For instance, Pelet is discovered to hide his "flint or steel under an external covering of velvet" (58). And even William's professorial role is a mask which disguises his own vulnerability and lack of confidence in his relations with his students. Thus he acts (in both senses of the word) quite haughty and contemptuous on his first day in M. Pelet's school because his French is not quite good enough to go into lengthy explanations at this point (52–53). One might say that his students' latent rebelliousness and lack of interest in their studies force William to assume such a mask. Yet he also wears the "garb of austerity" in dealing with Frances, his eager and beloved pupil, to "cloak" a "kindness as mute as watchful" (131). William's sternness, therefore, is not a simple deception; it defies consistent interpretation.[9] Hence the use of these two sciences in physical description is an attempt to objectify inherent mental qualities and bypass the surface manifestation of ordinary intercourse, in short, to pin down meaning.

Yet the antagonism towards language within the novel goes even further: finally, the characters resort to nonverbal communication as the most direct and truthful. While words often disguise true motives, the body, especially the eye, speaks for those who can read. For example, in the exchange between Hunsden and William following the latter's loss of position, William refuses to express in words his gratitude to Hunsden for precipitating a confrontation with William's brother, Edward. William perversely pretends that Hunsden has lost him the job he wanted. But,

> I could not repress a half-smile as I said this. . . .
> "Oh! I see!" said he, looking into my eyes, and it was evident he *did* see right down to my heart.
>
> (41)

William and Mlle. Reuter also communicate through eye language. After his first class she asks him about the three unruly girls who sit in the front row. His words are dismissive, and she ceases to question him,

> but her eye— . . . showed she was even with me; it let out a momentary gleam, which said plainly, "Be as close as you like, I am not dependent on your candour; what you would conceal I already know."
>
> (75)

And, of course, such non-verbal communication occurs throughout the novel between William and Frances, who begin to speak eye language immediately when William reads the appeal in Frances's eye to dictate more slowly on her first day in class (107).

Note that in each of these instances the characters may bypass the word through the exchange of looks, but insofar as William-narrator translates such exchanges, the narrative discourse does not similarly eschew verbalization. The recourse to eye language, then, merely exaggerates and thereby reveals the gap that always divides the perceptible (the characters' actions) from the intelligible (the narrator's interpretation) in the realistic text. However, just because that gap is so obvious here, the translation that spans it appears far-fetched: just *how* does a "momentary gleam" say all that? Certainly not "plainly." Again, the strain put upon the translation process exposes it *qua* process (as does the recourse to a fixed code of interpretation in the case of physiognomy).

On other occasions, however, the text offers no interpretation; it just reg-

isters. Examples include William's mysterious bout of hypochrondria following his marriage proposal to Frances and the strange wrestling match that
William and Hunsden engage in upon leaving Frances's house after Hunsden's
first meeting with her. Critics repeatedly complain about the irrelevance of
the hypochondria to the plot (see Martin 40; Ewbank 188). Even Crimsworth
asks, "Why did hypochondria accost me now?" (203). But the incident's
significance derives precisely from this irrelevance: it indicates the existence
of material so complex and contradictory that it defies rationalization by the
narrative discourse. So does the second incident. True, the struggle occurs
in part as a result of William's having misled Hunsden about Frances's supposed social inferiority. During their meeting Hunsden has learned the enor-
mous insufficiency of her description as a mere lacemender. (In other words,
the physical struggle is sparked by a statement that is *literally* accurate.)
However, this explanation of the incident is no more adequate than the description of Frances that ostensibly prompts it. After all, the two men end up
rolling over the pavement: their conflict is too fierce to be regarded as a mere
response to William's teasing. Moreover, William "*grappled* [Hunsden]
round the waist" (215), which means that however fierce, the struggle is also
an embrace.[10] Neither incident, then, is thoroughly integrated into the narrative. Consequently, the text forces the reader as well to strain against the
limits of discourse in an attempt to apprehend these strange relationships,
even at the risk of alienating him/her. Eagleton's criticism of Crimsworth's
defiance of the reader makes it clear that this risk is not negligible:

> Not even the reader must be allowed to slip under his guard; and this is why
> in reading his narrative we have the exasperated sense that he is telling us only
> what he wants us to know. . . . he treats the reader with something like the
> stiff, wary circumspection with which he handles Mdlle. Reuter.
>
> (79)

I do not happen to share Eagleton's exasperation because for me this
defiance is a mode of interrogating certain dominant narrative conventions.
And the antagonism to language expressed by the violent metaphors, the
negative presentation of characters and events, the use of phrenology and
physiognomy, and the attempt to replace speech with extra-verbal communication ultimately ties in with the use of pictures, especially the portrait,
throughout the narrative to designate material (that is, undischarged emotion)
which cannot be contained by the narrative discourse or accommodated by
the plot. Geoffrey Nowell-Smith, writing on melodrama, has suggested an
analogy between eruptions of such excesses in the narrative text and the

mechanisms of "conversion hysteria": in hysteria, the energy discharged by an idea that has been repressed is displaced onto the bodily symptom. The hysterical moment of the melodramatic text, which otherwise adheres to the principles of realistic representation, occurs at precisely those points where the displacement of emotion ruptures the realistic conventions (117).

Now the notion of the hysterical text is particularly interesting in light of the classic correlation between hysteria and femininity, which requires further elaboration at this point. Recent feminist theory demonstrates that the hysterical character is merely an exaggeration of the feminine norm, that the case histories of Anna O. and Dora simply present extreme pathological versions of that norm. Freud himself suggested as much: "In a whole series of cases the hysterical neurosis is nothing but an excessive overaccentuation of the typical wave of repression through which the masculine type of sexuality is removed and the woman emerges" ("Hysterical Attacks" 157).

The reason for the correlation between hysteria and femininity is the twofold prohibition imposed on the woman. Like the little boy, she must give up the mother to accommodate a third person, but this renunciation is problematic for her because she can neither substitute the father as the object of her desire nor identify with him. The either/or opposition is transformed in her case into a neither/nor, and she is twice barred from assuming the position of subject of desire. (The little boy's Oedipal itinerary, on the other hand, enables him to exchange his passive relation to the mother for the possibility of a different, active kind of sexual pleasure.) The hysterical symptom can be viewed, then, as an effect on the woman of this double-bind situation because as a sign, the symptom bypasses consciousness and ordinary language as it registers on the body the clash between the impulse to signify desire and the multiple cultural injunctions that block her access to the place and means of its articulation (Freud, "Hysterical Phantasies" 150).

It is tempting to consider this symptom as an alternative mode of signifying in view of the fact that the "cure" for hysteria is talking—the translation of unconscious wish into conscious discourse. However, insofar as such translation forces the hysteric to assume a position that conforms more closely to the culturally defined norms, certain distortions accompany the conscious articulation of the wish, which indicate that the hysteric is more the victim than the perpetrator of the "duplicity" that characterizes the hysteric's discourse. More specifically, the commonly reported scenarios of seduction by the father, which Freud only later identified as "the expression of the typical Oedipus complex in women" ("Femininity" 106), transpose fantasy into fact and invert the subject-object relation through the use of the passive voice so that her desire *for* the father is transformed into her seduction *by* him (Laplanche 33–34). It is only through recourse to such distortion that desires so socially unacceptable can surface in consciousness (which, incidentally, clarifies why Crimsworth's Oedipal relation to his mother's portrait is explicitly compared to fathers' pleasures in looking at their daughters). Thus the talking cure may alleviate the symptom but does not at all address the cultural imperatives that precipitated the disease in the first place. As Freud explained to his patients, he could help them only to transform their "hysterical misery into common unhappiness" (*Studies on Hysteria* 305).

For this reason, it is quite interesting that in so many cases of hysteria the treatment was not completed.[11] The instance of Dora is just the most famous of these. Peggy Kamuf argues that although Freud regarded this patient's abrupt termination of the sessions as an act of revenge designed to rob him of satisfaction in the success of his therapeutic efforts, it is possible, if we view the interruption from Dora's perspective, to see it as a protest or resistance to the submissive silence and passivity she could anticipate as the effect of her total cure and return to the norm (55).

Of course, this is mere speculation with regard to Dora, since in fact her perspective is not represented in Freud's case history. But it raises the issue of whether and how we can regard the hysterical symptom as a form of protest. Just what kind of resistance does it offer? Not a refusal of normative "feminine" identity in favor of some "other" sexuality, as perhaps Freud's references to the hysteric's bisexuality imply (see "Hysterical Phantasies" 150, 151). For the only "other" option offered by bisexuality is identification with a masculine position (as in the explanation of Dora's homosexual love for Frau K).

Resistance should rather be understood in the sense of questioning the interpretation that is imposed on the symptom, interrogating the ideology of the interpretation (Irigaray, *This Sex* 137). This means interrogating sexual identity *per se* by retraversing the history of the "feminine" subject as represented by the hysterical symptom, which Freud called a "memory symbol" because its particular form corresponds to some detail of the repressed phantasy ("Hysterical Phantasies" 149). An investigation of the relation between symptom and memory in Freudian theory might then be brought to bear on the analysis of a retrospective narrative like *The Professor*.

Freud observed that the correlation between the symptom and the repressed phantasy becomes obscured through the symptom's representing several phantasies simultaneously by means of the same material, that is, through *condensation*. . . . The phantasies thus made to coincide are often of quite different kinds, for instance, a recent wish and the re-activation of an infantile impression. . . .

("Hysterical Attacks" 153–54)

Also, symptoms can have several meanings in succession (*Dora* 70).

No wonder, then, that Freud found hysterics incapable of producing precise histories of their illness: their memories left gaps; connections remained incoherent; the sequence of events was uncertain. He regarded this impaired memory as *"a necessary correlate of the symptoms and one which is theoretically requisite"* (*Dora* 32, Freud's italics). He further maintained that the talking cure was designed to restore the memory:

> It is only towards the end of the treatment that we have before us an intelligible, consistent, and unbroken case history. Whereas the practical aim of the treatment is to remove all possible symptoms and to replace them by conscious thoughts, we may regard it as a second and theoretical aim to repair all damages to the patient's memory. These two aims are coincident. When one is reached, so is the other; and the same path leads to them both.[12]

(*Dora* 32)

But, in fact, this promise of total recall is never realized first of all because the pre-Oedipal phase of mother-attachment, deemed critical to the account of the hysteric's bisexuality, "has in analysis seemed . . . so elusive, lost in a past so dim and shadowy, so hard to resuscitate, that it seemed as if it had undergone some specially inexorable repression." This phase has been obscured insofar as the women Freud has analyzed "have been able to cling on to that very father-attachment in which they took refuge from the early phase," rendering insight into the pre-Oedipus phase "comparable in another field with the effect of the discovery of the Minoan-Mycenaean civilization behind that of Greece" ("Female Sexuality" 195, 196). Actually, the emphasis on the archaic quality of the relation to the mother is just a decoy. For the phase is *not* problematic simply or primarily for that reason. (As Irigaray demonstrates, the pre-Oedipal phase is already sexually inflected to privilege the masculine model.) Moreover, Freud fails to distinguish the connection between the phase and the etiology of hysteria from the relation of *all* women to the phase of mother-attachment. Thus his assertion that "both the phase and the neurosis . . . are characteristically feminine" ("Female Sexuality" 196) merely implies that all women are hysterical by some inherent predisposition: it explains nothing.

As for that relatively more accessible father attachment, it too resists total recall because it is not exempt from the operation of *Nachträglichkeit* or *deferred action,* even if Freud seems to repress its function in the quotation above which promises complete restoration of memory. As Laplanche and Pontalis remark, the English translation of the term is somewhat misleading. The term does not refer to the intervention of a time-lapse between stimulus and response but to a reworking or revision of psychic material at a later time and therefore to a complex temporal logic which undermines the linear determinism implicit in any straightforward narration of events (*Language of Psycho-analysis* 112–14). The notion is described in a number of Freud's texts, but it receives one of its fullest elaborations in the 1895 "Project for a Scientific Psychology," where it is associated with Freud's formulation of the concept of trauma as part of his seduction theory, which is also a theory of repression.

According to the theory, the symptom refers to an experience that was never present, not only because the existence of so many instances of actual seduction is doubtful, but also, and more importantly, because only the memory of the scene or event gives rise to the affect.[13] More specifically, in the "Project" Freud recounts two scenes brought to light in the analysis of a hysteric he calls Emma. In the earlier scene an adult (a shopkeeper) makes a sexual overture to the eight-year-old child, which she does not understand. (Hence the scene is not sexual *for her.*) The second scene, which is nonsexual but bears some incidental resemblance to the first (two shop assistants laugh at her clothes), activates the memory of the earlier scene, now understood because she has reached puberty in the interval. On this occasion she experiences a sexual release, which turns into anxiety and which is followed by her totally forgetting (repressing) the first scene. Freud writes,

> it is a highly noteworthy fact that [the sexual release] was not linked to the assault when it was actually experienced. Here we have an instance of a memory exciting an affect which it had not excited as an experience, because in the meantime changes produced by puberty had made possible a new understanding of what was remembered.
>   Now this case is typical of repression in hysteria. We invariably find that memory is repressed which has only become a trauma *after the event.*
>   (*Origins* 413, Freud's italics)

In other words, the notion of deferred action means that trauma cannot be located in a specific event because it is suspended between two temporally separated events as well as two registers of meaning: perception and consciousness. Freud thus assumes a psychical apparatus structured by a process of stratification, which renders any linear conception of causality untenable.[14]

Trauma, therefore, does not refer to the cause of the symptom in the form of a simple experience; rather, it is the after-affect of a process of interpretation. In short, *Nachträglichkeit* puts in question the primacy of event over significance (in the case of Emma, sexual *meaning* must be available to her in order for her to *experience* sexual release); indeed, it subverts the very idea of original event or primal scene.

The "Project," therefore, rules out any simple causal association of hysterical symptom with the pre-Oedipus (in the sense of pre-sexual) because it undermines the notion of simple causal relations on the one hand and specifies the hysterical symptom as the *deferred* effect of a *seduction* scenario on the other. It is perhaps significant that at the time of writing the "Project" Freud had not yet identified such seduction scenes with the feminine Oedipus complex nor predicated the special significance of an archaic relation of the daughter to the mother. Possibly because his theory of feminine sexuality was *not* at stake, he was able to elaborate the knowledge process that constitutes the feminine subject.

Interestingly, it is the very same retrospective procedure that produces castration anxiety in the little boy (for example, in the castration scene described in "Some Psychological Consequences of the Anatomical Distinction Between the Sexes") and marks his entry into the symbolic order and consciousness. It is this process which constructs the feminine subject as hysteric, which is to say impossible, because for her it is primarily a process of repression. The difference between *his* consciousness and access to language and *her* repression can be aligned with two different notions of cause in these scenes. Recall that in the castration scenario a cause is designated in the form of a sight that inaugurates the boy's castration anxiety; but in the hysteria scenario delineated in the "Project," the cause is missing insofar as trauma is conceived as a *relation* between events: trauma is not the cause but the *effect* of consciousness.

For Lacan the significance of this absence of cause in trauma is that it reveals the function of the real in relation to the symbolic as encounter "in so far as it is essentially the missed encounter," that is, as that which is "unassimilable." Lacan thus conceives of the real as *"en souffrance,"* a phrase that means "pending" or "in abeyance" as well as "in pain." Hence Lacan's definition of the real as "impossible" (*Fundamental Concepts* 55–56). Thus Lacan detaches the significance of trauma from the hysteria scenario and generalizes its application, which is to say that he assimilates the concept of trauma to the masculine model. (Significantly, most of his references are to the traumatic primal scene elaborated in the Wolfman case history.)

For Irigaray, on the other hand, hysteria is *not* displaced by the "real" in general as the "privileged place for preserving—but 'in latency,' 'in sufferance'—that which does not speak" (*This Sex* 136). Nor does she overlook the crucial distinction between the castration and hysteria scenarios; for her, the absence of cause in the latter indicates that the woman's relationship to the origin has been appropriated, the hysteria scenario thereafter being "condemned as so many 'bad' copies or gross caricatures of a 'good,' and valuable and valid, relationship to origin" (*Speculum* 60). For Irigaray it is feminine sexuality, not some generalized "real," that is "impossible": she demonstrates not *that* Lacan is ultimately wrong about the significance of trauma in the hysteria scenario but *how,* once again, he overlooks the sexual determination of that scene.

In this context, the hysterical moment in the text, specifically *The Professor,* clearly does not refer to the "return of the repressed" in the sense of a feminine essence that emerges in the content or a specifically feminine signifying practice that correlates with a particular literary form. Rather, the hysterical moment refers to those knots which cannot be comprehended by the realistic narrative system, which resist assimilation to consciousness and which therefore render totalization impossible. Invoking the logic whereby the exception proves the rule, the moment of hysterical rupture exposes the self-reflexive processes of realistic representation as processes that foreclose feminine subjectivity.

Surely it is not necessary to rehearse at this point the various strategies noted in the analysis of *The Professor* that bring to the surface the sexual determination of its procedures—the collapse of the oppositions whose implicit hierarchical organization insures the continuity of time, of space, of identity; the presentation of material that cannot be accommodated by the narrative discourse, and so on. But there is one aspect of the process that does require another word: the resistance of the reader.

The reader's function is crucial in realistic representation: all the reflexive structures within the text function to perpetuate the system by re-producing the same model of subjectivity—the masculine model. The reader is that subject. But what kind of subject/reader is constituted in *The Professor*? The reader, no less than the characters, becomes temporally disoriented on those occasions when the use of the present tense makes it difficult to discriminate past from present, narrator from protagonist.

Furthermore, in this novel the reader is denied omniscience first of all because his/her knowledge is subject to the limitations and fallibilities of Crimsworth's experience and memory. Of course, those limits apply to all autobiographical narrators (which is why there can be no simple correlation between narrative form and gender), but Crimsworth seems more unable than most to provide a smooth history (for example, the hypochondria incident). Secondly, this limitation is not strictly just a matter of the narrator's fallible memory and circumscribed experience: it also involves the reader's alienation. For the narrator's deliberate withholding of information keeps the reader at bay. Thus the identification mechanisms, which realism so heavily depends upon for the perpetuation of ideology and which can sometimes offer a distinct pleasure to compensate for the reader's limited access to knowledge, are here disrupted.

Disoriented, denied knowledge, denied identification—the reader's access to subjectivity is thus twice barred in this text. The reader's resistance to this foreclosure (evident, for example, in the harsh criticism leveled at the novel as noted above) is the measure of his/her determination by precisely those procedures in other, more realistic, representations. Paradoxically, then, the hysterical text alienates the reader only to implicate him/her more fully in the process of representation—especially its operation *in other texts* and contexts. For finally, the hysterical text shatters the frame that seals off the text and renders it an aesthetic object. The hysterical text reveals representation as the site of ideological/sexual conflict and production of the subject.

NOTES

1. My summary account of the premises of realism is based on Elizabeth Deeds Ermarth's excellent book-length study of the subject in *Realism and Consensus in the English Novel*, esp. 5, 10, 33–34.
2. This broad definition of empiricism, elaborated by Louis Althusser, includes Cartesian rationalism, eighteenth-century sensualist empiricism, and Hegelian idealism; despite differences in the status of the subject and the object which account for the formal differences among these philosophical strands, the basic structure remains the same: these variants all confuse the object of knowledge with the real object, whether through the conceptualization of the real as the result of thought (as in Hegel's speculative idealism) or through the reduction of thought about the real to the real itself (as in empiricist idealism) (Althusser 35).
3. In contrast, works of art that are not similarly arranged by a single, fixed viewpoint, for example Chinese or medieval painting, represent the essential qualities of objects as discrete from one another. Since form and position are not relative but absolute, such systems force the perceiver to relate to the various objects in the field individually yet simultaneously, thus producing at best a fragmented, discontinuous subjectivity.

4. My analysis of this essay is indebted to Mary Ann Doane's discussion of it in "Film and the Masquerade," 79.
5. See J. Hillis Miller 21, 22 for a discussion of temporal distance between protagonist and narrator in *Henry Esmond*.
6. My discussion of Wordsworth assumes Barbara Herrnstein Smith's elaboration of mimesis in poetry.
7. The word "tantalise" appears in the text (17) and explicitly defines William's difficulty in expressing desire as a matter of the distance imposed by vision. The word means "to torment with the sight of something desired but out of reach." The distance between William and the young ladies is too great for him to negotiate; he can relate only to objects that are close, like the portrait of his mother.
8. In addition to this specific quotation (46) I am indebted to John Berger's entire chapter in *Ways of Seeing* on the European tradition of nude painting and the conventions by which women are seen as spectacles appealing to masculine spectators.
9. This resistance to interpretation is precisely why the function of the mask (elaborated in Lacan's schema of the subject's determination in the visible by the gaze) corresponds to the function of the pronoun "I" in the verbal field. The inconsistency of meaning is also what distinguishes the subject's mask from the animal's camouflage in animal mimicry (*Fundamental Concepts* 107).
10. Recall that the dreaded hypochondria also embraces William, "taking [him] entirely to her death-cold bosom, and holding [him] with arms of bone" (202).
11. In his Letter to Wilhelm Fliess (21 September 1897) Freud complained of "the continual disappointment of my attempts to bring my analyses to a real conclusion, the running away of people who for a time had seemed my most favorably inclined patients . . ." (*Origins of Psychoanalysis* 215).
12. The account of the treatment of Anna O. describes more specifically how a controlled form of retrospection is being substituted for a hysterical representation of the memory (although the case history fails to report that this treatment was incomplete, that it was followed by Anna's hysterical pregnancy):

> Each individual symptom in this complicated case was taken separately in hand; all the occasions on which it had appeared were described in reverse order, starting before the time when the patient became bed-ridden and going back to the event which had led to its first appearance. When this had been described the symptom was permanently removed.
>
> (*Studies on Hysteria* 35)

13. Jean Laplanche, *Life and Death in Psycho-analysis*, 40. I am indebted to Chapter 2 as a whole for my account of Freud's seduction theory.
14. In a letter to Fliess (6 December 1896) Freud described this process of stratification:

> the material present in the shape of memory traces is from time to time subjected to rearrangement in accordance with fresh circumstances—is, as it were, transcribed. Thus, what is essentially new in my theory is the thesis that memory is present not once but several times over, that is registered in various species of "signs."

(*Origins of Psychoanalysis* 173)

WORKS CITED

Althusser, Louis and Etienne Balibar. *Reading Capital*. Trans. Ben Brewster. London: New Left Books, 1970.

Berger, John. *Ways of Seeing*. London: BBC & Penguin, 1972.

Brontë, Charlotte. *The Professor*. London & New York: Dent & Dutton, 1910.

Burkhart, Charles. *Charlotte Brontë: A Psycho-Sexual Study of Her Novels*. London: Gollancz, 1973.

Cixous, Hélène and Catherine Clement. *The Newly Born Woman*. Trans. Betsy Wing. Minneapolis: University of Minnesota Press, 1986.

Doane, Mary Ann. "Film and the Masquerade: Theorizing the Female Spectator." *Screen* 23 (Sept./Oct. 1982): 74–88.

————. "The Voice in the Cinema: The Articulation of Body and Space." *Yale French Studies* 60 (1980): 33–50.

Eagleton, Terry. *Myths of Power: A Marxist Study of the Brontës*. New York: Barnes & Noble, 1975.

Ermarth, Elizabeth Deeds. *Realism and Consensus in the English Novel*. Princeton, N.J.: Princeton University Press, 1983.

Ewbank, Inga-Stina. *Their Proper Sphere: A Study of the Brontë Sisters as Early Victorian Novelists*. London: Arnold, 1966.

Freud, Sigmund. *Dora: An Analysis of a Case of Hysteria*. Ed. Philip Rieff. New York: Collier, 1963.

————. "Female Sexuality." *Sexuality and the Psychology of Love*. Ed. Philip Rieff. New York: Collier, 1963.

————. "Femininity." *New Introductory Lectures in Psychoanalysis*. Trans. James Strachey. New York: Norton, 1965.

————. "General Remarks on Hysterical Attacks" (1909). *Dora: An Analysis of a Case of Hysteria*. Ed. Philip Rieff. New York: Collier, 1963.

————. "Hysterical Phantasies and their Relation to Bisexuality" (1908). *Dora: An Analysis of a Case of Hysteria*. Ed. Philip Rieff. New York: Collier, 1963.

————. *The Origins of Psychoanalysis: Letters to Wilhelm Fliess, Drafts and Notes: 1887–1902*. Trans. Eric Mosbacher and James Strachey. New York: Basic Books, 1954.

—————. "Some Psychological Consequences of the Anatomical Distinction Between the Sexes." *Sexuality and the Psychology of Love*. Ed. Philip Rieff. New York: Collier, 1963.

—————, and Joseph Breuer. *Studies on Hysteria: Standard Edition of the Complete Psychological Works*. Trans. James Strachey et al. Vol. 2. London: Hogarth, 1955.

Irigaray, Luce. *Speculum of the Other Woman*. Trans. Gillian C. Gill. Ithaca: Cornell University Press, 1985.

—————. *This Sex Which Is Not One*. Trans. Catherine Porter. Ithaca: Cornell University Press, 1985.

Kamuf, Peggy. *Fictions of Desire: Disclosures of Héloise*. Lincoln: University of Nebraska Press, 1982.

Kristeva, Julia. *Revolution in Poetic Language*. Trans. Margaret Waller. New York: Columbia University Press, 1984.

Kroeber, Karl. *Styles in Fictional Structure: The Art of Jane Austen, Charlotte Brontë, George Eliot*. Princeton, N.J.: Princeton University Press, 1971.

Lacan, Jacques. *Écrits: A Selection*. Trans. Alan Sheridan. New York: Norton, 1977.

—————. *The Four Fundamental Concepts of Psycho-analysis*. Trans. Alan Sheridan. New York: Norton, 1977.

Laplanche, Jean. *Life and Death in Psycho-analysis*. Trans. Jeffrey Mehlman. Baltimore: Johns Hopkins University Press, 1976.

—————, and J.-B. Pontalis. *The Language of Psycho-analysis*. Trans. Donald Nicholson-Smith. New York: Norton, 1973.

Martin, Robert B. *The Accents of Persuasion: Charlotte Brontë's Novels*. London: Faber & Faber, 1966.

Miller, J. Hillis. *The Form of Victorian Fiction: Thackeray, Dickens, Trollope, George Eliot, Meredith, and Hardy*. Notre Dame: University of Notre Dame Press, 1968.

Nowell-Smith, Geoffrey. "Minelli and Melodrama." *Screen* 18 (Summer 1977): 113–18.

Smith, Barbara Herrnstein. "Poetry as Fiction." *New Literary History* 2 (Winter 1971): 259–81.

Review of Brontë Studies, 1981–1987

Kathleen Blake

Haworth Parsonage is England's second most visited shrine of literary pil-grimage, after Stratford-Upon-Avon, Larry H. Peers reminds us in *Beyond Haworth*. Scholarship, too, keeps the faith. What J. Hillis Miller says of *Wuthering Heights* might be said of the whole Brontë canon: it "seems to have an inexhaustible power to call forth commentary and more commentary." A review of Brontë studies from 1981–1987 must necessarily be selective. So many books and chapters in books have been written that I cannot aim to cover journal articles as well. Not only do Emily and Charlotte Brontë continue to inspire many scholars and critics, but Anne Brontë has increased her following, and Branwell Brontë, too, has been the object of some devoted labor.

EDITIONS

Among important new editions are two added to the authoritative Clarenden Edition of the Novels of the Brontës, *Villette* and *The Professor,* both edited by Herbert Rosengarten and Margaret Smith. These offer full textual notes covering composition and successive editions, textual emendations and var-iants, and mss related to the novels themselves. And there are two important new editions of Charlotte Brontë's poetry, Tom Winnifrith, ed., *The Poems of Charlotte Brontë. A New Annotated and Enlarged Edition of the Shake-speare Head Brontë,* and Victor A. Neufeldt, ed., *The Poems of Charlotte Brontë, A New Text and Commentary.* Both of these are solid, though the Winnifrith work is the more readable, having far better print. Neufeldt includes more poems, listing a few mentioned by Charlotte or others which are still missing. The list of missing poems is longer in Winnifrith, largely because these have been left for Christine Alexander to publish in her edition of the juvenilia. Both collections provide an index of titles and first lines and notes mainly on the provenance of the poems. Neither offers much literary criticism nor really seeks to raise the repute of Charlotte as a poet. Neufeldt does not challenge the author's own low estimate of her poems, and Winnifrith concedes that Charlotte "was probably the worst poet in the family after her father." Brontë scholarship owes much to Winnifrith's comprehensive and reliable work in establishing the poetic record, not only for Charlotte, but also now for Branwell in *Poems of Patrick Branwell Brontë. A New Annotated and Enlarged Edition of the Shakespeare Head Brontë.*

We are comparably indebted to Christine Alexander for her work on the juvenilia. She is preparing a full *Edition of the Early Writings of Charlotte Brontë,* beginning with the volume on *The Glass Town Saga, 1826–1832.* Both Neufeldt and Winnifrith also acknowledge the great helpfulness of her *Bibliography of the Manuscripts of Charlotte Brontë.* I may mention here her clear and exact guide to *The Early Writings of Charlotte Brontë.* This orients us to the maze of mss extending from the Glass Town Saga and the chronicles of Angria to "Ashworth." Alexander has a scholar's belief that materials need not be overestimated to be worth presenting. She says "it would be wrong to exaggerate the importance of the juvenilia to the later work." In fact, she admires Charlotte's ability to turn from Angria's burning clime, to reduce her great numbers of characters, tighten up her loose plots, move from male to female narrators, seeking concision and realism.

Aside from various editions of the novels for general readers and students, other editions of note are Charlotte's *Something About Arthur,* ed. Christine Alexander; her *Leaf from an Unopened Volume, or the Manuscript of an Unfortunate Author: An Angrian Story,* ed. Charles Lemon; *The Juvenilia of Jane Austen and Charlotte Brontë,* ed. Francis Beer; *Selected Brontë Poems,* ed. Edward Chitham and Tom Winnifrith; another collection of *The Brontës: Selected Poems,* ed. Juliet R. V. Barker; and a reprint of the sisters' 1846 *Poems,* introduced by M. R. D. Seward.

REFERENCE WORKS

I have already mentioned Alexander's indispensable bibliography of Charlotte's juvenilia. Other bibliographies are by R. W. Crump, *Charlotte and Emily Brontë. A Reference Guide,* volumes covering 1846–1983, and Janet M. Barclay, *Emily Brontë Criticism 1900–1982. An Annotated Checklist.*

There are concordances to *Jane Eyre* and *Wuthering Heights* by Ruth Sabol and Todd K. Bender.

REPRINTS

Tom Winnifrith has introduced *The Life and Works of the Sisters Brontë*, a reprint of the 1899–1903 Haworth Edition of the *Works*, another measure of his industry and influence in Brontë studies. Q. D. Leavis's *Collected Essays* has been reprinted, including pieces on *Jane Eyre* and *Villette* of 1966 and 1972. Valerie Grosvenor Myer in her *Charlotte Brontë, Truculent Spirit* credits Leavis with significantly advancing the claim to greatness of Brontë's novels. There are other reprints indicative of continuing influences. Margot Peters's 1975 *Unquiet Soul: A Biography of Charlotte Brontë* and Helene Moglen's 1976 *Charlotte Brontë. The Self Conceived* have proved to have that kind of staying power, both with psychoanalytic and feminist dimensions.

A feminist critic kept current through reprinting is Nina Auerbach, whose earlier essays on Charlotte and Emily appear in her collected essays, *Romantic Imprisonment, Women and Other Glorified Outcasts*. Her 1979 treatment of Emily as an anti-romantic poet remains remarkable, considering Emily's reputation as a romantic. Another reprinted feminist critic shows the continuing influence of French psychoanalytic theory and deconstruction. This is Mary Jacobus, whose 1979 "The Buried Letter: *Villette*" appears in the collection of her essays, *Reading Woman, Essays in Feminist Criticism*.

Reprints appearing in a student text with the scope of influence of the Norton Critical Editions tell us something. Taking a sounding in Richard J. Dunn's revised Norton edition of *Jane Eyre*, we find the addition of feminist and Marxist selections—from Moglen's book, from Adrienne Rich's 1973 "Jane Eyre, The Temptations of a Motherless Woman," from Sandra M. Gilbert's and Susan Gubar's 1979 *The Madwoman in the Attic, The Woman Writer and the Nineteenth-Century Literary Imagination*, and from Terry Eagleton's 1975 *Myths of Power, A Marxist Study of the Brontës*.

BIOGRAPHY

All of the Brontës have inspired new biographical work, even Branwell. In *Profligate Son, Branwell Brontë and His Sisters* Joan Rees paints a picture close to what we might expect of the charming but ineffectual, dissembling, dissipated 5 foot 3 inch red-haired brilliant talker and favored son who brought himself to such a bad end. Rees advances some interesting facts and suppositions. She tells us of Branwell's lasting sense of loss for his sister Maria, and she associates his temper tantrums with *petit mal*. She draws effectively upon Branwell's notebooks and literary works and upon memoirs by his friends Francis Grundy and Francis Leyland. The most significant new interpretation lies in Rees's disagreement with Mrs. Gaskell's influential account in reckoning the blame in the disastrous Robinson affair. Rees is not so convinced of Mrs. Robinson's perfidy. For instance, she thinks there is more reason to believe that Branwell might invent the story of a change in Mr. Robinson's will to prevent the widow's marrying him than that Lydia Robinson should do so. Rees does not hold Mrs. Robinson responsible for Branwell's tragic decline. While this is fairly persuasive, another controversial new interpretation is less so. There is speculation on a possible homosexual episode between Branwell and Edmund Robinson, the son (a possible reason for Branwell's dismissal from the household rather than any adulterous affair). This remains very hypothetical.

If Branwell finds no apologist in Rees, Anne does in P.J.M. Scott, author of *Anne Brontë: A New Critical Assessment*. This is a critical biography that deplores the "ritual attention and dismissal" that has been allotted to Anne. Scott sometimes gushes—"Amazing, rich, profound, that metaphor!"—sometimes sounds a defensive note—Helen's expression of piety in *The Tenant of Wildfell Hall* is "not a choking, indigestible gobbet of sanctimoniousness." Scott's reason for admiring Anne is manifestly based on sharing her Christian viewpoint. He champions her all the more because the "blessed truths" she offers are not likely to be well received by modern readers—post-Marx, post-Wagner, post-Darwin. The issue of reader-response takes on a personal urgency in this work.

Edward Chitham's *A Life of Emily Brontë* is cooler, more cautious and scholarly. Chitham is a major Brontë scholar, collaborator with Winnifrith, for example, on *Selected Brontë Poems* and *Brontë Facts and Brontë Problems*. In this biography he stresses how little material there is to go on, and seeks to sort out the factual from the legendary. He is scrupulously exact about what we don't know—there is no record of when Emily began to walk—and what we do—the layout of Haworth Parsonage, including remodels, the regimen at Cowan Bridge School, the weather reports as compared to accounts of the weather in some of the poems. Chitham finds new interpretive possibilities in certain facts. Important for him is the evidence that Emily knew Shelley's work and that the figure of Shelley plays a role in her poetry. He also emphasizes her reading of the German romantics. He discusses her friendship with Louise Bassompierre at Brussels to moderate our impression of her social isolation. He argues the importance of her experience while a governess at Law Hill. The property had a history involving alienation from a natural heir by an adoptive one, paralleling a case in the Brontë's own family history and suggesting the case in *Wuthering Heights*. Chitham always tells us where facts stop and interpretation begins. He often pieces out facts persuasively, but not so when he gets into deeper psychoanalytic speculation. From slender evidence he surmises that Emily may have felt a sense of guilt for some school-time betrayal of Maria, especially after Maria died. On this he grounds his idea of a ruthlessness and self-punishment for it in some of Emily's behavior, from the way she beat her dog Keeper to the way she died. He thinks guilt over not doing more to avert Branwell's death may have been a factor in Emily's, while in her manner of dying she again showed her ruthless side in doing nothing to comfort Charlotte.

All of this is more rigorously argued than the biographical thesis that underlies Stevie Davie's footnote and bibliography-less *Emily Brontë. The Artist As a Free Woman*. For Davies, Emily's loss of her mother is the presumptive key to an art that represents the redeeming of all losses. Thus it is an art of memory, of retrieval of the past, of the renewing wind, of rebirth through mother nature, and rebirth of one generation in the next. Psychoanalytic and feminist tendencies join in a general way to make Davies extol the figure of the mother which she finds even in a man—Edgar caring for Catherine. This study shows the interest attaching to maternal relations (even where their importance for the author cannot be documented) as a biographical ground for critical analysis. This interest is also prominent in biographers and criticism of Charlotte Brontë.

While I must leave aside biographies of Charlotte by Winnifrith and Pauline Nestor that came out too late for me to consider, (along with Rebecca Fraser's *The Brontës,*) I may point here to Nestor's *Female Friendships and Communities, Charlotte Brontë, George Eliot, Elizabeth Gaskell*. This discusses women friends in Charlotte's life as well as fiction. Pairs of contrasting friends, Ellen Nussey and Mary Taylor, reveal her attraction towards both the conventional and the daring. The rupture between Brontë and Harriet Martineau curiously repeats itself in a rupture between Eliot and Martineau. The "homosocial" note is observed in letters to Ellen Nussey. But no very general conclusions are drawn from this or other matters in Nestor's book. She finds Brontë and Eliot narrower in their network of female relationships and more male-centered than Gaskell, who seems to hold the most appeal for her. There are more mixed and troubling elements in Brontë and Eliot, and Nestor somewhat oversimplifies in favor of positive readings of the one, negative ones of the other. She stresses the heroines' achievement of mutuality with men in Brontë's earlier novels and the achievement of personal self-sufficiency in her last.

I may also point here to John Maynard's *Charlotte Brontë and Sexuality,* returning to the biographical "maternity issue," and with this indicating the related issues of Brontë's degree of neurosis or conscious control as a person and writer. Maynard's work marks out the lines of a major biographical controversy, with strong implications for criticism as well. He challenges the idea that the trauma of Charlotte's early loss of her mother initiated a conflict of feelings over motherhood, which was exacerbated in other ways to the point of causing a psycho-pathology over her pregnancy that led to her death. In the appendix to his book Maynard contests the diagnosis of *hyperemesis gravidarum* advanced by Dr. Phillip Rhodes in his 1972 "A Medical Appraisal of the Brontës," which influenced the biographies of Peters and Moglen, and also Robert Keefe's 1979 critical study, *Charlotte Brontë's World of Death.* Maynard contends that the diagnosis is based on insufficient evidence. His own consultation with Dr. Gerson Weiss confirmed him in this conclusion, so that he advocates returning to the diagnosis of phthisis made by Charlotte's attending physician until we have better cause to overturn it. Maynard enters ardently into this controversy mainly because of his desire to lift the onus of neurosis from Brontë's life and work. He thinks it has been deepened by both psychoanalytic and feminist approaches. He gives an interesting indictment of the way feminist criticism has duplicated earlier Freudian tendencies by assuming that there must be something wrong with any woman who does anything notable and that the dynamic of her art is to be found in neurotic or out-of-control subconscious urges, such as rage, according to Gilbert and Gubar. Thus feminists are "more intent on showing how society has limited and warped women's achievements than in celebrating their successes." Throughout Maynard insists on Brontë's "maturity," and some of his readings rather overstate the case for the maturity of the heroine, for instance Lucy Snowe, whom Brontë herself calls morbid. But Maynard is important as a voice in the ongoing debate about the achievement of Charlotte Brontë as a conscious and deliberate artist. Q. D. Levis said she was, challenging those who would find in a work of hers "a document for the psychiatrist." Maynard challenges certain strains of Freudian and feminist analysis, as do other studies still to be covered.

SOURCES AND ANALOGS

For sources we can look close to home and far afield. Myer points out the plot affinities between *Jane Eyre* and Patrick Brontë's Sunday school tale, "The Cottage in the Wood." The influence of the English romantics is analyzed by Chitham, who stresses Shelley as a source for Emily, and Barry Qualls in *Secular Pilgrims of Victorian Fiction, The Novel As Book of Life* makes Carlyle the point of reference for Charlotte. Enid L. Duthie's *The Brontës and Nature* traces the romantic theme of nature in all the sisters' works. This book may have the most to offer on Anne, with her Wordsworthian devotion to the landscape of childhood memory, her attraction to the wild in nature, making her love the moors and also the sea. It is interesting to see how the sea comes to prevail as an image, and also to see how in her later poems in a hymn tradition nature becomes subordinated to the role of providing analogs for moral themes. Duthie has less that is new to say on Charlotte and Emily, on whose treatment of nature plenty has already been written. She observes that certain nature images, such as that of the sea in *Jane Eyre* and *Villette,* suggest "exploration of the depths of the subconscious." But Duthie does not get very deep herself in these much-plumbed seas.

Other literary traditions provide the terms for Jerome Beaty's "Jane Eyre at Gateshead: Mixed Signals in the Text and Context," Karen E. Rowe's "Fairy-born and Human-Bred, Jane Eyre's Education in Romance," and Lee R. Edward's *Psyche As Hero, Female Heroism and Fictional Form.* With admirable erudition Beaty shows the confluence of three traditions in *Jane Eyre:* that of the fictional autobiography with its "Byronism of personal feelings," that of the moral didactic tale for children, and of the spiritual biography derived from Bunyan and Defoe. These enable Brontë to reveal both the demands of the self and what it owes to others and to God. Rowe and Edwards judge Brontë by a feminist standard, the one approving, the other disapproving the story of a woman's life Brontë can tell through the literary traditions she has to draw on. Rowe argues that Jane initially follows fairy-tale models in her feminine quest, that she shifts into the mode of the adventuresome hero like Gulliver, but ends finding fulfillment within a Christian model of romance out of Shakespeare and Milton, one of equality in love and mutual need. Edwards finds the broad tradition of comedy ill adapted to liberate the heroine since comedy reintegrates its heroes into society through the marriage ending and is not very socially progressive. Thus Jane's desire for action goes unmet as she accepts the inheritance provided by the existing social order, and accepts the traditional fulfillment of marriage. She asserts her equality with Rochester but does not indict inequality as such. She is diminished as she is rewarded.

Certain studies seek to expand the frame of reference for the Brontës to make it not only English but European. This is the aim of Larry Peer in *Beyond Haworth, Essays on the Brontës in European Literature*. Unfortunately, his book is miscellaneous and minor. It seems more odd than anything else, say, to read that *Agnes Grey* employs techniques that create the first true *Bildungsroman* in English literature. A much more considerable contribution is Chitham's investigation into the extent of Emily's acquaintance with the German romantics. The study that goes furthest afield for cultural influences is *Emily Brontë and Beethoven, Romantic Equilibrium in Fiction and Music* by Robert K. Wallace. This is more intent on comparing the "motions of the spirit" of the composer and the writer than in proving Beethoven's direct influence on Brontë. After all, music plays no noticeable role in *Wuthering Heights*. Wallace insists most on the romantic emotion contained within classical construction that allies the work of these artists. He compares aspects of *Wuthering Heights* to three of Beethoven's piano sonatas from his different periods, in order to demonstrate programmatic kinship. And he is able to define some surprisingly technical similarities, such as abruptness and angularity of movement, the dramatic use of silence, and other devices of intensification. In the second half of his book Wallace goes on to demonstrate that Emily knew Beethoven's music before she went to Brussels, and that there she learned to appreciate and play it more. Beethoven was a "divinity" in Brussels musical circles, and Wallace documents the performances of his music that Emily might have attended or heard of. He also thinks Emily knew Anton Schindler's *Life of Beethoven* and could find in it motifs for use in her novel, including the intriguing episode of Beethoven's custody battle for a young nephew whom he desired to "shape." No opportunity for comparison is lost in this one-track study. But it's a new track.

Less novel but still highly revealing are studies of the Brontës' debt to the whole European gothic tradition. In "The Reconstruction of the Gothic Feminine Ideal in Emily Brontë's *Wuthering Heights*," Sydney McMillan Conger turns analysis of this tradition to feminist purposes in a quite straightforward manner. By comparison with the gothic heroine, Catherine is more complex and individualized, her conflicts more internalized. She is less submissive, less a victim, more a rebel, and she finds no resolution in a standard marriage ending. An interesting observation is that her celebrated love doctrine of the identity of lovers and their love unto death is no new thing in the gothic realm.

Margaret Homans is another feminist critic who takes up the issue of the gothic, but in a much more theoretically challenging way. Her "Dreaming of Children: Literalization in *Jane Eyre* and *Wuthering Heights*" appears in *The Female Gothic*, ed. Juliann Fleenor, and is also adapted for Homans's book, *Bearing the Word, Language and Female Experience in Nineteenth-Century Women's Writing*. In her book Homans elaborates a larger framework of thought, drawing especially on the psychological theories of Jacques Lacan and Nancy Chodorow, and she gives an additional piece on "The Name of the Mother in *Wuthering Heights*." The "literalization" issue remains crucial, as it joins with the "maternity issue" on which Homans is a major commentator.

Literalization manifests itself in two seemingly disparate forms—the conventions of the gothic and the theme of motherhood. In the gothic the subjective takes objective shape in a way that threatens the subject. A prime example is the objectification or literalization of Jane's thoughts while in the Red Room, as these give rise to the actual apparition of her uncle Reed. Though in her mind her uncle is a benign figure, such a gothic literalization of her internal thoughts is not. The ghostly Mr. Reed terrifies her.

In a peculiarly similar sense childbirth is the objectification of what was within the subject and is also threatening to the self, according to Homans. She draws upon the biographical view that sees Charlotte as ambivalent about motherhood. Jane's dreams of children are full of foreboding. She is loath to become a "new-born" self in marriage, and as a child of mother nature on the moors she nearly dies. Catherine Earnshaw does die in becoming part of maternal nature and in both going back to childhood and bearing a child. Homans's larger point is that women are endangered by literalization and stand to gain by participation in the figurative order, where the subject retains her priority. In *Bearing the Word* this becomes all the more evident in light of patriarchal tendencies to make woman the literal ground for what is figured, namely as the mother. The problem is that it is the mother's absence that makes possible the boy's entrance into the symbolic realm, according to Lacan, extrapolating from Freud. In such literalization is obliteration. Though in other parts of her book Homans explores a more positive potential for women in the literal, through the theories of Chodorow, this negative line is the one she pursues on the Brontës.

RELIGIOUS ISSUES

Myer performs a service in reminding theologically ill-informed modern readers that the legacy to the Brontës from their Church of England father and Methodist aunt was *not* Calvinist. Scott effectively reveals the attraction Anne Brontë holds for a Christian, and observes how loss of faith within the culture has lost her readers. Thomas Vargish in *The Providential Aesthetic in Victorian Fiction* also makes the point that religious themes are obvious enough in novelists like the Brontës but tend to be disregarded through lack of modern interest. Vargish calls for the exercise of historical imagination and protests against a too modernizing account of Victorian religious views, as in such a work of long-standing influence as J. Hillis Miller's *The Disappearance of God*. Vargish analyzes aspects of a providential aesthetic including coincidence, poetic justice, strongly marked design, and rounded-out plot. He makes the good point that didacticism need not seem opposed to realism aesthetically if reality itself were held to be didactic, that is, as teaching divine meanings. Vargish argues that from *Jane Eyre* to *Villette* we see a lessening faith in the intelligibility of providence, but not less faith that it exists, however obscure. As providence becomes more problematical, so do features of fictional form, like the happy ending. Vargish makes of Miss Marchmont's cry a religious keynote for *Villette*—''I cannot—*cannot*—see the reason.'' But because religious vision darkened, Vargish does not want us to read the Victorians as if they were not looking for God. Indeed. *Villette's* theme of submission to divine providence is often rather lightly passed over in favor of secular themes such as the woman question.

Qualls is another critic lending importance to religion, but compared to Vargish, he presumes its greater secularization in *The Secular Pilgrims of Victorian Fiction*. He compares the Brontë of *Jane Eyre* to Carlyle, especially in Jane's idea of trusting to God and herself, the God within the self, and also within nature. But it must be said that Charlotte did not actually lose her orthodox faith as Carlyle did; Qualls secularizes and modernizes her more than Vargish might like.

POLITICAL ISSUES

If we are not to overlook the religious, even less are we to overlook the political these days. The broad reason is a renewed historicism, a greater interest in the play of particular cultural forces in novels and less in the ''pure'' psychology of ''timeless'' characters. Feminist criticism represents an aspect and in good measure an initiator of such political awareness, belonging naturally within this category of criticism addressing political issues. Of course, psychological criticism remains strong, a category in itself, while also increasingly incorporating historical, political, and feminist awareness.

In the Rereading Literature series edited by Terry Eagleton appears James H. Kavanagh's *Emily Brontë*. This gives a social analysis of the dynamics of *Wuthering Heights* infused by Marxism, French poststructuralist psychoanalysis, and feminism. In Eagleton's summation, "Heathcliff and Nelly, then, square up one to another as violent antagonists on that battlefield which is Catherine's body, the one attempting to seduce her by the 'anarchy of desire,' the other striving to rescue her for patriarchy and social respectibility by a 'sadistic control.' " Heathcliff represents an energy of Oedipal desire that is, confusingly, that of both the capitalist and the dispossessed worker. In him the destabilizing dynamic of capitalism itself is seen, versus the forces of stabilization seen in Nelly. She is no nurturing foster-mother for Kavanagh—as, by way of contrast, she is for Margaret Kirkham in "Reading the Brontës." Rather, she is the "phallic mother," "the female figure who wields the phallic tools of the symbolic order." She pursues for herself and the family she watches over "a class project oriented towards moderate upward mobility within accepted parameters of class domination." In the cycle of destabilization and stabilization acted out by Heathcliff and Nelly appears the cycle of capitalism, and for the radical Kavanagh there is just as much if not more sadism in Nelly as in Heathcliff, as one might say, the one demanding the other. Such a political analysis of an endless, contentious dynamism stands in marked contrast, say, to the account of a final integration of contending forces put forth by H. M. Daleski in *The Divided Heroine: A Recurrent Pattern in Six English Novels*. Indeed, this study is unusual in the favor it shows to the second-generation lovers who can fit into society.

Compared to Kavanagh, Judith Lowder Newton is less fancy, more straightforwardly forceful in *Women, Power, and Subversion, Social Strategies in British Fiction 1778–1860*. She is, like him, historicist, aligned with the Marxist Eagleton, interested in money, class, and power along with gender. She analyzes *Villette* with a fine attention to the material base of power relations between men and women. She shows Brontë's "rejection of and counteradherence to the ideology of women's sphere," as, for instance, Lucy both exults in going out into the world and advancing her earning power and career and sometimes denigrates a successful professional woman like Madame Beck or one explicitly pursuing economic self-interest like Ginevra Fanshawe. Lowder Newton well observes how the declassing and impoverishment of the hero serve to balance out the power between the novel's lovers.

It seems a sign of Brontë's ambivalence that she does not carry through a plot of feminine autonomy in work beyond the middle of the book, where she makes a love plot carry the autonomy plot, and Lowder Newton considers the fulfillment in love and work at the end too good to be true.

It is very clear that feminist analysis is all over the place in Brontë studies, a factor in biographies and works on cultural sources, in the foregoing political commentaries and a number of the psychological commentaries that follow. It will further be seen to figure in reader-response criticism and deconstruction. But several works may be designated here.

My *Love the Woman Question in Victorian Literature, The Art of Self-Postponement* shares ground with other studies (such as Maynard's, among those already covered) in repudiating aspects of Freudian and deconstructive theory that validate the not-said, the unconscious subtext, almost more than the said in women's writing. In this view women's works are to be taken not as symptomatic of self-postponement, or repression, but as deliberate shapings of it, or art. This book also shares historicist grounds with a number of others, being especially concerned that modern Freudian and feminist meanings may be too easily read into supposed unwitting subtexts. The chapter on *Villette* treats the feminine need for love as shown by Brontë *in extremis,* and the dynamics of self-postponement that it generates. A woman in Lucy's situation, feeling the impossibility of satisfying her desire for love, seeks to suppress it, but finds suppression alike unsatisfactory. It leads to inertia, but this is too incomplete to be peaceful yet too complete to be easily broken. What is more, the inert self all the more needs outside impetus to activate it. Lucy, then, is still needy, and in the absence of a lover finds in the very pain of that absence what meets her need, what can stir her to feel alive. While this may not be a ''healthy'' psychological adaptation (of the sort Maynard wants to find in Brontë's novels), it is not to be condemned given the limited possibility of any ''cure'' of women's love sickness within the structures of Victorian society.

In *Victorian Women's Fiction: Marriage, Freedom, and the Individual,* Shirley Foster also finds it important to assert that the ambivalences of Brontë's novels are intended, and that significance is not primarily to be located in what she does not or cannot say. Brontë herself avows her ambivalence by giving *Villette* so ambiguous an ending. It does not deconstruct the novel but is part of its construction. Along these same lines Maggie Berg criticizes the amalgam of Freud and deconstruction within some Marxist as well as feminist Brontë criticism in her *Jane Eyre, Portrait of a Life.* Again, Foster's book, like mine, exposes the highly conflicted nature of women's feelings about love in Victorian fiction. It points to more skepticism than idealism concerning marriage in Brontë, while it observes that her heroines find it hard to "settle the bargain with celibacy."

PSYCHOLOGICAL ISSUES

A very fine study addressing *Repression in Victorian Fiction* is by John Kucich. It analyzes without condemning Victorian repression (in that being comparable to *The Art of Self-Postponement*). This is possible because of an historicist viewpoint, with a debt to Michel Foucault. Such historicizing connects psychological to social structures and thus can bring out political, including feminist, implications. Kucich wishes to dispel the characteristically modern stigmatization of repression by showing that it does not so much work to quell as actually to structure and affirm the nineteenth-century sense of self. We can see in Charlotte Brontë how "self-negating libido" and the consequent division of the self heighten feeling and exalt interiority. Thus even the losses of the self can be gain, "transformed into the spectacular force of solitary suffering." And reserve can be self-fulfillment. Kucich admirably analyzes how in reserve the self can feel its own forces and also find a power to exert over others. He helps us to understand the combativeness in such repressive characters as Brontë's, the fascinating dynamics of dominance and submission in her novels. He recognizes how the sexual power struggles that seem to threaten the heroines' selfhood at some fundamental level constitute it. It follows that Kucich questions the feminist impact of Brontë's works, since the losses and power struggles produced by gender and also class divisions (as in *Shirley*) become the almost necessary conditions for interiority, for individuality. Finally, Kucich is critical of the repression he does not want us too automatically to deplore. His main grounds are political, in that we see a psychology of self-negation, which might lead towards a collectivist social attitude, instead developing in the direction of a privatized individualism. The Victorian individual is weakened in its power to protest the social arrangements on which it also structures itself at a deep level.

There is some connection between Kucich's ideas and those of Karen Chase in *Eros & Psyche. The Representation of Personality in Charlotte Brontë, Charles Dickens, George Eliot*. This study, too, places psychology in an historical perspective, here by reference to nineteenth-century theories, such as that of phrenology in the case of Brontë. This study also may be said to make a case for repression. In the terms of the title eros signifies psychological energy, psyche psychological form or structure. According to Chase, Brontë explores and values the growth from simplicity to complexity in that structure and from Angria on shows the development of psyche that comes from erotic balking. Thus the desire of Zamorna, simple and always gratified, leads to nothing more, while women, the weaker and subordinate sex in Angria, develop a psychologically "more complex architecture of evasion, denial, compromise, restraint." Again, the feminist implications are very mixed if women gain psychologically by their disadvantages within the power relations of gender. Chase does not offer the critique of such implications that Kucich does, and is altogether less politically aware.

Other psychologically oriented works include Maynard's *Charlotte Brontë and Sexuality,* which, though it castigates the psychoanalytic critics who make Brontë out to be a neurotic, certainly employs Freudian theory, for instance, analyzing Jane Eyre's maturation in terms of the Electra complex she must overcome. Maynard is so devoted to the idea of an ultimate maturity that he doesn't always make sure the psychological solutions fit the psychological problems in his analysis. It could be made clearer how Jane's wanderings and finding of family, fortune, and so forth, help her over her Electra complex.

Quite opposite to Maynard's interpretation is Karen Ann Butery's in "Jane Eyre's Flight from Decision," an interesting if harsh application of Karen Horney's theories that finds Jane to be so fundamentally injured by early deprivation of love that she has no chance of healthy development. She is perpetually overcompensating, and in ways that hopelessly conflict with each other. In conflict are her needs to be free and to be loved, guided, and approved by others, and her needs to achieve moral perfection and resignation and to achieve happiness in love. Butery contends that Jane's compensations let her in for more problems. They breed rationalizations—as when she leaves Rochester and later St. John Rivers. That these are rationalizations Butery concludes from the fact that they are contradictory. Jane insists on a relationship of legal marriage in the first instance and one without in the second. Altogether she acts according to involuntary impulses and fails to make decisions. The great example of this is her responding to a magical, external "call" rather than herself determining to go back to Rochester. Butery understands how complex Brontë's character is, but might heed Maynard's request that critics "ease up in the face of life's complexity." She certainly makes no virtue of complexity in the manner of Chase.

Baruch Hochman in *The Test of Character, From the Victorian Novel to the Modern* is closer to doing that. For him, *Wuthering Heights* reveals that

violence is both a source and effect of love. He makes the interesting observation that a sharp sundering gives the occasion for Catherine to express her
love in her famous speech, and a reincorporation of what is sundered like
Catherine's and Heathcliff's must itself be violent.

Three other critics make use of newer psychoanalytic theories. They are
more feminist, and they share a focus on the psychic differences between the
sexes in their experiences of seeing, touching, and speaking. Dianne F. Sadoff
in *Monsters of Affection: Dickens, Eliot, & Brontë on Fatherhood* points out
the subordination of the female in the thinking of Lacan as well as Freud, but
goes on to use them along with their philosophical ally Jacques Derrida and
their French feminist adapters Luce Irigaray and Julia Kristeva. The male
principle of the father looms so large within this tradition that it is not surprising that Derrida finds a way to make paternity an issue in the "fort-da"
game that even the Oedipally obsessed Freud presents as hinging on relations
with the mother. According to Freud, the boy makes his wooden reel stand
for his mother so that when she goes away he can make it go and come back
again, giving him some sense of control in the early crisis of separation from
her. But with the help of Derrida and Lacan, Sadoff is willing to make the
reel, representative of the mother, represent the phallus, so as to make the
game part of the psychodrama of castration, whereby we get "the articulating
cut that makes language possible." Granted that fatherhood is an important
issue for the Brontës, but with theories like these Sadoff is bound to overstate
the case. Considering the interest in maternal relations that has been so strong
in Brontë studies, and the feminist coloring of this interest, it hardly seems
that Sadoff as a feminist Brontë scholar should be so utterly patrocentric. She
makes use of a notion of gender difference out of Irigaray and Kristeva that
orients men towards the visual, women towards voice and touch. However,
there are difficulties in applying this idea. Sadoff finds an advance towards
being her own master for Lucy in *Villette* when she can "speak rather than
spectate." But this is confusing. One problem is that speaking cannot offer
women a very definitive mastery if language itself is phallogocentric, per
Lacan. Furthermore, since mastery has hitherto been associated with spectating in the case of men, it is a question whether a woman should give it up.
Especially if a male mode like language can empower women, why not
spectating, too? I find myself caught in the nets and meshes of theory, unable
to answer these questions.

But it must be said that theory has proved stimulating in Brontë studies.
In *Woman Writing About Men* Jane Miller makes a point of the reversal of
the male gaze in *Villette*. Rather than being the object of men's vision, Lucy

makes men the objects of hers, and she also gains "faith . . . in her capacity to see herself." This is not expressed in highly theoretical terms, but it brings to mind an argument that is in Leslie W. Rabine's *Reading the Romantic Heroine, Text, History, Ideology,* except that here women are not learning to gaze more but men to gaze less. That is, the phallic economy of vision dominates the way men experience love in *Shirley,* whereas the women care more for the sharing of experiences, the intimacy of talking, than for their lovers as objects to look at. Specularization is critiqued, and men are shown as capable of giving up this patriarchal habit to some extent. However, Rabine finds specularization still at work in class relations, for in the battle scene at Moore's mill even women characters and the narrator view the workers in highly visual terms that objectify them.

READER RESPONSE CRITICISM

We have seen earlier in Myer, Scott, and Vargish how the readers' readiness (or lack of readiness) to respond to religious issues matters to the estimates of Anne and Charlotte Brontë's works. In other studies readership is a concern as well.

One kind of attention to the reader appears in Rachel M. Brownstein's *Becoming a Heroine, Reading About Women in Novels.* Brownstein explores what Charlotte Brontë's novels, among others, have offered her personally in the course of her own development. Thus she learned from Brontë that a woman can "feel the weight of her woman's life as serious," that a girl's character is not reducible to her sexual fate, that she can hoard her real self to herself, and in a way suggestive of self-postponement or repression "express her passionate uniqueness by suppressing it."

In Carla L. Peterson's *The Determined Reader, Gender and Culture in the Novel from Napoleon to Victoria* there is another kind of attention to the reader, here through a study of fictional protagonists as themselves readers. For instance, Jane is someone who reads, all the more so as an orphan and outsider who turns to books to search for herself. And reading can help her to find a way to relate herself to others, while it is at the same time socially isolating, and especially so for a girl. It may also teach her to subordinate herself according to such literary models as the fairy tale and religious texts. Here Peterson shares ground with students of the literary traditions that inform the novel. She takes the sanguine view (more like Rowe's than Edwards's) that Jane learns to resist assuming roles like those offered in male fictions,

and adapts her reading to serve a woman's story. Ultimately Jane becomes
a writer herself, and—in a detail pleasing to Peterson—is depicted reading
to a blinded Rochester at the end.

Yet another kind of attention to the reader is that of Brenda R. Silver in
"The Reflecting Reader in *Villette*." Hers is a fascinating study of narrative
techniques for constructing the kind of reader responses necessary for reception of a story like Lucy Snowe's. Silver employs the feminist narrative theory
of Nancy K. Miller to maintain that the implausible or awkward in the novel
seems so by the standards of conventional reading habits, masculine in bias.
Lucy must seek to reshape these conventional responses as she addresses her
implied reader. There is progress from early addresses to the reader conceived
as unsympathetic judge and jury. Before this tribunal Lucy uses a rhetoric
of defensiveness, irony, and disclaimers. She even hides information from
this reader—her recognition of Dr. John—as she does from other characters.
This is not an oddity that flaws the novel as has often been felt, nor is it to
be understood as part of the characterization of a repressive neurotic. It is a
sign that the ability to understand a woman like Lucy that is shown to be
lacking in most of the characters, may indeed be lacking in the reader, so
that she cannot afford to too freely expose herself in either case. But she
slowly evolves a conception of a reader whom she can address more openly,
in whom she can presume some sympathy and sense of mutuality. She need
no longer feel herself like "the half-drowned life-boatman [who] keeps his
own counsel, and spins no yarns." To spin out her yarn she needs someone
who can hear it. To develop then, she must develop ways to address the
reader that also develop that reader into a fit audience for her.

DECONSTRUCTIVE CRITICISM

After this review of so many Brontë studies it seems apt to conclude with
J. Hillis Miller's notion of "undecidability." Each interpretation—he is
speaking of *Wuthering Heights*—"tends to be plausible, but demonstrably
partial" though "presented with a certain certainty." His chapter on Emily
Brontë's novel in *Fiction and Repetition* holds forth no "univocal principle
of explanation." The secret truth is that there is no single secret truth at the
head of the chain of interpretations. Miller has the acutest awareness of a
reader's desire for complete and absolute understanding, illustrating this by
Lockwood's own desire to be given every detail of the tale, with nothing left
out, equivalent to the wish, if one were watching a cat lick herself, to see

the thing through without missing an ear. Yet Miller shows that the novel makes us miss ears. He examines passages that seem emblematic of the whole work, yet in not corresponding to each other imply different wholes and therefore no wholeness at all. As there is infinite duplication of meaning in the story—like Catherine's name swarming in Lockwood's consciousness as he falls asleep in her bed, like the interminable series of sins and parts of the sermon of which he dreams—so the reader contributes to the ever-multiplying interpretations of *Wuthering Heights,* repeating its own dynamic of endless repetition. Readings stand to the text as figures to what they figure, and Miller brilliantly analyzes the seductive frustrations of the figurative for Heathcliff in the novel. He finds in everything in the world a sign of Catherine and, as such, a sign that he has lost her. Miller tends to make us feel the frustration more than the pull in this by some little measure, though he seeks to balance out readers' regret at not penetrating to the mystery of meaning as against their sense of desecration should they do so.

Jay Clayton in *Romantic Vision and the Novel* finds a more overridingly positive value in the provisional nature of all figures seen in *Wuthering Heights.* Awareness of undecidability need not lead to a mode of radical scepticism and demystification, as is often the case in deconstruction. Rather, it may make us feel the strength of the dynamic of representation, which figures by its proliferating products the figure-making power. This is a romantic, apocalyptic power, for Clayton.

With two more vindications of figuration, we may console ourselves within the critical enterprise that multiplies ways of representing the Brontës. In "Passion, Narrative, and Identity in *Wuthering Heights* and *Jane Eyre,*" Tony Tanner reminds us that Catherine and Heathcliff die in their quest for an absolute that they prefer to the symbolic, that is, to the books that they so often reject. The mediation of language implies separateness from things in themselves and from other people. But Jane Eyre lives by accepting this, according to Tanner. Likewise, Margaret Homans finds a saving power for Jane when she begins to interpret things instead of merging with them, for example, figuring out the meaning of a light she sees on the moors instead of lying down to die there. Women improve their chances of life by emerging from the literal into the symbolic order, Homans says, and they may well beware of taking their place as the literal in men's minds, as that which only by being lacked makes the world significant. For Homans as well as Tanner, Catherine and Heathcliff find death in the end of figuration. So would Brontë studies, of course.

WORKS CITED 1981–1987

Alexander, Christine. *A Bibliography of the Manuscripts of Charlotte Brontë*. Westport: Brontë Society, Meckler, 1982.

—————. *The Early Writings of Charlotte Brontë*. Buffalo: Prometheus, and Oxford: Blackwell, 1983.

—————, ed. *An Edition of the Early Writings of Charlotte Brontë*, Vol. 1 *The Glass Town Saga 1826–1832*. Oxford: Blackwell, 1986.

—————, ed. *Something About Arthur*. By Charlotte Brontë. Austin: Humanities Research Center, University of Texas, 1981.

Auerbach, Nina. " 'This Changeful Life': Emily Brontë's Anti-Romance" (1979) in *Romantic Imprisonment, Women and Other Glorified Outcasts*. New York: Columbia University Press, 1986.

Barclay, Janet M. *Emily Brontë Criticism, 1900–1982, An Annotated Checklist*. Rev. ed. Westport: Meckler, 1984.

Barker, Juliet R. V., ed. *The Brontës: Selected Poems*. London: Dent, 1985.

Beaty, Jerome. "Jane Eyre at Gateshead: Mixed Signals in the Text and Context." *Victorian Literature and Society, Essays Presented to Richard D. Altick*. Ed. James R. Kincaid and Albert J. Kuhn. Columbus: Ohio State University Press, 1984.

Beer, Francis, ed. *The Juvenilia of Jane Austen and Charlotte Brontë*. Harmondsworth: Penguin, 1986.

Berg, Maggie. *Jane Eyre, Portrait of a Life*. Boston: Twayne, 1987.

Blake, Kathleen. "*Villette:* 'How Shall I Keep Well?' " *Love and the Woman Question in Victorian Literature, The Art of Self-Postponement*. Sussex: Harvester and Totowa, N.J.: Barnes & Noble, 1983.

Brownstein, Rachel M. *Becoming a Heroine, Reading About Women in Novels*. New York: Viking, 1982, and Harmondsworth: Penguin, 1984.

Butery, Karen Ann. "Jane Eyre's Flight from Decision." *Third Force Psychology and the Study of Literature*. Ed. Bernard Paris. Rutherford, N.J. and London: Fairleigh Dickinson University Press, 1986.

Chase, Karen. *Eros & Psyche, The Representation of Personality in Charlotte Brontë. Charles Dickens, George Eliot*. New York and London: Methuen, 1984.

Chitham, Edward. *A Life of Emily Brontë*. Oxford and New York: Blackwell, 1987.

—————, and Tom Winnifrith. *Brontë Facts and Brontë Problems*. London: Macmillan, 1983.

—————, and Tom Winnifrith, eds. *Selected Brontë Poems*. Oxford and New York: Blackwell, 1985.

Clayton, Jay. "*Wuthering Heights." Romantic Vision and the Novel*. London and New York: Cambridge University Press, 1987.

Conger, Sydney McMillan. "The Reconstruction of the Gothic Feminine Ideal in Emily Brontë's *Wuthering Heights.*" *The Female Gothic.* Ed. Juliann E. Fleenor. Montreal and London: Eden, 1983.

Crump, R. W. *Charlotte and Emile Brontë, A Reference Guide 1846–1983.* Boston: Hall, 1982–1986.

Daleski, H. M. *"Wuthering Heights,* The Whirl of Contraries." *The Divided Heroine, A Recurrent Pattern in Six English Novels.* New York and London: Holmes & Meier, 1984.

Davies, Stevie. *Emily Brontë, The Artist As a Free Woman.* Carcanet: Manchester, 1983.

Dunn, Richard J., ed. *Jane Eyre, Authoritative Texts, Backgrounds, Criticism.* 2nd ed. New York: Norton, 1987.

Duthie, Enid L. *The Brontës and Nature.* Basingstoke and London: Macmillan, 1986.

Eagleton, Terry. "Editor's Preface." Kavanagh.

————. *Myths of Power, A Marxist Study of the Brontës.* 1975. Selection in Dunn.

Edwards, Lee R. "Heroes into Heroines: The Limits of Comedy in *Emma, Jane Eyre,* and *Middlemarch.*" *Psyche as Hero, Female Heroism and Fictional Form.* Middletown, Conn.: Wesleyan University Press, 1984.

Foster, Shirley. "Charlotte Brontë, A Vision of Duality." *Victorian Women's Fiction: Marriage, Freedom, and the Individual.* London and Sydney: Croom Helm, 1985.

Gilbert, Sandra M., and Susan Gubar. *The Madwoman in the Attic, The Woman Writer and the Nineteenth-Century Literary Imagination.* 1979. Selection in Dunn.

Hochman, Baruch. *"Wuthering Heights:* Unity and Scope, Surface and Depth." *The Test of Character, From the Victorian Novel to the Modern.* Rutherford, N.J. and London: Fairleigh Dickinson University Press, 1983.

Homans, Margaret. "Dreaming of Children: Literalization in *Jane Eyre,*" and "The Name of the Mother in *Wuthering Heights.*" *Bearing the Word, Language and Female Experience in Nineteenth-Century Women's Writing.* Chicago and London: University of Chicago Press, 1986.

————. "Dreaming of Children: Literalization in *Jane Eyre* and *Wuthering Heights.*" *The Female Gothic.* Ed. Juliann. E. Fleenor. Montreal and London: Eden, 1983.

Jacobus, Mary. "The Buried Letter: *Villette.*" 1979. in *Reading Woman, Essays in Feminist Criticism.* New York: Columbia University Press, 1986.

Kavanagh, James H. *Emily Brontë.* Editor's preface by Terry Eagleton. Oxford: Blackwell, 1985.

Kirkham, Margaret. "Reading 'The Brontës' " in *Women Reading Women's Writing.* Ed. Sue Roe. New York: St. Martin's, and Sussex: Harvester, 1987.

Kucich, John. *Repression in Victorian Fiction, Charlotte Brontë, George Eliot, and*

Charles Dickens. Berkeley, Los Angeles, London: University of California Press, 1987.

Leavis, Q. D. *Collected Essays, The Englishness of the English Novel.* Ed. G. Singh. Vol. 1. Cambridge, London, and New York: Cambridge University Press, 1983.

Lemon, Charles, ed. *A Leaf from an Unopened Volume or the Manuscript of an Unfortunate Author: An Angrian Story.* By Charlotte Brontë. Haworth: Brontë Society, 1986.

Lowder Newton, Judith. *Women, Power, and Subversion, Social Strategies in British Fiction 1778–1860.* Athens: University of Georgia Press, 1981.

Maynard, John. *Charlotte Brontë and Sexuality.* Cambridge, London, and New York: Cambridge University Press, 1984.

Miller, J. Hillis. *Fiction and Repetition.* Cambridge, Mass.: Harvard University Press, 1982.

Miller, Jane. *Women Writing About Men.* New York: Pantheon, 1986.

Moglen, Helene. *Charlotte Brontë, The Self Conceived.* 1976. Madison: University of Wisconsin Press, 1984. Selection in Dunn.

Myer, Valerie Grosvenor. *Charlotte Brontë, Truculent Spirit.* London: Vision, and Totowa, N.J.: Barnes & Noble, 1987.

Nestor, Pauline. *Female Friendships and Communities, Charlotte Brontë, George Eliot, Elizabeth Gaskell.* Oxford: Clarendon Press, 1985.

Neufeldt, Victor A. *The Poems of Charlotte Brontë, A New Text and Commentary.* New York: Garland, 1985.

Peer, Larry H. *Beyond Haworth, Essays on the Brontës in European Literature.* Charles E. Merrill Monographs No. 8. Provo: Brigham Young University, 1984.

Peters, Margot. *Unquiet Soul: A Biography of Charlotte Brontë.* 1975. New York: Athenaeum, 1986.

Peterson, Carla L. "*Jane Eyre* and *David Copperfield*: Nature and Providence." *The Determined Reader, Gender and Culture in the Novel from Napoleon to Victoria.* New Brunswick and London: Rutgers University Press, 1987.

Qualls, Barry V. "The Terrible Beauty of Charlotte Brontë's 'Natural Supernaturalism'." *The Secular Pilgrims of Victorian Fiction, The Novel As Book of Life.* Cambridge, London, and New York: Cambridge University Press, 1982.

Rabine, Leslie W. *Reading the Romantic Heroine, Text, History, Ideology.* Ann Arbor: University of Michigan Press, 1985.

Rees, Joan. *Branwell Brontë and His Sisters.* London: Hale, 1986.

Rich, Adrienne. "Jane Eyre, The Temptations of Motherless Woman." 1973. Dunn.

Rosengarten, Herbert, and Margaret Smith, eds. *Villette, The Professor.* By Charlotte

Brontë. Clarendeon Edition of the Novels of The Brontës. Oxford: Clarendon Press, 1984, 1987.

Rowe, Karen E. "Fairy-Born and Human-Bred, Jane Eyre's Education in Romance." *The Voyage In, Fictions of Female Development.* Ed. Elizabeth Abel, Marianne Hirsch, Elizabeth Langland. Hanover and London: University Press of New England, 1983.

Sabol, Ruth, and Todd K. Bender. *A Concordance to Brontë's Jane Eyre.* New York and London: Garland, 1981.

—————. *A Concordance to Brontë's Wuthering Heights.* New York: Garland, 1984.

Sadoff, Dianne F. *Monsters of Affection, Dickens, Eliot, and Brontë on Fatherhood.* Baltimore and London: Johns Hopkins University Press, 1982.

Scott, P. J. M. *Anne Brontë: A New Critical Assessment.* London: Vision; and Totowa, N.J.: Barnes & Noble, 1983.

Seward, M.R.D., ed. *Poems by the Brontë Sisters.* Rpt. of 1846 *Poems.* London: Black, 1985.

Silver, Brenda R. "The Reflecting Reader in *Villette. The Voyage In, Fictions of Female Development.* Ed. Elizabeth Abel, Marianne Hirsch, Elizabeth Langland. Hanover and London: University Press of New England, 1983.

Smith. See Rosengarten.

Tanner, Tony. "Passion, Narrative, and Identity in *Wuthering Heights* and Jane Eyre, in *Contemporary Approaches to Narratives,* ed. Anthony Mortimer (Tübingen: Narr, 1984), pp. 9–23.

Vargish, Thomas. *The Providential Aesthetic in Victorian Fiction.* Charlottesville: University Press of Virginia, 1985.

Wallace, Robert K. *Emily Brontë and Beethoven, Romantic Equilibrium in Fiction and Music.* Athens and London: University of Georgia Press, 1986.

Winnifrith, Tom, intro. *The Life and Works of the Sisters Brontë.* Rpt. 1899–1903 Haworth Ed. New York: AMS Press, 1982.

—————, ed. *The Poems of Charlotte Brontë, A New Annotated and Enlarged Edition of the Shakespeare Head Brontë.* Oxford and New York: Blackwell, 1984.

—————, ed. *The Poems of Patrick Branwell Brontë, A New Annotated and Enlarged Edition of the Shakespeare Head Brontë.* Oxford: Blackwell, 1983.

—————. See also Chitham and Winnifrith

Recent Dickens Studies: 1987

George J. Worth

What follows will be a less comprehensive treatment of my subject than was
David Paroissien's "Recent Dickens Studies" review-essay for 1986. Working under tigher space limitations, not to mention the time constraints that
afflict us all, I have decided to devote my account of 1987 almost entirely
to general critical studies of Dickens and examinations of particular Dickens
novels. With considerable regret—but also, to be honest, with a sense of
relief, because my candidates for possible inclusion approached two hundred
in number, and I have the note cards to prove it—I am omitting editions,
adaptations, dissertations, compilations of previously published criticism, and
studies of minor works, parallels, sources, influences, and topography. Nor
will I even glance at those general studies, however valuable they may be,
in which Dickens gets only passing mention. My successor will no doubt
have much to say about the important biographical work on Dickens published
in 1988, and I will leave that pleasure to her: quantitatively, at least, those
pickings in 1987 were pretty slim.

Preferring Slearyan untidiness to Gradgrindian rigor, I am going to discuss
a couple of significant 1986 publications that were not included in the *Dickens
Studies Annual* survey for that year, N. N. Feltes's *Modes of Production of
Victorian Novels* and Carla Peterson's *The Determined Reader*. I will look
again, from somewhat different perspectives, at a couple of equally significant
pieces of work from "my" year that my indefatigable predecessor dealt with
prematurely, Rhoda Flaxman's *Victorian Word-Painting and Narrative* and
Suzanne Graver's "Writing in a 'Womanly' Way and the Double Vision of
Bleak House." Normally, though, I have not gone over 1987 ground that
David Paroissien has already covered so ably; this includes two very good
books that I have reviewed elsewhere, Juliet McMaster's *Dickens the Designer*
and Philip Bolton's *Dickens Dramatized*.

One of my earlier forerunners, Sylvia Manning, concluded her "Recent Dickens Studies: 1980" by expressing the hope that "Dickens critics will continue to avoid using language so as to offend the inimitable ghost" (*DSA* 10 [1982]: 262). Her "continue to" was too kind, as the rest of her penultimate paragraph made clear, and I am sorry to have to report that Dickens' spirit must have been at least as troubled in 1987 as he had been seven years before. To enumerate and document the linguistic sins of which Dickens critics—of course with many honorable exceptions—have been guilty would require a whole essay, if not a book, so let me merely mention a few of the most common: shaky grammar and syntax of a kind that used to bring a blush to the cheek of the young person teaching freshman English; circumlocution that would be the envy of a Barnacle or a Stiltstalking; a fondness for incantatory verbal tics like "I want to argue" (more than once I found myself scribbling in the margin "so go ahead already," or something less polite); and of course the several sorts of almost impenetrable jargon that seem to have become de rigueur in certain, closed, critical circles. One would like to think that something intellectually or imaginatively luminous lies behind such polluted mist, but the more one gropes and flounders one's way through verbal smog that is often as dense as Mr. Guppy's London particular the more one is inclined to doubt it.

And what, I wonder, would the shade of our author, who fought his own battles with publishers, have to say about the prevailing slovenliness that marks book and periodical production in the 1980s? Though he was inclined to be rather cavalier about proofreading, Dickens could be compulsive about details, and I suspect that his ghost would fly into a rage at encountering in a book by a famous scholar (who had better remain nameless here) put out by a prestigious university press (ditto) references not only to such of his characters as "Noah Claypo*ol*," "S*i*dney Carton," and "Monk" but also to such fiction-writing colleagues as "La*w*rence Sterne" and "Lo*ui*s Carroll"—all within fifty pages.

In the introduction to his *Repression in Victorian Fiction*, a book about which I will have more to say later, John Kucich defines his task as "the making visible of a fundamental . . . subtext" in the novels he examines rather than as the "imposition of theory on naive and groping texts" (17). Most interpreters of Dickens, today as in the past, would also claim to be exposing rather than imposing, often without sufficiently considering if the two kinds of activity can be so easily divorced from each other. For the critic necessarily approaches his or her material armed with *some* way of reading or relating texts, in the absence of which the criticism would turn out to be "naive" or "groping" or both. We may as well be candid about this need to lay our own conceptual structure over "texts" that contain conceptual structures of their own—rearranging pieces of the evidence to suit our argument, stressing some, neglecting some, changing the meanings of some by placing them in new contexts, perhaps inadvertently falsifying some because our Laputan concern with "theory" has led us to neglect mere details. (Even a formidable critic like Kucich occasionally gets simple facts wrong, and he is by no means the worst offender among those whose work will be surveyed here.) Nevertheless, I think we must try to avoid the sort of criticism that forsakes the reality of Dickens in order to concoct and caress a self-contained reality of its own—the sort of criticism that demands admiration of the critic's cleverness rather than of the novelist's genius. I am, of course, assuming that Dickens *had* genius (otherwise why do we spend our precious time on him?) and also that critics have more important things to do than glorify themselves or impress other critics (not to mention members of hiring, promotion and tenure, and salary committees).

For what and for whom, then, *should* critics write? Rather than answering that difficult question directly, I will mention here, out of its proper order, the most haunting single article I read in connection with my present assignment. Sylvia Sarrett's title says it all: "Why I Love Teaching the Gifted, Hated Seeing *Brazil,* and am Dropping *A Tale of Two Cities.*" She had accepted on faith what her professors taught her about the genius of Dickens and was deeply disappointed when her sophomore honors students at a high school in Tampa were not equally willing to accept what she tried to teach them. Then, having gone to see the movie *Brazil* because some highly regarded film critics had lauded it, she understood all too well her students' dislike of *A Tale of Two Cities.* The long-windedness of *Brazil,* its exaggerations, its allusiveness, and above all its self-consciousness aroused in her much the same kind of aversion, the same uneasy sense that the actual artistic product did not live up to the authoritative critical promise, that her bright and articulate teen-agers experienced in the presence of Dickens. Like them, she felt that she had been cheated and she resented it.

Now, I am fully aware that Sarrett's story raises all sorts of questions. One that I consider especially urgent is: How have we Dickens critics failed the Sylvia Sarretts of the world and their professors? Also: How much indirect blame must we bear for turning their students off Dickens? And, finally: Will there will be enough students in our colleges and schools reading Dickens a generation or two from now to support those academicians who want to write

Dickens criticism; and, if not, will we have helped to kill off our own progeny? (There are other, larger questions, but this is not the place to raise them.)

The gloomy mood in which Sarrett's essay had left me was aggravated by some other reading, totally unrelated to Dickens, that I did a few hours after my encounter with her. This was an article about recent criticism by Denis Donoghue in the *Times Literary Supplement* containing the following sentence:

> Literary theorists continue to offer large excruciations, misgivings about language, meaning, indeterminacy, form, and the politics of closure, but these 'techniques of trouble' are rarely enforced upon undergraduates, who have enough trouble reading and writing ordinary sentences.
>
> (*TLS*, 16–22 December 1988: 1399)

That struck a plangent chord, even though Donoghue's purpose in writing was very different from Sarrett's. Nor are his semi-literate undergraduates her high-IQ tenth-graders, but those young people do have something in common: they are all potential readers of Dickens, in whose lives the reading and enjoyment of Dickens could make a great difference, but to whom and whose teachers much of what passes for Dickens criticism today is utterly irrelevant.

I have cleared my throat, if not my mind. On to my appointed task.

I

Of all the books dealing with Dickens published in 1987, the furthest-reaching and most thought-provoking is Jerome Meckier's *Hidden Rivalries in Victorian Fiction*. Styling himself "the modern revaluator" (or, more modestly, "one"), Meckier sees Dickens as the central figure in what he calls "the realism wars," in the course of which mid-Victorian novelists competed with one another in validating and practicing what each took to be a faithful rendering of human experience, one that would be both recognizable to readers and conformable to nineteenth-century scientific doctrines.

Beginning in the 1850s and continuing for two decades, this generally covert contest described by Meckier repeatedly tested the mettle of such writers as Gaskell, Trollope, Eliot, and Collins, as well as Dickens himself, elevating their work to peaks of achievement they would not have scaled had each of them been working in artistic isolation. Disclosed, these rivalries lay bare some new oppositions and alignments—for instance, by disengaging Dickens from his putative struggle with Thackeray, here viewed as more his ally than his adversary—and pave the way for comparable struggles by twentieth-century British novelists.

In addition, Meckier persuasively challenges not only outdated simplistic definitions of realism but also more recently fashionable callings-into-question of the very possibility of realism. "A mind full of Bakhtin and Derrida is no substitute for a historical sense" (10), he points out dryly in his first chapter; in his last, he restates an earlier claim, by then amply supported, that "there were as many realisms in the nineteenth century as there were realists," adding that the chief common denominator among them was "the bravura assertion, by a prominent novelist or one who would soon be so, that his or her perspective was more realistic than any other, especially Dickens's" (273).

Taking liberties with chronology, Meckier begins by reading *Felix Holt* as "the classic instance of Victorian revaluation: a systematic revision, a complete redoing, of Dickens' *Bleak House*" (13)—without, however, explaining why Eliot waited thirteen years to do her demolition job or why it was as late as 1866 that "parodic reconstruction of a rival's world" became "an indispensable ingredient in the nineteenth-century British novel" (24–25). Eleven years before *Felix Holt,* Trollope's attack on an unwritten Dickens novel, *The Almshouse* by "Mr. Popular Sentiment," had turned *The Warden* into the "seminal" case of "parodic rewriting in Victorian fiction" (46) while the dust was still settling on another conflict involving Dickens, this one pitting him against Gaskell—a conflict that was much more complicated than one might infer from the fact that her *North and South* was serialized in *Household Words* after his *Hard Times,* for each partner in that remarkably combative-collegial relationship was keenly aware of what the other was, and had been, up to.

Though apparently more closely allied than Dickens and Gaskell, Dickens and Collins engaged in "a kind of creativity contest" (94) that Meckier regards as so fierce and protracted that he devotes three chapters and over a hundred pages to it. Simply put, *The Woman in White* emerges as Collins's attempt to outdo his mentor's work, especially *Bleak House* and *A Tale of Two Cities*; *Great Expectations* was Dickens' "effort to quell a sort of palace revolution by a subordinate trying to assume command of the melodramatic novel" (123); Collins returned to the attack, now also taking in *Great Expectations,* in *The Moonstone*; and Dickens effectively silenced Collins, while also getting in some last licks at Trollope, Gaskell, and Eliot, in the unfinished *The Mystery of Edwin Drood.*

It is Eliot who seems to have fired the last shot in "the realism wars," largely by outliving Dickens long enough to produce *Middlemarch* (as well as *Daniel Deronda*, which plays no role in Meckier's argument): Bulstrode's hypocrisy was her "revaluative revision" (210) of John Jasper's duplicity, and Dorothea and Lydgate represented other correctives to Dickens' dystopian view of potentially catastrophic self-division. But was Eliot's triumph over Dickens really conclusive? Meckier's last chapter maintains that, from a twentieth-century at least as much as from a nineteenth-century perspective, Dickens' brand of realism is as worthy of serious consideration as hers; that no final authority inheres in her Wordsworthian-gradualistic/evolutionary-utopian outlook; and that neither novelist—in fact no Victorian novelist—can be adequately understood without due attention to the "hidden rivalries" in which they were caught up. What gives Dickens his place of honor is the central position in which Meckier places him in this perpetual combat: always a favorite target by virtue of his prominence, but also a resourceful and effective fighter when stung into rebuttal.

There is much to admire in Meckier's clearly written, ably argued, copiously documented book. Still, he leaves himself open to objection, for example when he segues from bold conjecture into flat assertion as he frequently does in uncovering "hidden rivalries." What evidence, for instance, allows him to say that Eliot "*insist*[s] her Esther Lyon is above Esther Summerson" (99) or that Collins "*believes* that Mrs. Catherick's case better serves to typify providence's inherent sense of poetic justice than Lady Dedlock's does" (105; italics added in both quotations)? Meckier's readings can be tendentious, as when he calls Esther Summerson's discovery of her mother's corpse "the climactic revelation to which the preceding forty-eight chapters [of *Bleak House*] had built" (93), or when he follows Sue Lonoff in regarding Franklin Blake's theft of the moonstone from Rachel Verinder as "symbolic defloration" (136)—both debatable points on which he proceeds to build major arguments. When novelists fail to say what Meckier wants them to, he sometimes says it for them: for example, when he instructs Collins and Dickens how they should have made their cases in the prefaces to *The Moonstone* and *Bleak House*, or—most exhaustively and most ingeniously—when he bases his account of the unfinished half of *The Mystery of Edwin Drood*, which is at least as persuasive as anybody else's attempt to complete that novel, on his view of what Dickens "could" or "would" have written, had he lived, in order to outstrip *The Moonstone*. Such quibbles aside, however, *Hidden Rivalries in Victorian Fiction* must be placed among the few indispensable studies of the mid-Victorian novel.

Though he does not use Meckier's phrase, Fred Kaplan in his *Sacred Tears* also enlists Dickens in the nineteenth-century "realism wars" but in a role that is very different from the one in which Meckier casts him. According to Kaplan, Dickens did battle on the side of those who defended the almost universal existence and virtually indomitable potency of "innate moral sentiments" (29) against "the increasingly powerful forces of philosophical realism, which claimed that the ideal has no place either in life or in literature" (37). Ambiguous on this idealist's credentials as a realist, Kaplan grants that, on the one hand, "Dickens conceives of the external world as materially real" (54) and acessible to both the novelist and the characters he creates, but claims that, on the other hand, "Dickens throughout is basically non-mimetic" (59).

In concisely defining the philosophical bases of Dickens' sentimentality and tracing them back to their eighteenth-century roots—a task also performed, with more thorough relentlessness, by Wolfgang Herrlinger in *Sentimentalismus und Postsentimentalismus*—Kaplan renders a valuable service without, however, answering conclusively those in Dickens' lifetime or since who have been offended by this element in his fiction. Like "melodrama," "sentimentality" is a term whose unfavorable connotations cannot be explained away even by cogent historical or contextual arguments, nor is it at all clear that the sentimental Dickens can be absolved of either deliberate insincerity or accidental bad taste quite so readily as Kaplan appears to think. But it is good to have Kaplan's reminder that in Dickens, as in Thackeray, tears are not to be cynically dismissed as "water-works" to be turned on and off at will; rather they are, even in as hardened a fortune-hunter as Sophronia Lammle, to be interpreted as outward signs of widely shared inward moral sentiments and therefore to be respected, if not venerated, as vehicles of human communion.

Though treated along with two other "visually oriented books" in the *Dickens Studies Annual* review of 1986 publications, Rhoda Flaxman's 1987 *Victorian Word-Painting and Narrative* is worth another look here in the context of Meckier and Kaplan. Not as explicitly concerned as they are with nineteenth-century controversies surrounding realism, she does regard "word-painting" as a writer's attempt to render some sort of external reality in "passages of visually oriented description" (1). In Flaxman's view, Dickens—creator of "the most interesting word-paintings in the Victorian novel" (19)—goes significantly beyond such forerunners as Radcliffe and Scott in fusing descriptive passages with narrative, dramatic, and symbolic elements in his novels, bearing a marked resemblance to Tennyson in his growing ability to integrate such passages with other materials.

Flaxman refers occasionally to what she calls Dickens' "cinematic" ap-

proach to representation (29, 30, 32). This common and convenient, if an-
achronistic, way of regarding Dickensian descriptions is not without its perils,
as James R. Kincaid demonstrates in his "Viewing and Blurring in Dickens"
by references to several novels including two (*David Copperfield* and *Little
Dorrit*) of the three from which Flaxman draws most of her examples. What
Dickens is in fact representing, Kincaid insists, is often far from clear and
usually much more ambiguous than what a filmmaker finds in his novels.
For, like "interpretive commentary," says Kincaid, a film is "necessarily
an interpretation of an interpretation (or a non-interpretation), not a reflection. . . . Both, finally, are constructions, not reconstructions" (110).

How Dickens (re)constructed his brief stint of menial work in a shoe-polish
warehouse at the age of twelve has been a favorite topic among critics ever
since Edmund Wilson appropriated it from the domain of biography in his
landmark "Dickens: The Two Scrooges." Three 1987 books address this
question, each according it less than the due it has been given for the past
half-century.

In the opening sentence of the preface to *From Copyright to Copperfield,*
Alexander Welsh goes so far as to liken his book to "an assault on Warren's
Blacking warehouse." Though conceding that this famous "episode" in
Dickens's boyhood was "traumatic in some sense," Welsh denies that such
a trauma in itself can provide "the best ground for biographical criticism"
(vii), maintaining that it did not rise close enough to the surface of Dickens'
mind to be usable in his fiction until he was past thirty and that he confronted
it with increasing confidence and skill in the last three novels he wrote during
the 1840s: *Martin Chuzzlewit, Dombey and Son,* and *David Copperfield.*

The "*Copperfield*" in Welsh's title, then, signifies a culmination in one
phase of the novelist's career as he approached his fortieth year. The "*Copyright*" refers to the experience in Dickens's adult life that Welsh believes
triggered this phase—this "moratorium" as he calls it (10), borrowing the
term from Erik Erikson: Dickens' disturbing realization that he might have
been less than candid about the motives that led him to argue the case for
international copyright early in his 1842 trip to the United States. Despite his
vigorous disclaimers, could Dickens have been hoping, selfishly, for financial
gain?

The largely unconscious self-examination to which Dickens was brought
by such accusations from critics on both sides of the Atlantic, Welsh contends,
left its imprints on the three novels in a variety of ways that he describes with
his customary clarity and sophistication, establishing some surprising and
generally persuasive connections, both between Dickens' life and his creations

and among some of his characters. A final chapter carries the argument forward to rehearse and expand on the now widespread assessment of *Great Expectations* as a more honest reworking of the material that went into *David Copperfield* and as an implied challenge to what Dickens' "favourite child" among his novels seems to be saying.

Welsh's readings of all four novels are stimulating, but to the extent that they rest on psychoanalytic foundations they are necessarily speculative rather than conclusive. "The method of psychoanalysis often implies that less is more," Welsh correctly points out near the beginning (5): if it were demonstration rather exploration we were after, we might claim to be able to prove anything simply from the fact that there is no evidence for it, because silence, the absence (read withholding) of explicit evidence, must itself be regarded as significant. Welsh avoids that absurdity, of course, but he also fails to make it clear why the Dickens who was finding his identity during this moratorium should have relied as heavily as Welsh claims he did on earlier literary models: *Tartuffe* and *Paradise Lost* in *Martin Chuzzlewit, King Lear* in *Dombey and Son.*

Gwen Watkins, like Welsh, denies "that the blacking-factory episode was the great traumatic incident of [Dickens'] life from which all his later emotional difficulties proceeded" (11). Like Welsh, too, she sees Dickens' disillusionment during and immediately after his American journey of 1842 as the start of a major turning point in his career, and she believes that it was only in the mid-1840s that Dickens let subconscious preoccupations that went all the way back to his childhood assume major importance in his novels and other fiction.

But for Watkins the central fact in Dickens' early life was his parents', and especially his mother's, refusal or inability to give him the loving support any child needs if he is to develop into an emotionally whole adult. (Perhaps I should point out that it is Watkins, ignoring distinctions of gender, who consistently refers to "the child" and uses the masculine pronoun in such theoretical discussion as she provides.) As a result of this deprivation, she argues, Dickens, following a pattern later described by Karen Horney and others, invented a "second self"—a self designed "to gain love or approval" jeopardized by the actual or fancied exercise of the real, unconscious self—in a process that required "immense will-power" (9).

In Watkins's view, Dickens' second self was more or less in control while he wrote and published the early works that did indeed win him unprecedented acclaim. Beginning with *The Chimes,* however, she finds that themes welling up from his real self manifest themselves more and more strikingly in his writing: rejection by the mother and its consequences; the guilt-ridden child's sense that he had no right to be born; his impaired ability as he grows into manhood to love mature women; a special concern for the helplessness of other children; the creation of a new self out of the wreckage of the old; and the personality's tendency to split itself into parts that are at best uneasily aware of, and usually oblivious to, each other's existence.

Partly because her *Dickens in Search of Himself* tries to cover more ground and takes more chances than *From Copyright to Copperfield,* Watkins exposes the reader to more inconsistencies, self-contradictions, and unfortunate slips than does Welsh. Nevertheless, in its own agreeably unpretentious way her book sheds useful light on Dickens' work by confronting old questions—for example, his depictions of female and juvenile characters—in stimulating new ways. (Chapter 7 even offers yet another solution to *The Mystery of Edwin Drood,* as clever in its way as Meckier's.)

In his *Partings Welded Together* David Musselwhite also regards the 1840s as a major watershed for Dickens and, like Welsh and Watkins, he challenges Edmund Wilson's elevation of the Warren's Blacking experience into the central trauma of Dickens' life. For Musselwhite, the autobiographical fragment in which Dickens set down his anguish over that experience, supposedly for John Forster's eyes only, was a piece of disingenuous self-justification, an important document in the transformation of the anarchic "Boz" who "was fascinated by the surfaces of things, by the variegated play and heterogeneity of the world about him" into the much more tightly controlled "Dickens" who was preoccupied "with inner psychological states" (14), a process that reached its climax in *Dombey and Son,* the last novel of the decade, in which "Dickens" finally takes over.

Musselwhite regrets that victory, because he considers the "Boz" of the *Sketches* and *The Pickwick Papers* to be the better writer. Taking a larger view, he examines the course of Dickens' career as part of a general process whereby

> the exuberance and the threat of the forces let loose by the development of industrialism and the French Revolution [were] steadily but ineluctably worked within a new axiomatic, a new set of rules and constraints, of prescribed places and possibilities that made them both manageable and self-monitoring.
>
> (9)

Musselwhite, it will be clear, is a man with a thesis. But he is also an astute reader and a lively writer, whose eighty-four page chapter on Dickens is absorbing and whose use of other authorities (in the Dickens chapter primarily Gilles Deleuze and Felix Guattari) is gracefully subordinated to his own argument, indebted to them though it clearly is. And, not least important, his enjoyment of Dickens is overt, something that, sadly, I could not say about most of the critics whose work I have included in this survey.

Like Alexander Welsh and Gwen Watkins, Dirk den Hartog, in *Dickens and Romantic Psychology*, assumes that we can no longer accept the "idea of the adult self as autonomous" and that such complacent acceptance by the subject invites "retributive invasion from the more archaic depths of the psyche" (1). While acknowledging Dickens' own duality as a man, however, Den Hartog emphasizes the way he sees the novelist grappling with this issue in three of his major works—*Dombey and Son, Little Dorrit,* and *Great Expectations*—rather than what he takes to be the psychic roots of that duality. Den Hartog's concentration on the works instead of the man is in itself unexceptionable and even laudable, and it leads him to some useful local insights into the ways these three novels achieve their effects. But his choice of an interpretive model involves him, and his reader, in considerable confusion, which his slack writing and his publisher's casual copy-editing do nothing to alleviate.

Initially, Den Hartog's relating his position to Marshall Berman's argument in *All That is Solid Melts into Air* (1982) seems promising—though his misspelling of Berman's first name as "Marshal" (3 and passim) does diminish the reader's confidence right at the outset. For Berman sees "the experience of modernity" as a dialectic process involving a constant struggle between individualistic impulses and the desire for some kind of control to hold them in check, an ambivalence or ambiguity that can be profitably applied not only to Dickens himself but also to a number of the situations he presents in his fiction. It is when Den Hartog tries to view this conflict in "Romantic," "Wordsworthian" terms that the trouble starts. Not only is the concept of a single "Romantic Psychology" implied by his title highly questionable, but it is unclear on which side of the conflict Wordsworth's "metaphor of organic plant growth" (17) is to be placed or why Den Hartog lays so much stress on "the conservative implications" of what he infelicitously calls "the continuity idea" (89) derived from the second book of *The Prelude*.

The question of "continuity" is indeed important to an understanding of a number of the Dickensian characters Den Hartog treats, but one constantly wants to ask: "continuity" *with what?* It may be true, as Den Hartog argues, that Dombey had to overcome the "taboo on tenderness" (42; the term is Ian Suttie's) and that he had to experience "the emotional state of childhood anew" (53), but what evidence is there regarding Dombey's exposure to "tenderness" before the action of the novel begins or, for that matter, the kind of "childhood" he may have had? (How many children had Lady Macbeth?) What Den Hartog later calls Pip's un-Wordsworthian " 'bad' past" (132) is hardly a unique feature in the emotional development of these characters, as he implies.

Den Hartog calls *Great Expectations* "Dickens's most mature dialogue with Wordsworthian psychology, and his most mature exploration of the dialectic of the post-Romantic 'experience of modernity' " (126) because of the high degree of psychic integration he believes Pip achieves. His inconclusive conclusion—Dickens in *Great Expectations,* despite the advances it marks over *Dombey* and *Dorrit,* is still equivocating about some important questions, reluctant "to consciously acknowledge a radicalism of insight towards which his imagination is drawing him" (155)—seems to call for further exploration in Dickens' last two novels, but neither *Our Mutual Friend* nor *The Mystery of Edwin Drood* receives even the most cursory treatment in *Dickens and Romantic Psychology.*

In *Charles Dickens and the Form of the Novel,* Graham Daldry presents an author caught between the conflicting claims of two kinds of imagination, "an internal, individual and structuring imagination" and "an externally 'received', social, cultural and historical imagination" (1), a writer whose "works undertake to explore and, for the English novel at least, establish the possibilities and limitations of each of these approaches to the novel" (40). Conceding that he has "employed the terms 'fiction' and 'narrative' in a way which will perhaps seem unfamiliar" (1), Daldry uses the latter, as a noun and as an adjective, to refer to the "structuring" imagination, and the former, along with the adjective "fictive," to refer to the "externally 'received' " imagination. No one in the late 1980s had better dare object to a critic's right to use an "unfamiliar" vocabulary—whether a genuinely new one or an old one redefined and defamiliarized—but it is still legitimate to ask if those terms are clear and consistently used and if they strengthen the reader's understanding of the works to which they are applied. In the case of *Charles Dickens and the Form of the Novel,* the answer must, unfortunately, be No.

Confusion sets in as early as Daldry's introduction, where he tries to explain his use of "fiction" and "narrative" by appealing to supposedly comparable pairs of contrasting concepts in the writing of D. H. Lawrence, E. D. Hirsch, and Gillian Beer. Such explanations, however, do more to obfuscate than to clarify, as do some of Daldry's own synonyms—for example, his use of "genre" as an equivalent to "fiction" as he defines it. A similar disorientation results when Daldry tries to apply his "unfamiliar" terms to specific Dickens texts. To cite just one instance of many, for Daldry a narrator is anyone—author or character, narrator in the "familiar" sense or not—who tries to structure stories into plots. So in *Oliver Twist* he invites us to see Mr. Brownlow and Bill Sikes trying to exercise authorship/authority by shaping Oliver's and Nancy's stories into narratives that Brownlow and Sikes as narrators control. Partly because of the irresistible pressure of "fiction" on "narrative," he argues, such attempts are bound to fail; and so, therefore, does Dickens' second novel. What Daldry's readers must try to do is to square their sense of the narrative technique and effect of *Oliver Twist* with Daldry's often idiosyncratic version, and again and again, here and elsewhere, one is left with the sense that Daldry has been reading a different novel from the one one thinks one knows.

Daldry seems to be positing a Dickens who was searching purposefully for "a stable fictive voice" (96) and finding it in *Bleak House*; for a way "to demonstrate the powers, not of fiction, but of narrative" (131) and finding it in *Great Expectations*; and for a means of bringing "these opposing views together to achieve . . . the novel at its most extensive and comprehensive, and to provide us with a landscape which includes and extends those of the earlier novels" (164–165) and finally finding *that* in *Our Mutual Friend*. Never mind what Dickens may actually have been trying to do in many diverse works over the course of three highly productive decades or how Dickens' readers have perceived those works, singly or collectively: Daldry has used his "unfamiliar" terminology to organize and control what he himself would call a "narrative," an essentially self-referential account that excludes or contradicts much of the "fictive" material that others have seen in the "landscape" of Dickens' work. With less help from Daldry the stylist than we might hope for—he makes some heavy demands on our sense of logic and syntax—we end up with a clearer sense of the thesis of his book than of the novels by Dickens he treats.

An Austrian critic, Herbert Foltinek, is also concerned with the question of form in his *Charles Dickens und der Zwang des Systems*. His thorough readings of *Dombey and Son* and *Great Expectations* lead him to the conclusion that, for reasons of which Dickens was less aware than Daldry believes him to be, our novelist did, certainly in his artistic maturity, produce multi-layered but coherent narratives ("geschlossene Beziehungssysteme . . . in denen die Funktion jedes Einzelelements mehrfach bestimmt ist"; 7)—a conclusion that would have seemed more remarkable several decades ago than it did in 1987.

Beginning his book with an exercise in redefinition, as Graham Daldry does, John Kucich says that in *Repression in Victorian Fiction* he will not employ the term "repression" in the classic Freudian sense "as a function of unconscious resistance . . . that censors, displaces, and condenses dangerous material, driving it from the conscious into the unconscious, and producing the distortions of neurosis" (2), nor can he accept—fully or at all—the uses to which it has been put by others: Herbert Marcuse, Nina Auerbach, Carl Degler, Martha Vicinus, or Michel Foucault. Rather, Kucich conceives of repression as what he calls "a nineteenth-century strategy for exalting interiority," a generally productive mechanism whereby individuals are able to achieve "self-definition" (2) or "emotional autonomy" (2-3)—the cultivation of a private space in which to develop, a private arena within which to wage internal conflicts, relatively free of social pressures and also of the need to connect with the community. Elsewhere in his introduction, which is rough going for anyone who is neither conversant with nor especially interested in the psychological debates that he rehearses in considerable detail, Kucich rephrases his definition on several occasions, tending to preface each new formulation with a phrase like "that is to say" or "in other words" and quietly taking as many liberties with the commonly accepted meanings of terms like "erotic" and "libido" and their derivatives as he does with "repression"—strategies that make his argument no easier to follow.

Mercifully, Kucich puts such terminological hair-splitting behind him as he moves into the body of his book, in which he devotes separate chapters to examining the fiction of Charlotte Brontë, Eliot, and Dickens with a view to determining how each embodied repression, as understood by Kucich, in her or his work. In Dickens' novels, Kucich finds a complex relationship, "not a stable opposition at all" (203), between repression—desire for self-negation and desire for self-conservation—and passion. The two kinds of desire, in turn, are not simply opposed to each other as much as they are locked in "an inner complexity that would keep desires for both self-negation and self-conservation in play, synthesizing them without compromising one with the other" (225): truly, as Kucich puts it a page later, an "interminable subjective convolution."

Kucich's position, necessarily over-simplified in the foregoing summary, takes him to shrewd conclusions about some major issues in Dickens: for example, Dickens' treatment of death and the desire for it as the ultimate form of self-negation; his increasingly complex representations of the struggle between passion and repression; the growing "impoverishment of community" (215) in his novels; the changing uses he makes of hypocrisy, privacy, and invasions of privacy; his conferral of "social authority" (252 ff.) on such "self-reflexively, symmetrically repressed" (268) characters as Arthur Clennam; and the different ways in which repression works in female as opposed to male characters.

But, despite Kucich's acknowledgement of "the absolutely idiosyncratic nature of the resolutions [Dickens'] characters achieve" (249), he is too often prepared to tear such characters out of their contexts and pair them with each other to support his argument in ways that lead to distortion: John Jarndyce with Sydney Carton, for instance, or Arthur Clennam with Eugene Wrayburn, or John Harmon with Eugene Wrayburn. Other kinds of problems arise when Kucich applies his ideas to Dickens' novels: especially striking in a critic who has devoted many pages to deconstructing and reconstructing a sophisticated term like "repression" is his apparent inability to understand that the simple word "love" means very different things at different stages of David Copperfield's relationship with Agnes Wickfield or Eugene Wrayburn's relationship with Lizzie Hexam. And—unless I misread Kucich, which is entirely possible—his theoretical preconceptions lead him to interpret Twemlow's wonderful speech in the final chapter of *Our Mutual Friend* as meaning just the opposite of what it is usually taken to mean. Could this self-effacing man, surely a repressed character if ever there was one, really be articulating, with reference to Eugene's marriage to Lizzie, the "odd formula . . . that a dynamic suppression of one's feelings is a code by which gentlemen might be recognized" (270)?

The last general study of Dickens I must mention, because it bears the name of one of our most influential (and least self-effacing) critics, is Harold Bloom's introduction to the *Charles Dickens* volume in the Modern Critical Views series put out by Chelsea House. This is something of a disappointment, not so much because of its relative brevity, which is understandable given the occasion, as because of its nature as a peculiar collage of obiter dicta from Bloom and long quotations from Dickens and others, appropriate parts of which were recycled for use in the introductions to volumes on individual Dickens novels in the Modern Critical Interpretations series, also edited by Bloom and published by Chelsea House. It is not, regrettably, the kind of sustained presentation and defense of a thesis about Dickens that one would have hoped for from this source.

II

Both Paul Hoggart and N. N. Feltes are more interested in Dickens' first novel as a cultural document than as a literary text *per se*. Hoggart approaches *The Pickwick Papers*, and especially Mr. Pickwick himself, in terms of ideology as conveyed through Dickens' use of signs. Feltes uses the novel as the first of five texts—the later ones are *Henry Esmond, Middlemarch, Tess of the D'Urbervilles*, and *Howards End*—that he discusses in his Marxist analysis of "the material conditions for the production of Victorian novels generally" (ix).

Hoggart makes his point about the significance of *Pickwick* by contrasting it with some of the many plagiarisms, imitations, and adaptations that followed hard on its heels, mainly *The Penny Pickwick, Pickwick Abroad*, and *Pickwick in America*. Unlike Dickens' enormously successful work, which drew its readers from all segments of society, they were directed to a primarily working-class audience and adapted Dickens' material and his attitude toward it for that public. The resulting

> contrasts of style and tone between the various Pickwick texts, [Hoggart concludes,] stem from . . . deep-seated ideological differences . . . born of the processes by which social groups competed over a currency of cultural materials, whose meanings were reworked to establish senses of identity and social position in a rapidly changing world.
>
> (43)

For Feltes, *The Pickwick Papers* "marks the transition . . . from the petty-commodity production of books to the capitalist production of texts" (3). Understandably, given the premises from which he argues, he plays down the derivative features of *Pickwick* and stresses its originality, in the sense of "its specific historical determination": "Chapman and Hall can be recognized as the new publishers of industrial capitalism, just as Dickens can be seen as a free, professional writer and their mutual antagonistic struggle to produce a commodity-text analyzed as a whole process" (12). Less understandable is Feltes's failure to show how successful Dickens was in that "struggle," in which, quite apart from anything that can reasonably be called "historical determination," he generally came out the victor.

As old a crux in Dickens studies as the question of how he might have completed his last novel had he lived to do so is the question of why he inserted nine apparently discrete tales into his first. Jean Harris's answer is that the "overt assaults on father figures" in these interpolated stories "parallel a series of similar but covert attacks in the main narrative" (69) of *The Pickwick Papers*—an ingenious position, but one that disregards five out of nine of those short narratives and, more importantly, one that requires us to read the "main narrative" as a set of variations on the theme of Sam Weller's ousting by Tony and Sam's vicarious revenge through the depredations of the "impostorious" Stiggins. Harris makes a plausible case, but few readers will recognize her *Pickwick* as Dickens' or theirs.

The six essays—by K. J. Fielding, Morris Golden, Iain Crawford, Brian Rosenberg, Sylvia Manning, and Robert A. Colby—published in the "Oliver Twist 150th Anniversary Issue" of the *Dickens Quarterly* in June 1987 were reviewed last year, but another, by Michal Peled Ginsburg, deserves mention in this survey. Possibly owing its relative lucidity to its origin as a paper delivered at Santa Cruz in 1985, it points to the presence in *Oliver Twist* of two kinds of discourse: the non-standard, literal, mimetic "marked" language of lower-class criminals and the standard, figurative, rhetorical "unmarked" language of middle-class characters like Oliver himself. Ginsburg shows that the language of the narrator, too, is mixed: apparently committed to middle-class ideology, he departs from unmarked diction when under "the pressure that social relations exercise on individuals" (235) and in the process "goes beyond the ideological notions of objectivity and realism, to present a view of social reality as the arena where different languages enter a power struggle" (236).

"Lenticular curiosity" was Ruskin's contemptuous term for the Victorian preoccupation with what could be seen through the mechanical lenses of such devices as the camera, the telescope, and the microscope, often at the expense of what Ruskin called the "Moral Retina" and its perceptions. According to Michael Greenstein, Dickens moves beyond "lenticular curiosity" in *The Old Curiosity Shop* "by focusing on narrow spheres that lead ultimately to broader ethical concerns of the Moral Retina" (187). In an argument whose opacity is all the more remarkable because he ostensibly deals with vision, Greenstein directs his reader to the prominent use made in the novel of such apertures as windows and keyholes giving access to areas of experience and understanding that go beyond the physical. (When are commentators on *The Old Curiosity Shop*, like Greenstein, going to stop referring to Nell Trent's maternal grandparent as "grandfather Trent" [187] ?)

There is nothing opaque about G. Cordery's "The Gambling Grandfather in *The Old Curiosity Shop*," and he studiously and properly avoids giving him a surname. But what emerges from Cordery's article is an interpretation that would have given a nineteenth-century reader apoplexy and that manages to give pause even to a reasonably hard-bitten twentieth-century Dickensian: that pathetic old man, Cordery says, is consumed with "suppressed sexual desire for Nell," which manifests itself not only in his "compulsive or pathological'' gambling but also in his nocturnal theft of her money, which is really a ''symbolic rape'' (43), in Chapter 30. (David Musselwhite makes much the same point as part of a very different argument [192–193].) Remembering Lonoff and Meckier's interpretation of a comparable incident in *The Moonstone,* one is moved to wonder if it will ever again be possible to read a man's depriving a sleeping young virgin of a precious object as anything less than a sexual act. Apart from that flight of Freudian fancy, Cordery should be commended for making the point that Nell's grandfather may profitably be viewed ''as a precursor of Dickens' later and more mature portraits of repressed desires and disturbed states of mind'' (58).

Though very different from each other in purpose and scope, the two studies of *Barnaby Rudge* published in 1987 share some interesting features. Both Thomas Jackson Rice in the introduction to his excellent Garland *Annotated Bibliography* and Thelma Grove in her stimulating *Dickensian* article refer to the neglect from which Dickens' first historical novel has suffered; both—Rice, of course, at greater length—attempt to account for this neglect; and both exploit it, again in their necessarily different ways, in the service of future readers and researchers.

Not only is ''*Barnaby Rudge*'': *An Annotated Bibliography* shorter, at 845 entries, than the typical volume in the Garland series, but Rice has included more material that does not bear directly on his novel—about fifty percent by his own count—than any of his predecessors in compiling these useful works of reference. For he conceives of his task somewhat differently: as the putting together of ''a guide *for* research on BARNABY RUDGE, not simply a guide *to* studies of BARNABY RUDGE'' (xi). In his introduction and elsewhere, Rice points to ''genuine opportunities for original and valuable research'' (xxiv)—opportunities, as he says correctly, not to be found in any of Dickens' more-studied novels.

Few of the 251 entries Rice lists under ''Critical Studies'' have much of value to say about Barnaby himself; but Grove, a speech therapist by profession, applies her expertise to this odd character, whom she calls ''the first autistic hero in English literature'' (147), and demonstrates in fascinating detail how his behavior can be explained by the nine features of autism set forth by Leo Kanner and Mildred Creak in their definitive work on this condition. Surely without intending to assume such a role, Grove serves as a salutary model of how one should go about treating Dickens as a forerunner of scientific investigators who ''discovered'' and named traumas that he knew and described long before they did their research and wrote it up (the term ''autism'' did not come into use until about a century after the publication of *Barnaby Rudge*): she reads the novel scrupulously, without the kind of tunnel vision that Freudian critics, for example, often employ, and she is obviously more interested in sharing what she finds than in finding what she is looking for. Not so much because it is less shocking than Cordery's account of the grandfather in *The Old Curiosity Shop* as because Grove has subjected her novel to a much more balanced scrutiny, her modest article is considerably more persuasive than his.

The novel that succeeded *Barnaby Rudge, Martin Chuzzlewit,* begins with an elaborate "pedigree of the Chuzzlewit family" in the first chapter and ends with a lyrical apostrophe to Tom Pinch in the last. Both passages have been problematic for many readers, and three out of the four critics whose essays on *Martin Chuzzlewit* appeared in 1987 devote their attention to one or the other.

Kathleen Wales assigns more significance to the opening chapter than it is generally believed to have, insisting that, though *Chuzzlewit* is indeed the novel about selfishness that Dickens said it was, the self as it is manifested over and over again in those eight hundred-plus pages has to be understood in a context of family and inheritance. According to Wales, the chapter is not only "a parody of the whole framework of introductory geneaological [sic] histories popular in fiction of the 18c and early 19c" (170); it is also a necessary, self-mocking, "comical-satirical exposure of the Chuzzlewits as they really are" (171).

Some remarks about Tom Pinch, to whom H. Foltinek devotes a whole article, conclude Mary Rosner's examination of animal imagery in the novel. In her view, these frequent "allusions remind us that man does have a bestial nature no matter where he is" (131), whether in the English settings of most of *Martin Chuzzlewit* or in the American episodes, which these references help to integrate into the book. Jonas Chuzzlewit serves Rosner as the most striking illustration of her thesis. In the "tranquil, calm, and happy" Tom of the closing paragraphs, on the other hand, "the beast within" is denied, and for Rosner this constitutes proof that Tom is a "dissatisfying character . . . who clearly does not belong in this world" (140). Foltinek, who maintains that we ought to take Tom as seriously as Dickens did, would disagree, even though his thorough examination of Tom's role leads him to the concession that his place in *Chuzzlewit* "cannot be defined in exact terms" (201). Perhaps, Foltinek speculates, Tom, who is innocent of "ambition, self-regard, and envy," should be taken as an impersonation of "the hidden yearnings" of Dickens, "whose life, unlike that of his favourite, was never to become 'tranquil, calm, and happy' " (202).

In the most subtle of these articles on *Martin Chuzzlewit,* Norris Pope proposes that readers shift away from what Dorothy Van Ghent long ago called "the view from Todgers's" and see what happens if, instead, they use as their vantage point the nearby Monument. That enigmatic reminder of fire, plague, and suicide, which casts its giant shadow over the neighborhood in which Mrs. Todgers's celebrated boarding house is located, he suggests, is an even more powerful indicator of Dickens' troubled view of urban life.

In the first of three 1987 essays on *Dombey and Son* to be noticed here, N. N. Feltes returns us to the subject of realism in a discussion of the novel that is virtually unreadable by anyone not familiar with the theories of Michel Pêcheux and the arcane vocabulary in which he—or, rather, his translator, H. Nagpal—expresses them. (Feltes's other major source is *Language and Materialism* by Rosalind Coward and John Ellis; they, in turn, draw heavily on Jacques Lacan.) Denying Elizabeth Ermarth's claim that the realism of a novel like *Dombey* is a form of consensus, Feltes begins by asking, *"whose* consensus . . . is it, and whose, at any particular moment, is it not?" (297). Not surprisingly, when stripped of the vocabulary in which it is enshrouded Feltes's answer comes to little more than this: *Dombey and Son* reflects the sense of reality, with all the attendant class- and gender-based exclusions, of Dickens's mid-nineteenth-century bourgeois readers.

Much more accessible are two articles that agree on the need to go beyond parent-child relationships (must one really add, as Feltes no doubt would, in the "preconstructed" version of early-Victorian middle-class society that Dickens gives us?) if we are to understand Dickens' concerns in *Dombey and Son.* Lyn Pykett, attributing to Dickens an exaltation of "childlike innocence" (28) as the ideal state of human nobility, sees evidence in the novel that "satisfactory parent-child relations" cannot be achieved by anyone who is not in close touch with "the childhood state" (16). Mary Montaut looks past Edith's roles as Mrs. Skewton's daughter, Florence's stepmother, and indeed Dombey's second wife in order to present her, persuasively, as the focus of the novel's "main arguments about the role of women in the strongly patriarchal world of commercial capitalism" (142) and "the key to all the satires in the book" (152).

"Whether I shall turn out to be the hero of my own life, or whether that station will be held by anyone else, these pages must show," David Copperfield writes at the outset of Dickens' next novel. Not going quite so far as to claim that James Steerforth, rather than the first-person narrator, is "the hero," Edwin M. Eigner nevertheless makes a powerful case for reading *David Copperfield* as an "elegiac romance" (the term is Kenneth A. Bruffee's)—''a first-person retrospective narration recounting the death of a romantic figure who has captured the imagination of the less heroic narrator'' (39). That ''romantic figure,'' of course, is Steerforth.

In Eigner's judgment, Steerforth represents for David the gentility to which he aspires because it affirms the life he thinks he wants and denies the death he knows he dreads. As Eigner reminds us, other characters in the novel also regard Steerforth in this light; but, as things turn out, they are all—including David—mistaken. For Steerforth is revealed to be

> the false cultural hero of Victorian England, the romantic knight whom the narrator of one of the century's most significant elegiac romances must reject for himself and his age, so that he and his readers can find their true identities in the face of their otherwise overwhelming and paralyzing fear of death.
>
> (50)

A perceptive and retentive reader, Eigner subsumes a large amount of evidence from the novel, much of it well known but some of it neglected. What is exemplary about Eigner's argument is the way it opens up *David Copperfield* rather than constricting it to accommodate a particular theoretical/ideological bias.

Eigner is not convinced that David has totally rid himself of his ''fascination for Steerforth'' (56) when his narrative ends. Two other critics, Rosemary Mundhenk and Virginia Carmichael, agree that *David Copperfield* achieves a less than complete closure, though their reasons, like their arguments, are quite different from Eigner's. For Mundhenk, David is engaged in a ''struggle to deal with the complexity of memory'' (328) like that experienced by a number of others in the book, most notably Mr. Wickfield and Betsey Trotwood. David's task, she says, is ''to balance the tendency to submit to the oppression of remembrance and the inclination to suppress or distort painful memories'' (338); his success, though considerable, is not final. For Carmichael, David has ''two tasks'' to perform: ''expressing himself through mature work and love'' (654). She regards David's quest for ''social vocation'' as obviously successful but is less sure about his search for appropriate ''sexual bonding'' (654): his ''transcendentally ideal marriage'' with ''St. Agnes'' Wickfield is at best ''a problematic resolution'' (665) of that second problem.

Carmichael makes much of the fact that the French words ''*nom*'' and ''*non*'' are homonyms. Without bothering to consider whether or not this could have had any bearing on David's story as Dickens or David himself conceived of it, Carmichael insists that David's twin ''tasks . . . are enormously complicated by the violence with which the name and the no of his particular father are uttered'' (654), presumably referring to the influence not only of David's deceased biological father but also of his second "Pa," Mr. Murdstone. Though French, Gwenhaël Ponnau does not resort to such puns or to Carmichael's Lacanian terminology to construct an argument that also assigns great importance to the absent father of this "posthumous child," succinctly tracing the process by which David achieves an identity and a name through his encounters with a variety of doubles.

Resembling Ponnau in putting psychological theories to more discreet use than Carmichael, Carla Peterson approaches David's development primarily through his reading—fairy tales, picaresque novels, and (with a somewhat greater sense of strain) religious texts—and, later, through his writing, comparing him in the third chapter of *The Determined Reader* (82–131) with Jane Eyre. But, Peterson contends, David is also significantly different from Jane, both as a reader and as a writer. Less firmly in control of what he feels and what he does, David is "much less straightforward and more ambiguous" (124) than Jane as he moves from reading to writing: he cannot deal adequately with the transgressions of Emily or Steerforth, he cannot find appropriate role models in the masculine writers he has known (Dr. Strong, Mr. Micawber, and especially Mr. Dick), and he cannot write anything worth reading without feminine inspiration: Dora, "female nature" (that is, the "beautiful Swiss valley"; 127), and Agnes. Indeed, it is Agnes "who imposes order, structure, and meaning on the different events of David's life" and serves, "[i]n a sense," as the "true author" (129) of David's autobiography. Having begun, with Eigner, by asking if David is "the hero of [his] own life,'' we end encouraged by Peterson to wonder if indeed it is David's "own life" that we read.

The critical literature devoted to another of Dickens' narrators, Esther Summerson, must be more extensive than that dealing with any "real" nineteenth-century English woman writer of prose fiction except Austen, Emily Brontë, Charlotte Brontë, Gaskell, or Eliot, and at least two articles dating from 1987 must now be added to that seemingly endless list. Both Joseph Sawicki and Suzanne Graver ascribe great skill and even cunning to Esther as she succeeds in displacing the other, unnamed, presumably male narrator of *Bleak House* and gradually taking charge of the novel (Sawicki) and in revealing, even as she seemingly tries to conceal, an assertive as well as an accepting self (Graver). Each critic uses Esther to make a point: Sawicki that *Bleak House* is, at least in part, "about the way events are narrated, and who is in control of that narrative" (219) and Graver that Dickens, aware as he was that the social pressures of his day enforced "indirection" as "a strategy characteristic of women's writing," nevertheless set out "to celebrate a dutifully willed acceptance" of "Victorian womanly ideals" (4) in the troubled person of Esther. Though a third critic, Katherine Cummings, appears to be interested in some of the same questions considered by Sawicki and Graver, her treatment of the narrative method of *Bleak House* is a self-indulgent exercise in word-play rather than a genuine engagement with Dickens's novel and therefore will be passed over here in stunned silence. I gave up on Cummings after three tries. Life is too short.

In his useful little volume on *Bleak House* in Macmillan's The Critics Debate series, Jeremy Hawthorn discusses the dual narrative not once but twice: in the half reviewing critical approaches to *Bleak House* and again in the half concerned with the reader's ever-changing, ever-deepening response to the novel. Though Hawthorn addresses himself—in the words of the general editor of the series, Michael Scott—primarily to "students coming to advanced work in English for the first time" (7), he has worthwhile new things to say about this as about the other subjects he treats, for instance in calling attention to some of the implications and consequences of Esther's and the anonymous narrator's ignorance of each other's narratives. Perhaps *because* he is writing for such an audience, Hawthorn demonstrates admirably that, even in 1987, it is possible to be simultaneously lucid and up-to-date when dealing with critical questions of some complexity.

In a brief article, F. S. Schwarzbach attempts to explain Lady Dedlock's death in physiological as well as sociological terms: she caught smallpox, he presumes, in Chapter 16, at the same time and in the same place as Jo, who had led her to the pestilential graveyard where Hawdon was buried; and "as a member of a class very much connected with the Court of Chancery and like institutions" (164) she must bear responsibility for the appalling insanitary conditions that were thought to breed such deadly contagious diseases. Though Schwarzbach's logic is occasionally strained and his facts are not invariably straight, his thesis is persuasive.

Richard Fabrizio's thesis about *Hard Times* sounds promising. That novel, he says, is to be read less as "a satiric portrait of industrialization" than as "a keen description of the psyche forged out of socioeconomic conditions" (61). Life in Coketown has destroyed human and especially family relations, and people are no longer able to communicate effectively with those close to them. However, what could have been an instructive examination of how characters actually talk, or are unable to talk, to one another is not developed effectively. Throwaway references to akinesia, amphiboly, anastrophe, antonomasia, bradyphrasia, bradyphrenia, echolalia, prosopopeia, tachylalia, tachyphrasia, and tachyphrenia are no substitute for coherent argument, nor is Fabrizio's case strengthened by the more or less gratuitous cameo appearances of Greek deities, myths, and language and, toward the end, of the odd penis or vagina. For reasons that elude me, the essay contains two epigraphs, one from *The Way We Live Now* at the beginning of the first section and the other from *The Ordeal of Richard Feveral* (sic) at the beginning of the second. A more suitable motto might have been Stephen Blackpool's " 'Tis a' a muddle,'' especially since "Stephan,'' as he is called here on a couple of occasions, is one of those most deeply affected by the "Psychopathology'' of Fabrizio's title.

More conventionally, Edward Dramin views *Hard Times* as Dickens's protest against the allied evils of industrialism and Utilitarianism, with Blackpool, the victim of the former, representing "the nobility of which the working class is capable'' (211). Though another problematic character, Harthouse, seems to be "misallied with Utilitarianism,'' Dramin regards him as a personification of "both degenerate aristocracy and decadent Romanticism'' (210).

Neither James R. Zimmerman nor Carol A. Bock offers any startling new insights into Dickens' next novel, *Little Dorrit*. Zimmerman's image study sets out to show that Dickens went well beyond "conventional dark-equals-evil and light-equals-good'' oppositions and "a pattern of sun and shadow imagery which sets up both extreme sun and extreme shadow as negative attributes'' by carefully deploying an array of "five types of sun and shadow imagery,'' "systematically . . . highlighting the central characters and themes'' (94) throughout *Little Dorrit*. Bock examines Miss Wade's "The History of a Self-Tormentor'' (Chapter 21 of Book the Second) in conjunction with Dickens's short story "George Silverman's Explanation''; both first-person narratives embody features of the dramatic monologue, but, as she shows, there are important differences between them. Having been exposed to Miss Wade's heavily ironic account of her own life, the reader reaches a more sympathetic understanding of this deeply neurotic character, which is, however, subordinated to "our critical judgment of her personality'' (113). And this is appropriate, in Bock's view, for, unlike Silverman's self-contained "Explanation,'' "The History of a Self-Tormentor'' has a "didactic function within the . . . larger moral design'' (114) of a novel: it is "a cautionary tale which dramatizes the destructive consequences of imprisoning oneself within the narrow confines of an egocentric vision imposed upon life through a perverse assertion of personal will'' (116).

In the sixth chapter of his *Romantic Vision and the Novel,* Jay Clayton measures Amy Dorrit against the description of "threshold people" given by the anthropologist Victor Turner in his *The Ritual Process* and finds that she fits very well, in ways that serve to explain not only her elusive character but also the nature of the novel that bears her nickname as its title. A neo-Wordsworthian "liminal being" (123), she inhabits "the uncertain zone between two orders of existence" (124), "the real, everyday world" and "some Romantic fairy-tale realm" (128). Her "liminal status . . . mediates the complex relation between two opposed modes of discourse," for she helps Arthur to see that Mrs. Clennam's stern narrative ordering of experience is not the only, let alone the best, way to view his life: Amy's loving, healing way, marked by "the more elliptical—the unseen, the visionary—affinities of lyric" (131), offers him a necessary alternative, as he comes to understand by the end of the novel. A much more reductive reading of *Little Dorrit* is Jeff Nunokawa's rather labored effort to relate not only commercial transactions but also human relationships in the book to "Marx's conception of the character of capitalist possession" (328).

Not much was published about *A Tale of Two Cities* in 1987. Aside from Sylvia Sarrett's thunderclap, which I have already discussed, the only article I must note is one by Harry De Puy in *Cahiers victoriens & edouardiens* claiming that "Dickens reached back nearly eighteen years to find confinement imagery 'suitable' for *A Tale of Two Cities*" (39)—back, that is, to his impressions of three prisons (the Tombs in New York City, the House of Correction in Boston, and, especially, the Eastern Penitentiary in Philadelphia) that he visited during his North American tour of 1842. De Puy does not explain why Dickens would have found it necessary or expedient to borrow from his *American Notes* so long after he wrote them, nor are the comparisons De Puy invites the reader to make between passages from *A Tale of Two Cities* and their supposed originals from Dickens's earlier book very persuasive on the whole.

Great Expectations, by contrast, enjoyed a banner year, at least quantitatively, in 1987: I counted ten articles and two book chapters dealing with Dickens' thirteenth novel, and of course it was featured, sometimes prominently, in several of the general studies I mentioned in the first section of this review. There was also a whole book, by Bert Hornback, in Twayne's Masterwork Studies series; because it was discussed by David Paroissien last year, I will omit it. I will also hold my peace about one of the articles, J. S. Ryan's " 'The second Magwitch fortune' and His Second Daughter," which concerns

Michael Noonan's 1982 novel *Magwitch*: to include it would violate my own ban on adaptations.

The fullest account of Dickens' protagonist is Lars Hartveit's chapter on *Great Expectations* in his *Workings of the Picaresque in the British Novel*. He relates Pip to Dickens' self-image as "an abandoned child," the result of "an ejection which starts the picaro's career of wandering" (104). Using "the picaresque formula" wherever it suits his purpose, Dickens exposes "the dynamics of socio-moral transformation in a period which turned England into the workshop and commercial matrix of the world," but "Pip is never at ease in the new dispensation—the old always hampers his progress toward the success which is the aim of his climbing" (107). Hartveit usefully relates the picaresque features of *Great Expectations* to its allegorical, romance, and *bildungsroman* elements, and he demonstrates how "the traditional urge toward insider status" (129) cannot work for Pip given the social realities of his changing world.

More rigid if not more rigorous than Hartveit, Christopher Morris sets up a straw Pip, whose "conscience is functioning within an autonomous, continuous, achieved, created self" (941), so that he may proceed to deconstruct him. His real thesis seems to be that, like Pip's, all narrative more or less fraudulently "seeks to sustain the illusion of a signified" (952). If that is true—and who am I to say that it is not?—it applies as much to Morris's narrative as it does to Pip's or Dickens'. And where does that leave us? Unlike Morris, L. R. Leavis is willing to give credence to Pip, flawed and self-contradictory though both he and his life story as he tells it may be. Claire Slagter, in her pithy examination of "Pip's Dreams in *Great Expectations*," goes even further: not only does she see a Pip whose psychology deserves to be explored, but she also recognizes a narrative with a structure that deserves to be elucidated, and she makes good use of Pip's dreams as she strives to accomplish both tasks. And yet she goes not go too far: unlike some who have written on her subject, she understands, much as Dickens and his contemporaries would have, that we often "relive the experiences of the day as preoccupations recur to us in dreams" (180) and does not reach for her Freud the moment she sets about interpreting dreams.

Stanley Friedman also sticks close to Dickens's text as he seeks to justify his claim that Pip's discovery at the end of Chapter 50 that Magwitch is Estella's father should be regarded as the key to understanding the rest of his experience, including the revised ending. So does Paul Italia in his examination of *Great Expectations* for evidence that Dickens deliberately encouraged his readers to harbor the same misguided expectations as Pip, principally the "fairy-tale expectations" (233) that lead him to view, first, Miss Havisham as his fairy godmother and, later, after he gets over his shock at the convict's return from Australia, Magwitch as his fairy godfather—both characters who, he expects, will help him achieve his dream of union with Estella. Italia considers these "fairy-tale expectations" to be intimately bound up with socially sanctioned attitudes toward money, class, and sex as means of exercising power over others and believes that Dickens wanted to correct such dangerous attitudes in his readers as they are being corrected in the chastened Pip.

Carolyn Brown, on the other hand, apparently shares the widespread reluctance of contemporary critics to venture any judgment without appealing to somebody else's authority, the more authorities the better, and so the thirteen pages of her essay bristle with references to Jürgen Habermas, Hans Robert Jauss, Craig Owens, Marshall Berman (spelled correctly, though she insists on calling the mistress of Satis House "Miss Haversham"), Martin J. Wiener, Patrick Wright, Agnes Heller, Edward Said, and of course Sigmund Freud; the endnotes add Walter Benjamin, Raymond Williams, Michel Foucault, Jacques Donzelot, Toril Moi, Fredric Jameson, and Perry Anderson. All these serve as makeweights for a rudimentary account of Pip's emerging identity in a "modern" world that "is in a process of rapid social and textual transformation" (63), one that is "also (to me) an extraordinarily masculine world" in which women are present only to be incorporated into men, to be destroyed, or as narcissistic reflections" (61).

As we move away from Pip, we find Philip W. Martin's treatment of Miss Havisham and Mrs. Joe in the fourth chapter, "Secret Lives," of his *Mad Women in Romantic Writing* as heavily drenched in sexual politics as Carolyn Brown's contribution to the 1987 English Association *Essays and Studies*. (But he manages to get Miss Havisham's name right, most of the time.) Stripped of its rhetoric and its tiresome inclination to see phalluses sticking up everywhere, this is actually an intriguing study of two characters who are never brought together and seldom thought of together in *Great Expectations*. Martin maintains that both Miss Havisham, "who wishes to cripple Pip's emotional life," and his sister, "who mutilates Pip's body" (115), are punished by being brought down to a level even more abject than Biddy's. "The text's intention is clearly to enthrone Biddy at the centre of its moral enterprise, to praise her patience, tolerance and quiet acceptance of circumstances, and in order to do this it exploits myths of women's madness in new and possibly unique ways" (115–16).

Writing in *Hamlet Studies*, Stanley Friedman explores *Great Expectations* as the text that contains "the most conspicuous and extended mention" (86) of that play to be found in any Dickens novel. Most of the examples he cites concern Miss Havisham, to whom he attributes connections with the Ghost of Hamlet's father and also with Queen Gertrude. Taken together, they prove nothing, though Friedman may well be right in saying that for some readers such "parallels between *Hamlet* and *Great Expectations*" will serve to "intensify the tragic features of the novel" (89). Whether Dickens was aware of these "parallels" or not is a question that Friedman prudently leaves open.

Two notes in the Spring 1987 *Dickensian* have to do with the gestation period of *Great Expectations,* which began its run as a serial in *Harper's Weekly* on 24 November 1860 and in *All the Year Round* a week later. Kathleen Tillotson's examination of the front flyleaf of an edition of Johnson's *Dictionary* once owned by Dickens leads her to challenge the authenticity of the date "1856" on that page, which bears some memoranda pertaining to the novel in Dickens' hand. And my own reading of the *Uncommercial Traveller* sketch called "City of London Churches" published in *All the Year Round* on 5 May 1860 suggests that "at some level of his mind Dickens was laying the groundwork for the opening of his next novel in the spring of 1860, months before his first surviving reference to it" (20).

Two critics offer interesting arguments about *Our Mutual Friend* but tend to homogenize Dickens' last completed novel in the process. According to Audrey Jaffe, the narrator exercises his omniscience by creating in various characters and in all readers a sense that they understand and, at least to some degree, control what is happening in the various stories that comprise the plot; moreover, the surprise that ensues when characters and readers discover that they have been taken in produces complicated destabilizing and ultimately reconstitutive results. As Jaffe herself remarks, "the omniscient fantasy" (96) can be used for good purposes or bad, but there are more differences than she can deal with among the would-be manipulators in the novel. That master manipulator Charles Dickens himself made it very clear in the September 1865 postscript to *Our Mutual Friend* that he took a different view from Jaffe's of the distinction between *taking* readers in and *letting* them in on the truth. Margaret Flanders Darby examines Bella Wilfer, Lizzie Hexam, Sophronia Lammle, and Georgiana Podsnap as women struggling toward autonomy while displaying, each in her own way, "a subtle strength" (38) and situates all four "in a no-man's land between the opposing forces of the cultural expectations of their author's Victorian experience and his great sensitivity to the dramatic potential of character development in the world of his imagination" (25). What Darby has to say about Sophronia and Georgiana, especially about the "muted possibilities" (33) of the relationship between them, is more useful and original than her observations about Bella and Lizzie: it is doubtful that the former "begins as a delightful child" (26) or that the latter ends by marrying "a shadow of a man" (36).

The Mystery of Edwin Drood, finally, did not receive much critical attention in 1987, even though, as we have seen, both Jerome Meckier and Gwen Watkins weave it into the arguments of their books. H. R. F. Keating and LeRoy Lad Panek also treat it, briefly, in their studies of crime, mystery, and detective fiction. But the only article devoted to *Drood* is a short one, in *Notes and Queries,* in which Charles Forsyte points out that both Deputy's "curious chant" (43) of "Widdy widdy wen!" in Chapters 5 and 12 and the narrator's reference to "hot boiled beans and very good butter" in Chapter 18 come from popular nineteenth-century games, "Widdy" and "Beans and Butter," which Forsyte describes so as to make them yield some tantalizing clues about the roles of Deputy and Dick Datchery in Dickens' baffling fragment.

The observant reader will have noticed that one Dickens novel has gone unmentioned up to now: *Nicholas Nickleby,* which was not the focus of any 1987 critical study that I was able to discover. Much as I like Dickens' third novel—indeed, *because* I like it very much—I am not at all sure that this neglect was a bad thing. We will have to wait for solemn disquisitions on Nicholas's incestuous passion for Kate or the historically determined early-capitalist exploitation of the workers in Madame Mantalini's sweatshop. In the meantime, we can read, and enjoy, the ravings of the gentleman in the small clothes who lives next door to Mrs. Nickleby. He may be crazy, but he certainly knows how to reach an audience.

ACKNOWLEDGEMENT

Without Alan Cohn's checklists in the *Dickens Quarterly,* and without his cheerful service as a one-man short-order inter-library loan office, I could not have written this essay. Thank you, Alan.

WORKS CITED

Bloom, Harold. Introduction. *Charles Dickens.* Modern Critical Views. New York: Chelsea House, 1987. Pp. 1–27.

Bock, Carol A. "Miss Wade and George Silverman: The Forms of Fictional Monologue." *Dickens Studies Annual* 16 (1987): 113–26.

Brown, Carolyn. " 'Great Expectations': Masculinity and Modernity." In *Essays and Studies 1987: English and Cultural Studies: Broadening The Context.* Ed. Michael Green with Richard Hoggart. London: John Murray; Atlantic Highlands, N. J.: Humanities Press, 1987. Pp. 60–74.

Carmichael, Virginia. "In Search of *Beein': Nom/Non du Père* in *David Copperfield.*" *ELH* 54 (Fall 1987): 653–67.

Clayton, Jay. *Romantic Vision and the Novel.* Cambridge: Cambridge University Press, 1987.

Cordery, G. "The Gambling Grandfather in *The Old Curiosity Shop.*" *Literature and Psychology* 33. (1987): 43–61.

Cummings, Katherine. "*Bleak House*: Remarks on a Daughter's Da." *Style* 21 (Summer 1987): 237–58.

Daldry, Graham. *Charles Dickens and the Form of the Novel: Fiction and Narrative in Dickens' Work.* Totowa, N. J.: Barnes & Noble, 1986; London: Croom Helm, 1987.

Darby, Margaret Flanders. "Four Women in *Our Mutual Friend.*" *Dickensian* 83 (Spring 1987): 25–39.

De Puy, Harry. "American Prisons and *A Tale of Two Cities.*" *Cahiers victoriens & edouardiens* 25 (April 1987): 39–48.

Den Hartog, Dirk. *Dickens and Romantic Psychology: The Self in Time in Nineteenth-Century Literature.* London: Macmillan; New York: St. Martin's, 1987.

Dramin, Edward. *Light in a Dark Place: Romanticism in the Victorian Social-Political Novel: An Anthology.* Lanham, Md.: University Press of America, 1987.

Eigner, Edwin M. "Death and the Gentleman: *David Copperfield* as Elegiac Romance." *Dickens Studies Annual* 16 (1987): 39–60.

Fabrizio, Richard. "Wonderful No-Meaning: Language and the Psychopathology of the Family in Dickens' *Hard Times.*" *Dickens Studies Annual* 16 (1987): 61–94.

Feltes, N. N. *Modes of Production of Victorian Novels.* Chicago: University of Chicago Press, 1986.

————. "Realism, Consensus and 'Exclusion Itself': Interpellating the Victorian Bourgeoisie." *Textual Practice* 1 (Winter 1987): 297–308.

Flaxman, Rhoda L. *Victorian Word-Painting and Narrative: Toward the Blending of Genres.* Ann Arbor, Mich.: UMI Research Press, 1987.

Foltinek, Herbert. *Charles Dickens und der Zwang des Systems: Gestaltbildung und Geschlossenheit in den Romanen der Reife.* Vienna: Verlag der Österreichischen Akademie der Wissenschaften, 1987.

————. "The Other Hero of *Martin Chuzzlewit*: The Function of Tom Pinch in the Narrative and Thematic Structure of the Novel.'' *REAL: The Yearbook of Research in English and American Literature* 5 (1987): 171–203.

Forsyte, Charles. "Children's Games in *Edwin Drood.*" *Notes and Queries* NS 34 (March 1987): 43–46.

Friedman, Stanley. "Echoes of *Hamlet* in *Great Expectations.*" *Hamlet Studies* (Summer-Winter 1987): 86–89.

——————. "Estella's Parentage and Pip's Persistence: The Outcome of *Great Expectations.*" *Studies in The Novel* 19 (Winter 1987): 410–21.

Ginsburg, Michal Peled. "Truth and Persuasion: The Language of Realism and of Ideology in *Oliver Twist.*" *Novel* 20 (Spring 1987): 220–36.

Graver, Suzanne. "Writing in a 'Womanly' Way and the Double Vision of *Bleak House.*" *Dickens Quarterly* 4 (March 1987): 3–15.

Greenstein, Michael. "Lenticular Curiosity and *The Old Curiosity Shop.*" *Dickens Quarterly* 4 (December 1987): 187–94.

Grove, Thelma. "Barnaby Rudge: A Case Study in Autism." *Dickensian* 83 (Autumn 1987): 139–48.

Harris, Jean. " 'But He Was His Father': The Gothic and the Impostorious in Dickens's *The Pickwick Papers.*" In *Psychoanalytic Approaches to Literature and Film.* Ed. Maurice Charney and Joseph Reppen. Rutherford, N. J.: Fairleigh Dickinson University Press, 1987. Pp. 69–79.

Hartveit, Lars. *Workings of the Picaresque in the British Novel.* Oslo: Solum Forlag; Atlantic Highlands, N. J.: Humanities Press, 1987.

Hawthorn, Jeremy. *Bleak House.* The Critics Debate. Basingstoke: Macmillan, 1987.

Herrlinger, Wolfgang. *Sentimentalismus und Postsentimentalismus: Studien zum englischen Roman bis zur Mitte des 19. Jahrhunderts.* Tübingen: Max Niemeyer Verlag, 1987.

Hoggart, Paul. "Travesties of Dickens." In *Essays and Studies 1987: English and Cultural Studies: Broadening the Context.* Ed. Michael Green with Richard Hoggart. London: John Murray; Atlantic Highlands, N. J.: Humanities Press, 1987. Pp. 32–44.

Italia, Paul. "The Function of Expectation in Dickens' *Great Expectations.*" *Revista Canaria de Estudios Ingleses* No. 13/14 (April 1987): 231–39.

Jaffe, Audrey. "Omniscience in *Our Mutual Friend*: On Taking the Reader by Surprise." *Journal of Narrative Technique* 17 (Winter 1987): 91–101.

Kaplan, Fred. *Sacred Tears: Sentimentality in Victorian Literature.* Princeton, N. J.: Princeton University Press, 1987.

Keating, H.R.F. *Crime and Mystery: The 100 Best Books.* London: Xanadu; New York: Carroll & Graf, 1987.

Kincaid, James R. "Viewing and Blurring in Dickens: The Misrepresentation of Representation." *Dickens Studies Annual* 16 (1987): 95–111.

Kucich, John. *Repression in Victorian Fiction: Charlotte Brontë, George Eliot, and Charles Dickens.* Berkeley: University of California Press, 1987.

Leavis, L. R. "The Dramatic Narrator in *Great Expectations.*" *English Studies* 68 (June 1987): 236–48.

Martin, Philip W. *Mad Women in Romantic Writing.* Brighton: Harvester; New York: St. Martin's Press, 1987.

Meckier, Jerome. *Hidden Rivalries in Victorian Fiction: Dickens, Realism, and Revaluation.* Lexington: University Press of Kentucky, 1987.

Montaut, Mary. "The Second Mrs. Dombey." *Dickens Quarterly* 4 (September 1987): 141–53.

Morris, Christopher. "The Bad Faith of Pip's Bad Faith: Deconstructing *Great Expectations.*" *ELH* 54 (Winter 1987): 941–55.

Mundhenk, Rosemary. "*David Copperfield* and 'The Oppression of Remembrance.' " *Texas Studies in Literature and Language* 29 (Fall 1987): 232–41.

Musselwhite, David E. *Partings Welded Together: Politics and Desire in the Nineteenth-Century English Novel.* London: Methuen, 1987.

Nunokawa, Jeff. "Getting and Having: Some Versions of Possession in *Little Dorrit.*" in *Charles Dickens.* Modern Critical Views. Ed. Harold Bloom. New York: Chelsea House, 1987. Pp. 317–35.

Panek, LeRoy Lad. *An Introduction to the Detective Story.* Bowling Green: Bowling Green State University Popular Press, 1987.

Peterson, Carla. *The Determined Reader: Gender and Culture in the Novel from Napoleon to Victoria.* New Brunswick, N. J.: Rutgers University Press, 1986.

Ponnau, Gwenhaël. "Le héros du roman d'éducation et ses doubles: Le cas de David Copperfield." *Littératures* 16 (Spring 1987): 39–47.

Pope, Norris. "A View from the Monument: A Note on *Martin Chuzzlewit.*" *Dickens Quarterly* 4 (September 1987): 153–60.

Pykett, Lyn. "*Dombey and Son*: A Sentimental Family Romance." *Studies in the Novel* 19 (Spring 1987): 16–30.

Rice, Thomas Jackson. "*Barnaby Rudge*": An Annotated Bibliography. New York: Garland Publishing, 1987.

Rosner, Mary. "Reading the Beasts of *Martin Chuzzlewit.*" *Dickens Quarterly* 4 (September 1987): 131–41.

Ryan, J. S. " 'The second Magwitch fortune' and His Second Daughter." *Dickensian* 83 (Summer 1987): 106–09.

Sarrett, Sylvia. "Why I Love Teaching the Gifted, Hated Seeing *Brazil,* and Am Dropping *A Tale of Two Cities.*" *English Journal* 76 (April 1987): 56–58.

Sawicki, Joseph. " 'The Mere Truth Won't Do': Esther as Narrator in *Bleak House.*" *Journal of Narrative Technique* 17 (Spring 1987): 209–24.

Schwarzbach, F. S. " 'Deadly Stains': Lady Dedlock's Death." *Dickens Quarterly* 4 (September 1987): 160–65.

Slagter, Claire. "Pip's Dreams in *Great Expectations.*" *Dickensian* 83 (Autumn 1987): 180–83.

Tillotson, Kathleen. "*Great Expectations* and the Dartmouth College Notes." *Dickensian* 83 (Spring 1987): 17–18.

Wales, Kathleen. "The Claims of Kinship: The Opening Chapter of *Martin Chuzzlewit.*" *Dickensian* 83 (Autumn 1987): 167–79.

Watkins, Gwen. *Dickens in Search of Himself: Recurrent Themes and Characters in the Work of Charles Dickens.* Basingstoke: Macmillan; Totowa, N. J.: Barnes & Noble, 1987.

Welsh, Alexander. *From Copyright to Copperfield: The Identity of Dickens.* Cambridge, Mass.: Harvard University Press, 1987.

Worth, George J. "*The Uncommercial Traveller* and *Great Expectations*: A Further Note." *Dickensian* 83 (Spring 1987): 19–21.

Zimmerman, James R. "Sun and Shadow in *Little Dorrit.*" *Dickensian* 83 (Summer 1987): 93–105.

Index

437

Mad Women in Romantic Writing (Martin), 429

Male, Roy, R., 291

Managed Heart, The (Hochschild), 244

Manfred (Byron), 256, 257, 269, 271; and soliloquy, 256-72 *passim*

Manning, Sylvia, 404, 419

Marcus, Steven, 179, 186; and *Dombey and Son*, 205, 207, 213

Marcuse, Hervert, 416

Mariner's Chronicle, The (Duncan), 48

Martin Chuzzlewit (Dickens), 53, 54, 421; and animal imagery, 421; and the blacking warehouse, 410; and music, 102; and *Robinson Crusoe*, 51

Martin, Philip W.: *Mad Women in Romantic Writing*, 429

Martineau, Harriet, 125

Martineau, James: *The Life and Works of Dr. Priestley*, 125; and Unitarianism, 123, 125-28

Martz, Louis, 257

Mather, Cotton, 294, 295, 302; *Wonders of the Invisible World*, 293

Maurice, F. D.: *Theological Essays*, 137

Maynard, John, *Charlotte Brontë and Sexuality*, 386, 394

Meckier, Jerome, 412, 420, 431; *Hidden Rivalries in Victorian Fiction*, 406-09

Melville, Herman: *Moby Dick*, 80

Middlemarch (Eliot), 182, 408

Mill on the Floss, The (Eliot), 60, 61, 79, 80

Miller, Alice: *Drama of the Gifted Child, The*, 191-92

Miller, J. Hillis, 381; *The Disappearance of God*, 390; *Fiction and Repetition*, 397

Miller, Jane, *Woman Writing About Men*, 396

Miller, Nancy K., 228

Milton (Blake), 267

Milton, John, 257, 387; *Paradise Lost*, 50, 256, 293; *Paradise Regained*, 257

Minstrelsy of the Scottish Border (Scott): and Hawthorne, influence on, 277-303

Moby Dick (Melville), 73, 80

Modes of Production of Victorian Novels (Feltes), 403

Moglen, Helene: *Charlotte Brontë: The Self Conceived*, 383

Monsters of Affection: Dickens, Eliot, & Brontë on Fatherhood (Sadoff), 395

Montaut, Mary, 422

Morris, Christopher, 428

Moynahan, Julian, 199, 205, 206

Mudge, Bradford, 258

Mundhenk, Rosemary, 423

Murray, Grenville, 97

Musselwhite, David: *Partings Welded Together*, 412

Myer, Valerie Grosvenor: *Charlotte Brontë, Truculent Spirit*, 383

Myers, William, 230

Mystery of Edwin Drood, The (Dickens): 407, 408, 412; and music, 102

Myths of Power, A Marxist Study of the Brontës (Eagleton), 383

Nestor, Pauline: *Female Friendships and Communities, Charlotte Brontë, George Eliot, Elizabeth Gaskell*, 385

Neufeldt, Victor A., 381, 382

Newman, John Henry, 184

Newton, Judith Lowder: *Women, Power, and Subversion, Social Strategies in British Fiction 1778-1860*, 391

Nicholas Nickleby (Dickens), 5, 53, 159, 309

Nightingale, Florence, 186

North and South (Gaskell), 76; and *Household Words*, 407

Norton, Caroline: and *Barry Lyndon*, influence on, 338, 344-45; and *Diana of the Crossways*, heroine of, 340; and Dickens, 340; *English Laws*, 347-48, 349; *Letter to the Queen*, 347; the life of, 340-40; and *The Newcomes*, influence on, 338, 347-48; *A Plain Letter to the Lord Chancellor on the Infant Custody Bill*, 343, 344; *Separation of Mother and Child by the Custody of Infants Considered*, 342; and *Vanity Fair*, influence on, 338, 345-47

Nowell-Smith, Geoffrey, 370

Nunokawa, Jeff, 427

"Ode: Intimations of Immortality" (Wordsworth), 266

"Ode to a Nightingale" (Keats), 267

Old Curiosity Shop, The (Dickens), 53, 120, 187, and characterizations in, 19-35; and Providence, 24-35; and *Robinson Crusoe*, 50-51

Oliver Twist (Dickens), 63, 147, 415; and absence in, 9-10; and castration, metaphors of, 8; and characterizations in, 1-15; and clothing, 6-7; and discourse, 419; and hanging, motif of, 7-8; and Mary Hogarth, 33; and melodrama, 12; and memory, 102; and naming in, 12-13; and Nancy's death, 10-11; and Providence, 26, 29; and social class, 3-5, 6-7

Contents of Previous Volumes

Volume 4 (1975)

Dickens and Time: The Clock without Hands
STEPHEN L. FRANKLIN
Pickwick Papers: Humor and the Refashioning of Reality
MARGARET GANZ
Pickwick and Dickens: Stages of Development
STEVEN V. DANIELS
Dickens and Mayhew on the London Poor
ANNE HUMPHERYS
"Through a Glass Darkly": Esther Summerson and *Bleak House*
LAWRENCE FRANK
Sir Leicester Dedlock, Wat Tyler, and the Chartists: The Role of the
Ironmaster in *Bleak House*
HARVEY PETER SUCKSMITH
The Mysteries in *Bleak House*: A Psychoanalytic Study
GORDON D. HIRSCH
The Redeemed Feminine of *Little Dorrit*
EDWARD HEATLEY

Volume 5 (1976)

Dickens' HEROES, *heroes*, and heroids
LEONARD F. MANHEIM
Dickens' Romance: The Novel as Other
JAMES E. MARLOW
Dickens and Mrs. Stowe
H. L. KNIGHT
The Established Self: The American Episodes of *Martin Chuzzlewit*
EDWARD J. EVANS
David Copperfield: The Folk-Story Structure
CHRISTOPHER MULVEY
Dickens and Dombey: A Daughter After All
NINA AUERBACH
The Paradox of the Clown in Dickens
JOSEPH BUTWIN
Toward Jaggers
STANLEY TICK

Volume 8 (1980)

Volume 9 (1981)

Volume 15 (1986)

Volume 16 (1987)

* * *

Volume 17 (1988)

Volume 17 (1988)